Decisions with Multiple Objectives

Preferences and Value Tradeoffs

RALPH L. KEENEY

Institute of Safety and Systems Management
University of Southern California

and

HOWARD RAIFFA

Frank P. Ramsey Chair in Managerial Economics
Graduate School of Business and Kennedy School of Government
Harvard University

CAMBRIDGE
UNIVERSITY PRESS

Published by the Press Syndicate of the University of Cambridge
The Pitt Building, Trumpington Street, Cambridge CB2 1RP
40 West 20th Street, New York, NY 10011-4211, USA
10 Stamford Road, Oakleigh, Victoria 3166, Australia

First published in 1976 by John Wiley & Sons, Inc.
First published by Cambridge University Press 1993

Printed in Canada

Library of Congress Cataloging-in-Publication Data
Keeney, Ralph L., 1944–

Decisions with multiple objectives :   preferences and value
tradeoffs / Ralph L. Keeney and Howard Raiffa.

p.   cm.

Includes bibliographical references and index.

ISBN 0-521-44185-4 – ISBN 0-521-43883-7 (pbk.)

1. Multiple criteria decision making.   I. Raiffa, Howard, 1924–
II. Title.

T57.95.K43 1993	92–31874
658.4′03–dc20	CIP

A catalog record for this book is available from the British Library.

ISBN 0-521-44185-4 hardback
ISBN 0-521-43883-7 paperback

To
Tjalling C. Koopmans,
whose standards of excellence are
an inspiration to all who know him.

Contents

Preface to the Cambridge University Press Edition   xi

Preface to First Edition   xv

1. THE PROBLEM   1

1.1 Sketches of Motivating Examples   1

1.2 Paradigm of Decision Analysis   5

1.3 Comments About the Paradigm   7

1.4 Complex Value Problems   14

1.5 Classes of Examples and Methodological Nightmares   19

1.6 Organization of Remaining Chapters   26

2. THE STRUCTURING OF OBJECTIVES   31

2.1 Objectives and Attributes   32

2.2 Generation of Objectives and Attributes   34

2.3 Hierarchical Nature of Objectives   41

2.4 Sets of Objectives and Attributes   49

2.5 Proxy Attributes and Direct Preference Measurements   55

2.6 Summary and Perspective on the Practical Aspects of Specifying Objectives and Attributes   64

3. TRADEOFFS UNDER CERTAINTY   66

3.1 The Multiattribute Value Problem   66

3.2 Choice Procedures That Do Not Formalize Preference Structures   69

3.3 Structuring of Preferences and Value Functions   77

3.4 Preference Structures and Value Functions for Two Attributes   82

3.5   The Case of Three Attributes   100
3.6   The Case of More Than Three Attributes   108
3.7   Assessment of an Additive Value Function: An Abstract
      Hypothetical Example   117
3.8   Willingness to Pay   125
3.9   Brief Summary and Guide to Some Relevant Literature   129

4.   UNIDIMENSIONAL UTILITY THEORY   **131**
4.1   The Motivation for Utility Theory   131
4.2   Direct Assessment of Utilities for Consequences   140
4.3   Unidimensional Utility Functions   141
4.4   Risk Aversion   148
4.5   A Measure of Risk Aversion   159
4.6   Constant, Decreasing, and Increasing Risk Aversion   165
4.7   Proportional Risk Aversion   174
4.8   Monotonically Decreasing and Nonmonotonic Utility
      Functions   179
4.9   A Procedure for Assessing Utility Functions   188
4.10 Illustrations of the Assessment of Unidimensional Utility
      Functions   203
4.11 Explicating a Single Attribute by Means of Multiple
      Attributes   212
4.12 Conditional Unidimensional Utility Theory   214
4.13 Where We Stand   218

**5.   MULTIATTRIBUTE PREFERENCES UNDER
      UNCERTAINTY: THE TWO-ATTRIBUTE CASE**   **219**
5.1   Approaches for Multiattribute Assessment   219
5.2   Utility Independence   224
5.3   Additive Independence and the Additive Utility Function   229
5.4   The Implications of Mutual Utility Independence   232
5.5   Use of Certainty Equivalents   242
5.6   Utility Functions with One Utility-Independent Attribute   243
5.7   What to Do if No Independence Properties Hold   255
5.8   Assessment Procedure for Mulitattribute Utility
      Functions   261
5.9   Interpreting the Scaling Constants   271
5.10 The Assessment of a Utility Function in a Hospital
      Blood Bank   273

6. **MULTIATTRIBUTE PREFERENCES UNDER
    UNCERTAINTY: MORE THAN TWO ATTRIBUTES**   **282**
    6.1   Overview of the Chapter   282
    6.2   Utility Functions with Three Attributes   286
    6.3   The Multiplicative Utility Function   288
    6.4   The Multilinear Utility Function   293
    6.5   The Additive Utility Function   295
    6.6   Assessing Multiattribute Utility Functions 297
    6.7   A Fundamental Relationship Between Preferential
          Independence and Utility Independence   310
    6.8   Relationships Among Utility Independence Assumptions   316
    6.9   Decomposition of Multiattribute Utility Functions   319
    6.10 Additional Representation Theorems   324
    6.11 Hierarchical Structures and Conditional Preferences   332
    6.12 Summary   344
    Appendix 6A   Generalization of Preferential Independence and
                  Utility Independence   345
    Appendix 6B   Evaluating the Scaling Constant
                  in the Multiplicative Utility Function   347
    Appendix 6C   An Interactive Computer Program for
                  Assessing and Using Multiattribute Utility
                  Functions   349

7. **ILLUSTRATIVE APPLICATIONS**   **354**
    7.1   Air Pollution Control   355
    7.2   Preference Tradeoffs among Instructional Programs   365
    7.3   Fire Department Operations   377
    7.4   Structuring Corporate Preferences for Multiple
          Objectives   390
    7.5   Evaluating Computer Systems   408
    7.6   Siting and Licensing of Nuclear Power Facilities   412
    7.7   Other Applications   417

8. **AIRPORT DEVELOPMENT FOR MEXICO CITY:
    A CASE STUDY**   **436**
    8.1   The Problem   436
    8.2   Background Information   437
    8.3   Evolution of the Analysis   441
    8.4   The Static Model   442

8.5	Specifying the Possible Impacts of Each Alternative	445
8.6	Assessing the Multiattribute Utility Function	451
8.7	The Analysis	459
8.8	The Dynamic Analysis	463
8.9	Impact of the Results	470

9. PREFERENCES OVER TIME   **473**

9.1	Characteristics of the Time Problem	474
9.2	The Certainty Case: Value Functions over Time Streams	476
9.3	The Uncertainty Case: Utility Functions over Time Streams	488
9.4	Relaxing the Independence Assumptions	494
9.5	Uncertain Horizon	497
9.6	State-Dependent Utilities	501
9.7	Problems of Application	503
9.8	Time Resolution of Uncertainty	509
Appendix 9A.	Derivation of a Utility Function for Consumption and Lifetime	513

10. AGGREGATION OF INDIVIDUAL PREFERENCES   **515**

10.1	The Decision Maker as Synthesizer or Amalgamator	516
10.2	Aggregating Individuals' Preferences under Certainty	523
10.4	Additive Utility and Equity Considerations	532
10.5	Appraisal of the Independence Assumptions	536
10.6	Assessing Group Utility Functions	539
10.7	Uses of Multiattribute Utility Analysis for Groups	542

Bibliography	549
Index	561

Preface to the Cambridge University Press Edition

Way back in the mid-seventies when we wrote *Decisions with Multiple Objectives,* our objectives were clear. We aspired to develop a sound, practical theory for analyzing decisions with multiple, competing objectives; to make this theory and framework of thought accessible to a diverse audience of scholars and practitioners of the art of decision analysis; and to promote applications of multiattribute analysis. Today, our objectives are exactly the same. In the intervening sixteen years, the theory most relevant to applications has been augmented a little and the application of the theory has greatly expanded.

Decision analysis is widely recognized as a sound prescriptive theory. When a decision involves multiple objectives – and this is almost always the case with important problems – multiattribute utility theory forms the basic foundation for applying decision analysis. The theory explicitly addresses the value tradeoffs and uncertainties that are invariably at the center of multiple-objective decisions. The experience of numerous applications indicates that the theory available in 1976 is still the most relevant theory available today. The important addition since 1976 concerns value functions that address strength of preferences between pairs of consequences (see Dyer and Sarin, 1979; Bell and Raiffa, 1988).

The art of applying multiattribute utility has expanded in many directions since 1976. Collectively, decision scientists know much more today about identifying and structuring objectives and about measuring their achievement in terms of objectives. We are more skilled at assessing utility functions, and computer programs greatly assist analyses and sensitivity analysis. In addition, the use of structured values, both qualitative and quantitative, to help define decision situations, create alternatives, and communicate about decisions has been developed.

The identification and structuring of objectives essentially frames the decision being addressed. It sets the stage for all that follows. Recent work has developed techniques to involve relevant stakeholders in the process constructively, and to probe more deeply into the meaning, relevance, and relationships of objectives (see von Winterfeldt, 1987; Keeney, 1992). The computer program Logical Decision (Smith, 1989) is helpful in assessing utility functions. Given the utilities of possible consequences, Logical Decision, IDEA (Whitfield et al., 1989), Supertree (McNamee and Selona, 1990), Decision Programming Language (Call and Miller, 1990), and three programs by Kirkwood (1991) can analyze alternatives effectively.

Applications of decision analyses with multiple objectives have been summarized in several publications. Corner and Kirkwood (1991) has a comprehensive review of more than one hundred applications covering a broad range of fields including energy, manufacturing and services, public policy, and health care. A few earlier applications are discussed in depth in Bell, Keeney, and Raiffa (1977) and more recent applications, including personal decisions, are found in Keeney (1992). In the past decade, decision analysis involving multiple objectives has expanded to address the substance of important classes of problems more specifically. Examples of these are books that focus in-depth on siting major facilities (Keeney, 1980), the art and science of negotiation (Raiffa, 1982), and medical decisions (Sox, Blatt, Higgins, and Marton, 1988).

There should be significant interplay between descriptive studies of how people do process information and make decisions and prescriptive decision analysis to help people make decisions that are consistent with their values and understanding of the problem. Recently, there has been a major trend to incorporate the insights from descriptive studies into the prescriptive analyses to render them more effective and useful. Many of the descriptive concepts and ideas now used in prescriptive analysis are discussed in Kahneman, Slovic, and Tversky (1982), von Winterfeldt and Edwards (1986), Bell, Raiffa, and Tversky (1988), and Edwards (1992).

As stated in Section 1.3.3, we assumed in this book that the decision problem had been identified and the alternatives specified. However, we recognized that problem selection and alternative creation are critically important. Since our values indicate the reason we are interested in any decision situation, it seemed reasonable to use values as structured in this book to guide the thought process to select decisions and alternatives. This concept, called value-focused thinking (Keeney, 1992), is developed to create better alternatives for any decision problem that we face and to identify decision opportunities more appealing than the decision problems that confront us.

Teaching from This Book

It may be useful to perspective readers and teachers to suggest how we would revise this book if we spent the substantial time on such a revision, and what supplementary material we would use when teaching from the current version. The responses are essentially the same. Chapter 1 still is a useful introduction. Material in Chapter 2 on structuring objectives would be updated with material from Keeney (1992, Chapters 3 and 4). A discussion of the theory and results involving strength of preferences would be added to Chapter 3. The main theory in Chapters 4–6 and 9 would be changed only in a minor way. Specifically, we would focus a bit more on the art of assessing utility functions and the use of computers to assist the assessment. A Chapter 11 would be added to indicate how structured values can be used both to create alternatives and decision opportunities using value-focused thinking.

Chapter 10 on the aggregation of individual preferences would be substantially enhanced to account for several developments. The revision would include material on the structuring and combining of objectives in problems involving multiple stakeholders (von Winterfeldt, 1987; Keeney, 1992), the major advances in applying multiattribute utility in negotiation contexts (Raiffa, 1982), and the result that a group von Neumann utility function is consistent with assumptions analogous to Arrow's (Keeney, 1976). In other words, when strength of preferences and interpersonal values are explicitly addressed, there is a logical and consistent way to create a group utility function.

The major revisions of the book would have to do with the multitude of examples that could be presented along with those in Chapters 7 and 8. There are now so many good applications that we would carefully need to find a set that would illustrate the many key insights available from decision analyses with multiple objectives. This is precisely the difficult choice problem that we hoped to create when we originally wrote *Decisions With Multiple Objectives*. Thank you to the many original readers who applied the theory and helped make this problem a reality.

Ralph L. Keeney
Howard Raiffa

REFERENCES

Bell, D. E., R. L. Keeney, and H. Raiffa, eds. (1977). *Conflicting Objectives in Decisions*, Wiley, New York.

Bell, D. E., and H. Raiffa (1988). Marginal value and intrinsic risk aversion. In *Decision making: Descriptive, Normative, and Prescriptive Interactions*, D. E. Bell, H. Raiffa, and A. Tversky, eds., Cambridge University Press, Cambridge, pp. 384–397.

Bell, D. E., H. Raiffa, and A. Tversky, eds. (1988). *Decision Making: Descriptive, Normative, and Prescriptive Interactions*, Cambridge University Press, Cambridge.

Call, H. J., and W. A. Miller (1990). A comparison of approaches and implementations for automating decision analysis. *Reliability Engineering and Systems Safety,* 30, 115–162.

Corner, J. L., and C. W. Kirkwood (1991). Decision analysis applications in the operations research literature, 1970–1989. *Operations Research,* 39, 206–219.

Dyer, J. S., and R. K. Sarin (1979). Measurable multiattribute value functions. *Operations Research,* 27, 810–822.

Edwards, W., ed. (1992). *Utility Theories: Measurements and Applications,* Kluwer Academic Publishers, Dortrecht, Holland.

Kahneman, D., P. Slovic, and A. Tversky, eds. (1982). *Judgment Under Uncertainty: Heuristics and Biases,* Cambridge University Press, Cambridge.

Keeney, R. L. (1976). A group preference axiomatization with cardinal utility. *Management Science,* 23, 140–145.

Keeney, R. L. (1980). *Siting Energy Facilities,* Academic Press, New York.

Keeney, R. L. (1992). *Value-Focused Thinking,* Harvard University Press, Cambridge, Massachusetts.

Kirkwood, C. W. (1991). Computer programs for multiattribute evaluation. Technical Report DIS 91/92-7, Department of Decision and Information Systems, Arizona State University, Tempe.

McNamee, P., and J. Selona (1990). *Decision Analysis with Supertree, 2nd Edition,* Scientific Press, South San Francisco, California.

Raiffa, H. (1982). *The Art and Science of Negotiation,* Harvard University Press, Cambridge, Massachusetts.

Smith, G. R. (1989). *Logical Decision: Multi-Measure Decision Analysis Software,* Logical Decisions, Inc., Golden, Colorado.

Sox, H. C., M. A. Blatt, M. C. Higgins, and K. I. Marton (1988). *Medical Decision Making,* Butterworths, Boston, Massachusetts.

Whitfield, R. G., C. E. Swietlik, M. F. Warren, R. Fuja, M. J. Jusko, J. P. Peerenboom, and E. C. Johnson (1989). *IDEA-Interactive Decision Analysis: Users' Guide and Tutorial,* Technical Report ANL/EES-TM-378, Energy and Environmental Systems Division, Argonne National Laboratory, Argonne, Illinois.

von Winterfeldt, D. (1987). Value tree analysis: An introduction and an application to offshore oil drilling. In *Insuring and Managing Hazardous Risks: From Seveso to Bhopal and Beyond,* P. Kleindorfer and H. Kunreuther, eds., Springer, New York, 349–377.

von Winterfeldt, D., and W. Edwards (1986). *Decision Analysis and Behavioral Research,* Cambridge University Press, Cambridge.

Preface to First Edition

If we wanted the title of this book merely to convey the subject matter, it would be some horrendously complicated concoction such as: "On Cardinal Utility Analysis with Multiple Conflicting Objectives: The Case of Individual Decision making Under Uncertainty from the Prescriptive Point of View—with Special Emphasis on Applications but with a Little Theory Thrown In for Spice."

Our actual title, *Decisions with Multiple Objectives: Preferences and Value Tradeoffs* is longer than we think a title should ideally be, but, unfortunately, it is too short to prevent unjustified sales. Even in such a simple case, it is not so easy to *balance* among the conflicting objectives: convey the subject matter, minimize the length, and promote justified sales but prevent unjustified ones.

To an ever growing circle of people, "Decision Analysis" has carved out for itself a niche in the literature of operations research, systems analysis, management sciences, decision and control, and cybernetics. Decision analysis looks at the paradigm in which an individual decision maker (or decision unit) contemplates a choice of action in an uncertain environment. The approach employs systematic analysis, with some number pushing, which helps the decision maker clarify in his own mind which course of action he should choose. In this sense, the approach is not *descriptive,* because most people do not attempt to think systematically about hard choices under uncertainty. It is also not *normative* since it is not an idealized theory designed for the superrational being with an all-powering intellect. It is, instead, a *prescriptive* approach designed for normally intelligent people who want to think hard and systematically about some important real problems.

The theory of decision analysis is designed to help the individual make a choice among a set of *prespecified* alternatives. Of course, decision analysts do admit that an insightful generation of alternatives is of paramount importance, and they also take note of the often-overlooked fact that good analysis of a set of existing alternatives may be suggestive of ways to augment the set of alternatives. But this is a side point that is not suitable for development in a preface.

What is important here is that the usual analysis (after suitable modeling has been done) involves two distinctive features: an uncertainty analysis and a preference (or value or utility) analysis. There has been a great deal that has been written on the uncertainty phase: statistical validation of a model, uses of historical and experimental data for inference, the codification of judgmental estimates by the decision maker and by expert groups, and so on. In comparison with this voluminous literature on the uncertainty side little has been written about the value or preference side of the picture. The present book helps improve the balance.

At present, this gross imbalance is also unfortunately very much in evidence in applications. Several person-years of effort will be utilitzed developing, modifying, and verifying an elaborate simulation model that outputs the possible levels of several indicators of interest resulting from any particular policy. Perhaps the output is synthesized in terms of a few graphs or tables and a summary report is written for the *decision maker*. This decision maker then struggles for perhaps a week with the implications of the alternatives and then chooses an alternative. The score: person-years on the uncertainty side of the problem, a week on the preference side. We feel that the shifting of a little effort—perhaps only a few person-months—to the preference aspects could lead to significantly improved decision making in many situations. In this book, we suggest how you might constructively use more effort on the preference aspects of analysis.

An illustrative example can help set the stage. A decision-making unit must make a policy choice in a complicated environment. Imagine that the problem is so complicated that a computer-based simulation model is designed such that for each policy choice under review, a scenario can be generated that indicates how the future might unfold in time. Now suppose that the analyst effectively summarizes the relative desirability of any future scenario not by a single number but, let us say, by a dozen well-chosen numbers: some reflecting costs, others reflecting benefits. Since these output performance numbers may simultaneously deal with economic, environmental, social and health concerns, these summarizing indices will, in general, be in incommensurable units. To complicate matters, suppose that stochastic elements are involved in the simulation so that, for a single policy choice being investigated, repeated simulation runs result in different sets of summary performance measures. The joint probability distribution of these performance measures as made manifest through repeated realizations of the simulation will, in general, indicate that these 12 measures are probabilistically dependent. Now assume you are a harassed decision maker sitting in front of an output display device deluged with a mountain of conflicting information. You are confused. What should you do? How can you sort out the issues and start thinking systematically about your choice problem: which policy should you adopt in the real setting? We believe this book addresses your problem and has something constructive to say about it that is not merely platitudinous.

We are convinced of one thing: The decision maker cannot simply plug these incommensurate output performance measures into an objective formula that someone has proposed *ex ante* without any reference to the real-world meaning of the various measures. Instead, our prescriptions lead us in an opposite direction: we advocate that the responsible decision maker force himself to think hard about various value tradeoffs and about his attitudes toward risky choices and we suggest ways that this process can be systematically examined by dividing his complicated choice problem into a host of simpler choice problems.

The methodology will in a step-by-step fashion force the cooperating decision maker to articulate a rank ordering of all potential outcome vectors—in the illustrative example, an ordering of all 12-tuples. This rank ordering can be thought of as constituting a set of indifference curves plus an orientation in 12-space. But this is not enough since repeated simulations of the same policy will produce, because of stochastic elements, different 12-tuples. Our problem is a familiar one by now, and the utility theory of von Neumann–Morgenstern comes to the rescue. This theory tells us that in order to satisfy certain compelling behavioral desiderata, the decision maker must assign to each 12-tuple a single number, referred to as the utility of that 12-tuple, and this assignment must be such that:

1. The more preferred the 12-tuple the higher is the associated utility.
2. These utilities must be scaled in a way that justifies the maximization of expected utilities.

In order to evaluate the relative desirability of a given policy alternative, we then must (1) generate for each simulation run a set of output 12-tuples, (2) associate to each 12-tuple a utility, and (3) average the sequence of utilities generated by repeated runs for the same policy. Finally, we choose the policy that maximizes the expected utility. Built into the assignment of utilities are all the aspects of risk aversion or proneness that we feel are necessary to include. That this can be done and how it is done is the subject matter of utility theory, reviewed in Chapter 4.

Having stated our general approach, can it actually be done in practice? We argue yes, and we substantiate our case by citing many examples illustrating how it has already been done in practice. It's not easy to do; but what are the alternatives?

Outline of the Book

For conceptual purposes, the material presented can be partitioned into four main categories: (1) the *structuring* of multiple-objective problems: Chapters 1 and 2; (2) the *theory* of quantifying preferences over multiple objectives: Chapters 3 through 6; (3) the *applications* of that theory: Chapters 7 and 8; and (4) *special topics;* Chapters 9 and 10. We only briefly elaborate here since a more detailed outline is found in Section 1.6.

Chapter 1 introduces the subject matter of concern more systematically than has been done above. Our basic problem is phrased in terms of the analysis of decision trees instead of in terms of a stochastic simulation model, but the distinction for our purposes does not matter. In Chapter 2, we acknowledge that in a given context the set of objectives and attributes are not *given* for a problem. Some suggestions are made for generating and structuring appropriate sets of objectives.

The theory, Chapters 3 through 6, present techniques for quantifying preferences over multiple objectives. In order to obtain a von Neumann–Morgenstern utility function in such cases, one must address two separate issues: value trade-offs among objectives and attitudes toward risk. Chapter 3 looks at value trade-offs under conditions of certainty. Chapter 4 restricts itself to a single objective and introduces concepts and techniques that are needed in quantifying and assessing risk attitudes. This chapter essentially reviews single-attribute (i.e., uni-dimensional) utility theory. Chapters 5 and 6 consider both of these issues simultaneously; they present multiattribute (i.e., multidimensional) utility theory. Because of its length we divided this material into two segments: two attributes (Chapter 5) and more than two attributes (Chapter 6).

Multiattribute utility is already sufficiently developed to make worthwhile contributions to some important complex problems. Chapters 7 and 8 deal with applications that present support for this claim; many problems are discussed where preferences have been quanitified using multiattribute utility. These include structuring corporate objectives, examining operational policies of fire departments, allocating school-system funds, evaluating time-sharing systems, siting nuclear power facilities, treating medical problems such as cleft lip and palate, and so forth. In each case, we describe the problem context in which the preference assessments took place. We want to communicate some of the art as well as the theory and procedures of using multiattribute utility analysis. Chapter 8 discusses the theory and procedures developed in earlier chapters in a major case study: the development of airport facilities for Mexico City.

Chapters 9 and 10 on special topics examine preferences over time and aggregation of individual preferences, respectively. Each of these important problems can be cast and naturally studied in a multiattribute framework. As shown, many of the results of Chapters 3 through 6 are relevant to the *time* and *group* problems. These two problems are often added complicating features in multiple-objective problems.

Our Intended Audience

Decision making is of such a pervasive interest that it is hard for us to exclude any group. This book is certainly relevant to analysts, policy makers, policy advisors, economists, designers, engineers, and managers, among others. Meaningful and important applications can be found in business, public policy, engineering design, resource management, public health and medicine, educational management, and so on.

This is a big book and not all of it has to be read. There are parts, especially Chapter 6 and the latter part of Chapter 9, where the mathematics will be discouragingly complicated except for the mathematical pros. It would be helpful if the nonmathematical reader were already familiar with the rudiments of decision analysis as explicated by Raiffa (1968) or by books at a similar level such as Schlaifer (1969) and Brown et al. (1974).

Depending on interests, you may wish to read only a selection of the chapters. Chapters 1 and 2 on structuring the multiple-objective problem can be read with no prerequisite. Similarly, if you are willing to accept the abstract formulation of the problem, Chapters 3 through 6 are essentially self contained. Even within this group, the reader with some mathematical background could begin with either value tradeoffs (Chapter 3), unidimensional utility theory (Chapter 4), or multiattribute utility theory (Chapters 5 and 6). For a full understanding of the applications in Chapters 7 and 8, a knowledge of the main theoretical results of the book is required. However, a reader, interested in the domain of applicability of multiattribute utility and a feeling for how it is used in a specific context, could pick them up reading only Chapters 7 and 8. Before reading Chapters 9 or 10, it is advisable in most cases to at least glance through Chapters 3 through 6. However, a reader who feels at ease with the level of mathematics in these chapters could begin with either Chapter 9 or 10 and only refer back to the basic theory chapters when references indicate it may be worthwhile.

To our knowledge, there are no other books that overlap much in content with this one. However, most of the theoretical results have appeared in professional journals. Many of these results come from researchers other than ourselves. We have attempted to reference the original contributions appropriately so that you can easily trace the development of any particular topic. A large bibliography of these works is included following Chapter 10.

Ralph L. Keeney
Howard Raiffa

Laxenburg, Austria
May 1975

CHAPTER 1

The Problem

In an uncertain world the responsible decision maker must balance judgments about uncertainties with his or her preferences for possible consequences or outcomes. It's not easy to do and, even though we all have a lot of practice, we are not very good at it. Here we suggest formal techniques that will be helpful in this decision-making process. We concentrate on formalizing the preference or value side of the problem rather than developing procedures for the assessments of uncertainties. This doesn't mean that we think modeling of the uncertainties is unimportant. However, we feel that many capable scholars have already dealt with the modeling aspects of the kind of problems we have in mind; our efforts on the *value* side of the problem are meant to complement theirs. So, let's assume that the assessments of uncertainties are given, and let's worry about how we, as decision makers, can make sense out of our conflicting values, objectives, or goals and arrive at a wise decision. As one of our associates expressed it, "the aim of the analysis is to get your head straightened out!"

We suggest—or *prescribe*—how a decision maker (perhaps *you*) should think systematically about identifying and structuring objectives, about making vexing value tradeoffs, and about balancing various risks. The following sketches of problems will set the stage.

1.1 SKETCHES OF MOTIVATING EXAMPLES

1.1.1 Electrical Power versus Air Quality*

A mayor must decide whether to approve a major new electric power generating station. There is a need for more electricity, but a new station

* This example is discussed in detail in Section 7.1. That discussion uses the theoretical concepts introduced in the intervening chapters.

1

would worsen the city's air quality, particularly in terms of air pollutants such as sulfur dioxide, particulates, and nitrogen oxides. The mayor should be concerned with the effects that his actions will have on

The health of residents (morbidity and mortality).
The economic conditions of the residents.
The psychological state of the residents.
The economy of the city and the state.
Businesses.
Local politics.

These broad categories, and others, must be clarified and made more meaningful before measurements and evaluations can be made and before a delicate balancing of the possible impacts can be systematically undertaken. Even if the consequences of each possible action of the mayor could be foreseen with certainty, which is far from the true state of affairs, he would be faced with a complex value problem.

1.1.2 Location of an Airport*

What should Secretary Bracamontes, head of the Ministry of Public Works, recommend to President Echeverria regarding the development of future airport facilities in Mexico City? Should Mexico modernize its present facilities at Texcoco or build a new airport at Zumpango, north of the city? The decision is not a static one (Texcoco or Zumpango now!) but, instead, a dynamic one that considers phased developments over a number of years. There are many uncertainties, including the possibility of technological breakthroughs (e.g., noise suppressants, new construction methods for building runways on shallow lakes or marshlands, and a breakthrough on the increased maneuverability of commercial aircraft); the possibility of changes in demand for international travel; the possibility of future safety requirements being imposed by international carriers; and the like. But even if Secretary Bracamontes had a reliable clairvoyant, his problem of making a choice is still complex. He must balance such objectives as how to:

Minimize the *costs* to the federal government.
Raise the *capacity* of airport facilities.
Improve the *safety* of the system.
Reduce *noise* levels.
Reduce *access time* to users.
Minimize *displacement* of people for expansion.

* Chapter 8 is devoted entirely to this example.

Improve *regional development* (roads, for instance).
Achieve *political* aims.

These objectives are too vague at this stage to be operational. However, in making them more specific, the analyst must be careful not to inadvertently distort the sense of the whole.

1.1.3 Treatment of Heroin Addiction

Heroin addiction has reached alarming proportions in New York City and something must be done about it. But what? The problem has been studied and restudied, yet the experts differ widely in their proposed strategies. The reason is partly because the problem is so complex that experts honestly disagree about the implications of any specific treatment modality. Technically they differ on what a reasonable model of the phenomena should include and on what reasonable rates of flow from one category to another within the model should be. Therefore, their probabilistic predictions of the future vary. However, if these experts had crystal balls and their disagreements about uncertainties disappeared, the controversy would still continue. Now it would be focused on values only instead of on both values and uncertainties. The Mayor of New York City would like to:

Reduce the size of the addict pool (this is more complicated than it sounds since there are different types of addicts and tradeoffs must be made between the sizes of these categories).
Reduce costs to the city and its residents.
Reduce crimes against property and persons.
Improve the "quality of life"—whatever that may mean—of addicts and reduce their morbidity and mortality.
Improve the quality of life of nonaddicts, make New York City a more pleasant place to live, and reverse the disastrous trends of in-and-out migration of families and businesses.
Curb organized crime.
Live up to the high ideals of civil rights and civil liberties.
Decrease the alienation of youth.
Get elected to higher political office (perhaps the presidency?).

Sure, the problem is complicated, but the Mayor must act and, at least informally, combine assessments of uncertainties with value preferences*. As already mentioned, we will deal with the value side of these types of problems.

* See Moore (1973) for a formal attempt to examine various policy options concerning heroin use in New York City.

1.1.4 Medical Diagnostics and Treatment

Doctor William Schwartz,* Chief of Medicine at Tufts Medical School, makes the rounds of the wards with his students and insists on sharing his thought processes with them: "Well, for Z we can do this or this or this, and we must worry about the implications of our actions if she has disease state A or B or C. I think the chances are 0.2 that she has A, 0.4 that . . . . If we do this and that happens, then we'll learn so and so, which will revise my probabilities of A, B, C by . . . . But if that happens we must weigh the information we get with the possibility of side effects, discomfort, and costs to Z." And on and on. Very few doctors state their thought processes with such clarity. However, all doctors must constantly combine probabilities with value judgments. Some value judgments are not easy to make. Not only are costs to the patient to be considered, but also cost to the insurance companies, payments to the doctor, and utilization of scarce resources (doctors, nurses, surgical facilities, and hospital beds, for example). Doctor Schwartz must worry about pain, suffering, anxiety, the time of the patient's incapacitation, and the possibility of death. Then, societal externalities are involved in the value problem such as contagious effects, the information gained from one patient that can be useful in the treatment of other patients, and development of resistant bacterial strains. These societal considerations often create a conflict for the doctor: what's right for his patient may not be right for society. But all of these matters must be considered, and decisions must be made. Can the value side of the problem be systematically approached? We think so, but there is no "objectively correct solution." Subjective values must be inserted, and we will *develop a framework for assessing and quantifying these subjective values and systematically including them in the decision-making process.*

1.1.5 Business Problems

Most *routine* business problems do not involve complicated value issues. Profit (or even better, the net present value of a profit stream) may be *the index* to maximize. True, there might be difficulties in clarifying what is fixed cost and what is marginal, but generally these details are simple. However, top management does not become personally involved in most routine problems with a dollar-and-cents solution. The problems that filter up to management often involve ethics, tradition, identity, aesthetics, and personal values in contrast to corporate values. The more we study the problems of top management, the more we realize that these

---

* See Schwartz, Gorry, Kassirer, and Essig (1973).

so-called uncommon problems are not so uncommon, and the slogan "Maximize profits!" has operational limitations. We will see, however, that in business contexts it is often natural to scale nonmonetary intangibles into dollar values. We will be concerned with when is it legitimate to do this and how can it be done.

Top management is well aware that many of its strategic decisions involve multiple conflicting objectives and, therefore, it is simply *not* true that "qualitatively speaking, business decisions are simple because the objective function is crystal clear."

1.2 PARADIGM OF DECISION ANALYSIS

The simple paradigm of decision analysis* that we will study can be summarized in a five-step process.

PREANALYSIS. We assume that there is a unitary decision maker who is undecided about the course of action he or she should take in a particular problem. The problem has been identified and the viable action alternatives are given.

STRUCTURAL ANALYSIS. The decision maker structures the qualitative anatomy of his problem. What choices can he make now? What choices can he defer? How can he make choices that are based on information learned along the way? What experiments can he perform? What information can he gather purposefully and what can he learn during the normal course of events without intentional intervention? These questions are put into an orderly package by a decision tree (Fig. 1.1). The decision tree has nodes that are under the control of the decision maker

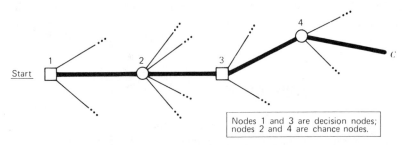

Nodes 1 and 3 are decision nodes; nodes 2 and 4 are chance nodes.

Fig. 1.1. Schematic form of a decision tree.

* See, for example, Brown, Kahr, and Peterson (1974), Howard (1968), Raiffa (1968), Schlaifer (1969), Tribus (1969), or Winkler (1972).

(i.e., the square nodes) and nodes that are not under his full control (i.e., the circled nodes). We refer to these two nodes as *decision* nodes and *chance* nodes.

UNCERTAINTY ANALYSIS. The decision maker assigns probabilities to the branches emanating from chance nodes. These assignments are made by artfully mixing various techniques and procedures based on past empirical data, on assumptions fed into and results taken from various stochastic, dynamic models, on expert testimony (duly calibrated, to take into account personal idiosyncracies and biases resulting from conflict of interest positions), and on the subjective judgments of the decision maker. The assignments should be checked for internal consistencies.

So that there is no confusion resulting from the special schematic decision tree in Fig. 1.1, we include the possibility that certain chance nodes can have a set of outcomes represented by a continuum in a singular or higher-dimensional space.

UTILITY OR VALUE ANALYSIS. The decision maker assigns utility values to consequences associated with paths through the tree. In Fig. 1.1 one possible path (from Start to point C) is shown. In an actual problem, there would be associated with this path various economic and psychological costs and benefits that affect the decision maker and others whom the decision maker considers as part of his decision problem. The cognitive impacts are conceptually captured by associating with each path of the tree a *consequence* that completely describes the implications of that path. The decision maker should then encode his preferences for these consequences in terms of cardinal utility numbers.* This measurement not only reflects the decision maker's ordinal rankings for different consequences (e.g., C' is preferred to C'' which is preferred to C'''), it also indicates his relative preferences for lotteries over these consequences. For example, in Fig. 1.2, we consider a problem of choice between act a' and a'' that is translated into a choice between lottery l' and l''. The decision maker must assign numbers to consequences (such as u_i' to C_i' and u_j'' to C_j'') in such a manner that he feels that

$$(a' \text{ is preferred to } a'') \Leftrightarrow \left(\sum_{i=1}^{m} p_i' u_i' > \sum_{j=1}^{n} p_j'' u_j'' \right).$$

In other words the assignment of utility numbers to consequences must be such that the maximization of *expected utility* becomes the appropriate criterion for the decision maker's optimal action.

OPTIMIZATION ANALYSIS. After the decision maker structures his problem, assigns probabilities, and assigns utilities, he calculates his optimal

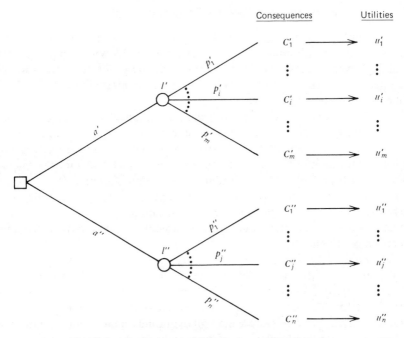

Consequences   Utilities

Fig. 1.2. A choice problem between two lotteries.

strategy—the strategy that maximizes expected utility. This strategy indicates what he should do at the start of the decision tree and what choice he should make at every decision node he can possibly reach along the way. There are various techniques an analyst can employ to obtain this strategy, but the simplest is the dynamic programming algorithm of averaging-out-and-folding-back, with which we assume the reader is already familiar.†

1.3 COMMENTS ABOUT THE PARADIGM

Is this a reasonable paradigm for the problems we stated at the outset: air-quality control, airport location, treatment modalities for heroin addiction, medical diagnostics and treatment, and strategic business problems?

---

* We assume that the reader has some familiarity with cardinal utility theory. However, in Chapter 4, we review aspects of the theory that will be needed.
† See, for example, Raiffa (1968), p. 21–27 and 71–74.

1.3.1   Unitary versus Group Decision Making

Throughout most of this book we assume that there is a unitary decision maker. Shouldn't we be more concerned with group decision making? Aren't most public decisions and many business decisions an intricate composite of different choices made by many individuals? Let's take an example.

New York City is concerned with the poor quality of air being breathed by its residents. Should the city government impose more stringent limits on the sulfur content of fuels burned in the city for space heating and power generation? Many people are involved in this problem: the mayor, the city council, the Environmental Protection Agency, lobbyists for power companies, local politicians, and the citizens, for example. Any *postdescription* purporting to explain what happened in the past certainly must involve many individuals. Descriptively it is a group, interactive decision problem.

But wait!

We are not trying to *describe* what has been done but *prescribe* what should be done.* Let's first clarify for whom we are prescribing. Who is the client for our proposed analysis? Suppose it is an agency head. He alone surely does not dictate what will eventually happen but he might be asked to make a proposal to the mayor, for instance. Suppose he's confused about whether he *should* offer proposal A or B or C. The agency head has a decision problem, doesn't he? *He* might want to analyze systematically what *he* should do. He must consider what others might do and perhaps he might want to view the actions of the mayor and the city council as part of the uncertainties confronting him. One individual's decisions may be another individual's uncertainties.

We emphasize that decisions (as we use the term) do not have to be grandiose end determinations. There are more modest decisions: should an individual vote for passage of a bill, propose an amendment, or apply political pressure? If an individual has choices to make, we consider him to be the decision maker. Thus, there are many decision problems in the public sector where the decision maker can be viewed as a well-specified, identifiable, unitary entity. Now some of these decision makers might want to analyze their particular problem systematically. We want to effectively adapt the previously mentioned decision paradigm to help this decision maker.

---

* Clearly there is much overlap of interest between the prescriptive and descriptive viewpoints. Over the past 25 years, the contributions of many people concerned with descriptive aspects of decision making has had a significant impact on prescriptive decision analysis. Four excellent reviews of this work are Edwards (1954, 1961), Slovic and Lichtenstein (1971), and Fischer and Edwards (1973).

1.3.2   Personal Conviction, Advocacy, and Reconciliation

We approach problems as if we were an undecided decision maker who has to decide which course of action he should take. He knows that some of his snap judgments may later be wrong; he might change his mind after deeper reflection. He also recognizes that when a problem is decomposed into parts, he might initially give answers to a series of questions that turn out to be internally inconsistent. When this occurs we assume that the decision maker will want to scrutinize his answers carefully and perhaps change some of his earlier responses so that the total pattern of modified responses is consistent and seems reasonable to him. Only if he can structure his preliminary responses in a coherent fashion will we be able to use deductive analysis to carry him to the next step. The spirit is one of Socratic discovery—of *unfolding* what you really believe, of *convincing* yourself, and of *deciding*.

We have found, in many of our consulting contacts, that decision makers undertake formal decision analyses with their minds already made up. They view the formal analysis as a kind of window dressing. We are not against this; instead, we emphasize the class of problem situations where the unitary decision maker has not as yet made up his mind. However, there is often a legitimate purpose for doing careful analyses even if the decision maker has already decided what to do. First, there is the problem of *psychological* comfort: he might want the security of having a formal analysis to corroborate his unaided intuition. Second, he might want to use the formal analysis to help the *communication* process. Third, there is the question of *advocacy*: he might have to justify his conclusions to others or to convince others of the reasonableness of his proposed action. In addition, there is always the possibility that these postdecision analyses will uncover new insights that result in a different alternative—one that is perceived as better than the original.

An analysis done solely to convince yourself might be quite different from an analysis done for advocacy purposes. A personal analysis might very well incorporate very sensitive information, such as assessments of potential future actions of political associates, an economic value placed on the life of a human being, and value tradeoffs between the benefits to various identifiable groups. On the other hand, an advocacy document must often be intentionally vague on such issues. When an analysis is put on public display you can hardly expect your adversaries to give up without a fight. They will carefully scrutinize the reasoning and seek out the soft spots. Unfortunately, this means that it is often impolitic to base a decision on a formal analysis that includes subjective feelings if the analysis will be disclosed to a critical public audience. This is not the place for us to request moral obligation from government officials or ask that they be open and honest and share their real analyses with other government officials, agencies, and concerned citizens. Again, we are concerned primarily with helping confused decision makers make up their minds.

There is another reason why you might do a formal analysis of a decision problem even though your mind is already made up. Although our proposal might be considered to be a variation of an advocacy role, we think of it as a *reconciliation* process. For example, suppose a mayor must make a decision and two agencies strongly recommend different alternatives. The rhetoric is sharp and divisive, the protagonists are eloquent and able, and the situation is so complex that there is apparent merit on each side. How can the decision maker weigh the arguments and make a responsible decision?

A formal analysis that attempts to break down the overall problem into component parts can often help this reconciliation process. Perhaps the parties can decide what they agree about and what they disagree about. Perhaps they can further break down areas of disagreement in a manner that would highlight fundamental sources of differences of opinion. Would more information help sort out the merits of the two positions? Could they agree on additional objective (or subjective) evidence that could help them decide? Or is it not a matter of assessing uncertainties but rather of differing value judgments? Perhaps here is where the mayor could exert his own overriding value structure.

We don't want to appear excessively naive by implying that formal analysis is the key to the reconciliation process. We are well aware that, in some circumstances, the more confusion that abounds the easier it is to establish a compromise. Still, in principle, we think that familiarization can sometimes facilitate reconciliation. Chapter 8 discusses an example of such an undertaking in which both of us were involved as consultants. We were only partially successful.

1.3.3 Preanalysis and the Iterative Nature of an Analysis

We assume that the decision maker's problem has been identified and viable action alternatives are prespecified. In practice this does not mean that the preliminaries are not crucially important. By creative insight, not only must we recognize that a problem exists, we must be intuitive about what types of problems are worth attempting to analyze.

Complex problems, especially in societal contexts, tend to have spill-over effects in all directions. Thus, bounding a problem is critically important. We know the dangers of suboptimization, but if problems are not bounded in some way, they remain hopelessly intractable. The process of identifying and bounding a problem area is intimately connected with the generation of alternative decision choices to be considered. When we assume that the alternative decision strategies are prespecified, we seriously misrepresent the art of formal analysis. In practice, the process is iterative. The analyst might bound his problem one way only to find that he's in an impossible morass; so he backs up and redefines his problem area by bounding it differently and generating new restricted alternatives. Or, in the course of the analysis, he sees that his conclusions are sensitive to a facet of the problem that has not been delicately enough modeled. If this happens, he may redefine the problem. We believe that a careful analysis of the problem often triggers a line of thought that generates action alternatives that might have been overlooked. Yes, we do recognize the iterative nature of the overall process of analysis but for our purposes, with all due apologies, we assume that the preanalysis stage has been completed.

We think that even experienced analysts often fail to sufficiently exploit the usage of *adaptive* and *process-oriented* action alternatives. Not only is it important for the analyst to know what must be done now and what he can defer to the future, it is also critically important that he recognize the possibility that future actions could depend on information learned along the way. A dynamic strategy for action should be adaptive and exploit the gradual, time-dependent unfolding of uncertainties. The decision-tree framework is especially suitable for thinking about such alternatives. However, it does not help us with process alternatives. Let us explain.

"You analysts want to decide on everything," a nameless voice exhorts. "Why decide at all? Let the contending factors address the issues in an open, democratic process." That advice is often right. Establishing a *process* may be the creative new alternative to which we alluded. Still, someone might have to decide whether decision *strategy* A or B or decision *process* C or D should be adopted. And that is a decision problem. Furthermore, if process C is selected, among the many decision makers who will influence the actual outcome there may be a confused, analytically minded person who wants to straighten out his mind with our framework.

We do not deny that it is often desirable to institute an advocacy process for resolving complex issues in the public domain. However, we do not think that this assertion necessarily diminishes the usefulness of the decision analytic framework. It may, of course, influence the nature of the problems to be analyzed or the identity of the decision maker who employs these tools. Finally, on the subject of process, we think that the decision analytic framework can, in some cases, structure the process of debate and action.

1.3.4 Subjective Values and Formal Analyses*

It is almost a categorical truism that decision problems in the public domain are very complex. They almost universally involve multiple conflicting objectives, nebulous types of nonrepeatable uncertainties, costs and benefits accruing to various individuals, businesses, groups, and other organizations—some of these being nonidentifiable at the time of the decision—and effects that linger over time and reverberate throughout the whole societal superstructure. It would be nice if we could feed this whole mess into a giant computer and program the superintellect to generate an "objectively correct" response. It just can't be done! You can go only so far without introducing subjective attitudes—no matter how hard you squeeze the available objective data, it won't come close to providing courses of action for complex problems. Indeed, a purely "objective" analysis might fall so far short of providing guidelines for decision making that the output of the analysis may not pass the threshold of relevancy. We believe that complex social problems—and, for that matter, complex *business* problems—demand the consideration of subjective values and tradeoffs. It is not whether subjective elements should be considered, but whether they should be articulated and incorporated into a formal, systematic analysis. The choice is between *formal analysis* and *informal synthesis* and this metadilemma does not have an obvious solution.

We have often heard that formal analysis is inappropriate for complex problems, since these problems require subjective evaluations. They do, but formal decision analysis is ready to receive such subjective evaluations as inputs for the decision algorithm. The trouble with formal analysis is *not* that subjective evaluations cannot be accommodated into the framework but that there is a demand for *too many* subjective inputs; and although decision makers argue for inclusion of subjective evaluations, they are most reluctant to write these evaluations down.

Many people feel that we should be wary of analysts that try to quantify the unquantifiable. Let us remember, however, that it is also wrong for us not to learn how to quantify the quantifiable. The question is: *What is quantifiable?* An art expert might be hard pressed to give an objective formula for ranking the quality of paintings; nevertheless, he might be able to rank order these paintings saying, in effect, that given a choice between two paintings he would prefer one over the other. And, where we have rank orders, numbers can't be far behind. Our artist might even be willing to put a price tag on each painting, thereby quantifying one

* Subsections 1.3.4 and 1.3.5 liberally adapt material from Keeney and Raiffa (1972).

aspect of his subjective judgment. This sort of quantification is not done by means of an objective formula but by subjective introspection. Is it legitimate to work with such numbers? We do it all the time. As analysts we must learn how to incorporate such soft, squishy considerations as aesthetics, psychic factors, and just plain fun into our analyses. If we don't, the hard will drive out the soft and efficiency—very narrowly interpreted— will prevail.

However, the quantification of these subjective factors cannot be done frivolously. They should be generated by making the best use of the accumulated experience and expertise available. And on problems of public concern, such as power plant siting, this quantification should undergo the scrutiny of independent "experts" as well as the concerned public.

1.3.5 Strategic versus Repetitive Decisions

Some individuals feel that formal analysis is appropriate for repetitive operational decisions, for example, "Where should we send the sanitation trucks today?" "What procedures should be used for operating airport runways in order to minimize travel delays?" "What should we charge for breakfast cereal WOW?" But these same individuals think analysis is impossible for such one-of-a-kind, strategic decisions as "Should we dispense methadone to heroin addicts?" "Should we spend 200 million dollars for research on nuclear breeder reactors?" "Should the Mexican government build a new airport miles from Mexico City or modernize the old?" "Should Corporation X internationalize its marketing operations?" No one claims it is easy to analyze complicated strategic problems, but we believe that many of these strategic questions are amenable to systematic attack.

1.3.6 Implementation, Postanalysis, and Other Considerations

Other than the very few brief remarks we are about to make in this paragraph, we will say nothing about another critical aspect of an integrated analysis: the *implementation* phase. By this we mean all those indispensable activities required to execute the chosen strategy resulting from a given analysis. This includes the communication of instructions, the delineating of responsibilities, the establishment of incentives and rewards, the punishment of willful deviations, the monitoring of the system, the systematic collection of data, the creation or adaption of a management information system, the dissemination of reports, the further refinement of the model, identification of new key variables, and creation of new alternatives that were overlooked. In practice, it is artificial to completely separate the identification and analysis of a problem from its implementation. Clearly what's needed once again, is iteration. If a suggested solution cannot be implemented realistically, the analysis must be redone with some attention paid to constraints imposed by the implementation phase.

How do good analyses get done? How can you choose good analysts? Should you use outside consultants or an inside group? Where in the organization hierarchy should an analytical capability be created? How does the introduction of an analytical team shake up an existing bureaucracy? Our contribution to this is silence—except to say that the decision whether or not to do formal analysis cannot be divorced from organizational structure, personal incentives of the people involved, and quality of the analysts.

We hope that our nonexistent treatment of these crucial considerations of the analytical process does not belittle their importance. Indeed we won't be insulted if you claim that we have only scrutinized a part of the entire problem, because we are doing this with some awareness.

1.4   COMPLEX VALUE PROBLEMS

1.4.1   Simple versus Complex Value Problems

Consider a decision maker who has already decided on the identification and bounding of his problem and has generated the set of alternative actions he wishes to evaluate. Let's assume that he has structured his problem in the form of a decision tree and assigned probabilities to all the branches of chance nodes. We enter where he is encoding his preferences for consequences. Let's turn back to Fig. 1.1 and look at one path through the decision tree and consider consequence C, depicted at the terminus of the path. In some problems it is possible to objectively assign a single number to each consequence C that adequately describes the full implications of that path. For example, in a business problem the single numerical value might be a monetary one that fully reflects all financial considerations with no other considerations to worry about. In a medical context, a single summary number might be a cure rate for a given disease. In such problems consequences are adequately described in terms of an objective, single, numerically scaled attribute. Suppose that the value associated with consequence C' is $X(C') = x'$ and with C'' is $X(C'') = x''$. Here x' and x'' are real numbers. Also assume that C' is preferred to C'' when and only when $x' > x''$. (This last assumption is made for convenience and can be trivially generalized.) Problems of this kind will be called *simple value* problems in contrast to *complex value* problems. In complex value problems, consequences at the ends of the tree *cannot* be adequately described objectively by a single attribute (e.g., money). Our main concern is with complex value problems.

Simple value problems would be conceptually easy to solve if there were no uncertainties involved, if there were no chance moves in the tree. This would then be a straightforward maximization problem with a well-specified payoff function. There is another way of saying this. Imagine a decision problem abstracted in the form of a decision tree. If a decision maker had the services of a clairvoyant, or as a colleague of ours, John Lintner, puts it, "if he had a phone line to the Lord," would his problem be conceptually simple? It would if every consequence were already described in terms of a single attribute. He would just choose that strategy leading to the highest x payoff.

In Fig. 1.3 we schematically show a section of a decision tree with one path that ends in consequence C_i'. Now let's suppose that C_i' can be adequately described in objective terms only by means of n numbers: x_{i1}', $x_{i2}', \ldots, x_{in}'$. We can think of the number x_{ij}' as the performance measure of consequence C_i' on the jth attribute scale. When the decision maker contemplates taking action a' in Fig. 1.3, he is led to consider the lottery l' that, with probability p_i', results in a consequence described by an n-tuple $\mathbf{x}_i' \equiv (x_{i1}', \ldots, x_{in}')$, where the i subscript ranges over the number of branches of the chance node. More technically, lottery l' can be interpreted as a discrete probability distribution with outcomes in an n-dimensional space. The decision maker must clarify in his own mind which one of these n-dimensional distributions he would rather choose. This is *no easy task*. How can he think systematically about this?

If the decision maker had a clairvoyant his problem would not become trivially simple. It would be easier to be sure, since there would be no uncertainties, but he would still be faced with a complex value problem: given possible ending consequences $C_1, C_2, \ldots, C_q$ where C_i is described in terms of $\mathbf{x}_i = (x_{i1}, \ldots, x_{in})$, which consequence should he prefer? This choice problem involves complex value tradeoffs.

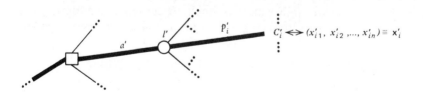

Fig. 1.3. Section of a tree resulting in a complex consequence.

Let's return to the uncertainty case as depicted in Fig. 1.3. Formally the problem can be answered by the introduction of a utility function u that would associate to each n-tuple a single real number. Let $u(x'_{i1}, \ldots, x'_{in})$ be denoted by u'_i. In this case the relative desirability of lottery l' would be given by $\sum_i p'_i u'_i$, the expected utility of lottery l'. In terms of expected utilities we can now work backwards through the tree in order to pick out the optimal strategy. Pretty easy. The rub is, of course, it isn't so easy to find an appropriate utility function u. Some would say it's impossible to do this in a responsible manner. Our task is to indicate techniques that you might employ in discovering an appropriate u function. We will discuss some basic principles for decomposing the overall complex value problem into more manageable and "thinkable" component parts. We feel that some of these principles are so basic that they might profitably be employed by some analysts to partially structure their value problem even though they might be reluctant to completely determine an overall utility function. How far you should formalize your value problem depends on many factors: it's importance, the need to convince others, your training, and the availability of techniques that can be employed in the thought process.

1.4.2 Is Utility Analysis Necessary?

Those who have worked on problems in decision analysis can readily testify that it's hard enough to get responsible utility functions for a single, numerically scaled attribute (e.g., assets) and, furthermore, such techniques are rarely used in practice. Should anybody take seriously, then, an endeavor that tries to obtain a responsible utility function for higher-dimensional space? If you haven't completely succeeded in one-dimensional space why go higher? Never mind that there are many mathematical theorems to prove and that it's a fertile field of new theoretical development. Can the theory to be developed have any practical value? We think so—here's why.

First consider the unidimensional case. Suppose that the decision maker must decide between actions A and B which result in the probabilistic, monetary payoff distributions shown in Fig. 1.4. It's not immediately clear which distribution should be chosen, and a formal analysis could be made by introducing a utility function u and then comparing

$$\bar{u}_A = \int u(x) f_A(x)\, dx \qquad \text{and} \qquad \bar{u}_B = \int u(x) f_B(x)\, dx.$$

In practice, this bit of formality is usually sidestepped. Instead, the decision maker looks at the distributions f_A and f_B which, in the uni-

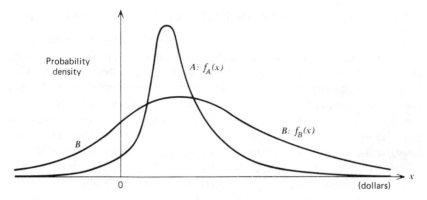

Fig. 1.4. Comparison of two distributions of payoffs.

dimensional case as contrasted to the multidimensional case, can be visually interpreted. He then subjectively reacts to the whole distribution and makes a choice unaided by formal utility analysis. We would prefer to introduce the formality of a utility function if we were responsible for the decision, because we have trained ourselves to think hard about what we want our utility function to be, and thus we would feel more comfortable with the derived results than with an intuitive, unaided choice. But experience has also shown us that our attitude is not commonly shared, even among business executives who have been adequately exposed to the concepts of utility analysis. In the unidimensional case they can circumvent the formal approach by acting intuitively to easily comprehended alternatives.

Now let's contrast the above unidimensional case with a choice involving many attributes. Actions A and B lead to complicated distributions not over a single x but over n-tuples $(x_1, \ldots, x_n)$. No longer is it possible to draw the distributions in a simple manner and the mind boggles at the complexity. No wonder that in practice decision makers introduce pragmatic simplifications, such as "Let's just look at the most important attribute and forget the others," or, Let's not worry about uncertainties but take some value of central tendency for each attribute and set up aspiration levels on each of these attributes." Decisions are made on the basis of ad hoc, heuristic simplifications. We believe that many, though not necessarily all, of these decision makers would be better served if they systematically probed their value structure and created for themselves a derived utility function. How this can be done, will be the subject matter of this book.

1.4.3 The Use of Hypothetical Questions in Assessments

We ask simple hypothetical questions involving easy-to-comprehend probability distributions to obtain the preferences of the decision maker. These questions focus on the basic preferential attitudes of the decision maker. The answers to these hypothetical questions are consistently put together to provide the information necessary to arrive at a specific utility function. Our feeling is that it is easier for the decision maker to understand his own preferences and articulate them in a form useful for constructing his utility function by answering questions in these simple contexts rather than in complex situations. In checking the consistency of any utility function, we suggest a comparison of the implications of the utility function with the decision maker's responses to "more realistic" probability distributions as a first step toward ascertaining whether the use of hypothetical questions contributed to a systematic error in the utility function.

Critics of decision analysis often attack the use of hypothetical questions in the assessment procedure. However, for any problem, every question concerning preferences addressed to the decision maker—other than "Which of your real options do you prefer?"—is hypothetical by definition. It appears that if we want any structured analysis of the problem, hypothetical questions will necessarily have to be asked concerning parameters in any model—probabilities of various outcomes, preferences, and the like. Thus, if analysis is deemed worthwhile, an important point is the degree of hypothetical questioning and not whether any hypothetical questions should be used.*

Of course, the particular phraseology of the hypothetical questions should be in a vernacular that's comfortable to the decision maker. [See, e.g., Grayson (1960).] The trick is to be as realistic as possible but still to pose hypothetical questions that are easily understood and precise. Compromises, of course, have to be made and an analyst often has to go to artful extremes when his respondent has a low threshold for hypothesizing. For some problems we might begin with more complex, more realistic questions involving many of the critical issues of the problem and work toward simpler questions focusing on single critical issues. In the

---

* It has been suggested that by observing how a decision maker *does* make decisions, his preference structure can be derived. If these "revealed preferences" are to be used for normative purposes we must assume the decision maker has made "optimal" decisions in the past. Another assumption is that we can separate the decision maker's perceptions (i.e., probabilities) in previous problems from his preferences (utilities). It seems to us that these two assumptions lead one to conclude that the "revealed preferences" alone simply do not provide enough information to specify a decision maker's preference structure, especially when interdependent uncertainties and multiple objectives are involved.

process, it may be possible to sensitize the decision maker to these individual issues and increase his capacity for thinking hard about the "hypothetical" questions involving them. This might clarify his thinking.

1.5 CLASSES OF EXAMPLES AND METHODOLOGICAL NIGHTMARES

We have a twofold purpose in this section. First we cite a few broad categories of methodological problems that fall in our domain of concern. In contrast to the motivating examples we have already mentioned (e.g., air pollution, power generation, heroin addiction, and airport location), we now look at categories of problems that are organized by methodological type—problems such as cost-benefit and cost-effectiveness analysis, analyses involving time streams of payoffs (e.g., discounting), and analyses of such awesome consequences as death. Second, we mention briefly several issues that we feel are crucially important and relevant to our domain of discourse but that we do not do justice to in this book. We refer to these as methodological nightmares.

Let us consider an abstraction of a real problem that results in a decision tree where each consequence C is described in terms of n attributes $X_1, \ldots, X_n$.

1.5.1 Private Decisions or Individual Cost-Benefit Analyses

Mr. Smith is the decision maker and his actions will affect only himself. When he totes up the ledger resulting from any action he might take, he might be concerned with various costs and obligations that will accrue to him (assume for the time being that these costs and obligations are immediate) and with various benefits in terms of money, prestige, power, sense of community responsibility, and so on. In an example of this type we might have the following identifications:

$X_1 \equiv$ Out-of-pocket costs to Smith.
$X_2 \equiv$ Measurement of time commitment.
$X_3 \equiv$ Monetary rewards.
$X_4 \equiv$ Combined index of psychological satisfaction (other than financial).

Now there are many questions that will immediately come to mind that we do not want to address until Chapter 2. How should one generate these objectives? What about overlaps? What about measurement problems (e.g., with X_4)? What about completeness? What about uniqueness of the set of attributes? What could be done with the evaluations if they were made? And so on.

You might want to anticipate some of the discussions in Chapter 2 by thinking of various categories of individual choice problems. What would be a reasonable set of attributes to consider in the choice of (1) a job, (2) a house, (3) a car, (4) a spouse, (5) a birth-control technique (if any), (6) a college [see Hammond (1965)], (7) a summer vacation?

1.5.2 The Case of the Altruistic Dictator—A Social Welfare Problem

In contrast to the preceding example, let's imagine that Ms. Tate must decide what she, as an agency head, should do. She is concerned with the way in which her actions will affect the costs and benefits to diverse individuals, business firms, and other organizations. She is also not completely altruistic because she must worry about the implications to her agency and to herself in particular. Her decision might be complicated by the fact that she might not know how a segment of the public really feels about a given societal modification. True, she (or others) can ask them (or a sample of them) but it's not always easy to do.

Jan Acton (1970) conducted a door-to-door sample survey in which he asked heads of households what they would be *willing to pay* for an emergency coronary care unit in their community. Well, this presented many problems. Most people just weren't willing to take time to try to understand what the issues were. Even if they did, it's not clear they knew how to think in a reasonable manner about such a complex issue. But even if they took the time, and could think straight about their own interests, what about *honesty*? After all, why is this guy asking me this question?

Then there is also the problem of present versus future tastes. Ms. Tate might be firmly convinced that her subjects really don't know what's good for themselves. They don't know that if they only listened long enough to classical music they'd eventually like it. Sure those misguided dupes voted against the bond issue for improved schools, but if they *only knew* what a good school system is really like, then they would have voted for the bond issue. The populace is not interested in pollution now since they are more interested in the wherewithal for daily survival, but in time things will improve and then they will be concerned with air quality.

The methodological issues these points raise are devilish to work with. Still, decisions must be made.

1.5.3 Cost-Effectiveness and Cost-Benefit Analyses

Consider a given decision problem where one possible consequence resulting from a given action (or strategy) can be adequately described in terms of a *cost C*, and *r benefit* measures $B_1, B_2, \ldots, B_r$. In this case it will be easier to think of the description in the form $(c, b_1, \ldots, b_r)$ where a lower-case letter designates a specific amount of the respective measure rather than in the less suggestive but more neutral notation $(x_1, \ldots, x_{r+1})$. It is important to understand that these benefit measures may be in different units of measurements so that you cannot simply add them up. For example, B_3 may measure man-hours of work saved and B_7 may measure the architectural quality of a given building.

Leaving aside uncertainty for a moment, we can imagine that any agency head has a specified amount c^* that he may spend on projects. His objective is to accept all projects that in totality, do not exceed his cost constraint c^* and, subject to that, will yield a desirable portfolio of joint benefits. This problem is difficult to make more precise since the various benefits are in incommensurable units and not much can be done with coalescing these separate entities.

In *cost-effectiveness* analysis no attempt is made to combine the various benefit measures into a single, composite benefit measure. In a cost-effectiveness analysis, one might investigate the following problem: "Characterize various sets of projects that yield at least $b_1^*, b_2^*, \ldots, b_r^*$ on the respective benefit measures." Here the so-called *aspiration levels* $b_1^*, \ldots, b_r^*$ are usually preassigned. Are there feasible sets of projects that will meet these combined aspirations? If not, change some of the b_i^*'s. If yes, investigate whether you can selectively raise some of the aspiration levels. Of course, this leaves out of the formal analysis two important relevant considerations:

1. How should the aspiration levels be selected in the first place? What should the tradeoffs be among them?
2. How can all this be generalized to bring in the everpresent problem of uncertainties?

In *cost-benefit* analysis, we condense the benefits $B_1, \ldots, B_r$ into a single composite measure, for example, B_0. One usual technique is to introduce a set of conversion factors $w_1, w_2, \ldots, w_r$ and then define

$$b_0 \equiv w_1 b_1 + \cdots + w_i b_i + \cdots + w_r b_r.$$

Of course the units of measurement of the w_i's are such that the individual summands $w_1 b_1, w_2 b_2, \ldots, w_r b_r$ are all in commensurable units. The trick, in practice, is to find suitable conversion factors. Often this is done by an objective market mechanism or by subjectively inputing dollar prices of monetary worth to various measures (e.g., \$500 to keep each child off the street during the summer months).

If we use a cost-benefit analysis, and if we disregard uncertainties for a moment, then the kth project can be evaluated by the pair $[c^{(k)}, b_0^{(k)}]$ where $c^{(k)}$ and $b_0^{(k)}$ represent the cost and the composite benefit measures.

Imagine having a list of possible projects with cost and composite benefit measures for each. Now *if* the problem is "Select a subset of projects to maximize the sum of benefits subject to the constraint that the total cost does not exceed a preassigned c^*," then the analysis calls for the ranking of the projects according to benefit-cost ratios R_k [i.e., $b_0^{(k)}/c^{(k)}$ for the kth project] and accepting projects in order until the cutoff c^* is reached. Let's ignore the problem of indivisibilities, what to do with a fractional project.

It is much easier to arrive at definitive answers using cost-benefit analyses than cost-effectiveness analyses. Therefore, it is not surprising that many studies use this route. Be careful to observe the legitimacy and the reasonableness of the transformations that condense $b_1, \ldots, b_r$ into b_0 and then condense c and b_0 into R. All too often, in practice, important benefits are not included in the listing because it is not clear how a market mechanism can be conjured up to "price out" this particular benefit. We're thinking here of such benefits as aesthetics, psychological well-being, and security, among others.

We think that there are several difficulties with both cost-effectiveness and cost-benefit studies. Both suffer from an inability to cope with uncertainties in an operationally reasonable or theoretically sound manner. That's not to say that ingenious efforts have not been made. But, by and large we believe the utility approach is a more systematic way of handling these uncertainties. Admittedly we pay the price of increased complexity. Also, as we emphasize in Section 3.8, it is *not always appropriate* to condense an r-tuple of benefits $(b_1, \ldots, b_r)$ by means of a simple linear weighting rule

$$w_1 b_1 + \cdots + w_i b_i + \cdots + w_r b_r,$$

or even by a generalized-linear rule

$$w_1 g_1(b_1) + \cdots + w_i g_i(b_i) + \cdots + w_r g_r(b_r)$$

using suitably chosen nonlinear functions (transformations) $g_1, \ldots, g_r$. The legitimacy of these procedures will be systematically analyzed throughout this book.

1.5.4 Temporal Considerations: Present versus Future

Our society is often accused of selling its future generations short. In an attempt to ameliorate our immediate woes we often exacerbate our future problems. Analysts must constantly make tradeoffs between what is right for the present generation and what is right for future generations. Some think that we're worse off today than we were in the past and that this trend is likely to continue. Others feel that future generations will be better off than we are today and that it's reasonable to borrow from the future to improve the present. What obligations do we have to future generations? Should the future be given more weight just because there will be more people in the future than in the present? It seems that as our time perspective unfolds, our spatial concerns grow too: today and tomorrow, it's our family; in the decades ahead, it's our country; in the centuries ahead, it's the world's population; and in the millenia, it's the planet Earth.

On a more mundane level, government agencies are concerned with finding an appropriate rate of discount. Should we do research on the development of a new nuclear breeder reactor? A lot depends on whether we use a 5, 10, or 15% rate of discount. Or is any discount rate appropriate? Let's look at what these problems involve.

Consider a decision problem where one possible consequence can be (just adequately) described in terms of a *stream* of costs $c_1, c_2, \ldots, c_t, \ldots$, one for each time period t, and of r different streams of benefits:

$$\text{Benefit stream of type 1:} \quad b_{11}, b_{12}, \ldots, b_{1t}, \ldots$$

$$\cdot$$
$$\cdot$$
$$\cdot$$

$$\text{Benefit stream of type } i: \quad b_{i1}, b_{i2}, \ldots, b_{it}, \ldots$$

$$\cdot$$
$$\cdot$$
$$\cdot$$

$$\text{Benefit stream of type } r: \quad b_{r1}, b_{r2}, \ldots, b_{rt}, \ldots.$$

We are not complicating things here needlessly. This is the prototypical problem found in most cost-effectiveness and cost-benefit analyses of social problems.

In order to make the mass of numbers

$$\begin{bmatrix} c_1, & c_2, & \ldots, & c_t, & \ldots \\ b_{11}, & b_{12}, & \ldots, & b_{1t}, & \ldots \\ \cdot & \cdot & \cdot & \cdot & \\ \cdot & \cdot & \cdot & \cdot & \\ \cdot & \cdot & \cdot & \cdot & \\ b_{r1}, & b_{r2}, & \ldots, & b_{rt}, & \ldots \end{bmatrix}$$

associated with any consequence more manageable, and therefore more "thinkable," various reduction procedures are employed. For example, in cost-benefit analyses it is customary, as indicated previously, to combine benefits of various types into a composite benefit. In this more complicated example, one would then proceed this way *for each period.* Thus we can let $B_{.1}^0$ be the combined benefit of the column of benefits in the first period, $B_{.2}^0$ for the second period, and so on.* This reduction leads to a simpler summary of the consequence, that is,

$$\begin{bmatrix} c_1, & c_2, & \ldots, & c_t, & \ldots \\ b_{.1}^0, & b_{.2}^0, & \ldots, & b_{.t}^0, & \ldots \end{bmatrix}.$$

In this display we merely have time streams of costs and composite benefits. The usual procedure at this point is to coalesce each of the time streams into a *present value.* Since future costs are less painful than present costs (e.g., we could put money in the bank today and get back more in the future), discounting is usually employed and the present value of the cost-stream is

$$\sum_t \frac{c_t}{(1+\lambda)^t}$$

where λ is the effective period-to-period interest rate. Many government agencies use a λ value of .10 and argue that it has something to do with the time value of capital funds in the private sector. In a similar manner we can also discount the composite-benefit stream.

Another alternative would be for each project to collapse, for each i, the benefit stream of type i: $B_{i1}, \ldots, B_{it}, \ldots$, to get a present value $B_{i.}^0$ of the ith stream. One would then compare the present value of the cost stream with the r values $(b_{1.}^0, \ldots, b_{i.}^0, \ldots, b_{r.}^0)$. And this reduced form now presents us with a problem that is discussed in Section 1.5.3.

Are these reduction procedures reasonable? Are there alternatives? If discounting is used how should we think of a reasonable discount level to use? Should the discount factors be constant from period to period? What about uncertainties? Should we discount expected values? Is it reasonable to raise the discount rate to account for uncertainties? Should we discount streams of physical quantities (as is commonly done with money values) or should we first transform these physical measurements into psychological values or utilities before the discounting takes place?

We are not going to answer all of these questions because many

---

* In the notation $B_{.t}^0$ think of the zero as an aggregating or collapsing indicator and the subscript as indicating that in this case the collapsing is done over types of benefits for time period t.

answers will be the "It depends..." type, but we will provide a conceptual framework that can be applied to value problems of temporal tradeoffs.

1.5.5 The Value of a Life

There are a number of problems, in surprisingly different contexts, where descriptions of consequences may involve dire happenings, like human death and suffering. It's not very comfortable thinking about such problems, and therefore we often act in such matters without sufficient reflection. Who likes to play God? If we all abdicate our responsibilities to think hard about such matters as "the value of a life" and allow decisions to be made by chance, we may inadvertently contribute to a lot of human anguish.

The problems we cited at the beginning of this chapter (e.g., electrical power generation versus pollution, location of an airport, treatment of heroin addiction, medical diagnostics) all involve, in one way or another, considerations that involve life-and-death matters. There are other classes of problems, more complicated from an ethical point of view, that we have decided to ignore: abortion, population control, euthanasia, and genetic engineering, for example. Not that these problems cannot be thought about in the framework we will develop, but we haven't sorted out our thoughts on these topics clearly enough to subject them to the perusal of an audience in today's highly, emotionally charged arena.

Let's simplify our discussion a bit and consider the case where a decision maker must choose among several life-saving programs. For a cost of x dollars he can achieve a certain probability distribution of saved lives. In a public setting it's important to think of alternative uses of funds. If we save lives by spending more money to keep people alive on kidney machines, are the alternatives "more milk for the malnourished," "better dental care for the needy," or "more money for military research?"

We have a cherished symbolism about the "sanctity of a single life." But perhaps our morality has gone astray when it comes to numbers. Emotionally we get choked up about a little girl getting killed—especially if we can see her picture—but we do not feel emotionally touched by thousands of people being wiped out by a tidal wave or an earthquake. Somehow we must learn that our grief should rise monotonically with the magnitude of a catastrophe. Numbers are important.

Charles Fried (1970) pointed out that as a society, we are romantic sentimentalists. We're willing to spend a lot more money on rescue than on prevention—more to save trapped miners and marooned astronauts than to save many more statistical anonymous lives. If we conjure up a face, we can empathize with the victim.

If a public official acts to save lives, he gets more kudos if he can point to 10 specific identifiable persons who have been saved than if he can prove conclusively that 1000 lives have been saved but can't identify who these people are.

The problem of identifiability and partial identifiability comes up all the time in circumstances less dramatic than in life-or-death matters. In counting up the benefits of Program A it's really helpful to know that John Smith and Mary Doe have been helped. If Program B benefits many more people than Program A, but if these people can't be brought together or identified easily, then, descriptively speaking, Program A will beat out Program B in a competition for survival. As a society we must learn how to respect such numbers more.

1.5.6 Group Decisions

In many situations, it is not an individual but, instead, a group of individuals who collectively have the responsibility for making a choice among alternatives. Such a characterization is referred to as a group decision problem. With each group decision, there is the crucial metadecision of selecting a process-oriented strategy by which the group decision is to be made. A general strategy for this may be first to obtain each individual's preferences for the alternatives, and then to combine these in some reasonable manner to achieve the group's preferences. With this framework, the essence of the group metadecision is how to integrate the individual's preferences.

It should be clear by now that we feel that often the methodology and procedures discussed in this book would be helpful to the separate individuals in specifying their preferences, whether ordinal or cardinal, for the alternatives. We also believe that, in some cases, the procedures of multiattribute preference theory discussed here might be useful in providing a process by which group decision can be responsibly made. Thus, the implications of the concepts and methodology for use in group decision processes and suggestions for implementation are included in the book.

1.6 ORGANIZATION OF REMAINING CHAPTERS

To help explain the organization of this book we consider the following abstraction. Assume that associated with each action of the (unitary) decision maker—the individual who really wants to make up his mind—

there will be a resulting consequence. We shall partition this class of problem by means of the following double dichotomy:

1. First, is it a problem under *certainty* or *uncertainty*? If it is in the uncertainty category, then we shall assume that to each action there is a well-specified probability distribution over the possible resulting consequences. To the subjectivist—often referred to as a "Bayesian"—this is not any loss of generality for he, if called on, can always generate (at least conceptually) such a probability distribution. For the objectivist, the existence of a well-specified probability distribution does, admittedly, restrict the generality of our abstraction.

2. Second, is it a *single-* or *multiple*-attribute problem? That is, can the typical consequence be adequately described in terms of a single attribute (e.g., money, degree of pain, or number of lives saved), or is more than one descriptor needed?

The most general case we will consider—and the case that is of primary interest to us—is when the consequence of an action is both uncertain and multidimensional. Let's label it $\tilde{\mathbf{x}}$ where the tilde ($\tilde{\ }$) represents uncertainty (some might prefer to view the tilde as the sign for random variable) and the boldface $\mathbf{x}$ represents a vector in contrast to a scalar.

We shall distinguish four cases as exhibited in Fig. 1.5. When the consequence is both certain and unidimensional the analysis is clear, at least conceptually: we merely choose the feasible alternative that maximizes the given single objective measure. Of course, in practice, if the alternatives are numerous and constraints are given in terms of a set of mathematical restrictions, we might be hard pressed to find the optimum. The entire range of mathematical programming techniques might have to be employed. But still, the problem is conceptually straightforward and, as such, we will not deal with that case here.

Chapter 3—we'll come back to Chapter 2 shortly—deals with the case

	Single attribute	Multiple attribute
Certainty	x	$\mathbf{x}$
Uncertainty	$\tilde{x}$	$\tilde{\mathbf{x}}$

Fig. 1.5. Double dichotomy of decision problems.

of certainty when there is more than one descriptor. This can be thought of as complex value analysis under certainty. Much of this book's flavor comes through in this analysis. Basically the problem boils down to the following: How can we systematically think about ranking a set of consequences when each consequence is described in terms of performance values on many attributes? The problem of subjective tradeoffs must be met in earnest in these discussions. We don't suggest a magic objective formula to grapple with these tradeoffs but we do suggest several concrete procedures that might be employed to help probe and articulate basic values or tastes.

In Chapter 4 we generalize to the uncertainty case but at the same time specialize to the case where there is only one descriptor. The uncertain consequence associated with an action can now be labeled by $\tilde{x}$ rather than by $\tilde{\mathbf{x}}$. In this chapter we present a general review of what is now known as the theory of risky choice, cardinal utility theory, or von Neumann–Morgenstern utility theory. An elementary version of this material can be found in Chapter 4 of Raiffa (1968), but the discussion here is more analytic and surveys some of the considerable progress that has been made in the last few years. In order to describe succinctly the problem examined in this chapter, suppose that to each action there is a probability distribution of an as-yet-unknown monetary reward. You, as decision maker, are called on to rank order such probability distributions and, as such, you must implicitly characterize your attitudes toward gambling situations. What kind of a risk taker are you?

In Chapters 5 and 6 the consequences are both uncertain and multidimensional, and the techniques developed in Chapters 3 and 4 for the two special cases (certainty-complex and uncertainty-simple) come into play here but collectively they do not quite satisfy our needs. Additional techniques are developed to handle the difficulties introduced by the interactions between uncertainty and multidimensionality. We have, a bit arbitrarily, divided the subject matter into two chapters because of the overall length. Chapter 5 deals primarily with utility functions over two attributes whereas Chapter 6 copes with more complicated multiple-attribute structures.

Now let us back up and briefly describe the contents of Chapter 2. This chapter starts by establishing some basic vocabulary: goals, objectives, attributes, evaluators, measures of performance, subjective scales, and so on. some of these terms will be part of our technical vocabulary and we must establish a common understanding of their meanings, at least as we shall use the terms. We then focus our attention to perhaps the most creative part of our subject matter—but, unfortunately, one that is difficult to describe systematically: How should we generate the objectives and attributes in concrete problems? After all, these objectives are not, in practice, delivered to the decision maker on the proverbial platter, but he or she must, literally, create them. The best way we know how to deal with this is to describe some concrete cases and illustrate how you might think about pertinent objectives.

We would like the set of objectives to be complete but yet we do not want to encumber ourselves with a lot of trivial considerations that do not add up to anything significant as far as making decisions is concerned. You will see that the generation of a suitable set of attributes is not unique and, as such, you must understand what considerations should be involved in a choice between alternatives. But you can't decide on what constitutes a desirable set of objectives without understanding what could be done with these objectives after they have been thought up. This involves an understanding of how various attributes can be evaluated, how redundancies can be handled, how parts of the problem can be isolated from other parts, how values get intertwined with probabilistic assessments, how inconsistencies may be rectified, and how calculations can be made in order to select a wise course of action. In short, when choosing a set of attributes to consider, you must worry about what comes next, and therefore you must have some appreciation of the contents of Chapters 3–6. But yet in Chapters 3–6 we assume, for the most part, that a set of attributes has already been determined. It is not until you come to Chapters 7 and 8 that the separate parts get integrated.

In Chapter 7 we look at a series of concrete problems and discuss how you might generate suitable sets of attributes describing the possible consequences, but now, unlike Chapter 2, we can also discuss whether these attribute sets can be manipulated in a tractable fashion. In particular we shall consider such problems as:

1. Should New York City lower the legal limit on the sulfur content of fuel oils burned within the city?
2. How should budget allocations be made among diverse activities of an educational program?
3. Which response strategies available to an urban fire department result in the best overall deployment of service?
4. How can we evaluate the quality of service of a computer system?
5. Can the process of siting and licensing of nuclear power facilities be significantly improved?
6. What policies should management adopt to "best" achieve the objectives of a corporation?

Chapter 7 emphasizes how the ideas of previous chapters have been used on various aspects of some complex problems and suggests the relevance of these same concepts and techniques to other strategic issues.

It is in Chapter 8 that we discuss a case from start to finish. The problem concerns selecting a strategy for developing the major airport facilities of Mexico City to the year 2000. This study serves two purposes. First, it further illustrates the applicability of many of the techniques and procedures developed in earlier chapters to a very important "typical" problem, typical of those one-of-a-kind strategic problems with so many atypical features. Second, the Mexico City airport study indicates the integration of and interconnections among different aspects of the analyses: defining and structuring the problem, modeling possible impacts of various alternatives, specifying the value judgments of the Mexican Ministry of Public Works, and so on. The larger setting within which the analysis occurred is also discussed.

Chapters 9 and 10 contain two very important methodological problems that can be naturally cast and studied within a multiattribute framework. These are, respectively, "preferences over time" and "group preferences and the social welfare problem," both of which were outlined in Section 1.5. The analytical results of Chapters 3–6 are relevant to either situation if the appropriate assumptions are satisfied. Thus, concerning temporal preferences, we may obtain a utility function for consequences of the form $(x_1, x_2, \ldots)$, where x_i indicates the consequence in time period i. In the group interpretation, it would be desirable to assign an overall group utility for each consequence $(u_1, u_2, \ldots, u_n)$, where u_j indicates the utility of the jth group member, $j = 1, 2, \ldots, n$. In both Chapters 9 and 10, we present brief surveys of previous work on the respective problems, an interpretation of multiattribute utility in the contexts of concern, and a discussion of procedures for implementing the multiattribute results within these contexts.

CHAPTER 2

The Structuring of Objectives

Let us start with the decision paradigm mentioned in Chapter 1, where we abstract a decision problem into the form of a decision tree as shown in Fig. 2.1. At each tip of the tree there is a consequence C that characterizes the full cognitive impact of that position point in time and space. The decision maker is called on not only to rank the consequences at the tips of the tree but also to evaluate the strengths of his preferences and his attitudes toward risk in terms of a utility function defined on these consequences. This is not an easy task. As a step in this evaluation procedure we imagine that the decision maker first describes each consequence C in terms of an ordered set of r numerical evaluators or descriptors. These r evaluators presumably make the abstract consequence C a bit more concrete. Instead of making a paired comparison between C and C' in the abstract, it may be easier to think of the comparison between

$$X_1(C), \ldots, X_i(C), \ldots, X_r(C) \quad \text{and} \quad X_1(C'), \ldots, X_i(C'), \ldots, X_r(C'),$$

where $X_i(C)$ refers, for example, to the "level" (to be defined more accurately later) of the consequence C as evaluated by X_i. If this is a worthwhile step to take, these r evaluators must in some sense be an adequate representation of the consequences they purport to describe.

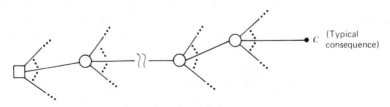

(Typical consequence)

Fig. 2.1. Schematic decision tree.

31

2.1 OBJECTIVES AND ATTRIBUTES

There are no universal definitions of the terms objective, goal, attribute, measure of effectiveness, standard, and so on, so we begin this section by indicating in an informal manner how these terms will be used in this book. We will illustrate our terminology in problems similar to the motivating examples in Chapter 1.

2.1.1 Some Illustrations

AIR POLLUTION. Because of excessive levels of pollution in a certain city, the authorities might be interested in, or have an *area of concern* in, "the threatened well-being of the residents of the city." A broad overall *objective* corresponding to this area of concern is to "improve the well-being of the residents." Such a broad objective provides little if any insight into which of a number of alternative programs may be best or even worthwhile to pursue. It does, however, provide a useful starting point for specifying detailed objectives in more operational terms.

For example, two more detailed objectives, or *lower-level objectives* as we will refer to them, might be to "reduce the emissions of pollutants from sources within the city" and "improve the citizen's attitude toward their air quality." The first of these subobjectives might further be broken into three lower-level objectives: "reduce sulfur dioxide emissions," "reduce emission of nitrogen oxides," and "reduce the particulate emissions." For each of these lowest-level objectives we might want to associate an *attribute* that will indicate the degree to which alternative policies meet this objective.

The objective, "reduce sulfur dioxide emissions," may be measured by an attribute, "tons of sulfur dioxide emitted per year." This attribute is measured with a scalar quantity, and thus is referred to as a *scalar attribute*. Similarly, scalar attributes for our other two lower-level emission objectives might be in "tons of nitrogen oxides emitted per year" and "tons of particulate emitted per year." Together these three scalar quantities could be represented as a vector measuring the degree to which the next level objective, "reduce the emissions of pollutants from sources within the city," is met. Thus, the composite of the three scalar attributes is referred to as a *vector attribute*.

The objective "improve the public's attitude toward their air quality" may be measured by an attribute "percent of residents alarmed by the city's air pollution." In each of these cases, the attribute provides a scale for measuring the degree to which its respective objective is met.

THE POSTAL SERVICE.   Suppose the overall objective of the Postal Service is "to provide efficient, dependable service to the users of the system and to the government." There are many possibilities for subobjectives, or lower-level objectives. These include "minimize total transit times for parcels and letters," "maximize the percentage of mail delivered (i.e., avoid losses)," "minimize the total cost of handling the mail," and "provide services to the government." The cost objective may be broken into "minimize direct mailing costs to users," and "minimize the cost to government," the government being ultimately responsible for all postal service expenses.

For the first objective—to minimize total transit time for parcels and letters—a rather obvious attribute is "the time in days from sender to receiver." However, it may be more appropriate to decompose "mail" into categories where the kth category refers to a particular destination at a particular time of year. Let us denote by X_k the attribute "the time in days that a randomly selected letter of category k is in transit from sender to receiver." For a given alternative this attribute will have a frequency distribution. In some examples we might want to summarize this distribution in terms of a single summary number (e.g., the mean, or an adjusted mean, or another more sophisticated index that reflects the nature of the tails of the distribution). If we follow this thought, the kth category will be summarized by a single number x_k, and if the categories k range from 1 to K, then the objective "minimize transit time for parcels and letters" will be evaluated by the vector attribute $(x_1, \ldots, x_k, \ldots, x_K)$.

The problem of finding an attribute, most likely a vector attribute, to indicate the degree to which alternatives meet the objective "provide service to government" may be very difficult. Aspects of this include facilitating communication among all citizens, informing citizens of their government's activities, and providing employment for thousands of people. Even if we do effectively spell out a set of lower-level objectives in this case, it will be difficult to identify useful attributes for each. Such problems are discussed throughout this chapter.

2.1.2   Terminology: Objectives, Attributes, and Goals

It is very likely that objectives, as we use the term, will conflict with each other in that the improved achievement with one objective can only be accomplished at the expense of another. For example, most businesses and public services have objectives like "minimize cost" and "optimize the quality of service." Since better service can often only be attained for a price, these objectives conflict. It may be possible in some cases to simultaneously increase achievement on both objectives relative to the current situation. That is, a better strategy, in terms of all objectives, may exist. However, at some point we will be faced with the proposition that further achievement on one objective can only be accomplished at the expense of achievement on the other.

An objective generally indicates the "direction" in which we should strive to do better. Recall the Postal Service *objective* "minimize total transit time for a given category of mail," which was measured in terms of the *attribute* "days." Since it is unlikely that transit times would be reduced to zero, we could always strive to do better. Let us contrast this objective and its associated attribute with a so-called *goal*. For this problem, a goal may be "deliver at least 90% of the parcels and letters within two days." A goal is different from an objective in that it is either achieved or not.

Goals are useful for clearly identifying a level of achievement to strive toward. President Kennedy's stated goal in 1961 was to reach the moon by 1970. This goal would either be achieved or not. It is much easier to inspire people, including oneself, to climb a mountain when it has a summit than when there is none. However, for our subject matter we feel that objectives are more relevant than goals for evaluating alternatives in strategic decision problems. This does not mean that the use of goals is not a useful tactical device for implementing an action program. We shall confine our language to objectives and attributes and minimize the usage of the term "goal."

2.2   GENERATION OF OBJECTIVES AND ATTRIBUTES

In practice there is considerable interplay in the creative process of generating objectives and selecting attributes for these objectives. Before pursuing the interrelationships in depth, it is necessary to first consider objectives and attributes separately.

2.2.1   Some Techniques for Generating Objectives

Let us suggest some guidelines that may be helpful in generating objectives for a specific problem. As a starting point, assume that one objective has been specified, such as the overall objective "improve the well-being of the residents" in the air-pollution problem. Clearly, in this case it would be desirable to be more specific about such a broad objective. Answering the question, "What is meant by "well-being of the residents?" would better specify the objectives. For instance, you might include health and economic conditions as part of well-being. Each of these conditions may be broken down further.

MacCrimmon (1969) suggests the following approaches for generating objectives: (a) examination of the relevant literature, (b) analytical study, and (c) casual empiricism. "Examination of the literature" should be clear. If others have faced problems similar to yours, perhaps they have documented some objectives that are relevant to your problem. "Analytical study" suggests that by building a model of the system under consideration and identifying relevant input and output variables, suitable objectives will become obvious. This might be useful for picking up objectives that were originally omitted either by oversight or intention. Some objectives originally regarded as insignificant might seem important after considering the results of various studies with the model. The third suggestion, "casual empiricism," includes observing people to see how, in fact, they are presently making decisions relevant to the problem. How do they rationalize their actions? What do they talk about? For instance, in selecting objectives for choosing among alternate housing developments, you might observe how people choose among currently available options. This may provide some indication of relevant objectives.

Surveys may be useful in selecting objectives for public decision making. Individuals who will be affected by a certain decision can be asked what objectives should be included in a study. Such a process might generate many "low-level" objectives. In such a case, we would want to utilize these lower-level objectives to specify broader objectives. For instance, if one objective were "to not feel nauseated by the smog," this might be translated into a broader objective by answering the question "Why is it important that one not feel nauseated?" Feeling nauseated indicated some adversity affecting people's health, so a broader objective might be to "improve the health of the specified population."

In many instances, it may be useful to have a group of knowledgeable experts identify the objectives in a problem area. The board of directors in business firms often plays this role of setting objectives. In recent years, especially in technological and scientific problem areas, both government and private industry have begun to use the "panel of experts," a group of people with expertise in the area of interest, to generate the objectives.

2.2.2 Illustrations*

SCIENTIFIC OBJECTIVES OF NASA.   An ingenious approach was utilized in specifying objectives for the National Aeronautics and Space Administration to use in evaluating the scientific merit of alternative plans for space

* Precisely speaking, the two studies briefly described in this section do not specify *objectives* as we defined them. In our terms they identified *areas of concern* from which one could generate objectives. For this section, we have retained the terminology of the cited works.

Table 2.1

Generating Scientific Objectives for a Space Program

Action Phrase	Target Feature	Target Subject
Characteristic circulation patterns in	The photosphere of	The sun
Measure tidal deformations of	The surface of	The moon
Establish the structure of	The interior of	Jupiter
Measure relativistic time dilations in	————	The space environment

exploration. The scientific objectives were first grouped into five main subareas: (1) earth and its environment, (2) extraterrestrial life, (3) the solar system, (4) the universe, and (5) space as a laboratory. Then lists of what were called action phrases, target features, and target subjects were developed. The idea can best be explained by referring to Table 2.1, which is reprinted from Dole et al. (1968a). One would try each of the combinations (action phrase, target feature, target subject) and then ask, "Is this one of the scientific objectives of a space program?" If the grouped words were an objective, it was included in the list. If the words were meaningless, then they were omitted. Thus, for instance, "Establish the structure of the interior of the sun" was an objective, whereas "Measure tidal deformations of the space environment" was not an objective. This procedure generated 1030 lower-level objectives. The complete results are in Dole et al. (1968b).

THE LOUISVILLE STUDY.* In Louisville, Kentucky, a group of citizens representing diverse segments of the community, who worked closely with the mayor, identified areas of concern and selected objectives for public policy. This Mayor's Citizens Advisory Committee identified 10 major areas of concern that were further divided into 35 lower-level aims representing interests of the city of Louisville. These "goals" are indicated in Table 2.2.

Table 2.2 provides an excellent point to further articulate objectives. Consider area of concern C6, "Insure the optimal utilization of all land." This identifies land utilization as important and, almost by definition, everyone would want optimal utilization. However, this very likely means different things to different people. What is optimal utilization? This difficult problem should perhaps be answered by the Mayor's Citizens Advisory Committee or another such group with the assistance of the

* For details, see Schimpeler et al. (1969).

Table 2.2

Areas of Concern to Residents of Louisville, Kentucky

Major Objectives[a]	Lower-Level Objectives
A. Public safety program development	1. Insure safe public facilities 2. Provide for adequate public safety regulations and their enforcement 3. Provide for the removal of contaminants
B. Public utility and transportation development	1. Minimize maintenance costs of public utilities 2. Insure maximum effectiveness of public utilities by design and locational consideration 3. Develop a balanced, effective, and integrated transportation system that provides for the accessibility requirements of each land use
C. Economic development programs	1. Develop public improvement programs within available financial resources 2. Maintain highest equitable property values 3. Insure effective utilization of mineral, vegetation, air, and water resources 4. Establish strong economic base through commerce that will bring money into the community 5. Establish trade development that provides maximum convenience to consumers 6. Insure the optimal utilization of all land 7. Achieve increased disposable income for all people
D. Cultural development	1. Preserve historic sites and areas of natural beauty 2. Promote adequate public libraries, museums, and cultural activities 3. Protect meaningful local tradition and encourage civic pride
E. Health program development	Establish the mechanism for adequate preventive and remedial health programs and facilities
F. Education program development	Develop education facilities and opportunities for citizens at every level
G. Welfare program development	1. Eliminate injustice based on discrimination 2. Develop needed public welfare programs 3. Encourage development of religious opportunities 4. Develop an aesthetically pleasing environment
H. Recreation program development	1. Establish open space programs 2. Provide adequate recreational facilities utilizing parks, rivers, and lakes
J. Political framework	1. Improve the framework (channels, systematic use) for citizens' participation in government functions 2. Establish equitable taxation policies (bases, mixes, rates)

Table 2.2 (continued)
Areas of Concern to Residents of Louisville, Kentucky

Major Objectives[a]	Lower-Level Objectives
J. Political framework (*continued*)	3. Achieve efficient governmental administration representative of all citizens
	4. Develop adequate government staffs and personnel programs (high job standards, reasonable salary ranges, effective delegation of authority)
	5. Establish sound governmental fiscal programs
	6. Develop an effective, long-range metropolitanwide planning process
	7. Establish effective control mechanisms
K. Housing development	1. Encourage rehabilitation and conservation neighborhood programs
	2. Provide adequate low-cost housing
	3. Develop neighborhood units
	4. Promote a wide variety of housing as required within the community

[a] More precisely, Areas of Concern.

city's property tax authorities. The identification of such open problems is one of the contributions made by a formal specification of objectives.

Once a "first-cut" list of objectives is published, it also can be used by all interested parties and individuals as a base for constructive criticism and improvement. This type of recapitulation should help generate more objectives for a given problem but, equally important, it has the beneficial effect of getting concerned individuals to think actively about a complex problem that is relevant to them.

2.2.3 Specification of Attributes

To describe completely the consequences of any of the possible courses of action in a complex decision problem requires volumes. In the air quality example a consequence would cover who got sick when, how badly they felt, when they recovered, the economic impact on each individual due to pollution, and all related psychological, physical, and economic impacts. This would certainly be complete. However, information in this form is not useful for decision-making purposes. Summary statistics are needed to reduce this morass to a useful, manageable form.

To be useful to the decision maker, an attribute should be both comprehensive and measurable. An attribute is *comprehensive* if, by knowing the level of an attribute in a particular situation, the decision maker has a clear understanding of the extent that the associated objective is achieved. An attribute is *measurable* if it is reasonable both (a) to obtain a probability distribution for each alternative over the possible levels of the attribute—or in extreme cases to assign a point value—and (b) to assess the decision maker's preferences for different possible levels of the attribute, for example, in terms of a utility function or, in some circumstances, a rank ordering.* Furthermore, we would like to accomplish both these tasks without taking an inordinate amount of time, cost, or effort. Thus, to some extent, comprehensiveness refers to the appropriateness of the attribute on theoretical grounds: Does it give us the information we would like to have, regardless of whether we can get it? And measurability refers to the practical considerations: Can we get the necessary assessments?

A comprehensive attribute should be relevant to the particular alternative courses of action under consideration and not subject to other extraneous considerations. For instance, suppose one objective of a proposed law requiring all travelers to wear seat belts in all vehicles at all times is to reduce vehicle casualties. In this case, the attribute "number of casualties in automobiles per year" would not be comprehensive, because it is difficult to differentiate the effects of this attribute due to wearing seat belts from the effects due to other factors, such as the number of accidents.

As another example, suppose the overall objective of a government "stop smoking campaign" is "to improve the health of the nation." Then the attribute "number of deaths due to smoking" is not comprehensive because it offers no information about those who are sick or disabled due to smoking. Whenever we consider attributes involving how many people are sick, injured, and so on, the problem of precision must be dealt with. For example, in a transportation problem where one objective is to decrease injuries, the attribute "number of injuries" is not precise because the definition of injury is not clear. This is regardless of whether all injuries, using any specified definition, should be considered as equally important. Because of the imprecision, different people might assign different levels to the number of injuries even though they had access to the same information.

In many cases, choosing an attribute will not be difficult if the objective is clear. If a businessman's objective is to maximize profits, then profits

---

* We are implicitly assuming that all other attributes are held fixed at specified levels. It could be that preferences for different levels of an attribute might shift when the other attribute levels are changed. This is discussed fully in later chapters.

measured in dollars would be a logical attribute. Knowing the profits for a particular endeavor would indicate how much the objective "maximize profits" is achieved. If a freight shipping firm wanted to deliver all shipments on time, a reasonable attribute might be the delay time in the arrival of the shipment. In a medical context, a major objective might be to keep a patient alive, in which case the attribute "probability of death" would be appropriate. A number could be assigned to the delay time of shipments, profits, and the probability of death; whereas the respective *objectives* per se cannot be quantified.

2.2.4 Subjective Attribute Scales

Many attributes we intuitively think of using are objective (as opposed to subjective) in nature.* By this, we mean there already exists a commonly understood scale for that attribute and its levels are objectively measurable. However, there are objectives for which no objective index exists and, in such cases, a subjective index must be constructed.

Consider the businessman who wishes to "maximize profits" and "increase prestige." As mentioned previously, an obvious attribute for the first objective is the objective index "profits, measured in dollars." However, since there is no objective scale for prestige, we are obliged to establish a subjective index for this objective. A first step could establish a 10-point ordered scale from "desultory low" to the "pinnacle of world-renowned esteem," for example. We would then subjectively assign consequences, ranked from worst to best, to several identification points along this scale. In some circumstances we might have to assess probability distributions and establish a cardinal utility measure over this scale. The literature in psychometrics is replete with examples that establish such scales but the motivation for that literature is quite distinct from ours. Nevertheless, in this book we build up from that methodological base.

We cite here only one example of a subjectively assessed scale. (See section 7.7.5 for another example.) Huber, Sahrey, and Ford (1969) asked a number of experienced, professional personnel of a large hospital to subjectively evaluate 12 hypothetical hospital wards on a scale from 0 to 100. They asserted that their results strongly indicate that professionals can develop and reliably use subjective evaluation models. In our work, if we were to use such a scale in conjunction with other scales in a multiattribute problem, we would be obliged to structure this scale

---

* Note that we use the terms *objective* and *subjective* to describe two types of attributes, both of which are used to indicate the degree to which *objectives* are met. However, we shall not facetiously define a "subjective" or worry about achieving it.

internally in such a manner that it would mesh *externally* with other scales. This leads to the problem of conjoint measurement, which we will discuss in Chapter 3.

There are, of course, difficulties in using subjectively defined attribute scales, and depending on context it may be important to go to creative, fanciful extremes in order to get an objective base. In Section 2.5, we discuss the notion of *proxy* attributes, which alleviates some of these difficulties.

2.3 THE HIERARCHICAL NATURE OF OBJECTIVES

Suppose you have thought hard about the objectives in a given problem and have produced a list that encompasses all the areas of concern. No doubt the different objectives will vary widely in their scope, explicitness, and detail, and be inconsistent. How can you bring some structure to this list of objectives? Often these objectives can be structured in a meaningful way by the use of a *hierarchy*. Almost everyone who has seriously thought about the objectives in a complex problem* has come up with some sort of hierarchy of objectives.

2.3.1 Constructing the Hierarchy

How is a hierarchy constructed from an original list of objectives? And how do we recognize if, in fact, "holes" are present in such a hierarchy? The concepts of specification and means–ends discussed by Manheim and Hall (1967) help here. Specification means subdividing an objective into lower-level objectives of more detail, thus clarifying the intended meaning of the more general objective. These lower-level objectives can also be thought of as the means to the end, the end being the higher-level objective. Thus, by identifying the ends to very precise objectives (the means), we can build the hierarchy up to higher levels.

When we go up the hierarchy, there is the natural stopping point at the all-inclusive objective. This objective is extremely broad and indicates the reason for being interested in the problem, but it is often too vague for any operational purpose. For example, as seen in Fig. 2.2, the overall objective used by Manheim and Hall for evaluating passenger transportation facilities for serving the Northeast Corridor in 1980 was "the good

---

* For example, Manheim and Hall (1967), MacCrimmon (1969), Raiffa (1969), Miller (1970), Gearing et al. (1974), the NASA study [Dole et al. (1968a)], and the Mayor's Citizens Advisory Committee of Louisville [Schimpeler et al. (1969)].

42

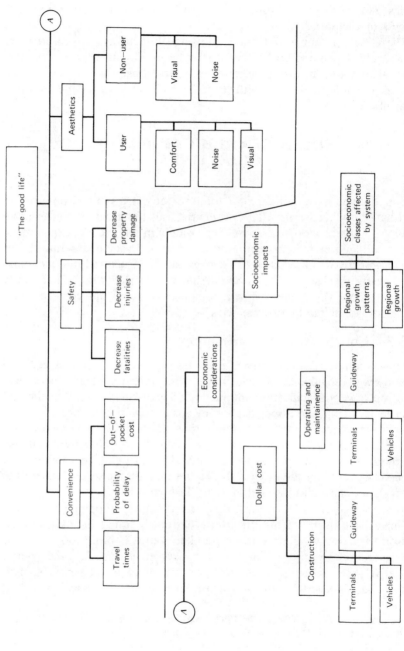

Fig. 2.2. A hierarchy of objectives for evaluating passenger transportation facilities for the northeast corridor in 1980.

life." However, when we go down a hierarchy, there is no obvious point where we stop specifying the objectives. Our judgment must be used to decide where to stop the formalization by considering the advantages and disadvantages of further specification. If this were not done, and the hierarchy were carried to absurd lengths, we would end up with an astronomical set of objectives. In planning passenger transportation in the Northeast Corridor, we could say that each affected individual (maybe 50 million of them) had a subhierarchy representing only themselves in the overall hierarchy of system objectives. Of course, no one would advocate such an approach, but the point of all this is that we must be pragmatic about the level of detail or specification we are prepared to assess.

2.3.2 How Far to Formalize?

How far should the objectives hierarchy be extended? It depends a great deal on what will be done next with the hierarchy. Are we going to identify attributes for each of the objectives? This is related to the qualitative versus quantitative growth of the hierarchy to be discussed and to the concept of direct preference measurements. Are we willing to use subjective indices of effectiveness, or do we prefer objective ones? This question depends partially on who the decision maker is and who is performing the analysis and for what purpose.

When dividing an objective into subobjectives, at any level, care must be taken to insure that all facets of the higher objective are accounted for in one of the subobjectives. However, we must guard against a proliferation of the hierarchy in the lateral direction as well as the vertical. For instance, if we ended up with hundreds of lower-level objectives, which are specifiers of a higher-level objective, some of these might be so insignificant relative to others that they could be excluded from the formal analysis without leading the decision maker astray. Still, care must be exerted in discarding objectives lest the remainder become seriously noncomprehensive.

Ellis (1970) introduces a "test of importance" to deal with this problem. Before any objective is included in the hierarchy, the decision maker is asked whether he feels the best course of action could be altered if that objective were excluded. An affirmative response would obviously imply that the objective should be included. A negative response would be taken as sufficient reason for exclusion. Naturally, we must avoid excluding a large set of attributes, each of which fails the "test of importance" but which collectively are important. As the analysis proceeds, and the decision maker gains further insight into his problem, it is worthwhile to repeat the test of importance with the excluded objectives. If the decision maker has a change in mind, then some objectives and their associated attributes must be added to the problem and certain parts of the analysis repeated.

2.3.3 Qualitative Proliferation of the Objectives Hierarchy

In this book our ultimate aim in a specific applied context is not merely to generate a good objectives hierarchy for the problem. We use this hierarchy as a step along the way in a decision analytical framework. In Chapter 3, we shall begin to talk about preference tradeoffs between attributes and quantifying our preferences. Numbers will play a big role in the ensuing analysis. Let us consider, for example, the abstracted schematic version of the hierarchy shown in Fig. 2.3. In this hierarchy there are 13 lower-level objectives; let their associated attributes be Z_1, $Z_2, \ldots, Z_{13}$. Thus a given consequence of the decision problem could be described by a 13-tuple $(z_1, z_2, \ldots, z_{13})$. We might formalize a utility function in this 13-dimensional space and thus assign values such as $u(z_1, z_2, \ldots, z_{13})$. But this is not necessary in order to proceed. As an alternative, we might quantify preferences at a much higher level of aggregation. For example, it may be better to work directly with the attributes X_1 and X_2, where X_1 is a subjectively assessed composite of Z_1 to Z_5 and X_2 of Z_6 to Z_{13} (see Fig. 2.3). Instead of engaging the utility analysis at the level of

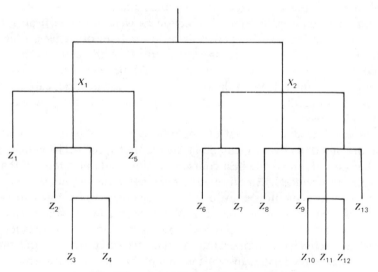

Fig. 2.3. An abstract objectives hierarchy.

$(z_1, z_2, \ldots, z_{13})$, utility assignments for entities of the form (x_1, x_2) could be used. Of course, in this case for a given consequence C, the values of $X_1(C) = x_1$ and $X_2(C) = x_2$ might have to be subjectively assessed.

We can use the hierarchy in a manner that is convenient to ourselves and embark on a further analysis by introducing utility assignments at various levels of the hierarchy. However, if we were going to quantify our preferences at the X_1, X_2 level, why proliferate the hierarchy down to the Z_1–Z_{13} level? Because the *qualitative* structuring of the objectives associated with X_1 and X_2 might help us to think more clearly about X_1 and X_2. In other words, the vertical depth of the proliferation of the hierarchy does not necessarily force us to quantify our preferences down to this level of detail. The hierarchy after a given level may serve merely as a qualitative checklist for items to consider.

Extending the hierarchy for qualitative purposes can be illustrated using one of the major objectives of the air pollution problem cited in Chapter 7. For the objective "achieve the best political solution," a subjective index to indicate the degree of achievement was used. However, to stimulate thinking about the assessment of this subjective index, it may be desirable to specify the major objective further. For instance, we could identify some subobjectives of this major objective such as to "improve relations with the City Council," to "gain the support of certain political groups," to "maintain good terms with the landlords" who must buy fuel to heat their buildings, and to "transmit the idea that the City Administration is concerned about the welfare of its residents and the environment of the area." If we were to assess utilities directly for the major objective, preferences and likelihoods relating directly to the lower-level objectives need not be assessed, and therefore we do not need to identify measures of effectiveness for them. Thus, many of the considerations that might extend an objectives hierarchy for *quantitative* reasons are not relevant to the case where certain parts of the hierarchy are to be used for *qualitative* reasons only.

2.3.4 Subjective versus Objective Measures Revisited

The more an objectives hierarchy is subdivided, the easier it usually is to identify attribute scales that can be objectively assessed. When the hierarchy is limited, we often must resort to subjective measures of effectiveness. To illustrate this point, consider another objective in the air pollution problem of Chapter 7: "to improve the physical health of the New York City residents." Other than a subjective index, no single measure could be found to indicate the degree to which this objective is met. The difficulty was that both mortality and morbidity effects of various kinds were important. Thus, the subobjectives "decrease mortality" and "decrease morbidity" were specified, and objective clinical measures of effectiveness were identified for each.

As a second example consider the design of a new transportation system and concentrate on one objective within the hierarchy: "maximize passenger comfort." There is no readily available engineering index that can capture the essence of this feature. But if we specified comfort in terms of types of comfort (e.g., smoothness or ride, quality of light, maneuverable space, and background noise) we could assign engineering and physical measurements to most of the subobjectives that were introduced, giving specificity to the objective "passenger comfort."

2.3.5 Who is the Decision Maker? The Need to Convince Others. Reconciliation of Viewpoints

Let us again suppose that a qualitative objectives hierarchy is shown as in Fig. 2.3. If the decision maker is his own analyst, and he does not have to convince anyone of the correctness of his action, it may be convenient for him to subjectively assign assessed values for the X_1 and X_2 attributes and to synthesize in his mind, in a purely informal manner, the consideration of any further detail (such as the further specification of the Z's).

However, when the single decision maker and his analyst work apart from each other, the problem becomes more involved. In this situation, the analyst presumably presents his results and recommendations to the decision maker, who then chooses an alternative course of action. Thus, to better support his work, the analyst will most likely specify formally the objectives hierarchy in greater detail. He will want to use objective indices rather than subjective ones whenever possible in the interest of "objectivism." The analyst might be forced down to the Z level rather than remain at the subjective X level.

If the sole decision maker has to convince others of the correctness of his decision, as well as to straighten his own mind out, he may be well advised to go as far as he can with jointly held objective conceptions, and this may force him to push the hierarchical analysis down to the objective Z attributes. But this also works another way. The more involved the analysis, the harder it may be to explain it to others, and therefore it may be easier to work at the X level than the Z level.

Let us now see how an analyst serving multiple clients might handle the problem. He might develop the hierarchy down to the Z level and obtain objective engineering measurements for the Z attributes—measurements that might be accepted by all his clients. Of course, the trouble will come at the next stage of the analysis when the various attribute n-tuples, in this case $(z_1, z_2, \ldots, z_{13})$, have to be rank ordered and scaled (perhaps with utilities) by the various decision makers. But at least the analyst could postpone that consideration while he tries to synthesize the commonly held objective features of the problem.

Now suppose that two or more decision makers project the hierarchy down to the X level, and suppose that they disagree on their overall rankings (or utilities) for consequences. In a reconciliation process it may be desirable to understand *why* they disagree. One way of proceeding is to break down the problem further—in this case to further specify the meanings of the X attributes in terms of the Z levels. Then probe the values on some of the Z-attributes holding the other Z values fixed. Later we shall introduce various qualitative independence assumptions concerning preferences for multiple attributes, and even though the decision makers might differ in their quantitative tradeoffs, they often might conceivably hold qualitatively similar viewpoints that could help probe their differences. Of course, in some circumstances reconciliation could not be achieved by such rational analyses. Indeed there are many cases where reconciliation is only achieved by creative obfuscation. We like to think that the complementary set of circumstances is not a null set. In Chapter 8 we shall discuss these issues further in an actual case.

2.3.6 Nonuniqueness of the Objectives Hierarchy

As mentioned earlier, the objectives hierarchy for a particular problem is not unique. It can be varied simply by changing the degree to which the hierarchy is formalized. However, even if the degree of formalization remains unchanged (in the sense that the number of lowest-level objectives is the same), the objectives hierarchy can be significantly varied. Whether one arrangement is better than another is mainly a matter of the particular points the decision maker and the analyst wish to make. Two alternative analyses of employment possibilities, reviewed in Section 7.7, provide a fascinating example of such considerations. With different hierarchies, different tradeoffs facing the decision maker can be more easily identified and illustrated.

There is another example where the specific display of the hierarchy may be exploited—the times when some of the lower levels of the hierarchy can be pruned because further distinction does not matter. For example, imagine that, for a heroin problem (like the one outlined in Chapter 1), you might at times wish to distinguish between the effects on different sexes and age groups. If the lowest level makes the differentiation between effects on males and females, and if for particular alternatives the decision maker is not concerned about these separate effects, the two attributes associated with these objectives can effectively be coalesced into one.

2.3.7   An Illustrative Example: Choice of a Transportation System

To illustrate some of the ideas discussed in this section, reconsider the objectives hierarchy for the Northeast Corridor transportation system in Fig. 2.2.

As you can see, the overall objective is to acquire "the good life." Clearly we would not expect to find a single attribute for this overall objective. This was divided into four objectives: "provide maximum convenience," "provide maximum safety," "provide an aesthetically pleasing transportation system," and "minimize system costs and promote regional economic development." To be complete, these four objectives should include all the aspirations of the individuals responsible for the decision that must be made.

Next, the test of importance is applied to each objective to determine whether or not it should be included in the formal analysis. Since it is fairly obvious here that each objective should be kept in the analysis, we do not emphasize the approach at this point.

Let us now take the objective "provide maximum convenience" and attempt to find an attribute that expresses the degree to which this objective is met. Convenience implies that service should be fast, dependable, and economical, at the very least, and no apparent single attribute satisfying the criteria of Section 2.2 includes all of these facets of convenience. Therefore, we might choose to subdivide this objective further.

Now that we have decided to specify "convenience" to a greater degree, it is necessary to consider a suitable set of subobjectives. For example, we might want to:

1. Minimize travel time.
2. Minimize departure delays.
3. Minimize arrival delays.
4. Minimize fare costs.
5. Provide easy access to the system.

Since we want to have as few final attributes as possible, we try to generate the minimum number of subobjectives each time this process is carried out. Of course, we must make sure that the list includes all relevant considerations. In this situation, let us consider the possibility of combining some of the five objectives listed above. We might reasonably think that easy access to the system means we can get to the system quickly, and then combine objectives 1 and 5 to minimize door-to-door travel time. Whether this would be appropriate in a specific problem would depend on the situation at hand. We should look for ways of combining objectives in this manner. For argument's sake, let us agree that objectives 1 and 5 are combined.

Let us also agree that no other combinations are apparent; the next step is to apply the test of importance to each of the remaining four subobjectives. We start with "minimize door-to-door travel time." Is this objective important enough to possibly influence the final decision? It seems entirely reasonable that this objective would be important. Therefore, we will keep it in our hierarchy of objectives. The same conclusion is reached for "minimize fare costs."

Objectives "minimize departure delays" and "minimize arrival delays" may be different. For example, we could reason that leaving on schedule and arriving on schedule is not much different from leaving an hour late and arriving on schedule. That is not to say that it is not inconvenient to wait for late departures, but that departure delays might not be particularly serious in themselves. Much of the importance of delayed departure results from its causal effect on total travel time, and total travel time is already included in our analysis. Finally, we ask whether arrival delays, in addition to their impact on total travel time, are important enough to influence the alternative courses of action chosen. A negative response means that this attribute has failed to make the test of importance, and it need not be considered explicitly in any ensuing analysis of this problem.

As a result, we have ended up with two subobjectives of "convenience":

1. Minimize door-to-door travel time.
2. Minimize fare costs.

Now we try to find a meaningful attribute for each of these. In this case, the attributes "door-to-door travel time in minutes" and "fare cost in dollars" are likely candidates. Of course, this brings up two problems: to whom and from where do these times and costs apply.

Unfortunately, even when we have resolved the problems just mentioned, the process is not complete. The procedure illustrated above must be repeated for the three remaining lower-level objectives, those concerning safety, aesthetics, and economic and regional impact.

2.4 SETS OF OBJECTIVES AND ATTRIBUTES

Sections 2.2 and 2.3 discussed building the objectives hierarchy and selecting an attribute for each of the lowest-level objectives. These two topics were considered in isolation. Now we ask the broader question: Is the set of objectives and their associated attributes appropriate for the problem? In this regard, we shall define five properties—we should say "objectives"—that are desirable for selecting a set of attributes.

2.4.1 Desirable Properties of a Set of Attributes

It is important in any decision problem that the set of attributes be *complete*, so that it covers all the important aspects of the problem; *operational*, so that it can be meaningfully used in the analysis; *decomposable*, so that aspects of the evaluation process can be simplified by breaking it down into parts; *nonredundant*, so that double counting of impacts can be avoided; and *minimal*, so that the problem dimension is kept as small as possible. Let us be specific about these properties.

COMPLETENESS. A set of attributes is *complete* if it is adequate in indicating the degree to which the overall objective is met. This condition should be satisfied when the lowest-level objectives in a hierarchy include all areas of concern in the problem at hand and when the individual attributes associated with each of the lowest-level objectives in this hierarchy satisfy the comprehensiveness criterion specified in Section 2.2.

There is another way to view the property of completeness. We have associated with each lowest-level objective a single scalar attribute that takes on real values. Suppose an overall objective in the hierarchy has been subdivided into two subobjectives, and scalar attribute X_1 has been associated with the first of these and scalar attribute X_2 with the second. We can measure the overall objective with a vector attribute Y, which is a composite of attributes X_1 and X_2. A specific value of attribute Y will be a two-tuple (x_1, x_2), where x_i is a specified value of X_i. Now, to say that the set of attributes X_1 and X_2 is complete is to say that the vector attribute Y is comprehensive. To generalize, a set of n attributes is *complete* if, by knowing the value of the n-dimensional vector attribute associated with the overall objective, the decision maker has a clear picture about the extent to which the overall objective is met.

Here is an example of a "good decision analysis gone astray" because the attribute set was not complete (written for one of us as an undergraduate thesis). The problem concerned the alternative course of actions to be followed after graduation, including joining the military service, going to graduate school, or accepting a civilian job. The attributes included financial aspects, future flexibility, and so on, but the author did not feel comfortable with the implication of his own formal study. The fault was that the analysis contained no considerations for the romantic life of the individual, and this factor was important enough to change the overall implications. He did not deem it suitable at first to bring sex into his attribute hierarchy. Clearly, with many people, such aspects should be considered before signing up for work on the North Slope of Alaska or in a nuclear submarine for a five-year stay. But in subsequent trials he learned how to become more honest himself and he finally reached a point where the formal analysis felt right to him and acted accordingly. He referred to this experience as a cheap and orderly way to psychoanalyze oneself.

OPERATIONAL. A set of attributes must be operational. This implies many different things depending somewhat on the intended use of the analysis. Basically, since the idea of decision analysis is to help a decision maker choose a best course of action, the attributes must be useful for that purpose. The attributes must be meaningful to the decision maker, so that he can understand the implications of the alternatives. They should also facilitate explanations to others, especially in cases where the main purpose of the study is to make and advocate a particular position. Consider the mayor of a large city, who is appraising alternatives for handling solid wastes. It may not be possible for him, in a publicly discussed study, to include an attribute like "annual number of tons of untreated solid waste dumped into the ocean" even though this amount might be extremely important. If the analysis were to be released, inclusion of the attribute might make the mayor too politically vulnerable. The analyst and decision maker must be aware of the many nontechnical problems that may render a set of attributes as nonoperational. Some of these issues are discussed in Keeney and Raiffa (1972).

DECOMPOSABLE. A formal decision analysis requires that we quantify both the decision maker's preferences for consequences and his judgments about uncertain events. For a problem with n attributes, this means assessing an n-attribute utility function as well as joint probability distributions for the relevant uncertainties. Because of the complexity involved, these tasks will be extremely difficult, if not impossible, for decision problems in which the dimensionality n is even modestly high (e.g., 5) unless the set of attributes is *decomposable*. By this we mean that the aforementioned tasks can be broken down into parts of smaller dimensionality. For instance, if the problem involves five attributes, it might be possible to break the assessments into two parts, one involving two attributes and one involving three. This idea, in the case of preferences, is one of the central themes of this book and is discussed in detail in Chapters 3–6.

NONREDUNDANCY. We do not want redundancies in our final set of attributes—the attributes should be defined to avoid double counting of consequences. For example, if we were evaluating a portfolio with investments in companies A and B, the attributes "income from company A" and "income from investments" are clearly redundant since income from company A is counted in both attributes. We should only use "income from investments" or "income from company A" and "income from company B" to avoid the redundancy. A more subtle example is discussed in McKean (1958) in conjunction with the allocation of water resources. Two attributes he considered were "increase in farm income" and "increase in livestock yield." These may be redundant in that the latter may be important only by virtue of its impact on the former.

This second illustration points out a common way that redundancies creep into a set of attributes. The problem is that the means–ends relationships of the objectives are not clearly indicated, and attributes are included that are associated with both means and ends objectives.

Another way in which redundancies enter sets of attributes is when some attributes represent variables that are inputs to a system and others represent variables that are outputs. One example of such a problem is the evaluation of space vehicles. An input might be "weight" and an output might be "thrust" required to break out of the earth's gravitational field. Again, weight may only be important because of its implications on thrust.

MINIMUM SIZE.   Subject to the four criteria for sets of attributes just discussed, it is desirable to keep the set as small as possible. Each time an objective is subdivided, possibilities for excluding important concerns occur. In addition, the difficulties in obtaining joint probability distributions and quantifying multiattribute preferences increase greatly as the number of attributes increases.

In some problems, it is possible to combine attributes and thus reduce the dimensionality. For example, in the two-company portfolio problem, the decision maker may not be concerned with whether his income comes from company A or company B, in which case the single attribute "income from investments" would be appropriate.

The minimum size of a set of attributes is obviously 1. One grandiose objective, suitably chosen, could be complete, and if we did not require that the set of attributes be operational, we could always pick such an objective.* However, it should be clear that, in most complex decision problems, this would not make the problem more tractable. Here, as in

---

* In Section 4.11 we discuss an example where a single attribute is both comprehensive and objectively measurable but, nevertheless, the attribute had to be partitioned into several lower-level attributes in order for these to become operationally meaningful to the decision maker.

most problems of the real world, we often want to fulfill conflicting objectives and, since this is an ideal we cannot achieve, we must engage in vexing tradeoffs—a theme that is repeated throughout this book.

2.4.2 Nonuniqueness of a Set of Attributes

A set of attributes is not unique for a specific problem nor is it unique even for a specific objectives hierarchy. To illustrate this, consider the objective of an airline "to provide frequent service between Los Angeles and San Francisco." To measure this objective, we might use the number of flights per day, the maximum time between scheduled flights, or the average time between scheduled flights. In fact, the first and third suggested attributes are deterministically related. If n is the number of flights in a day and t is the average time in hours between flights, then $t = 24/n$.

As a second example, suppose X represents the crimes solved in one area and Y represents the crimes solved in another. Then, if we were interested in the impact on crime in both of these areas, we could include X and Y in our total set of attributes. However, the average number of crimes solved, $(X + Y)/2$, and the difference in crime solved in the two areas, $X - Y$, could be used equally well. It should be clear that a knowledge of the effects of a program on these two attributes is equivalent to a knowledge of the effects on X and Y. The choice of which is a better set to use depends on the future uses of the analysis, and particularly on assessments of probabilities and utilities.

2.4.3 An Illustrative Example: Medical Treatment

Here we try to tie together many of the properties discussed in the preceding subsections: These properties are connected in many ways, as we will show. Also, quite naturally, the degree that a certain set of attributes meets one metaobjective might only be improved at the expense of the degree that it meets other metaobjectives.

Consider a simplification of the medical problem discussed in Chapter 1. A doctor about to perform a critical operation on a patient may have the overall objective to "do the best for the patient." We will avoid asking whose objective, the doctor's or the patient's, for the time being. Suppose this objective is divided into "minimize costs" and "avoid death." Then, as we have discussed, the attributes of total cost in dollars and the probability of death might be used for these objectives, respectively. Therefore, if we define the overall objective as Y and costs in dollars as X_1 and probability of death as X_2, we have $Y = X_1 \times X_2$. Is Y complete? Since we have considered at length the desirable properties of attributes for lowest-level objectives, let us assume that attributes X_1 and X_2 satisfy these criteria. Whether Y is complete now reduces to whether the objectives "minimize costs" and "avoid death" cover all important aspects of the problem. As indicated in the beginning of Section 2.2, whether we conclude that all important aspects of a problem are included in a set of objectives is mainly a matter of resourcefulness in selecting additional objectives and judgment.

In our example, we might believe that the amount of pain and suffering that the patient might undergo would be important enough to influence decisions and thus should be represented by an objective. This might be formalized by including an objective to "minimize pain." With this, we would have three subobjectives under the overall objective. The original two were not complete.

A next step would be to assign a measure of effectiveness to the objective "minimize pain." As suggested earlier, this would likely be very difficult because of our inability to measure pain. It might be possible, however, to set up a subjective index appropriate for this purpose.* However, care must be taken to insure that this index is meaningful to the patient and/or the doctor. Otherwise, it would not be operational.

As a consequence, we may be forced to search for another attribute to indicate the degree of pain that is operational and possesses the other desired properties to the degrees possible. In this case, the "number of days which the patient must stay in bed" might be useful as such an attribute. While this clearly does not directly indicate the degree of pain, it is related, in some manner, to the amount of pain suffered by the patient. Such attributes, called proxy attributes, are discussed in detail in Section 2.5.

Suppose the patient and the doctor could meaningfully use a subjective index for "minimize pain" and suppose this, along with days in bed, cost, and probability of death, were suggested as a set of four attributes for the problem. In this case, you might argue that days in bed may be eliminated from the list because it is redundant with the pain index. This would also reduce the number of attributes by one, which is desirable, of course. Someone else may suggest eliminating the pain index in favor of number of days in bed for the same reason. Which of these suggestions is better would have to be weighed by the decision maker, and his choice should depend on how much the remaining three attributes satisfy the various desirable properties for a set of attributes.

Going further, we might decide that the particular circumstances of this

---

* An interesting effort in this same spirit is the development of a severity-of-burn index by Gustafson and Holloway (1974). The work is briefly described in Kneppreth et al. (1974).

problem make it such that the total cost is very closely related to the number of days in bed. This may also be directly related to the pain. Thus, it might be possible to eliminate both cost and the subjective pain index from the original list of four attributes and still end up with a complete, operational set of attributes: "the number of days in bed" and "the probability of death." This would have no redundancies and be of minimal reasonable size.

The discussion of the preceding few paragraphs should clearly bring out the point that sets of attributes are not unique. We have suggested several combinations that might serve for a particular medical problem.

2.5 PROXY ATTRIBUTES AND DIRECT PREFERENCE MEASUREMENTS

In this section we discuss an age-old problem confronting analysts: "...but what if we have specified an adequate objectives hierarchy and we just cannot find reasonable attributes for some of the lower-level objectives? We cannot go on subdividing objectives forever as you might suggest. And if we did this long enough, each of the objectives would fail to satisfy the test of importance; consequently they would be eliminated in further analysis, and we would have no attributes for some aspects of the hierarchy." What can be done?

In many cases, we can use *proxy attributes* and *direct preference measurements*. These two concepts provide us with methods for surmounting the difficulties posed. Their use, however, opens up additional ways that flaws can enter the analysis, but without them we can often only continue working on "half a problem." Let us discuss what we mean by these two concepts and when and how they should be used.

2.5.1 What are Proxy Attributes?

A *proxy attribute* is one that reflects the degree to which an associated objective is met but does not directly measure the objective. Thus, proxy attributes *indirectly* measure the achievement on a stated objective. It could be argued that essentially all attributes are proxy attributes because nothing can be absolutely measured. There are just varying degrees to which an objective is directly measured. Instead of getting into a philosophical discussion that would not be very fruitful, let us illustrate some points with an example.

Some mathematical symbolism might help here. Suppose that in a given context we have a rather natural set of lower-level objectives measured by attributes $X_1, \ldots, X_i, \ldots, X_n$. Let us further assume that it would be relatively easy for the decision maker to state his preferences for attribute evaluations of the form $\mathbf{x} = (x_1, \ldots, x_n)$. But now let us assume that it is impossible because of measurement reasons to use the set of X attributes. For example, in a decision concerning environmental standards we might be concerned with a set X of health attributes associated with different levels of pollution. We might simply not know very much about the linkage between a constellation of pollution levels, let us call these levels $\mathbf{y} = (y_1, \ldots, y_j, \ldots, y_r)$—where y_j might, for example, be the annual tonnage of particulate matter that is injected into the air over New York City—and the ultimate health levels $\mathbf{x} = (x_1, \ldots, x_n)$. Now, for each $\mathbf{y}$ we could assign a probability distribution for the uncertain $\tilde{\mathbf{x}}$ associated with that $\mathbf{y}$. If $u_X(\mathbf{x})$ designated the utility for the composite health levels $\mathbf{x}$, we could calculate an induced utility function u_Y over $\mathbf{y}$ levels by taking

$$u_Y(\mathbf{y}) = E_{X|\mathbf{y}} u_X(\tilde{\mathbf{x}}),$$

where the operator $E_{X|\mathbf{y}}$ expects out the uncertain quantity $\tilde{\mathbf{x}}$ (a random variable) using the *conditional* probability distribution over $\tilde{\mathbf{x}}$ given $\mathbf{y}$. In schematic form this is depicted in Fig. 2.4. The branch $\mathbf{y}$ leads to a chance fork of $\mathbf{x}$ possibilities, really a continuum of $\mathbf{x}$ possibilities in n space. We then assign a utility value $u_X(\mathbf{x})$ for each end position and average these utilities over the $\tilde{\mathbf{x}}$ fan using the conditional probability distribution for $\tilde{\mathbf{x}}$ *given* $\mathbf{y}$. At position B in Fig. 2.4 we then obtain the induced utility value $u_Y(\mathbf{y})$. This is repeated for each $\mathbf{y}$. Now we can proceed in the usual way—backwards—by putting a probability distribution over $\tilde{\mathbf{y}}$ and averaging-out back to position A, and so on.

A situation where this procedure may be particularly desirable is when decisions are made to "improve life" in terms of the X attributes, but where the entire impact of the decision can be specified by its impact on the Y attributes. Use of the induced utility function u_Y could then greatly

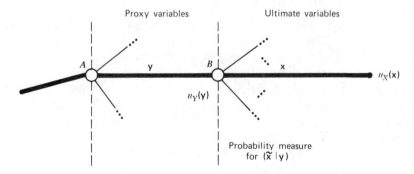

Fig. 2.4.   **An induced utility function** u_Y.

reduce the total effort involved, since one major part of the model, once it has been done, can be neglected except for prudent periodical reviews.

When there are several X attributes and only one Y attribute, we are effectively evaluating a multiattribute problem with the much simpler unidimensional framework. An air quality example where Y designates a single variable influenced by the decision alternatives is one plausible situation where this may occur.

But now let us suppose that we cannot responsibly assign a distribution to the chance fork B. In this case we can then subjectively assess our preferences or utilities for y configurations *directly*. Thus in using proxy variables y instead of the "ultimate" variables x we suppress, in Fig. 2.4, the chance fork emanating from B and use our mind as an informal synthesizer for directly assessing the $u_Y(\cdot)$ function.

Decision makers using the same proxy variables y might differ in their u_Y assignments because they might differ on (a) the u_X assignments, (b) the probability distribution of $(\tilde{x} \mid y)$, or (c) discrepancies arising from the informal synthesis of utilities and probabilities.

2.5.2 Example: Emergency Ambulance Service

The overall objective of an emergency ambulance system might be to "deliver patients to the hospital in the best possible conditions under the circumstances." Since there is no obvious attribute for this objective, suppose it is subdivided into "minimize the likelihood of death on arrival at the hospital" and "minimize the likelihood of arrival in critical condition." The proportion of patients dead on arrival and the proportion arriving in critical condition might be reasonable attributes for these objectives. However, the question of what is a critical condition would be difficult. Furthermore, a patient might receive the best care and treatment possible and still die en route to the hospital. In that case, the result should not be attributed to the competency of the ambulance service. But how would we differentiate this case from one where poor service contributed to the patient's death? It might not be possible to identify suitable attributes that directly indicate the extent to which the objectives are achieved.

Faced with the problem of analyzing emergency ambulance systems, both Savas (1969) and Stevenson (1972) have used the proxy attribute "response time." They defined this as the time between receipt of a call for an ambulance and arrival of an ambulance at the scene. The "delivery time," the time between receipt of the call and arrival of the patient, is another important proxy attribute used in ambulance studies. The premise is that shorter response times and delivery times will help achieve the overall objective of an emergency ambulance system. And, because of this relationship, they may be used as attributes that reflect the degree to which this objective is achieved.*

2.5.3 The Mind as an Informal Synthesizer

When we use proxy attributes, the decision maker must process additional information in his mind when he chooses the best alternative. He must informally decide to what extent the objectives are met by the different levels of achievement as indicated by the proxy attributes.

The point is clarified by expanding on the ambulance example. Consider Fig. 2.5, which represents a simplified model of an emergency ambulance system. Our input variables are:

$N \equiv$ The number of ambulances.
$K \equiv$ The location of ambulances.
$M \equiv$ Quality and quantity of personnel in the system.

Although this may be vague, we would only complicate the discussion by being more specific. What we would like to do is measure the extent that the objectives are met in terms of attributes X and Y, which represent the proportion of the patients arriving at the hospital dead and in critical condition, respectively. These can be designated the output of the system. The decisions control the inputs, and achievement is measured by the outputs.

However, we just argued that it might not be practical to use X and Y for evaluating the decisions and, as an alternative, we suggested using response time R and delivery time T for this evaluation. If our model gave us everything we wanted, we could get probability density functions for X and Y conditional on each possible decision. But it does not give us this, so we must settle for probability density functions over R and T. Now X and Y have some probabilistic relationship to R and T, which we will designate by

$$x = f_1(r, t, e_3)$$

and

$$y = f_2(r, t, e_4),$$

---

* Response time has been used as a proxy attrubute in analyzing other emergency services. For example, Larson (1972) uses police response time in evaluating various allocation strategies in urban police departments, and Carter and Ingall (1970) use the response times of the various pieces of equipment answering calls for service in comparing operational policies available to the New York City Fire Department. See Section 7.3 for an attempt to aggregate the response times of these various pieces of equipment into an overall index of the quality of response to fires.

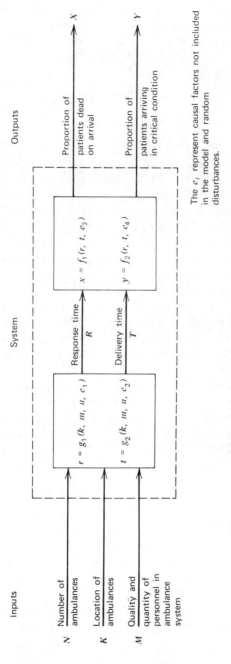

Fig. 2.5. Proxy attributes in a simplified model of an emergency ambulance system.

Inputs

N — Number of ambulances

K — Location of ambulances

M — Quality and quantity of personnel in ambulance system

System

$r = g_1(k, m, n, c_1)$

$t = g_2(k, m, n, c_2)$

Response time R

Delivery time T

$x = f_1(r, t, c_3)$

$y = f_2(r, t, c_4)$

Outputs

Proportion of patients dead on arrival — X

Proportion of patients arriving in critical condition — Y

The c_i represent causal factors not included in the model and random disturbances.

where the e_i represent causal factors, other than response time and delivery time, and random disturbances.* Our model does not indicate what f_1 and f_2 are, and this is why we cannot get the probability density functions for X and Y. Actually both R and T are functions of N, K, and M and the model gives us

$$r = g_1(k, m, n, e_1)$$

and

$$t = g_2(k, m, n, e_2)$$

where g_1 and g_2 are those functions.

What do we lose by using R and T rather than X and Y to evaluate the various courses of action? Presumably, when we ask the decision maker to express his preferences for different amounts of R and T, he does this by considering the effects that R and T have on X and Y. But this requires an understanding of $f_1(r, t, e_3)$ and $f_2(r, t, e_4)$, or at least an understanding of how different values of R and T contribute to the overall objective of getting patients to the hospital in the best possible condition under the circumstances. Essentially, the introduction of proxy attributes requires that some of the modeling of the system be done in the decision maker's head. This is what we would often like to avoid, because there is too much information in complex problems to handle effectively this way. However, when it is unavoidable, careful thinking may permit the decision maker to express a useful set of relationships between proxy attributes and the original objectives. It is probably safe to say that, in general, when a smaller part of the model must be implicitly considered by the decision maker, the quantified preferences more accurately reflect his true preferences for the basic objectives. For this reason, Hatry (1970) cautions against the excessive use of proxy attributes even though they might be easier to handle analytically or might be easily accessible.

Attributes R and T might still be useful even if the set X, Y is not complete. For example, suppose that a third attribute Z representing "annual cost of the ambulance system" is needed. Again, there may be problems using X and Y on a practical problem, but Z itself may be adequate for cost considerations. In such a case, R and T might again be collectively proxy for X and Y, the service considerations, and the set R, T, and Z may reasonably satisfy our criteria for a set of attributes.

Suppose, in the ambulance problem, that we could not build an analytical or simulation model of any sort; that is, we could not relate the inputs to the outputs or to any sets of proxy attributes that we felt might be appropriate for the problem. In this case, the decision maker might

---

* Lower-case letters will represent specific amounts of variables and attributes. That is, a specific value of response time R will be r.

have to consider the entire model in his head by relating the possible levels of inputs to achieving the stated objective. The decision maker must assess his preferences over various levels of K, M, and N by considering their effect on X and Y. And so, these three variables can be thought of as another set of proxy attributes that we might need to "fall back on" in our analysis. This indicates two points. First, there is no unique set of proxy attributes, and second, the proxy attributes can come in degrees. That is, some sets of proxy attributes are more closely related to the basic objectives than are other sets.

2.5.4 Common Proxy Attributes

Earlier in this section, we remarked that all attributes might be proxy attributes because there is nothing that measures completely and precisely all that we are interested in. But clearly some are "less proxy" than others. Here we point out a couple of attributes that are so conventionally used that we often do not think of them as proxy attributes.

The best examples of this are the attributes "total wealth," "income," or "profits" that are associated with the very commonly stated objective "maximize profits." However, is the basic objective to accumulate dollars for their own sake, or for other things such as consumer goods, the power to implement ideas, and so on, which dollars help one to achieve? Probably, in many cases, the latter are more important, so profits can be thought of as a proxy attribute.

Another similar example concerns the "share of the market" that many large firms use in evaluating their relative position. But this might often be a proxy attribute for such intangibles as prestige and power. Or "share of the market" may be a proxy for future profits, which may be a proxy for other more basic attributes.

For many problems, it is imperative to introduce proxy attributes in order to handle operationally some very messy difficulties.

2.5.5 Direct Preference Measurements

With both proxy attributes and subjective indices, we need to obtain a probability distribution for the various possible levels of the attribute, to assess a utility function over these levels, and finally to calculate the expected utility over the attribute for each course of action.* The result would be a single number (expected utility over attribute Y) for each course of action indicating the preferences for that course of action relative to the others as far as that particular objective was concerned. In

---

* More precisely we should consider *conditional* utilities and expected *conditional* utilities of Y given different levels of other attributes.

some instances, it may be virtually impossible to assess these probability distributions and the conditional utility function. When this is true, the decision maker may prefer (or perhaps be forced for lack of alternatives) to directly assign a utility index on a particular attribute for each of the various courses of action under consideration.

To illustrate the idea with a simple example, let us take a business with two objectives: "maximize profit" and "maximize goodwill." Let X and Y designate the respective attributes for these objectives. For X, the measure "profits in dollars" may be chosen, but there appears to be no clear objective index for Y. Three options for handling this are a subjective index, a proxy attribute, or direct preference measurements. With a subjective index, the procedure should now be reasonably clear. We attempt to establish a scale of goodwill meaningful in the context of our problem. Then, for each alternative, probability distributions are assessed to describe the possible impact in terms of Y, and a utility function is assessed over the Y attribute. Expected conditional utilities— conditional on the X attribute being held constant—can then be calculated for each alternative and used in the ensuing analysis.* With a proxy attribute, the process still involves assessing probability distributions over Y—now a proxy attribute—for each alternative and a conditional utility function. Then again, conditional expected utilities are calculated for each alternative. With direct preference measures, the story is different. The decision maker must directly assign the conditional expected utilities for achieving the objective "maximize goodwill." This avoids the formalism of specifying an attribute for goodwill, assessing conditional probability distributions, and assessing the conditional utility function. However, it clearly requires hard and thoughtful input on the decision maker's part.

Some direct preference measurements are used by Miller (1969) in structuring the decision process for choosing among various employment opportunities. He used three attributes to describe continuing aspects of the jobs that would make them desirable. These were personal interest in the technical content of the job, degree of variety implicit in the job, and the amount of training in management skills realizable from the job. Preferences for four different jobs were assessed directly along each of these three attributes. Another use of direct preference measurements is discussed in the dynamic analysis of the Mexico City airport study, described in Chapter 8.

---

* Throughout this subsection, we implicitly assume that the X attribute is held fixed. In Chapter 5, concepts are introduced indicating when it is reasonable to calculate expected utility conditionally for one attribute while the other attributes are fixed at convenient levels.

2.5.6 Some Comments on Proxy Attributes and Direct Preference Measurements

When it is necessary to use proxy attributes, or direct preference measurement, it is important to find attributes with which the decision maker is familiar. For instance, fire department officials are accustomed to thinking in terms of response times. When we ask a fire official for his preferences, he will presumably be able to relate the response times to achievement of the basic objectives in a meaningful way. Similarly, one might expect a politician to directly assign preferences for alternatives in terms of the attribute "political effects." Essentially, in both cases, we are asking the decision maker to distill his years of experience in providing these preferences. The more accustomed the decision maker is to thinking in terms of the attribute, the more easily he will be able to express preferences, and the more likely he will understand the complex relationships between the attribute, the alternatives, and the basic objectives.

A second point is probably very obvious to most readers. That is, for every proxy attribute we suggest, we can easily find an associated "proxy objective." For instance, the objective "minimize the emergency ambulance response time" is a proxy objective. We point this out because confusion on this matter can easily result in a redundant set of attributes for a problem. If we build an objectives hierarchy for the ambulance problem with "minimize response time," "minimize the proportion of arrivals dead at the hospital," and "minimize the proportion of arrivals in critical condition," and so on, we are likely to end up with redundancies in the final set of attributes.

Finally, note that, in most of our examples, improving performance in terms of the proxy attributes contributes to meeting the basic objectives. For instance, a lower response time contributes to "getting the patient to the hospital in the best possible condition." In some problems, it may be more convenient to look at performance on proxy attributes that are improved by meeting the basic objectives. For instance, one objective of a municipal sanitation service might be "to keep the streets clean." An attribute that might directly measure this would be "pounds of dirt and garbage per hundred yards of street." Such proxy attributes as "number of garbage pickups per week" and "time between street cleanings" indicate performance that contributes to accomplishing the basic objective. On the other hand, a proxy attribute such as "the number of citizen complaints about dirty streets per week" also indirectly indicates the level of service provided. In this case, however, presumably better service in terms of the basic objective *causes* better performance as measured by the proxy attribute.

2.6 SUMMARY AND PERSPECTIVE ON THE PRACTICAL ASPECTS OF SPECIFYING OBJECTIVES AND ATTRIBUTES

To attempt any formal analysis of a complex decision problem requires an articulation of the decision maker's objectives and an identification of attributes useful for indicating the extent that these objectives are achieved. Unfortunately these objectives and attributes are not simply handed to us in an envelope at the beginning of an analysis. The intertwined processes of articulating objectives and identifying attributes are basically creative in nature. Thus, it is not possible to establish a step-by-step procedure that leads one in the end to a meaningful set of objectives and attributes.

What we have tried to accomplish in this chapter is to establish guidelines that may be useful in carrying out the necessary thought processes. At one end of the spectrum—the input side—suggestions were included to help the decision maker and/or analyst probe his mind when facing the problems of obtaining objectives. At the other end of the spectrum, a set of criteria were suggested for the quality of the output of the objective and attribute generation processes. This output—the set of attributes—is crucial in the ensuing analysis. Since it is not usually the case that nice objective attributes are available to measure all the objectives in a complex problem, three specific procedures for handling such problems—subjective indices, proxy attributes, and direct preference measurements—were introduced and illustrated.

Before concluding this chapter, let us try to put some of the ideas we have discussed into proper perspective. Perhaps the biggest shortcoming of going through many examples such as we have done is that, inevitably, the overall feeling for what we are trying to do does not come through as well as the specific points used for illustrations (although the former is more important than the latter). This is mainly because much realism is lost in reducing the problem into written form and again in trying to distill that to bring out specific points. Without this reduction of scope, our ideas would probably be lost in the multitudes of words necessary to adequately describe all the relevant aspects of the problem. In establishing a meaningful objectives hierarchy and associated set of attributes for a complex problem, we can bring forth many factors we have not explicitly considered here. The process of specifying the objectives is not done in a vacuum. At the same time, we may have relevant information about what data are accessible, the quality and quantity of other available resources (e.g., computers), various types of constraints that are in force (e.g., time, politics), the range of alternative courses of action, and so on. All of these factors might significantly affect the objectives hierarchy and choice of attributes.

The message should be clear. Although we have offered some guidelines that will hopefully facilitate the selection of an objectives hierarchy and associated attributes, we view our work as far from complete. It would be erroneous to assume that any of our suggestions can replace serious thinking and resourcefulness.

CHAPTER 3

Tradeoffs Under Certainty

Many complex decision problems involve multiple conflicting objectives. It is often true that no dominant alternative will exist that is better than all other alternatives in terms of all of these objectives. Perhaps some of the original alternatives can be eliminated from further consideration because they are dominated, but generally you simply cannot maximize several objectives simultaneously. You cannot maximize benefits and at the same time minimize costs; you cannot necessarily maximize yield and minimize risk; nor can you share a pie by giving the maximum amount to each child. The literature is replete with high-sounding rhetoric where an advocate cries out for doing "best" for everybody, in every possible way, in the shortest time, with the least inconvenience, and with the maximum security for all. Ah, for the simplicity of the romanticist's dream world!

3.1 THE MULTIATTRIBUTE VALUE PROBLEM

Our problem is one of value tradeoffs. In this chapter we see what can be done about systematically structuring such tradeoffs. In essence, the decision maker is faced with a problem of trading off the achievement of one objective against another objective. If there is no uncertainty in the problem, if we know the multiattribute consequence of each alternative, the essence of the issue is, "How much achievement on objective 1 is the decision maker willing to give up in order to improve achievement on objective 2 by some fixed amount?" If there is uncertainty in the problem, the tradeoff issue remains, but difficulties are compounded because it is not clear what the consequences of each of the alternatives will be.

The tradeoff issue often becomes a personal value question and, in

66

those cases, it requires the subjective judgement of the decision maker. There may be no right or wrong answers to these value questions and, naturally enough, different individuals may have very different value structures. If the tradeoff issue requires deep reflection—and we believe it often does in complex problems—there are two possibilities for resolving the issue: (1) the decision maker can informally weigh the tradeoffs in his mind or (2) he can formalize explicitly his value structure and use this to evaluate the contending alternatives. Of course, there are mixtures of intermediary possibilities between these two extremes. In this chapter, we discuss some techniques to help a confused decision maker formalize his or her own value structure. These provide a framework of thought that can be used by the decision maker to assist him in articulating his preferences.

3.1.1 Statement of the Problem

Let a designate a feasible alternative and denote the set of all feasible alternatives by A. To each act a in A we will associate n indices of value: $X_1(a), \ldots, X_n(a)$. We can think of the n evaluators $X_1, \ldots, X_n$ as mapping each a in A into a point in an n-dimensional consequence space, as shown in Fig. 3.1.

We often talk about some *attribute* X, such as the aesthetic appeal of a design, and about an evaluator X of this attribute. We will unashamedly use the same symbol X for the attribute in question and the evaluator of that attribute. It will be clear what we are talking about and sometimes it is just plain convenient not to draw distinctions between these two concepts.

In this chapter, the n attributes are given. But, of course, we must keep in mind that in practice, we have to design and create these attributes that purport to describe the consequences of actions. The ideas of Chapter 2 may be useful for this task.

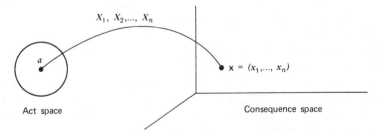

Fig. 3.1. The mapping of acts into consequences.

Observe that if $(x_1, x_2, \ldots, x_n)$ is a point in the consequence space, we will never compare the magnitudes of x_i and x_j, for $i \neq j$, since in most situations this would be meaningless because attributes X_i and X_j may be measured in totally different units.

Roughly the decision maker's problem is to choose a in A so that he will be happiest with the payoff $X_1(a), \ldots, X_n(a)$. Thus we need an index that combines $X_1(a), \ldots, X_n(a)$ into a scalar index of preferability or value. Alternatively stated, it is adequate to specify a scalar-valued function v defined on the consequence space with the property that

$$v(x_1, x_2, \ldots, x_n) \geqq v(x_1', x_2', \ldots, x_n') \Leftrightarrow (x_1, x_2, \ldots, x_n) \succeq (x_1', x_2', \ldots, x_n'),$$

where the symbol $\succeq$ reads "preferred or indifferent to." We refer to the function v as a *value function*. The same construct has many other names in the literature—ordinal utility function, preference function, worth function, or utility function. Given v, the decision maker's problem is to choose a in A such that v is maximized. The value function v serves to compare various levels of the different attributes indirectly, through the effects the magnitudes x_i, $i = 1, \ldots, n$, have on v.

3.1.2 Organization and Perspective of the Chapter

Our main consideration is how to structure and assess a value function v. It would be nice if we could find some function, call it f, with a simple form such that

$$v(x_1, x_2, \ldots, x_n) = f[v_1(x_1), v_2(x_2), \ldots, v_n(x_n)],$$

where v_i designates a value function over the single attribute X_i. Some of the constructions of v in this chapter do exactly this.

However, before delving deeply into this problem, we shall first discuss some concepts that do not require complete formalization of the preference structure. In some cases, this may give us enough information for a responsible decision. Then we consider the structure of value functions where there are two, three, and more than three attributes, respectively. This is followed by a detailed illustration of the assessment of a multiattribute value function.

Much of this chapter is expository in nature. Many of the concepts and results discussed are due to Debreu (1960), Gorman (1968a, 1968b), Krantz et al. (1971), Leontief (1947a, 1947b), Luce and Tukey (1964), Pruzan and Jackson (1963), and Ting (1971). When important results are stated, they will be designated as theorems for easy reference, but in many cases the formal proofs will be omitted since the proofs are accessible in the original works. We will, however, try to capture the ideas of these theorems with several "informal proofs." One price we pay for this is that assumptions such as continuity, differentiability, essentiality, and solvability, which are often utilized in the formal proofs, are sometimes ignored in our informal ones. Essentially we assume exactly what is necessary to make our reasoning work, and we concentrate on only the simplest nonpathological cases. Later, where our work becomes less expository, we become a bit more formal and careful.

Section 3.9 provides you with a brief guide to the literature on multiattribute value functions.

In summary then, this chapter looks at the certainty case—the case where associated to each alternative there is a certain known consequence in n space. In ensuing chapters we will look at the probabilistic case—the case where we only know the associated payoff in the consequence space in probabilistic terms. Techniques developed for the certainty case will prove useful also for the probabilistic case.

3.2 CHOICE PROCEDURES THAT DO NOT FORMALIZE PREFERENCE STRUCTURES

Let acts a' and a'' have consequences

$$\mathbf{x}' = (x'_1, \ldots, x'_i, \ldots, x'_n) \quad \text{and} \quad \mathbf{x}'' = (x''_1, \ldots, x''_i, \ldots, x''_n)$$

where

$$X_i(a') \equiv x'_i \quad \text{and} \quad X_i(a'') \equiv x''_i, \quad \text{for} \quad i = 1, \ldots, n.$$

Furthermore, let us assume throughout this section that preferences* increase in each X_i.

3.2.1 Dominance

We say that $\mathbf{x}'$ *dominates* $\mathbf{x}''$ whenever

$$\text{(a)} \quad x'_i \geq x''_i, \quad \text{all } i, \quad (3.1)$$

and

$$\text{(b)} \quad x'_i > x''_i, \quad \text{for some } i. \quad (3.2)$$

If $\mathbf{x}'$ dominates $\mathbf{x}''$, then the act a'' is a *noncontender* for "best," since a' is at least as good as a'' for every evaluator [given by (3.1)], and strictly better for at least one [given by (3.2)].

* More formally, in terms of vernacular to be introduced later, we assume that each X_i is preferentially independent of the complementary set of attributes (see Section 3.5), and that preferences increase in each X_i.

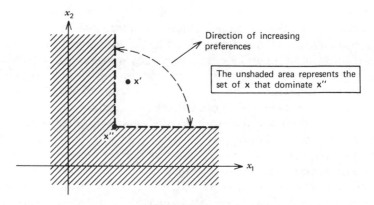

Fig. 3.2. Dominance with two attributes.

In the case $n = 2$, we can plot the points $\mathbf{x}'$ and $\mathbf{x}''$ as in Fig. 3.2 and we see that $\mathbf{x}'$ dominates $\mathbf{x}''$ if and only if $\mathbf{x}'$ is "northeast" of $\mathbf{x}''$.

Observe that the idea of dominance exploits only the *ordinal* character of the numbers in the consequence space (i.e., given two numbers $x'_i = 6$ and $x''_i = 3$ we are interested in the relationship that $x'_i > x''_i$) and not the *cardinal* character of these numbers (i.e., the fact that the difference between 10 and 6 is greater than the distance from 6 to 3 or that 6 is twice 3). Also observe that dominance does not require comparisons between x'_i and x''_j for $i \neq j$.

3.2.2 The Efficient Frontier

For any (feasible) act $a \in A$ there is an associated consequence $\mathbf{x}$ in n space (i.e., the evaluation space) where $x_i \equiv X_i(a)$, all i. Let R be the set of consequences in n space that are associated with acts in A; the set R is the so-called range-set of the vector X of evaluators $X_1, \ldots, X_n$ that are defined on the domain A.

Figure 3.3 depicts various range-sets, R, when $n = 2$. We shall have occasion to discuss these qualitatively different cases.*

The set of consequences of R that are *not dominated* will be called the *efficient frontier of R*. It is also known as the "Pareto optimal set." In Fig.

---

* We don't want to be too fussy about mathematical details but somehow we must rule out pathological cases or else we will get into trouble. We assume that the region R is bounded and that it contains all of its boundary points. That is, we definitely want to rule out the case where there is a sequence of points $\mathbf{x}^{(1)}, \mathbf{x}^{(2)}, \ldots, \mathbf{x}^{(m)}, \ldots$ in R such that each point in the sequence dominates the preceding consequence, and where the sequence approaches some point $\mathbf{x}^*$ that does *not* belong to R.

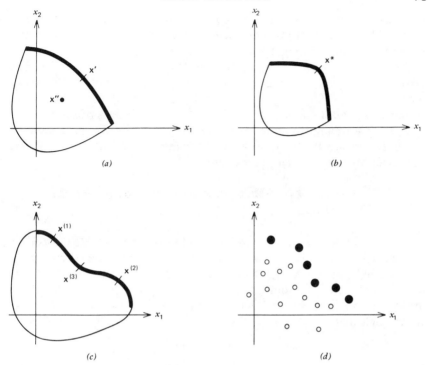

Fig. 3.3. The efficient frontier for various sets of consequences with two attributes.

3.3*a*, *b*, and *c*, the efficient frontiers are darkened. Thus in Fig. 3.3*a* the choice of **x″** can be ruled out because there is the consequence **x′** in the efficient frontier which dominates **x″**. In Fig. 3.3*c* the consequence **x**$^{(3)}$ is efficient (i.e., lies on the efficient frontier) even though it lies in a local valley, so to speak. In Fig. 3.3*d* the set *R* consists of discrete consequences and the efficient points are marked with an overlaying heavy dot. The cases depicted in Fig. 3.3*a* and *b* are the easiest to handle analytically, since the sets of consequences are convex and the efficient frontiers continuous. Notice, however, that the concept of convexity introduces *cardinal* (as opposed to ordinal) notions.

In some cases where the efficient set can be drawn it might be pretty obvious which **x** should be chosen. For example, in Fig. 3.3*b* the point **x*** naturally suggests itself because we must sacrifice so much of one attribute to gain so little of another attribute when moving slightly from **x***. Admittedly, we are implicitly using cardinal concepts in making this last remark, but the natural units for the X_1 and X_2 evaluators might make such cardinal tradeoffs manifestly clear. We are not saying this is necessarily so; just that it might be.

For values of $n > 3$ we cannot picture R and its efficient frontier. The next two sections describe two ways the decision maker can "move around" on an efficient frontier in order to locate a point that seems reasonably good. Later sections will describe procedures a decision maker can use to formally structure his preferences for points in the evaluation space. But meanwhile let us look at what can be done without completely specifying such a preference structure.

3.2.3 Exploring the Efficient Frontier: Use of Artificial Constraints*

The decision maker is faced with the following problem. He must select an act $a \in A$ so that he will be "satisfied" with the resulting n-dimensional payoff: $X_1(a), X_2(a), \ldots, X_n(a)$. One procedure he might employ is to think of some "aspiration levels" $x_1^o, x_2^o, \ldots, x_n^o$ for the n attributes and pose the well-defined, mathematical problem: Is there an $a \in A$ such that

$$X_i(a) \geq x_i^o, \qquad \text{for} \qquad i = 1, \ldots, n? \tag{3.3}$$

Is it possible to satisfy these joint aspirations? If not, then the decision maker can change his joint aspirations to some point $x_1', x_2', \ldots, x_n'$. If yes, that is, if an act a^+ exists that satisfies (3.3), then, although we know that

$$X_i(a^+) \geq x_i^o, \qquad \text{for} \qquad i = 1, \ldots, n,$$

we still do not know that the point

$$(X_1(a^+), X_2(a^+), \ldots, X_n(a^+))$$

is efficient. It may be dominated. We might continue our probing procedure by setting up another aspiration level $(x_1', \ldots, x_n')$ where

$$x_i' = X_i(a^+) + \Delta_i, \qquad i = 1, \ldots, n$$

and where the increment Δ_i is chosen in an ad hoc, intuitive manner that is a combination of wishful thinking and realism. Thus in an iterative manner the decision maker can investigate the frontier or "almost frontier" of R. By informally keeping his preferences in mind, he can choose a

---

*Some references covering topics briefly discussed in this subsection are Dyer (1972), Geoffrion, Dyer, and Feinberg (1972), Kornbluth (1973), Roy (1971), and Schroeder (1974).

succession of aspiration levels that can move him around the region R until he reaches the limits of his patience, or until he figures that the expected gain of continuing the probing procedure is not worth the effort in time and cost of analysis.

Perhaps a more satisfactory variation of this procedure consists of setting aspirational levels for all attributes but one. for example, suppose the decision maker selects aspiration levels $x_2^o, x_3^o, \ldots, x_n^o$ and seeks an $a \in A$ that satisfies the imposed constraints

$$X_i(a) \ge x_i^o, \quad \text{for} \quad i = 2, 3, \ldots, n \quad (3.4)$$

and maximizes $X_1(a)$.

This maximization problem is in the form of the "standard optimization problem." If there is no feasible solution [i.e., no $a \in A$ that satisfies (3.4)], then obviously the set of aspirations $x_2^o, \ldots, x_n^o$ has to be changed. But even if a feasible solution exists, the decision maker may be surprised at the maximum value of $X_1(a)$. If it is either too small or too large (as compared to what he "expected") he might want to change the original aspiration levels $x_2^o, \ldots, x_n^o$ and iterate the procedure.

Let the maximum of $X_1(a)$ subject to constraints $a \in A$ and (3.4) be denoted by $M_1(x_2^o, \ldots, x_n^o)$. The notation emphasizes the point that the maximum depends on the aspiration levels $x_2^o, \ldots, x_n^o$. It is often the case that, as a by-product of the solution procedure of the standard optimization problem, we get the local rate of change of M_1 as each of the constraints is released (all others remain fixed). In mathematical terms we obtain the partial derivatives

$$\frac{\partial}{\partial x_j^o} M_1(x_2^o, \ldots, x_n^o)$$

for $j = 2, \ldots, n$. Now the decision maker has a lot of information at his disposal. He chooses $x_2^o, \ldots, x_n^o$ and then, as a result of the analysis, he obtains

$$M_1(x_2^o, \ldots, x_n^o) \quad \text{and} \quad \frac{\partial}{\partial x_j^o} M_1(x_2^o, \ldots, x_n^o) \quad \text{for} \quad j = 2, \ldots, n.$$

He now has to decide either to remain satisfied with what he has or probe further. If he decides to continue his search for a "satisfactory" solution he might wish to single out an index j and investigate the behavior of

$$M_1(x_2^o, \ldots, x_{j-1}^o, x_j, x_{j+1}^o, \ldots, x_n^o)$$

as a function of x_j. That is, he might choose to keep intact all the previous constraints (other than x_j^o) and systematically observe what happens to M_1 as x_j moves over a given range. He does this even though he already knows the value of M_1 at x_j^o and the derivative at this point, because this

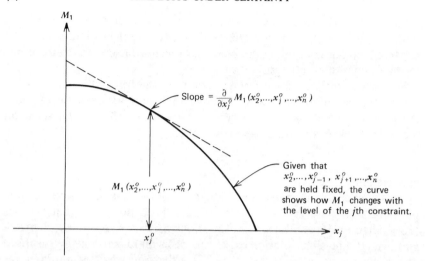

Fig. 3.4. Exploring the efficient frontier using artificial constraints.

additional information may be useful, and the cost of the additional analysis may be quite small. Figure 3.4 shows one possible result of such an analysis.

The above investigative, probing procedure is ad hoc; it is not precisely programmed. It requires a series of creative judgments from the decision maker. He has to decide on aspiration levels, on special investigations of the sensitivity of payoffs (e.g., M_1) to his arbitrarily imposed constraints, on setting new aspiration levels, and so on; finally, he must decide when to be "satisfied" and stop. This probing procedure involves a continuing interaction between analyzing what is *achievable* and what is *desirable*. It proceeds incrementally, where the choice of each step is decided by the decision maker, who must constantly weigh informally in his mind what he would *like* to get and what he thinks he might be *able* to get. Interactive computer programs have been written to help make this iterative probing operational. In the next subsection we discuss another way of exploring the efficient frontier in n space.

3.2.4 Exploring the Efficient Frontier: Use of Variable, Linear-Weighted Averages*

In this section we pose an auxiliary mathematical problem, the solution of which will result in the identification of some point on the efficient

---

* For procedures that generate the entire efficient frontier using linear programming, see Zeleny (1974). Also see Zionts and Wallenius (1976).

frontier. By modifying the auxiliary problem, the decision maker can move along the efficient frontier until he is satisfied with the result.

For any $a \in A$ we assume, as before, there is the payoff $X_1(a), \ldots, X_n(a)$. Let

$$\boldsymbol{\lambda} = (\lambda_1, \lambda_2, \ldots, \lambda_n) \qquad (3.5a)$$

be any n-tuple for which

$$\lambda_i > 0, \quad \text{all } i \qquad (3.5b)$$

and

$$\sum_{i=1}^{n} \lambda_i = 1. \qquad (3.5c)$$

Define the auxiliary problem as follows: choose $a \in A$ to maximize

$$\sum_{i=1}^{n} \lambda_i X_i(a). \qquad (3.6)$$

We also state the problem in an equivalent fashion as follows: choose $x \in R$ to maximize

$$\sum_{i=1}^{n} \lambda_i x_i. \qquad (3.7)$$

This auxiliary problem is in the form of a standard optimization problem. Let $\mathbf{x}^o = (x_1^o, \ldots, x_n^o)$ be a solution to this auxiliary problem. We now assert that $\mathbf{x}^o$ must lie on the efficient frontier. Suppose it did not; then there would be an $\mathbf{x}'$ belonging to R that would dominate $\mathbf{x}^o$. But this cannot be, since in that case

$$\sum_{i=1}^{n} \lambda_i x_i' > \sum_{i=1}^{n} \lambda_i x_i^o$$

and therefore $\mathbf{x}^o$ would not be a maximizer of $\sum \lambda_i x_i$.

Hence corresponding to an n-tuple $\boldsymbol{\lambda}$ satisfying (3.5), the maximizer of $\sum \lambda_i x_i$ (for $\mathbf{x}$ in R), results in a point $\mathbf{x}^o$ that lies on the efficient frontier.

The geometry of this analysis is shown in Fig. 3.5 for $n = 2$, when $\boldsymbol{\lambda} = (.8, .2)$. The point $\mathbf{x}^o$ is a maximizer of

$$.8x_1 + .2x_2.$$

The line through $\mathbf{x}^o$ of the form

$$.8x_1 + .2x_2 = k$$

(for a suitably chosen k) must be tangential to R at $\mathbf{x}^o$, since this line obviously contains $\mathbf{x}^o$ and no point of R can be to the right of this line (otherwise, $\mathbf{x}^o$ would not be a maximizer of $.8x_1 + .2x_2$).

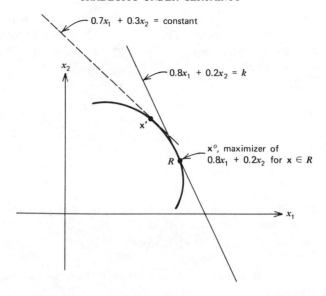

Fig. 3.5. Exploring the efficient frontier using linear weighting.

Now the decision maker can ask himself whether he wants to settle for $\mathbf{x}^o = (x_1^o, x_2^o)$ or explore the efficient frontier further. He knows that at $\mathbf{x}^o$ he can move along the frontier of R trading off Δ units of X_1 for approximately 4Δ units of X_2. That tradeoff is only precisely true in a limiting sense but for practical purposes we can think of 1 to 4 as the (local) marginal rate of substitution of X_1 for X_2 at the frontier point $\mathbf{x}^o$. Suppose the decision maker, on reflection, feels that the value of x_2^o is too low in comparison with x_1^o (i.e., he would be willing to give up some X_1 to get more X_2). He can then resolve the auxiliary problem by looking for a maximizer of, for example,

$$.7x_1 + .3x_2,$$

for $\mathbf{x} \in R$. If $\mathbf{x}' = (x_1', x_2')$ is such a maximizer, then $\mathbf{x}'$ will also be on the efficient frontier of R and $\mathbf{x}'$ will lie northwest of $\mathbf{x}^o$ as seen in Fig. 3.5. At $\mathbf{x}'$ the (local) marginal rate of substitution will be Δ units of X_1 for $7\Delta/3$ units of X_2, and so on.

Of course, if $n = 2$, the efficient frontier can be pictured. The real power of the technique can best be appreciated for higher values of n where the geometry can only be imagined but not drawn. For example, if the choice of $\boldsymbol{\lambda} = (\lambda_1, \ldots, \lambda_n)$ gives rise to the associated maximizer $\mathbf{x}^o = (x_1^o, \ldots, x_n^o)$, and if x_i^o appears to be unsuitably low, then the auxiliary maximization problem can be recycled with an increased value of λ_i. This will result in an increase (to be precise, it will not result in a decrease) in the optimal level x_i in the new maximization problem. The decision maker must decide when to be satisfied by looking at the points he has already obtained on the efficient frontier. By manipulating the λ_i's he can always move to different points on that frontier. Once again he is asked informally to balance what he would *like* to get with what he *thinks he can achieve*. If the efficient frontier is convex, with no local dips or valleys, the procedure that manipulates the λ_i's can generate any point on the frontier. In the nonconvex case, special techniques can be employed to map out these dips, but since this procedure is not in the mainstream of our concern, we will not explore these variations.

It is possible to proceed further. We might want to formalize some variation of the above iterative procedure and prove convergence to an optimum. Of course, if we do this, we would have to imagine that there is a complete ordering of the points in n space that is called on at each step of the iteration in order to guide the choice of each incremental adjustment. Since this approach does not generalize readily to the probabilistic case which is, after all, our main orientation, we shall not pursue the numerous analytical points emanating from the discussion in this subsection.

3.3   STRUCTURING OF PREFERENCES AND VALUE FUNCTIONS

We now discuss a new topic, one that formalizes the decision maker's preferences for points in the consequence space. As is commonly done in economics, we initially forget about the set of achievable points in n space (i.e., the set R in the Section 3.2) and discuss the decision maker's preferences for consequences in n space whether they actually belong to R or not. Only after formalizing these preferences do we then investigate the problem of finding a point in R that will yield the greatest preference.

3.3.1 Lexicographical Ordering

As our first illustration we examine an approach that we believe is more widely adopted in practice than it deserves to be: lexicographical ordering. However, it is simple and it can easily be administered. Our objection is that it is naively simple.

A lexicographical ordering is like the ordering found in a lexicon or dictionary: $a' > a''$ if and only if:

(a) $X_1(a') > X_1(a'')$

or

(b) $X_i(a') = X_i(a'')$, $i = 1, \ldots, k$,   and $X_{k+1}(a') > X_{k+1}(a'')$,
for some $k = 1, \ldots, n-1$.

In other words, we assume that the evaluators $X_1, \ldots, X_n$ are ordered according to importance. Act a' is preferred to a'' if it merely has a higher score on X_1, regardless of how well or poorly it does on other evaluators. Only if there is a tie on X_1 does evaluator X_2 come into consideration. Only if there is a tie on X_1 and X_2 does evaluator X_3 come into consideration, and so on. Naturally, we can generalize this formulation by permuting the prominence of the evaluators. We can, for example, make X_3 most important, followed by X_1, and so on.

Notice that if $\mathbf{x}'$ and $\mathbf{x}''$ are distinct points in an evaluation space, they cannot be indifferent with a lexicographical ordering.

A lexicographical ordering is easy to understand and, in some (very rare!) cases, it might reflect the "true" beliefs of the decision-making unit. However, it is our belief that, leaving aside "administrative ease," it is rarely appropriate. But, of course, administrative ease, is an important metaevaluator in its own right and cannot be ignored. Thus we do observe cases where lexicographical orderings are employed.

A VARIANT OF LEXICOGRAPHICAL ORDERING WITH ASPIRATION LEVELS. Suppose we order the evaluators in importance and for convenience let us use the natural ordering $1, 2, \ldots$. For each evaluator X_i set an aspiration level x_i^o and posit the following rules: $a' > a''$ whenever

(a) $X_1(a') > X_1(a'')$ and $X_1(a'') < x_1^o$

(i.e., X_1 overrides all else as long as X_1 aspirations are not met), or

(b) $X_1(a') \geq x_1^o$
$X_1(a'') \geq x_1^o$
$X_2(a') > X_2(a'')$ and $X_2(a'') < x_2^o$

(i.e., if X_1 aspirations are met, then X_2 overrides all else as long as X_2 aspirations are not met) and so forth.

If all aspiration levels are met, then we may be willing to give up some of X_1 for a suitably large increase in X_2, and so on. In this ordering system two distinct points $\mathbf{x}'$ and $\mathbf{x}''$ might be indifferent provided that $x_j' > x_j^o$ and $x_j'' > x_j^o$, for all j.

Again we feel that such an ordering procedure, if carefully scrutinized, will rarely pass a test of "reasonableness," but for administrative purposes such an ordering might indeed be imposed.

In what follows we deal only with preference structures that are less dogmatic in this sense: if $\mathbf{x}'$ is an interior point of R, then for a suitably small decrease in x_i' there will be a suitably large compensating increase in x_j'. In two space, this means that every point $\mathbf{x}$ lies on an indifference curve.

3.3.2 Indifference Curves

Figure 3.6 depicts an example of how a decision maker might structure his preferences for points in a two-dimensional evaluation space. This example assumes that the decision maker does not care whether he achieves $\mathbf{x}'$ or $\mathbf{x}''$, and this is portrayed by having both $\mathbf{x}'$ and $\mathbf{x}''$ on the same *indifference curve*. The point $\mathbf{x}'''$ is preferred to $\mathbf{x}'$ (by the decision maker) and therefore $\mathbf{x}'''$ lies on a higher (or more preferred) indifference curve.

We imagine that through any point $\mathbf{x}$ in an n-dimensional consequence space there is an indifference surface connecting all points that are indifferent to $\mathbf{x}$. These indifference surfaces will be curves for $n = 2$. We shall assume throughout that, in the opinion of the decision maker, any two points $\mathbf{x}^{(1)}$ and $\mathbf{x}^{(2)}$ are *comparable* in the sense that one, and only one, of the following holds:

(a) $\mathbf{x}^{(1)}$ is indifferent* to $\mathbf{x}^{(2)}$ (written: $\mathbf{x}^{(1)} \sim \mathbf{x}^{(2)}$),
(b) $\mathbf{x}^{(1)}$ is preferred to $\mathbf{x}^{(2)}$ (written: $\mathbf{x}^{(1)} > \mathbf{x}^{(2)}$),
(c) $\mathbf{x}^{(1)}$ is less preferred than $\mathbf{x}^{(2)}$ (written: $\mathbf{x}^{(1)} < \mathbf{x}^{(2)}$).

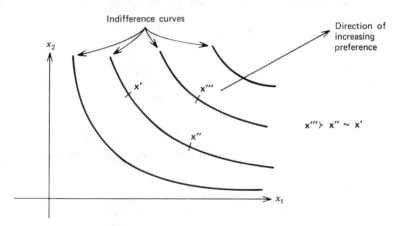

Fig. 3.6. A set of indifference curves.

---

*Less elliptically, and more grammatically, we could say that the decision maker is indifferent between $\mathbf{x}^{(1)}$ and $\mathbf{x}^{(2)}$.

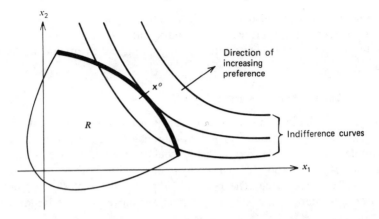

Fig. 3.7. The consequence x^o is the best consequence in R.

We write $\mathbf{x}^{(1)} \gtrsim \mathbf{x}^{(2)}$ to mean "not $[\mathbf{x}^{(1)} < \mathbf{x}^{(2)}]$" and assume all the relations $\sim, >, \gtrsim$ to be *transitive*.

A *preference structure* is defined on the consequence space if any two points are comparable and no intransitivities exist. We assume, also, that the decision maker believes that in a specified decision context there is a particular preference structure that is appropriate for him.

Once the decision maker has specified his preference structure he can proceed to formalize his problem: Find $a^o \in A$ such that

$$X(a^o) \gtrsim X(a), \qquad \text{for all } a \in A$$

where

$$X(a) \equiv [X_1(a), X_2(a), \ldots, X_n(a)].$$

Or, alternatively stated: find $\mathbf{x}^o \in R$ such that

$$\mathbf{x}^o \gtrsim \mathbf{x}, \qquad \text{for all } \mathbf{x} \in R.$$

Figure 3.7 depicts the geometry of this maximization problem.

3.3.3 Value Functions

A function v, which associates a real number $v(\mathbf{x})$ to each point $\mathbf{x}$ in an evaluation space, is said to be a *value function* representing the decision maker's preference structure provided that

$$\mathbf{x}' \sim \mathbf{x}'' \Leftrightarrow v(\mathbf{x}') = v(\mathbf{x}''), \tag{3.8a}$$

and

$$x' > x'' \Leftrightarrow v(x') > v(x'').$$ (3.8b)

Some typical examples of value functions for $n = 2$ are

$$v(\mathbf{x}) = c_1 x_1 + c_2 x_2, \qquad \text{where } c_1 > 0, \quad c_2 > 0,$$

$$v(\mathbf{x}) = x_1^\alpha x_2^\beta, \qquad \text{where } \alpha > 0, \quad \beta > 0,$$

$$v(\mathbf{x}) = c_1 x_1 + c_2 x_2 + c_3 (x_1 - b_1)^\alpha (x_2 - b_2)^\beta.$$

If v is a value function reflecting the decision maker's preferences, then his problem can be put into the format of the standard optimization problem: Find $a \in A$ to maximize $v[X(a)]$.

We shall see later that there is a subtle interplay between formulating a preference structure and finding a corresponding value function. Indeed, we may employ value functions to *help* a decision maker articulate his preferences.

3.3.4   Indifference Curves and Value Functions

Given a value function v, any two points $\mathbf{x}'$ and $\mathbf{x}''$ such that $v(\mathbf{x}') = v(\mathbf{x}'')$ must be indifferent to each other and must lie on the same indifference surface. Hence we see that given v it is possible, in principle, to find the indifference surfaces. More generally we see that a knowledge of v *uniquely* specifies an entire preference structure. The converse, however, is not true: a preference structure does *not uniquely* specify a value function.

Definition. The value functions v_1 and v_2 are *strategically equivalent,* written $v_1 \sim v_2$, if v_1 and v_2 have the same indifference curves and induced preferential ordering.

Suppose v_1 is a value function consistent with a given preference structure. Then if $T(\cdot)$ is any strictly monotonically increasing real-valued function (of a real variable), as depicted in Fig. 3.8, and if we now define $v_2(\mathbf{x}) \equiv T[v_1(\mathbf{x})]$, then it is immaterial whether we choose $a \in A$ to maximize v_1 or v_2. The value functions v_1 and v_2 are strategically equivalent.

For example, if all x_i are positive and

$$v_1(\mathbf{x}) = \sum_i k_i x_i, \qquad k_i > 0, \qquad \text{all } i,$$

then

$$v_2(\mathbf{x}) = \sqrt{\sum_i k_i x_i}$$

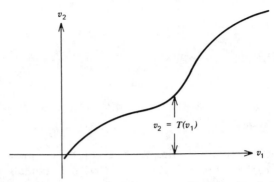

Fig. 3.8. **A monotonically increasing real-valued function T relating two strategically equivalent value functions v_1 and v_2.**

and

$$v_3(\mathbf{x}) = \log\left(\sum_i k_i x_i\right)$$

would be strategically equivalent to v_1. All three functions are representations of the same preference structure. Indeed, for operational purposes, given v we will want to choose T such that the value function $T(v)$ is easy to manipulate mathematically.

3.4   PREFERENCE STRUCTURES AND VALUE FUNCTIONS FOR TWO ATTRIBUTES

For notational convenience we label the two attributes as X and Y instead of X_1 and X_2. We repeat that X and Y shall each be assumed to be positively oriented: the more of any component the better, given any fixed level of the other component.

3.4.1   The Marginal Rate of Substitution

Suppose that you are given a concrete problem where X and Y are specified desirable attributes and you are asked: If Y is increased by Δ units, how much does X have to decrease in order for you to remain indifferent? Clearly, in many instances, your answer depends on the levels x of X and y of Y. If, at the point (x_1, y_1), you are willing to give up $\lambda\Delta$ units of X for Δ units of Y, then we will say that the *marginal rate of substitution* of X for Y at (x_1, y_1) is λ. In other words, λ is roughly the

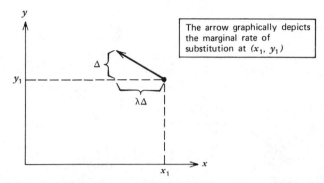

Fig. 3.9.   The marginal rate of substitution of X **for** Y **at** (x_1, y_1) **is** λ.

amount of X you are just willing to "pay" for a unit of Y, given that you presently have x_1 of X and y_1 of Y (see Fig. 3.9). Strictly speaking we should take the limit as Δ approaches 0. Throughout we assume that we are in a well-behaved world where all functions have smooth second derivatives.

The marginal rate of substitution at (x_1, y_1), as we are using it, is the negative reciprocal of the slope of the indifference curve at (x_1, y_1). Thus, if we have indifference curves, then we can calculate local substitution rates.* In this section we develop some methods for doing the reverse: that is, we think about how marginal rates of substitution can help us construct indifference curves.†

3.4.2   The General Case

We now investigate how marginal rates of substitution might depend on the levels of X and Y, that is, on (x_1, y_1). A straightforward procedure is

---

* *Mathematical digression*: If the indifference curve through (x_1, y_1) is given by

$$v(x, y) = c,$$

then the marginal rate of substitution λ at (x_1, y_1) can be obtained from the following formula:

$$\lambda = -\frac{dx}{dy}\bigg|_{x_1, y_1} = \frac{v_y'(x_1, y_1)}{v_x'(x_1, y_1)}$$

where v_x' and v_y' are the partial derivatives of v with respect to the first and second arguments, respectively.

† MacCrimmon and Toda (1969) introduce a procedure for determining indifference curves and present experimental results. An interactive computer program for utilizing the procedure and related experience with its use are found in MacCrimmon and Siu (1974), [see also Toda (1974)].

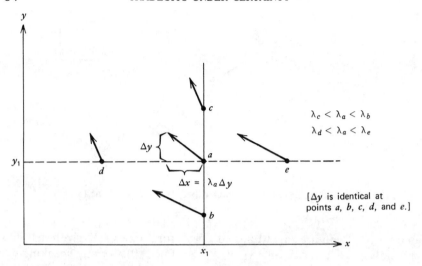

Fig. 3.10. The marginal rate of substitution as a function of X and Y.

(1) to hold x_1 fixed and look at the substitution rates as a function of y_1, and (2) to hold y_1 fixed and look at the substitution rates as a function of x_1.

For example, suppose the substitution rate at (x_1, y_1), the point a in Fig. 3.10 is λ_a. If we hold x_1 fixed, we might find that the substitution rates increase with a decrease in Y and decrease with an increase in Y. This is illustrated at points b and c in Fig. 3.10. The changes in the substitution rates mean that the more of Y we have, the less of X we would be willing to give up to gain a given additional amount of Y. In Fig. 3.10 we see that for the same increase in Y, the sacrifice of X is less at c than at b.

Similarly, if we hold y_1 fixed, we might find that the substitution rates decrease with decreasing X and increase with increasing X. This is illustrated at points d and e in Fig. 3.10. Thus we see that additional units of X become less important relative to Y the higher the x value, and that we are therefore willing to substitute more X per additional unit of Y. This behavior is consistent with indifference curves of the shape given in Fig. 3.6.

In many applications it is convenient to let X stand for monetary consequences. Now in this case, if $(x', y') \sim (x'', y'')$, then we can say that the decision maker is *just willing to pay* an amount $x'' - x'$ for a change of Y from y' to y'', when the monetary change taken place from the base of

x'. If h is a positive amount it definitely does *not* follow that, in general,

$$[(x', y') \sim (x'', y'')] \qquad \text{implies} \qquad [(x'+h, y') \sim (x''+h, y'')].$$

That is, the amount that the decision maker is just willing to pay for a change from y' to y'' depends on the monetary base from which he is starting. It generally is not possible to "price out" a change from y' to y'' without specifying the absolute level of X. The next two subsections consider those special cases where changes in Y can be "priced out" independently of the X starting position. A more general discussion of "willingness-to-pay" arguments is found in Section 3.8.

3.4.3   Constant Substitution: The Case of Linear Indifference Curves

An extreme special case of substitution rates occurs when the substitution rate at (x_1, y_1) does not depend on the values x_1 and y_1. That is, the local substitution rate is also the *global* substitution rate, applicable at any point and to substitutions in any amounts. In this case, the indifference curves are of the form

$$x + \lambda y = \text{constant}, \qquad\qquad (3.9)$$

and a suitable value function for this preference structure is

$$v(x, y) = x + \lambda y. \qquad\qquad (3.10)$$

Since in this case the local substitution rate is the global substitution rate, when assessing λ, the analyst does not have to ask localized questions involving small changes in x and y. The decision maker can base his assessment of λ on sizeable, psychologically meaningful changes in x and y.

Sometimes a decision maker may think that for his problem the substitution rates should be constant, but he may have difficulty assigning a value to λ. In practice it may not be necessary to determine λ exactly. For example, in a problem involving the choice of one of several actions, the decision maker might calculate λ intervals, such that action a_1 is best if

$$\lambda \leq \lambda_1,$$

action a_2 is best if

$$\lambda_1 < \lambda \leq \lambda_2,$$

and so on. Figure 3.11 illustrates such intervals.

In some problem, it may be clear that, although the exact value of λ is unknown, λ falls in the interval (λ_2, λ_3) and thus a_3 is best. If λ is close to

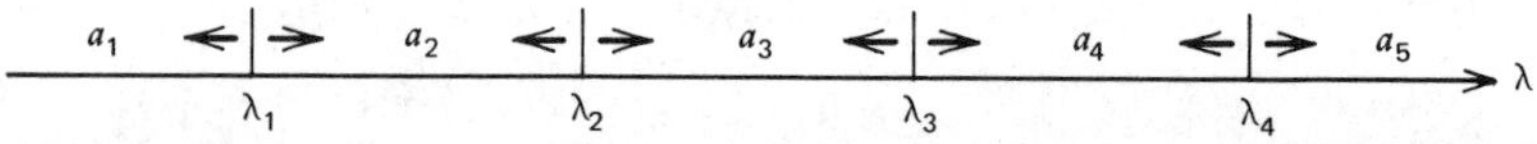

$$a_1 \quad \Leftarrow | \Rightarrow \quad a_2 \quad \Leftarrow | \Rightarrow \quad a_3 \quad \Leftarrow | \Rightarrow \quad a_4 \quad \Leftarrow | \Rightarrow \quad a_5$$
$$\lambda_1 \qquad\qquad \lambda_2 \qquad\qquad \lambda_3 \qquad\qquad \lambda_4 \qquad \lambda$$

Fig. 3.11. The optimal act as a function of the substitution rate λ.

λ_2 it may not be clear whether λ is greater than or less than λ_2 and thus whether a_2 or a_3 should be chosen. But in this case, a_2 and a_3 are almost at a standoff, so it may not be necessary to worry too much about which one is chosen, and certainly $a_1, a_4,$ and a_5 can be eliminated from consideration.

3.4.4 Constant Substitution Rates with a Transformed Variable

Suppose that the marginal rate of substitution λ at (x_1, y_1) depends on y_1 but not on x_1. That is, suppose that the amount the decision maker is willing to pay in X units for additional Y units depends on the level of Y but not on the level of X. (Even if this supposition is not exactly true, it may be true approximately for x values in a given range of concern, and a convenient "lie" may not be inappropriate.) Four typical substitution rates for this case are illustrated in Fig. 3.12.

An example of the kind of composite value function that produces this pattern of local substitution rates is

$$v(x, y) = x + v_Y(y), \tag{3.11}$$

where we use the symbol $v_Y(\cdot)$ to indicate a function of single variable y.

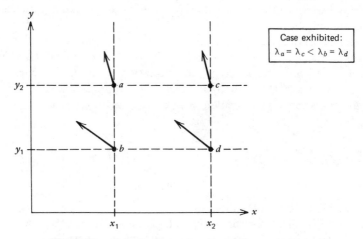

Fig. 3.12. Substitution rates depending on y but not x.

If a decision maker feels that substitution rates depend on y but not on x, how can this qualitative requirement help in the assessment of an appropriate v function? We now show in this case that v may be expressed as in (3.11).

If you are at (x_1, y_1), how much should you be willing to pay in X units to increase Y from y_1 to y_2? To answer this, let the marginal rate of substitution (x, y) be denoted by $\lambda(y)$, which shows the dependence of λ on y but not on x. As a first-order approximation, for a small Δ increment in Y, you should be just willing to spend $\lambda(y)\Delta$ in X units. Therefore, to go from y_1 to y_2 you should be just willing to pay in X units the amount

$$\int_{y_1}^{y_2} \lambda(y)\, dy.$$

Let y_0 be the minimum value of Y that is of concern in our problem. Define the function

$$v_Y(y') = \int_{y_0}^{y'} \lambda(y)\, dy. \tag{3.12}$$

The function v_Y can be thought of as the global substitution function between Y and X. In terms of the v_Y function, the decision maker is indifferent between

$$(x_1, y_1) \quad \text{and} \quad (x_1 - [v_Y(y_2) - v_Y(y_1)], y_2).$$

That is, an increase from y_1 to y_2 is worth $v_Y(y_2) - v_Y(y_1)$ in X units.

We have just informally argued an important result.

Theorem 3.1. *The marginal rate of substitution between X and Y depends on y and not on x if and only if there is a value function v of the form*

$$v(x, y) = x + v_Y(y), \tag{3.13}$$

where v_Y is a value function over attribute Y.

Pruzan and Jackson (1963) offer a slightly different presentation of this same result.

ASSESSMENT OF v_Y. The measurement problem associated with (3.13) boils down to an appropriate assessment of v_Y. It is usually difficult for subjects to give meaningful quantitative responses for small changes in attribute levels. Thus, in most circumstances, the analyst should *not* assess v_Y by first assessing $\lambda(y)$ and then using (3.12). Instead, he should get at v_Y another way, and if he then wants to find $\lambda(y)$, he can invert (3.12) to calculate

$$\lambda(y) = \frac{d}{dy} v_Y(y). \tag{3.14}$$

One way to obtain v_Y is to arbitrarily set $v_Y(y_0) = 0$. With this choice of origin we can now interpret $v_Y(y)$ as the amount (in X units) that the decision maker is willing to pay to go from y_0 to y. Thus the analyst can, in principle, obtain direct assessments of v_Y at selected points $y_1, y_2, \ldots$ and "fair in" a curve. The analyst might be well advised, however, to first attempt to learn more about the qualitative structure of v_Y before getting involved in quantitative details. For example, it is often true that the decision maker would be willing to pay less and less for a positive, fixed change of Δ units in Y as the value of y increases. In other words he might feel that

$$v_Y(y+\Delta) - v_Y(y) < v_Y(y) - v_Y(y-\Delta), \quad \text{all } y, \Delta > 0; \tag{3.15}$$

it is worth less to go from y to $y+\Delta$ than from $y-\Delta$ to y, regardless of the value of y or Δ (positive). A qualitative determination of the appropriateness of (3.15) implies that v_Y is strictly concave—that is, it exhibits, in the language of classical economics, a decreasing marginal evaluation. [Notice that we shun the expression decreasing marginal "utility" because we use the term "utility" in a different fashion (see Section 4.4).] If the analyst learns that an appropriate shape for v_Y is concave, as shown in Fig. 3.13, then he can draw v_Y reasonably accurately if he ascertains numerical values for just a few points.

In order not to leave the impression that v_Y is necessarily concave, let us consider another common type of qualitative structure for v_Y. Imagine that the decision maker feels that there is some small interval about a level y_1, for example, where things go "critical." Going from $y_1 - \Delta$ to

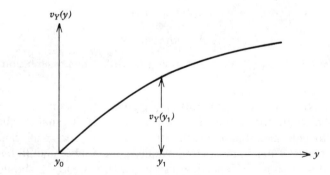

Fig. 3.13. A concave value function for attribute Y.

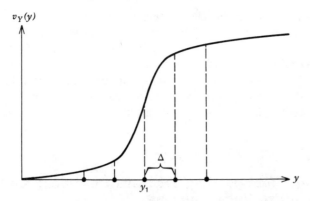

Fig. 3.14.   A value function that is not concave.

$y_1 + \Delta$ might be much more important than going from $y_1 + \Delta$ to $y_1 + 3\Delta$ or going from $y_1 - 3\Delta$ to $y_1 - \Delta$. By qualitative probing, the analyst might ascertain that this decision maker's v_Y curve is shaped somewhat like the one depicted in Fig. 3.14.

CHANGE OF SCALE FOR LINEARIZATION.   If the marginal rate of substitution depends on y but not on x, then the indifference curves will be horizontal translates of each other. One indifference curve can generate the other by just sliding it horizontally as shown in Fig. 3.15a. The indifference curves can be "straightened out" by changing the Y variable to a Z variable using the function v_Y. Thus, if we define

$$z = v_Y(y), \qquad (3.16)$$

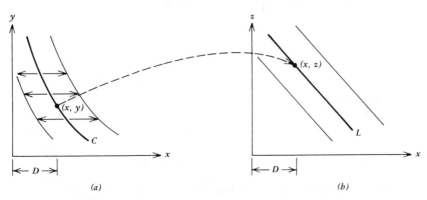

Fig. 3.15.   A change of scale to linearize indifference curves.

then the point (x, y) in Fig. 3.15a becomes (x, z) in Fig. 3.15b where z and y are related by (3.16). The indifference curve C in Fig. 3.15a is transformed into the straight line L with slope -1 in Fig. 3.15b.

In the transformed coordinates x and z, the indifference curves are parallel straight lines. There is no constant substitution rate between X and Y but there is a constant substitution rate (of 1) between X and Z where $z = v_Y(y)$. In the (x, z) evaluation space an appropriate value function is

$$v(x, z) = x + z. \qquad (3.17)$$

3.4.5 The Corresponding Tradeoffs Condition: An Additive Value Function

In general the marginal rate of substitution at (x_1, y_1) depends on the level of x_1 and on the level of y_1. It may be, however, that we can transform the X scale into a W scale and the Y scale into a Z scale such that the substitution rate at (w_1, z_1) would not depend on the level of w_1 or z_1. Then we would have the constant substitution rate case discussed in Section 3.4.3.

AN ADDITIVE VALUE FUNCTION. Consider four points $A:(x_1, y_1)$, $B:(x_1, y_2)$, $C:(x_2, y_1)$, and $D:(x_2, y_2)$ as shown in Fig. 3.16. Suppose the

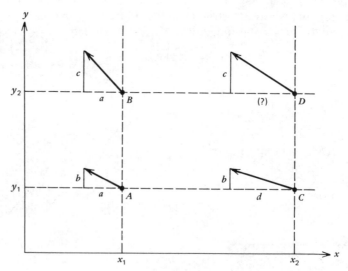

Fig. 3.16. Substitution rates consistent with an additive value function when ? equals amount d.

following holds:

1. At (x_1, y_1) an increase of b in Y is worth a payment of a in X;
2. At (x_1, y_2) an increase of c in Y is worth a payment of a in X;
3. At (x_2, y_1) an increase of b in Y is worth a payment of d in X.

At (x_2, y_2) an increase of c in Y is worth what payment in X? If it is worth a payment of d in X (i.e., in Fig. 3.16 the question mark (?) is answered d), and if this holds regardless of the values of x_1, x_2, y_1, y_2, a, b, c, and d, then we say that the *corresponding tradeoffs condition* is satisfied. This test provides us with necessary and sufficient conditions for an important result. But first let us define the concept of additivity, which will simplify the statement of the next result.

Definition. A preference structure is *additive* if there exists a value function reflecting that preference structure that can be expressed by

$$v(x, y) = v_X(x) + v_Y(y).$$

If a given preference structure, for example, has a value function

$$v_1(x, y) = (x - \alpha_1)^{\alpha_2}(y - \beta_1)^{\beta_2},$$

then that preference function would be additive since then

$$\log v_1(x, y) = \alpha_2 \log (x - \alpha_1) + \beta_2 \log (y - \beta_1)$$

and an additive v can be defined as $\log v_1$.

Theorem 3.2. *A preference structure is additive and therefore has an associated value function of the form*

$$v(x, y) = v_X(x) + v_Y(y), \tag{3.18}$$

where v_X and v_Y are value functions if and only if the corresponding tradeoffs condition is satisfied.

Clearly, given the additive value function (3.18), the corresponding tradeoffs condition is met. However, the converse, proven by Luce and Tukey (1964), is much more difficult to show. In the next subsection, where a conjoint scaling procedure is used to illustrate the assessment of the additive value function, a plausibility proof of Theorem 3.2 is given. A formal proof is not given here.

3.4.6 Conjoint Scaling: The Lock-Step Procedure

Suppose that the corresponding tradeoffs condition is met, implying the existence of v_X and v_Y. How might we go about finding them? One procedure we might adopt is the following.

Let x_0 and y_0 be the lowest values of X and Y under consideration.

1. Define

$$v(x_0, y_0) = v_X(x_0) = v_Y(y_0) = 0. \qquad (3.19)$$

This sets up the origin of measurement.

2. Choose $x_1 > x_0$ and arbitrarily set $v_X(x_1) = 1$. This sets up the unit of measurement.

3. Ask the decision maker to give a value of Y (e.g., y_1) such that

$$(x_1, y_0) \sim (x_0, y_1),$$

where $\sim$ stands for "is indifferent to." Define $v_Y(y_1) = 1$.

4. Ask the decision maker to give a value of X (e.g., x_2) and a value of Y (e.g., y_2) such that

$$(x_2, y_0) \sim (x_1, y_1) \sim (x_0, y_2).$$

Define

$$v_X(x_2) = v_Y(y_2) = 2.$$

5. A necessary condition for this scaling procedure to work is that

$$(x_1, y_2) \sim (x_2, y_1).$$

But, as is easily seen from Fig. 3.17, this condition holds if the corresponding tradeoffs condition works. Compare Fig. 3.17 with Fig. 3.16 and

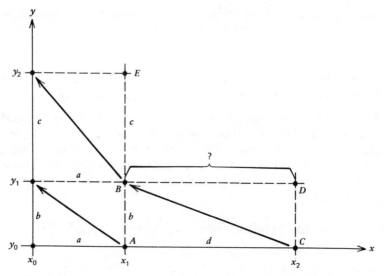

Fig. 3.17. Conjoint scaling with an additive preference structure.

identify points labeled A, B, C, and D in each. In Fig. 3.17, the corresponding tradeoffs condition implies that the distance in X units from B to D must be d and therefore points D and E are indifferent.

6. Assuming step 5 is passed, ask the decision maker to choose (x_3, y_3) such that

$$(x_3, y_0) \sim (x_2, y_1) \sim (x_1, y_2) \sim (x_0, y_3).$$

define

$$v_X(x_3) = v_Y(y_3) = 3.$$

7. As in step 5, a necessary condition for this scaling procedure to work is that

$$(x_3, y_1) \sim (x_2, y_2) \sim (x_1, y_3).$$

You might want to check that the above is implied by the corresponding tradeoffs condition.

8. Continue in the same manner as above.

9. Plot these few points, as in Fig. 3.18, fair in smooth v_X and v_Y curves and agree tentatively to let

$$v(x, y) = v_X(x) + v_Y(y).$$

10. As a precautionary measure check a few pairs of points for "reasonableness." To this end let us define x_k and y_k such that

$$v_X(x_k) = v_Y(y_k) = k.$$

Now we can check, for example, if

$$(x_1, y_0) \sim (x_{.5}, y_{.5}).$$

If not, you might alter the points $(x_{.5}, 0.5)$ and $(y_{.5}, 0.5)$ on the v_X and v_Y curves.

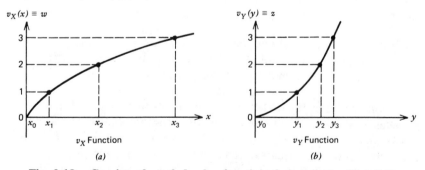

Fig. 3.18. Consistently scaled value functions for attributes X and Y.

Notice how the v_X and v_Y functions are *intrinsically intertwined*; we cannot interpret completely one without the other.

The above method of generating v_X and v_Y constitutes a constructive heuristic (almost) proof showing that the validity of the corresponding tradeoffs condition implies the existence of an additive preference structure. The construction was only demonstrated on a grid of points and we would have to subdivide the intervals (e.g., by a "halving technique") and sprinkle in some continuity somewhere to complete the proof. Note also the implicit use of a "solvability condition" that is not formally stated: We selected, for example, x_0, y_0, and x_1 and then glibly assumed the existence of y_1 that solved the indifference equation

$$(x_0, y_1) \sim (x_1, y_0).$$

Similarly we obtained x_2 and y_2 as solutions to indifference equations.

3.4.7 An Alternative Conjoint Scaling Procedure: The Midvalue Splitting Technique

Two preliminary definitions will facilitate the presentation of an alternate procedure for assessing v_X and v_Y. Assume that the corresponding tradeoffs condition is valid.

Definition. The pair (x_a, x_b) is said to be *differentially value-equivalent* to the pair (x_c, x_d), where $x_a < x_b$ and $x_c < x_d$, if whenever we are just willing to go from x_b to x_a for a given increase of Y, we would be just willing to go from x_d to x_c for the same increase in Y. Or, restated, if at any point y' of Y we are willing to "pay" the same amount of Y for the increase of X from x_a to x_b as for the increase from x_c to x_d, then (x_a, x_b) is differentially value-equivalent to (x_c, x_d).

Definition. For any interval $[x_a, x_b]$ of X its *midvalue* point x_c is such that the pairs (x_a, x_c) and (x_c, x_b) are differentially value-equivalent.

Observe two things about this definition. First, to define a midvalue point x_c of $[x_a, x_b]$ we exploited the existence of a second attribute Y. Second, if the decision maker, starting at y', is willing to give up in Y the same amount to go from x_a to x_c as from x_c to x_b, then the same condition ($c = c'$ in Fig. 3.19) must prevail starting at any other level y'' *provided* that the corresponding tradeoffs condition holds. The argument can be readily seen from Fig. 3.19. We label points A, B, C, D to help the reader make the necessary correspondences with Fig. 3.16.

Let the range of X be $x_0 \le x \le x_1$, of Y be $y_0 \le y \le y_1$, and assume that

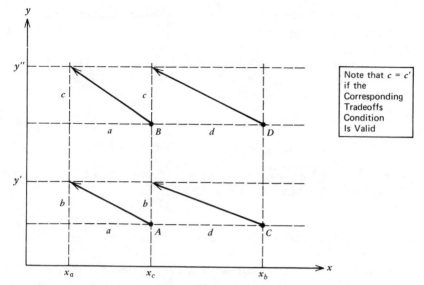

Fig. 3.19. The existence of the midvalue point x_c requires the corresponding tradeoffs condition.

the corresponding tradeoffs condition is passed.* We now seek a value function v that can be expressed in the form

$$v(x, y) = \lambda_1 v_X^*(x) + \lambda_2 v_Y^*(y),\qquad (3.20)$$

where

    (a) $v_X^*(x_0) = 0$ and $v_X^*(x_1) = 1,$ (3.21a)

    (b) $v_Y^*(y_0) = 0$ and $v_Y^*(y_1) = 1,$ (3.21b)

    (c) $\lambda_1 > 0,$ $\lambda_2 > 0,$ and $\lambda_1 + \lambda_2 = 1.$ (3.21c)

The assessment procedure is as follows:

1. Obtain v_X^* as follows. (1) Find the midvalue point of $[x_0, x_1]$; call it $x_{.5}$ and let $v_X^*(x_{.5}) = .5$. (2) Find the midvalue point, $x_{.75}$, of $[x_{.5}, x_1]$ and let $v_X^*(x_{.75}) = .75$. (3) Find the midvalue point $x_{.25}$ of $[x_0, x_{.5}]$ and let $v_X^*(x_{.25}) = .25$. (4) As a consistency check, ascertain that $x_{.5}$ is the midvalue point of $[x_{.25}, x_{.75}]$; if not, juggle the entries to get consistency. (5) Fair in the v_X^* curve passing through points (x_k, k)

---

  * In this subsection the subscripts on the symbols x and y are used differently than they were used in the previous subsection. We also now assume that v is bounded.

for $k = 0$, 1, .5, .75, .25 and perhaps additional points obtained by a midvalue splitting technique.

2. Repeat the same process for v_Y^*.
3. Find the scale factors λ_1 and λ_2: Choose any two (x, y) pairs that are indifferent, for example, (x', y') and (x'', y''). We then have

$$v(x', y') = v(x'', y'')$$

or

$$\lambda_1 v_X^*(x') + \lambda_2 v_Y^*(y') = \lambda_1 v_X^*(x'') + \lambda_2 v_Y^*(y'').$$

Since $v_X^*(x')$, $v_Y^*(y')$, $v_X^*(x'')$ and $v_Y^*(y'')$ are now known numbers and since $\lambda_1 + \lambda_2 = 1$ we can solve for λ_1 and λ_2.

3.4.8   A Hypothetical Illustrated Assessment

In order to demonstrate the interaction process between an analyst and decision maker, we present below an imaginary dialogue between an interrogator and a very cooperative respondent.

In the natural units of attributes X and Y, assume that $X(a)$ ranges over the interval 7 to 92 and $Y(a)$ ranges over the interval -9 to 8. For convenience let us choose $x_0 = 0$, $x_1 = 100$, $y_0 = -10$, $y_1 = 10$, which are consistent with the scaling conventions of (3.21).

Question	Hypothesized Answer
1. Suppose Y is at 0 and X at 20. If Y were decreased by 1 unit how much more X would you need to just offset it? Don't be exact, give a rough answer.	I would want to move to $x = 25$.
2. Keep Y at 0 and let X be at 60. How much would 1 unit of Y buy of X at this point? Again, all I want is a rough answer.	Say $x = 70$.
3. All right. At $y = 0$ it would cost roughly 1 unit of Y to push you from $x = 20$ to 25 and from 60 to 70. Is that right?	Yes, roughly.

Question	Hypothesized Answer
4. O.K. Now think hard about this one. At another value of Y, say at $y = 5$ would you pay the same amount to go from $x = 20$ to 25 as from 60 to 70?	What's hard about that? I already said I would pay the same for the change 20 to 25 as for the change 60 to 70. But the absolute amount of Y I would pay would depend on the level of Y I'm at. I might pay 1 unit of Y at $y = 0$ and 3 units of Y at $y = 5$. Is that O.K.?
5. Sure. That's reasonable.	

(At this point, the interrogator might presume that the corresponding tradeoffs condition is satisfied even though, strictly speaking, he must be sure that the same type of response would be forthcoming for more general values of X and Y. also at this point the interrogator might query the respondent about concavity or convexity of the functions v_X and v_Y. This is omitted for the sake of brevity. The interrogator next proceeds to describe the midvalue point of any interval.)

Question	Hypothesized Answer
6. Suppose you're at $y = 0$. Would you pay more of Y to change X from 0 to 50 or 50 to 100?	I would pay more to go from 0 to 50.
7. More to go from 0 to 10 or 10 to 100?	More to go from 10 to 100.
8. Give me a value, x' say, such that you would give up the same in Y to go from 0 to x' as from x' to 100.	About $x' = 20$.
9. In our language then, 20 is the midvalue point between 0 and 100. We label 20 by $x_{.5}$. What is your midvalue point between 20 and 100?	Let's say 45. I'd pay the same to go from 20 to 45 as 45 to 100.
10. In that case $x_{.75} = 45$. What is your midvalue point between 0 and 20?	Oh, about 7.
11. Fine. This means that $x_{.25} = 7$. Does 20 seem like a good midvalue between 7 and 45?	Sure.

Question	Hypothesized Answer
12. Now let's turn to the Y value. What is the midvalue point between -10 and 10?	Say, -2.
13. The midvalue between -2 and 10?	Say, 3.
14. The midvalue between -10 and -2?	-7.

(The analyst now plots these few points as shown in Fig. 3.20 and fairs in v_X and v_Y curves.)

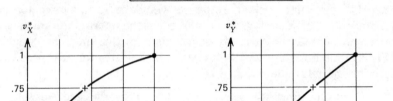

Fig. 3.20. The assessed value functions for attributes X and Y.

15. I have to trouble you for a few more questions. Which (x, y) pair would you prefer, $(0, 10)$ or $(100, -10)$? In other words, if you were at $(0, -10)$ would you rather push Y up to its limit of 10 or X up to its limit of 100?

The X variable is more critical. I would rather have $(100, -10)$ than $(0, 10)$.

(This answer implies that $\lambda_1 > \lambda_2$.)

16. O.K. then. Give me a value x such that you are indifferent between $(x, -10)$ and $(0, 10)$. In other words, I'm asking

I don't know. I would say about 60. But I feel awfully woozy about that.

Question

you to consider the following. Imagine that you're at $(0, -10)$. How much would you have to push X up to be equivalent to Y going from -10 to 10.

(The analyst draws the Fig. 3.21.)

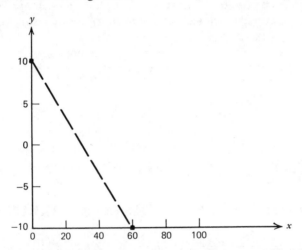

Fig. 3.21. Specifying the value tradeoffs between X and Y.

If we assume that $(60, -10)$ is indifferent to $(0, 10)$ then we have

$$v(60, -10) = v(0, 10),$$

or

$$\lambda_1 v^*_X(60) + \lambda_2 v^*_Y(-10) = \lambda_1 v^*_X(0) + \lambda_2 v^*_Y(10).$$

Since

$$v^*_X(60) = .85, \quad v^*_Y(-10) = v^*_X(0) = 0, \quad \text{and} \quad v^*_Y(10) = 1,$$

this implies

$$.85\lambda_1 = \lambda_2;$$

and, since $\lambda_2 = 1 - \lambda_1$, we have

$$\lambda_1 = \frac{1}{1.85} = .54 \quad \text{and} \quad \lambda_2 = .46.$$

Or perhaps we should say, "λ_1 is a woozy .54."

We could think of this procedure as a first approximation to a suitable value function v. Now let us look at a few pairs that have the same v values and ask the decision maker whether he would consider these pairs to be roughly indifferent. In other words we still might want to "fine tune" the v_X^* and v_Y^* curves and the λ_1, λ_2 values. Furthermore, if the λ_1 value (remember $\lambda_2 = 1 - \lambda_1$) were deemed the "weakest link of the chain," it might be appropriate to do sensitivity or break-even analyses with respect to the λ_1 value. It is important to observe that it would not be possible to run such sensitivity studies on λ_1 without the preliminary structuring of the problem. This is often the case: *in order to run sensitivity studies for certain critical variables, one often has to structure the less sensitive part of the problem in a precise manner.*

If the decision maker has hard-formed judgments, it may often be the case in practice that a value function cannot be found of the form

$$v(x, y) = v_X(x) + v_Y(y).$$

Nonetheless, such a value function may hold approximately. In other cases, it may be important for ease of analysis to create a value function of this form. The decision maker may begin the conjoint-scaling procedure and see along the way if the checking conditions are plausible.

3.5 THE CASE OF THREE ATTRIBUTES

We can straightforwardly generalize the results we obtained in Section 3.4 to the case of three evaluating criteria. Instead of the two evaluators X and Y we consider the three evaluators X, Y, and Z. The evaluators map any act a in the act space into a point $[X(a), Y(a), Z(a)]$ in the three-dimensional consequence space.

3.5.1 Conditional Preferences

We begin by considering a *conditional preference structure* in the (x, y) space given an assumed value of Z (e.g., z').

Definition. Consequence (x', y') is *conditionally preferred to* (x'', y'') given z' if and only if (x', y', z') is preferred to (x'', y'', z').

Conditional indifference is defined analogously and thus we can talk about conditional indifference curves in the (x, y) space given z'.

Generally, the conditional preference structure for attributes X and Y, given the value of the Z attribute is z', depends on the value z'. For example, the marginal rate of substitution at some point (x_1, y_1) might depend on z'. In some cases, however, the conditional preference structure in the (x, y) space given z' may not depend on z'. We are thus led to the following definition:

Definition. The pair of attributes X and Y is *preferentially independent* of Z if the conditional preferences in the (x, y) space given z' do not depend on z'.

Notice that if the pair $\{X, Y\}$ is preferentially independent of Z, then the substitution rate between X and Y at the point (x_1, y_1) given z' does not depend on z', for all x_1, y_1, and z'. Thus, the set of indifference curves in X, Y space does not depend on z'. Furthermore, because of the preferential independence condition, these curves have the same preference ordering.

Suppose that the pair $\{X, Y\}$ is preferentially independent of Z. In this case we can say that *if*

$$(x_1, y_1, z') \gtrsim (x_2, y_2, z'),$$

where the symbol $\gtrsim$ is read "is preferred or indifferent to," *then*

$$(x_1, y_1, z) \gtrsim (x_2, y_2, z), \qquad \text{for all } z.$$

The following two examples indicate cases of possible preferential independence.

Suppose the three attributes of a proposed construction project are

Q = Quality

T = Time to completion (negatively oriented)

C = Cost (negatively oriented)

In some circumstances the value tradeoffs between quality and time to completion may not depend on the cost of the project. In this case $\{Q, T\}$ would be preferentially independent of C. Also, we might find that, given a quality level q', the preference structure in the (time, cost) subspace does not depend on the particular level of q'; in other words, $\{T, C\}$ may be preferentially independent of Q. Similarly, $\{Q, C\}$ may be preferentially independent of T. Whether or not any one of these preferential independent assertions would, in fact, be valid depends on the particular setting of the problem.

A second example concerns a proposed program with attributes

B_1 = Benefit of type 1

B_2 = Benefit of type 2

C = Cost (negatively oriented)

If the two types of benefits must be kept in balance, then $\{B_1, C\}$ would not be preferentiaily independent of B_2 and $\{B_2, C\}$ would not be preferentially independent of B_1. However, it might be plausible to expect that $\{B_1, B_2\}$ would be preferentially independent of C.

3.5.2 Reduction of Dimensionality

How can we exploit, in our measurement techniques, the fact that a particular decision maker may feel that $\{X, Y\}$ is preferentially independent of Z? In the next section we develop special techniques for the case where each pair of attributes is preferentially independent of the remaining attribute. But now let us assume that all we can justify is that $\{X, Y\}$ is preferentially independent of Z. Here is one way we might proceed.

Consider the conditional preference structure for X and Y, given some value z'. Observe that the particular value z' is really immaterial because of our hypothesis of preferential independence. We shall only consider the special case where each of the conditional indifference curves in the (x, y) space intersects some line $y = y'$ for a suitably chosen y'. We shall refer to y' as a *base* value for Y. (If no such y' exists, then the procedure we are about to describe will have to be modified a bit.) Now the indifference curve through a typical point (x, y) will intersect the line $y = y'$ at some value (x', y') as shown in Fig. 3.22. Observe that x' depends on the choice of y' and on the point (x, y). In order to emphasize this observation we write

$$x' = T(x, y; y').$$ \hfill (3.22)

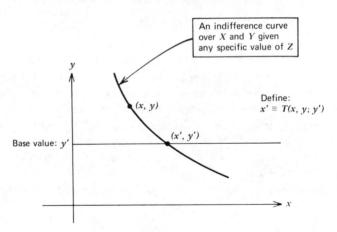

Fig. 3.22. **Exploiting preferential independence to reduce the dimensionality of a problem.**

Also notice that in terms of three-space, we have

$$(x, y, z) \sim (x', y', z), \qquad \text{for all } z. \qquad (3.23)$$

Hence the preferential comparison of any two triplets

$$(x_1, y_1, z_1) \qquad \text{versus} \qquad (x_2, y_2, z_2)$$

can be transformed into the preferential comparison of

$$(x_1', y', z_1) \qquad \text{versus} \qquad (x_2', y', z_2)$$

where

$$x_1' = T(x_1, y_1; y') \qquad \text{and} \qquad x_2' = T(x_2, y_2; y').$$

Thus our overall measurement task now reduces formally to a consideration of our conditional preference structure for $\{X, Z\}$ given the level of Y is y'. Instead of comparing

$$(x_1, y_1, z_1) \qquad \text{and} \qquad (x_2, y_2, z_2)$$

in three-space, we now must make the conditional comparison of

$$(x_1', z_1) \qquad \text{and} \qquad (x_2', z_2)$$

given y'. We have essentially used our hypothesis to reduce one three-dimensional comparison to two-dimensional comparisons.

SOME WORDS ABOUT THE TRANSFORMATION T. Let the set of acts be labeled $A = \{a_1, \ldots, a_i, \ldots, a_n\}$. Once again assume that $\{X, Y\}$ is preferentially independent of Z. If n is small, then for each a_i it may not be outlandish to ask the decision maker directly for a value $X'(a_i)$ such that he is conditionally indifferent between

$$[X(a_i), Y(a_i)] \qquad \text{and} \qquad [X'(a_i), y'].$$

Answers to these n questions may be a lot easier to obtain than to get the full conditional preference structure in the (x, y) plane.

If n is very large, this procedure is not operational. If, however, in the (x, y) plane we can justify a value function v of the form

$$v(x, y) = v_X(x) + v_Y(y)$$

(see Section 3.4.5), then $x' = T(x, y; y')$ will be such that

$$v_X(x') - v_X(x) = v_Y(y) - v_Y(y'),$$

and this may be a feasible operation to implement.

If n is large and no simple v function can be assumed, then we're in trouble; but it isn't hopeless. We might, for example, choose a reasonable number of points $(x_1, y_1), \ldots, (x_j, y_j), \ldots, (x_m, y_m)$, for $m = 10$, for example, and by direct questioning get for each j a value x'_j where

$$(x'_j, y') \sim (x_j, y_j)$$

or equivalently where

$$x'_j = T(x_j, y_j; y').$$

By carefully investigating the dependence of x'_j on x_j and y_j (remember y' is fixed for all j), we might create a reasonable, simple compromise function T that fits the data reasonably well and can be used to extrapolate an x' value for any other (x, y) pair. We shall not even begin to enumerate the myriad of techniques that can be employed for this type of data-fitting procedure.

Of course, if $\{X, Y\}$ is preferentially independent of Z, then instead of bringing each y to a base position y' and defining x' by (3.22) and (3.23), we could bring x to a base position x', for example, and define y' to be such that

$$(x, y, z) \sim (x', y', z), \quad \text{for all } z.$$

This reduction would then be followed by a conditional preference analysis of Y and Z given $x = x'$. We must be imaginative in choosing the most convenient reduction procedure. There are still other possibilities. For example, suppose in a given context it is natural to expect y to be approximately a multiple h of x. In this case for any (x, y) pair we might choose a value x' such that

$$(x, y, z) \sim (x', hx', z), \quad \text{for all } z.$$

This reduction would then be followed by a conditional preference analysis of X and Z given the understanding that y is not free but is always an h multiple of x.

3.5.3 Mutual Preferential Independence and the Existence of an Additive Value Function*

If preferences for (x, y, z) triplets are consistent with a v function of the additive form

$$v(x, y, z) = v_X(x) + v_Y(y) + v_Z(z),$$

then clearly

    (a) $\{X, Y\}$ is preferentially independent of Z,

    (b) $\{X, Z\}$ is preferentially independent of Y,

    (c) $\{Y, Z\}$ is preferentially independent of X.

---

* We assume throughout this section that all three evaluators are essential, that is, the preference structure cannot be fully described using only two of the three evaluators.

What is much more important, however, and quite surprising, is that the converse is true.

Theorem 3.3.   *A value function v may be expressed in an additive form*

$$v(x, y, z) = v_X(x) + v_Y(y) + v_Z(z), \qquad (3.24)$$

where v_X, v_Y, and v_Z are single-attribute value functions, if and only if $\{X, Y\}$ is preferentially independent of Z, $\{X, Z\}$ is preferentially independent of Y, and $\{Y, Z\}$ is preferentially independent* of X.

This result was first proven by Debreu (1960). A slightly more general proof is found in Krantz et al. (1971). Since formal proofs do appear in the literature, our discussion will avoid formalities and merely attempt to illustrate the plausibility of the result. Before proceeding, we will define an important term.

Definition.   If each pair of attributes is preferentially independent of its complement, the attributes are *pairwise preferentially independent.*

In short, Theorem 3.3 says that additivity coimplies pairwise preferential independence.

Something is truly remarkable about Theorem 3.3. Remember that in order to get an additive representation for two evaluators X and Y we had to impose the stringent corresponding tradeoffs condition. Nothing of the sort is required here. If all we know is that $\{X, Y\}$ is preferentially independent of Z, then we cannot say that conditional preferences for X and Y will satisfy the corresponding tradeoffs condition. But once we assume pairwise preferential independence, then the conditional preference structure for any pair of evaluators, given any level of the remaining evaluator, clears the corresponding tradeoffs hurdle. Without giving a formal proof of these assertions, let's see how these assertions can be made plausible.

Recall how we constructed the v_X and v_Y functions using the conjoint scaling technique for two evaluators. (See Section 3.4.6.) We first arbitrarily chose values x_0, y_0, and x_1. Then, we successively used the decision maker's preferences to generate y_1, x_2, and y_2. Up to that point no requirement was made of the corresponding tradeoffs condition. The first place that this condition had to be invoked was to justify the indifference of (x_1, y_2) and (x_2, y_1). Now how does bringing in Z and imposing pairwise preferential independence avoid this condition? Well let's back

---

* The condition that each pair of attributes must be preferentially independent of the remaining attribute will be weakened in the next subsection. Roughly, any two of the three preferential independence assumptions will be shown to imply the third.

up a bit and start the measurement process from the beginning for three evaluators.

1. First choose x_0, y_0, and z_0 and let

$$v(x_0, y_0, z_0) = v_X(x_0) = v_Y(y_0) = v_Z(z_0) = 0.$$

2. Next arbitrarily choose x_1 and define y_1 and z_1 such that

$$(x_1, y_0, z_0) \sim (x_0, y_1, z_0) \sim (x_0, y_0, z_1).$$

   Let

$$v_X(x_1) = v_Y(y_1) = v_Z(z_1) = 1.$$

3. Now notice how mutual preferential independence works to allow us to conclude that

$$(x_1, y_1, z_0) \sim (x_1, y_0, z_1) \sim (x_0, y_1, z_1).$$

   For example, from step 2 we know that (x_1, y_0) and (x_0, y_1) are conditionally indifferent given z_0. Hence they must be conditionally indifferent given z_1, or $(x_1, y_0, z_1) \sim (x_0, y_1, z_1)$.
   Similarly from step 2 we know that $(x_1, z_0) \sim (x_0, z_1)$ given y_0, and therefore, from the preferential independence of $\{X, Z\}$ from Y, it is true also given y_1. But this implies $(x_1, y_1, z_0) \sim (x_0, y_1, z_1)$.

4. Next define x_2, y_2, and z_2 such that

$$(x_2, y_0, z_0) \sim (x_0, y_2, z_0) \sim (x_0, y_0, z_2) \sim (x_1, y_1, z_0).$$

Now we are ready to discuss the crucial point that we referred to earlier: How do we know, without a corresponding tradeoffs condition, that

$$(x_2, y_1, z_0) \sim (x_1, y_2, z_0)?$$

The trick is to show that

$$(x_2, y_1, z_0) \sim (x_1, y_1, z_1)$$

and

$$(x_1, y_2, z_0) \sim (x_1, y_1, z_1),$$

and by transitivity of indifference we're home. We know that

$$(x_2, y_0, z_0) \sim (x_1, y_0, z_1),$$

and since $\{X, Z\}$ is preferentially independent of Y, we can freely change y_0 to y_1 for the above indifference relation. This shows that

$$(x_2, y_1, z_0) \sim (x_1, y_1, z_1).$$

We complete the demonstration by showing in an analogous manner that

$$(x_1, y_2, z_0) \sim (x_1, y_1, z_1).$$

While the above argument is far from being a proof it should make the theorem seem much less mysterious—even transparent. But, of course, there is a big gap between heuristic plausibility and a formal proof.

3.5.4   Weakening the Additivity Assumptions

We are interested in results such as Theorem 3.3 mainly to take a set of fundamental assumptions—in this case the preferential independence assumptions—about a decision maker's preferences and from these, ascertain a specific convenient mathematical expression consistent with these preferences. In any problem, we first try to check for the appropriateness of the conditions and then assess subjectively the decision maker's value function. Thus, it is important to reduce the number of conditions implying a particular functional form for our preferences. The following result is operationally useful for this purpose.

Theorem 3.4.   *If*
(*a*) $\{X, Y\}$ *is preferentially independent of* Z, *and*
(*b*) $\{Y, Z\}$ *is preferentially independent of* X,
then
(*c*) $\{X, Z\}$ *is preferentially independent of* Y.

A formal proof of Theorem 3.4 is found in Gorman (1968a). Here, let us try to provide some intuitive insights into this result.

In Fig. 3.23 let the points A and B have a common y coordinate and assume $A \sim B$. To show that $\{X, Z\}$ is preferentially independent of Y, we must show that if we modify the y coordinate of A and B (keeping the y coordinates equal) then the modified points remain indifferent. First choose a point C that has an x coordinate in common with A and a z coordinate in common with B such that $C \sim A \sim B$. Now since $A \sim C$ and $\{Y, Z\}$ is preferentially independent of X, it follows that $D \sim E$. Also, since $B \sim C$ and $\{X, Y\}$ is preferentially independent of Z, it follows that $D \sim F$. Hence, by transitivity, we have $E \sim F$. Now we started with $A \sim B$ and have shown that if we change the common y coordinate by an amount Δ the resulting points F and E are indifferent. This does not prove our result since the distance Δ is chosen in a special way and is not arbitrary. But now we can repeat the process on E and F, and so on. In order to gain another degree of flexibility we also could have started the process with a point such as G where $G \sim A \sim B$. Thus we see that if we simultaneously slide the points A and B to any one of several specified y levels, the resulting points remain indifferent. We can repeat the argument using other points on the indifference curve through A and B and spread them out in such a way that we obtain additional points on the indifference curve through points E and F. Now we might reasonably

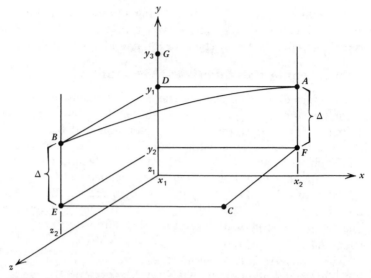

Fig. 3.23. A graphical argument to illustrate a relationship among preferential independence conditions.

suspect that with a sprinkling of continuity and differentiability thrown in, the result we want should follow. It does.

3.6. THE CASE OF MORE THAN THREE ATTRIBUTES

Let $X_1, \ldots, X_i, \ldots, X_n$ be n evaluators that map any act a into a point $[X_1(a), \ldots, X_i(a), \ldots, X_n(a)] = X(a)$ in an n dimensional consequence space. We shall continue to assume that for any two points $\mathbf{x}'$ and $\mathbf{x}''$ in the consequence space that either $\mathbf{x}' \gtrsim \mathbf{x}''$ or $\mathbf{x}'' \gtrsim \mathbf{x}'$—if both hold, then we say that $\mathbf{x}' \sim \mathbf{x}''$ and if not $[\mathbf{x}' \gtrsim \mathbf{x}'']$ holds, we say that $\mathbf{x}'' > \mathbf{x}'$—and that the preference relation $\gtrsim$ is transitive.

We shall have occasion in what follows to examine a point $\mathbf{x}$ by concentrating on a designated subset of its attributes as an entity and on the complementary set of attributes as an entity. For example, if $n = 5$ then we might want to partition $\mathbf{x}$ into two subvectors (x_1, x_3, x_4) and and (x_2, x_5). If we let

$$\mathbf{y} = (x_1, x_3, x_4)$$

and

$$\mathbf{z} = (x_2, x_5),$$

then we can think of $\mathbf{x}$ as displayed as the pair $(\mathbf{y}, \mathbf{z})$ where $\mathbf{y}$ involves attributes X_1, X_3, and X_4 and $\mathbf{z}$ involves attributes X_2 and X_5. More generally we shall talk about

$$\mathbf{x} = (\mathbf{y}, \mathbf{z})$$

where $\mathbf{y}$ represents those components of $\mathbf{x}$ on a previously specified subset of the indices $\{1, \ldots, n\}$ and $\mathbf{z}$ represents $\mathbf{x}$ on the complementary set of indices. Without any loss of generality we can always permute the indices so that we can think of $\mathbf{y}$ as representing $\mathbf{x}$ on the first s indices and $\mathbf{z}$ as representing $\mathbf{x}$ on the last n-s indices so that

$$\mathbf{y} = (x_1, \ldots, x_s) \quad \text{and} \quad \mathbf{z} = (x_{s+1}, \ldots, x_n).$$

In a natural manner we shall also extend this convention to talk about partitioning the attributes into two sets

$$Y = \{X_1, \ldots, X_s\} \quad \text{and} \quad Z = \{X_{s+1}, \ldots, X_n\}.$$

Definition. We shall say that $\mathbf{y}'$ is *conditionally preferred or indifferent to* $\mathbf{y}''$ *given* $\mathbf{z}'$ if and only if

$$(\mathbf{y}', \mathbf{z}') \succeq (\mathbf{y}'', \mathbf{z}').$$

Thus, we can talk about the conditional preference structure among attributes Y given that the complementary attributes are held fixed at $\mathbf{z}'$.

3.6.1 Preferential Independence

Definition. The set of attributes Y is *preferentially independent of the complementary set* Z if and only if the conditional preference structure in the $\mathbf{y}$ space given $\mathbf{z}'$ does not depend on $\mathbf{z}'$. More symbolically, Y is preferentially independent of Z if and only if for some $\mathbf{z}'$,

$$[(\mathbf{y}', \mathbf{z}') \succeq (\mathbf{y}'', \mathbf{z}')] \Rightarrow [(\mathbf{y}', \mathbf{z}) \succeq (\mathbf{y}'', \mathbf{z})], \quad \text{all } \mathbf{z}, \mathbf{y}', \mathbf{y}''.$$

For example, there may be several benefit attributes and several cost attributes, and it *may* happen (this will not necessarily be the case!) that the conditional preferences among various packages of benefit levels may not depend on the particular costs involved. If the benefit vector $\mathbf{y}'$ is deemed better than the benefit vector $\mathbf{y}''$ at cost $\mathbf{z}'$, the same may hold at any other cost, $\mathbf{z}$. In this case we would say elliptically that "benefits are preferentially independent of costs."

If the decision maker feels that the set of attributes Y is preferentially independent of the set of complementary attributes Z, then he can concentrate his efforts on structuring his preferences among $\mathbf{y}$'s holding $\mathbf{z}'$ fixed, knowing full well that this effort does not have to be repeated for different levels of $\mathbf{z}$. In this case it is meaningful for the decision maker to structure a value function v_Y defined on $\mathbf{y}$'s without having to specify a particular $\mathbf{z}'$. In particular v_Y, to be a valid value function, must be such that

$$(\mathbf{y}', \mathbf{z}) \gtrsim (\mathbf{y}'', \mathbf{z}) \Leftrightarrow v_Y(\mathbf{y}') \geq v_Y(\mathbf{y}''). \qquad (3.25)$$

If Y is preferentially independent of Z we shall write $\mathbf{y}' \gtrsim \mathbf{y}''$ to mean $(\mathbf{y}', \mathbf{z}) \gtrsim (\mathbf{y}'', \mathbf{z})$ for all $\mathbf{z}$. Similarly, the notation $\mathbf{y}' \sim \mathbf{y}''$ means $(\mathbf{y}', \mathbf{z}) \sim (\mathbf{y}'', \mathbf{z})$.

If Y is preferentially independent of Z it does *not* necessarily follow that Z is preferentially independent of Y. However, the following holds.

Theorem 3.5. *If Y is preferentially independent of Z, then*

$$[(\mathbf{y}', \mathbf{z}') \gtrsim (\mathbf{y}', \mathbf{z}'')] \Rightarrow [(\mathbf{y}, \mathbf{z}') \gtrsim (\mathbf{y}, \mathbf{z}'')]$$

for all $\mathbf{y} \sim \mathbf{y}'$.

Proof. The result follows from the following string of relations which follow from the hypotheses and the meaning of preferential independence:

$$(\mathbf{y}, \mathbf{z}') \sim (\mathbf{y}', \mathbf{z}') \gtrsim (\mathbf{y}', \mathbf{z}'') \sim (\mathbf{y}, \mathbf{z}''). \qquad \blacktriangleleft$$

The above theorem says that if Y is preferentially independent of Z, then the conditional preference structure in the Z space given $\mathbf{y}$ depends on $\mathbf{y}$ only through its indifference surface. If v is an appropriate value function of argument $(\mathbf{y}, \mathbf{z})$ then the above theorem also says that if Y is preferentially independent of Z, then $v(\mathbf{y}, \mathbf{z})$ depends on $\mathbf{y}$ via its value function $v_Y(\mathbf{y})$.

If Y is preferentially independent of Z, and if also Z is preferentially independent of Y, then the preference structures in the $\mathbf{y}$ and $\mathbf{z}$ spaces can be considered separately. In particular, in this case, if v, v_Y, *and* v_Z are appropriate value functions of arguments $(\mathbf{y}, \mathbf{z})$, $\mathbf{y}$, and $\mathbf{z}$, respectively, then we have

$$v(\mathbf{y}, \mathbf{z}) = f[v_Y(\mathbf{y}), v_Z(\mathbf{z})].$$

Operationally, this means that the decision maker can structure his preferences for $\mathbf{y}$'s, without worrying about $\mathbf{z}$'s, and for $\mathbf{z}$'s, without worrying about $\mathbf{y}$'s. Then he must worry about tradeoffs between $v_Y(\mathbf{y})$ and $v_Z(\mathbf{z})$, which is a problem we analyzed in Section 3.4 where we considered the case of two evaluators. We are thus led to the following question: If $v_Y(\mathbf{y}) = v_Y^0$ and $v_Z(\mathbf{z}) = v_Z^0$, how much are you (the decision maker) willing to give up in v_Y units to increase v_Z from v_Z^0 to v_Z'? The trouble with this question is that the value functions v_Y and v_Z are not necessarily intuitively meaningful, they are only meaningful up to monotone transformations. Well, what can be done? One suggestion is the following: Suppose that

$$Y \equiv \{X_1, X_2, \ldots, X_s\}$$

and

$$Z \equiv \{X_{s+1}, X_{s+2}, \ldots, X_n\}.$$

Choose typical values $x_2^o, \ldots, x_s^o, x_{s+2}^o, \ldots, x_n^o$ and consider the conditional preference structure in the (x_1, x_{s+1}) space given $x_2^o, \ldots, x_s^o, x_{s+2}^o, \ldots, x_n^o$. This is a "thinkable" task.

If, for example, in this subspace

$$(x_1', x_{s+1}') \sim (x_1'', x_{s+1}'')$$

given $x_2^o, \ldots, x_s^o, x_{s+2}^o, \ldots, x_n^o$, then this would mean that in the v_Y, v_Z space we would have

$$(v_Y(x_1', x_2^o, \ldots, x_s^o), v_Z(x_{s+1}', x_{s+2}^o, \ldots, x_n^o))$$
$$\sim (v_Y(x_1'', x_2^o, \ldots, x_s^o), v_Z(x_{s+1}'', x_{s+2}^o, \ldots, x_n^o)).$$

Roughly, we can help structure indifference curves in the v_Y, v_Z space by examining tradeoffs between a pair of components, one from the Y set and one from the Z set, holding all other components fixed.

3.6.2 Mutual Preferential Independence and the Existence of an Additive Value Function

Definition. The attributes $X_1, \ldots, X_n$ are *mutually preferentially independent* if every subset Y of these attributes is preferentially independent of its complementary set of evaluators.

Recall from the previous section concerning the three attribute case that mutual preferential independence implied the existence of an additive value function.* The result is also valid for cases with more than three attributes.

Theorem 3.6. *Given attributes $X_1, \ldots, X_n$, $n \geq 3$, an additive value function*

$$v(x_1, x_2, \ldots, x_n) = \sum_{i=1}^{n} v_i(x_i) \qquad (3.26)$$

(*where v_i is a value function over X_i*) *exists if and only if the attributes are mutually preferentially independent.*

Formal proofs of this theorem are found in Debreu (1960), Fishburn (1970), and Krantz et al. (1971). Pruzan and Jackson (1963) also state this result. Since we have already informally argued through the three attribute case, we avoid repeating the essential arguments here.

---

* In the next subsection, it is shown that, for three or more attributes, pairwise preferential independence is equivalent to mutual preferential independence.

Furthermore, the argument for $n > 3$ can be made to depend on the argument for $n = 3$ by partitioning $X_1, \ldots, X_n$ into three vector variables and using the additivity results for the three-dimensional case.

In the next section, we assess in detail a four-attribute value function in a hypothetical setting. This again brings out some of the flavor of the relationship between preferential independence conditions and additive value functions.

3.6.3 Weakening the Additivity Assumptions

Theorem 3.6 is very useful because the additive value function is about as simple as we can find. However, as it is now written, the number of preferential independence conditions that we would need to verify gets astronomically large as n gets even modestly large, for example, 10. Clearly, for a general n, there are $n(n-1)/2$ pairs of attributes that must be preferentially independent of their respective complements, and this says nothing about the triples of attributes, and the like. Fortunately, results in Leontief (1947a, 1947b) and in Gorman (1968a, 1968b) save us much potential work. Let us first state this result and then discuss its use.

Theorem 3.7. *Let Y and Z be subsets of the attribute set $S \equiv \{X_1, X_2, \ldots, X_n\}$ such that Y and Z overlap, but neither is contained in the other, and such that the union $Y \cup Z$ is not identical to S. If Y and Z are each preferentially independent of their respective complements, then the following sets of attributes:*

$$(i) \qquad Y \cup Z,$$

$$(ii) \qquad Y \cap Z,$$

$$(iii) \qquad Y - Z \quad and \quad Z - Y,$$

$$(iv) \qquad (Y - Z) \cup (Z - Y),$$

are each preferentially independent of their respective complements.

Consult Gorman (1968a) for a formal proof of this result.*

To gain insight into the meaning of Theorem 3.7, let us assume that $S = \{X_1, X_2, X_3, X_4\}$, $Y = \{X_1, X_2\}$, and $Z = \{X_2, X_3\}$. The theorem says that if $\{X_1, X_2\}$ and $\{X_2, X_3\}$ are preferentially independent of $\{X_3, X_4\}$ and

---

* If each of $Y_1, Y_2, \ldots, Y_m$ is a subset of $S \equiv \{X_1, X_2, \ldots, X_n\}$, and is preferentially independent of its complement, we can repeatedly use Theorem 3.7 to obtain all the implied preferential independence conditions and therefore to simplify the resulting value function as much as possible. A general result in this spirit is proven in Section 6.9 using the "utility independence" analog to Theorem 3.7.

$\{X_1, X_4\}$ respectively, then

(i) The union $Y \cup Z$, that is, $\{X_1, X_2, X_3\}$, is preferentially independent of X_4.

(ii) The intersection $Y \cap Z$, which is X_2, is preferentially independent of its complement $\{X_1, X_3, X_4\}$.

(iii) X_1 as $Y - Z$ and X_3 as $Z - Y$ are preferentially independent of their respective complements.

(iv) $\{X_1, X_3\}$ is preferentially independent of $\{X_2, X_4\}$.

The two most important parts of Theorem 3.7 for application are (i) and (iv). These two results permit us to reduce the number of requisite preferential independence conditions necessary to invoke the additive value function of Theorem 3.6 to $n-1$, where n is the number of attributes.

The informal proof of Theorem 3.4 in 3.5.4 lends some insight into why part (iv) of Theorem 3.7 is true. However, let us try to suggest why part (i) is valid.

The essence of the proof can be shown from considering the special case where we let

$$\mathbf{x} = (x_1, x_2, x_3, x_4)$$

and consider the case where

$$Y = \{X_1, X_2\}, \qquad Z = \{X_2, X_3\}.$$

If both Y and Z are preferentially independent of their complementary sets, we shall now show that

$$Y \cup Z = \{X_1, X_2, X_3\}$$

is also preferentially independent of its complementary set. We must show

$$[(x_1', x_2', x_3', x_4^*) \gtrsim (x_1'', x_2'', x_3'', x_4^*)]$$
$$\Rightarrow [(x_1', x_2', x_3', x_4) \gtrsim (x_1'', x_2'', x_3'', x_4)], \qquad \text{all } x_4. \quad (3.27)$$

That is if $(x_1', x_2', x_3') \gtrsim (x_1'', x_2'', x_3'')$ given x_4^*, it is also true given any x_4. Let x_1''' be such that

$$(x_1''', x_2'') \sim (x_1', x_2'). \quad (3.28)$$

Note that this assertion makes sense since $\{X_1, X_2\}$ is preferentially independent of its complementary set.*

---

* Here we assume that x_2' and x_2'' were chosen so that a x_1''' satisfying (3.28) exists. The solvability and continuity assumed throughout this chapter (see Section 3.1) imply this existence.

From the hypothesis of (3.27) and (3.28) we have

$$(x_1''', x_2'', x_3', x_4^*) \succsim (x_1'', x_2'', x_3'', x_4^*). \qquad (3.29)$$

But since $\{X_1, X_3\}$ is preferentially independent of $\{X_2, X_4\}$, (3.29) implies, for any x_4, that

$$(x_1''', x_2'', x_3', x_4) \succsim (x_1'', x_2'', x_3'', x_4). \qquad (3.30)$$

By (3.28) together with the hypothesis that $\{X_1, X_2\}$ is preferentially independent of its complement, we find

$$(x_1', x_2', x_3', x_4) \sim (x_1''', x_2'', x_3', x_4). \qquad (3.31)$$

From (3.31), (3.30), and transitivity we get the right-hand side of (3.27). This proves our assertion.

Corollary. *If every pair of attributes is preferentially independent of its complementary set, then the attributes are mutually preferentially independent.*

The argument can be formalized using part (i) of Theorem 3.7 by mathematical induction: if it's true for any subset of k attributes ($k \geq 2$) it can be shown to be true for $k+1$ evaluators. The details are omitted.

3.6.4   Selecting Preferentially Independent Sets of Attributes

Note that as a result of Theorem 3.7, there are numerous possible combinations of preferentially independent sets of attributes that imply mutual preferential independence among the members of $\{X_1, X_2, \ldots, X_n\}$. A simple combination is that $\{X_i, X_{i+1}\}$ be preferentially independent of its complement for $i = 1, 2, \ldots, n-1$.

In order to see how this works, let $n = 5$ and assume that each of the sets

$$\{X_1, X_2\}, \qquad \{X_2, X_3\}, \qquad \{X_3, X_4\}, \qquad \{X_4, X_5\}$$

has the preferential independence (PI) property, that is, each is preferentially independent of its complement. We then conclude from Theorem 3.7 part (iv), that

$$\{X_1, X_3\}, \qquad \{X_2, X_4\}, \qquad \text{and} \qquad \{X_3, X_5\}$$

also have the PI property. Repeating, we next get that

$$\{X_1, X_4\} \qquad \text{and} \qquad \{X_2, X_5\}$$

have the PI property. Finally, we see that $\{X_1, X_5\}$ also has the PI property. Thus we see that each pair has the PI property, and we know from the previous corollary that therefore every triplet must have the PI property and so on.

Another set of $n-1$ assumptions that implies mutual preferential independence among $\{X_1, X_2, \ldots, X_n\}$ is that the pairs $\{X_1, X_i\}$, $i = 2, 3, \ldots, n$, are each preferentially independent of its complement. The reasoning is similar to the one above.

As a more involved example, suppose there are five attributes $\{X_1, X_2, \ldots, X_5\}$ and that the following sets are preferentially independent of their complements:

(a) $\{X_1, X_2\}$,

(b) $\{X_2, X_3\}$,

(c) $\{X_1, X_2, X_3, X_4\}$,   and

(d) $\{X_2, X_3, X_4, X_5\}$.

It is a simple matter to show that (a)–(d) imply mutual preferential independence. Together (a) and (b) imply that $\{X_1, X_2, X_3\}$ is preferentially independent of $\{X_4, X_5\}$, which when combined with (d), implies by part (iii) of Theorem 3.7 that $\{X_4, X_5\}$ is preferentially independent of its complement. By the same reasoning, (a) and (d) imply that $\{X_3, X_4, X_5\}$ is preferentially independent of $\{X_1, X_2\}$, which together with (c) implies that $\{X_3, X_4\}$ is preferentially independent of $\{X_1, X_2, X_5\}$. Thus we see that $\{X_i, X_{i+1}\}$, $i = 1, 2, 3, 4$, are preferentially independent of their respective complements from which mutual preferential independence among the X_i directly follows.

Clearly, in practice, it would not be reasonable to check directly for all possible preferential independence conditions. A little judgment on which conditions are most likely to yield useful results could facilitate the assessment process considerably. Ting (1971) suggests a few guidelines that may help in this. An important one is to look for natural attribute groups. For instance, in dealing with siting a nuclear power plant, the first level of disaggregation in the objectives hierarchy may specify the overall objective in terms of consideration for monetary costs, environmental impact, human health, and political factors. Each of these may be further specified and involve multiple attributes. However, it may be natural at this first level to have the decision maker ascertain that his preferences for attributes in various combinations of these groups do not depend on the other groups' levels. Perhaps at this point, we could conclude the existence of an additive value function defined over these four major attribute groups,

$$v(m, e, h, p) = v_M(m) + v_E(e) + v_H(h) + v_P(p),$$

where M, E, H, and P represent monetary, environmental, health, and political considerations, respectively. We could then try to utilize the preferential independence concept on the attributes within each grouping and hopefully further specify the decision maker's value structure.

In Section 3.8, we discuss the technique of pricing-out nonmonetary variables. For certain problems, this approach, which involves separately considering each nonmonetary attribute paired with a monetary attribute, may be reasonably natural for identifying preferential independence conditions. More details concerning verification procedures for preferential independence are given in Section 6.6.

3.6.5   Value Functions With Partial Additivity

Even when mutual preferential independence does not hold, the existence of any preferential independence properties that do hold may help in structuring the value function.

Theorem 3.8.   *Given* $\{X_1, X_2, X_3, X_4\}$, *if* $\{X_1, X_2\}$ *and* $\{X_2, X_3\}$ *are preferentially independent of their respective complements, a value function* v *exists of the form*

$$v(x_1, x_2, x_3, x_4) = f(y, x_4) \tag{3.32}$$

where $y = v_1(x_1) + v_2(x_2) + v_3(x_3)$ *and* f *is increasing in its first variable.*

A proof of this result is in Gorman (1968a).

Note that $v_1(x_1) + v_2(x_2) + v_3(x_3)$ can be thought of as a conditional additive value function over attributes X_1, X_2, and X_3 given that X_4 is fixed at a convenient level. This level does not matter since by the conditions of Theorem 3.8, it follows from Theorem 3.7 that $\{X_1, X_2, X_3\}$ is preferentially independent of X_4.

Since the X_i in Theorem 3.8 can designate vector attributes, the theorem represents a general attribute case. It is important to realize that this result can be used several times, perhaps corresponding to different levels in the objectives hierarchy, in structuring the same value function.

3.6.6   Using the Additive Value Function

As illustrated in earlier two-attribute assessments of the additive value function, rather than using the form

$$v(x_1, x_2, \ldots, x_n) = \sum_{i=1}^{n} v_i(x_i) \tag{3.33}$$

directly, when v is bounded, it may be more convenient to scale v and each of the single-attribute value functions from zero to one. Thus, we will have the additive value function of the form

$$v(x_1, x_2, \ldots, x_n) = \sum_{i=1}^{n} \lambda_i v_i(x_i), \qquad (3.34)$$

where v and v_i, $i = 1, 2, \ldots, n$, in (3.34) are scaled from zero to one and

$$\sum_{i=1}^{n} \lambda_i = 1, \qquad \lambda_i > 0. \qquad (3.35)$$

Equations (3.33) and (3.34) are both additive value functions and given consistent scaling, they are equivalent. The assessment of (3.34) is illustrated in Section 3.7.

3.7 ASSESSMENT OF AN ADDITIVE VALUE FUNCTION: AN ABSTRACT HYPOTHETICAL EXAMPLE*

In this section we illustrate, with an example, how a decision maker might assess an additive value function over four attributes.

Suppose that you, the decision maker, have to choose from among 75 alternative acts and that each act can be evaluated in terms of four attributes. Table 3.1 summarizes these evaluations. for example, act A_1 has a score of 7.5 on attribute X_1, a score of 344 on attribute X_2, a score of .47 on X_3, and 12.15 on X_4. For act A_i, the recorded scores are x_{1i}, x_{2i}, x_{3i}, and x_{4i} on attributes X_1 to X_4 respectively. Let us assume that attributes Table 3.1 summarizes these evaluations. For example, act A_1 higher scores on each of these attributes, but assume that attribute X_4 is negatively oriented in that you would prefer lower scores.†

Your problem is: Given performance evaluations of these 75 acts on these four attributes, which act should you single out as being best for you? That is, how can you systematically probe your feelings about these attributes so that you could force yourself to articulate your underlying preference structure?

For the time being observe, however, that A_{75} cannot be a serious contender for "best" since A_1 is better than A_{75} on each of the four attributes—remember that for the fourth attribute, 12.15 is better than 12.92. In technical jargon A_{75} is dominated by A_1.

* In Section 7.2, we discuss the work of James Roche, who utilized the procedures illustrated here for evaluating alternative instructional programs in a public school system.

† This assertion implicitly assumes that each attribute, taken individually, is preferentially independent of its complement.

Table 3.1

Performance Measures of Alternative Acts on Four Attributes

| Act | Attributes | | | |
	$X_{1(\nearrow)}$	$X_{2(\nearrow)}$	$X_{3(\nearrow)}$	$X_{4(\searrow)}$
A_1	7.5	344	.47	12.15
A_2	3.7	268	.79	12.20
.	.	.	.	.
.	.	.	.	.
A_i	x_{1i}	x_{2i}	x_{3i}	x_{4i}
.	.	.	.	.
.	.	.	.	.
A_{75}	6.7	250	.24	12.92
Lowest (rounded down)	2.0	200	.15	12.00
Highest (rounded up)	9.0	400	.90	13.50

Note that act A_1 dominates act A_{75}

Performance profile of A_1: (7.5, 344, .47, 12.15)

On the bottom of Table 3.1 note that the 75 entries under attribute X_1 lie within the interval from 2.0 to 9.0. The entries under attribute X_2 lie in the interval 200 to 400. Similarly the ranges for attributes X_3 and X_4 are recorded. Observe once again that for attribute X_4 no act is better than 12.00 or worse than 13.50.

The four numbers x_{1i}, x_{2i}, x_{3i}, and x_{4i} associated with act A_i can be thought of as the profile of A_i and the profiles of acts A_1 and A_2 are shown in Fig. 3.24.

3.7.1 Legitimacy of the Additivity Value Function

Now let us suppose that you, the decision maker, feel that any pair of attributes is preferentially independent of the others. Thus, for example, suppose that the tradeoffs for attributes X_2 and X_3, *keeping the levels of attributes X_1 and X_4 fixed*, do not depend on the particular values of these fixed levels, and so on for each pair of attributes. Now, as we indicated in Section 3.6, your preferences, if they are to be fully articulated in a manner consistent with the above preferential independence assumptions, can be characterized by a value function v of the form

$$v(x_1, x_2, x_3, x_4) = \sum_{j=1}^{4} \lambda_j v_j(x_j),$$

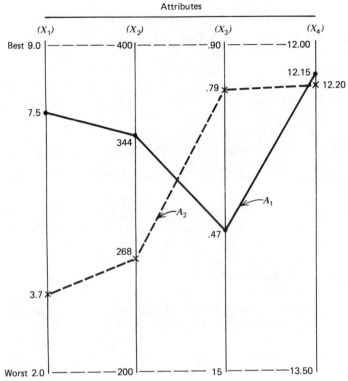

Fig. 3.24. Performance profiles of acts A_1 and A_2 for a hypothetical example.

where

(a) $v_j(\text{worst } x_j) = 0,$ $v_j(\text{best } x_j) = 1,$ $j = 1, \ldots, 4;$

(b) $0 < \lambda_j < 1,$ $j = 1, \ldots, 4;$

(c) $\sum_{j=1}^{4} \lambda_j = 1.$

We can think of the function v_j defined over the attribute score x_j as the jth *component* value function and the λ_j as the weight associated with attribute X_j. For our illustrative example, we note, from Table 3.1, that the worst x_1 score is 2.0 and the best is 9.0. We will see later that the determination of the λ_j weights are intimately related to the ranges of the scales.

The problem you now face is to determine appropriate v_j functions and λ_j weights. By so doing you will have articulated your underlying preference structure for **x** profiles.

3.7.2 Assessment of Component Value Functions

One procedure for determining the v_1, v_2, v_3, and v_4 functions is described and illustrated in Subsection 3.4.7. Let us merely illustrate in sketch form how we might assess v_1.

First we normalize v_1 by letting $v_1(2.0) = 0$ and $v_1(9.0) = 1$. We then seek the subjective midvalue point, let us call it $m_{.5}$, of the interval 2.0 to 9.0. That is we want to find the value $m_{.5}$ for which $v_1(m_{.5}) = .5$. We ask for that knife-edge point where the intervals $(2.0, m_{.5})$ and $(m_{.5}, 9.0)$ are differentially value-equivalent. The value $m_{.5}$ is such that *if*

$$(2.0, b, c, d) \sim (m_{.5}, b', c', d')$$

then

$$(m_{.5}, b, c, d) \sim (9.0, b', c', d').$$

If we give up a certain amount of attributes X_2, X_3, and X_4—for example, by going from (b, c, d) to (b', c', d')—to go from 2.0 to $m_{.5}$, we should be willing to give up exactly the same amount to go from $m_{.5}$ to 9.0.

Let's say that the midvalue point of 2.0 to 9.0 is 4.0. We then go through the same procedure for determining the midvalue point of the interval 2.0 to 4.0. Let's say it is 2.8 so that $v_1(2.8) = .25$. Similarly let the midvalue point of the range 4.0 to 9.0 be 5.7, so that $v_1(5.7) = .75$. These points can now be plotted as shown in Fig. 3.25 and a curve v_1 can be faired through these five points. Alternatively, more midvalue points could be determined before fairing in the curve. It depends on how much

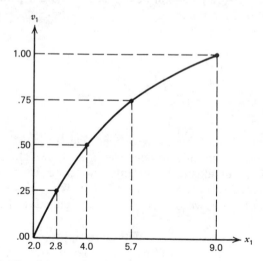

Fig. 3.25. Assessment of the component value function v_1.

accuracy is needed. We repeat the point we made earlier: it may be desirable to run consistency checks (e.g., finding the midpoint of 2.8 to 5.7) and to police the inconsistencies so that a coherent set of compatible responses is obtained. In addition, we may wish initially, before specific numbers are chosen, to check in a qualitative way whether v_1 is concave, convex, or is perhaps more complicated in shape.

3.7.3 Assessment of Scaling Constants

Some special notation should help our discussion of the λ_j's. For the jth attribute let w_j represent the *worst* value and b_j the *best* value. Then for positively oriented scales we would have $w_j \le x_j \le b_j$. Let I be the complete set of attribute indices; in our example $I = \{1, 2, 3, 4\}$. Let T be a subset of I and $\bar{T}$ be the complementary set to T, or $\bar{T} = I - T$. Let $\mathbf{x}^T$ be that profile where all the component x_j's are equal to b_j for $j \in T$ and equal to w_j for $j \in \bar{T}$. Thus, for example if $T = \{2, 3\}$, then

$$\mathbf{x}^T = \mathbf{x}^{\{2,3\}} = (w_1, b_2, b_3, w_4).$$

Since $v_j(w_j) = 0$ and $v_j(b_j) = 1$, we know that

$$v(\mathbf{x}^T) = \sum_{j \in T} \lambda_j$$

so when $T = \{2, 3\}$, then $v(\mathbf{x}^T) = \lambda_2 + \lambda_3$. Also define

$$\lambda(T) \equiv \sum_{j \in T} \lambda_j.$$

Notice that when T consists of the single-element set $\{j\}$ we have

$$v(\mathbf{x}^{\{j\}}) = \lambda_j = \lambda(\{j\}).$$

We want to suggest techniques for determination of the λ_j's. First, rank the profiles $\mathbf{x}^{\{1\}}, \ldots, \mathbf{x}^{\{4\}}$. Suppose, for example, that you feel that

$$\mathbf{x}^{\{2\}} > \mathbf{x}^{\{1\}} > \mathbf{x}^{\{4\}} > \mathbf{x}^{\{3\}}.$$

This would imply that for you

$$\lambda_2 > \lambda_1 > \lambda_4 > \lambda_3.$$

Next, you could try to get more refined inequalities by comparing say

$$\mathbf{x}^{\{2\}} \qquad \text{versus} \qquad \mathbf{x}^{\{1,3,4\}}.$$

If, in this paired comparison, $\mathbf{x}^{\{2\}}$ were preferred then we could infer that $\lambda_2 > .5$.

Observe that when you are asked to compare $\mathbf{x}^T$ to $\mathbf{x}^S$ you are essentially asked this question: "Suppose the $\mathbf{x}$ profile were at the worst case, (w_1, w_2, w_3, w_4), and you had the option of improving some of the w_j's from the worst to the best position. Would you rather improve the levels of the attributes in the subset T or subset S?"

This method of analysis usually only provides inequalities for the λ_j's. In some special cases precise numerical values can be deduced if there are indifferences. For example, if $\mathbf{x}^{\{T\}}$ and $\mathbf{x}^{\{\bar{T}\}}$ are indifferent, then $\lambda(T) = .5$. But this is not the usual case.

Let us continue with the special case where

$$\lambda_2 > \lambda_1 > \lambda_4 > \lambda_3.$$

Now compare the two profiles,

$$(w_1, x_2, w_3, w_4) \qquad \text{versus} \qquad \mathbf{x}^{\{1\}},$$

and manipulate the level of x_2 until indifference is reached. Suppose this occurs at $x_2 = 350$; that is, suppose

$$(2.0, 350, .15, 13.50) \sim (9.0, 200, .15, 13.50).$$

Then we have

$$v(2.0, 350, .15, 13.50) = v(9.0, 200, .15, 13.50)$$

or

$$\lambda_2 v_2(350) = \lambda_1,$$

and since it is assumed that the component v_2 function has already been assessed, we can find $v_2(350)$. Suppose it is

$$v_2(350) = .6,$$

so that

$$.6\lambda_2 = \lambda_1. \tag{3.36}$$

Similarly, we can determine the proportional relationships between λ_4 and λ_2, and between λ_3 and λ_2. Assume in particular that

$$(2.0, 240, .15, 13.50) \sim (2.0, 200, .15, 12.00)$$

and

$$v_2(240) = .4,$$

so that

$$.4\lambda_2 = \lambda_4; \tag{3.37}$$

also assume that

$$(2.0, 210, .15, 13.50) \sim (2.0, 200, .90, 13.50)$$

and

$$v_2(210) = .1,$$

so that

$$.1\lambda_2 = \lambda_3. \tag{3.38}$$

From (3.36), (3.37), (3.38), and

$$\lambda_1 + \lambda_2 + \lambda_3 + \lambda_4 = 1,$$

we conclude that

$$\lambda_1 = .286, \qquad \lambda_2 = .476, \qquad \lambda_3 = .048, \qquad \lambda_4 = .190.$$

We repeat that it may be desirable to ask additional questions thereby getting an over-determined system of equations, fully expecting that the set of responses would be inconsistent in practice. These inconsistencies can be used by the analyst to "force" the decision maker to rethink through his preferences. Hopefully, reasons for the original inconsistencies can be found, and from this a consistent set of preferences established.

3.7.4   Additional Comments on the λ Function

The λ function defined on subsets of I satisfies the usual rules of a probability measure:

(a) $\lambda(T) \geq 0,$ for $T \subset I$;

(b) $\lambda(I) = 1$;

(c) $\lambda(S \cup T) = \lambda(S) + \lambda(T),$ if S and T are disjoint.

Thus finding the λ function is related to the problem of finding suitable probability assignments over a finite sample space. Very often in assigning the weighting measure λ, just like in assigning a probability measure, it is not natural to initially assign weights at the atomic level, that is, to assign numbers for $\lambda_1, \lambda_2, \ldots$. Instead, it may be more appropriate to make initial assignments to subsets [e.g., to assign values to $\lambda(T)$ for special subsets] and to make conditional assignments. For example, consider a 10-attribute case with the hierarchical structure shown in Fig. 3.26. In this case let

$$I = \{1, 2, \ldots, 10\}$$
$$A = \{1\}, \qquad B = \{2, 3, 4\}, \qquad C = \{5, 6\}, \qquad D = \{7, 8, 9, 10\},$$
$$E = A \cup B, \qquad F = C \cup D.$$

In such a hierarchical example, it might be natural to compare

$$\lambda(E) \qquad \text{versus} \qquad \lambda(F)$$
$$\lambda(A) \qquad \text{versus} \qquad \lambda(B)$$
$$\lambda(C) \qquad \text{versus} \qquad \lambda(D).$$

Taking our cue from probability theory, let us also define conditional

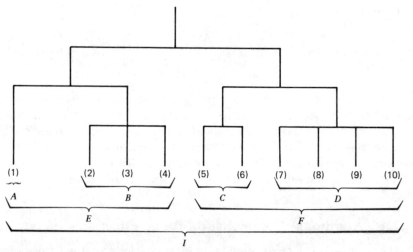

Fig. 3.26. The hierarchical structure of objectives used in evaluating scaling constants.

weighting functions, such as

$$\lambda(B \mid E) = \frac{\lambda(B)}{\lambda(E)} \quad \text{for } B \subset E,$$

where $\lambda(B \mid E)$ gives the "weighting importance" of attribute set B within the subset E, or the conditional weighting of B within E.

In hierarchical attribute sets with many attributes it is critically important to isolate components of the problem and to make conditional assessments. In Fig. 3.27, we have created some hypothetical conditional assignments. for example, we have let

$$\lambda(E) = .6 \quad \text{and} \quad \lambda(F) = .4,$$
$$\lambda(A \mid E) = .5 \quad \text{and} \quad \lambda(B \mid E) = .5,$$
$$\lambda(\{2\} \mid B) = .5, \quad \lambda(\{3\} \mid B) = .3, \quad \text{and} \quad \lambda(\{4\} \mid B) = .2,$$
$$\lambda(C \mid F) = .8 \quad \text{and} \quad \lambda(D \mid F) = .2,$$

and so on.

To find λ_3, we have

$$\lambda_3 = \lambda(\{3\} \mid B) \cdot \lambda(B \mid E) \cdot \lambda(E)$$
$$= .3 \times .5 \times .6 = .09.$$

In a similar manner we get all the individual λ_j's, which are displayed in the second row from the bottom in Fig. 3.27.

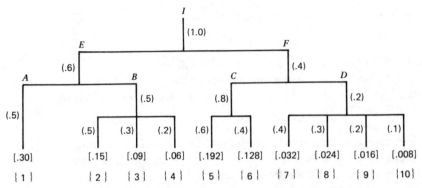

Fig. 3.27. Hypothetical scaling constants in a hierarchical structure.

In this problem it might be clear, for example, how to assign conditional weights within subsets E and F, but it might be hard to apportion weights between E and F. *But an ability to structure part of the problem might make it possible to run meaningful sensitivity analyses on those critical assessments that are the hardest to make.* This comment about sensitivity analysis—and others like it—are especially important if there is more than one decision maker involved in the decision process.

3.8 WILLINGNESS TO PAY

Consider an attribute structure with a monetary attribute M, measured in monetary units m, and with other attributes $X_1, X_2, \ldots, X_n$. Paired comparisons are then of the form

$$(m_1, x_1^1, \ldots, x_n^1) \quad \text{versus} \quad (m_2, x_1^2, \ldots, x_n^2),$$

or, more compactly,*

$$(m_1, \mathbf{x}^1) \quad \text{versus} \quad (m_2, \mathbf{x}^2).$$

3.8.1 Pricing Out

In many contexts—but we insist not all!—it is natural to proceed by "costing out" or "pricing out" the $\mathbf{x}$ components. For example, we might single out some particular $\mathbf{x}$ profile (e.g., $\mathbf{x}^*$) and ask:

"Starting from the profile $(m_o, \mathbf{x}^o)$ how much would you just be willing to pay to alter $\mathbf{x}^o$ to the base case $\mathbf{x}^*$?"

* We employ the asymmetric notation $(m_1, \mathbf{x}^1)$ because we reserve subscripts on $\mathbf{x}$ for components and we shall need super primes on the m.

We want to find the value m_o' in the indifference equation

$$(m_o', \mathbf{x}^*) \sim (m_o, \mathbf{x}^o).$$

The willingness to pay would then be $m_o' - m_o$.

If we had to evaluate a limited number of alternatives $(m_i, \mathbf{x}^i)$ for $i = 1$ to N, and if we determined for each i a value m_i' such that

$$(m_i', \mathbf{x}^*) \sim (m_i, \mathbf{x}^i), \qquad i = 1, \ldots, N,$$

then we could rank the N alternatives in terms of the numbers m_1' to m_N'.

This procedure becomes even more attractive under a special structure. for example, in the indifference equation

$$(m_o', \mathbf{x}^*) \sim (m_o, \mathbf{x}^o),$$

the willingness to pay for changing $\mathbf{x}^o$ to $\mathbf{x}^*$ might (in a special case) not depend on the level m_o. This simplifies things. However, if this is not the case, and if the number N of alternatives is large, then the dependence of $m_o' - m_o$ on m_o becomes a particularly bothersome complication.

If the dimensionality of $\mathbf{x}$ is large, it is helpful to price out the transformation of $\mathbf{x}^o$ to $\mathbf{x}^*$ in stages. For example, we might want first to consider the component x_j and modify it to the base x_j^*. We are then led to the indifference equation

$$(m_o', x_1^o, \ldots, x_{j-1}^o, x_j^*, x_{j+1}^o, \ldots, x_n^o) \sim (m_o, \mathbf{x}^o).$$

In general without special assumptions the willingness to pay $m_o' - m_o$ will depend not only on x_j^o and x_j^* but also on m_o, and on $x_1^o, \ldots, x_{j-1}^o, x_{j+1}^o, \ldots, x_n^o$. If, however, the monetary attribute M and attribute X_j, taken as a pair, are *preferentially independent* of the complementary set of attributes, then we can "price out" the change from x_j^o to x_j^* without worrying about the levels of the other attributes. We still, of course, have to worry about the initial monetary level m_o.

If the pair $\{M, X_j\}$ is preferentially independent of the complementary set for each j, then we can price out the attributes in sequence. For example, suppose

$$(m_o + \Delta_1, x_1^*, x_2^o, x_3^o, \ldots) \sim (m_o, x_1^o, x_2^o, x_3^o, \ldots),$$

so that Δ_1 is what we "pay" for the transformation of x_1^o to x_1^*; in general Δ_1 will depend on m_o (but not on $x_2^o, x_3^o, \ldots$). Next suppose that

$$(m_o + \Delta_1 + \Delta_2, x_1^*, x_2^*, x_3^o, \ldots) \sim (m_o + \Delta_1, x_1^*, x_2^o, x_3^o, \ldots)$$

so that Δ_2 is the price we "pay" for transforming x_2^o to x_2^* and this will depend, with the assumptions we have made, on $m_o + \Delta_1$, on x_2^o, and on x_2^* but not on the other x's, and so on. When we price out the transformation of x_j^o to x_j^*, it will, unfortunately, depend on $m_o + \Delta_1 + \cdots + \Delta_{j-1}$, unless of course we explicitly assume otherwise.

If, in general, the pair $\{M, X_j\}$ is preferentially independent of the complementary set of attributes for all j, *and if* the quantity Δ_j in the indifference equation

$$(m_o + \Delta_j, x_1^o, \ldots, x_{j-1}^o, x_j^*, x_{j+1}^o, \ldots, x_n^o) \sim (m_o, \mathbf{x}^o)$$

does *not* depend on m_o, for each j, life becomes especially attractive. Then we can price out the transformation of x_j^o to x_j^* without first determining in a sequential order the values of $\Delta_1, \Delta_2, \ldots, \Delta_{j-1}$.

In some circumstances it may not be possible to assume that $\{M, X_j\}, j = 1, 2, \ldots, n$, is pairwise preferentially independent of the complementary set of attributes. In some contexts we might be able to partition the X attributes into two subsets, Y and Z, so that in a suggestive notational fashion we can express

$$(m, \mathbf{x}) \qquad \text{as} \qquad (m, \mathbf{y}, \mathbf{z}).$$

If the attribute set $\{M, Y\}$ is preferentially independent of Z, we can price out a transformation of $\mathbf{y}^o$ to $\mathbf{y}^*$ and in doing so we would not have to worry about the $\mathbf{z}^o$ levels.

The willingness to pay procedure has its virtues. It is easy to explain, and that in itself should not be underestimated. Unfortunately, in practice, the procedure in its simplest form (i.e., the direct pricing out of each component) is often applied indiscriminately without verifying the necessary validating assumptions:

1. The money attribute taken together with any other single attribute is preferentially independent of the complementary set of attributes.
2. The marginal rate of substitution between money and any other attribute does not functionally depend on the monetary level.

We point out that *even if* the above assumptions make sense in a given context it does not necessarily follow that the willingness to pay procedure should be followed. In many cases it may be too difficult and too unnatural to try to price out a transformation of $\mathbf{x}^o$ to $\mathbf{x}^*$ or even of x_j^o to x_j^*. In some circumstances it may be more natural to directly attempt to specify the preference structure as discussed in sections 3.3–3.7.

For some interesting examples where willingness-to-pay arguments are used in a multiattribute context, see several of the publications of the Decision Analysis Group of Stanford Research Institute: Matheson and Roths (1967), Stanford Research Institute (1968), Boyd et al. (1971), and Howard, Matheson, and North (1972).

3.8.2　Dominance and Extended Dominance

There are many tricks we can use for processing preferences, short of establishing a full value function, and it is hopeless here to try to be very systematic about describing many of these tricks. But we emphasize a point that has been exploited by us in practice. It is not easy to make the kinds of tradeoffs that we have been glibly describing. If we could avoid making some of these vexing tradeoffs, then this should be exploited. One obvious device is to exploit the concept of *dominance* introduced in Section 3.2. If we compare

$$\mathbf{x}' = (x_1', \ldots, x_n') \quad \text{and} \quad \mathbf{x}'' = (x_1'', \ldots, x_n'')$$

and if x_j' is preferred to x_j'' for all j (or preferred or indifferent for all j and strictly preferred for some j) then $\mathbf{x}''$ can be eliminated as a contender if $\mathbf{x}'$ is available. Getting rid of dominances may solve the problem. Fine, *if* this is the case!

Now suppose that we try the above reduction by dominance and the decision problem is not resolved—the usual situation. Furthermore suppose that we can partition $\mathbf{x}$ into $(\mathbf{y}, \mathbf{z})$ and let us suppose that we can "price-out" $\mathbf{y}$'s in terms of the $\mathbf{z}$'s by transforming each $\mathbf{y}$ to some base (e.g., $\mathbf{y}^*$). That is, for the ith alternative $(\mathbf{y}_i, \mathbf{z}_i)$, we solve the indifference equation

$$(\mathbf{y}_i, \mathbf{z}_i) \sim (\mathbf{y}^*, \mathbf{z}_i')$$

for $\mathbf{z}_i'$. Let us assume this is repeated for $i = 1, \ldots, N$. Now once again we can investigate dominance relations among the restrictive profiles, $\mathbf{z}_1', \ldots, \mathbf{z}_N'$. Of course, this latter type of *extended dominance* does incorporate the subjective reduction of $(\mathbf{y}_i, \mathbf{z}_i)$ to $(\mathbf{y}^*, \mathbf{z}_i')$ for $i = 1, \ldots, N$.

If the processes of dominance and extended dominance help to isolate a best alternative, then this would be a welcome bonus. More generally, however, the elimination of alternatives have other beneficial effects: with a reduction in the number of alternatives there is likely to be a diminution in the size of the interval range required for each of the scalar attribute scales. And this restriction in the sizes of the intervals makes it more palatable to adopt various assumptions such as preferential independence (and other variations to be introduced later). To illustrate this last point suppose we consider the case of three attributes and are contemplating whether or not it is legitimate to assume that attributes 1 and 2 are preferentially independent of attribute 3. This might be a reasonable assumption to utilize (a palatable lie) provided that the range of values of attribute 3 is sufficiently narrow. We might not be able to make this convenient assumption if the third attribute varies widely.

And here is where some preliminary work on dominance and especially extended dominance may have a significant impact.

3.9   BRIEF SUMMARY AND GUIDE TO SOME RELEVANT LITERATURE

This chapter presented techniques for assessing multiattribute value functions. Once the decision maker articulates a value function, which implies a preference ordering over all multidimensional evaluations, the subsequent analysis must then examine the set of technologically achievable evaluations and choose a best evaluation in this set. The two processes—determination of achievability and articulation of a preference structure—can be kept separate and fused at the very end of the analysis. We concentrate almost exclusively on the latter of these two processes. However, at the beginning of this chapter we described a very informal mechanism for intertwining these two processes: first we find a point on the efficient frontier of achievable evaluations and then move around this frontier in a manner that improves our preferences at each step. This is done in a rather ad hoc manner that does not require a full specification of our preference structure. While this procedure may sometimes be effective in some special, highly structured problems (e.g., in linear programming problems with more than a single linear objective function), in most of the applied problems dealt with in this book, this informal, interactive search procedure is not very useful—especially when probabilistic concerns are introduced. We therefore concentrate our attention on the aspect of the decision problem dealing with the articulation of preferences. We do it also in a manner that will enable us later on to bring in probabilistic considerations.

Sections 3.4–3.6 provide a number of representation theorems that break down the assessments of the value function into component parts. The key concept in all these reduction techniques is *preferential independence*. Because there is considerable power in the implications of overlapping sets of attributes being preferentially independent of their complements, the two-attribute case cannot be dealt with nearly as nicely as are cases with three or more attributes. Most of the important representation theorems provided conditions for expressing the value function v in the additive form

$$v(x_1, x_2, \ldots, x_n) = \sum_{i=1}^{n} v_i(x_i),$$

where the v_i are consistently scaled single-attribute value functions. A complete example illustrating the assessment of such a function is given in Section 3.7.

A common practice of many analysts is to "price out"—that is, bring down to a standard level—all the nonmonetary attributes into a (single) monetary attribute. A comparison of alternatives is then made only in terms of the "adjusted" levels of the monetary attribute. The requisite assumptions necessary for such an approach to be valid are strong. The assumptions are discussed in Section 3.8.

Most of this chapter is expository in nature, since as indicated throughout, the fundamental results are due to others. We have refrained from giving formal proofs but on occasion we supplied insights with "almost proofs." Formal proofs of the theorems have been referenced to the original articles and the technical literature.

We now present a cursory review of the literature. This is merely to suggest some sources where an interested reader may search for more depth than provided here. We will, however, try to mention some classic works that are directly relevant.

Leontief (1947a, 1947b) investigated properties of functions of several variables that provided for separability, breaking the original function down into one defined over distinct subsets of the original variables. His results were local in nature rather than global. Debreu (1960) provided the first axiomatization implying the existence of an additive value function for three or more attributes using an elegant topological proof. An alternative algebraic proof of additivity was given by Luce and Tukey (1964) in their paper introducing "conjoint measurement" for the two-attribute case. Several extensions to conjoint measurement were made by Krantz (1964), Luce (1966), and Tversky (1967). For a complete summary of this field we highly recommend *Foundations of Measurement* by Krantz, Luce, Suppes, and Tversky (1971). In a general measurement context, this book also presents representation theorems for a number of more general value functions than those considered in this chapter. This includes the large class of value functions that can be represented by polynomial structures. A recent addition to this class of literature is Fishburn (1975).

An important contribution toward separating the assessment of a value function into a number of component parts is Gorman (1968a). His results allow us to greatly reduce the number of conditions necessary to imply that a value function is additive, thus, making the techniques more operational. Ting (1971) discusses many techniques for decomposing the assessment of preferences and suggests some guidelines for verifying the assumptions necessary to use the results.

CHAPTER 4

Unidimensional Utility Theory

The general problem addressed can be stated simply. A decision maker must choose among several alternatives $A_1, A_2, \ldots, A_m$, each of which will eventually result in a consequence describable in terms of a single attribute X. The decision maker does not know exactly what consequence will result from each of the various alternatives, but he can assign probabilities to the various possibilities that might result from any course of action. What should he do?

4.1 THE MOTIVATION FOR UTILITY THEORY*

The power of the concept of utility and the grounds for our interest in it is as follows. If an appropriate utility is assigned to each possible consequence and the expected utility of each alternative is calculated, then the best course of action is the alternative with the highest *expected utility*. Different sets of axioms that imply the existence of utilities with the property that expected utility is an appropriate guide for consistent decision making are presented in von Neumann and Morgenstern (1947), Savage (1954), Luce and Raiffa (1957), Pratt, Raiffa, and Schlaifer (1965), and Fishburn (1970). The next subsection informally reviews the basic ideas of the theory.

In terms of our double dichotomy of Chapter 1 depicted in Fig. 4.1, the problem in this chapter is a special case of the general problem of Chapter 3 in that we are concerned with only one unidimensional

* Sections 4.1–4.8 present an expository account of much of the standard literature of single-attribute utility theory. This account draws heavily on the research work in the last 15 years of Robert Schlaifer, Kenneth Arrow, John Pratt, and Richard Meyer. Readers who are thoroughly familiar with the concepts and results in Pratt (1964) may wish to skim these sections briefly.

	Unidimensional	Multidimensional
Certainty		Chapter 3
Uncertainty	Chapter 4	Chapters 5 and 6

Fig. 4.1. Double dichotomy of decision problems.

attribute, but it is a generalization in that uncertainty is now involved. One might ask why, when Chapters 1 and 2 argue that most important real-world problems require more than one attribute to adequately summarize consequences, do we allocate a chapter solely to the unidimensional case? We have three reasons. First, a thorough understanding of unidimensional utility theory and the associated techniques in implementing the theory is essential for work on the multiattribute problem involving uncertainty; second, there are some important problems where one scalar attribute may be adequate; and third, we shall show that many multidimensional utility problems can be reduced to unidimensional ones by using some of the techniques of the previous chapter. These are expanded on later in this section.

4.1.1   Basic Fundamentals of Utility Theory

We are assuming that most of our readers are familiar with the basic fundamentals of utility theory but, as a review to some and a short introduction to others, we offer the following.

Suppose we start out with just n consequences labeled $x_1, x_2, \ldots, x_n$. It is immaterial at this point what the underlying scales of these x's are. Each x could be a scalar, a vector, or a paragraph of prose describing this consequence. It is important, however, that the decision maker can rank the consequences in order of his preference, and we shall assume the labeling is such that x_1 is less preferred than x_2, which is less preferred than x_3, and so on. In symbols, we assume

$$x_1 < x_2 < x_3 < \cdots < x_n. \tag{4.1}$$

Now suppose the decision maker is asked to express his preferences for probability distributions over these consequences. For example, the decision maker is asked to state his preference between acts a' and a'' where

1. Act a' will result in consequence x_i with probability p'_i, for $i = 1, 2, \ldots, n$. Of course, $p'_i \geq 0$, all i, and $\sum_i p'_i = 1$.

2. Act a'' will result in consequence x_i with probability p_i'', for $i = 1$, $2, \ldots, n$. Again, $p_i'' \geq 0$, all i, and $\sum_i p_i'' = 1$.

Notice that there is an infinity of potential probability distributions over this finite set of consequences. Now suppose the decision maker asserts that, for each i, he is indifferent between the following two options:

Certainty Option: Receive x_i.
Risky Option: Receive x_n (the best consequence) with probability π_i and x_1 (the worst consequence) with the complementary probability $1 - \pi_i$.

Let us denote the risky option by $\langle x_n, \pi_i, x_1 \rangle$. Furthermore, the decision maker is consistent in that he assigns $\pi_n = 1$ and $\pi_1 = 0$, and the π's are such that

$$\pi_1 < \pi_2 < \cdots < \pi_n. \tag{4.2}$$

Comparing (4.2) with (4.1), we can see that the π's can be thought of as a numerical scaling of the x's.

The fundamental result of utility theory is that the *expected value* of the π's can also be used to numerically scale probability distributions over the x's. To illustrate the reasoning, let us reconsider the choice between act a' (which results in x_i with probability p_i') and act a'' (which results in x_i with probability p_i''). If we associate to each x_i its scaled π_i value then the expected π scores for acts a' and a'', which we label by $\bar{\pi}'$ and $\bar{\pi}''$, are

$$\bar{\pi}' = \sum_i p_i' \pi_i$$

and

$$\bar{\pi}'' = \sum_i p_i'' \pi_i.$$

There are compelling reasons for the decision maker to rank order act a' and a'' in terms of the magnitudes of $\bar{\pi}'$ and $\bar{\pi}''$. The argument briefly follows. Take act a'. It results with probability p_i' in consequence x_i. But x_i is considered by the decision maker as indifferent to a π_i chance at x_n and complementary chance at x_1. So, in effect, act a' is equivalent to giving the decision maker a $\bar{\pi}'$ chance at x_n and a complementary chance at x_1. Similarly, a'' yields a chance of $\bar{\pi}''$ at x_n and a complementary chance at x_1. This completes the argument, which rests heavily on the *substitution* of the risky option $\langle x_n, \pi_i, x_1 \rangle$ for each x_i. The pros and cons of this substitution idea, which lies at the core of utility theory, are discussed in Raiffa (1968).

Now, if we transform the π's into u's by means of a positive linear transformation,

$$u_i = a + b\pi_i, \qquad b > 0, \qquad i = 1, \ldots, n,$$

then we have

$$u_1 < u_2 < \ldots < u_n$$

and it is easy to see that for probabilistic choice (such as between a' and a'') the expected u values rank order a' and a'' the same way as the expected π values. For example,

$$\bar{u}' = \sum_i p_i' u_i = \sum_i p_i'(a + b\pi_i) = a + b\bar{\pi}'.$$

If, however, we were to transform the π's into a new scale, call it w, by a monotone transformation other than a positive linear transformation, then the w's would reflect preferences for the simple consequence x_1, $x_2, \ldots, x_n$ but would not necessarily reflect preferences for probabilistic alternatives such as a' and a''.

If someone is sold on the merits of the above argument as we are, then the critical issue becomes: How can appropriate π values be assessed in a responsible manner? This is really the essence of our problem. If the x's are scalars, there are, as we shall see in this chapter, ways of thinking about the assessment problem that exploit this underlying structure. Subsequent chapters describe techniques for structuring the assessment problem when the x's are vectors.

4.1.2 Alternative Approaches to the Risky Choice Problem

Does the decision maker need the full power of utility theory to make choices among risky alternatives? Can he get by, in practice, with less formal machinery, or can he circumvent the use of subjective judgements altogether and use more objective measures such as means and variances?

Of course, in special cases, we can get by with less paraphernalia than is needed for the maximization of expected utility. Suppose the possible impacts of two alternatives A and B can be described by the probability density functions f_A and f_B in Fig. 4.2a or, alternatively, by the cumulative probability distributions in Fig. 4.2b, where we have denoted the attribute of importance as X. Let F_A and F_B denote the cumulative distribution functions of A and B, respectively. Notice from Fig. 4.2b that the probability that any outcome is x or less is greater for alternative A than for alternative B. Thus, if we just knew, for instance, that more of X is preferred to less of X, it would be appropriate to conclude that B

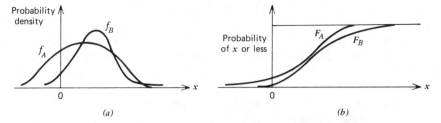

Fig. 4.2. An illustration of probabilistic dominance.

should be preferred to A. In such a case we say alternative A is *probabilistically dominated* by alternative B. When such situations occur, we can use less information than contained in the complete utility function over X to make responsible, consistent decisions. This conclusion would not be visually apparent, however, from Figure 4.2a. Of course, we are not always lucky enough to be able to invoke probabilistic dominance.

There are cases where two cumulative distribution functions F_A and F_B for alternatives A and B intersect (so that no probabilistic dominance is present) but where a bit of subjective informal common sense might help in making a choice without much ado. Often we merely have to look at F_A and F_B and, without any formal procedures whatsoever, come to a comfortable decision. But, again, this depends usually on extreme differences. Life is often more complicated. We would like to probe our basic feelings more systematically—and here, of course, the full power of utility theory comes to the forefront. But let us look first at some so-called objective procedures.

One simple proposal is to use the *expected value* of the uncertain outcome as a guide. Here we require only a knowledge of the probability distributions to calculate the expected value for each alternative. For specific problems, this may be appropriate. However, many decision makers would probably not be different between the following acts:

Act $A \equiv$ earn \$100,000 for sure.

Act $B \equiv$ earn \$200,000 or \$0, each with probability 0.5.

Act $C \equiv$ earn \$1,000,000 with probability 0.1 or \$0 with probability 0.9.

Act $D \equiv$ earn \$200,000 with probability 0.9 or lose \$800,000 with probability 0.1.

Notice that for each of the acts, the expected amount earned is exactly \$100,000, and so the expected value of the consequence would not be an appropriate criterion for a decision maker with a preference among these acts.

A possible criticism of this illustration might point out that "Naturally act A is preferred to the others, since there is no uncertainty associated with the outcome. However, if a measure of uncertainty, such as the variance of the possible outcome, was used in addition to the expected outcome, we should be able to correctly order preferences for alternatives." This claim seems plausible, but it is not always correct. Simple calculation will show that both acts C and D have the same expected outcomes and variances and, therefore, any evaluation scheme based on just the mean and variance of the outcome would necessarily imply indifference between acts C and D. Various investigations have indicated that many people do have a preference between C and D; therefore, no criterion based solely on means and variances can correctly represent their preferences.

Even if some *mean-variance criterion* seems appropriate for evaluating alternatives in a specific problem, we must establish an appropriate preference order over the two attributes "expected outcome" and "outcome variance." This task, which may require assessing a value function over these two attributes, could be more involved than originally assessing a utility function over the single outcome attribute.

There are many other ad hoc schemes that can be found in the literature but, to our mind, no proposal other than maximization of expected utility withstands the scrutiny of careful examination. Let us cite one further proposal. Let the uncertain outcome resulting from a given alternative be denoted by $\tilde{x}$. This proposal suggests that the distribution of $\tilde{x}$ be summarized by two indices:

1. $\alpha = P[\tilde{x} \leq x_0]$, the probability that $\tilde{x}$ is less than some critical aspiration level x_0.
2. $\beta = E[\tilde{x} \mid \tilde{x} \geq x_0]$, the conditional expectation of $\tilde{x}$, given that $\tilde{x}$ attains the *aspiration level* x_0.

The analyst can then compute the pair (α, β) for each alternative and set up a simple two-dimensional value function. For example, we might want to maximize β subject to the condition that $\alpha \leq .05$. Ad hoc procedures of this kind can be easily destroyed by citing extreme examples, but then the retort usually is: "Oh, in such extreme examples we would modify our (α, β) proposal by imposing another constraint such as $\cdots$" There have been endless debates of this kind in the literature and suffice it to say, here, that we become more and more committed to the principle of maximization of expected utility, the younger we get and the more arguments we hear. Of course, this in itself should not be a compelling argument to you, but we are reporting what we feel is a relevant empirical fact.

4.1.3 Relevance of Unidimensional Utility Theory to Multiattribute Problems

Our motivation stated above for introducing unidimensional utility theory concerns mainly the usefulness for the concept of utility itself and relies on the fact that this usefulness can be easily illustrated with the unidimensional case. There is another very important reason. In many of the techniques we shall describe for assessing multiattribute utility functions, an essential component part is the assessment of unidimensional utility functions over single attributes. That is, our procedures often provide a basis for reducing the problem of assessing a multiattribute utility function into one of assessing some consistently scaled unidimensional utility functions. A thorough knowledge of unidimensional utility theory is needed for this task.

For instance, although the consequences of a problem may only be adequately described in terms of n attributes, it may be possible, using the techniques discussed in Chapter 3, to reduce the dimensionality of the attribute space from n to $(n-1)$. If $n=2$, we then have a unidimensional problem. If $n>2$, successive reduction of the dimensionality may lead us to the unidimensional case.

In Chapter 3, the techniques discussed suggested procedures for obtaining a value function $v(\mathbf{x})$ for all possible outcomes $\mathbf{x}$. Since value is unidimensional and $v(\mathbf{x}') = v(\mathbf{x}'')$ if and only if $\mathbf{x}'$ and $\mathbf{x}''$ are equally preferable, it is appropriate to assess a utility function $u[v(\mathbf{x})]$ over the unidimensional attribute "value" and thus associate a utility with each possible consequence $\mathbf{x}$. One way that this can be done is discussed in Section 5.1.

An alternate approach that does not require the assessment of a value function requires instead the verification of assumptions implying a specific form of the *utility* function. The simplest example of this in two dimensions is the additive utility function $u(y, z) = u_Y(y) + u_Z(z)$, where u_Y and u_Z are consistently scaled unidimensional utility functions. The point is that both $u_Y(y)$ and $u_Z(z)$ can be assessed using the techniques discussed in this chapter.

The assumptions needed to justify an additive form such as

$$u(x_1, \ldots, x_n) = \sum_i k_i u_i(x_i)$$

or various multiplicative forms such as

$$u(x_1, \ldots, x_n) = \prod_i [\alpha_i + \beta_i u_i(x_i)],$$

require various utility independence assumptions to be introduced in Chapters 5 and 6. However, even in cases where such independence does not hold, we shall often have to introduce conditional univariate utility functions, for example, the conditional utility of x_i given that a summary index Y is at level y°.

In summary, univariate utility functions will be an essential ingredient in all the multivariate theory to be developed in ensuing chapters.

4.1.4 Examples of Unidimensional Decision Problems

Let us cite some examples where one attribute might adequately summarize consequences for decisional purposes. A company's objective is to maximize profits. In this case, the attribute chosen to describe consequences might be incremental cash flow, monetary asset position, net monetary profit, or the like. One attribute may be better than another in that the decision maker can more easily express his preferences over different amounts of that attribute. The choice of which attribute to use is obviously subjective and left largely to the discretion of the analyst with consultation of the decision maker.* The question of how to choose an attribute, whether or not it is sufficient to describe consequences, and so on, was discussed in detail in Chapter 2.

Many of the concepts covered in this chapter use money as the unidimensional attribute. The main reasons for this are (1) many of the past interests and results in utility theory deal with this special case, and (2) most readers have already thought about or could think about their preferences for various amounts of money. Therefore, a better intuitive feeling for the concepts of preference and risk introduced in the chapter will likely be developed using money as the primary attribute than if a less familiar attribute were used in illustrations. However, the concepts to be introduced are relevant to other unidimensional problems of importance. Let us indicate a few examples.

The emergency services, such as ambulance, police, and fire, respond to requests for help by dispatching an emergency vehicle (ambulance, etc.) to the scene "as soon as possible." An obvious choice of a measure of

---

* In business contexts, it is often preferable to use assets instead of incremental flows because it helps avoid some idiosyncratic behavior (e.g., the zero illusion) in the assessment procedures, and also it is easier to examine dynamic problems. See Schlaifer (1969), pages 163–165.

effectiveness in this case is *response time,* the elapsed time from receipt of the call requesting help to arrival on the scene of an emergency vehicle. Larson (1972) and Savas (1969) have chosen this attribute in some of their work on police systems and ambulance services, respectively.

In many queuing situations, whether they involve automobiles at toll booths or customers at a checkout counter, the objective is good service, and this might be measured in terms of the attribute "delay time." Another queuing problem concerns the congestion occurring at the major airports. Here, a prime objective of the people responsible for operating these airports is the efficiency of runway operations. Blumstein (1959). Odoni (1972), and others have built analytical models of landing and departure operations; they measure effectiveness of the various operating policies in terms of "the number of runway operations per hour," and this becomes the single attribute of concern.

In a medical context, basic univariate attributes might be the cure rate of some medical treatment, the number of severe side effects that result from use of a drug, and so on.

As a final example, consider the following unpleasant situation. A country is seized by an epidemic, and the medical director of the country must choose an alternative for curtailing the death caused by this epidemic. An attribute that would describe the consequences of his actions might be number of deaths caused by the epidemic. In a variation of this problem the underlying attribute might be the probability that "severe consequences" will occur.

4.1.5 Outline of This Chapter

In the next section, a direct method of assigning utilities to consequences is presented. This method is not operationally adequate when there are many consequences, since the direct method requires a subjective input from the decision maker for each assignment of utility, and there may be too many such inputs to handle practically. In these situations, it may be desirable and necessary to construct a utility function u that assigns a utility $u(x)$ to any possible consequence x over a continuous range of possibilities. Sections 4.3–4.7 develop a framework for examining *monotonically increasing* utility functions defined on a real-valued variable—that is, for cases where more of the variable is preferred to less. This framework is extended to decreasing and nonmonotonic utility functions in Section 4.8. The next two sections, respectively, suggest a procedure for assessing unidimensional utility functions and report examples of such assessments. Sections 4.11 and 4.12 extend the ideas of the chapter to conditional unidimensional utility theory and provide a transition to the multiattribute case considered in Chapters 5 and 6.

4.2 DIRECT ASSESSMENT OF UTILITIES FOR CONSEQUENCES

Let us denote the possible consequences of a decision as $x_1, x_2, \ldots, x_N$. Then, because utility is relative and not absolute, to establish an origin and unit of measure, we can arbitrarily assign utilities to two of the consequences and then assess utilities for the other consequences relative to those two. This procedure is probably easier to illustrate if we define x^o and x^* as a least preferred and a most preferred consequence. The use of "a least preferred" instead of "the least preferred" indicates there could be more than one consequence with the same degree of preference.

Now, to set our scale, let us assign

$$u(x^*) = 1 \quad \text{and} \quad u(x^o) = 0,$$

and assess for each other consequence x, a probability π such that x is indifferent* to the lottery $\langle x^*, \pi, x^o \rangle$, yielding a π chance at x^* and a $(1 - \pi)$ chance at x^o. Then, because the utility of x must equal the expected utility of the lottery, we assign

$$u(x) = \pi u(x^*) + (1 - \pi)u(x^o) = \pi.$$

If utilities were assessed in this manner for all x's, there would be many possible consistency checks. For instance, let x', x'', and x''' designate an increasing preference sequence, and let the alternative x'' for certain be indifferent to the lottery $\langle x''', p, x' \rangle$; then, for consistency, p must be such that

$$u(x'') = pu(x''') + (1 - p)u(x'),$$

or

$$p = \frac{u(x'') - u(x')}{u(x''') - u(x')}.$$

In problems with only a few possible consequences—maybe even up to 50—this direct assessment technique may be appropriate. However, we feel that in problems with many consequences, where there is a natural ordering for the underlying x's, an alternative approach is often better. The procedure involves fixing the utilities of a few consequences as above and then fitting a curve, that is, a utility function, to these. As we will see in the next five sections, the shape and functional form of the utility function tells us a great deal about the basic attitudes of the decision maker toward risk. Therefore, our general approach is to start with these

* Less elliptically we should say, "Let the decision maker be indifferent between x and the lottery."

basic attitudes toward risk, establish functional forms of utility functions exhibiting these properties, and then choose a specific utility function using a few assessed points. This will become clearer in what follows.

4.3 UNIDIMENSIONAL UTILITY FUNCTIONS

Let us introduce some *qualitative* characteristics of utility functions. Each characteristic implies a certain attitude of the decision maker with regard to his preferences for consequences and lotteries. By expressing these attitudes mathematically, restrictions on the utility function implied by these attitudes can be analytically derived. Provided the decision maker subscribes to a certain attitude, his utility function is restricted to a degree and, therefore, the actual assessment of his utility function is simplified. Furthermore, it then becomes possible to do sensitivity and break-even analyses.

4.3.1 Monotonicity

Often a very reasonable characteristic is monotonicity. When monetary asset position is appropriate to summarize consequences, most (if not all) decision makers prefer a greater amount to a lesser amount. In this case, if u represents a utility function for monetary assets X, then due to the nature in which utility functions are assessed,

$$[x_1 > x_2] \Leftrightarrow [u(x_1) > u(x_2)]. \tag{4.3}$$

Now consider the preferences for response time to calls for ambulance service. It seems quite reasonable to assume a smaller response time is always preferred to a larger one. In this case, if t is a specific response time and u again represents the utility function, then

$$[t_1 > t_2] \Leftrightarrow [u(t_2) > u(t_1)]. \tag{4.4}$$

Therefore, we say that the utility function for response time is *monotonically decreasing*.

We can easily transform from a decreasing to an increasing utility function simply by changing the attribute. For example, suppose that instead of measuring ambulance service in terms of response time, we define a "standard response time" as 15 minutes and use the attribute "standard minutes saved in response" to measure service. For a particular call for service, if we let y be the standard minutes saved in response and define it by

$$y \equiv 15 - t,$$

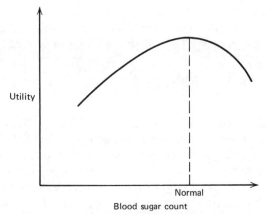

Fig. 4.3. A nonmonotonic utility function.

where t is the previously defined response time, then preferences clearly are increasing in y and, therefore, the utility function for our new attribute Y is increasing. This is true whether or not the "standard minutes saved in response" is ever negative (i.e., response time is greater than 15 minutes).

It is clear that we can easily change from an increasing to a decreasing utility function by switching the measure of effectiveness. Perhaps the most intuitive example of this involves measuring the operations of a business concern in terms of either profits or opportunity losses. It is safe to assume that preferences are increasing in profits and decreasing in opportunity losses.

Let us suggest a situation where the utility function is not monotonic. In a medical context, a patient may be having problems with sugar in his blood. The doctor in charge may have a variety of alternatives to try to solve the problem. The blood sugar count may be used as the measure of effectiveness. There is some "normal" blood sugar count that is desired. Below the normal, the less the blood sugar count, the worse the situation is; above the normal, larger blood sugar counts are less preferred than smaller ones. In this case, preferences are monotonically increasing up to the normal level and monotonically decreasing afterward. Such a utility function is illustrated in Fig. 4.3.

4.3.2 The Certainty Equivalent and Strategic Equivalence

The concept of the *certainty equivalent* is basic to utility theory. It is introduced now, since it will be used frequently in the presentation of the various risk characteristics of utility functions in the following sections.

Let L be a lottery yielding consequences $x_1, x_2, \ldots, x_n$ with probabilities $p_1, p_2, \ldots, p_n$, respectively. We will denote the uncertain consequence (i.e., a random variable) of the lottery by $\tilde{x}$ and the expected consequence by $\bar{x}$ where, of course,

$$\bar{x} \equiv E(\tilde{x}) = \sum_{i=1}^{n} p_i x_i. \tag{4.5}$$

The expected utility of this lottery is

$$E[u(\tilde{x})] = \sum_{i=1}^{n} p_i u(x_i), \tag{4.6}$$

which is an appropriate index to maximize in choosing among lotteries.

Definition. A *certainty equivalent* of lottery L is an amount $\hat{x}$ such that the decision maker is indifferent between L and the amount $\hat{x}$ for certain. Therefore, $\hat{x}$ is defined by

$$u(\hat{x}) = E[u(\tilde{x})], \quad \text{or} \quad \hat{x} = u^{-1} E u(\tilde{x}). \tag{4.7}$$

Note that the certainty equivalent of any lottery is unique for monotonic utility functions.

When the attribute X of interest is monetary asset position, then a certainty equivalent of a lottery is referred to as a certainty monetary-asset equivalent. If X is a response time, the certainty equivalents are more appropriately called certainty response-time equivalents. However, since it will always be clear from the context of the discussion, we choose to use just the term "certainty equivalent" without further specification.

Historically, much of the development of unidimensional utility theory and, therefore, certainty equivalents, has been concerned with the utility for money. For this case, the terms *cash equivalent* and *selling price* of a lottery are often found in the literature. Both terms mean the certainty equivalent of a lottery with consequences representing monetary amounts.*

Although it is perhaps obvious, the following point must be made. Notice that the expected consequence and certainty equivalent defined by (4.5) and (4.7), respectively, were concerned with a lottery having a discrete number of possible consequences. When the possible consequences of a lottery are described by a probability density function f, then

---

* The *buying price* of a lottery with monetary consequences is another term frequently found in the literature. It is defined as the largest amount of money the decision maker would pay for a lottery given his present asset position. Only in special circumstances is the buying price equal to the selling price of a lottery. See Chapter 4, Section 11 of Raiffa (1968).

the expected consequence $\bar{x}$ of that lottery is clearly

$$\bar{x} = E(\bar{x}) = \int xf(x)\,dx$$

and a certainty equivalent $\hat{x}$ is the solution to

$$u(\hat{x}) = E[u(\bar{x})] = \int u(x)f(x)\,dx.$$

Before presenting some examples, it is important to introduce the concept of strategic equivalence.

Definition. Two utility functions, u_1 and u_2, are *strategically equivalent*, written $u_1 \sim u_2$, if and only if they imply the same preference ranking for any two lotteries.

From the definition it follows, of course, that if $u_1 \sim u_2$, the certainty equivalents for any particular lottery implied by u_1 and u_2 are the same. Symbolically,

$$u_1 \sim u_2 \Rightarrow u_1^{-1}Eu_1(\bar{x}) = u_2^{-1}Eu_2(\bar{x}), \qquad \text{for all } \bar{x}.$$

It is straightforward to show that if for some constants h and $k > 0$,

$$u_1(x) = h + ku_2(x), \qquad \text{for all } x,$$

then $u_1 \sim u_2$.

We now assert the converse.

Theorem 4.1. *If $u_1 \sim u_2$, there exists two constants h and $k > 0$ such that*

$$u_1(x) = h + ku_2(x), \qquad \text{for all } x. \tag{4.8}$$

Proof. Let x be any value in $[x^\circ, x^*]$ and let $x \sim \langle x^*, \pi, x^\circ \rangle$ so that

$$u_i(x) = \pi u_i(x^*) + (1 - \pi)u_i(x^\circ), \qquad \text{for } i = 1, 2. \tag{4.9}$$

Letting $i = 2$ in (4.9) and solving for π we get

$$\pi = \frac{u_2(x) - u_2(x^\circ)}{u_2(x^*) - u_2(x^\circ)}. \tag{4.10}$$

Substituting this value of π into (4.9) for $i = 1$ we get the desired result. ◄

Strategically equivalent utility functions have identical implications for action. Let us present some examples.

Example 4.1. Let $u(x) = a + bx \sim x$, $b > 0$. Suppose the decision maker is faced with a lottery described by the probability density function *f.* Then the expected consequence is

$$\bar{x} = E[\bar{x}] = \int xf(x)\, dx,$$

and the certainty equivalent $\hat{x}$ is found from

$$u(\hat{x}) = E[u(\bar{x})] = E[a + b\bar{x}] = a + b\bar{x}.$$

Since $u(\hat{x}) = a + b\hat{x}$, it follows that $\hat{x} = \bar{x}$. This example shows that if the utility function is linear, the certainty equivalent for any lottery is equal to the expected consequence of that lottery. ∎

Example 4.2. Let $u(x) = a - be^{-cx} \sim -e^{-cx}$, where $b > 0$, and suppose the decision maker is faced with a 50–50 lottery yielding either x_1 or x_2, written $\langle x_1, x_2 \rangle$. The expected consequence $\bar{x}$ is $(x_1 + x_2)/2$. The certainty equivalent is the solution to

$$u(\hat{x}) = E[u(\bar{x})]$$

or, equivalently, the solution to

$$-e^{-c\hat{x}} = -\frac{e^{-cx_1} + e^{-cx_2}}{2}.$$

Completing the calculations for a few cases, we obtain Table 4.1

Table 4.1

Certainty Equivalents for
Lotteries $\langle x_1, x_2 \rangle$ Using
$u(x) \sim -e^{-cx}$

c	x_1	x_2	$\bar{x}$	$\hat{x}$
1.0	0	10	5	.69
1.0	10	20	15	10.69
1.0	20	30	25	20.69
.2	0	10	5	2.85
.2	10	20	15	12.85
.2	20	30	25	22.85
.1	0	10	5	3.8
.1	10	20	15	13.8
.1	20	30	25	23.8

Now suppose the lottery is described by the uniform probability density function

$$f(x) = \begin{cases} \dfrac{1}{x_2 - x_1}, & x_1 \leq x \leq x_2 \\ 0, & \text{elsewhere.} \end{cases}$$

The expected consequence is clearly $(x_1 + x_2)/2$, and the certainty equivalent is found by solving

$$u(\hat{x}) = \int_{x_1}^{x_2} (-e^{-cx}) \left(\frac{1}{x_2 - x_1} \right) dx$$

or

$$-e^{-c\hat{x}} = \left(\frac{1}{x_2 - x_1} \right) \left(\frac{e^{-cx_2} - e^{-cx_1}}{c} \right).$$

Completing the calculations for a few cases, we obtain Table 4.2. ∎

From Tables 4.1 and 4.2, it appears that if all the consequences of a lottery are increased by a fixed amount, the certainty equivalent is increased by that same amount. This is an important property of the exponential utility function.

Theorem 4.2. *If* $u(x) = -e^{-cx}$ *and* $\hat{x}$ *is the certainty equivalent for a lottery* $\tilde{x}$, *then* $\hat{x} + x_0$ *is the certainty equivalent for the lottery* $\tilde{x} + x_0$.

Proof. The certainty equivalent $\hat{x}'$ for the second lottery solves

$$-e^{-c\hat{x}'} = E[u(\tilde{x} + x_0)]$$
$$= E[-e^{-c(\tilde{x} + x_0)}]$$
$$= e^{-cx_0} E[-e^{-c\tilde{x}}].$$

But, by definition,

$$-e^{-c\hat{x}} = E[-e^{-c\tilde{x}}],$$

so

$$-e^{-c\hat{x}'} = e^{-cx_0}(-e^{-c\hat{x}}) = -e^{-c(\hat{x} + x_0)}$$

from which it follows that $\hat{x}' = \hat{x} + x_0$. ◀

Table 4.2

Certainty Equivalents for Uniform Lotteries Using $u(x) \sim -e^{-cx}$

c	x_1	x_2	$\bar{x}$	$\hat{x}$
1.0	0	10	5	2.30
1.0	10	20	15	12.30
1.0	20	30	25	22.30
.2	0	10	5	4.2
.2	10	20	15	14.2
.2	20	30	25	24.2
.1	0	10	5	4.58
.1	10	20	15	14.58
.1	20	30	25	24.58

Example 4.3.   Let $u(x) = \log (x + b)$, $x > -b$. The expected conse-quence for lottery $\langle x_1, x_2 \rangle$ is $(x_1 + x_2)/2$ as before. The certainty equivalent is the solution to

$$\log (\hat{x} + b) = \frac{\log (x_1 + b) + \log (x_2 + b)}{2},$$

which is

$$\hat{x} = \sqrt{(x_1 + b)(x_2 + b)} - b$$

A few cases are cataloged in Table 4.3.   ■

One can see from Table 4.3 that for every lottery, the certainty equival-ent is always less than the expected consequence. However, for any particular value of b, this difference grows smaller as the consequences x_1 and x_2 are increased by a fixed amount. Later in this chapter, we shall devote a good deal of attention to utility functions that imply such a behavior for the certainty equivalents.

Example 4.4.   The first three examples have all concerned monotoni-cally increasing utility functions. Let us consider the decreasing utility function $u(x) = -x^2$, $x \geq 0$,   and   calculate   the   expected   conse-quences and certainty equivalents for $\langle 0, 10 \rangle$ and $\langle 10, 20 \rangle$. The expected consequences are clearly 5 and 15, respectively. The certainty equivalent for $\langle 0, 10 \rangle$ is the solution to

$$-\hat{x}^2 = -\frac{0^2 + 10^2}{2} = -50.$$

Thus, $\hat{x} = 7.07$. Similarly, the certainty equivalent for $\langle 10, 20 \rangle$ is found to be 15.8. This means that the decison maker is indifferent between

Table 4.3

Certainty Equivalents for
Lotteries $\langle x_1, x_2 \rangle$ Using
$u(x) \sim \log (x + b)$

b	x_1	x_2	$\bar{x}$	$\hat{x}$
1	0	10	5	2.32
1	10	20	15	14.2
1	20	30	25	24.5
11	0	10	5	4.2
11	10	20	15	14.5
11	20	30	25	24.7
21	0	10	5	4.5
21	10	20	15	14.7
21	20	30	25	24.8

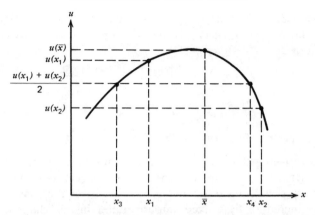

Fig. 4.4. The certainty equivalents using a nonmonotonic utility function.

obtaining $x = 7.07$ for certain and the lottery $\langle 0, 10 \rangle$, and that he is indifferent between obtaining $x = 15.8$ for certain and the lottery $\langle 10, 20 \rangle$.

∎

The examples have illustrated calculation of the certainty equivalents for some representative lotteries. However, they dealt only with monotonic utility functions. But what about the nonmonotonic case? In this situation, the certainty equivalent may not even be unique. Refer to Fig. 4.4 and consider a 50–50 lottery between x_1 and x_2. A certainty equivalent is any consequence whose utility equals the expected utility of the lottery $[u(x_1) + u(x_2)]/2$. As we can see from Fig. 4.4, both x_3 and x_4 are certainty equivalents for $\langle x_1, x_2 \rangle$ and, in fact, one of these does not even fall between the two possible consequences of the lottery.

4.4 RISK AVERSION

In this and the next four sections, we introduce various basic attitudes toward risk and illustrate their implications on the functional form of the utility function. In order to maintain a continuity in the presentation and to help the reader develop an intuitive understanding for these concepts, the Sections 4.4–4.7 concern only monotonically *increasing* utility functions. And, for the same reasons, much of our discussion will concern the cases involving a monetary attribute, such as "net assets" or "incremental income." However, as we have stressed earlier, the concepts are equally valid for nonmonetary attributes. Section 4.8 then extends the risk concepts to situations with decreasing and nonmonotonic preferences.

4.4.1 A Definition of Risk Aversion

Intuitively, we think of a risk-averse person as one who prefers to behave conservatively. Consider a decision maker facing a lottery yielding either a consequence x' or a less preferable consequence x'', with equal probability. Obviously, the expected consequence $\bar{x}$ of this lottery is $(x' + x'')/2$. Now suppose the decision maker is asked to state his preference between receiving $\bar{x}$ for certain and the lottery $\langle x', x'' \rangle$. If the decision maker prefers the certain consequence $\bar{x}$ to the lottery $\langle x', x'' \rangle$ with the same expected consequence, then the decision maker is actually saying he prefers to avoid the risks associated with the lottery. That is, although $\bar{x}$ and $\langle x', x'' \rangle$ have the same expected consequences, he prefers $\bar{x}$, since there is no risk associated with it, whereas there is risk associated with the outcome of the lottery. When a decision maker has this type of attitude toward all lotteries, we say he is *risk averse*. Let us formalize this notion.

Definition. A decision maker is *risk averse* if he prefers the expected consequence of any nondegenerate lottery to that lottery.*

In such a situation, the utility of the expected consequence of any lottery must be greater than the expected utility of that lottery. So, if the possible consequences of a lottery are represented by $\bar{x}$, we are risk averse if, for all nondegenerate lotteries,

$$u[E(\bar{x})] > E[u(\bar{x})]. \tag{4.11}$$

Theorem 4.3. *A decision maker is risk averse if and only if his utility function is concave.*

Proof. Consider a lottery that yields either x_1 with probability p or x_2 with probability $(1-p)$, $0 < p < 1$. The expected consequence is $\bar{x} = px_1 + (1-p)x_2$. For risk averse utility functions, from (4.11),

$$u[px_1 + (1-p)x_2] > pu(x_1) + (1-p)u(x_2), \qquad 0 < p < 1,$$

which is the definition of (strict) concavity.

To prove the converse (done only for the finite case), consider lottery $\bar{x}$ yielding x_i with probability p_i, for $i = 1, \ldots, m$, where no $p_i = 1$. Since u is strictly concave, we know that

$$u\left[\sum_{i=1}^{m} p_i x_i\right] > \sum_{i=1}^{m} p_i u(x_i).$$

This inequality is just (4.11) for the finite case, so u is risk averse. ◀

---

* A nondegenerate lottery is one where no single consequence has a probability of one of occurring.

Operationally, it may be unrealistic to check condition (4.11) for all nondegenerate lotteries to determine whether or not one is risk averse. To help matters, there is the related corollary.

Corollary. *A decision maker who prefers the expected consequence of any 50–50 lottery* $\langle x_1, x_2 \rangle$ *to the lottery itself is risk averse.*

Proof. It follows from the premise that

$$u(\bar{x}) = u(\tfrac{1}{2}x_1 + \tfrac{1}{2}x_2) > \tfrac{1}{2}u(x_1) + \tfrac{1}{2}u(x_2), \qquad \text{all } x_1 \neq x_2$$

which implies u is concave.   ◀

Digression. As we learn in every basic economics course, the economist's concept of *decreasing marginal utility* implies that the *utility function* is concave and conversely. Here, *utility function* is in italics because it is a completely different construction from the von Neumann–Morgenstern utility function that we are considering in this chapter. The distinction seems important enough to deserve a brief digression.

When the economist says "his marginal utility for attribute X is decreasing," he means that the difference in units of utility, called utiles—which are never explicitly defined—because of an incremental change of X from x to $x+1$ decreases as x increases. No probabilistic notions are introduced, and any expected utility calcuated from such a *utility function* has no particular interpretation as it does in the case of von Neumann–Morgenstern utility functions.

As an example of our economist's *utility function* with decreasing marginal utility, suppose we considered 8 utiles as the utility of one day of skiing, 14 utiles for two days, 18 utiles for three days, and so on. Then we could say the first day is worth 8 utiles, the second an additional 6, and the third another 4. The marginal utility of each additional day of skiing is decreasing. However, if we had a choice between two days of skiing for sure or a lottery yielding either one or three days with equal likelihood, we could not say which option should be preferred using the *utility function.* This is so even though the expected number of utiles for the lottery is 13, whereas it is 14 for the sure two days skiing. The concept of "expected utiles" has *no* meaning. The utility functions we are talking about in this chapter are completely different from the economist's *utility function.* Knowing one implies very little about the other. One can easily be convex and the other concave for the same attribute.

Let us return to our decision maker and suppose he did not wish to behave conservatively. In fact, suppose the decision maker preferred any lottery to the expected consequence of that lottery. That is, he was more than willing to accept the risks associated with any lottery. This type of individual is said to be risk prone.

Definition. A decision maker is *risk prone* if he prefers any nondegenerate lottery to the expected consequence of that lottery.

For such an individual, the utility of the expected consequence must be less than the expected utility of the lottery, that is,

$$u[E(\tilde{x})] < E[u(\tilde{x})]. \tag{4.12}$$

Because of the similarity to the preceding assertion, we state Theorem 4.4, without proof.

Theorem 4.4. *A decision maker is risk prone if and only if his utility function is convex.*

There is an alternative way in which we could have defined risk aversion for increasing utility functions. However, since this definition would not be valid for other cases, we chose (4.11) to define risk averse and to state the alternative as Theorem 4.5.

Theorem 4.5. *For increasing utility functions, a decision maker is risk averse if and only if his certainty equivalent for any nondegenerate lottery is less than the expected consequence of that lottery.*

Proof. Assume he is risk averse. Then, from (4.11),

$$u[E(\tilde{x})] > E[u(\tilde{x})].$$

But, by the definition of a certainty equivalent, we know that

$$u(\hat{x}) = E[u(\tilde{x})],$$

so

$$u[E(\tilde{x})] > u(\hat{x}).$$

Since the utility function is increasing, clearly

$$E(\tilde{x}) > \hat{x}.$$

Now, to go the other way, assume that

$$E(\tilde{x}) > \hat{x}.$$

Then, because the utility function is increasing,

$$u[E(\tilde{x})] > u(\hat{x}) = E[u(\tilde{x})],$$

which completes the proof. ◀

For *increasing* utility functions we make the following definition.

Definition. The *risk premium* RP of a lottery $\tilde{x}$ is its expected value minus its certainty equivalent. In symbols we have

$$\text{RP}(\tilde{x}) = \bar{x} - \hat{x} = E(\tilde{x}) - u^{-1}Eu(\tilde{x}).$$

where u^{-1} is the inverse of u.

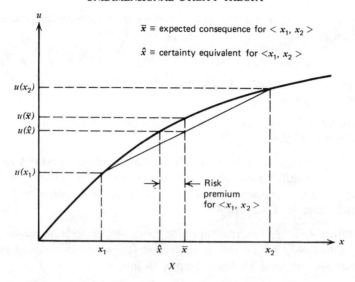

Fig. 4.5. An increasing utility function exhibiting risk aversion.

Theorem 4.6.   *For increasing utility functions, a decision maker is risk averse if and only if his risk premium is positive for all nondegenerate lotteries.*

The proof is omitted, since it follows directly from the definition of the risk premium.

It may be illustrative to work through a couple of examples. Refer to Fig. 4.5 for an illustration of the certainty equivalent and risk premium for $\langle x_1, x_2 \rangle$ using a risk-averse utility function.

Example 4.5.   From Table 4.1, we see that using the utility function $u(x) = -e^{-.2x}$, the certainty equivalent for $\langle 0, 10 \rangle$ is 2.85 and the expected consequence is 5.0. Thus, the risk premium is $(5.0 - 2.85)$ or 2.15. Similarly, the certainty equivalent for $\langle 20, 30 \rangle$ is 22.85 and the expected consequence is 25.0, so again the risk premium is 2.15. ∎

Example 4.6.   Given $u(x) = \log(x + 30)$, for $x > -30$, we find the certainty equivalent for $\langle -20, -10 \rangle$ to be -15.857; the risk premium is $[-15 - (-15.857)]$, or .857. The risk premiums for the lotteries $\langle -25, -15 \rangle$ and $\langle -29, -19 \rangle$ would be 1.34 and 2.68 respectively. Note that if, for example, x were to be interpreted in units of thousands of dollars, then the number 30 would refer to $30,000. ∎

Intuitively, the risk premium is the amount of the attribute that the decision maker is willing to "give up" from the average (i.e., the amount less than the expected consequence) to avoid the risks associated with the particular lottery.

When the decision maker is faced with an unfavorable lottery, that is, one that is less preferable than the status quo, it is natural to ask how much would he "pay" in terms of attribute X to avoid accepting this lottery.

Definition. The *insurance premium* IP for a lottery $\tilde{x}$ is the negative of the certainty equivalent of the lottery. In symbols,

$$\text{IP}(\tilde{x}) = -\hat{x} = -u^{-1}Eu(\tilde{x}).$$

If, for example, the lottery $\tilde{x}$ has a certainty equivalent of $-\$5000$, then the insurance premium is \$5000. The decision maker should just be willing to give up \$5000 to rid himself of the financial responsibility of the lottery.

In the last example, assume that $x = 0$ is equivalent to doing nothing, that is, the status quo. Then $\langle -20, -10 \rangle$ is an unfavorable lottery since its expected utility is less than the utility of the status quo. Since the decision maker is indifferent between $\langle -20, -10 \rangle$ and its certainty equivalent -15.857, he should be willing to pay 15.857 to eliminate his responsibility for the lottery $\langle -20, -10 \rangle$. Therefore 15.857 is the insurance premium for $\langle -20, -10 \rangle$.

4.4.2 Restricting the Form of the Utility Function

Before going any deeper into the theory, let us illustrate how monotonicity and risk aversion can be exploited to simplify greatly the assessment of a utility function. Suppose we wish to assess a utility function u for attribute X, and the decision maker has indicated that his preferences increase monotonically in X and that he is risk averse.

To begin, we choose x_1 and x_2, where $x_2 > x_1$, and we arbitrarily assign $u(x_1)$ and $u(x_2)$ subject to the restriction that $u(x_2) > u(x_1)$. This is permissible, since utility functions are unique up to positive linear transformations. By plotting the points $[x_1, u(x_1)]$ and $[x_2, u(x_2)]$ on the graph in Fig. 4.6a, we can see the decision maker's utility function is limited to the nonshaded area. Consider point 3 in the figure. If the utility function passed through this point, then part of the function would necessarily not be concave. But, since the decision maker is risk averse, his utility function must be concave; therefore, it cannot pass through point 3. Similarly, if the decision maker's utility function passed through point 4, monotonicity would be violated, since $x_4 > x_2$ and $u(x_4) < u(x_2)$.

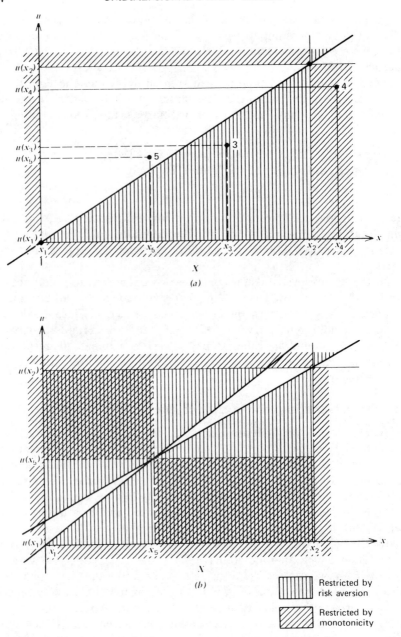

Fig. 4.6.   Restrictions placed on a utility function by monotonicity and risk aversion.

Now suppose we question the decision maker to find his certainty equivalent for the lottery yielding either x_1 or x_2, each with probability $\frac{1}{2}$. Denoting this certainty equivalent by x_5, we have one additional point, $[x_5, u(x_5)]$, on the utility function, where

$$u(x_5) = \frac{u(x_1) + u(x_2)}{2}.$$

After plotting this point on the graph of Fig. 4.6a, we use the same logic as before to restrict the decision maker's utility function to the nonshaded region of Fig. 4.6b. As can be seen from the figure, by empirically evaluating the utility of only one consequence, the shape of the utility function can be restricted quite a degree by exploiting the qualitative characteristics of monotonicity and risk aversion.

The same type of reasoning can be used to bound the certainty equivalents of a lottery. Perhaps this can best be illustrated with an example.

Example 4.7. Let us say $x_1 = 0$, $x_2 = 100$, and $x_5 = 40$ in Fig. 4.6. Furthermore, assume we had arbitrarily set $u(0) = 0$ and $u(100) = 1$, so $u(40) = 0.5$. Then, as we can see in Fig. 4.7, by elementary geometric

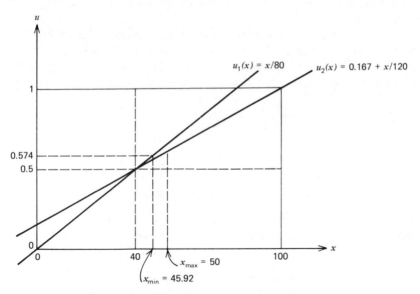

Fig. 4.7. Bounding the certainty equivalent using risk aversion and monotonicity.

reasoning, any monotone, risk-averse utility function must lie between

$$u_1(x) = \frac{x}{80}$$

and

$$u_2(x) = 0.167 + \frac{x}{120}.$$

Suppose we want to bound the certainty equivalent for the lottery described by the probability density function $f(x)$ where

$$f(x) = \begin{cases} \dfrac{1}{50}, & 25 \le x \le 75 \\ 0, & \text{elsewhere.} \end{cases}$$

To get an upper bound on the certainty equivalent for a lottery, in general we could obtain an upper bound on its expected utility and find the largest value of x that could possibly have this utility. Because of risk aversion, Theorem 4.5 implies the certainty equivalent can be no greater than 50. However, for the specific lottery, note from Fig. 4.7 that it is possible that the utility function be linear from $x = 25$ to $x = 75$. Since the probability density specifies possible outcomes only in this range, the certainty equivalent could be as high as 50, the expected outcome. Hence, the lowest upper bound on the certainty equivalent for our lottery, call it x_{max}, is 50.0.

To find a lower bound on the certainty equivalent, we could first get a lower bound on the expected utility of this lottery, and then find the smallest value of x that could possibly have this utility. Clearly, regardless of what the actual utility function u is, the expected utility of the lottery

$$E[u(\tilde{x})] = \int_{25}^{75} u(x)f(x)\, dx$$

$$\ge \int_{25}^{40} u_1(x)f(x)\, dx + \int_{40}^{75} u_2(x)f(x)\, dx,$$

so

$$E[u(\tilde{x})] \ge 0.122 + 0.452 = 0.574.$$

As can be seen from Fig. 4.7, the smallest possible amount x, call it x_{min}, that could have a utility equal to 0.574 results when $u(x) = u_1(x)$, and it is found by solving

$$u_1(x_{min}) = \frac{x_{min}}{80} = 0.574.$$

This gives us

$$x_{min} = 45.92,$$

and x_{min} is a lower bound on the "true" certainty equivalent of our lottery. It is not necessarily the greatest lower bound, since x_{min} was calculated using $u = u_1$ in the range $x \geq 40$, whereas $u = u_2$ was used in this range to calculate the minimum utility for the given probability density. Tighter bounds could probably be found. ∎

However, our purpose in this example was not to find the tightest possible bounds on the certainty equivalent, but to illustrate how some rather powerful inferences can be made from a limited amount of information about a decision maker's preferences and to become more familiar with some of the concepts we will be using regularly.

4.4.3 The Risk-Prone Case*

Let us now take a look at the opposite of a risk-averse decision maker, that is, a risk-prone one.

Theorem 4.7. *For increasing utility functions, a decision maker is risk prone if and only if his certainty equivalent for any nondegenerate lottery is greater than the expected consequence of that lottery.*

The proof is omitted because of its similarity to the corresponding proof for the risk-averse case.

Recall that the risk premium was defined as the expected consequence minus the certainty equivalent for increasing utility functions. Following directly from this definition, we have Theorem 4.8.

Theorem 4.8. *For increasing utility functions, a decision maker is risk prone if and only if his risk premium is negative for all nondegenerate lotteries.*

The proof is omitted. However, let us illustrate this result with an example.

Example 4.8. Consider a risk-prone utility function of the form $u(x) = .2x^2$ as illustrated in Fig. 4.8 and let us calculate the expected consequence, certainty equivalent, and risk premium for the lottery $\langle 4, 12 \rangle$. Clearly, the expected consequence is

$$\bar{x} = \frac{4 + 12}{2} = 8.$$

The expected utility of this lottery is

$$\tfrac{1}{2}u(4) + \tfrac{1}{2}u(12) = \tfrac{1}{2}(.2 \times 16) + \tfrac{1}{2}(.2 \times 144) = 16,$$

---

* This subsection examines the *risk-prone* case in a manner analogous to the *risk-averse* case. It is included primarily for reference purposes and may be skipped.

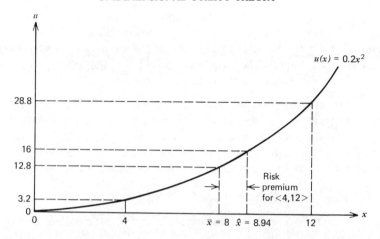

Fig. 4.8. An increasing utility function illustrating risk proneness.

so its certainty equivalent $\hat{x}$ is the solution to

$$.2(\hat{x})^2 = 16.$$

Solving this, we find $\hat{x} = 8.94$. The risk premium, $\bar{x} - \hat{x}$, is then easily found to be $-.94$. ■

A risk-prone individual is one who is "willing to gamble." In laboratory experiments and in operational situations in the real world, different researchers have found certain decision makers to be risk prone. For instance, Grayson (1960), by measuring several oil wildcatters' utility functions for money, found some of them to have this characteristic. In other words, these oil wildcatters were willing to risk their stakes on a lottery (i.e., drilling for oil) with an expected return less than their stakes, but that might result in a very large return (i.e., striking oil). This large return represented the opportunity for a "new way of life," and this made the gamble worthwhile to many wildcatters. Aspects of Grayson's work are discussed in Section 4.10.

Given that the decision maker's preferences are increasing and that he is risk prone, and given the certainty equivalent for one 50–50 lottery, we could bound his utility function as we did for the risk-averse individual. Also, we could calculate bounds for the certainty equivalent of any other lottery using the procedure illustrated in Example 4.7. However, since the ideas are similar to the previous case, another example would not be particularly illustrative, so we omit it.

4.5 A MEASURE OF RISK AVERSION*

Now that the usefulness of risk aversion is established, we will direct our attention toward a measure of this property for increasing utility functions. We would like a measure of risk aversion to indicate when one decision maker is more risk averse than another in that for any specified lottery, his risk premium is greater than that of the other decision maker.

Consider the lottery $\langle x + h, \ x - h \rangle$ where h is a specified amount of X. Intuitively, it seems that the more concave the utility function u is about x, the larger the risk premium $\pi(x, h)$ for the lottery $\langle x + h, x - h \rangle$ will be. However, this notion is quickly dismissed by viewing Fig. 4.9. As can be seen, although u'', the second derivative of u with respect to x, is different for the two utility functions, the risk premium is the same. Therefore, the magnitude of u'' provides no insight into our attitudes toward risk. With good hindsight, we can see, of course, that this is true, since utility functions that are positive linear transformations of each other are strategically equivalent.

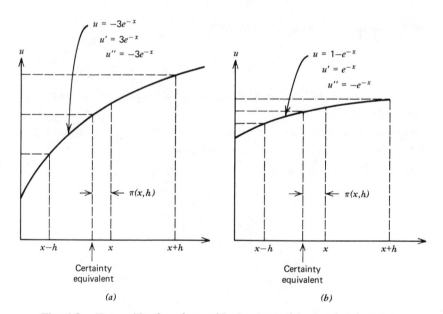

Fig. 4.9. Two utility functions with the same risk-aversion function.

---

* The reader is strongly urged to read Pratt (1964), which is the original source for much of what is discussed in this and the following two sections. See also Arrow (1971).

The sign of u'' does provide some information, however. If u'' is negative for all x, then u must be concave and, therefore, risk averse. On the other hand, if u'' is positive for all x, then u is convex, implying that the decision maker is risk prone. Thus it seems reasonable to take u'' into account in some way in a measure of risk aversion.

Let us proceed in the same manner that led to the development of a measure of risk aversion. It seemed desirable that such a measure should, among other things, (1) indicate whether a utility function is risk averse or risk prone (which can be done with u'') and (2) be identical for strategically equivalent utility functions. Following this theme for strategically equivalent utility functions u_1 and u_2, clearly $u_2 = a + bu_1$, so that $u_2' = bu_1'$, and $u_2'' = bu_1''$. From this, we can observe that $u_2''/u_2' = u_1''/u_1'$, and thus it seems that a relevant measure of aversion to risk might be the ratio of u'' and u'. This was tried, and it was discovered that such a measure had many desirable properties.

Definition. The *local risk aversion* at x, written $r(x)$, is defined by

$$r(x) \equiv -\frac{u''(x)}{u'(x)}. \qquad (4.13)$$

Operationally, it is useful to note that

$$r(x) = -\frac{d}{dx}[\log u'(x)]. \qquad (4.14)$$

The risk aversion function* preserves all that is essential concerning u while eliminating the arbitrariness.

Theorem 4.9. *Two utility functions are strategically equivalent if and only if they have the same risk-aversion function.*

Proof. Let $u_1(x) = a + bu_2(x)$, $b > 0$. Clearly, $u_1'(x) = bu_2'(x)$ and $u_1''(x) = bu_2''(x)$, so

$$r_1(x) \equiv -\frac{u_1''(x)}{u_1'(x)} = -\frac{bu_2''(x)}{bu_2'(x)} \equiv r_2(x).$$

To prove the converse, notice from (4.14) that

$$-r(x) = \frac{d}{dx}[\log u'(x)].$$

Integrating both sides gives us

$$\int -r(x)\, dx = \log u'(x) + c,$$

---

* Whenever $r(\cdot)$ is discussed, we are assuming that $u(\cdot)$ is twice continuously differentiable.

where c is an integration constant. Exponentiating this, we find

$$e^{-\int r(x)\,dx} = e^{\log u'(x)+c} = e^c u'(x).$$

And, finally, integrating again,

$$\int e^{-\int r(x)\,dx} dx = \int e^c u'(x)\,dx = e^c u(x) + d.$$

Since $e^c > 0$ and d are constants, $r(x)$ specifies $u(x)$ up to positive linear transformations. ◀

4.5.1 Interpreting the Risk Aversion Function

Let us try to build up an intuitive interpretation for the risk-aversion function. Let x_0 denote the decision maker's initial endowment of a given attribute X, and now consider adding to x_0 a lottery $\tilde{x}$ involving only a small range of X with an expected consequence $E(\tilde{x})$ equal to zero. Also, let $\pi(x_0, \tilde{x})$ be the decision maker's risk premium* for $x_0 + \tilde{x}$. By definition of the certainty equivalent,

$$u(x_0 - \pi) = E[u(x_0 + \tilde{x})]. \tag{4.15}$$

Using Taylor's formula to expand both sides of (4.15), we find that

$$u(x_0 - \pi) = u(x_0) - \pi u'(x_0) + \frac{\pi^2}{2!} u''(x_0) + \cdots \tag{4.16}$$

and

$$E[u(x_0 + \tilde{x})] = E\left[u(x_0) + \tilde{x}u'(x_0) + \frac{1}{2!}\tilde{x}^2 u''(x_0) + \frac{1}{3!}\tilde{x}^3 u'''(x_0) + \cdots \right]$$

$$= u(x_0) + \frac{1}{2} E[\tilde{x}^2] u''(x_0) + \frac{1}{3!} E[\tilde{x}^3] u'''(x_0) + \cdots \tag{4.17}$$

Equating (4.16) and (4.17) and neglecting the higher-order terms gives us

$$-\pi u'(x_0) \approx \tfrac{1}{2} E[\tilde{x}^2] u''(x_0). \tag{4.18}$$

Realizing that $E[\tilde{x}^2]$ is the variance σ_x^2 of the lottery $\tilde{x}$, since $E(\tilde{x}) = 0$, and rearranging (4.18), we find that

$$\pi(x_0, \tilde{x}) \approx \tfrac{1}{2}\sigma_x^2 r(x_0), \tag{4.19}$$

where $r(x_0)$ is defined by (4.13). Thus, starting with an initial level x_0, the

---

* A cautionary word about a possible notational confusion is in order. We use the notation $\pi(x, \tilde{x})$ as the risk premium for the lottery $(x + \tilde{x})$. When $\tilde{x}$ is the special lottery $\langle -h, h \rangle$, we use the symbolism $\pi(x, h)$ instead of $\pi(x, \langle -h, h \rangle)$ for the risk premium of the lottery $x + \langle -h, h \rangle$ or, equivalently, of the lottery $\langle x - h, x + h \rangle$.

decision maker's risk premium for a small-ranged lottery with $E(\tilde{x}) = 0$ is $r(x_0)$ times half the variance of $\tilde{x}$ to a first approximation. Stated another way, the risk aversion $r(x_0)$ is twice the risk premium per unit variance for such lotteries.

Let us now work through a couple of examples to gain a better feeling for the risk aversion function.

Example 4.9. To find the risk-aversion function for $u(x) = a - be^{-cx}$, $b > 0$, we calculate $u'(x) = cbe^{-cx}$ and $u''(x) = -c^2be^{-cx}$; therefore, from (4.13),

$$r(x) \equiv -\frac{u''(x)}{u'(x)} = -\frac{-c^2be^{-cx}}{cbe^{-cx}} = c.$$

Using the same utility function, in Table 4.1 we displayed the expected consequence $\bar{x}$ and certainty equivalents $\hat{x}$ for three different lotteries of the form $\langle x_1, x_2 \rangle$ for three different values of c. Using this, it is easy to calculate the risk premium π for all these lotteries. This is done in Table 4.4. Notice that for any particular value of c, the risk premium for lotteries of the form $\langle x, x + 10 \rangle$ are the same. Also, notice that as c gets smaller, the risk premiums for the same lottery get smaller, and that all the risk premiums are positive. ∎

Observations such as these might lead one to wonder what kind of general statements can be implied about the decision maker's preferences from a knowledge of the risk aversion function.

Theorem 4.10. *If r is positive for all x, then u is concave and the decision maker is risk-averse.*

Table 4.4
The Risk Aversion Function for $u(x) = a - be^{-cx}$

c	x_1	x_2	$\bar{x}$	$\hat{x}$	π	$r(x)$
1.0	0	10	5	.69	4.31	1.0
1.0	10	20	15	10.69	4.31	1.0
1.0	20	30	25	20.69	4.31	1.0
.2	0	10	5	2.85	2.15	.2
.2	10	20	15	12.85	2.15	.2
.2	20	30	25	22.85	2.15	.2
.1	0	10	5	3.8	1.2	.1
.1	10	20	15	13.8	1.2	.1
.1	20	30	25	23.8	1.2	.1

Proof. Assume r is positive. Now, since u' is always positive (u is increasing), $u''(x)$ must be negative. This implies that u is concave, which implies that the decision maker is risk averse.   ◀

And, as you might expect, the analog is also true.

Theorem 4.11. *If r is negative for all x, then u is convex and the decision maker is risk-prone.*

Let u_1 and u_2 be utility functions with risk aversion r_1 and r_2, respectively. Then, from (4.19), we can see that if $r_1(x_0) > r_2(x_0)$ at a particular point x_0, the risk premium $\pi_1(x_0, \tilde{x})$ for a small range lottery $\tilde{x}$ with $E(\tilde{x}) = 0$ is larger than the corresponding risk premium $\pi_2(x_0, \tilde{x})$. However, a more important result, which holds for any lottery, is the following.

Theorem 4.12. *If $r_1(x) > r_2(x)$ for all x, then $\pi_1(x, \tilde{x}) > \pi_2(x, \tilde{x})$ for all x and $\tilde{x}$.*

(In other words, if u_1 has a unifomally larger *local* risk aversion than u_2, then the risk premium for any lottery $x + \tilde{x}$ is larger with u_1 than with u_2. This means that a uniform local condition has a natural global implication.)

Proof.* Assume $r_1(x) > r_2(x)$. Therefore,

$$r_2(x) - r_1(x) = -\frac{d}{dx}[\log u_2'(x)] + \frac{d}{dx}[\log u_1'(x)]$$

$$= \frac{d}{dx}\left[\log \frac{u_1'(x)}{u_2'(x)}\right].$$

is negative. It follows that $\log[u_1'(x)/u_2'(x)]$ is decreasing. Note that

$$\frac{d}{dt} u_1(u_2^{-1}(t)) = \frac{u_1'(u_2^{-1}(t))}{u_2'(u_2^{-1}(t))},$$

which is also decreasing in t, since $\log[u_1'(x)/u_2'(x)]$ is. Therefore, $u_1(u_2^{-1}(t))$ is a concave function of t.

Working the other direction, by definition,

$$\pi_i(x, \tilde{x}) = x + E[\tilde{x}] - u_i^{-1} E u_i(x + \tilde{x}), \qquad i = 1, 2.$$

Then, simply subtracting, we find

$$\pi_1(x, \tilde{x}) - \pi_2(x, \tilde{x}) = u_2^{-1} E u_2(x + \tilde{x}) - u_1^{-1} E u_1(x + \tilde{x})$$

$$= u_2^{-1} E[\tilde{t}] - u_1^{-1} E u_1(u_2^{-1}(\tilde{t}))$$

---

* This proof, which is given in Pratt (1964), is mathematically more involved than the rest of this section. The details of the proof are not required in later discussions.

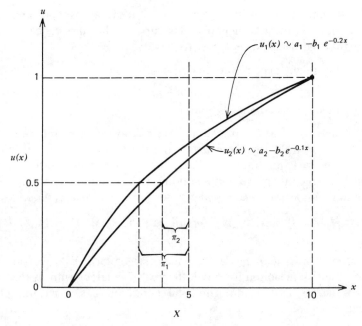

Fig. 4.10. The relationship between the risk premium and the risk-aversion function.

where $\bar{t} = u_2(x + \tilde{x})$. Since $u_1(u_2^{-1}(t))$ is concave, from Jensen's inequality,* we have

$$E[u_1(u_2^{-1}(\tilde{t}))] < u_1(u_2^{-1}[E(\tilde{t})]).$$

Substituting this into the previous expression, we find that

$$\pi_1(x, \tilde{x}) - \pi_2(x, \tilde{x}) > u_2^{-1}E(\tilde{t}) - u_1^{-1}u_1u_2^{-1}[E(\tilde{t})]$$
$$> u_2^{-1}E(\tilde{t}) - u_2^{-1}[E(\tilde{t})]$$
$$> 0$$

which is the desired result. ◀

It should be pointed out that the above result required no restrictions on the sign of r_1 or r_2. Thus, the statement is valid for both risk-averse and risk-prone decision makers.

An illustration of the implications of the preceding result seems appropriate. In Example 4.9, we showed that the risk-aversion function for

---

* See William Feller, *An Introduction to Probability Theory and Its Applications*, Vol. 2., Wiley, New York, 1966.

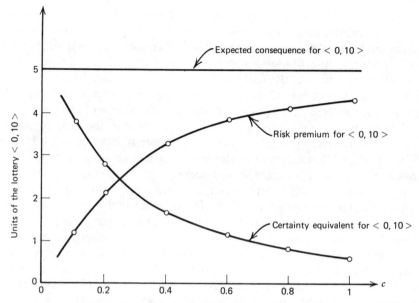

Fig. 4.11.   Relationship between the risk-aversion function and the risk premium with $u(x) = -e^{-cx}$**.**

$u(x) = a - be^{-cx}$ was c. Table 4.4 indicated that the risk premium for $\langle 0, 10 \rangle$ was 2.15 when $c = 0.2$ and 1.2 when $c = 0.1$. This is illustrated in Fig. 4.10 where we let $u_1(x) = a_1 - b_1 e^{-0.2x}$, $u_2(x) = a_2 - b_2 e^{-0.1x}$, and set $u_1(0) = u_2(0) = 0$ and $u_1(10) = u_2(10) = 1$ for reference. Our result states that since $r_1(x) > r_2(x)$ for all x, then π_1 for $\langle 0, 10 \rangle$ must be greater than π_2 for $\langle 0, 10 \rangle$. Figure 4.10 verifies this.

In Fig. 4.11, we go one step further and plot the risk premium and the certainty equivalent for $\langle 0, 10 \rangle$ using $u(x) = -e^{-cx}$ as a function of c (the risk-aversion function). As we expected, the risk premium for the lottery increases and the certainty equivalent decreases as the risk aversion increases. For all values of c, the risk premium plus the certainty equivalent must equal the expected consequence, which is always 5.

4.6   CONSTANT, DECREASING, AND INCREASING RISK AVERSION

In previous sections we have spoken of a risk premium $\pi(x, \tilde{x})$ for lottery $\tilde{x}$ given reference point x, i.e., for lottery $(x + \tilde{x})$. A very interesting question is what happens to $\pi(x, \tilde{x})$ as x increases. For greater amounts of x, is the decision maker's risk premium larger or smaller? Often a decision maker may be able to state that as x increases, the risk premium he would be willing to pay for $\tilde{x}$ decreases. As we shall show in this section, such attitudes put strong restrictions on the functional form of the utility function. By working directly with the utility function u, it is difficult to determine whether such preference attitudes are implied. However, they are very apparent from the risk-aversion function r.

For an increasing utility function, let us consider the risk premium $\pi(x, h)$ for the lottery $\langle x + h, x - h \rangle$ for a risk-averse individual. Clearly, π is positive for all amounts of x. However, it might be reasonable that the risk premium for this lottery should decrease as x increases. To illustrate a situation where such an attitude might be relevant, suppose x represents a specific monetary asset position of a decision maker and h is some monetary amount. It seems to be empirically true for many people that as their assets increase, they are only willing to pay a smaller risk premium for a given risk. Their reasoning is that as they become richer, they can better afford to take a specific risk, and therefore will forgo less to avoid it. The same reasoning implies that the insurance premium associated with an unfavorable lottery (i.e., one less preferable than the status quo) decreases as we get richer and increases as we get poorer.

Let us formalize this attitude, which is intuitively appealing for many decision makers.

Definition. An individual is said to be *decreasingly risk averse* if (1) he is risk averse, and (2) his risk premium $\pi(x, \tilde{x})$ for any lottery $\tilde{x}$ decreases as the reference amount x increases.

With our present tools, it would be all but impossible to determine whether a specific utility function implied such an attitude. To accomplish such a task would require an exhaustive check for all possible lotteries $\tilde{x}$. Fortunately, Pratt proves an important result that gets us out of this difficulty and makes the concept of decreasing risk aversion operationally significant.

Theorem 4.13. *The risk-aversion function r for utility function u is decreasing if and only if the risk premium $\pi(x, \tilde{x})$ is a decreasing function of x for all $\tilde{x}$.*

Proof. Theorem 4.12 states if $r_1(x) > r_2(x)$, then $\pi_1(x, \tilde{x}) > \pi_2(x, \tilde{x})$ for all $\tilde{x}$. Applying this to $u_1(x) \equiv u(x)$ and $u_2(x) \equiv u(x + k)$ for positive and negative k proves the "if" and "only if" parts of this assertion, respectively. ◀

As we will soon see, many of the "traditional" candidates for a utility function, such as the exponential and quadratic utility functions, are not appropriate for a decreasingly risk-averse decision maker. Thus the characteristic of decreasing risk aversion places strong restrictions on the shape (i.e., functional form) of one's utility function. If we know that the decision maker desires his utility function to be decreasingly risk averse, then this constraint significantly simplifies the assessment of his utility function. Some examples are appropriate.

Example 4.10.   Consider the exponential utility function $u(x) = -e^{-cx}$, $c > 0$. In Example 4.2 we illustrated and later proved that the risk premium $\pi(x, \tilde{x})$ associated with any lottery $\tilde{x}$ does not depend on x when $u(x) = -e^{-cx}$. Thus, although this utility function implies risk aversion, it clearly does not imply decreasing risk aversion, since $\pi(x, \tilde{x})$ is constant, not decreasing, for any $\tilde{x}$.   ∎

The following theorem stated without proof, expresses this attitude in a more general fashion.

Theorem 4.14.   *The risk aversion r is constant if and only if $\pi(x, \tilde{x})$ is a constant function of x for all $\tilde{x}$.*

Definition.   A decision maker is *constantly risk averse* if r is a positive constant, risk neutral if r is zero, and *constantly risk prone* if r is a negative constant.

Theorem 4.15 indicates the strong restrictions these conditions place on the shape of a utility function.

Theorem 4.15.

$$u(x) \sim -e^{-cx} \Leftrightarrow r(x) \equiv c > 0. \qquad (\textit{constant risk aversion}), \qquad (4.20)$$

$$u(x) \sim x \Leftrightarrow r(x) \equiv 0. \qquad (\textit{risk neutrality}), \qquad (4.21)$$

$$u(x) \sim e^{-cx} \Leftrightarrow r(x) \equiv c < 0. \qquad (\textit{constant risk proneness}). \qquad (4.22)$$

Proof.   If $u(x) \sim -e^{-cx}$, using definition (4.13), $r(x) = c$. Now, if $r(x) = c > 0$, from (4.14),

$$\frac{d}{dx}[\log u'(x)] = -c.$$

Integrating and exponentiating both sides gives

$$e^{-cx} = e^{\log u'(x)+d} = e^d u'(x),$$

where d is a constant of integration. Integrating again yields

$$\int e^{-cx} \, dx = -\frac{e^{-cx}}{c} = e^d u(x) + h,$$

where h is another constant of integration. From this, clearly, $u(x) \sim -e^{-cx}$. The other proofs are similar. ◀

This result says, for instance, that if the decision maker is constantly risk averse, his utility function *must* be of the form (4.20). Knowing this, we need only determine the value of parameter c in order to specify his utility function completely. This can easily be done by determining the certainty equivalent of any one lottery. However, the sophisticated analyst would employ consistency checks in his assessments, so the procedure may not be as simple as it appears. The problem of assessing utility functions is considered in Section 4.9.

Since we are still interested in finding a decreasingly risk-averse family of utility functions, let us examine the following.

Example 4.11. Consider the *quadratic utility function*

$$u(x) = a + bx - cx^2, \tag{4.23}$$

where $b > 0$, $c > 0$, and x is constrained to amounts less than $b/2c$, since the utility function is decreasing beyond this point. Taking derivatives, we find $u'(x) = b - 2cx$ and $u''(x) = -2c$, so the risk-aversion function is

$$r(x) \equiv -\frac{u''(x)}{u'(x)} = \frac{2c}{b - 2cx}. \tag{4.24}$$

Since $r > 0$ for all x, clearly u is risk averse, but r *increases* as x *increases*, so u is certainly *not* decreasingly risk averse. We see that *the quadratic utility function is not appropriate to use when decreasing risk aversion is a compelling desideratum.* ■

Aside from possessing the property of risk aversion, the quadratic utility function is often used in the literature because the expected utility of a lottery yielding uncertain consequence $\tilde{x}$ depends only on the mean $\bar{x}$ and variance σ^2 of $\tilde{x}$. That is,

$$\begin{aligned}
E[u(\tilde{x})] &= E[a + b\tilde{x} - c\tilde{x}^2] \\
&= a + b\bar{x} - c(\sigma^2 + \bar{x}^2) \\
&= u(\bar{x}) - c\sigma^2.
\end{aligned}$$

As indicated in Section 4.1, in general, we do not think it is reasonable to base decisions solely on the mean and variance of the possible consequences. This example gives us motivation for the following definition.

Definition. A decision maker is *increasingly risk averse* if (1) he is risk averse, and (2) his risk premium $\pi(x, \tilde{x})$ increases in x for any specific lottery $\tilde{x}$.

Theorem 4.16 relates such an attitude to the risk-aversion function.

Theorem 4.16. *The risk-aversion function r is increasing if and only if $\pi(x, \tilde{x})$ is increasing in x for any $\tilde{x}$.*

The proof, which is similar to preceding ones, is omitted.

Recall from (4.24) that r for the quadratic utility function is increasing in x. Since that utility function is also risk averse, it follows that it is increasingly risk averse. Since this attitude implies, for instance, that a person should be willing to pay higher insurance premiums to avoid certain unfavorable lotteries when he becomes richer, we would normally not expect many decision makers to subscribe to it. However, provided this condition held, it could, and should, be exploited to simplify the assessment of the utility function.

Finally, we arrive at a decreasingly risk-averse utility function.

Example 4.12. Consider the *logarithmic utility function* $u(x) = \log(x + b)$, discussed in Example 4.3. Taking derivatives, we find $u'(x) = 1/(x + b)$ and $u''(x) = -1/(x + b)^2$, so

$$r(x) = -\frac{u''(x)}{u'(x)} = \frac{1}{x + b}.$$

Clearly, $r(x)$ is positive and decreasing in x for all $x > -b$. Therefore, $u(x)$ is a decreasingly risk-averse utility function over this range of x.   ∎

Let us digress and see where we stand. We have looked at increasing risk aversion, constant risk aversion, and decreasing risk aversion. Intuitive arguments and experience tell us that the increasing case is of little interest, and we have essentially discussed what is important concerning the constant case. However, more must be said about the decreasing case. We would like a few simple families of utility functions with a rich variety of specific members. Then, provided an individual wished to be decreasingly risk averse, we could hypothesize a particular family of utility functions and concentrate on selecting the specific member appropriate to the situation in question. The following useful result allows us to construct such classes of utility functions.

Theorem 4.17. *A utility function, which is the weighted sum of two or more utility functions that are decreasingly or constantly risk averse on the interval $[x^\circ, x^*]$, is itself decreasingly or constantly risk averse on $[x^\circ, x^*]$*

UNIDIMENSIONAL UTILITY THEORY

and, except on subintervals where the weighted utility functions have equal and constant risk aversion, it is decreasingly risk averse.

Proof. Let $u = u_1 + ku_2$, $k > 0$. Then,

$$r = -\frac{u''}{u'} = -\frac{u_1'' + ku_2''}{u_1' + ku_2'}$$

$$= \frac{u_1'}{u_1' + ku_2'} r_1 + \frac{ku_2'}{u_1' + ku_2'} r_2,$$

which is differentiated to yield

$$r' = \frac{u_1'}{u_1' + ku_2'} r_1' + r_1 \frac{(u_1' + ku_2')u_1'' - u_1'(u_1'' + ku_2'')}{(u_1' + ku_2')^2}$$

$$+ \frac{ku_2'}{u_1' + ku_2'} r_2' + r_2 \frac{(u_1' + ku_2')ku_2'' - ku_2'(u_1'' + ku_2'')}{(u_1' + ku_2')^2}$$

$$= \frac{u_1'r_1' + ku_2'r_2'}{u_1' + ku_2'} + \frac{r_1[k(u_2'u_1'' - u_1'u_2'')] + r_2[k(u_1'u_2'' - u_2'u_1'')]}{(u_1' + ku_2')^2}$$

$$= \frac{u_1'r_1' + ku_2'r_2'}{u_1' + ku_2'} - \frac{k(r_1 - r_2)^2 u_1'u_2'}{(u_1' + ku_2')^2}.$$

Since $u_1' > 0$, $u_2' > 0$, $r_1' \leq 0$, and $r_2' \leq 0$, we see that $r' < 0$ and, therefore, the assertion is true for the case $u = u_1 + ku_2$. The general case, $u = \sum_{i=1}^{n} c_i u_i$, $c_i > 0$, follows from repeated application of the proof. ◀

Let us illustrate the applicability of this result with an example.

Example 4.13. What is the risk aversion for $u(x) = -e^{-ax} - be^{-cx}$, where a, b, and c are positive constants? If we define $u_1(x) = -e^{-ax}$ and $u_2(x) = -e^{-cx}$, then $u(x) = u_1(x) + bu_2(x)$. Also, we know that $r_1(x) = a$ and $r_2(x) = c$. Therefore, from Theorem 4.17, it follows that $u(x)$ must be constantly risk averse if $a = c$ and decreasingly risk averse if $a \neq c$. This can be validated directly. Suppose $a = c$; then $u(x) = -e^{-ax} - be^{-ax} = -(1+b)e^{-ax}$, which we know is constantly risk averse. If $a \neq c$, $u'(x) = ae^{-ax} + bce^{-cx}$ and $u''(x) = -a^2 e^{-ax} - bc^2 e^{-cx}$, so

$$r(x) = \frac{a^2 e^{-ax} + bc^2 e^{-cx}}{ae^{-ax} + bce^{-cx}}, \tag{4.25}$$

whose derivative is negative. Therefore, $u(x)$ is indeed decreasingly risk averse. ∎

The utility function of the preceding example is frequently used in actual assessment of preferences. Let us consider it in more detail to

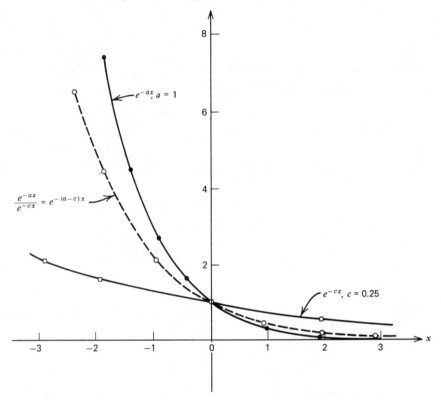

Fig. 4.12. **The behavior of the component exponentials of the utility function** $u(x) = -e^{-ax} - be^{-cx}$.

further our intuitive understanding of decreasing risk aversion. To develop a feeling for the risk aversion $r(x)$ in (4.25) as a function of x, we must first look at the behavior of e^{-ax} and e^{-cx}. Without loss of generality, let us assume $a > c$. Both e^{-ax} and e^{-cx} are graphed in Fig. 4.12 with $a = 1$ and $c = 0.25$. Both terms have large positive values for large negative amounts of x, decrease but remain positive for all x, are less than one for positive x, and asymptotically approach zero as x grows large. Their ratio, that is, $e^{-ax}/e^{-cx} = e^{-(a-c)x}$, is perhaps more revealing. It, too, is plotted in Fig. 4.12 and is clearly of the same shape as the original two functions. Thus, e^{-cx} is very small compared to e^{-ax} for large negative values of x, they are equal at $x = 0$, and e^{-ax} is small compared to e^{-cx} for large positive values of x.

With this background, let us look at the risk aversion for $u(x) = -e^{-ax} - be^{-cx}$, $a > c$ in more detail. From (4.25), $r(0) = (a^2 + bc^2)/(a + bc)$,

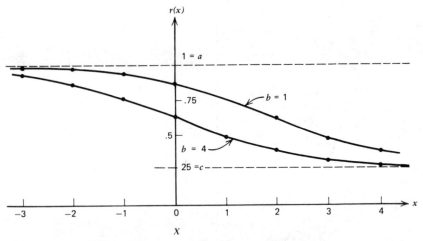

Fig. 4.13. The risk aversion $r(x)$ for the utility function $u(x) = -e^{-x} - be^{-0.25x}$.

which is less than a but greater than c. For large negative amounts of x, since e^{-cx} is small compared to e^{-ax}, we find that

$$r(x) = \frac{a^2 e^{-ax} + bc^2 e^{-cx}}{ae^{-ax} + bce^{-cx}} \approx \frac{a^2 e^{-ax}}{ae^{-ax}} = a.$$

The limit of $r(x)$ as x goes to minus infinity is a. For large positive amounts of x, we know that e^{-ax} is small compared to e^{-cx}, so

$$r(x) \approx \frac{bc^2 e^{-cx}}{bce^{-cx}} = c.$$

The limit of $r(x)$ as x approaches plus infinity is c.

A graph of $r(x)$ as a function of x for $a = 1.0$, $c = 0.25$, and two different values of b is shown in Fig. 4.13. The general shape of each curve is as we just described. The risk aversion $r(x)$ is decreasing in x and always between $r_1(x) = a$ and $r_2(x) = c$, where $u(x) = u_1(x) + bu_2(x)$. The weighting factor b determines the rate at which $r(x)$ approaches the lower asymptote c. The higher the b the quicker the curve approaches c as x increases. Notice that $r(x)$ given $b = 1$ is larger than $r(x)$ given $b = 4$ for all amounts of x. From Theorem 4.12, we know the risk premium for any lottery $\tilde{x}$ using $u(x) = -e^{-ax} - b_1 e^{-cx}$ will be larger than the risk premium for $\tilde{x}$ with $u(x) = -e^{-ax} - b_2 e^{-cx}$ if and only if $b_2 > b_1$.

Another example of a decreasingly risk-averse utility function seems appropriate.

Table 4.5
Some Common Decreasingly Risk-Averse Utility Functions

$u(x)$	Restrictions	$r(x)$	Decreasing Risk-Averse Range
$\log(x+b)$	–	$\dfrac{1}{x+b}$	$x \geq -b$
$(x+b)^c$	$0<c<1$	$-\dfrac{(c-1)}{x+b}$	$x \geq -b$
$(x+b)^{-c}$	$c>0$	$\dfrac{c+1}{x+b}$	$x \geq -b$
$x+c\log(x+b)$	$c>0$	$\dfrac{c}{(x+b)(x+c+b)}$	$x > -b$
$-e^{-ax}-be^{-cx}$	$a,\,b,\,c,>0$	$\dfrac{a^2 e^{-ax}+bc^2 e^{-cx}}{ae^{-ax}+bce^{-cx}}$	all x
$-e^{-ax}+bx$	$a,\,b>0$	$\dfrac{a^2 e^{-ax}}{ae^{-ax}+b}$	all x

Example 4.14. What is the risk aversion for $u(x) = -e^{-ax} + bx$, where a and b are positive. If we let $u_1(x) = -e^{-ax}$ and $u_2(x) = x$, then $r_1(x) = a$ and $r_2(x) = 0$ so, from Theorem 4.17, $u(x)$ must be decreasingly risk averse. To prove this directly, we have $u'(x) = ae^{-ax} + b$ and $u''(x) = -a^2 e^{-ax}$, giving

$$r(x) = \frac{a^2 e^{-ax}}{ae^{-ax} + b}.$$

Experience from the preceding example tells us $r(x)$ is approximately equal to a for large negative amounts of x, decreases to $a^2/(a+b)$ at $x = 0$, and asymptotically approaches zero as x grows larger. ∎

Because of the fundamental importance of decreasingly risk-averse utility functions in utility theory, we catalog some of the more common ones in Table 4.5. This list, of course, is not exhaustive.

4.6.1 Decreasing Risk Proneness*

It is probably evident by now that we could categorize risk-prone utility functions as decreasingly risk prone, constantly risk prone, or increasingly

---

*This section is included for completeness and for reference purposes. It can be omitted without impairing the continuity of the development.

risk prone. We have already mentioned the second of these, but let us discuss the first to make sure the concepts are clear.

Definition. An individual is *decreasingly risk prone* if (1) he is risk prone, and (2) his risk premium $\pi(x, \tilde{x})$ for any lottery $\tilde{x}$ increases as the reference amount x increases. Recall that $\pi(x, \tilde{x})$ for risk-prone utility functions is always negative.

Theorem 4.18 provides an operational method for examining decreasingly risk-prone utility functions.

Theorem 4.18. *The utility function u is decreasingly risk prone if and only if the associated risk aversion r is negative and increasing.*

The proof is omitted because of its similarity to previous ones. Let us illustrate the result with a simple example.

Example 4.15. Consider the utility function $u(x) = x^2$. Since $u'(x) = 2x$ and $u''(x) = 2$, the associated risk aversion $r(x) = -1/x$. This is clearly negative and increasing for positive x, so $u(x)$ is decreasingly risk prone for that range of x. The expected utility of $\langle 1, 3 \rangle$ is 5, from which the certainty equivalent for $\langle 1, 3 \rangle$ is found to be 2.24. The associated risk premium is -0.24. Likewise, the risk premiums for $\langle 2, 4 \rangle$ and $\langle 3, 5 \rangle$ are -0.17 and -0.12, respectively. As expected, they are increasing. ∎

4.7 PROPORTIONAL RISK AVERSION

In this section, another concept concerning risk is examined: proportional risk aversion. And as we have often done earlier, the ideas will be introduced in the context of preferences for monetary consequences. Again, however, the theory is relevant in other contexts.

Consider the situation of an investor who has an amount x_0 he can invest in any one of a set of investment plans $\{I_\alpha\}$. If he chooses investment I_α his resulting asset position (his gross payoff) will be $x_0 \tilde{z}_\alpha$ where $\tilde{z}_\alpha$ is a nonnegative random variable. Thus if the investor has utility function u, defined on assets rather than on incremental monetary values, so that 0 now refers to "ruin" rather than the status quo, then he will choose that investment I_α to maximize $E[u(x_0 \tilde{z}_\alpha)]$. Throughout this section, we assume increasing preferences for assets.

For example, consider the class of investments where the investor puts up a proportion m of his assets on a double-or-nothing bet where the probability of winning is p and of losing is $1 - p$. The outcome of his investment can then be depicted as follows:

$$(1-m)x_0 + 2mx_0 = (1+m)x_0$$

$$(p) \text{ win}$$

$$\text{lose} (1-p)$$

$$(1-m)x_0$$

Thus this investment leads to a payoff of $x_0 \tilde{z}_m$ where

$$\tilde{z}_m = \begin{cases} 1+m & \text{with probability } p \\ 1-m & \text{with probability } 1-p. \end{cases}$$

4.7.1 Investments Independent of Asset Position

We now consider four special classes of utility functions for which the optimal investment plan does *not* depend on the initial asset position x_0. These are shown to be the *only* utility functions that enjoy this property. As motivation, consider two examples.

Example 4.16. Let $u(x) \sim x$, the linear utility function. The decision maker should choose I_α to maximize his expected utility. In this case

$$\max_\alpha Eu(x_0 \tilde{z}_\alpha) = \max_\alpha E(x_0 \tilde{z}_\alpha)$$
$$= x_0 \max_\alpha E(\tilde{z}_\alpha),$$

so that the optimal investment does *not* depend on the amount x_0 to be invested. For later purposes we observe that for $u(x) \sim x$, we have

$$xr(x) \equiv -x \frac{u''(x)}{u'(x)} = 0, \qquad \text{for all } x. \qquad \blacksquare$$

Example 4.17. Suppose $u(x) = x^{1-c}$ for $0 \neq c < 1$. Then the expected utility of the optimal investment is

$$\max_\alpha Eu(x_0 \tilde{z}_\alpha) = \max_\alpha E(x_0 \tilde{z}_\alpha)^{1-c}$$

$$= x_0^{1-c} \max_\alpha E(\tilde{z}_\alpha^{1-c})$$

so that again the optimal investment does *not* depend on the amount x_0 to be invested. For this case observe that

$$xr(x) \equiv -x \frac{u''(x)}{u'(x)} = c.$$

Note that when $c < 0$, since x is nonnegative, then r is negative so u is risk prone. When $c > 0$, u is risk averse. $\blacksquare$

With this as background we shall now prove the following theorem and corollary.

Theorem 4.19. *If in any class of investments the optimal investment plan does not depend on the amount to be invested and if a risk averse u is "well behaved," then $x\,r(x)$ is constant.**

Proof. Suppose p is a fixed number where $1/2 < p < 1$. Consider the class of investments described earlier where

$$\tilde{z}_m = \begin{cases} 1+m \\ 1-m \end{cases} \text{ with probability } \begin{matrix} p \\ 1-p \end{matrix}$$

and $0 \le m \le 1$. Now

$$Eu(x_0 \tilde{z}_m) = pu[x_0(1+m)] + (1-p)u[x_0(1-m)].$$

To find the maximum m to invest (assuming it is an internal maximum) we differentiate with respect to m and set the result equal to zero, getting

$$pu'[x_0(1+m)] = (1-p)u'[x_0(1-m)], \text{ all } x_0.$$

Now by the hypothesis, the value of m that satisfies the above is constant for all x_0. Letting

$$K = \frac{1-p}{p}, \qquad x = x_0(1-m), \qquad \text{and} \qquad \lambda = \frac{1+m}{1-m},$$

we get

$$u'(\lambda x) = Ku'(x), \qquad \text{for all } x.$$

But then

$$\lambda u''(\lambda x) = Ku''(x),$$

and dividing the above two equations, we get

$$-\lambda x \frac{u''(\lambda x)}{u'(\lambda x)} = -x \frac{u''(x)}{u'(x)}$$

or

$$\lambda x r(\lambda x) = x r(x), \qquad \text{for all } x.$$

Now using the existence of $\lim x r(x)$ as $x \to 0$ we must prove $x r(x)$ is constant. Suppose, to the contrary, that

$$x_1 r(x_1) \neq x_2 r(x_2).$$

_____
* By "well behaved" we mean u is twice differentiable, and

$$\lim_{x \to 0} -x \frac{u''(x)}{u'(x)}$$

exists.

Then we have

$$\frac{x_1}{\lambda^n} r\!\left(\frac{x_1}{\lambda^n}\right) = x_1 r(x_1) \neq x_2 r(x_2) = \frac{x_2}{\lambda^n} r\!\left(\frac{x_2}{\lambda^n}\right).$$

Taking the limit as $n \to \infty$ in the above (observing that $\lambda > 1$), we contradict the existence of $\lim xr(x)$ as $x \to 0$.

If the optimal m is not an internal maximum, then the optimal $m = 0$ or 1. But both these cases can be ruled out: the case $m = 0$ by observing that u behaves like a linear function in the small and $E(\tilde{z}_m) > 1$; the case $m = 1$ by observing that since u is risk averse there is an asset amount x_0 that is preferred to a gamble giving a p chance at x_0 and a complementary chance at 0. (For this last argument think of p as a value such as .51.) This completes the proof. ◀

Corollary. The following are equivalent:

(i) $xr(x)$ is constant.
(ii) $u(x) \sim \log x$, or x^{1-c} for $0 \neq c < 1$, or $-x^{-(c-1)}$ for $c > 1$, or $u(x) \sim x$.
(iii) The optimum investment plan is independent of assets.

By Examples 4.16 and 4.17 (plus analogous examples for $u \sim \log x$ and $u \sim -x^{-(c-1)}$, $c > 1$), we see that (ii) $\to$ (iii) and (ii) $\to$ (i). The above theorem demonstrates that (iii) $\to$ (i). It remains to show that (i) $\to$ (ii).

Proof. From

$$xr(x) = -x \frac{d}{dx}[\log u'(x)] = c,$$

we have

$$\frac{d}{dx} \log u'(x) = -\frac{c}{x},$$

or

$$\log u'(x) = -c \log x + \text{constant}, \qquad \text{for } c \neq 0,$$
$$\sim \log x^{-c}, \qquad \text{for } c \neq 0.$$

It follows that

$$u'(x) \sim x^{-c}, \qquad \text{for } c \neq 0.$$

For $c = 0$, it is easy to show that $u'(x) \sim k$, where $k > 0$. Thus we have

$$u(x) \sim \begin{cases} x & \text{for } c = 0, \\ x^{1-c} & \text{for } c < 1, \quad c \neq 0, \\ \log x & \text{for } c = 1, \\ -x^{-(c-1)} & \text{for } c > 1. \end{cases} \qquad (4.26)$$

This completes the proof of the corollary. ◀

Definition. The expression

$$xr(x) \equiv -x \frac{u''(x)}{u'(x)},$$

is called the *proportional local risk aversion* at x.

To interpret this, consider the following two options:

1. *Certainty option.* Receive asset position $x(1 - \pi^*_{x,m})$ for certain.
2. *Risky option.* Receive with equal probabilities asset positions $x(1+m)$ or $x(1-m)$.

If the decision maker is indifferent between these options, the expression $\pi^*_{x,m}$ can be thought of as the *proportional risk premium*. Now using (4.18), and noting the risk premium $\pi = x\pi^*_{x,m}$ we get

$$\lim_{xm \to 0} \frac{x\pi^*_{x,m}}{x^2 m^2} = -\frac{1}{2} \frac{u''(x)}{u'(x)} = \frac{1}{2} r(x)$$

or

$$\lim_{m \to 0} \frac{\pi^*_{x,m}}{m^2} = \frac{1}{2} xr(x),$$

and thus we get the term *proportional* local risk aversion for $xr(x)$.

4.7.2   Specifying the Parameter in Utility Functions Exhibiting Constant Proportional Risk Aversion

Given that the decision maker ascertains that he wants to use a utility function with constant proportional risk aversion, how can he operationally determine the appropriate parameter c?

Let the decision maker's current endowment of the given attribute be x_0. We ask him to compare the two options:

1. The status quo, that is, x_0 for certain.
2. A 50–50 lottery that will either double his endowment to $2x_0$ or reduce it to ρx_0.

If he is indifferent between options 1 and 2 when $\rho = 1/2$, then $c = 1$ or $u(x) \sim \log x$. If we keep $\rho = 1/2$ and he prefers option 1, then $c > 1$; if he prefers option 2, then $c < 1$. Suppose the decision maker is indifferent between the two options for $\rho > 1/2$, the case where $c > 1$. Then c can be evaluated using $u(x) = -x^{-(c-1)}$ from (4.26) by solving the equation

$$-x_0^{-(c-1)} = \tfrac{1}{2}[-(\rho x_0)^{-(c-1)} - (2x_0)^{-(c-1)}]$$

or

$$2 = \rho^{-(c-1)} + 2^{-(c-1)}.$$

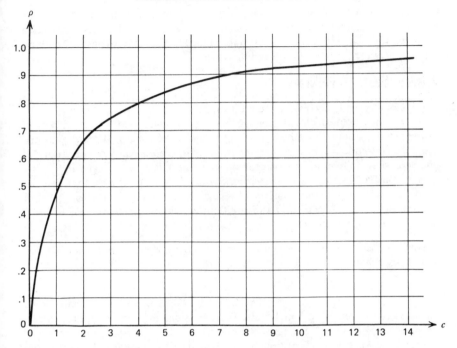

Fig. 4.14. Determining the parameter c in utility functions exhibiting constant proportional risk aversion.

For $\rho < 1/2$, the case where $c < 1$, we must solve the equation

$$x_0^{1-c} = \tfrac{1}{2}[(\rho x_0)^{1-c} + (2x_0)^{1-c}]$$

or

$$2 = \rho^{1-c} + 2^{1-c}.$$

A plot of c against ρ is illustrated in Fig. 4.14. Thus if ρ were .8 for example, c could be read as equal to 4 and then $u(x) \sim -x^{-3}$.

4.8   MONOTONICALLY DECREASING AND NONMONOTONIC UTILITY FUNCTIONS*

In this section, we extend the concepts of risk introduced in the last four sections to monotonically decreasing and nonmonotonic utility functions. The former case will be considered first, and the order of presentation will be the same as for monotonically increasing utility functions. The concepts of risk aversion and

* Once again this section is included primarily for reference purposes. It can be skipped without impairing the continuity of the development.

risk proneness are defined, a measure of risk aversion is introduced, and increasing, decreasing, and constant risk aversion are discussed. The last subsection concerns the nonmonotonic case. Proofs of results that are analogous to those presented in earlier sections are omitted here.

4.8.1 Risk Aversion

For monotonically decreasing preferences, a person is *risk averse* if he prefers the expected consequence of any nondegenerate lottery to that lottery. Then, of course, if the utility function u represents such preferences, the utility of the expected consequence must be greater than the expected utility of the lottery. If one prefers [is indifferent to] every nondegenerate lottery to its expected consequence, then he is said to be *risk prone* [*risk neutral*]. As with the increasing case, we need not try to verify the property of risk aversion by checking every possible degenerate lottery. A necessary and sufficient condition for this to hold is that it holds for all 50–50 lotteries.

Theorem 4.20.   *A decision maker is risk averse [risk prone, risk neutral] if and only if his monotonically decreasing utility function is concave [convex, linear].*

Figure 4.15 illustrates these cases.

Before proceeding further, let us suggest a couple of problems that involve monotonically decreasing preferences. First, consider the response times to calls for ambulance service. Because of the manner in which response time relates to the patient's condition, it is reasonable to assume that for any response time t, the certainty of t would be preferred to the 50–50 chance at $t-1$ or $t+1$. Hence, $u(t) > [u(t-1) + u(t+1)]/2$, from which it follows that the decision maker's utility function is concave.

A second illustration concerns response times to calls for police service. In this

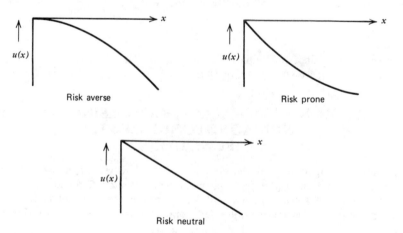

Risk averse

Risk prone

Risk neutral

Fig. 4.15. Risk properties of monotonically decreasing utility functions.

situation, the decision maker may not prefer a sure response time t to a lottery $\langle t+1, t-1 \rangle$ for any t. The reasoning might be that the probability of apprehending a criminal decreases very quickly as the response time increases. This means that $u(t) < [u(t-1) + u(t+1)]/2$, which implies u is convex and risk prone. The decision maker is willing to gamble in this situation in order to have a reasonable chance of obtaining a small response time.

So far, the definitions and results stated in this section have been identical to those given for the monotonically increasing case. Now we explain a few differences. Recall that for increasing utility functions, the certainty equivalent had to be less than the expected consequence of a lottery for a risk-averse individual. Just the opposite is true for risk-averse decreasing utility functions. Furthermore, in the context of increasing utility functions, the risk premium, defined as the expected consequence minus the certainty equivalent, represented the amount the decision maker would be willing to give up (from the expected consequence) in order to avoid the risks associated with a particular lottery. To keep this connotation for decreasing utility functions, we are forced to change the definition of the risk premium for the decreasing case. In this context, we define the *risk premium* of a lottery as the certainty equivalent minus the expected consequence of that lottery. Then, it follows that the risk premium is again the amount the decision maker is willing to give up (from the expected consequence) in order to free himself of the responsibilities of a particular lottery.

Theorem 4.21 *For decreasing utility functions, a decision maker is risk averse if and only if his risk premium is positive for all nondegenerate lotteries.*

An example may be helpful.

Example 4.18. Consider the risk-averse, decreasing utility function of the form $u(x) = -e^{.1x}$ illustrated in Fig. 4.16. Let us find the expected consequence,

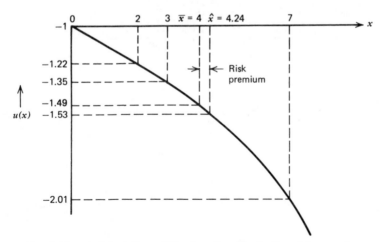

Fig. 4.16.   A decreasing utility function illustrating risk aversion.

certainty equivalent, and risk premium for a lottery yielding either $x = 2$, $x = 3$, or $x = 7$, each with a probability of 1/3. The expected consequence is

$$\bar{x} = \tfrac{1}{3}(2 + 3 + 7) = 4,$$

and the expected utility is

$$E[u(\tilde{x})] = \tfrac{1}{3}(-e^{.1(2)} - e^{.1(3)} - e^{.1(7)}) = -1.528.$$

Therefore, the certainty equivalent $\hat{x}$ is such that

$$-e^{.1\hat{x}} = -1.528.$$

Solving this, we find $\hat{x} = 4.24$. The risk premium, $\hat{x} - \bar{x}$, is then .24. ∎

Now let us consider risk proneness.

Theorem 4.22. *For decreasing utility functions, the following are equivalent:*

1. *A decision maker is risk prone.*
2. *The certainty equivalent is less than the expected consequence of any non-degenerate lottery.*
3. *The risk premium for all nondegenerate lotteries is negative.*

To help illustrate this result, consider

Example 4.19. Suppose $u(x) = e^{-.2x}$, and we are interested in the certainty equivalent and risk premium for $\langle 0, 10 \rangle$.

The expected utility of this lottery is

$$E[u(\tilde{x})] = \tfrac{1}{2}(e^{-.2(0)} + e^{-.2(10)}) = .568.$$

Calculating the certainty equivalent $\hat{x}$ from

$$e^{-.2\hat{x}} = .568,$$

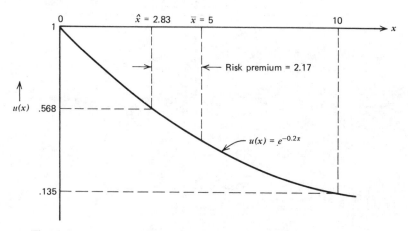

Fig. 4.17.   A decreasing utility function illustrating risk proneness.

we find $\hat{x} = 2.83$. Since the expected consequence $\bar{x} = 5$, the risk premium $\hat{x} - \bar{x}$ is -2.17 (see Fig. 4.17). ∎

4.8.2 A Measure of Risk Aversion

By a development similar to that for increasing utility functions, we can show that a relevant measure of risk aversion for decreasing utility functions is

$$q(x) \equiv \frac{u''(x)}{u'(x)} = \frac{d}{dx}[\log (u'(x))]. \qquad (4.27)$$

Notice that $q(x)$ is defined almost the same as $r(x)$ in Section 4.5; only a minus sign is different. The reason for this is, as you will see in the examples, is motivated by the following result.

Theorem 4.23. *If q is positive for all x, then u is concave and the decision maker is risk averse.*

Proof. Assume that $q(x)$ is positive. Then since $u'(x)$ is negative for decreasing utility functions, $u''(x)$ must be negative implying $u(x)$ is concave, implying that the decision maker is risk averse. ◀

The idea is then consistent with the case of increasing utility functions; positive risk aversion means the decision maker is risk averse.

Theorem 4.24. *Two utility functions are strategically equivalent if and only if they have the same risk-aversion function.*

This says the arbitrariness of a utility function as to scale and origin is eliminated by the risk-aversion function although our attitudes toward risk are retained.

The next theorem links this risk-aversion function q (which represents the decision maker's risk attitude toward small lotteries with a zero-expected consequence) to his risk attitudes toward any lottery. But first let us define $\pi_i(x, \bar{x})$ as the risk premium for lottery $x + \bar{x}$ given a utility function with risk function q_i.

Theorem 4.25. *If $q_1(x) > q_2(x)$ for all x, then $\pi_1(x, \bar{x})$ is larger than $\pi_2(x, \bar{x})$.*

Some examples seem appropriate to illustrate these results.

Example 4.20. In Example 4.4, we showed, using $u(x) = -x^2$, the certainty equivalents for $\langle 0, 10 \rangle$ and $\langle 10, 20 \rangle$ were 7.07 and 15.8, respectively. The risk premiums are then 2.07 for $\langle 0, 10 \rangle$ and .8 for $\langle 10, 20 \rangle$. Using (4.27) we find the risk-aversion function for $u(x) = -x^2$ to be $q(x) = 1/x$. This is positive for $x \geq 0$, so we expect risk premiums for lotteries with consequences in this range to be positive. Our results follow this pattern.

Notice that q is decreasing. Thus the risk aversion in the 0-10 range is greater than the risk aversion in the 10-20 range. Thus, you would expect that risk premiums for a particular lottery $\bar{x}$ in the 0-10 range would be greater than those for an equivalent lottery, $\bar{x} + 10$, in the 10–20 range. The risk premiums for $\langle 0, 10 \rangle$ and $\langle 10, 20 \rangle$ exhibit this relationship. ∎

Example 4.21. What is the risk aversion for $u(x) = -e^{.1x}$? Working directly from the definition (4.27),

$$q(x) = \frac{u''(x)}{u'(x)} = \frac{-(.1)^2 e^{.1x}}{-.1 e^{.1x}} = .1.$$

In Example 4.18, we used this utility function and found the risk premium for the lottery yielding either $x = 2$, $x = 3$, or $x = 7$ with probability 1/3 was .24. Since q is positive, we expected this risk premium to be positive. ∎

Example 4.22. Suppose that $u(x) = e^{-.2x}$, and we are interested in the risk-aversion function. From the definition

$$q(x) = \frac{u''(x)}{u'(x)} = \frac{(.2)^2 e^{-.2x}}{-.2 e^{-.2x}} = -.2.$$

Notice that this is negative. In Example 4.19, we used the same utility function and found the risk premium for $\langle 0, 10 \rangle$ to be -2.17, also negative. ∎

This example is an indication of an important result.

Theorem 4.26. *If $q(x)$ is negative for all x, then $u(x)$ is convex and the decision maker is risk prone.*

In Section 4.3, we discussed the possibility of changing attributes in such a manner that the utility function for a new attribute increased when the utility function for the present attribute decreased. Let us consider the effects of such a transformation on the risk aversion of the decision maker. Suppose Y is the attribute of concern and $u(y) = -e^{cy}$ where c is positive. Note that $u(y)$ is decreasing and risk averse with $q(y) = c$. Let us define $x = y^* - y$, for all y, where y^* is a standard amount of Y. Let $u_1(x)$ be the utility for x and define it by

$$u_1(x) \equiv u(y^* - x) = -e^{c(y^* - x)} = -(e^{cy^*}) e^{-cx}.$$

Since e^{cy^*} is just a positive constant,

$$u_1(x) \sim -e^{-cx},$$

which is increasing with risk aversion $r(x) = c$. The conclusion is that although a transformation was used to change from a decreasing to an increasing utility function, the decision maker's attitudes toward risk were not affected by this change.

Let us try to generalize this concept.

Theorem 4.27. *If a transformation of the form $x = y^* - y$ is made to change from a decreasing utility function $u(y)$ to an increasing utility function $w(x)$, the risk aversion $q(y)$ associated with $u(y)$ and the risk aversion $r(x)$ associated with $w(x)$ must be such that $r(x) = q(y^* - x)$, or equivalently, $q(y) = r(y^* - y)$.*

In other words, the risk aversion function associated with a particular consequence—either x or y—is not changed by the stated transformation.

Proof. By definition, $q(x) = u''_y(y)/u'_y(y)$ where the subscript designates differentiation with respect to y. An appropriate utility function for x is $w(x) = u(y^* - x)$. Taking derivatives of $w(x)$ with respect to x, we find

$$w'_x(x) = \frac{d}{dy}[u(y^* - x)]\frac{dy}{dx} = u'_y(y)(-1)$$

and

$$w''_x(x) = \frac{d}{dx}[w'_x(x)] = \frac{d}{dy}[-u'_y(y)]\frac{dy}{dx} = -u''_y(y)(-1).$$

Substituting these into $r(x) = -w''_x(x)/w'_x(x)$, we have

$$r(x) = -\frac{u''_y(y)}{-u'_y(y)} = \frac{u''_y(y)}{u'_y(y)} = \frac{u''_y(y^* - x)}{u'_y(y^* - x)}.$$

Thus $r(x) = q(y^* - x)$. Substituting variables, $q(y) = r(y^* - y)$. ◀

4.8.3 Increasing, Constant, and Decreasing Risk Aversion

The most important category of decreasing utility functions probably contains those that are increasingly risk averse. Let us formally define what we mean by this category, and then argue its importance. In decreasing utility functions, an individual is *increasingly risk averse* if (a) he is risk averse, and (b) his risk premium $\pi(x, \tilde{x})$ for any lottery $\tilde{x}$ increases as the reference amount x increases. Notice that the words used to define "increasingly risk averse" in this case are the same as the ones used to define this concept for monotonically increasing utility functions. However, since the risk premium is defined differently for these cases, the definitions of increasingly risk averse are different.

To be increasingly risk averse implies that the risk premium that a decision maker would be willing to pay to avoid the lottery $\langle x - h, x + h \rangle$ increases as x is increased. This might be quite reasonable if X represented costs, for example. For smaller amounts of X, the decision maker could afford to take the lottery, but as x increased, he might be forced to avoid the same lottery since the potential high cost might cause severe financial problems.

The same reasoning applies to decision problems within fire departments, where X represents the response time to a fire. A chief may prefer $\langle 1, 3 \rangle$ to a response time of 2.2 minutes, and also prefer 4.2 minutes to $\langle 3, 5 \rangle$. In other words, he would not be willing to pay a .2 minute risk premium to avoid $\langle 1, 3 \rangle$, but he would pay this premium to avoid $\langle 3, 5 \rangle$. The chief wants to behave more conservatively when dealing with larger response times, so his utility function must be increasingly risk averse.

Another consideration is as follows. Suppose the decision maker's utility function for X *is* decreasing and he is increasingly risk averse. Then, if we transform to an attribute Y, where a specific value $y = x^* - x$, the decision maker's utility function for Y will be increasing and decreasingly risk averse. That is, the increasingly risk-averse category of decreasing utility functions corresponds to the decreasingly risk-averse category of increasing utility functions.

Theorem 4.28.   *If decreasing utility function $u(x)$ is increasingly risk averse and if $y = x^* - x$, the utility function $w(y)$ is increasing and decreasingly risk averse.*

Proof. If $q(x)$ is the risk aversion for $u(x)$ and $r(y)$ is the risk aversion for $w(y)$, the result follows directly from Theorem 4.27.   ◀

Thus the intuitive reasoning given for decreasing risk aversion concerning increasing utility functions is relevant to the current case.

All of the important results of Section 4.6 have analogs for decreasing utility functions. An example is the following.

Theorem 4.29.   *The risk aversion $q(x)$ for utility function $u(x)$ is increasing [constant, decreasing] if and only if the risk premium $\pi(x, \tilde{x})$ is an increasing [constant, decreasing] function of x for all $\tilde{x}$.*

Let's try to find some simple examples of increasingly risk averse utility functions.

Example 4.23.   Suppose that $u(x) = -e^{cx}$, $c > 0$. Then clearly $u'(x) = -ce^{cx}$ and $u''(x) = -c^2 e^{cx}$, so the risk aversion is $q(x) = c$. Certainly $u(x)$ is decreasing and risk averse, but $q(x)$ is constant, not increasing.   ∎

This example motivates some definitions and a generalization of the result. A decision maker is *constantly risk averse* if $q(x)$ is a positive constant, *constantly risk neutral* if $q(x)$ is zero, and *constantly risk prone* if $q(x)$ is a negative constant. As with increasing utility functions, these conditions place strong restrictions on the shape of the utility function.

Theorem 4.30.

$$u(x) \sim -e^{cx} \Leftrightarrow q(x) = c > 0 \qquad \textit{(constant risk aversion)},$$

$$u(x) \sim -x \Leftrightarrow q(x) = 0 \qquad \textit{(risk neutrality)},$$

$$u(x) \sim e^{cx} \Leftrightarrow q(x) = c < 0 \qquad \textit{(constant risk proneness)}.$$

Provided the assumptions implying such a utility function were valid, we only have to determine the certainty equivalent of one simple lottery in order to specify the entire utility function.

Example 4.24.   Consider the quadratic utility function of the form

$$u(x) = a - bx - cx^2,$$

where $b > 0$, $c > 0$, and $c \geq -(b/2c)$. This last condition is necessary since u is only decreasing in this range. It is a simple matter to calculate

$$q(x) \equiv \frac{u''(x)}{u'(x)} = \frac{2c}{b + 2cx},$$

from which we can see that $q(x)$ is positive but decreases as x increases.   ∎

In Example 4.24, u is decreasingly risk averse. To define this idea more precisely, we say a person is *decreasingly risk averse* if (a) he is risk averse, and (b) his risk premium $\pi(x, \tilde{x})$ decreases in x for any lottery $\tilde{x}$. Such an attitude is, by definition, opposite of increasingly risk averse.

Example 4.25. Suppose that $u(x) = \log (b - x)$. Then, $u'(x) = -1/(b - x)$ and $u''(x) = -1/(b - x)^2$, so $q(x) = 1/(b - x)$. Clearly $q(x)$ is positive and increasing in x for $x < b$. This implies $u(x)$ is increasingly risk averse for $x < b$. ∎

Example 4.26. Let $u(x) = -e^{ax} - be^{cx}$, where $a > 0$, $b > 0$, and $c > 0$. If $a = c$, then $u(x) = -(1 + b)e^{cx}$, which is constantly risk averse as we have shown. If $a \neq c$, then $u'(x) = -ae^{ax} - bce^{cx}$ and $u''(x) = -a^2 e^{ax} - bc^2 e^{cx}$, so

$$q(x) = \frac{a^2 e^{ax} + bc^2 e^{cx}}{ae^{ax} + bce^{cx}}.$$

In this case, the risk aversion $q(x)$ is always positive and increasing in x. Thus $u(x)$ is increasingly risk averse if $a \neq c$. Assuming that $a < c$, which we can do without loss of generality, the risk aversion is slightly larger than a for large negative amounts of x, increases to $(a^2 + bc^2)/(a + bc)$ at $x = 0$, and approaches c as x becomes positively large. ∎

In this example, we used a general result analogous to one for increasing utility functions.

Theorem 4.31. *A utility function, which is the weighted sum of two or more utility functions that are increasingly or constantly risk averse on the interval $[x^\circ, x^*]$, is increasingly risk averse on $[x^\circ, x^*]$ except on subintervals where the weighted utility functions have equal and constant risk aversion. Then it is constantly risk averse.*

Note that in Example 4.26, if we set $u_1(x) = -e^{ax}$ and $u_2(x) = -e^{cx}$, then $u(x)$ is a weighted sum: $u(x) = u_1(x) + bu_2(x)$. Now u_1 and u_2 are each constantly risk averse. If they don't have equal risk-aversion functions, that is, if $a \neq c$, then u must be increasingly risk averse, and if they do have equal risk-aversion functions, then clearly u must be constantly risk averse.

As we did with increasing utility functions, we could categorize the monotonically decreasing utility functions that are risk prone as increasingly risk prone, constantly risk prone, or decreasingly risk prone. Also we could define and investigate proportional risk aversion in the context of monotonically decreasing utility functions. However, at this point, we feel the exercise would provide little, if any, insight, therefore it is omitted.

4.8.4 Nonmonotonic Utility Functions

Our definitions for risk averse and risk prone are the same for nonmonotonic preferences as they were for the monotonic cases. Specifically, we are risk averse if we prefer the expected consequences of any nondegenerate lottery to the lottery itself; we are risk prone if we prefer any nondegenerate lottery to its expected consequence.

Theorem 4.32. *For nonmonotonic preferences, a decision maker is risk averse [risk prone] if and only if his utility function is concave [convex].*

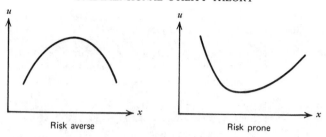

Fig. 4.18.   Risk properties of nonmonotonic utility functions.

Examples of risk averse and risk prone nonmonotonic utility functions are given in Fig. 4.18.

As illustrated earlier in Section 4.3, the certainty equivalent for nonmonotonic utility functions is not necessarily unique. Because of this, there are no alternative definitions for risk aversion and risk proneness in terms of the certainty equivalent as there were for monotonic utility functions. Also, the risk premium cannot be usefully defined for nonmonotonic utility functions. In addition, for nonmonotonic utility functions, the first derivative of $u(x)$ is zero for at least one value of x. Hence, a measure of risk aversion similar to the $r(x)$ and $q(x)$ in the monotonic cases would not be defined for all x. Perhaps an alternative definition of a local risk aversion exists for this case, but this seems to be academic. For operational problems, a reasonable approach would be to divide the range of the attribute into intervals so that preferences are monotonic in each interval and then treat each interval separately using the theory relevant to the respective cases.

4.9   A PROCEDURE FOR ASSESSING UTILITY FUNCTIONS

From the heading of Section 4.9. you might think it contains a general procedure, applicable to *anyone* at *any time*. But, in fact, it contains "a procedure for assessing utility functions" applicable to *some* of the people *some* of the time, *maybe*.

To make sure that you do not misunderstand, note that we did not state that you cannot evaluate a utility function for the decision maker in most problems. We did state, however, that the procedure that is discussed now is not necessarily appropriate in many cases. This is mainly because the assessment of utility functions is as much of an art as it is a science and, therefore, no single set of rules can be laid down that invariably result in a utility function. In fact, not only are there many different techniques* for evaluating utility functions, there are also many variants

---

*For example, see Mosteller and Nogee (1951), Davidson, Suppes, and Siegel (1957), Becker, DeGroot, and Marschak (1964), and Schlaifer (1969).

of each of these. Also, the technique that might be best in a certain situation is very hard to predict and depends on the particular decision maker and the context of the problem, plus many less obvious factors. Thus, this section does not contain a generally applicable procedure simply because it doesn't exist.

The *basic* ideas, however, that one uses in assessing a utility function remain more or less the same for all the procedures. That is, regardless of the technique being used to assess a utility function, the specific points or objectives that must be considered and accomplished by any assessment procedure are essentially the same. To help clarify this, let us divide procedures into the following five steps:

1. Preparing for assessment.
2. Identifying the relevant qualitative characteristics.
3. Specifying quantitative restrictions.
4. Choosing a utility function.
5. Checking for consistency.

The different assessment procedures result from the numerous ways of carrying out each of these five steps. Although this division allows us to emphasize exactly what goes into the assessment of a utility function, in practice the distinctions between certain steps may not be so clear.

Before beginning the main discussion, we emphasize that the detail given here is much greater than would be required for the assessment of a given decision maker's utility function. The analyst, being aware of all the small points described, will no doubt find it convenient to skip many of them in most circumstances. For example, the preliminaries to assessment may be omitted when dealing with someone familiar with decision analysis, since, the purpose of step 1 is to insure that analyst and decision maker are speaking the same language.

4.9.1   Preparing for Assessment

Recall from Chapter 1 that the paradigm of decision analysis is divided into five steps: preanalysis, structuring the problem, assessing the judgmental probability distributions, assessing preferences for consequences, and maximizing expected utility. Before assessing the preferences, we would have explained the concept of decision analysis to the decision maker and, with his help, structured the problem. Thus, we assume that the decision maker realizes the reason for assessing his preferences and is sufficiently motivated to think hard about his feelings for the various consequences. It is at this point that we begin to assess his utility function.

Before any assessments are made, it should be clear to the decision maker that we are interested in *his* preferences. It must be understood that there are no *objectively correct preferences*, the preferences of importance represent the subjective feelings of the decision maker. If, at any time, the decision maker feels uncomfortable with any of the information he has offered about his subjective feelings, it is perfectly all right—in fact, it is necessary for a correct analysis—for him to change his mind. This is one purpose of decision analysis: to require the decision maker to reflect on his preferences and hopefully straighten them out in his own mind.

Let us clarify something at this point. Experience has shown that many individuals fall into certain standard traps when they assess utility functions for the first time. They respond to certain hypothetical questions and perhaps even feel comfortable about their responses. But then they are aghast at some of the implications of their judgmental inputs. The experienced analyst may wish to point out these implications to the assessor and by various compromises help guide him over these troublesome rough spots. Now, of course, there is a danger in doing this since we are seeking the decision maker's preferences and not the analyst's, but some healthy tensions might force the decision maker to think a bit more deeply about his problem. If the intervention of the analyst is crude and overpowering, then, of course, the whole process of trying to organize the decision maker's preferences into a coherent whole is subverted.

In this chapter on *unidimensional* utility theory we deal with the case where each possible consequence of any act can be adequately described in terms of a single attribute. Let X be the evaluator function, which associates to a consequence Q the real number $x = X(Q)$. It is crucial that the decision maker understands the orientation of the scale: Are higher x numbers more or less desirable? Do preferences increase with x up to a point and then decrease?

In some contexts the attribute X may be quite natural and the x scale can be given in natural physical units like monetary assets, share of the market, lives saved, or time elapsed. In other contexts the values on the x scale may involve such subjective appraisals as an index for comfort, aesthetics, and functionality. No matter how we find the x values we ask whether we prefer a consequence x_1 to consequence x_2.

Next, we limit the region over which we must assess preferences to as small a region as reasonable. From the problem structure, the decision maker should be able to bound the possible amount that x could assume. Then we would choose x^o and x^* so that any possible x is bounded by x^o below and x^* above. These values should be chosen for convenience and meaningfulness to the decision maker. For instance, if x ranged from 0 to 8.75 in the specific units, we might define $x^o = 0$ and $x^* = 10$. A value of $x^* = 10,000$, for example, probably would have little meaning to the

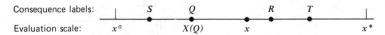

Fig. 4.19. The evaluation space for a single attribute.

decision maker. The preferences that we eventually assess must only be those for consequences x with $x^o \le x \le x^*$.

As a final check on the decision maker's understanding of how consequences are represented as real numbers, we ask whether or not he prefers consequence T to consequence S in Fig. 4.19, where the points S and T should be chosen so that it is clear to us, the analyst, that the decision maker would almost certainly prefer a particular one. If the decision maker's preference in this case agrees with the expected result, we proceed to assess the utility function. If not, we ask the decision maker to clarify his reasoning and perhaps then repeat some or all of the familiarization process.

Enough has been said about the preliminaries. The basic idea is to acquaint the decision maker with the framework that we use in assessing his utility function.

All these preliminaries are theoretically trivial, and you might feel that we are talking down to you by emphasizing the obvious. However, we have made many errors ourselves in helping others assess utility functions and very often it is these simplistic preliminaries that foul up the procedure.

4.9.2   Identifying the Relevant Qualitative Characteristics

At an early stage in the assessment process we want to determine whether or not the utility function u is monotonic. Referring to Fig. 4.19, we ask the decision maker if S or Q is preferable. Suppose Q is preferred to S. Then we might ask whether T is preferred to R; again, assume it is. More such questions may be appropriate, but finally we ask: "If x_k is greater than x_j, is x_k always preferred to x_j?" For example, from the previous responses, we would probably expect a yes answer, implying that $u(\cdot)$ is monotonically increasing in x. If this did not agree with our own understanding of the consequence, we should offer our reasoning to the decision maker and recheck his preferences. This is designed to educate the decision maker (not to bias him) and hopefully, it forces him to think hard about his preferences.

Next, we want to determine whether u is risk averse, risk neutral, or risk prone. First we ask the decision maker if he prefers $\langle x+h, x-h \rangle$ or x

for arbitrarily chosen amounts of x and h. If he prefers the lottery, we have reason to believe he might be risk prone, whereas if he prefers the expected consequence x, we believe he might be risk averse. The same question should be repeated using many different amounts for either x or h while keeping the other amount fixed. If the lotteries are chosen to cover the entire range of possible consequences and if the expected consequence is always preferred, it is reasonable to assume that the decision maker is risk averse. In similar circumstances, if the lottery is always preferred, he is risk prone. And, of course, indifference between each lottery and its expected consequence indicates risk neutrality. For a mathematically sophisticated decision maker who preferred x to the initial lottery $\langle x+h, x-h \rangle$, we simply ask: "If x and h are allowed to vary over the range of possible consequences, would you always prefer x to $\langle x+h, x-h \rangle$?" An affirmative response is a sufficient condition for risk aversion.

The less sophisticated decision maker may require a more specific version of this procedure. For example, we might divide the range of attribute X into 10 equal segments, where division points are denoted by $x_0, x_1, \ldots,$ and x_{10}, respectively. This notation is illustrated in Fig. 4.20. Now we ask the decision maker whether or not he prefers $\langle x_2, x_0 \rangle$ or x_1. For risk aversion, x_1 should be preferred. Similarly we ask for preferences between $\langle x_{i+1}, x_{i-1} \rangle$ and x_i for $i = 2, 3, \ldots, 9$. If u is risk averse, the certain consequence (which is the expected consequence) should be preferred to the lottery in all these cases. Given that the decision maker answered all the questions in this manner, we would be justified in assuming that he is risk averse. If he always preferred the lottery, we assume that he is risk prone.

It is now useful to determine if u is increasingly, decreasingly, or constantly risk averse. One method to do this involves finding the certainty equivalent $\hat{x}_1$, such that the decision maker is indifferent between $\hat{x}_1$ and $\langle x_2, x_0 \rangle$. One procedure for evaluating such a cecainty equivalent is given in the next subsection. We also want to determine the certainty equivalent $\hat{x}_i$, which is indifferent to $\langle x_{i+1}, x_{i-1} \rangle$ for $i = 2, 3, \ldots, 9$. For increasing utility functions, if the risk premium $(x_i - \hat{x}_i)$ decreases [increases, is constant] as i increases, then u is decreasingly [increasingly, constantly] risk averse. It may be difficult to determine the $\hat{x}_i$'s precisely, but the decision maker should be able to answer qualitatively whether $(x_i - \hat{x}_i)$ is increasing, decreasing, or remaining constant as i

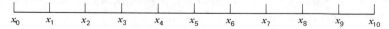

$x_0 \quad x_1 \quad x_2 \quad x_3 \quad x_4 \quad x_5 \quad x_6 \quad x_7 \quad x_8 \quad x_9 \quad x_{10}$

Fig. 4.20. The notation used in ascertaining risk properties.

increases without actually specifying the amounts of the $\hat{x}_i$'s. It is possible that $(x_i - \hat{x}_i)$ may increase in certain regions of X and decrease in other regions. This information is also valuable.

For the more sophisticated subject the analyst might ask him for his risk premium for a lottery of the form $\langle x - h,\ x + h \rangle$ for a specific x and h. Then the subject would be asked how this risk premium would behave as x is increased with h held fixed. If, as is often the case for monetary assets, this risk premium decreases as x increases, then there is a strong presumption of decreasing risk aversion. In implementing this procedure we can often ascertain that the subject is decreasingly risk averse without ever forcing him to give a specific numerical value for the risk premium of any specific lottery $\langle x - h,\ x + h \rangle$. It is encouraging to note how often subjects feel comfortable with these qualitative questions.

We have just illustrated a few ways of determining some possible qualitative characteristics of u—monotonicity, risk aversion, decreasing risk aversion, and so on. These methods have proved to be important in many decision problems. In other problems, however, a characteristic of main interest may be proportional risk aversion.

In a similar style, the analyst should be able to devise a simple technique to ascertain which proportional risk characteristics apply. Such a technique should take into consideration the problem context and the abilities of the decision maker.

After the qualitative characteristics have been identified, we need to assess quantitative utility values for a few points on X. The analyst could either then fair in a "smooth" utility function satisfying the qualitative characteristics and quantitative assessments, or perhaps assess appropriate parameter values for an appropriate family of utility functions that exhibit the qualitative specifications already elicited from the subject. Let us consider these quantitative assessments.

4.9.3   Specifying Quantitative Restrictions

Step 3 in assessing a utility function is determining some quantitative restrictions. That is, we want to fix the utilities of a few particular points on the utility function. This usually involves determining the certainty equivalents for a few 50–50 lotteries. Refer to Fig. 4.21 for the meaning of the consequences x_a, x_b, and so on, and assume we want to determine the certainty equivalent for $\langle x',\ x'' \rangle$.

Fig. 4.21.   A convergence technique for assessing a certainty equivalent.

We begin by asking the decision maker whether he prefers $\langle x', x'' \rangle$ or x_a. The consequence x_a is chosen such that a particular answer is expected. Suppose the decision maker prefers the lottery to x_a and this agrees with our expectation. Then we ask the decision maker whether he prefers $\langle x', x'' \rangle$ or x_b, where x_b is chosen so that we expect that x_b would be preferred. Assume that this is true. Next, we inquire about the preferences of $\langle x', x'' \rangle$ relative to x_c. Since x_c is "near" x_a, we expect somewhat that the lottery will be preferred to x_c, but perhaps not. We continue with this convergence procedure until a consequence $\hat{x}$ is reached so that $\langle x', x'' \rangle$ and $\hat{x}$ are equally desirable (or undesirable) to the decision maker.*

If the decision maker indicates any preferences that we do not feel represent his "true" preferences, this should be pointed out and discussed again. Provided that the assessments are correct in the sense that the decision maker really is indifferent between $\hat{x}$ and $\langle x', x'' \rangle$, then $\hat{x}$ is the certainty equivalent for that lottery. And, of course, the utility assigned to $\hat{x}$ must equal the expected utility of $\langle x', x'' \rangle$. More specifically, we set

$$u(\hat{x}) = \tfrac{1}{2}u(x') + \tfrac{1}{2}u(x'').$$

Using this procedure, we can determine the certainty equivalents for some lotteries that will help us specify the decision maker's utility function. In particular, suppose we are interested in a utility function $u(\cdot)$ for all x such that $x_0 \leq x \leq x_1$. The reason for this notational change will soon be clear.

A reasonable first step would be to assess the certainty equivalent $x_{.5}$ for the lottery $\langle x_1, x_0 \rangle$. Then, clearly

$$u(x_{.5}) = \tfrac{1}{2}u(x_1) + \tfrac{1}{2}u(x_0). \tag{4.28}$$

Next, we assess the certainty equivalents for $\langle x_1, x_{.5} \rangle$ and $\langle x_{.5}, x_0 \rangle$, which we will designate as $x_{.75}$ and $x_{.25}$, respectively. And, obviously,

$$u(x_{.75}) = \tfrac{1}{2}u(x_1) + \tfrac{1}{2}u(x_{.5}) \tag{4.29}$$

and

$$u(x_{.25}) = \tfrac{1}{2}u(x_{.5}) + \tfrac{1}{2}u(x_0). \tag{4.30}$$

Suppose the decision maker's preferences are increasing in x and that $x_1 > x_0$, then we can arbitrarily set

$$u(x_0) = 0 \tag{4.31}$$

and

$$u(x_1) = 1. \tag{4.32}$$

---

* The questions should be asked so that the decision maker understands them and finds them reasonable. For a good example of this, see the work of Grayson (1960), which is briefly discussed in Section 4.10.

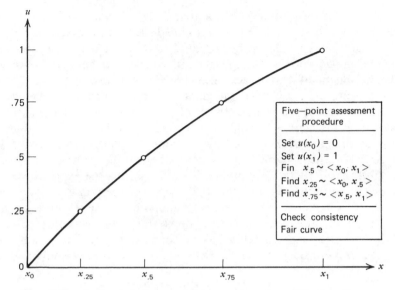

Fig. 4.22. A five-point assessment procedure for utility functions.

Substituting these into (4.28), (4.29), and (4.30), we easily obtain

$$u(x_{.5}) = .5, \tag{4.33}$$

$$u(x_{.75}) = .75, \tag{4.34}$$

and

$$u(x_{.25}) = .25. \tag{4.35}$$

Equations (4.31)–(4.35) fix five points on the utility function for X as shown in Fig. 4.22. A utility function with the previously specified qualitative characteristics can be faired through these points.

Before this is done, however, some simple consistency checks should be included in the procedure. For instance, we can assess the decision maker's certainty equivalent $\hat{x}$ for $\langle x_{.75}, x_{.25} \rangle$. For consistency, $\hat{x}$ should equal $x_{.5}$ since $u(x_{.5}) = .5$ and

$$u(\hat{x}) = \tfrac{1}{2}u(x_{.75}) + \tfrac{1}{2}u(x_{.25}) = .5.$$

Also, we now have the necessary information for a simple check on whether the utility function is risk averse or risk prone. For increasing u, recall that the certainty equivalents $x_{.25}$, $x_{.5}$, and $x_{.75}$ are less than the expected consequences of their respective lotteries if u is risk averse. These certainty equivalents must be larger than the expected consequences if u is risk prone. For monotonically decreasing utility functions, as previously discussed, the reverse is true.

When these consistency checks reveal inconsistent preferences, the discrepancies should be pointed out to the decision maker, and part of the assessment procedure must be repeated to iron out the differences and obtain consistent preferences. This iterative procedure hopefully results in a better statement of the decision maker's preferences.

Before proceeding further, the great amount of overlap between identifying the qualitative characteristics of a utility function and specifying qualitative restrictions should be explicitly mentioned. For example, suppose that in checking the risk aversion of utility function $u(\cdot)$ for $0 \le x \le 1000$, the decision maker states that 400 is the certainty equivalent for the lottery $\langle 1000, 0 \rangle$. We note this and ask, "Is the expected consequence always preferred to a lottery?" A positive response indicates that the decision maker is risk averse. Next suppose that he is constantly risk averse, so his preferences could be represented with the utility function $u(x) = -e^{-cx}$. Since this function has only one parameter c, we do not need to get any more quantitative restrictions since we already know that

$$u(400) = \tfrac{1}{2}u(1000) + \tfrac{1}{2}u(0).$$

From this we can calculate a value for c. Of course, it is often prudent to make consistency checks on this value. In Section 4.7, we indicated how the one-parameter families of constant proportional risk-averse utility functions can be assessed with the answer to one question. This also illustrates the interaction among the steps of a utility assessment—steps that we have already identified mainly for discussion purposes.

We now raise two points about assessments that are discussed by Schlaifer (1969). The consequences used to assess utility functions must be psychologically real to this decision maker. For example, if we are interested in assessing someone's utility function for monetary amounts between zero and $20,000, he should not be asked to consider consequences like $1 million. This consequence might be inconceivable to him and inconsistent assessments would likely result. For the same monetary utility function, assessing the certainty equivalent for $\langle \$0, \$10 \rangle$ would not likely provide very useful information, since any extrapolation of the result to the range of interest would have little relevance.

4.9.4 Choosing a Utility Function

After we have determined some qualitative and quantitative characteristics of the utility function, we must determine whether these assessments are consistent. That is, does a utility function exist that simultaneously satisfies all of them? If there is such a utility function, how restrictive are these assessments, and how should an appropriate utility function be determined? If there is no such utility function, how should we obtain a consistent set of assessments?

One method for answering these questions first involves finding a parametric family of utility functions that possesses the relevant characteristics (such as risk aversion) previously specified for the decision maker. Then using the quantitative assessments, that is, the certainty equivalents, we try to find a specific member of that family that is appropriate for the decision maker. The information on certainty equivalents is used to specify values for the parameters of the original family of utility functions. If we are lucky, we will find a utility function satisfying all the qualitative and quantitative assessments simultaneously. Unfortunately, no general procedure exists either for determining whether a given set of qualitative and quantitative assessments are consistent or indicating an appropriate functional form of the utility function when the assessments are consistent. To our knowledge, the most advanced work on these problems is that of Meyer and Pratt (1968), who have answered these questions for some important cases.*

The first situation concerns the case where certainty equivalents for some simple lotteries are given and regions of risk aversion and risk proneness specified. They prove that a utility exists satisfying these assessments, provided that certain linear constraints are satisfied. Finding bounds for the acceptable utility function is essentially a linear programming problem.

The second important case is when the decision maker is decreasingly risk averse and an arbitrary number of certainty equivalents is given. Meyer and Pratt develop and illustrate an algorithm that checks the consistency of these assessments and bounds the possible utility functions satisfying the constraints.

As a simple illustration of several points, suppose that the decision maker's utility function was monotonically increasing in x and decreasingly risk averse. From Section 4.6, we know a family of utility functions that satisfies these characteristics is

$$u(x) = h + k(-e^{-ax} - be^{-cx}), \qquad (4.36)$$

where a, b, c, and k are positive constants. Using (4.36) to evaluate the utilities of the consequences in (4.31)–(4.35) will give us five equations with five unknowns. Then, provided that these equations can be solved subject to the restrictions on the parameters, they will give us the specific

---

*Meyer and Pratt answer consistency questions in two situations concerning increasing utility functions. Using their methods, it would be a straightforward exercise to obtain results analogous to theirs for decreasing utility functions.

member of (4.36) that represents the decision maker's preferences.* If they have no solution the analyst is faced with implictly weighing the disadvantages of choosing an "almost appropriate" utility function against the disadvantages of further search for a "more appropriate" utility function, with a knowledge that a further search might not improve matters. Thus, in many situations, choosing a utility function subject to the given constraints is somewhat of a heuristic search process. Unfortunately, we cannot offer any clear-cut procedures for solving such a problem. However, if we have obtained a utility function that satisfies almost all of the constraints, and that is not grossly incompatible with any of the others, then because of the subjectiveness of utility assessments, it seems appropriate for the decision maker to further investigate this utility function.†

Finally, we discuss utility functions that are not monotonic. The theory for this case is not so nice but, operationally, the problem is only a little more difficult than cases where the utility function is monotonic. Suppose our preferences for X increase up to x_m and then decrease. A reasonable way to quantify these preferences is to assess one utility function $u_1(x)$ for $x \leq x_m$ and another $u_2(x)$ for $x \geq x_m$. Obviously $u_1(x)$ is monotonically increasing in x and $u_2(x)$ is monotonically decreasing, and the theory previously discussed is applicable to those cases. The only remaining problem would be to scale u_1 and u_2 correctly. First we fix one point on each utility function by setting $u_1(x_m) = u_2(x_m)$. Second, we determine $x' < x_m$ and $x'' > x_m$ so that the decision maker is indifferent between x' and x''. Then, of course, we set $u_1(x') = u_2(x'')$, which fixes a second point on each utility function. Having completed this, a utility function valid for all x is

$$u(x) = \begin{cases} u_1(x), & x \leq x_m \\ u_2(x), & x \geq x_m. \end{cases}$$

4.9.5   Checking for Consistency

There are many different consistency checks that can be used to detect errors in the decision maker's utility function. By error, we mean that the utility function that we have assessed for him does not represent his true preferences. We discuss two consistency checks in this subsection. With

---

* See Section 4.10.3 for a brief description of a computer program that addresses this problem.

† Hammond (1974) indicates that in some situations, an easy-to-use simple utility function can be substituted for a more complex utility function that is not precisely known.

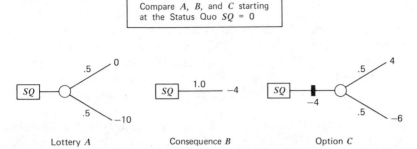

Lottery A   Consequence B   Option C

Fig. 4.23. A consistency check which generates intransitivities to promote reconsideration.

these checks (and those discussed throughout this section*) as a guide, the decision analyst should have no trouble developing other checks designed to uncover discrepancies in a utility function.

One generally useful check involves asking the decision maker his preference between any lottery and any consequence, or between two lotteries. In both cases, the expected utility of the preferred situation must be greater in order to be consistent.

A more "subtle" consistency check is illustrated by the following example. Suppose the decision maker's utility function is assessed over the attribute "incremental monetary assets," so that zero is the status quo. And let us suppose we want $u(x)$ for $-100 \leq x \leq 100$. Experience has indicated that, often in practice, the decision maker may seem to be risk averse in the entire range except for small negative amounts (e.g., for $-10 \leq x \leq 0$) where he has indicated that he would rather face the lottery $A \equiv \langle -10, 0 \rangle$ than take the sure consequence $B \equiv -4$. Note that consequence B is essentially a *payment* of 4 units. The analyst may be a bit skeptical about the appropriateness of the risk behavior and probe its implications with the decision maker. Suppose an option C—where the decision maker pays 4 units and then *immediately* faces the lottery $\langle -6, 4 \rangle$—is displayed, along with A and B. The options A, B, and C are illustrated in Fig. 4.23.

We already know that the decision maker indicated $A > B$. Then he is asked for his preference between B and C. He responds, "In both situations, I must first pay 4 units. Then with B, I am finished. However, with C, I must face the additional lottery $\langle -6, 4 \rangle$ which has a negative

---

* For instance, earlier in this section, two techniques for determining whether a person is risk averse were described: one concerned preferences between lotteries and their expected consequences and the other involved evaluating certainty equivalents of some lotteries. Either of those can be used as a consistency check of the other.

expected value of -1. My preference is clear; I prefer B." Therefore $B > C$.

But now, the analyst asks, "Compare A and C and give consideration to the total impact to yourself." Thinking out loud, the decision maker says, "Lottery A is clear, I either get -10 or 0 with a 50–50 chance. For C, I lose 4 and then either gain it right back or lose 6 more. I guess with C, I also either get -10 or 0 with a 50–50 chance, so I should be indifferent between A and C."

The result should be clear: the decision maker prefers A to B and B to C, but then C is indifferent to A. An intransitivity has been created. When this is pointed out, most subjects are a little surprised and indicate they do not want such inconsistencies in their preference structure. On reflection, subjects often will feel comfortable maintaining that $B > C$ and $C \sim A$. Thus they are forced to conclude that $B > A$. This can lead to a removal of the risk-prone segment of the utility function in the $-10 \le x \le 0$ range. The decision maker ends up better understanding his preferences and in the process, *helps himself* to "straighten out his head."

Obviously, for utility functions implying a complex preference structure, both the need and opportunity for meaningful consistency checks increase. As mentioned before, if the checks produce discrepancies with the previous preferences indicated by the decision maker, these discrepancies must be called to his attention and parts of the assessment procedure should be repeated to acquire consistent preferences. Once a utility function is obtained, which the decision maker and the analyst feel represents the true preferences of the decision maker, they can proceed with the analysis.

4.9.6 Using the Utility Function

In this subsection, we consider two practical topics that are useful in sensitivity analysis. This ties in with the consistency checks and with the entire assessment procedure since it helps indicate how precise our assessments must be.

SIMPLIFYING THE EXPECTED UTILITY CALCULATIONS. We often deal with utility functions that have exponential terms. For instance, a common example is the constantly risk-averse utility function for X of the form

$$u(x) = -e^{-cx}, \qquad (4.37)$$

where c is a positive constant. Another very important example is the decreasingly risk averse utility function

$$u(x) = -e^{-ax} - be^{-cx}, \qquad (4.38)$$

where a, b, and c are positive constants. There is a simple method to calculate expected utility when such utility functions are valid and when the possible consequences are described with a probability distribution function.

The exponential transform $T_x(s)$ for a probability distribution function $f(x)$ that is defined by

$$T_x(s) \equiv E[e^{-sx}] = \int_{-\infty}^{\infty} e^{-sx} f(x) \ dx, \tag{4.39}$$

where $\int$ indicates summation for discrete distributions, has been calculated for most common probability distribution functions. Table 4.6 gives a partial list. Given a utility function of the form (4.37) and a course of action resulting in a random outcome $\tilde{x}$ described by probability distribution f, the expected utility of this course of action can easily be calculated by observing from (4.39) that

$$E[u(\tilde{x})] = \int_{-\infty}^{\infty} u(x)f(x) \ dx$$

$$= \int_{-\infty}^{\infty} -e^{-cx} f(x) \ dx = -T_x(c). \tag{4.40}$$

If the utility function was of the form (4.38), the expected utility could be calculated from

$$E[u(\tilde{x})] = \int_{-\infty}^{\infty} (-e^{-ax} - be^{-cx})f(x) \ dx$$

$$= -T_x(a) - bT_x(c). \tag{4.41}$$

In a similar manner, the *Mellin transfrom* $M_x(s)$ for a probability distribution $f(x)$ is defined by

$$M_x(s) \equiv E[x^s] = \int_{-\infty}^{\infty} x^s f(x) \ dx. \tag{4.42}$$

This transform has also been tabulated for many common probability distributions and could be used in expected utility calculations where the utility function contains powers of x.

PARAMETRIC ANALYSES.   The sophisticated analyst usually includes a *sensitivity analysis* in his work. For decision problems, this might mean that the sensitivity of the best decision to parameters of the utility function be determined. For example, suppose from his characteristics we found that a decision maker's preferences would be quantified by the utility function

$$u(x) = 1 - e^{-cx}. \tag{4.43}$$

Table 4.6
Exponential Transforms of Some Common Probability Distributions

Probability Distribution	$f(x)$	$T_x(s) \equiv E[e^{-sx}]$
Beta	$\dfrac{\Gamma(a+b)}{\Gamma(a)\Gamma(b)} x^{a-1}(1-x)^{b-1}, \quad 0 \le x \le 1; \quad a>0, \quad b>0$	$1 \div \displaystyle\sum_{n=1}^{\infty} \dfrac{(-s)^n (a)(a+1)\cdots(a+n)}{n!(a+b)(a+b+1)\cdots(a+b+n)}$
Binomial	$\dfrac{n!}{x!(n-x)!} p^x (1-p)^{n-x}, \quad x=0,1,\ldots,n; \quad 0<p<1$	$(pe^{-s}+1-p)^n$
Cauchy	$\dfrac{1}{\pi} \dfrac{a}{a^2+(x-b)^2}, \quad -\infty < x < \infty; \quad a>0$	$e^{-bs-a|s|}$
Exponential	$\lambda e^{-\lambda x}, \quad x \ge 0; \quad \lambda>0$	$\dfrac{\lambda}{\lambda+s}$
Gamma	$\dfrac{\lambda}{\Gamma(r)} (\lambda x)^{r-1} e^{-\lambda x}, \quad x \ge 0; \quad \lambda>0, \quad r>0$	$\left(\dfrac{\lambda}{\lambda+s}\right)^r$
Geometric	$p(1-p)^{x-1}, \quad x=1,2,\ldots; \quad 0<p<1$	$\dfrac{pe^{-s}}{1-(1-p)e^{-s}}$
Normal	$\dfrac{1}{\sigma\sqrt{2\pi}} e^{-[(x-\bar{x})^2/2\sigma^2]}, \quad -\infty < x < \infty; \quad \sigma>0$	$e^{-s\bar{x}+s^2\sigma^2/2}$
Poisson	$\dfrac{\lambda^x e^{-\lambda}}{x!}, \quad x=0,1,\ldots; \quad \lambda>0$	$e^{\lambda(e^{-s}-1)}$
Uniform	$\dfrac{1}{b-a}, \quad a \le x \le b; \quad a<b$	$\dfrac{e^{-sa}-e^{-sb}}{s(b-a)}$

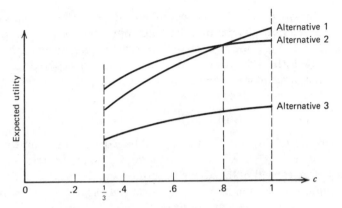

Fig. 4.24. Parametric analysis using $u(x) = -e^{-cx}$.

However, suppose he also had difficulty in specifying certainty equivalents for lotteries, and thus our confidence in the value of parameter c might not be too great. His certainty equivalents for different lotteries may have led to quite different values of c between one-third and one, for example.

In such a case, the appropriateness of a sensitivity analysis is clear. First, we would evaluate the expected utilities of each course of action as a function of parameter c. If there were three possible courses of action, a plot of this might be shown as in Fig. 4.24. With such information, alternative 3 would immediately be eliminated from further consideration since it is dominated by both alternatives 1 and 2. If $c < .8$, alternative 2 is best; otherwise alternative 1 should be chosen. Now rather than specify the exact value of c to solve the decision problem, we only need to determine whether c is larger or smaller than .8. This should be an easier assessment task than our former one.

4.10 ILLUSTRATIONS OF THE ASSESSMENT OF UNIDIMENSIONAL UTILITY FUNCTIONS

The purpose of this section is to illustrate with examples the assessment of some unidimensional utility functions. It is by no means meant to be a catalog of the work on this problem. In fact, to illustrate the state of the art, we emphasize more recent work at the expense of some earlier investigations that helped pave the way to our present status. However, we briefly mention two of these initial efforts.

One of the pioneering attempts to measure utility functions was that of Mosteller and Nogee (1951). In a laboratory setting, an individual was offered his choice between accepting a monetary lottery $\langle h, p, k \rangle$, a lottery yielding h cents with probability p or costing k cents with probability

$1 - p$. During the course of the experiment, the same lottery was offered several times. From this the proportion of times the lottery was accepted was calculated. By using this procedure and varying h while holding p and k constant, the amount of money h_0 where the acceptance proportion was one-half determined. Then zero (not accepting the lottery) was taken as the certainty equivalent for $\langle h_0, p, k \rangle$, so

$$u(0) = pu(h_0) + (1 - p)u(k) \qquad (4.44)$$

where u is the subject's utility function. The experimenters arbitrarily set $u(0) = 0$ and $u(k) = -1$ and used (4.44) to calculate the relative preference of h_0. By repeating the above procedure for seven different values of p, the utilities of seven experimental points were specified from which the subject's utility function was graphed.

Another important contribution to the measurement of utility functions was given by Davidson, Suppes, and Siegel (1957), who attempted to improve the work just described. One of their major criticisms of Mosteller and Nogee's experiment was that almost every choice offered to the subject involved choosing between accepting or rejecting a lottery. Thus, one alternative had uncertainty and participation in the experiment associated with it, while the other alternative involved no uncertainty or participation. If a subject were biased either toward or against gambling or participation, this procedure could have led to distorted results. A second criticism concerned the fact that Mosteller and Nogee used objective probabilities as if they were the subjective probabilities perceived by the subjects. To deal with these problems, Davidson, Suppes, and Siegel offered their subjects choices between lotteries, which hopefully canceled out distortion resulting from preferences for gambling and participation, and experimentally determined the subject's subjective probabilities.

The purpose of both of these experiments was to test the appropriateness of the expected utility decision model with regard to small sums of money. In both cases, their results established that utility functions could be measured in laboratory settings, at least for small sums of money. They also pointed out some of the "do's and dont's" in assessing utility functions. They did not demonstrate that meaningful utility functions could be assessed for decision makers faced with real-world decision problems.

4.10.1 Preferences of Oil Wildcatters

Grayson (1960) was one of the first to assess utility functions in an operational situation. He spent considerable time quantifying the preferences for money of a number of oil wildcatters engaged in exploratory search for gas and oil. Grayson offered a hypothetical drilling venture to a wildcatter, who was asked to accept or reject it on the basis of the investment required, potential payoff, and probability of success.

For instance, the operator was asked whether he would invest \$20,000 in a venture that had a potential gross payoff of \$100,000 if it were successful and had a .4 probability of success. If the answer was yes, the probability of success was lowered until the operator was indifferent between accepting and rejecting the venture. If the investment was originally rejected, the probability of success was raised to the indifference probability.

If this indifference probability is p, then

$$u(0) = pu(\$80,000) + (1-p)u(-\$20,000). \tag{4.45}$$

By arbitrarily setting two points on the utility function, a third point was empirically evaluated using (4.45). This procedure was repeated for a large number of ventures, thus providing many points on the wildcatter's preference curve. Finally a "best fit" curve (determined visually) was drawn through these points.

Before presenting a specific example of Grayson's work, two comments on his work are in order. First, no attempt was made to exploit the general characteristics of utility functions such as risk aversion. Of course, seminal research in this area did not appear until after Grayson's work. Second, as pointed out by Grayson, inconsistencies in an operator's preferences were not brought to his attention for possible modification except in one case. For this operator, William Beard of Beard Oil Company, these inconsistencies were reduced to a nominal level.

Mr. Beard's utility function for money on October 23, 1957 is illustrated in Fig. 4.25. The points marked by O on the figure were empirically determined by Grayson. Kaufman (1963) later found that an "astoundingly good" fit to this empirical data is the *logarithmic utility function*

$$u(x) = -263.31 + 22.093 \log(x + 150,000), \qquad x > -150,000 \tag{4.46}$$

where x represents the change in Mr. Beard's asset position in dollars.

It is evident from Fig. 4.25 that u is monotonically increasing and risk averse. Also, by calculating the risk aversion

$$r(x) = -\frac{u''(x)}{u'(x)} = \frac{1}{x + 150,000}, \tag{4.47}$$

it is clear that u is decreasingly risk averse. If it had been possible to determine beforehand that Mr. Beard subscribed to these characteristics,

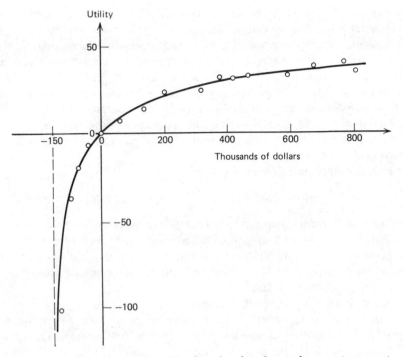

Fig. 4.25. William Beard's utility function for change in monetary assets.

the number of empirical evaluations required to accurately assess his utility function would have been considerably smaller.

4.10.2   Preferences of Business Executives

Another large effort to assess utility functions was conducted by Swalm (1966). He interviewed approximately 100 people from various corporations in an attempt to evaluate their corporate utility function for money experimentally. That is, he was interested in the utility function they used to make corporate decisions as differentiated from personal decisions. The intent of this work was to describe—not prescribe—how these people made corporate decisions.

The first step in each interview was to familarize the decision maker with the concept of utility theory. Then his "planning horizon," defined as twice the maximum amount he might recommend be spent in any one year, was determined. The utility functions were assessed for consequences up to the planning horizon, since it was felt amounts greater than this would not be meaningful fo the decision maker.

The type of questioning used to empirically evaluate points on the utility curve involved choices between simple 50–50 lotteries with two consequences and another consequence for certain. The certain consequence was then adjusted in succeeding questions until the decision maker was indifferent between it and the lottery (i.e., the certainty equivalent for the lottery was found). By arbitrarily setting the utility for the consequences of this lottery, the utility assigned to the certainty equivalent was easily found. The certainty equivalent was then used in new lotteries to fix the utilities of other consequences. A number of points on the utility function involving both gains and losses were specified in this manner. Finally a smooth curve was fitted to the data.

Throughout the questioning, the alternatives available to the decision maker were made as realistic as possible. As an example quoted from Swalm:

"Suppose your company is being sued for patent infringement. Your lawyer's best judgment is that your chances of winning the suit are 50–50; if you win, you will lose nothing, but if you lose, it will cost the company $1,000,000. Your opponent has offered to settle out of court for $200,000. Would you fight or settle?"

Two of Swalm's conclusions were particularly interesting. First, he found that businessmen did not attempt to maximize expected dollar income in situations involving risk and that cardinal utility was "at least a step in the right direction." Second, most junior executives made company decisions in a manner that put their own interests before the company's.

Spetzler (1968) quantified the preferences of a number of business executives from one company in an attempt to evaluate a corporate utility function. His objective was to develop a corporate risk policy for capital investment decisions. A major part of this work concerned assessing utility functions for 36 managers of this firm, including all the top executives. The initial interview with each individual was to acquaint him with the concept and need for quantifying his preferences and to determine which risk characteristics represented his attitude. To accomplish this, the decision makers were given an investment opportunity yielding a present value of x_s net dollars if it succeeded and x_f net dollars if it failed. The probability of success p was also given, and the decision maker chose whether to accept such an investment. The probability p was then varied to find the indifference probability p_o where the decision maker was indifferent between accepting and rejecting the project. By repeating this procedure for 20 different investment opportunities at each of two company investment levels, $3 and $50 million per investment, a number of points on a utility function were empirically determined for each decision maker.

From the questioning, Spetzler found that each of the decision makers was risk averse. He assumed that they should also be decreasingly risk averse. Then, using a least-square error approach, decreasingly risk averse utility functions of the form

$$u(x) = a + b \log (x + c), \qquad b > 0, \qquad (4.48)$$

were fitted to the empirical utility points. Using the resulting "best-fit" utility function, adjusted indifference probabilities were calculated for each investment, and these were discussed with the respective decision makers. Many of the individuals felt that these adjustments more adequately expressed their preferences than did their original responses. However, some did not, so a more flexible utility function,

$$u(x) = a + b \log (x + c - d \, |x|), \qquad b > 0, \qquad 0 \le d < 1, \quad (4.49)$$

was tried. This function still satisfied all the original risk characteristics except for a break at the origin. By repeating the procedure just described, using (4.49) to calculate adjusted indifference probabilities, Spetzler found that a few decision makers were still not satisfied. Thus, to partially smooth this break at the origin, he added another parameter while maintaining the decreasing risk aversion property. The newly revised utility function was

$$u(x) = a + b \log \{x + c - d[(x^2 + f^2)^{1/2} - f]\}, \qquad (4.50)$$

where $b > 0$, $0 \le d < 1$, $f > 0$, and $\{x + c - d[(x^2 + f^2)^{1/2} - f]\} > 0$ for all possible amounts of x. The adjusted indifference probabilities calculated using the best-fit utility function of form (4.50) were not only acceptable to each decision maker but on reflection these were, in all cases, preferred to his original assessments. For certain values of parameters c, d, and f, we can prove that u is decreasingly risk averse, but for some individuals the best-fit utility function violated this condition.

By using both qualitative risk characteristics and quantitative assessments, Spetzler developed utility functions that adequately expressed the preferences of a number of decision makers faced with real-world investments problems. The value of consistency checks, which in this case involved the repeated interviewing of the decision makers concerning the adjusted indifference probabilities, is particularly evident from this work.

4.10.3   Computer Programs to Assess Preferences for Money

Quite a different approach has been used at the *Harvard Business School* since 1966. Several computer programs (see Schlaifer (1971)) are used to assess utility functions of different forms that are consistent with various input data specifying both qualitative and quantitative characteristics of the utility function. Here, as an illustration, we briefly discuss the first program, which computes a decreasingly risk-averse utility function of the form

$$u(x) = -e^{-ax} - be^{-cx}, \qquad a > 0, \qquad bc > 0, \qquad (4.51)$$

consistent with a decision maker's certainty equivalents for three 50–50 lotteries. If no consistent function exists, this is indicated by the program. By presenting the decision maker with three 50–50 lotteries where the consequences have equal spread, it is easy to check the appropriateness of the decreasingly risk-averse assumption.

For example, suppose we are assessing a decision maker's utility function for change in monetary asset position between−$1000 and $3000. We begin by asking his certainty equivalents for lotteries ⟨$0,−$1000⟩, ⟨$1000, $0⟩, and ⟨$2500, $1500⟩. If his certainty equivalent for the second lottery is greater than $500, we know that he is risk prone for this region at least and, therefore, not decreasingly risk averse. Another decision maker faced with the same three lotteries might give his certainty equivalents as −$550, $400, and $1850, respectively. Clearly this decision maker is risk averse since his risk premiums (the expected monetary values minus the certainty equivalents) are positive. However, he is increasingly risk averse since the risk premiums increase as the potential payoffs increase. For both of these cases, a utility function of form (4.51) would not be appropriate.

Suppose a third decision maker's certainty equivalents were −$650, $400, and $1950, respectively. This decision maker is decreasingly risk averse. By using (4.51) and equating the utilities of the certainty equivalents to the expected utilities of the respective lotteries, we get three equations with three unknowns, a, b, and c. The computer solves for these unknowns and outputs the resulting utility function. Even when the three certainty equivalents are consistent with a decreasingly risk averse utility function, there may not be a utility function of form (4.51) that both fits these data and is decreasingly risk averse for all amounts of x. For instance, if both $b < 0$ and $c < 0$, the resulting utility function becomes risk prone for x greater than some amount. If the decision maker's operational range of x includes part of the risk-prone range, we must either try a different functional form for the utility function or repeat this procedure with a different set of input lotteries.*

The research program on the assessment of utilities at the Harvard Business School has the following pragmatic orientation: the researchers assume that a time–sharing, interactive computer terminal can be used during the interrogation procedure. The respondent is first asked a series of qualitative questions that establish the qualitative structure of his utility curve. Next one or two hypothetical numerical questions are posed and the respondent can give either explicit numerical values or ranges of values. At any stage in the protocol the computer program checks for internal consistency of the past responses, and for any hypothetical lottery the program is prepared to compute the possible range of certainty equivalents for that lottery that is consistent with the input data. In practice, then, we can often resolve our actual choice problem without fully defining a single utility function. With some familiarity with the programs the respondent can run his own sensitivity tests and, in so doing, build up a sense of confidence in the procedure. And in cases where the sensitivity analysis undermines our sense of security it is better that this be overt rather than covert.

4.10.4 Preferences in a Hospital Blood Bank

A final example of an empirically evaluated utility function in a context quite different from the previous examples concerns the operation of a hospital blood bank. One of the important measures of effectiveness for evaluating hospital blood bank inventory policies is blood shortage. Here, shortage is defined as blood requested by a doctor that could not be assigned from the hospital inventory. As part of a larger effort, which is discussed in detail in Section 5.10, a utility function was assessed for

---

* A great deal of empirical investigation has shown that there is a serious deficiency in the above-described assessment protocol. Subjects tend to be too risk-averse in the small and therefore when a utility function is fitted to certainty equivalents of three successive gambles like ⟨$0, -$1000⟩, ⟨$1000, $0⟩, ⟨$2500, $1500⟩, the implications are often not satisfactory in the large; that is, the fitted utility functions exhibit unacceptably large risk premiums for lotteries with a large spread. If we reverse the process and ask for certainty equivalents of lotteries with large spread, and then fit a utility function with positive, decreasing risk aversion to these answers, we often find that the computed risk premiums for gambles with small spread are smaller than the subjects think appropriate. Most of the subjects however, who think hard about these inconsistencies gradually become less risk-averse in the small. It is often the case that subjects, after working interactively at a computer console for a time, can reconcile their inconsistencies and they feel that they have taught themselves an important lesson about how they want to behave. As a consequence, some subjects cancel their automobile collision insurance and take out more term insurance on their lives.

percent of blood shortage in a year, that is, the percent of all blood requested by doctors that could not be assigned from hospital inventory at a particular hospital. In this shortage situation, a special order for the particular type of blood is placed with a central blood bank, professional donors may have to be called, an operation may be postponed, and so on, but only in extremely rare circumstances would a death result from shortage as we have defined it.

The person whose preferences were assessed was the nurse in charge of ordering blood at The Cambridge Hospital in Cambridge, Massachusetts.

First it was established that, in this hospital, shortage would never exceed 10 percent of the units demanded. The problem was then to evaluate a utility function for shortages between 0 and 10 percent.

Clearly, preferences decreased as percent shortage increased so the utility function had to be monotonically decreasing. the certainty equivalent for the 50–50 lottery $\langle 0, 10 \rangle$ yielding 0 or 10 percent shortage was found to be 6.5 percent shortage. Next, the certainty equivalents for the lotteries $\langle 0, 6.5 \rangle$ and $\langle 6.5, 10 \rangle$ were found to be 4 and 8.5, respectively. With these responses, it was reasonable to assume the decision maker was risk averse and this was confirmed with additional consistency checks.

For simplicity, a constantly risk averse utility function was fitted to the data. As can be seen from Fig. 4.26, the utility function

$$u(x) = \frac{1}{2.67} (1 - e^{.13x}) \qquad (4.52)$$

fits the empirical data quite closely.

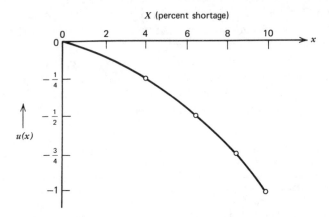

Fig. 4.26. A utility function for blood shortage.

4.10.5 Summary

The first attempts to evaluate utility functions were made in laboratory settings. These experiments indicated that preferences could be quantified and provided some experience with the assessment procedures. Building on this work, utility functions for decision makers faced with operational decisions were next determined by fitting a curve to a number of empirically evaluated utility points. Since the appearance of Pratt's paper on risk aversion in 1964, qualitative characteristics of utility functions have been exploited to complement the quantitative certainty equivalent information. This has led to both a simplification of procedures for assessing utility functions and resulted in utility functions that more accurately express the decision maker's preferences.* In Chapters 7 and 8, additional examples illustrating the assessment of unidimensional utility functions and their relevance to multiattribute problems are given.

4.11 EXPLICATING A SINGLE ATTRIBUTE BY MEANS OF MULTIPLE ATTRIBUTES

In later chapters of this book we consider ways of coping with preferences and utilities for consequences that can only be described with multiple attributes. We investigate techniques that reduce multidimensional problems down to unidimensional problems, thus enabling us to apply the techniques of this chapter. But, as we show in this section, there are examples where the reverse procedure may need to be employed. It is sometimes constructive to expand what is seemingly a unidimensional problem into a multidimensional one. Let us explain this by an example.

Norman Toy (1971), in his doctoral thesis, investigated how such individuals as ourselves or other academics should manage their retirement pension funds. Take the example of a professor whose sole source of income after retirement will come from Social Security payments and the retirement funds of his university. He typically has a range of options each year: he can choose to invest the funds set aside for his later retirement years in fixed-interest bonds (or comparatively fixed), or invest

---

* Recent work by Tversky (1975) and other experimental psychologists working in descriptive decision theory indicate that assessors inadvertently bias responses by the forms of questions they pose—for example, by asking for certainty equivalents for lotteries. These psychological insights will undoubtedly help analysts design better assessment protocols in the future. We have learned a great deal about the assessment of utilities over the past few years and we suspect that as time goes on the interrogation procedure will become less complicated and less subject to dysfunctional biases.

a portion (within bounds) of these funds in equities whose future values depend on the visissitudes of the stock market. His choice can appreciably affect his post retirement life-style. Not only does the professor have to worry about the uncertainties of the stock market but also about inflation rates, about the longevity of his spouse, and so on. A natural way to approach the problem is to assess a utility function for total wealth at retirement. Toy asked his subjects these questions: Would you rather have a total retirement fund of $150,000 for certain or a 50–50 chance at $100,000 or $250,000? This question, if taken really seriously, is terribly difficult to answer. It depends on many things: What is the inflation rate? That's not so conceptually difficult: we can normalize all amounts to today's price index. How certain can one be that a spouse will be alive to share those retirement years? This complication can be handled, as is done in Section 4.12, by assessing utility function for total wealth at retirement *conditional* on the spouse surviving and on not surviving. But still the problem is not easy to think about—even if we condition the outcome by the status of family obligations. We are forced to think hard about the implications of different monetary amounts in our post retirement standard of living. Wealth in itself can be a surrogate for consumption streams that can be purchased with that level of wealth. It is further complicated by the fact that without the availability of inflation-free annuities, we cannot be certain of which consumption stream we will enjoy (or perhaps not enjoy) starting from a given wealth position.

Toy grappled with this problem in several ways. In one informal approach he had his subjects simulate choices to be made in their post retirement years. The simulation exercise took place at a time-sharing computer terminal. Take the case of the professor who retires with a retirement fund of $150,000 when he is 67 years and his wife is 66. He must decide in year 1 (first year after retirement) how much to consume, how much to put into stocks, and how much into bonds. Toy's interactive computer model had a built-in simulator of inflation rates, the equity and bond market, and longevity rates based on actuarial tables for the male and female partners. The subject is asked to decide year by year what he wants to do (how much he wishes to consume and to invest) and then the computer obligingly handles all the accounting in the probabilistically simulated world. Sooner or later one of the partners dies and the spouse carries on. Since the environment is uncertain, it is important to experience many runs with the same initial conditions before generating an appreciation of what it means to be left with a retirement fund of $150,000. Since the year-by-year process is slow to simulate, Toy allowed his subjects to choose various strategies over time that obviated the need to make these time consuming simulated year-by-year decisions. By means of this simulated experience, Toy's subjects become better prepared to respond more responsibly to hypothetical questions about wealth at retirement.

In a more formal approach to this problem Toy investigates his subject's utility preferences over consumption streams, a process that involves multidimensional assessments, and he then deduced by this means a *derived* utility function over the *surrogate unidimensional variable*: wealth at retirement. Richard (1972) and Oksman (1974) discuss the same problem in a more systematic, rigorous, analytical fashion. Their work is based on the path-breaking results of Richard Meyer, which concern utility assessments of consumption streams over time (discussed in Chapter 9).

To summarize this discussion: in certain contexts there may be a consequence that can be described quite naturally by a unidimensional attribute, but it may not be natural to assess a utility function directly over this attribute. Instead we might have to seemingly complicate the analysis by introducing multiple attributes, over which it may be more natural to assess preferences.

4.12 CONDITIONAL UNIDIMENSIONAL UTILITY THEORY

This section illustrates directly the relevance of unidimensional utility theory to multiattribute utility problems and, as such, begins a transition to later chapters.

4.12.1 State-Dependent Preferences

As before, let us assume that the decision maker's choice of an act a determines the probability distribution of an uncertain payoff $\tilde{x}$. But now let us assume that in reacting to simple lotteries with various x payoffs the decision maker is concerned about which state of the world, $w_1, \ldots, w_j, \ldots, w_r$ will prevail. To take a simple example, if x represents the decision maker's wealth at retirement 20 years from now, his certainty equivalent for a 50–50 gamble between x_1 and x_2 might depend on the status of the health of his wife and himself. He can, of course, answer the question keeping in mind the possible states of health and their probabilities, but instead of answering the question in an *unconditional* or marginal sense, he may feel more comfortable thinking about the question *conditionally* on each state, and then combining these conditional evaluations to get an unconditional evaluation.

We simplify by assuming that the choice of act a affects the probability distribution of $\tilde{x}$ but not of $\tilde{w}$. Let

$$P(\tilde{w} = w_j) = p_j, \quad \text{for } j = 1, \ldots, r. \tag{4.53}$$

We assume, however, that the decision maker's utility function u depends on both x and w. He wishes to choose the act a to

$$\max_{a \in A} E_a u(\tilde{x}, \tilde{w}), \tag{4.54}$$

where the expectation operator E_a depends on a since the probability distribution of $\tilde{x}$ (not of $\tilde{w}$) depends on a. How can the decision maker think systematically about constructing his two-dimensional $u(\cdot, \cdot)$ function? That is the issue. We hope to demonstrate the usefulness of unidimensional utility theory to this question.

Let us examine our problem in terms of the decision tree in Fig. 4.27. At move 1, the decision maker chooses an act a from A; at move 2, Chance chooses x from a distribution that depends on a; at move 3, Chance chooses w_i with probability p_i (for $i = 1, \ldots, r$) independently of the choices at moves 1 and 2. The consequences resulting from the path (a, x, w_i) has a utility $u(x, w_i)$.

We define the *unconditional* utility of x to be

$$\bar{u}(x) = \sum_{i=1}^{r} u(x, w_i) p_i \tag{4.55}$$

and, for the purpose of making a decision at move 1, the unidimensional *unconditional* utility function $\bar{u}(\cdot)$ is all that is necessary to know. If the decision maker can directly assess $\bar{u}$, fine; but he still might prefer to find $\bar{u}$ indirectly through a set of conditional assessments.

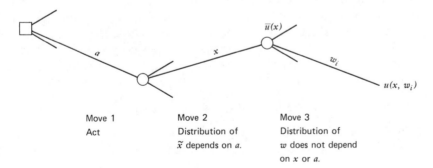

Move 1	Move 2	Move 3
Act	Distribution of $\tilde{x}$ depends on a.	Distribution of w does not depend on x or a.

Fig. 4.27.   A decision tree illustrating state-dependent preferences.

4.12.2   Conditional Assessments

Assume that we are concerned with a range of x values that fall in the interval* from x^o to x^*. If the decision maker knew that w_i were to prevail then let him be indifferent between obtaining x for certain and obtaining the lottery that yields x^* with probability $\pi_i(x)$ and x^o with probability $1 - \pi_i(x)$. Schematically,

$$x \sim \begin{array}{c} \overset{\pi_i(x)}{\diagup} x^* \\ \diagdown_{1-\pi_i(x)} x^o \end{array} \quad , \qquad given\ w_i. \qquad (4.56)$$

In other words $\pi_i(\cdot)$ is the decision maker's *conditional* utility function for x values given the state w_i, normalized by the requirements $\pi_i(x^o) = 0$ and $\pi_i(x^*) = 1$. Clearly π_i is a unidimensional utility function.

In principle, at least, we can think of the utility function in two attributes $u(\cdot, \cdot)$ and it must be such that for any i there are constants c_i and $b_i > 0$ where

$$u(x, w_i) = c_i + b_i \pi_i(x), \qquad \text{for all } x, \qquad (4.57)$$

and for $i = 1, \ldots, r$. Thus in order to assess $u(\cdot, \cdot)$ it is not enough to assess the r conditional utility functions $\pi_1(\cdot), \ldots, \pi_r(\cdot)$, we must somehow also assess the scaling constants $c_1, b_1, c_2, b_2, \ldots, c_r, b_r$. That is our next concern.

From (4.55) and (4.57) we observe that

$$\bar{u}(x) = \sum_{i=1}^{r} [c_i + b_i \pi_i(x)] p_i$$

$$= \sum_{i=1}^{r} c_i p_i + \sum_{i=1}^{r} b_i \pi_i(x) p_i. \qquad (4.58)$$

But for decision purposes we can ignore the constant term on the right-hand side of (4.58) and thus we see that we do *not* have to determine the c_i's. This is a tremendous help because otherwise we would have to ask such questions as: "If you were at position (x, w_i), how much, in terms of attribute X, would you be willing to give up in assets to modify w_i to w_j?" Fortunately we can avoid such questions.

4.12.3   Conditional Certainty Equivalents

For any act a let the resulting payoff be denoted by the uncertain quantity $\tilde{x}^{(a)}$. The conditional certainty equivalent for $\tilde{x}^{(a)}$ given w_i,

---

* This assumption can easily be relaxed but is made for convenience.

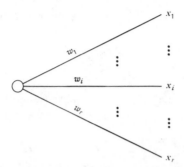

Fig. 4.28. A lottery where the consequence depends on the state w.

denoted by $\hat{x}_i^{(a)}$, satisfies the relation

$$\pi_i[\hat{x}_i^{(a)}] = E_a \pi_i[\tilde{x}^{(a)}]. \qquad (4.59)$$

Hence any act a can be evaluated by the r-tuple of conditional certainty equivalents $[\hat{x}_1^{(a)}, \ldots, \hat{x}_r^{(a)}]$. In practice if we have only a few acts to choose from we might wish to directly assess $\hat{x}_i^{(a)}$ for all i and a without formalizing the conditional utility functions π_i for $i = 1, \ldots, r$. But now the problem boils down to tradeoffs or substitution rates among the r conditional certainty-equivalent values.

Let us now consider the lottery, which will yield a certain amount x_i if w_i prevails, for $i = 1, \ldots, r$, illustrated in Fig. 4.28. Let us characterize this lottery by the symbol $\langle x_1, \ldots, x_i, \ldots, x_r \rangle$; our task is to structure the decision maker's preferences in this evaluation space. If we let

$$\langle \mathbf{x}' \rangle \equiv \langle x_1', \ldots, x_r' \rangle \qquad \text{and} \qquad \langle \mathbf{x}'' \rangle \equiv \langle x_1'', \ldots, x_r'' \rangle,$$

then by (4.58) we see that

$$\langle \mathbf{x}' \rangle \geq \langle \mathbf{x}'' \rangle \Leftrightarrow \sum_{i=1}^{r} b_i p_i \pi_i(x_i') \geq \sum_{i=1}^{r} b_i p_i \pi_i(x_i'') \qquad (4.60)$$

Recall, however, that we still have to develop a method for determining the appropriate b_i values.

Let us compare the following two lotteries.

Lottery L': the return is x^+ for each state w_1 to w_r.
Lottery L'': the return is x^+ for each state w_1 to w_r except for states w_i and w_j; the return for w_i is $x^+ + \alpha_i$, for w_j is $x' - \beta_j$.

Now suppose the decision maker adjusts α_i and β_j so that L'' is indifferent to L'. Then from (4.60) we have

$$b_i p_i \pi_i(x^+) + b_j p_j \pi_j(x^+) = b_i p_i \pi_i(x^+ + \alpha_i) + b_j p_j \pi_j(x^+ - \beta_j). \qquad (4.61)$$

Since in (4.61) the α_i and β_j values are known, it is a simple matter to solve for the ratio

$$\frac{b_i p_i}{b_j p_j}.$$

If, for example, we repeatedly use this pairwise indifference procedure by letting $i = 1$ and $j = 2, \ldots, r$ successively then we can determine the ratios

$$\frac{b_1 p_1}{b_j p_j}, \quad \text{for } j = 2, \ldots, r. \tag{4.62}$$

Now, since u in (4.57) can be arbitrarily scaled, there is no loss of generality in letting $b_1 p_1 = 1$. Using this and (4.62), we can determine the appropriate scaling constants $b_1, \ldots, b_r$. Observe also that if we wish to do so, we can always suppress the formal determination of the p_i's. But, of course, the tradeoff question between the lotteries in Fig. 4.27 does implicitly require the decision maker to weigh in his mind the chances of w_i and w_j.

There are other procedures one might use to elicit information about the b's. Indeed, in practice it would be desirable to ask probing questions from various vantage points and investigate consistency and sensitivity. Our aim here is not to examine this problem in any great detail but to give a nontrivial example where conditional unidimensional utility functions are introduced and combined.

4.13 WHERE WE STAND

Many of the important aspects of utility theory have been introduced in this chapter. The theory necessary to make the concept of utility operationally useful has been discussed in detail, methods for assessing unidimensional utility functions have been described, and examples where utility functions have been assessed in operational situations illustrated. The conditional unidimensional utility theory introduced in the proceeding sections begins to bridge the gap between unidimensional and multiattribute utility theory. Only with a firm understanding of the fundamentals in this chapter can we begin to tackle the main problem of concern in Chapters 5 and 6: the structure and assessment of multiattribute utility functions.

CHAPTER 5

Multiattribute Preferences Under Uncertainty: The Two-Attribute Case

In this and the following chapter, the ideas developed and the results presented are useful for assessing multiattribute utility functions. The main results are representation theorems that specify the functional form of the utility function when certain assumptions concerning the decision maker's preferences are appropriate. We shall develop reasonable preference assumptions, determine when such assumptions are appropriate, and assess the resulting utility functions.

Many of the concepts of importance in multiattribute utility theory can be illustrated with the two-attribute problem. Therefore, to avoid unnecessary complications and detail, we focus on this case in Chapter 5. Assessments involving three or more attributes are addressed in Chapter 6. However, the material in this first section is relevant to both situations.

5.1 APPROACHES FOR MULTIATTRIBUTE ASSESSMENT

We shall assume that an objectives hierarchy has been specified and that attributes $X_1, X_2, \ldots, X_n$ have been identified and are appropriate for the problem. If x_i designates a specific level of X_i, then our task is to assess a utility function* $u(\mathbf{x}) = u(x_1, x_2, \ldots, x_n)$ over the n attributes.

---

* To be consistent with our past use, we should refer to the utility *function* as u or $u(\cdot)$ and not $u(\mathbf{x})$ which, strictly speaking, is the value of u at $\mathbf{x}$. But we believe our occasional sloppiness in notational use will simplify the presentation a little and will not cause any real confusion—perhaps a bit of aesthetic displeasure.

The utility function u has the salient characterizing property that, given two probability distributions A and B over multiattribute consequences $\tilde{\mathbf{x}}$, *probability distribution A is at least as desirable as B if and only if*

$$E_A[u(\tilde{\mathbf{x}})] \geq E_B[u(\tilde{\mathbf{x}})], \tag{5.1}$$

where E_A and E_B are the usual expectation operators taken with respect to distribution measures A and B, respectively.* This merely asserts that expected utility is the appropriate criterion to use in choosing among alternatives.

As a special degenerate case of (5.1) we conclude that *alternative $\mathbf{x}^A$ is at least as desirable as $\mathbf{x}^B$ if and only if*

$$u(\mathbf{x}^A) \geq u(\mathbf{x}^B). \tag{5.2}$$

In our presentation, we shall differentiate between cases when a value function over the attributes has already been determined and when it has not. The value function can be exploited in determining the utility function.

5.1.1   Assessing a Utility Function Over the Attribute "Value"

Recall from Chapter 3 that a value function $v(\mathbf{x}) = v(x_1, x_2, \ldots, x_n)$ over n attributes assigns a ranking to all possible consequences. It is a function that satisfies the special case (5.2) required of a utility function. And so, by definition, a utility function is a value function, but a value function is not necessarily a utility function.†

Chapter 3 indicated several methods that might be used to acquire the value function $v(\mathbf{x})$. Because this function assigns a scalar "value" to each consequence $\mathbf{x}$, we can consider V as the scalar attribute "value" that takes on levels designated by v. Furthermore, since $v(\mathbf{x}^A) > v(\mathbf{x}^B)$ if and

---

*If probability distribution A is defined in terms of a joint probability density function $f_A(\cdot)$ in R_n, Euclidean n-space, then,

$$E_A[u(\tilde{\mathbf{x}})] \equiv \int_{R_n} u(\mathbf{x}) f_A(\mathbf{x}) \, d\mathbf{x}.$$

†Unfortunately, there is no standardized terminology for what we have chosen to call value functions and utility functions. In the literature, our value functions are sometimes referred to as worth functions, ordinal utility functions, preference functions, Marshallian utility functions, and even utility functions. Similarly, our utility functions are referred to as preference functions, cardinal utility functions, von Neumann utility functions, probabilistic utility functions, and utility functions. Although clearly we cannot be consistent with all the existing literature, we shall try to be internally consistent with our own use of value functions and utility functions as we have defined them.

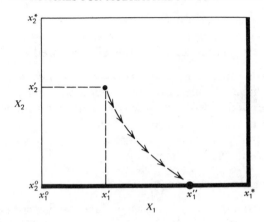

Fig. 5.1.   Assigning utility to consequences when a value function is known.

only if the decision maker finds $\mathbf{x}^A$ preferable to $\mathbf{x}^B$, the utility function over V must be monotonically increasing. Therefore, any of the ideas discussed in Chapter 4 for assessing unidimensional utility functions are appropriate for assessing $u[v(\mathbf{x})]$.

Operationally, the problem is not quite the same, however, since different levels of V per se do not have a physical interpretation to the decision maker. The techniques of Chapter 4 are useful in assessing $u[v(\mathbf{x})]$, but usually we must fall back on the interpretations of the original attributes $X_1, X_2, \ldots, X_n$ in order to implement the assignment task. This idea can probably best be illustrated with a simple example.

Example 5.1.   Consider Fig. 5.1 and suppose a value function $v(x_1, x_2)$ has been specified over the attribute space $X = X_1 \times X_2$ for $x_i^o \leq x_i \leq x_i^*$, $i = 1, 2$. For convenience assume that v is continuous and increasing in both X_1 and X_2. Also, for any consequence (x_1', x_2'), let us assume that there is a consequence of either form (x_1, x_2^o) for $x_1^o \leq x_1 \leq x_1^*$ or of the form (x_1^*, x_2) for $x_2^o \leq x_2 \leq x_2^*$ that is indifferent to (x_1', x_2'). The loci of all points of the form (x_1, x_2^o) or (x_1^*, x_2) are indicated in the figure by heavy lines. Thus, if we had a utility function u defined for all points of the form (x_1, x_2^o) or (x_1^*, x_2), it would be easy to extend u to all points (x_1, x_2) in the domain of concern. If $v(x_1', x_2')$ equals $v(x_1'', x_2^o)$, then clearly $u(x_1', x_2')$ must be assigned to equal $u(x_1'', x_2^o)$, which is already known.

The problem then boils down to the assessment of u over the heavy lines in Fig. 5.1, but this is a much easier task than assessing u over all X. Furthermore, the techniques of Chapter 4 can be directly applied to assess the two one-attribute (conditional) utility functions $u_1(x_1, x_2^o)$ as a function of x_1 and $u_2(x_1^*, x_2)$ as a function* of x_2. The only additional difficulty is that u_1 and u_2 must be consistently scaled to yield an appropriate u. Procedures for doing this are discussed in Section 5.8. ■

The generalization to more than two attributes is conceptually simple. We assess a number of one-attribute (conditional) utility functions over the X_i attributes and consistently scale these utility functions to form one utility function u over a subspace of X. Then, for each $\mathbf{x}^a$ to which u is not directly assigned, we find an $\mathbf{x}^b$ with a u assigned, such that $v(\mathbf{x}^a) = v(\mathbf{x}^b)$, and then set $u(\mathbf{x}^a) = u(\mathbf{x}^b)$.

5.1.2 Direct Assessment

Now consider the case where the value function has not been specified over X. If there are only a few possible consequences $\mathbf{x}^1, \mathbf{x}^2, \ldots, \mathbf{x}^R$, it may be reasonable to assign a utility to each of these directly. We set the utility of two of the consequences and evaluate the others in terms of the first two (or other consequences with utilities already assigned). For example, if we define $\mathbf{x}^o$ to be the least preferable of $\{\mathbf{x}^1, \mathbf{x}^2, \ldots, \mathbf{x}^R\}$ and $\mathbf{x}^*$ to be the most preferable of this set, then we can arbitrarily set

$$u(\mathbf{x}^o) = 0 \quad \text{and} \quad u(\mathbf{x}^*) = 1. \tag{5.3}$$

For each $\mathbf{x}^r$, we empirically assess a probability π_r such that $\mathbf{x}^r$ is indifferent to the lottery yielding either $\mathbf{x}^*$ with probability π_r or $\mathbf{x}^o$ with probability $(1 - \pi_r)$. By equating expected utilities, it follows that

$$u(\mathbf{x}^r) = \pi_r, \quad \text{all } r. \tag{5.4}$$

This approach is reasonable for perhaps up to 50 consequences, although with this size the procedure would be very tedious, and we would need many consistency checks to develop confidence in the assessments. Note that the basic idea is identical to that used in Chapter 4 for directly assessing utilities of consequences. The only difference is that the stimuli, the $\mathbf{x}^r$'s, are now vectors instead of scalars.

In situations where there are many possible $\mathbf{x}$ consequences contained in X, for which utilities are needed, the same approach could be used to assign utilities to a number of consequences in X. A curve-fitting procedure, interpolation, extrapolation, or the like, could then be utilized to acquire utilities for all the other consequences. Especially when X represents a continuum in multiattribute space, such a procedure has three major practical shortcomings: (1) it fails to exploit the basic preference

---

* Once again we apologize for our notational inconsistencies. We could talk about the functions $u_1(\cdot, x_2^o)$ and $u_2(x_1^*, \cdot)$ but, at times, it is more natural for us in this chapter to use the notation in the text.

structure of the decision maker, (2) the requisite information is difficult to assess and (3) the result is difficult to work with in expected utility calculations and sensitivity analysis. The ideas presented in the following section are motivated by these inadequacies.

5.1.3 Qualitative Structuring of Preferences

The basic approach utilized in this and the next chapter is (1) to postulate various sets of assumptions about the basic preference attitudes of the decision maker, and (2) to derive functional forms of the multiattribute utility function consistent with these assumptions. To use the results, we must first verify whether some of the assumptions are valid for the particular problem at hand, and then we must assess a utility function consistent with the verified assumptions. The motivation for this procedure is that it addresses the shortcomings of the more direct approach suggested in the last section. The basic preference attitudes of the decision maker are exploited in specifying a utility function, and the actual assessment is simplified. Note that this is exactly the same approach used in Chapter 3 to assess value functions and in Chapter 4 to assess unidimensional utility functions.

The assumptions investigated are felt to be operationally significant and relevant to many decision problems. Of fundamental importance in identifying simple representations of individual preferences is the verification and exploitation of certain independence properties that may exist among the decision maker's preferences for various amounts of different attributes. Ideally, we would like to obtain a representation of the utility function such that

$$u(x_1, x_2, \ldots, x_n) = f[f_1(x_1), f_2(x_2), \ldots, f_n(x_n)], \qquad (5.5)$$

where f_i is a function of attribute X_i only, for $i = 1, 2, \ldots, n$, and where f has a simple form, an additive or multiplicative form, for example. When this is possible, the assessment of u can be greatly simplified. The fruitfulness of this approach, both in theoretical terms and in applications, is illustrated in this and the remaining chapters.

5.1.4 Outline of the Chapter

Chapter 5 develops two-attribute utility functions. First, the concepts of independence and their theoretical implications are presented. Then a procedure for assessing such utility functions is suggested. Finally, the detailed assessment of a utility function in a real-world setting is presented.

For notational convenience we shall denote the generic point in two-space as (y, z) instead of the more cumbersome (x_1, x_2). The utility function $u(y, z)$, which is a two-attribute utility function when written in this form, may have more than two dimensions. For instance, if Y is a two-dimensional vector attribute and Z is a three-dimensional vector attribute, then $u(y, z)$ can be interpreted as five-dimensional utility function. All the results of this chapter are appropriate for all two-attribute utility functions, regardless of the dimensionability of each of the arguments. However, for conveneience, we often will treat Y and Z as undimensional, scalar attributes.*

5.2 UTILITY INDEPENDENCE

One of the fundamental concepts of multiattribute utility theory is that of *utility independence*. Its role in multiattribute utility theory is similar to that of probabilistic independence in multivariate probability theory. Here and in Chapter 6, much attention will be concentrated on utility independence and its implications for the following reasons.

1. Various utility independence conditions imply that the multiattribute utility function must be of a specified form. These forms include many possibilities for the final shape of the utility function, including situations involving an interaction of preference among the attributes, and yet these independence assumptions simplify greatly the assessment of the original utility function.
2. The utility independence assumptions are appropriate in many realistic problems, and they are operationally verifiable in practice.
3. Utility functions exploiting utility independence have been used in a number of important problems. Chapter 8 presents the details of one such problem concerning the development of the airport facilities of the Mexico City Metropolitan Area. Other problems in which utility independence has been used are covered in less detail in Chapters 7 and 9.
4. Utility independence might help structure a problem and thus make it easier to run sensitivity analyses.
5. The decision maker can effectively delegate different parts of his assessment problems to different groups of advisors when utility independence is ascertained.

---

* Throughout, we shall use y and z, instead of the more conventional **y** and **z** to represent what may be either scalar or vector consequences.

6. Systematic exploration of utility independence assumptions is an appropriate step in conflict analysis and resolution. In group decision problems, the decision makers might have different utility functions but they might jointly agree on the appropriateness of various utility independence assumptions. They can then better concentrate on those critical aspects of their problem where they disagree and examine various compromises. By better understanding their differences they might also be able to generate new action alternatives.

The concept of utility independence can be viewed as a specialization of the concept of preferential independence, which was exploited in Chapter 3.

5.2.1 Definition of Utility Independence

We begin with a definition of utility independence in the two-attribute case. Let the attribute space X be partitioned into Y and Z such that $X = Y \times Z$ and denote a typical point in the attribute evaluation space by (y, z). Let us assume that

$$y^o \leq y \leq y^* \qquad \text{and} \qquad z^o \leq z \leq z^*. \tag{5.6}$$

In analyzing a problem of this kind it is natural first to look at various unidimensional conditional utility functions. For example, we might investigate the conditional utility function for various y values given z^o; that is, the utility function along the heavy line in Fig. 5.2. We may then inquire whether the decision maker's utility function shifts strategically if

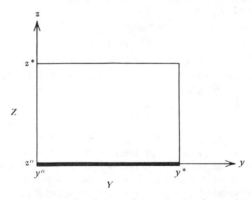

Fig. 5.2. Preferences over the heavy line may be interpreted as conditional preferences for Y levels given z^o.

the given z-level changes from z^o. We are led to such questions as, "If z is held fixed throughout at z^o, what is your certainty equivalent for a 50–50 gamble yielding values y_1 and y_2, say?" Let us suppose the answer is $\hat{y}$, so that

$$(\hat{y}, z^o) \sim \begin{array}{c} \overset{.5}{\diagup} (y_1, z^o) \\ \underset{.5}{\diagdown} (y_2, z^o) \end{array}$$

Now we ask: "If z were held fixed at some other fixed value, say z', would your certainty equivalent $\hat{y}$ shift?"

In a surprisingly large number of contexts it does not shift. The certainty equivalent $\hat{y}$ would depend solely on the y_1 and y_2 values and *not* on the fixed z value. If this condition is valid for any fixed y_1 and y_2, the conditional utility functions $u(\cdot, z^o)$ and $u(\cdot, z)$ would be strategically equivalent. Therefore, from Theorem 4.1, we know that all the conditional utility functions along horizontal cuts in Fig. 5.2 would be positive linear transformations of each other. In particular we would have

$$u(y, z) = g(z) + h(z)u(y, z') \tag{5.7}$$

for all y and z, where $g(\cdot)$ and $h(\cdot) > 0$ only depend on z and not on y. Of course, the functional form of $g(\cdot)$ and $h(\cdot)$ will depend on the particular z' chosen. Note that if (5.7) holds for one z', then it must be valid for any other level.

Definition. We shall say that Y is *utility independent* of Z when conditional preferences for lotteries on Y given z do not depend on the particular level of z.

From this definition we immediately see that Y is utility independent of Z if and only if (5.7) holds.* When Y is utility independent of Z the conditional utility function over Y given z does not *strategically* depend on z. Whenever this condition prevails, we can elliptically talk about the utility function for Y without referring to any particular z. Already we have a great deal of structure to exploit!

---

* An alternative interpretation of utility independence is as follows. Given that Y is utility independent of Z, we know all utility functions of the form $u(\cdot, z)$ are strategically equivalent. If y is scalar and if the second derivative of $u(\cdot, z)$ with respect to y is continuous, we can define a conditional local risk aversion function over Y, for each z, analogous to that in Section 4.5. When Y is utility independent of Z, the local risk-aversion function defined on Y for fixed z will not depend on z. The converse is also true. See Keeney (1973d) and Pollak (1973).

Similarly, it is natural to investigate whether Z is utility independent of Y. If we hold the Y-level fixed at y', for example, and consider preferences for lotteries over Z, do these preferences depend on y'? If not, then Z is utility independent of Y, and we can talk about the utility function for Z without worrying about a dependence on y'.

In practice it is natural to investigate at an early stage whether Y is utility independent of Z and whether Z is utility independent of Y. Notice that all cases are possible: neither holds, one holds without the other, or both hold. To show that this is mathematically possible, let us consider the following utility functions.

1. $u(y, z) = \dfrac{y^\alpha z^\beta}{y + z}$
2. $u(y, z) = g(z) + h(z)u_Y(y)$
3. $u(y, z) = k(y) + m(y)u_Z(z)$
4. $u(y, z) = k_1 u_Y(y) + k_2 u_Z(z) + k_3 u_Y(y)u_Z(z)$
5. $u(y, z) = [\alpha + \beta u_Y(y)][\gamma + \delta u_Z(z)]$
6. $u(y, z) = k_Y u_Y(y) + k_Z u_Z(z)$

In case 1, neither attribute is utility independent of the other. In case 2, Y is utility independent of Z, but not vice versa. In case 3, Z is utility independent of Y, but not vice versa, and in cases 4, 5, and 6, each is utility independent of the other. We shall investigate representation theorems in what follows so that we shall be able to recognize from purely qualitative considerations whether a particular form is appropriate. Naturally, these representation results will materially affect the assessment protocol.

Utility independence is important because it is a necessary and sufficient condition for us to speak about a single utility function over one of the attributes. When Y is utility independent of Z, there is a single utility function over Y. In this case, preferences for varying amounts of Y can be assessed after fixing Z at any convenient level. When Y is not utility independent of Z, then it is not meaningful to speak of a utility function over Y, and assessment of $u(\cdot, \cdot)$ becomes much more difficult. In this case, the *conditional utility function* for Y given $z = z'$ and the conditional utility function for Y given $z = z''$, that is, $u(\cdot, z')$ and $u(\cdot, z'')$, respectively, are not strategically equivalent. Each must be assessed separately and completely, since knowing one may imply little about the other.

5.2.2 Getting a Feeling for Utility Independence

Before proceeding, let us try to understand how utility independence helps us out considerably in the assessment of utility functions. If we are

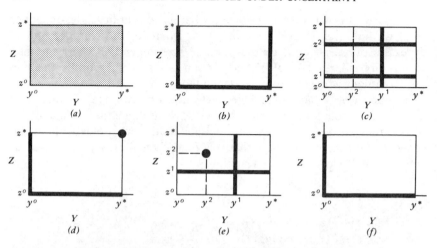

Fig. 5.3. Exploiting utility independence to simplify the assessment of the utility function.

interested in preferences over (y, z) such that $y^o \le y \le y^*$ and $z^o \le z \le z^*$ then, in the absence of any simplifying assumptions, we must directly assess the utility function u over the entire shaded region of Fig. 5.3a.

However, suppose that Y is utility independent of Z. Then the general shape of the conditional utility functions $u(\cdot, z)$ cutting across Y for various levels of z must be positive linear transformations of each other. Therefore, as we shall see later, we can get enough information to completely specify u by knowing the utilities of the darkened consequences in Fig. 5.3b. This means we would have to assess and consistently scale three one-attribute conditional utility functions.

To take another case, if Z is utility independent of Y, and Y is not utility independent of Z, we can, for example, completely specify u by consistent assessment of the three one-attribute conditional utility functions in Fig. 5.3c. In this case, the conditional utility functions $u(y, \cdot)$ cutting across Z for various levels of y are all positive linear transformations of each other. To illustrate this using the notation of the figure, we know that

$$u(y^2, z) = k_1 + k_2 u(y^1, z), \qquad \text{all } z. \qquad (5.8)$$

The conditional utility function $u(y^1, \cdot)$ is known because it is assessed, and the k_1 and k_2 are found by evaluating (5.8) at (y^2, z^1) and (y^2, z^2), two consequences whose utilities are known. The resulting simple equations are then easily solved. More about this later.

Now suppose that Y and Z are utility independent of each other, a condition that we will define as *mutual utility independence*. Then, taking Fig. 5.3b as a starting point, we can see that the two conditional utility functions $u(y°, \cdot)$ and $u(y^*, \cdot)$, as functions of z, must be positive linear transformations of each other. Therefore, instead of assessing $u(y^*, \cdot)$ for all z, we just need, for instance, the utilities of two points on the curve to fix the correct transformation. The implication is that, if Y and Z are mutually utility independent, we need only consistently assess two conditional utility functions and the utility of (y^*, z^*) to specify u completely. The consequences whose utilities are needed are blackened in Fig. 5.3d.

Actually, when mutual utility independence holds, we have the freedom to choose any arbitrary conditional utility functions $u(\cdot, z^1)$ and $u(y^1, \cdot)$ and the utility of any arbitrary consequences (y^2, z^2) to specify $u(y, z)$ for all y, z. This freedom can be used to select y^1, z^1, y^2, and z^2 to simplify the decision maker's assessment problem. That is, he may feel more comfortable assessing $u(\cdot, z^1)$ than $u(\cdot, z°)$, because his accumulated experience with consequences of the form (y, z^1) may be considerably greater. Figure 5.3e indicates what needs to be assessed in this case.

If mutual utility independence holds, and if an additivity assumption also holds, which we will describe later, we can completely assess $u(y, z)$ for all (y, z) using only the two conditional utility functions darkened in Fig. 5.3f. This is the simplest two-attribute utility function that we can have without simplifying the form of the one-attribute conditional utility functions or without making various tradeoff assumptions, such as a constant rate of substitution, discussed in Chapter 3. Thus, in some sense, the darkened information in Fig. 5.3f represents the minimum actual information that needs to be assessed to specify $u(y, z)$ for all (y, z).

In the following sections, we begin discussing different forms of the utility function implied by the various sets of assumptions beginning with the simplest case (Fig. 5.3f). After presenting the results, we suggest procedures for verifying the requisite assumptions and assessing such utility functions; lastly we illustrate the techniques with a real-world example.

5.3   ADDITIVE INDEPENDENCE AND THE ADDITIVE UTILITY FUNCTION

The additive utility function that has the form

$$u(y, z) = k_Y u_Y(y) + k_Z u_Z(z),$$

where k_Y and k_Z are positive scaling constants, allows us to add the separate contributions of the two attributes to obtain the total utility. It is the best known of the multiattribute utility functions and important both because of its relevance to some real problems and its relative simplicity.

As we can easily verify, and as indicated in the previous section, the additive utility function implies that Y and Z are mutually utility independent. However, the converse is *not* true. Mutual utility independence does *not* imply that the utility function is additive.* The assumptions, in addition to mutual utility independence, which imply that the two-attribute utility function is additive, are presented in Section 5.4. Here, an alternative set of assumptions about the decision maker's preferences that allow us to use the additive utility function is discussed.

Necessary and sufficient conditions for the existence of an additive utility function can be stated using the concept of additive independence. Unfortunately, this terminology is not universal, and what we refer to as the "additive independence" condition has been referred to elsewhere as "independence." However, the adjective "additive" is needed to differentiate it from other independence conditions that we have introduced.

Definition. Attributes Y and Z are *additive independent* if the paired preference comparison of any two lotteries, defined by two joint probability distributions on $Y \times Z$, depends only on their marginal probability distributions.

The above condition is written in the form stated because it is easy to generalize. In two dimensions, as we shall soon verify, an equivalent condition for Y and Z to be additive independent is that the lotteries

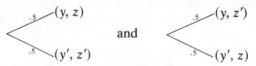

must be equally preferable (i.e., indifferent) for all (y, z) given an arbitrarily chosen y' and z'. Note that in each of these two lotteries, there is a one-half probability of getting either y or y' and a one-half probability of getting either z or z'. The only difference is how the levels of Y and Z are combined. From this is should be clear that it is not meaningful to have Y additive independent of Z, but Z not additive independent of Y. The property is reflexive, which is not the case with the other independence conditions we shall discuss.

---

* For example, if $u(y, z) = y^\alpha z^\beta$, $1 \le y \le 10$, $1 \le z \le 10$, then Y and Z are mutually utility independent, but u is not additive. Taking logarithms, we get $\log u(y, z) = \alpha \log y + \beta \log z$, which is clearly additive. However, this $\log u$ is not a utility function, since it is not a positive linear transformation of u. On the other hand, $\log u$ is an appropriate value function, since it preserves the ordering of the consequences (y, z).

5.3.1   A Fundamental Result of Additive Utility Theory

The following result is due to Fishburn (1965a), but presented slightly differently here.

Theorem 5.1.   *Attributes Y and Z are additive independent if and only if the two-attribute utility function is additive. The additive form may be written either as*

$$u(y, z) = u(y, z^o) + u(y^o, z), \qquad (5.9)$$

or as

$$u(y, z) = k_Y u_Y(y) + k_Z u_Z(z) \qquad (5.10)$$

where

1. $u(y, z)$ *is normalized by* $u(y^o, z^o) = 0$ *and* $u(y^1, z^1) = 1$ *for arbitrary* y^1 *and* z^1 *such that* $(y^1, z^o) > (y^o, z^o)$ *and* $(y^o, z^1) > (y^o, z^o)$.
2. $u_Y(y)$ *is a conditional utility function on Y normalized by* $u_Y(y^o) = 0$ *and* $u_Y(y^1) = 1$.
3. $u_Z(z)$ *is a conditional utility function on Z normalized by* $u_Z(z^o) = 0$ *and* $u_Z(z^1) = 1$.
4. $k_Y = u(y^1, z^o)$.
5. $k_Z = u(y^o, z^1)$.

Proof.   Clearly, additive independence implies indifference between the two lotteries* $\langle (y, z), (y^o, z^o) \rangle$ and $\langle (y, z^o), (y^o, z) \rangle$, since they have the same marginal probability distribution on the attributes. Equating the expected utilities of these two lotteries gives us

$$\tfrac{1}{2}u(y, z) + \tfrac{1}{2}u(y^o, z^o) = \tfrac{1}{2}u(y, z^o) + \tfrac{1}{2}u(y^o, z). \qquad (5.11)$$

If we arbitrarily set $u(y^o, z^o) = 0$, (5.9) follows directly from (5.11). Defining

$$u(y, z^o) = k_Y u_Y(y) \qquad (5.12)$$

and

$$u(y^o, z) = k_Z u_Z(z), \qquad (5.13)$$

to allow for free scaling of the one-attribute utility functions, and substituting these into (5.11) yields the result (5.10).

To prove the other half of the theorem, that an additive utility function implies additive independence, note that the expected utility of any lottery using (5.9) or (5.10) depends only on the marginal probability distributions for Y and Z. Therefore, preferences among such lotteries

---

* We remind the reader that the lottery denoted by $\langle A, B \rangle$ has consequences A and B each with probability one half.

cannot depend on the joint probability distribution of Y and Z, so the two attributes are additive independent.   ◀

The assumptions required for the justification of an additive utility function are rather restrictive. They allow for no interaction of the decision maker's preferences for various amounts of the two attributes. Often, we might expect the desirability of various amounts of one attribute to depend on the specified level of the other attribute. For instance, consider a farmer with preferences for various amounts of sunshine and rain because of the impact this will have on the season's crops. Here, we might expect that the farmer's preferences for various amounts of sunshine to be different depending on whether there had been only a little rain or much rain. Such an interaction of preferences cannot be expressed with the additive utility function. In the subsequent sections, we will present some more general two-attribute utility functions that do allow for certain types of interaction.

In Section 5.8 we discuss procedures and techniques that can be employed to (1) verify additive independence and (2) assess the appropriate unidimensional utility functions and scaling constants.

5.4 THE IMPLICATIONS OF MUTUAL UTILITY INDEPENDENCE

In this section we derive functional forms for evaluating the utility function $u(y, z)$ when attributes Y and Z are mutually utility independent. First, it is illustrated how this assumption restricts the form of $u(y, z)$. Then the manner in which the resulting utility function accounts for possible interactions in the decision maker's preferences for the two attributes is discussed.

The theorems and proofs in this and the following sections are presented in terms that indicate exactly what must be empirically assessed to specify the utility function. The results stated are consequently a bit more "bulky" than would be the case if we just wanted to prove the mathematical result and to ignore the assessment aspect.

Throughout Chapters 5 and 6, algebraic proofs will be given for the theorems. While this demonstrates the result for the general case we had in mind, it does not communicate as much of an intuitive feeling for the result as is possible with alternative less formal proofs. With a loss of some generality, more natural proofs can be given for the results. So, in some cases, especially here where we begin to discuss utility independence, we will offer a more intuitive, less formal proof in addition to the main algebraic one.

From (5.7), we see that the assumption of mutual utility independence can be mathematically represented by

$$u(y, z) = c_1(z) + c_2(z)u(y, z_0), \qquad \text{for all } y, z, \qquad (5.14)$$

for an arbitrarily chosen z_0, and

$$u(y, z) = d_1(y) + d_2(y)u(y_0, z), \qquad \text{for all } y, z, \qquad (5.15)$$

for an arbitrarily chosen y_0. Equation (5.14) says that Y is utility independent of Z and (5.15) says that Z is utility independent of Y.

5.4.1   The Multilinear Utility Function

When Y and Z are mutually utility independent, then $u(y, z)$ can be expressed by the multilinear representation[*]

$$u(y, z) = k_Y u_Y(y) + k_Z u_Z(z) + k_{YZ} u_Y(y) u_Z(z),$$

where u, u_Y, and u_Z have a common origin and are consistently scaled by the scaling constants $k_Y > 0$, $k_Z > 0$, and k_{YZ}. Since the dimensionality of the utility functions u_Y and u_Z is less than the dimensionality of the original utility function u, its assessment is simplified when the stated assumptions hold.

A geometrical interpretation of the result for the case where Y and Z are scalar attributes is shown in Fig. 5.4. Our result says that subject to

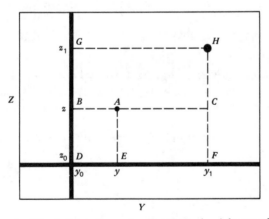

Fig. 5.4. Mutual utility independence implies that $u(y, z)$ is completely specified from the utilities of the heavy shaded consequences.

[*] Because there are just two attributes, we could have referred to this utility function as the bilinear utility function. Since the representation is generalized to n attributes in Chapter 6, we have chosen to use the general term "multilinear" in this chapter, also.

the requisite assumptions, the utility of any consequence in the specified consequence space is uniquely determined by the relative utilities of the consequences along the heavy lines and at the heavy point in the figure.

To see why this is true, refer to Fig. 5.4 and follow these steps:

1. Consistently assess $u(\cdot, z_0)$, $u(y_0, \cdot)$, and $u(y_1, z_1)$.
2. For any point Q (where Q can assume values $A, B, \ldots, H$) denote the value of u at Q by u_Q. Let A represent the generic point (y, z) and denote $u(y, z)$ as u_A.
3. Express u_A in terms of u_B and u_C. This follows from the relationship of u_D, u_E, and u_F, since Y is utility independent of Z.
4. We know u_B but not u_C. Therefore, express u_C in terms of u_F and u_H, using the fact that Z is utility independent of Y and using the utilities u_D, u_B, and u_G.
5. The utility u_A is now expressed in terms of the known utilities u_B, u_F, and u_H.

If A were not originally chosen to fall within the region "cornered" by D, F, G, and H, slightly different steps—using identical reasoning—would be required. With this motivation, we prove the following.

Theorem 5.2. *If Y and Z are mutually utility independent, then the two-attribute utility function is multilinear. In particular, u can be written in the form*

$$u(y, z) = u(y, z_0) + u(y_0, z) + ku(y, z_0)u(y_0, z), \qquad (5.16)$$

or

$$u(y, z) = k_Y u_Y(y) + k_Z u_Z(z) + k_{YZ} u_Y(y)u_Z(z), \qquad (5.17)$$

where

1. *$u(y, z)$ is normalized by $u(y_0, z_0) = 0$ and $u(y_1, z_1) = 1$ for arbitrary y_1 and z_1 such that $(y_1, z_0) > (y_0, z_0)$ and $(y_0, z_1) > (y_0, z_0)$.*
2. *$u_Y(y)$ is a conditional utility function on Y normalized by $u_Y(y_0) = 0$ and $u_Y(y_1) = 1$.*
3. *$u_Z(z)$ is a conditional utility function on Z normalized by $u_Z(z_0) = 0$ and $u_Z(z_1) = 1$.*
4. *$k_Y = u(y_1, z_0)$.*
5. *$k_Z = u(y_0, z_1)$.*
6. *$k_{YZ} = 1 - k_Y - k_Z$ and $k = k_{YZ}/k_Y k_Z$.*

Proof. Let us set the origin of $u(y, z)$ by

$$u(y_0, z_0) = 0. \qquad (5.18)$$

Evaluating (5.14) at $y = y_0$,

$$u(y_0, z) = c_1(z) + c_2(z)u(y_0, z_0) = c_1(z). \qquad (5.19)$$

Substituting (5.19) into (5.14) and evaluating at an arbitrary $y_1 \neq y_0$,

$$u(y_1, z) = u(y_0, z) + c_2(z)u(y_1, z_0)$$

or

$$c_2(z) = \frac{u(y_1, z) - u(y_0, z)}{u(y_1, z_0)}. \tag{5.20}$$

Using (5.19) and (5.20) in (5.14), we now have

$$u(y, z) = u(y_0, z) + \frac{u(y_1, z) - u(y_0, z)}{u(y_1, z_0)} u(y, z_0), \quad \text{all } z. \tag{5.21}$$

Similarly, by evaluating (5.15) successively at $z = z_0$ and at an arbitrary $z_1 \neq z_0$, it becomes

$$u(y, z) = u(y, z_0) + \frac{u(y, z_1) - u(y, z_0)}{u(y_0, z_1)} u(y_0, z), \quad \text{all } y. \tag{5.22}$$

Evaluating (5.22) at $y = y_1$ and substituting this into (5.21), we conclude that

$$u(y, z) = u(y_0, z) + \frac{\left[u(y_1, z_0) + \dfrac{u(y_1, z_1) - u(y_1, z_0)}{u(y_0, z_1)} u(y_0, z) - u(y_0, z) \right]}{u(y_1, z_0)}$$

$$\times u(y, z_0)$$

$$= u(y_0, z) + u(y, z_0) + \left[\frac{u(y_1, z_1) - u(y_1, z_0) - u(y_0, z_1)}{u(y_1, z_0)u(y_0, z_1)} \right]$$

$$\times u(y_0, z)u(y, z_0). \tag{5.23}$$

Equation (5.23) can be written as (5.16), where k is an empirically evaluated constant defined by

$$k = \frac{u(y_1, z_1) - u(y_1, z_0) - u(y_0, z_1)}{u(y_1, z_0)u(y_0, z_1)}. \tag{5.24}$$

To provide for arbitrary scaling of the conditional utility functions, we can define u_Y and u_Z such that

$$k_Y u_Y(y) = u(y, z_0) \quad \text{and} \quad k_Z u_Z(z) = u(y_0, z), \tag{5.25}$$

where k_Y and k_Z are positive scaling constants and where u_Y and u_Z are scaled as stated in the theorem. Then, substituting (5.25) into (5.16) and defining $k_{YZ} = k k_Y k_Z$ gives us (5.17). From (5.18) and (5.25), it follows that the origins of u_Y and u_Z must be

$$u_Y(y_0) = 0 \quad \text{and} \quad u_Z(z_0) = 0,$$

respectively. It is important to realize that there are no other restrictions on the functional forms of the conditional utility functions u_Y and u_Z. ◄

5.4.2   Use of Isopreference Curves*

Because the decision maker may be unaccustomed to thinking in terms of a particular attribute, it may be difficult to assess one of the conditional utility functions required to use (5.16). However, we might be able to obtain an isopreference curve, that is, a set of all consequences that are equally desirable to the decision maker. In this section, we show that an iso-preference curve may be substituted for one of the conditional utility functions required by Theorem 5.2, provided it covers the same range.

A geometrical interpretation of the result is shown in Fig. 5.5 for the case where Y and Z are scalar attributes. We prove that if Y and Z are mutually utility independent, then $u(y, z)$ is uniquely determined in the specified consequence space by assessing a conditional utility function along the vertical heavy line, a utility for the heavy point in the figure and the isopreference curve.

1. Determine u on L in Fig. 5.5 setting $u_C = 0$ and assess u_P for consequence P.

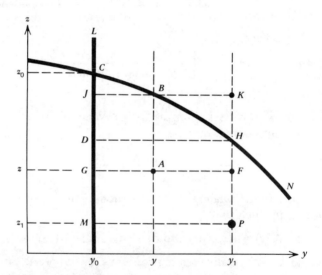

Fig. 5.5.   Mutual utility independence implies that $u(y, z)$ is completely specified from the utilities of the heavy shaded consequences.

---

* This section describes another way of assessing a utility function when each attribute is utility independent of the other. It exploits the existence of an assessed isopreference curve. The section can be skipped without interfering with the reading of the remainder of the chapter. However, other sections using isopreference curves should then also be skipped. These sections will be appropriately designated.

2. Then u along the isopreference curve N must be a zero.
3. Select A with arbitrary coordinates (y, z).
4. Express u_F in terms of u_H and u_P, using the fact that Z is utility independent of Y and using u_D, u_G, and u_M.
5. Similarly, express u_K in terms of u_H and u_P using u_J, u_D, and u_M.
6. Express u_A in terms of u_G and u_F, using the fact that Y is utility independent of Z and the relationship of u_J, u_B, and u_K.

Since u_G and u_F are known, the reasoning is complete. If A had not been in the region cornered by C, H, P, and M, a slightly altered proof using the same reasoning would be required.

Theorem 5.3. *If Y and Z are mutually utility independent, then*

$$u(y, z) = \frac{u(y_0, z) - u(y_0, z_n(y))}{1 + ku(y_0, z_n(y))} \qquad (5.26)$$

where

1. $u(y_0, z_0) = 0$
2. $z_n(y)$ *is defined such that* $(y, z_n(y)) \sim (y_0, z_0)$
3. $k = \dfrac{u(y_0, z_1) - u(y_1, z_1) - u(y_0, z_n(y_1))}{u(y_1, z_1)u(y_0, z_n(y_1))}$ $\qquad (5.27)$

where (y_1, z_1) *is arbitrarily chosen such that* (y_0, z_0) *and* (y_1, z_1) *are not indifferent.*

Proof. Let us define $z_n(y)$ to be such that the set $\{(y, z_n(y)); \text{ all } y\}$ is an isopreference curve over all Y. We can set the utility level of the isopreference curve* and the origin of $u(y, z)$ by

$$u(y, z_n(y)) = 0. \qquad (5.28)$$

Let us designate $z_n(y_0)$ as z_0. Then, of course,

$$u(y_0, z_0) = 0,$$

which is consistent with our origin in Theorem 5.2. Therefore, we can evaluate (5.16) at $(y, z_n(y))$ and solve for $u(y, z_0)$ to find

$$u(y, z_0) = \frac{-u(y_0, z_n(y))}{1 + ku(y_0, z_n(y))}. \qquad (5.29)$$

---

*For any y, we only need to determine one $z_n(y)$ such that (5.28) holds in order to specify $u(y, z)$.

Now, substituting (5.29) into (5.16) and rearranging, we get

$$u(y, z) = u(y_0, z) + \frac{-u(y_0, z_n(y))}{1 + ku(y_0, z_n(y))} + ku(y_0, z)\left[\frac{-u(y_0, z_n(y))}{1 + ku(y_0, z_n(y))}\right]$$

$$= \frac{u(y_0, z) - u(y_0, z_n(y))}{1 + ku(y_0, z_n(y))}. \tag{5.30}$$

To determine k from (5.24), we need to know $u(y_1, z_0)$. We can assess $u(y_1, z_1)$ for an arbitrary (y_1, z_1) such that it is not indifferent to (y_0, z_0). Substituting this into (5.30) yields

$$u(y_1, z_1) = \frac{u(y_0, z_1) - u(y_0, z_n(y_1))}{1 + ku(y_0, z_n(y_1))}$$

which, after rearranging, gives us the desired result (5.27).   ◄

5.4.3 The Multiplicative Representation

The multilinear form

$$u(y, z) = u(y, z_0) + u(y_0, z) + ku(y, z_0)u(y_0, z) \tag{5.16}$$

of Theorem 5.2 has a strategically equivalent multiplicative representation provided that $k \neq 0$. To this end, let*

$$\begin{aligned}
u'(y, z) &= ku(y, z) + 1 \\
&= ku(y_0, z) + ku(y, z_0) + k^2 u(y_0, z)u(y, z_0) + 1 \\
&= [ku(y, z_0) + 1][ku(y_0, z) + 1] \\
&= u'(y, z_0)u'(y_0, z). \tag{5.31}
\end{aligned}$$

When $k > 0$, then $u'(y, z_0)$ and $u'(y_0, z)$ are conditional utility functions for Y and Z, respectively. When $k < 0$, they are just the negative of the respective utility functions. Thus, *if two attributes are mutually utility independent, their utility function can be represented by either a product form, when $k \neq 0$, or an additive form, when $k = 0$.*

5.4.4 The Additive Representation

It would be interesting to know when k in (5.16) is zero. In this case the multilinear representation reduces to the additive representation discussed in Section 5.3. The following theorem clarifies this.

Theorem 5.4. *If Y and Z are mutually utility independent and if*

$$\langle (y_3, z_3), (y_4, z_4) \rangle \sim \langle (y_3, z_4), (y_4, z_3) \rangle$$

---

* The prime superscript on u does not denote "derivative."

for some y_3, y_4, z_3, z_4, *such that* (y_3, z_3) *is not indifferent to either* (y_3, z_4) *or* (y_4, z_3), *then*

$$u(y, z) = u(y, z_0) + u(y_0, z)$$

where $u(y, z)$ *is normalized by*

1. $u(y_0, z_0) = 0$

and

2. $u(y_1, z_1) = 1$ *for arbitrary* y_1 *and* z_1 *such that* $(y_1, z_0) \succ (y_0, z_0)$ *and* $(y_0, z_1) \succ (y_0, z_0)$.

Remark A. Given the above hypotheses, an alternative form of the utility function is given by (5.17) with its usual normalizations and with $k_{YZ} = 0$.

Remark B. The difference between Theorems 5.1 and 5.4 should be clarified. In Theorem 5.1 we require that $\langle (y, z), (y', z') \rangle \sim \langle (y, z'), (y', z) \rangle$ for *all* (y, z). Theorem 5.4 requires this indifference condition to hold for *only one* set of four points. However, of course, Theorem 5.4 also requires mutual utility independence.

Proof. Equating the expected utilities of the lotteries, we have

$$\tfrac{1}{2}u(y_3, z_3) + \tfrac{1}{2}u(y_4, z_4) = \tfrac{1}{2}u(y_3, z_4) + \tfrac{1}{2}u(y_4, z_3).$$

Evaluating these terms using (5.16), canceling and transposing, we find

$$k[u(y_0, z_3) - u(y_0, z_4)][u(y_3, z_0) - u(y_4, z_o)] = 0.$$

Since $u(y_3, z_3) \neq u(y_3, z_4)$, because of utility independence, $u(y_0, z_3) \neq u(y_0, z_4)$, and similarly, $u(y_3, z_0) \neq u(y_4, z_0)$. Therefore, k must be zero and (5.16) reduces to the additive representation.

From Theorem 5.4, it should be clear that additive independence implies mutual utility independence, but the converse is not true. Additive independence is obviously the stronger condition.

Corollary.* *Given the same conditions as the Theorem 5.4, $u(y, z)$ is completely specified by*

1. $u(y_0, z)$, *a conditional utility function for Z, for arbitrary y_0;*
2. *An isopreference curve over all Y.*

Proof. In this case, $k = 0$, and (5.26) becomes

$$u(y, z) = u(y_0, z) - u(y_0, z_n(y)). \qquad \blacktriangleleft$$

---

* This corollary should also be skipped if the reader did not read Section 5.4.2.

5.4.5   Interpretation and Implications of Parameter k

There is an interesting manner in which to interpret the parameter k. Consider the two 50–50 lotteries $\langle A, C \rangle$ and $\langle B, D \rangle$ illustrated in Fig. 5.6. We shall assume that preferences are increasing in both Y and Z in the figure. If this were not originally the case, simple transformations as indicated in Chapter 4 could be used to meet this requirement. Using the multilinear utility function (5.16) to calculate expected utilities, it is easy to show that

$$\left[\langle A, C \rangle \left\{ \begin{matrix} > \\ \sim \\ < \end{matrix} \right\} \langle B, D \rangle \right] \Leftrightarrow k \left\{ \begin{matrix} > \\ = \\ < \end{matrix} \right\} 0.$$

In some sense, consequences A and C are such that we either get a high level of both Y and Z or a low level of each. On the contrary, with B and D, we either get a high level of Y or Z, but not a lot (or a little) of both. Thinking about it this way, if $\langle A, C \rangle$ is preferred, it is as if we need an increase of Y to *complement* an increase in Z in going from A to C. Otherwise the full worth of the increase in Z could not be exploited. On the other hand, to prefer $\langle B, D \rangle$ implies that it is important to do well in

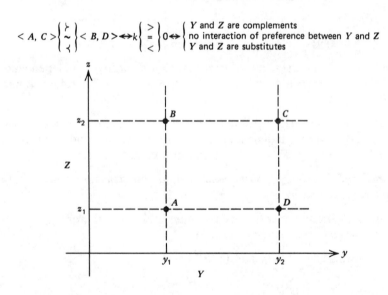

Fig. 5.6. **Using lotteries $\langle A, C \rangle$ and $\langle B, D \rangle$ to interpret the interaction term in the multilinear utility function.**

terms of at least one attribute and, given a high level of Y, the increased preference due to an increase in Z is not so much. Thus Y and Z can be thought of as *substitutes* for each other.

Two simple illustrations may help clarify the idea. First, suppose the president of a corporation has two large divisions operating in entirely different markets. She may be interested in profits of division 1, represented by Y, and profits of division 2, represented by Z. Achievement on these attributes would likely be substitutes for each other. If division 1 was doing well financially, the president would likely not be as concerned about division 2, as in the case when division 1 is doing poorly. If either division was quite successful, the corporation as a whole would probably live comfortably.

To illustrate a complementary case, consider the general who is fighting a battle on two fronts. Attribute Y and Z represents the performance on the respective fronts. Here, if either of the fronts break, the consequence may be almost as bad as if both break. In such a case, success on both fronts or failure on both fronts would likely be preferred by the general to success on one and failure on the other. Therefore, these attributes have a complementary effect. Complementarity, as we have used it here, is just a formalization, although somewhat weakened, of the saying "a chain is only as strong as its weakest link."

Further insight into the implications of parameter k can be seen if we rewrite (5.16) as

$$u(y, z) = u(y, z_0) + u(y_0, z)[1 + ku(y, z_0)]. \tag{5.32}$$

From (5.32), it is clear that if $u(y_0, z)$ is increasing in z,

$$k\begin{Bmatrix} < \\ = \\ > \end{Bmatrix} 0 \Rightarrow \frac{\partial u(y, z)}{\partial z}\bigg|_{y=y_1} \begin{Bmatrix} > \\ = \\ < \end{Bmatrix} \frac{\partial u(y, z)}{\partial z}\bigg|_{y=y_2} \qquad \text{for } u(y_2, z_0) > u(y_1, z_0).$$

Thus, if k is negative (positive, zero), and $u(y_0, z)$ is increasing, the increase in utility caused by an incremental increase in Z is smaller (greater, the same) for more preferred amounts of Y. In this sense, k again may be interpreted as a parameter that indicates the manner in which the amount of one attribute affects the value of the other attribute. If k is positive, more preferred amounts of Y *complement* more preferred amounts of Z. Just the reverse is true where k is negative. Here, we can consider more preferred amounts of Y and Z as being *substitutes* for each other. And in the additive case when $k = 0$, there is no interaction of preference between Y and Z.

5.5   USE OF CERTAINTY EQUIVALENTS

Recall that if we have a lottery* $(\bar{y}, z)$, the certainty equivalent for $\bar{y}$ given z is defined as the amount $\hat{y}_z$ such that

$$u(\hat{y}_z, z) = E[u(\bar{y}, z)] \qquad (5.33)$$

where $\hat{y}_z$ generally will depend on the level z. Because the expected utility $E[u(\bar{y}, z)]$ of the lottery in (5.33) is difficult to interpret physically, it is often easier for the decision maker to comprehend the situation by considering the equivalent certain consequence $(\hat{y}_z, z)$. It would be especially convenient if the certainty equivalent for lotteries on Y did not depend on the level of Z; we can then simply write $\hat{y}$ without the subscript z. It is easily seen that if Y is utility independent of Z, then for the lottery $(\bar{y}, z)$ the certainty equivalent for $\bar{y}$ given z does not depend on z. The converse is also true provided that the hypothesis holds for all probability distributions associated with $\bar{y}$.

Consider the lottery represented by $(\bar{y}, \bar{z})$ where Y and Z are mutually *utility* independent. We do *not* assume, however, that random variables $\bar{y}$ and $\bar{z}$ are *probabilistically* independent. Then, using (5.16), expected utility can be calculated from

$$E[u(\bar{y}, \bar{z})] = E[u(\bar{y}, z_0)] + E[u(y_0, \bar{z})] + kE[u(\bar{y}, z_0)u(y_0, \bar{z})], \quad (5.34)$$

since the expected value of a sum is the sum of the expected values. In the cases where Y and Z are also probabilistically independent, (5.34) becomes

$$E[u(\bar{y}, \bar{z})] = E[u(\bar{y}, z_0)] + E[u(y_0, \bar{z})] + kE[u(\bar{y}, z_0)]E[u(y_0, \bar{z})], \quad (5.35)$$

which can be reduced using (5.33) to

$$E[u(\bar{y}, \bar{z})] = u(\hat{y}, z_0) + u(y_0, \hat{z}) + ku(\hat{y}, z_0)u(y_0, \hat{z}) = u(\hat{y}, \hat{z}). \quad (5.36)$$

This is formalized in the following theorem.

Theorem 5.5. *Given a lottery of the form $(\bar{y}, \bar{z})$, separate certainty equivalents $\hat{y}$ and $\hat{z}$ for $\bar{y}$ and $\bar{z}$, respectively, may be calculated using the marginal probability distributions on $\bar{y}$ and $\bar{z}$ to form a joint certainty equivalent $(\hat{y}, \hat{z})$ for $(\bar{y}, \bar{z})$, provided either*

1. The attributes are mutually utility independent and probabilistically independent, or

2. The attributes are additive independent.

---

* A lottery over $Y \times Z$ with an uncertain outcome $\bar{y}$ coupled with a certain outcome z will be denoted by $(\bar{y}, z)$. We assume that a probability measure is known for the uncertain quantity (random variable) $\bar{y}$.

That condition 1 is sufficient is proved by (5.36). When additive independence holds, $k = 0$ in (5.34), from which the desired result immediately follows.

5.6   UTILITY FUNCTIONS WITH ONE UTILITY-INDEPENDENT ATTRIBUTE*

In the previous sections, we have been concerned with representing and assessing two-attribute utility functions when assumptions at least as strong as mutual utility independence hold. In this section, we look at the implication of the weaker assumption, where only one attribute is utility independent of the other. It is shown that the two-attribute utility function can be specified by either three conditional utility functions, or two conditional utility functions and an isopreference curve, or one conditional utility function and two isopreference curves. Special cases of these results, including the additive and multilinear utility functions, are indicated.

For all the work in this section, we will denote the attributes as Y and Z and assume that Z is utility independent of Y. That is, for any arbitrary y_0,

$$u(y, z) = c_1(y) + c_2(y)u(y_0, z), \qquad c_2(y) > 0, \qquad \text{all } y. \qquad (5.37)$$

5.6.1   Assessments In Terms of Three Conditional Utility Functions

Let us begin with an illustration of what we shall prove. If Z is utility independent of Y, then $u(y, z)$ is completely specified by two arbitrary conditional utility functions for Y and one conditional utility function for Z, subject to consistent scaling. To see this in the case where Y and Z represent scalar attributes, consider Fig. 5.7. If we consistently assess the utilities along the heavy lines in the figure, we will have enough information to assign the utility to every consequence. For example, consider an arbitrary point A with coordinates (y, z). The utility of A can be expressed as a linear combination of the utilities u_B and u_C where the weights are determined (since Z is utility independent of Y) by the values of u_D, u_E, and u_F.

As an alternative way of looking at the same proof, consider any vertical line at arbitrary point y. The utility function $u(y, \cdot)$ must be

---

* Material in this section is adapted from Keeney (1971).

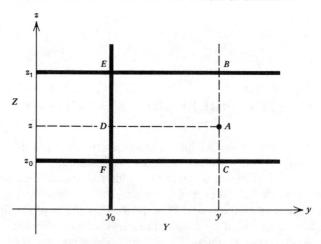

Fig. 5.7. Z **utility independent of** Y **implies that** $u(y, z)$ **is completely specified from the utilities of the heavy shaded consequences.**

strategically equivalent to the function $u(y_0, \cdot)$, which is given. The utilities at B and C serve to normalize $u(y, \cdot)$.

Let us formalize this argument.

Theorem 5.6. *If Z is utility independent of Y, then*

$$u(y, z) = u(y, z_0)[1 - u(y_0, z)] + u(y, z_1)u(y_0, z), \qquad (5.38)$$

where $u(y, z)$ is normalized by $u(y_0, z_0) = 0$ and $u(y_0, z_1) = 1$.

Proof. We can define z_0 and z_1 to insure $u(y_0, z_1) > u(y_0, z_0)$ and then arbitrarily set the origin and unit of measure of $u(y, z)$ by

$$u(y_0, z_0) = 0 \qquad (5.39)$$

and

$$u(y_0, z_1) = 1. \qquad (5.40)$$

Since Z is utility independent of Y, (5.37) holds. Evaluating (5.37) at $z = z_0$ and using (5.39), we find

$$u(y, z_0) = c_1(y) + c_2(y)u(y_0, z_0) = c_1(y). \qquad (5.41)$$

Combining (5.41) and (5.37) and evaluating at $z = z_1$,

$$u(y, z_1) = u(y, z_0) + c_2(y)u(y_0, z_1),$$

and using (5.40), we conclude

$$c_2(y) = u(y, z_1) - u(y, z_0). \qquad (5.42)$$

Now, (5.41) and (5.42) can be substituted into (5.37) to give

$$u(y, z) = u(y, z_0) + [u(y, z_1) - u(y, z_0)]u(y_0, z)$$
$$= u(y, z_0)[1 - u(y_0, z)] + u(y, z_1)u(y_0, z),$$

which is the desired result.   ◄

It should be noted that $u(y_0, \cdot)$, $u(\cdot, z_0)$, and $u(\cdot, z_1)$ are conditional utility functions. Equations (5.39) and (5.40) specify the origin and unit of measure of $u(y_0, \cdot)$ and fix one point on the $u(\cdot, z_0)$ and $u(\cdot, z_1)$ curves. One other point on each of the latter two conditional utility functions must be evaluated empirically in order to set their units of measure equal to that of $u(y_0, \cdot)$ and thus insure consistency of the unit of measure of $u(\cdot, \cdot)$. This can be done by finding a consequence (y_0, z_2) that is indifferent to a consequence (y_2, z_0). Therefore, $u(y_0, z_2)$ equals $u(y_2, z_0)$, which specifies a second point on $u(\cdot, z_0)$, thereby fixing its unit of measure. Similarly, we can find a (y_0, z_3) that is indifferent to (y_3, z_1) to consistently fix the unit of measure of $u(\cdot, z_1)$.

To provide a better understanding of (5.38), we offer graphical illustrations of two special cases. First, let us assume that Y is two dimensional, that is, $y \equiv (x_1, x_2)$, and Z is one dimensional. For this case, Theorem 5.6 states that provided Z is utility independent of Y, $u(y, z)$ can be specified by assessing two two-dimensional conditional utility functions, $u(\cdot, z_0)$ and $u(\cdot, z_1)$, and the one-dimensional conditional utility function $u(y_0, \cdot)$. Referring to Fig. 5.8a, this means we must assess the relative utilities of the shaded consequences to specify $u(\cdot, \cdot)$.

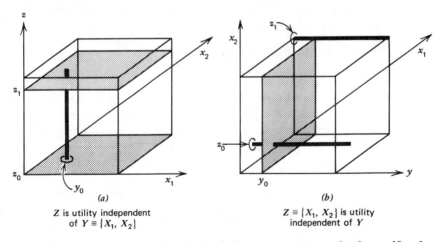

(a)

Z is utility independent
of $Y \equiv \{X_1, X_2\}$

(b)

$Z \equiv \{X_1, X_2\}$ is utility
independent of Y

Fig. 5.8.   Assessing utilities for the shaded consequences completely specifies the utility function.

As a second illustration, suppose Y is one dimensional and $z \equiv (x_1, x_2)$. In this case, the theorem states that $u(\cdot, \cdot)$ is specified by two one-dimensional conditional utility functions, $u(\cdot, z_0)$ and $u(\cdot, z_1)$, and the two-dimensional conditional utility function $u(y_0, \cdot)$, provided that Z is utility independent of Y. Thus, to determine $u(\cdot, \cdot)$ in this case, one must assess the relative utilities of the consequences shaded in Fig. 5.8b.

5.6.2 Substitution of One Isopreference Curve for One Conditional Utility Function*

In certain problems, it may be more convenient to assess an isopreference curve than a conditional utility function. We prove that, in evaluating $u(y, z)$, an isopreference curve may be substituted for either a conditional utility function for Y or Z provided that it covers the same range.

Theorem 5.7. If Z is utility independent of Y, then

$$u(y, z) = u(y, z_0) + \left[\frac{u(y_0, z_1) - u(y, z_0)}{u(y_0, z_n(y))} \right] u(y_0, z) \tag{5.43}$$

where

1. $u(y_0, z_0) = 0$
2. $z_n(y)$ is defined such that $(y, z_n(y)) \sim (y_0, z_1)$ for an arbitary z_1.

[*Remark Before Proof:* Thus to implement the results of this theorem we must ascertain that Z is utility independent of Y, assess the function $u(\cdot, z_0)$ and $u(y_0, \cdot)$, and determine one isopreference curve with a full range of y's.]

Proof. We will set the origin of $u(y, z)$ by

$$u(y_0, z_0) = 0, \tag{5.44}$$

and define $z_n(y)$ so that the set $\{(y, z_n(y)): \text{all } y\}$ is an isopreference curve over all Y. Since the curve $\{(y, z_n(y)): \text{all } y\}$ must intersect the line $\{(y_0, z): \text{all } z\}$, we can denote the intersection point as (y_0, z_1) and set the utility level of the isopreference curve by

$$u(y, z_n(y)) = u(y_0, z_1). \tag{5.45}$$

Evaluating (5.37) at $z = z_0$ and at $z = z_n(y)$, we respectively find

$$u(y, z_0) = c_1(y) + c_2(y)u(y_0, z_0) = c_1(y) \tag{5.46}$$

---

*The remainder of Section 5.6 can be omitted without interfering with the continuity of the presentation.

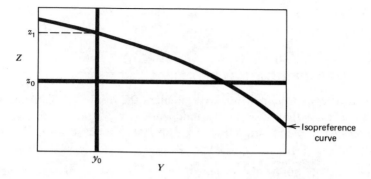

Fig. 5.9. Z **utility independent of** Y **implies that** $u(y, z)$ **is completely specified from the utilities of the heavy shaded consequences.**

and

$$u(y, z_n(y)) = u(y_0, z_1) = c_1(y) + c_2(y)u(y_0, z_n(y))$$
$$= u(y, z_0) + c_2(y)u(y_0, z_n(y)).$$

or

$$c_2(y) = \frac{u(y_0, z_1) - u(y, z_0)}{u(y_0, z_n(y))}. \tag{5.47}$$

Substituting (5.46) and (5.47) into (5.37), we obtain (5.43).   ◄

In the special case when the isopreference curve goes through (y_0, z_0) (i.e., the case where $z_1 = z_0$), $u(y_0, z_1) = 0$ and (5.43) simplifies to

$$u(y, z) = u(y, z_0)\left[1 - \frac{u(y_0, z)}{u(y_0, z_n(y))}\right]. \tag{5.48}$$

The geometrical interpretation of Theorem 5.7 in the case where Y and Z are scalar attributes is given in Fig. 5.9. To specify $u(\cdot, \cdot)$ we must consistently assess the utilities of the consequences covered by heavy lines in the figure.

It is also of interest to use an isopreference curve in place of the conditional utility function for Z in the assessment of $u(\cdot, \cdot)$. Let us formalize this with

Theorem 5.8. *If* Z *is utility independent of* Y, *then*

$$u(y, z) = \frac{u(y, z_0)u(y_n(z), z_1) - u(y, z_1)u(y_n(z), z_0)}{u(y_n(z), z_1) - u(y_n(z), z_0)} \tag{5.49}$$

where

1. $u(y_0, z_0) = 0,$ $z_1 \neq z_0,$
and

2. $y_n(z)$ is defined so that $(y_n(z), z) \sim (y_0, z_0)$.

[*Remark Before Proof:* Thus to implement the results of this theorem we must ascertain that Z is utility independent of Y, assess the functions $u(\cdot, z_0)$, $u(\cdot, z_1)$, and determine one isopreference curve with a full range z's.]

Proof. Let us define the origin of $u(y, z)$ as the point where the iso-preference curve, $\{(y_n(z), z) : \text{all } z\}$, crosses the line $\{(y, z_0) : \text{all } y\}$. This must occur at some y, call it y_0, and thus

$$u(y_n(z), z) = u(y_0, z_0) = 0.$$

Furthermore, we can set the unit of measure by $u(y_0, z_1) = 1$. Thus, since Z is utility independent of Y, we can use (5.38) to evaluate $u(y_n(z), z)$ to yield

$$u(y_n(z), z) = 0 = u(y_n(z), z_0)[1 - u(y_0, z)] + u(y_n(z), z_1)u(y_0, z),$$

which, after rearranging, becomes

$$u(y_0, z) = \frac{-u(y_n(z), z_0)}{u(y_n(z), z_1) - u(y_n(z), z_0)}. \qquad (5.50)$$

Substituting (5.50) into (5.42) we get the result (5.49).   ◀

A geometrical illustration of Theorem 5.8 is given in Fig. 5.10 for the case where Y and Z are scalar attributes. Expression (5.49) gives us a

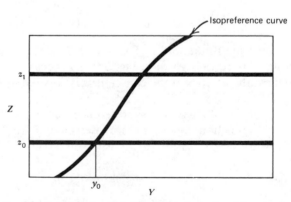

Fig. 5.10. Z **utility independent of** Y **implies that** $u(y, z)$ **is completely specified from the utilities of the heavy shaded consequences.**

method of evaluating $u(\cdot, \cdot)$ from the relative utilities of the consequences along the heavy lines in the figure. From the orientation of the isopreference curve in Fig. 5.10, it should be clear that preferences must be increasing in one attribute and decreasing in the other.

5.6.3   Use of Two Isopreference Curves

It is possible to substitute an isopreference curve for each of the conditional utility functions for Y necessary to implement (5.38). To this end, we prove the following theorem.

Theorem 5.9.   *If Z is utility independent of Y, then*

$$u(y, z) = \frac{u(y_0, z) - u(y_0, z_m(y))}{u(y_0, z_n(y)) - u(y_0, z_m(y))}, \tag{5.51}$$

where

1. *$u(y, z)$ is normalized by $u(y_0, z_0) = 0$ and $u(y_0, z_1) = 1$.*
2. *$z_m(y)$ is defined such that $(y, z_m(y)) \sim (y_0, z_0)$.*
3. *$z_n(y)$ is defined such that $(y, z_n(y)) \sim (y_0, z_1)$.*

[*Remark Before Proof:*   To implement this theorem, we must ascertain that Z is utility independent of Y, assess the function $u(y_0, \cdot)$, and determine two isopreference curves with the full range of y's.]

Proof.   Let us define $z_m(y)$ and $z_n(y)$ such that the sets $\{(y, z_m(y)): \text{all } y\}$ and $\{(y, z_n(y)): \text{all } y\}$ represent two isopreference curves over all Y. Both isopreference curves must intersect the line $\{(y_0, z): \text{all } z\}$, so we can set the origin and unit of measure of $u(\cdot, \cdot)$ and define z_0 and z_1 by

$$u(y, z_m(y)) = u(y_0, z_0) = 0 \tag{5.52}$$

and

$$u(y, z_n(y)) = u(y_0, z_1) = 1. \tag{5.53}$$

By evaluating $u(y, z_m(y))$ and $u(y, z_n(y))$ using (5.38) we find, respectively,

$$u(y, z_m(y)) = 0 = u(y, z_0)[1 - u(y_0, z_m(y))] + u(y, z_1)u(y_0, z_m(y)) \tag{5.54}$$

and

$$u(y, z_n(y)) = 1 = u(y, z_0)[1 - u(y_0, z_n(y))] + u(y, z_1)u(y_0, z_n(y)). \tag{5.55}$$

Equations (5.54) and (5.55) are two equations with two unknowns, which can be solved to yield

$$u(y, z_0) = \frac{-u(y_0, z_m(y))}{u(y_0, z_n(y)) - u(y_0, z_m(y))} \tag{5.56}$$

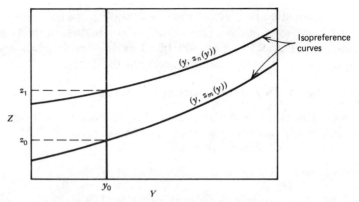

Fig. 5.11. Z **utility independent of** Y **implies that** $u(y, z)$ **is completely specified from the utilities of the heavy shaded consequences.**

and

$$u(y, z_1) = \frac{1 - u(y_0, z_m(y))}{u(y_0, z_n(y)) - u(y_0, z_m(y))}. \tag{5.57}$$

Substituting (5.56) and (5.57) into (5.38), we obtain

$$u(y, z) = \frac{-u(y_0, z_m(y))[1 - u(y_0, z)] + [1 - u(y_0, z_m(y))]u(y_0, z)}{u(y_0, z_n(y)) - u(y_0, z_m(y))} \tag{5.58}$$

from which (5.51) follows after canceling terms.   ◀

When Y and Z both represent scalar attributes, Theorem 5.9 can be illustrated geometrically as shown in Fig. 5.11. We have proven that provided Z is utility independent of Y, $u(\cdot, \cdot)$ is specified by assessing the relative utilities of the consequences along the heavy lines.

A utility function gives us a measure of the decision maker's attitude toward risky or uncertain situations. To assess the utility function, the decision maker must specify his preferences for lotteries. An isopreference curve, on the other hand, yields no information about the decision maker's attitudes toward risk and can be assessed by comparing certain consequences only. Thus, since only one conditional utility function is necessary to implement (5.58), the decision maker's attitudes toward risks involving both uncertain Y and Z can be specified by considering risky situations involving only uncertain Z.

5.6.4 Special Cases: The Additive and Multilinear Form

As proven in Section 5.4, if Y and Z are mutually utility independent,

$$u(y, z) = u(y, z_0) + u(y_0, z) + ku(y, z_0)u(y_0, z), \tag{5.59}$$

where k is an empirically evaluated constant. It would be interesting to know what additional conditions must hold for the results of this section to reduce to the form (5.59) or to the additive utility function. To this end, we prove two results that can be thought of as corollaries to Theorem 5.6.

Corollary 1. *Given Z is utility independent of Y, it is a necessary and sufficient condition for $u(y, z)$ to be of form (5.59) that*

$$u(y, z_1) = a + bu(y, z_0), \qquad (5.60)$$

for arbitrary $z_1 \neq z_0$, where a and $b > 0$ are constants.

[*Remark Before Proof:*   In other words, this corollary states that if Z is utility independent of Y, in order to get the multilinear utility function (5.59), we do not have to assert that *all conditional* utility functions $u(\cdot, z)$ be strategically equivalent. It is enough that there be merely a single pair, say $u(\cdot, z_0)$ and $u(\cdot, z_1)$, that are strategically equivalent.]

Proof.   For sufficiency, let us substitute (5.60) into (5.38) giving

$$u(y, z) = u(y, z_0)[1 - u(y_0, z)] + [a + bu(y, z_0)]u(y_0, z)$$
$$= u(y, z_0) + au(y_0, z) + (b - 1)u(y, z_0)u(y_0, z). \qquad (5.61)$$

Since $u(y_0, z_0) = 0$ in (5.39), evaluating (5.61) at $y = y_0$ yields

$$u(y_0, z) = 0 + au(y_0, z) + 0$$

so

$$a = 1. \qquad (5.62)$$

Substituting this result into (5.61) and defining $k \equiv b - 1$, we get (5.59).

To prove that (5.60) is a necessary condition for (5.59), we only need to observe that (5.59) implies

$$u(y, z_1) = u(y_0, z_1) + [1 + ku(y_0, z_1)]u(y, z_0),$$

and that $u(y_0, z_1)$ and $[1 + ku(y_0, z_1)]$ are constants.   ◀

Corollary 2.   *Given that Z is utility independent of Y, $u(y, z)$ is additive if and only if $\langle (y_0, z_0), (y, z_1) \rangle$ is indifferent to $\langle (y_0, z_1), (y, z_0) \rangle$ for all y.*

Proof.   Equating expected utilities of the two lotteries,

$$\tfrac{1}{2}u(y_0, z_0) + \tfrac{1}{2}u(y, z_1) = \tfrac{1}{2}u(y_0, z_1) + \tfrac{1}{2}u(y, z_0), \text{ for all } y. \qquad (5.63)$$

Recalling that the origin and unit of measure of $u(y, z)$ in (5.38) were set by $u(y_0, z_0) = 0$ and $u(y_0, z_1) = 1$, we can substitute these into (5.63) to give

$$u(y, z_1) = 1 + u(y, z_0). \qquad (5.64)$$

Expression (5.64) is the necessary and sufficient condition for the multilinear form stated in Corollary 1. Noting for this case that $a = 1$ and $b = 1$, the additive utility function follows directly from (5.61).   ◄

Recall from Section 5.3 that, in general, additivity follows from an assumption that

$$\langle (y_0, z_0), (y, z) \rangle \sim \langle (y_0, z), (y, z_0) \rangle \tag{5.65}$$

for all y and z given some arbitrarily chosen y_0 and z_0. Corollary 2 states that if we can assume that Z is utility independent of Y, then additivity follows if we set $z = z_1$ and the above assumption holds for all y given the arbitrarily chosen y_0, z_0, and z_1. Earlier in Theorem 5.4, we proved that if mutual utility independence holds, then the additive utility function follows if $y = y_1$ and $z = z_1$ are both set and assumption (5.65) is valid for the single set of four values y_0, z_0, y_1, and z_1.

5.6.5   Use of Certainty Equivalents

As before, a certainty equivalent $\hat{y}$ for $\tilde{y}$ in the lottery $(\tilde{y}, z)$ is defined by the relation

$$u(\hat{y}, z) = E[u(\tilde{y}, z)].$$

When Z is *utility* independent of Y and when $\tilde{y}$ and $\tilde{z}$ are *probabilistically* independent, the expected utility of $(\tilde{y}, \tilde{z})$ using (5.38) is

$$\begin{aligned} E[u(\tilde{y}, \tilde{z})] &= E[u(\tilde{y}, z_0)]\{1 - E[u(y_0, \tilde{z})]\} + E[u(\tilde{y}, z_1)]E[u(y_0, \tilde{z})] \\ &= u(\hat{y}_0, z_0)[1 - u(y_0, \hat{z})] + u(\hat{y}_1, z_1)u(y_0, \hat{z}), \end{aligned}$$

where $\hat{y}_0$ and $\hat{y}_1$ are, respectively, the certainty equivalents for $\tilde{y}$ when $z = z_0$ and $z = z_1$, and $\hat{z}$ is the certainty equivalent for $\tilde{z}$.

The use of certainty equivalents for evaluating lotteries is discussed in more detail in Section 5.5. The basic explanation for their applicability is as follows. Utility independence allows us to express the expected utility of a lottery with more than one uncertain attribute in terms of the expected utilities of lotteries involving only one uncertain attribute. Probabilistic independence allows us to calculate expected utility over these latter lotteries by evaluating the expected utility over each component of the terms separately. Thus we have an expression for expected utility of the multiattribute lottery in terms of the expected utilities of one-variable lotteries. A certainty equivalent may then be substituted for the uncertain attribute in these simple lotteries, which should greatly facilitate interpretation of the implications of the lottery.

5.6.6   Utility Independence as an Approximation Technique

Even if neither attribute is utility independent of the other, the utility representation (5.38), which was derived using the assumption that just one of the attributes was utility independent of the other, may provide a good approximation for the true utility function.

The basis for our argument is that (5.38) gives us five degrees of freedom in assessing $u(y, z)$, whereas the multilinear formulation of (5.16) gives us four degrees of freedom, and the additive formulation of (5.10) offers only three degrees of freedom in assessing $u(y, z)$. Consider the two-dimensional illustrations in Fig. 5.12.

The degrees of freedom are shown on the figure as heavy lines or points. The two consequences marked "0" represent the consequences chosen to establish the origin and unit of measure of $u(y, z)$.

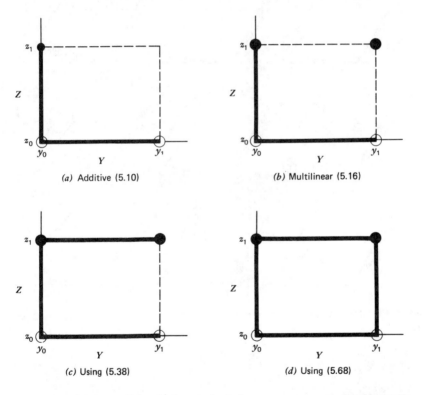

Fig. 5.12.   **Assigning utilities for heavy shaded consequences completely specifies the utility function in the cases indicated.**

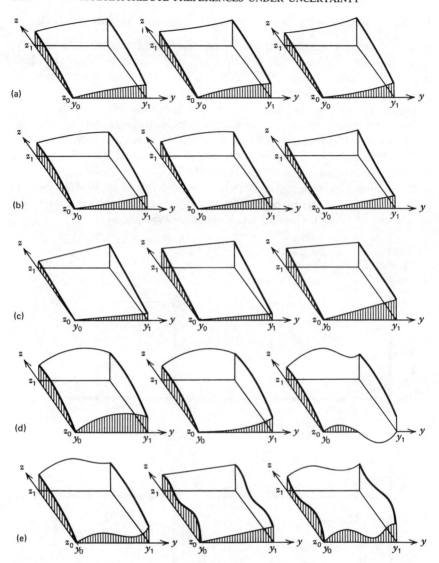

Fig. 5.13.   Different shapes of utility functions $u(y, z)$ **where** Z **is utility indepen-dent of** Y.

Using the additive form, we can then arbitrarily determine the following:

(a) The shape of $u(\cdot, z_0)$, a conditional utility function for Y.
(b) The shape of $u(y_0, \cdot)$, a conditional utility function for Z.
(c) The unit of measure of $u(y_0, \cdot)$ relative to that of $u(\cdot, z_0)$ by assessing $u(y_0, z_1)$.

These are the three degrees of freedom of the additive representation.

With the multilinear form, we have, in addition to (a), (b), and (c), the freedom to fix

(d) The unit of measure of $u(\cdot, z_1)$, a conditional utility function for Y, by assessing $u(y_1, z_1)$.

Using (5.38), we can add to this list the freedom to evaluate

(e) The shape of $u(\cdot, z_1)$.

In Fig. 5.13, we illustrate some of the general shapes of $u(y, z)$ that we can obtain using (5.38). The common restriction on each utility function is that all the conditional utility functions over Z must be strategically equivalent. In each of the 15 drawings, two such functions are darkened. Note however that the $u(\cdot, z)$ can have many shapes. Rows A and B in Fig. 5.13 illustrate the effect of varying the shapes of $u(\cdot, z_0)$, $u(\cdot, z_1)$, and $u(y_0, \cdot)$. Various combinations of convex and concave conditional utility functions are shown.

With row C, we intend to illustrate the freedom created by selecting the units of $u(\cdot, z_0)$ and $u(\cdot, z_1)$. Finally, in rows D and E, we wish to point out that there are no restrictions, such as monotonicity or certain risk properties, on the conditional utility functions. To repeat, the only restriction on the forms of $u(\cdot, \cdot)$ in Fig. 5.13 is that $u(y, \cdot)$ has the same general shape (i.e., is strategically equivalent to) as $u(y_0, \cdot)$ for all values of y.

5.7 WHAT TO DO IF NO INDEPENDENCE PROPERTIES HOLD*

Suppose we have ascertained, using assessment techniques discussed in the next section, that neither Y or Z is utility independent of the other. Then clearly, since mutual utility independence is a necessary condition

---

* You may wish to omit this entire section, but we suggest that you at least quickly read the introduction of the section before proceeding to Section 5.8.

for additive independence, none of the functional forms of two-attribute utility functions discussed in the preceding sections are strictly appropriate. Furthermore, suppose we have tried to implement the techniques discussed in Chapter 3 to reduce the dimensionality of the problem. These did not help either. However, we still want to quantify the decision maker's preferences. The question is, what can we do to obtain a reasonable u over $Y \times Z$ for decision making? Several possibilities exist including:

1. Transformation or adjustment of Y and Z to new attributes that might allow exploitation of utility independence properties.
2. Direct assessment of $u(y, z)$ by acquiring utilities of several consequences in the range of $Y \times Z$, and then using interpolation, extrapolation, and curve fitting.
3. Application of various of the results in preceding chapters over subsets of the $Y \times Z$ space, and then consistently scaling them.
4. Development or use of existing more complicated assumptions about the decision maker's preference structure that imply more general utility functions.

Let us clarify these options. The relative desirability of one approach versus another, of course, is very much a function of the problem at hand.

5.7.1 A Transformation of Attributes

It may be possible to select an alternative set of attributes and proceed to analyze the problem with this new set. Unfortunately, in this case the questions raised in Chapter 2 concerning the appropriateness of the set of attributes, such as completeness and measurability, must be reconsidered. Furthermore, it may be necessary to repeat much of the analysis, including perhaps probabilistic assessments. To avoid this, perhaps we can choose the new attributes that will have some simple functional relationship to the original ones. Then, almost all of the analysis already completed will be directly applicable.

As a simple illustration, let Y and Z designate measures of the crime rates in the two sections of a city, respectively. It may be that there is a complicated preference structure for (y, z) pairs. The relative ordering of lotteries for criminal activity in one section may depend very much for political reasons on the level of crime in the other section. However, suppose we define $S \equiv (Y + Z)/2$ and $T \equiv |Y - Z|$. Then S may be interpreted as some kind of an average crime index for the city and T is an indicator of the balance of criminal activity between the two sections. Attributes S and T are functionally related to Y and Z. If we are given probability distributions over Y and Z, we could derive probability distributions over S and T. In addition, although there may be no simplifying preference assumptions in $Y \times Z$ space, such properties may exist in $S \times T$ space.

Example 5.2. Suppose that *no utility independence properties* exist among the original attributes Y and Z. Still it may be possible to define new attributes $S \equiv Y + Z$ and $T \equiv Y - Z$ that do possess independence properties. For instance, S and T might be additive independent with the form

$$u(s, t) = s^2 + t. \tag{5.66}$$

In this case the assessment of (5.66) should not be too difficult.

Notice that

$$\begin{aligned} u^*(y, z) &\equiv u[s(y, z), t(y, z)] = (y + z)^2 + (y - z) \\ &= y^2 + y + z^2 - z + 2yz, \end{aligned}$$

which illustrates that indeed no utility independence properties existed between Y and Z. ∎

5.7.2 Direct Assessment of $u(y, z)$

This procedure is essentially that discussed in subsection 5.1.2. We pick two consequences as reference points and assign utilities to these. Then using reference lotteries and empirical assessments of the decision maker, utilities are successively assigned to a number of consequences throughout $Y \times Z$. Utilizing a curve-fitting technique, a utility can be assigned to all possible consequences.

5.7.3 Employing Utility Independence Over Subsets of $Y \times Z$

The idea is simple: just subdivide the consequence space into parts such that various of the functional forms of preceding sections are appropriate. We must be careful to insure consistent scaling on $u(y, z)$.

Example 5.3. Suppose we want to assess $u(y, z)$, $y' \le y \le y''$ and $z' \le z \le z''$ where preferences are increasing in both attributes. For $y \le y_0$, Z is utility independent of Y, so from (5.42), if we set $u_1(y_0, z') = 0$ and $u_1(y_0, z'') = 1$, then

$$u_1(y, z) = u_1(y, z')[1 - u_1(y_0, z)] + u_1(y, z'')u_1(y_0, z),$$
$$y \le y_0, \quad z' \le z \le z''.$$

For the rest of the original region, suppose Y is utility independent of Z, so if we set $u_2(y_0, z') = 0$ and $u_2(y'', z') = 1$, then

$$u_2(y, z) = u_2(y_0, z)[1 - u_2(y, z')] + u(y'', z)u(y, z'),$$
$$y \geq y_0, \quad z' \leq z \leq z''.$$

Since both u_1 and u_2 have the same origin, then in order to consistently scale u_1 and u_2 we need only determine a scaling constant λ defined by

$$\lambda = \frac{u_2(y_0, z'')}{u_1(y_0, z'')}.$$

In this case a consistent utility function for all $Y \times Z$ is

$$u(y, z) = \begin{cases} \lambda u_1(y, z), & y \leq y_0, \quad z' \leq z \leq z'' \\ u_2(y, z), & y \geq y_0, \quad z' \leq z \leq z''. \end{cases} \quad \blacksquare$$

5.7.4   Weaker Assumptions on the Preference Structure*

This subsection indicates several models more general than those of the previous sections. As is evident and expected, the requisite assumptions for these utility functions are more complex than those used earlier. The advantage is clear. Such models are more likely to be appropriate for a specific decision maker's preference structure and, therefore, less likely to misrepresent it. The disadvantage is operational. It is more difficult both to verify the assumptions of the more general models and to assess $u(y, z)$ once they are verified. This tradeoff must inevitably be considered in selecting a model for one's utility function.

REVERSING PREFERENCES.   If Z is utility independent of Y, then

$$u(y, z) = c_1(y) + c_2(y)u(y_0, z), \tag{5.67}$$

where $c_2(y)$ must be greater than zero. This implies that the preference order over lotteries on Z will always be the same regardless of the amount y. Suppose we allow $c_2(y)$ to also be negative or zero. Then if $c_2(y') < 0$, the preference order on lotteries over Z given y' is exactly reversed from this order given y_0. If $c_2(y') = 0$, then we are indifferent between all lotteries over Z given y'. Fishburn (1974) allowed for these reversals of preference and indifference and derived results analogous to those in Section 5.4.

A GENERALIZATION OF UTILITY INDEPENDENCE.   The most general result we have discussed so far is (5.38), which requires two one-attribute utility

---

* In this subsection, we will be quite informal. The purpose is (1) to communicate a flavor for some generalizations of material presented earlier in this chapter that have been developed, and (2) to indicate sources for this work.

functions over Y and one one-attribute utility function over Z. Necessary and sufficient conditions have been developed that require two one-attribute utility functions over each of Y and Z. Then $u(y, z)$ is determined by assessing adequately scaled utility functions over the heavy lines of Fig. 5.12d. The result is that

$$u(y, z) = u_Y(y) + u_Z(z) + f_Y(y)f_Z(z). \tag{5.68}$$

The requisite assumptions and proof for (5.68) along with a discussion of scaling the functions u_Y, u_Z, f_Y, and f_Z is found in Fishburn (1974).

PARAMETRIC DEPENDENCE.   As indicated in Section 5.2, if Z is utility independent of Y, then our attitude toward risk in terms of lotteries over Z is independent of Y. Kirkwood (1976) developed parametric dependence, which eliminates this restriction, but requires the preferences over Z for different amounts of Y to be representable by members of the same parametric family of utility functions. For instance, if preferences over Y are increasing and constantly risk averse for all z, but the degree of risk aversion varies, we have

$$u(y, z) \sim -e^{-y\theta(z)}, \qquad \theta(z) > 0. \tag{5.69}$$

Equation (5.69) indicates that all conditional utility functions over Y depend on z through the parameter $\theta(z)$. In this case Y is parametrically dependent on Z. More formally, we say that Y is *parametrically dependent* on Z if the conditional utility functions over Y given different levels of z depend on z only through a parameter θ. This means that

$$u(y, z) = d_1(z) + d_2(z)u_{Y|z}[y \mid \theta(z)], \tag{5.70}$$

where $d_2(z) > 0$ and $u_{Y|z}$ indicates a conditional utility function over Y given z.

The following result provides an intuitive flavor of the use of parametric dependence.

Theorem 5.10.   *If Y is parametrically dependent on Z, then $u(\cdot, \cdot)$ is completely determined by three consistently scaled utility functions on Z given levels of y and one utility function on Y given z.*

Instead of a formal proof, refer to Fig. 5.14 for the basis of an informal one. Theorem 5.10 says that, subject to the stated conditions, the utility of any point can be assigned given the consistently scaled utilities of the darkened lines. From $u(\cdot, z_0)$ we know the functional form of the utility function $u(\cdot, z)$ for all z. To determine the value of the parameter for a particular z, we just use the utilities of (y_0, z), (y', z), and (y_1, z). Then $u(\cdot, z)$ is scaled by $u(y_0, z)$ and $u(y_1, z)$, which allows us to assign a utility to any (y, z).

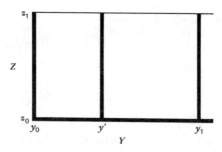

Fig. 5.14. When Y is parametrically dependent on Z, the utility function $u(y, z)$ is completely specified by the utilities over the heavy shaded consequences.

Obviously the parametric dependence concept could be extended to include families of utility functions involving two parameters rather than one. Then it would not be difficult to derive results analogous to Theorem 5.10. For instance, the only change in Theorem 5.10 would be that four conditional utility functions over Z, one more than before, would need to be assessed. Similarly, results making use of both parametric dependence and utility independence can be derived. Kirkwood (1972) presents some of these.

SUMMARY STATE DESCRIPTORS. Let us terminate this section with one further generalization that will be further developed in Chapter 9. Consider the two attributes Y and Z but now assume that Z is multidimensional. In some circumstances the conditional utility function $u(\cdot, z)$ on Y might depend on (the multidimensional) z only through some summary state description, say $\theta(z)$. In some cases the range of θ might be unidimensional. For example, suppose we are concerned with time streams of consumption. The utility of future consumption starting from a point in time t_0 might depend on past and present consumption. But, as an approximation, we might be able to assume that the utility for future consumption depends only on the past through the present consumption at t_0. Hence the consumption stream up to and including time t_0 can be effectively summarized by the state description: consumption at t_0. This example is a natural analogy of the concept of Markovian dependence from conventional probabilistic analysis. Other weak forms of probabilistic dependence also have analogies in the utility domain. In other words, if we cannot assume as reasonable various utility independence notions, we can introduce weak forms of *utility dependence*. As far as we know this research direction has hardly been begun. (See Section 6.10, Bell (1975a) and Meyer (1975).)

As indicated at the beginning of this subsection, with the greater generality of the utility functions comes the greater complexity of utilizing them. For many problems, the simpler models are likely "good enough" approximations even if they are not precisely valid. However, for those problems where this is not the case, it is important to realize how to add generality to the model and still keep the assessment task within bounds.

5.8 ASSESSMENT PROCEDURE FOR MULTIATTRIBUTE UTILITY FUNCTIONS

After reading the unidimensional case in Chapter 4, it should come as no surprise to the reader that we feel that we cannot identify a series of steps that, when followed, will result in a properly assessed multiattribute utility function. As in the previous case, the process requires a good deal of foresight and improvisation. Before assessing any preferences or utilities, we assume that the analyst (or interrogator) has properly set the stage for the decision maker or his delegated expert. In particular, we assume that the respondent realizes the purpose of the exercise and is sufficiently motivated to think hard about his feelings for the various consequences.

It is at this point that we begin to assess his utility function. As with the one-attribute case, the assessment procedure can be segmented for discussion purposes to highlight various aspects that must be completed. Although our discussion will focus on two-attribute utility functions, the basic ideas are relevant to all multiattribute utility assessments. The sequence we might follow in determining a utility function can be described in five stages:

1. Introducing the terminology and ideas.
2. Identifying relevant independence assumptions.
3. Assessing conditional utility functions or isopreference curves.
4. Assessing the scaling constants.
5. Checking for consistency and reiterating.

5.8.1 Introducing the Terminology and Ideas*

Suppose we have structured the decision problem and specified two attributes Y and Z, which are adequate to describe the consequences.

---

* In Section 4.9, we discussed an assessment procedure for assessing single-attribute utility functions. The preliminaries to assessment were essentially the same as those discussed in this subsection, since the purpose in both cases is to make sure the decision maker understands the process and its motivation. The basic ideas are included here to make this section a complete unit.

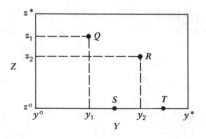

Fig. 5.15. A two-attribute consequence space.

Then we must assess a utility function over all possible (y, z) consequences. A consequence space should be illustrated* as in Fig. 5.15 as a
graphical aid to the decision maker.

Before any assessments are made, it should be clear to the decision
maker that the preferences we are interested in are his. It must be
understood that there are no objectively correct preferences, that the
preferences of importance represent the subjective feelings of the decision maker. At any time if the decision maker feels uncomfortable with any
of the information he has offered about his subjective feelings, it is
perfectly all right—in fact, it is necessary for a correct analysis—for him
to change his mind. This is one of the purposes of a utility analysis, that
is, to help the decision maker think hard about his preferences and
hopefully straighten them out in his mind.

Now, the analyst—let's assume this role for ourselves—must make sure
that the decision maker understands the consequence-space representation
of Fig. 5.15. By consequence Q we mean the consequence where $y = y_1$
and $z = z_1$. Then we might ask what is meant by consequence R. The
answer, of course, is $y = y_2$ and $z = z_2$. The decision maker should realize
the directions in which y and z increase in Fig. 5.15.

Next, it is helpful to limit the region over which we must assess
preferences to as small a region as possible. From our earlier involvement
in structuring the problem with the decision maker, we should already
know the maximum and minimum amounts that both y and z could
assume. Then we would choose a y^o, y^*, z^o, and z^* such that for all
possible (y, z),

$$y^o \leq y \leq y^* \quad \text{and} \quad z^o \leq z \leq z^*.$$

---

* The figures and examples in the text in this section concern scalar attributes in order to
simplify the presentation. All of the suggestions do generalize for vector attributes, although
clearly the problem then becomes more involved.

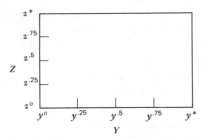

Fig. 5.16. A graphical aid for verifying additive independence conditions.

The values should be chosen for convenience and meaningfulness to the decision maker. For instance, if y ranged from 0 to 8.75 in the specific units, we might define $y^o = 0$ and $y^* = 10$. A value of $y^* = 10,000$, for example, probably would have little meaning to the decision maker. The preferences that we eventually assess must only be those for consequences (y, z) with $y^o \leq y \leq y^*$ and $z^o \leq z \leq z^*$. This is the region shown in Fig. 5.15.

As a final check on the decision maker's understanding of the consequence space representation, we might ask him whether or not he prefers consequence T to consequence S in Fig. 5.15. The points S and T should be chosen such that it is clear to us, the analyst, that the decision maker would almost for sure prefer a particular one. If the decision maker's preference in this case agreed with the expected result, we could proceed to more difficult questions. If not, the decision maker's reasoning should be pursued, and perhaps the familiarization process should be repeated, in part or in full.

Enough has been said about the preliminaries. The basic idea is to acquaint the decision maker with the framework that we use in assessing his utility function.

5.8.2 Identifying Relevant Independence Assumptions

Here we discuss procedures to verify whether Y and Z are additive independent and if either attribute is utility independent of the other.

ADDITIVE INDEPENDENCE. Suppose we wish to assess preferences over the consequence space $y^o \leq y \leq y^*$ and $z^o \leq z \leq z^*$ as shown in Fig. 5.16. As defined in Section 5.3, Y and Z are additive independent if and only if the lotteries

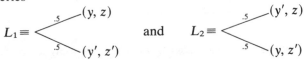

are indifferent for all amounts of y, z given a specific y', z'. So the obvious method to verify additive independence is to select a y' and z' and see if indifference between L_1 and L_2 holds for some (y, z) pairs.

Practically speaking, if Y and Z are divided into four equal subsections by $\{y^o, y^{.25}, y^{.5}, y^{.75}, y^*\}$ and $\{z^o, z^{.25}, z^{.5}, z^{.75}, z^*\}$, respectively, as indicated in Fig. 5.16, and if L_1 is indifferent to L_2 for each possible (y, z) pair taken from these two groups of five, then it seems justified to assume that Y and Z are additive independent.

An alternative procedure to check for additive independence involves first trying to verify that Y and Z are mutually independent.

Recall that mutual utility independence is a necessary but not a sufficient condition for additive independence. If Y and Z are mutually utility independent, they are additive independent if there exists a y_1, y_2, z_1, and z_2 such that

$$L_3 \equiv \overset{.5 \quad (y_1, z_1)}{\underset{.5 \quad (y_2, z_2)}{<}} \quad \text{and} \quad L_4 \equiv \overset{.5 \quad (y_1, z_2)}{\underset{.5 \quad (y_2, z_1)}{<}}$$

are equally desirable, where neither (y_1, z_2) or (y_2, z_1) are indifferent to (y_1, z_1). On the other hand, if there exist any L_3 and L_4 so that they are not indifferent, then clearly additive independence cannot hold.

UTILITY INDEPENDENCE. Again, suppose we have two scalar attributes, Y and Z, and wish to assess preferences over $y^o \leq y \leq y^*$ and $z^o \leq z \leq z^*$ as shown in Fig. 5.17. The letters P, Q, R, S, and so on designate consequences referred to in the discussion.

To verify whether Y is utility independent of Z, begin by asking the decision maker if he prefers $\langle P, Q \rangle$, a lottery yielding either P or Q with equal probability, or S. The consequence S is chosen so a particular answer is expected. Suppose the decision maker prefers $\langle P, Q \rangle$ to S and

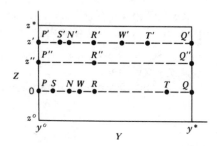

Fig. 5.17. A graphical aid for verifying whether Y is utility independent of Z.

this agrees with our expectations. Then we ask the decision maker whether he prefers $\langle P, Q \rangle$ or T, where T is chosen so that we expect T is preferred to $\langle P, Q \rangle$. Next, we inquire about the preferences of $\langle P, Q \rangle$ relative to W. Since W is "near to" S, we somewhat expect that $\langle P, Q \rangle$ will be preferred to W, but perhaps not. This convergence procedure is continued to consequence R defined such that $\langle P, Q \rangle$ and R are equally desirable (or undesirable) to the decision maker. Thus, R is a certainty equivalent for the lottery $\langle P, Q \rangle$.

If the decision maker indicates any preferences that we do not feel are consistent with his "true" preferences, this should be pointed out and discussed again.

Notice from Fig. 5.17 that consequences P, Q, R, S, T, and W all had a common amount of Z and only differed in their amount of Y. Now we move our concentration to the set of consequences with a different amount of Z in common (e.g., z') and ask similar questions. First we want to determine whether or not the decision maker prefers T' to $\langle P', Q' \rangle$. To avoid a repetition of the previous answers without thinking about the current questions, T' should be chosen such that the amount of Y, and not only the amount of Z, in T and T' are different. Suppose the decision maker prefers T' to $\langle P', Q' \rangle$. Then we ask about his preferences between $\langle P', Q' \rangle$ and S', between $\langle P', Q' \rangle$ and W', and eventually determine R' such that $\langle P', Q' \rangle$ is indifferent to R' for the decision maker. If R' and R have a common amount of Y (i.e., R' lies directly above R in Fig. 5.17), then we begin to think Y might be utility independent of Z. What we have so far determined is that the relative preferences of P, Q, and R and the relative preferences of P', Q', and R' are the same.

Again we repeat the procedure for another amount of Z (e.g., z'') and hopefully find that R'', a certainty equivalent for $\langle P'', Q'' \rangle$, has a common amount of Y with R and R'. If this is the case, we can feel reasonably confident that Y is utility independent of Z. The assumption can be further checked following the same procedure to determine a consequence N indifferent to $\langle P, R \rangle$ and a consequence N' indifferent to $\langle P', R' \rangle$, for example. If Y is utility independent of Z, then N and N' must have a common amount of Y.

Finally, we ask the decision maker: if

(i) $\langle (y^*, z'), (y^\circ, z') \rangle$ is indifferent to (y', z'), and
(ii) $\langle (y^*, z''), (y^\circ, z'') \rangle$ is indifferent to (y', z''),

then can we conclude that

$$\langle (y^*, z), (y^\circ, z) \rangle \text{ is indifferent to } (y', z) \text{ for all } z?$$

The answer must be "Yes" if Y is to be utility independent of Z. Finally, for any arbitrary y_1, y_2, and y_3, if $\langle (y_1, z), (y_2, z) \rangle$ is indifferent to (y_3, z) for a particular value of z, will the same relation hold for all possible values of Z? A "Yes" answer to this definitely implies that Y is utility independent of Z.

Another way of verifying that Y is utility independent of Z might go as follows.

"Consider a 50–50 lottery between y_1 and y_2 for a fixed level of z, for example, $z = z_1$," our analyst asks the decision maker. "Look at the figure on the page in front of you. Now think hard about what y amount you would want for certain, *always* keeping z_1 fixed, so that you are indifferent between the certainty amount and the 50–50 lottery. Reflect on this problem for a while" . . . . "O.K.," the analyst continues, "Now when you were thinking about your break-even y, was it important to you to keep in mind the level of z? Suppose we let $z = z_2$ instead of z_1—would it have made any difference?"

Now if the answer was "No, it would not," then the analyst should check with the respondent whether this could be assumed to be generally the case if y_1 and y_2 were changed and if z_1 and z_2 were changed. If this is verified, then we could assume that Y is utility independent of Z.

If, in our original set of questions, we found that R and R' did not have a common amount of Y, then assuming R and R' correctly represented the decision maker's preferences, Y could not be utility independent of Z. However, since utility independence is not reflexive, Z may yet be utility independent of Y. Even if this is not so, if the amounts of Y in R and R' are "reasonably" close to each other, we might approximate the true utility function by assuming Y to be utility independent of Z and assessing a utility function accordingly.

Suppose we label the certainty equivalent of the lottery $\langle (y', z), (y'', z) \rangle$ by $(\hat{y}_z, z)$. Often, in practice, the decision maker might feel there is a slight dependence of $\hat{y}_z$ on z but it might be a convenient "lie" to set $\hat{y}_z$ equal to a fixed value for all z *provided* that the *relevant* range of z is small. Therefore, in practice, it is often crucially important to be able to restrict the range set of an attribute such as Z. One way of achieving this restriction is by eliminating acts that are dominated or "practically" dominated by others. By restricting the domain of Z, we can make an idealized abstraction—or lie—such as, Y *is utility independent of* Z more palatable. This issue was discussed in Subsection 5.6.6.

5.8.3   Assessing Conditional Utility Functions

The conditional utility functions $u_Y(\cdot)$ over Y and $u_Z(\cdot)$ over Z may be either multidimensional or unidimensional. That is, the arguments y and z, respectively, may be vectors or scalars. If they are vectors, hopefully we can further decompose the utility function using the independence properties discussed in this and the next chapter in order to decrease the dimensionality of utility functions which must be directly assessed. If this is not possible, then some of the ideas of Sections 5.1 or 5.7 must be utilized.

On the other hand if the conditional utility functions are unidimensional, then the procedures discussed in Chapter 4 are appropriate. If this is the case, and if the previously suggested procedure to verify utility independence was used, then we already have a number of certainty equivalents, which are appropriate in assessing the conditional utility functions. Obviously, this information, and any other obtained in verifying independence assumptions, should be utilized wherever possible.

5.8.4   Assessing the Scaling Constants

In all the models in this chapter, the form of the utility function $u(y, z)$ has been specified in terms of a number of conditional utility functions over either Y or Z and scaling constants. For example, with the multilinear utility function discussed in Section 5.4,

$$u(y, z) = k_Y u_Y(y) + k_Z u_Z(z) + k_{YZ} u_Y(y) u_Z(z), \qquad (5.71)$$

there is one conditional utility function for each of Y and Z and three scaling constants: k_Y, k_Z, and k_{YZ}. Both of the utility functions in (5.71) can be scaled from 0 to 1 since the scaling constants are used to insure internal consistency.

The basic idea for evaluating the three scaling constants is to obtain a set of three independent equations with three unknowns, which are then solved to obtain the k's. These equations can be generated from certainty considerations, probabilistic considerations, or a combination of both. For example, using certainty scaling, if consequences (y_1, z_1) and (y_2, z_2) are indifferent, then equating these utilities using (5.71), we have

$$k_Y u_Y(y_1) + k_Z u_Z(z_1) + k_{YZ} u_Y(y_1) u_Z(z_1) = k_Y u_Y(y_2) + k_Z u_Z(z_2)$$
$$+ k_{YZ} u_Y(y_2) u_Z(z_2). \qquad (5.72)$$

Both u_Y and u_Z are known, since we are assuming they have already been assessed, so (5.72) is one equation with at most three unknowns. Using probabilistic scaling, suppose (y_3, z_3) is indifferent to the lottery $\langle (y_1, z_1); p; (y_2, z_2) \rangle$, which yields (y_1, z_1) with probability p and (y_2, z_2) with the complementary probability $1 - p$. Then, equating expected utilities,

$$u(y_3, z_3) = p u(y_1, z_1) + (1 - p) u(y_2, z_2), \qquad (5.73)$$

which, when combined with (5.71), yields an equation involving k_Y, k_Z, and k_{YZ} as the only unknowns. Clearly, using either or both certainty and probabilistic scaling, we can generate three independent equations with the three k's as unknowns. Let us illustrate this.

Consider again the multilinear utility function (5.71) where the origins of u, u_Y, and u_Z are

$$u(y^o, z^o) = 0, \qquad u_Y(y^o) = 0, \qquad \text{and} \qquad u_Z(z^o) = 0. \qquad (5.74)$$

And suppose we are interested in preferences over the consequence space where $y^o \le y \le y^*$ and $z^o \le z \le z^*$. For illustration purposes, let us further assume that preferences are increasing in both Y and Z so the utility functions can be scaled by

$$u(y^*, z^*) = 1, \qquad u_Y(y^*) = 1, \qquad \text{and} \qquad u_Z(z^*) = 1. \qquad (5.75)$$

Using (5.75) to evaluate (5.71) at (y^*, z^*), we find, for consistency, that

$$1 = k_Y + k_Z + k_{YZ}. \qquad (5.76)$$

Furthermore evaluating (5.71) at (y^*, z^o) and (y^o, z^*), respectively, gives us

$$u(y^*, z^o) = k_Y \qquad \text{and} \qquad u(y^o, z^*) = k_Z. \qquad (5.77)$$

As a starter, let us first try to see which is larger: k_Y or k_Z? This could be done, for instance, by asking the decision maker whether he preferred (y^*, z^o) or (y^o, z^*). From (5.77), if the former is preferred, then $k_Y > k_Z$; if the latter is preferred, then $k_Z > k_Y$; and if they are indifferent, then $k_Y = k_Z$. Suppose we find $k_Y > k_Z$. Then we can look for an amount y' such that decision maker is indifferent between (y', z^o) and (y^o, z^*). Equating their utilities using (5.71) yields

$$k_Z = k_Y u_Y(y'), \qquad (5.78)$$

where $u_Y(y')$ is known. To help the decision maker identify y', we might present him with a specific choice between (y, z^o) and (y^o, z^*) with y fixed. If the first consequence were preferred to the second, y would be decreased and the binary choice reoffered; if the second consequence were preferred, y would be increased and the procedure repeated. With this approach, one should soon converge to y'. Equation (5.78) is the result of certainty scaling.

For an example of probabilistic scaling, suppose that, using techniques discussed in Chapter 4, we assessed the indifference probability π_Y, so that (y^*, z^o) is indifferent to $\langle (y^*, z^*); \pi_Y; (y^o, z^o) \rangle$. Using (5.71) and equating expected utilities, we find

$$k_Y = \pi_Y. \qquad (5.79)$$

The system of (5.76), (5.78), and (5.79) has three unknowns, which can be solved for k_Y, k_Z, and k_{YZ}. For $\pi_Y = .5$ and $u_Y(y') = .8$, we easily conclude that

$$k_Y = .5, \qquad k_Z = .4, \qquad \text{and} \qquad k_{YZ} = .1. \tag{5.80}$$

Let us generalize the ideas here. All our two-attribute formulations in this chapter express $u(y, z)$ in terms of conditional utility functions over the individual attributes and scaling constants. Thus, if there are N and M conditional utility functions over Y and Z, respectively, and if there are R scaling constants, we can write

$$u(y, z) = f[u_Y^1(y), \ldots, u_Y^N(y), u_Z^1(z), \ldots, u_Z^M(z), k_1, k_2, \ldots, k_R]. \tag{5.81}$$

where f is specified. The utility functions in (5.81) can all be scaled from 0 to 1 since the scaling constants provide overall consistency.

Thus to evaluate the R scaling constants, we must generate R independent equations and solve. As illustrated, each equation can be generated from certainty considerations or probabilistic considerations.

One operational problem of concern is how to avoid redundancy in the equations. In practice, our understanding of the problem and knowledge of the functional form of the utility function are probably the best guards against a large number of redundant equations. When a redundancy does occur, we need to empirically generate another equation that is not redundant to substitute for a redundant one. To illustrate this, let us return to the preceding example.

Suppose that after (5.78) had been determined, we assessed a y'' and z'' such that (y'', z^o) and (y^o, z'') were equally desirable. Then, equating expected utilities,

$$k_Y u_Y(y'') = k_Z u_Z(z''). \tag{5.82}$$

Clearly (5.76), (5.78), and (5.82) are three equations with three unknowns, but (5.78) and (5.82) are not independent of each other. Both are concerned with setting the scaling between u_Y and u_Z. To get around this, we can obviously use probabilistic scaling as we did in the original example. If we preferred to use certainty scaling, we could assess y'' so that (y'', z^*) is indifferent to (y^*, z^o). Then, of course,

$$k_Y = k_Y u_Y(y'') + k_Z + k_{YZ} u_Y(y''), \tag{5.83}$$

where $u_Y(y'')$ is known. Now (5.83) is independent of both (5.78) and (5.82). So, for example, (5.76), (5.78), and (5.83) can be solved for k_Y, k_Z, and k_{YZ}, and (5.82) can be used to check the consistency of the resulting $u(y, z)$.

5.8.5 Checking for Consistency and Reiterating

There are many different consistency checks that can be used to detect errors in the decision maker's utility function. By an error, we mean that the utility function that we have assessed for him does not represent his preferences when it is tested by hypothetical examples. Three such consistency checks are suggested in this section. With these as a guide, the decision analyst should have no trouble developing other checks designed to uncover discrepancies in the utility function.

One method to check the validity of a utility function involves paired comparisons of various consequences. Concerning a utility function $u(y, z)$, we might ask the decision maker if he prefers (y_1, z_1) to (y_2, z_2). If so, then $u(y_1, z_1)$ should be greater than $u(y_2, z_2)$ to be consistent. This type of check can be repeated as many times as it is felt useful. It might be wise to start with some easy comparisons and work up to more difficult ones. This acquaints the decision maker with the technique before really pressing his judgment for difficult choices among consequences.

A more systematic way of doing this would be to use the u function on $Y \times Z$ to generate a family of indifference curves in the $Y \times Z$ plane—we are assuming here, of course, that Y and Z are each unidimensional. Then the decision maker could reflect whether these indifference curves seem reasonable to him.

Another check on the utility function is to determine empirically whether the decision maker is risk averse on positive rays of the form (y, cy) where $c > 0$. We might ask him what consequence (y_1, cy_1) is indifferent to $\langle (y_2, cy_2), (y_3, cy_3) \rangle$. For the case where $u(y, cy)$ is increasing in y, if y_1 is less than $(y_2 + y_3)/2$, we might expect he is ray risk averse. From Section 4.4, we have the theory to determine if the decision maker is risk averse on this and any other positive rays. If we do decide he is ray risk averse, for the case where preferences are increasing in Y and Z, then using the theory in Section 4.5, it should be clear that to be consistent $u'(y, cy)$ must be positive and $u''(y, cy)$ negative for all y, where u' and u'' denote first and second derivatives with respect to Y. If he is not ray risk averse, then obviously $u(y, z)$ should not possess ray risk aversion.

In cases where the utility function is of a special form, a particular consistency check may be applicable. For example, if $u(y, z)$ is of the multilinear form (5.16) of our preceding example, we can choose any y_1, y_2, z_1, and z_2 such that

$$u(y_2, z_0) > u(y_1, z_0), \tag{5.84a}$$

and

$$u(y_0, z_2) > u(y_0, z_1), \tag{5.84b}$$

and check the sign of parameter k_{YZ} in the following manner. We ask the decision maker whether he prefers $L_1 \equiv \langle (y_2, z_2), (y_1, z_1) \rangle$ or $L_2 \equiv \langle (y_2, z_1), (y_1, z_2) \rangle$. If L_1 is preferred to L_2, then k_{YZ} must be positive; if the lotteries are indifferent, k_{YZ} must be zero, and if L_2 is preferred to L_1 then k_{YZ} should be negative. Also, if L_1 is preferred to L_2 for any set of y_1, y_2, z_1, and z_2 satisfying (5.84), it must hold for all such sets satisfying (5.84). More is said concerning this point in Section 5.4.

In practice, the imagination of the analyst will not be strained in an attempt to develop efficient and effective consistency checks. And, as mentioned before, if the consistency checks produce discrepancies with the previous preferences indicated by the decision maker, these discrepancies must be called to his attention and parts of the assessment procedure should be repeated to acquire consistent preferences. Once we obtain a utility function that the decision maker and the analyst feel represents the true preferences of the decision maker, we may proceed with the analysis. Of course, if the respondent has strong, crisp, unalterable views on all questions and if these are inconsistent, then we would be in a mess, wouldn't we? In practice, however, the respondent usually feels fuzzier about some of his answers than others, and it is this degree of fuzziness that usually makes a world of difference. For it then becomes usually possible to generate a final coherent set of responses that does not violently contradict any strongly held feelings. Finally, if the decision maker and his analyst remain a bit squeamish about accepting any "compromise" utility function, then they can always embark on a sensitivity analysis.

5.9 INTERPRETING THE SCALING CONSTANTS

It is not easy to interpret the scaling constants since they depend on the choices of y^o, y^*, z^o, and z^* which depend on the possible consequences of the problem. Let us illustrate our discussion with the additive function

$$u(y, z) = k_Y u_Y(y) + k_Z u_Z(z), \qquad (5.85)$$

where

$$u(y^o, z^o) = 0, \qquad u_Y(y^o) = 0, \qquad u_Z(z^o) = 0, \qquad (5.86)$$

and

$$u(y^*, z^*) = 1, \qquad u_Y(y^*) = 1, \qquad u_Z(z^*) = 1. \qquad (5.87)$$

Then, for consistency, clearly

$$k_Y + k_Z = 1. \qquad (5.88)$$

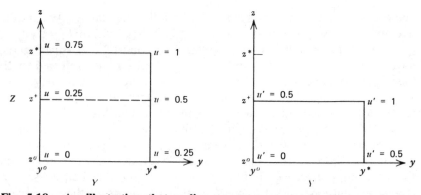

Fig. 5.18. An illustration that scaling constants cannot be interpreted as an indicator of attribute importance.

If we have assessed $k_Y = .25$ and $k_Z = .75$, we *cannot* say that Z is three times as important as Y. In fact, we cannot conclude that attribute Z is more important than Y. Going one step further, it is not clear how we would precisely define the concept that one attribute is more important than another. We can say, however, that starting from the point (y^o, z^o), if we would rather change z^o to z^* than change y^o to y^*, then $k_Z > k_Y$, and vice versa. If, for instance, y^o and y^* are close together, meaning the range of Y is relatively small, then k_Y may be small but still the Y attribute may be mighty important. Changing the range of y^o to y^* will necessarily change the value of k_Y. Because of the consistency condition (5.88), the scaling constant k_Z will also change. To better illustrate the point suppose, in comparing jobs, attribute Y refers to monetary rewards and all jobs under consideration pay almost the same amount, so y^o and y^* are close together; then k_Y may be small but this does not mean that money is unimportant to the decision maker. As y^o and y^* become closer and closer, the value of k_Y approaches zero. Clearly when using an additive utility function in such situations, the pay would have little influence on the final choice of a job, but we can still not conclude that money is not important.

To illustrate the point graphically, consider Fig. 5.18, which exhibits two consequence spaces,* both of which could be used to evaluate the same problem provided all possible consequences fell within the smaller of the two. Furthermore, suppose the additive utility function is appropriate. If the utility function $u(y, z)$ scaled from 0 to 1 is assessed over (y, z) for $y^o \le y \le y^*$ and $z^o \le z \le z^*$, we might find, for instance, that

$$u(y, z) = k_Y u_Y(y) + k_Z u_Z(z) \qquad (5.89)$$

---

*For simplicity, we assume that preferences are increasing in both Y and Z.

where $k_Y = .25$, $k_Z = .75$, and u_Y and u_Z are also both scaled 0 to 1. And since $u_Z(z^+)$ must fall between 0 and 1, let us assume it is 1/3. Therefore, from (5.89), note that

$$u(y^o, z^+) = u(y^*, z^o) = .25. \tag{5.90}$$

Now suppose that we had originally decided to assess preferences over (y, z), where $y^o \leq y \leq y^*$ and $z^o \leq z \leq z^+$ using $u'(y, z)$. The additive utility function

$$u'(y, z) = k'_Y u'_Y(y) + k'_Z u'_Z(z), \tag{5.91}$$

where each of the utility functions can be scaled by

$$u'(y^o, z^o) = 0, \qquad u'_Y(y^o) = 0, \qquad u'_Z(z^o) = 0 \tag{5.92}$$

and

$$u'(y^*, z^+) = 1, \qquad u'_Y(y^*) = 1, \qquad u'_Z(z^+) = 1, \tag{5.93}$$

then holds. For consistency, clearly

$$1 = k'_Y + k'_Z \tag{5.94}$$

and since (y^o, z^+) and (y^*, z^o) are indifferent from (5.90), utilities can be equated using (5.91), (5.92), and (5.93) to yield

$$k'_Y = k'_Z. \tag{5.95}$$

Combining (5.94) and (5.95), we see that

$$k'_Y = k'_Z = .5.$$

Now if we insist on interpreting the scaling constants as indicators of the importance of their respective attributes, then obviously from u, we must conclude that Z is three times as important as Y. And for the exact same attributes, using u', we conclude that Y and Z are equally important. This may be overemphasizing the point that scaling constants *do not* indicate the relative importance of attributes, but because this misinterpretation is so common, we thought a little overindulgence might be in order.

5.10 THE ASSESSMENT OF A UTILITY FUNCTION IN A HOSPITAL BLOOD BANK*

This section ties together the ideas of this chapter and illustrates our method for assessing multiattribute utility functions. This is done using a

---

* Several parts of this section were adapted from Keeney (1972b).

specific problem—one concerned with blood bank inventory control. The suggestions of Section 5.8 are followed in assessing the preferences of the decision maker in a hospital blood bank over the shortage–outdating consequence space. Although the example involves only two attributes, the general method described is applicable to a wide range of problems requiring multiattribute utility functions. Additional examples are discussed in Chapters 7, 8, and 9.

5.10.1   The Blood Bank Inventory Control Problem

To motivate the assessment of the utility function presented below, we briefly discuss the blood bank inventory control problem, and formulate it in the decision-theoretic framework. Jennings (1968) developed a detailed model of a whole-blood inventory system for a blood bank in a hospital and examined the control of such a system. Various operating policies were evaluated in terms of blood shortage and blood outdating. Shortage is the blood requested by a doctor that could not be assigned from the hospital inventory. In this situation, a special order for the particular type of blood is placed with a central blood bank, professional donors may have to be called, an operation may have to be postponed, and so on, but only in extremely rare circumstances would a death result from shortage as defined here. Outdated blood is the blood not used during its legal lifetime, which currently is 21 days in most hospitals.

One basic decision that must be made in hospital blood banks is what type of daily inventory ordering policy is best for each of the blood types. In this section the problem is analyzed for any one blood type. The decision maker must choose among the courses of action denoted by A_i where $i = 1, 2, \ldots, n$. For each A_i there is a probability distribution for consequences described in terms of Y and Z, which represent shortage and outdating, respectively. More specifically, shortage can be stated in terms of yearly percent of units demanded and not filled from stock, and outdating can be measured in terms of yearly percent of units that outdate. The probability distributions can be obtained by simulation using a model such as Jennings' and from empirical records kept by the blood bank.

The structure of the inventory problem is illustrated in Fig. 5.19, where the notation $(\tilde{y}_i, \tilde{z}_i)$ is used to designate the uncertain consequence of act A_i. The decision maker should choose an act based on the assessed probability distributions of the paired random variables and his preferences for the various consequences.

A PERSPECTIVE.   The experiences recounted below are those of one author (Keeney) who contacted the doctor in charge of the blood bank at

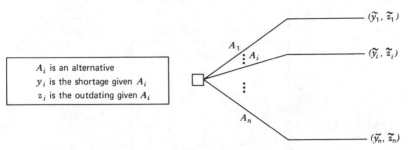

Fig. 5.19. The blood bank problem.

the Cambridge Hospital in Cambridge, Massachusetts. As part of a doctoral dissertation concerned with utility independence and assessing utility functions, the main purpose of the visit was to see whether the property of utility independence could be exploited in assessing utility functions. Thus certain approaches that an analyst might take on a consulting assignment were not followed. Aside from considerations of whether the problem was the "real problem," and so on, we cite two major shortcomings of this work if it had been a consulting assignment. (1) No attempt was made to exploit the value structure, using ideas such as those discussed in Chapter 3, before diving headfirst into the utility structure with probabilistic questioning. (2) Practically no concern was given to whether the decision maker was assessing preferences by considering only impacts to herself, or whether she included her perceived viewpoint of the impacts to patients, doctors, the hospital, and the public.

Notwithstanding the above facts, we do feel that the process of assessment described below does provide a good indication of the general procedure.

5.10.2   Assessing the Utility Function

INTRODUCING THE TERMINOLOGY AND IDEAS.   On a first visit, Jennings' work was discussed with the doctor and the nurse in charge of ordering blood, and the importance of assessing preferences over the shortage-outdating space was indicated. On a subsequent visit the preferences of the nurse were assessed.* In the interim, she had read Jennings (1968) and developed a good understanding of the purpose of the interviews. Before

---

* The nurse's preferences were used since she had responsibility for ordering whole blood for the blood bank. As indicated, the issue of whether her preferences appropriately represent those of the doctors and patients is ignored. Presumably, the nurse's preferences are influenced by her perceived preferences of the community served by the blood bank.

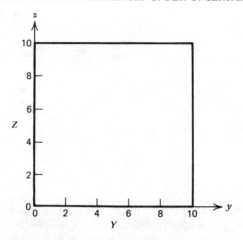

Fig. 5.20. The shortage-outdating consequence space.

assessing the preferences, the purpose of utility theory was explained to the decision maker, and the meanings of the chosen measures of effectiveness were made clear. Thus, the decision maker realized the purpose of assessing her preferences and was motivated sufficiently to think hard about her feelings concerning the various consequences.

Before assessing her preferences, it was determined that the shortage would never exceed 10 percent of the units demanded and that outdating would not exceed 10 percent of the total units stocked during a year. Thus the consequence space was limited, as shown in Fig. 5.20. A check was made to ensure that the decision maker knew what was meant by a point (y, z) in the consequence space. When it was clear that the decision maker completely understood the basic ideas, it was possible to begin assessing preferences. At this time, it was stressed that there were no objectively correct or incorrect answers to the questions that would be asked.

VERIFYING RELEVANT INDEPENDENCE ASSUMPTIONS. It was necessary to check whether Y (shortage) was utility independent of Z (outdating). This was done with the aid of Fig. 5.21 where $P, Q, R, S, \ldots$ represent consequences. And as before, the notation $\langle P, Q \rangle$ will mean a lottery yielding either P or Q with equal probability. The decision maker was asked if she preferred $\langle P, Q \rangle$ or S. The consequences S was chosen by the questioner to make the question relatively simple. She preferred S, as one would intuitively expect. Next she was asked to choose between $\langle P, Q \rangle$ and T, and she chose $\langle P, Q \rangle$; this also was a relatively easy question.

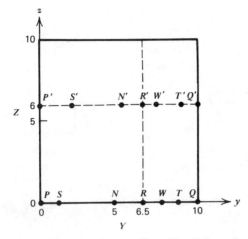

Fig. 5.21.   Test used to verify utility independence.

Progressively more difficult questions were posed about preferences be-tween $\langle P, Q \rangle$ and N, $\langle P, Q \rangle$ and W, and so on, and eventually her preferences "converged" to the fact that $\langle (0, 0), (10, 0) \rangle$ was indifferent to $(6.5, 0)$. Then the same types of questions were repeated using $\langle P', Q' \rangle$ instead of $\langle P, Q \rangle$, and an indifference between $\langle (0, 6), (10, 6) \rangle$ and $(6.5, 6)$ was established. In fact, the decision maker stated that she did not see why the 6.5 *should* be different from the previous answer. In response to a general question she stated that the 'same was true for any level of Z held constant for all consequences. It was thus concluded that Y was utility independent of Z. In a similar manner, Z was found to be utility independent of Y. Thus, the attributes were mutually utility independent, and the multilinear utility function previously discussed was applicable.

ASSESSING CONDITIONAL UTILITY FUNCTIONS.   Next, a conditional utility function for $(y, 0)$ was assessed.* It was easy to establish that preference was monotonically decreasing in y. Previously the lottery $\langle (10, 0), (0, 0) \rangle$ was shown to be indifferent to $(6.5, 0)$. In addition $\langle (6.5, 0), (0, 0) \rangle$ was indifferent to $(4, 0)$, and $\langle (10, 0), (6.5, 0) \rangle$ to $(8.5, 0)$. Thus, it was felt that the conditional utility function for $(y, 0)$, which will be denoted by $u_Y(y, 0)$, was risk averse.

After arbitrarily setting the origin and unit of measure of $u_Y(y, 0)$ by

$$u_Y(0, 0) = 0 \tag{5.96}$$

* Less elliptically, we could say that a conditional utility function over the domain $\{(y, 0) : 0 \le y \le 10\}$ was assessed. Instead of $(y, 0)$ in the text, the purist might prefer $(\cdot, 0)$.

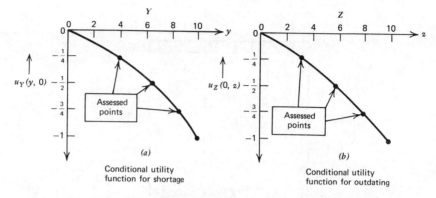

Fig. 5.22. The utility functions in the blood bank problem.

and

$$u_Y(10, 0) = -1, \qquad (5.97)$$

the points on the utility function were plotted as indicated in Fig. 5.22a. For simplicity, a utility function of the form $b(1 - e^{cy})$ was chosen. Using $\langle(10, 0), (0, 0)\rangle \sim (6.5, 0)$, the parameter c was specified. Parameter b was then determined using (5.97) giving the result

$$u_Y(y, 0) = \frac{1}{2.67}(1 - e^{.13y}) \qquad (5.98)$$

shown in the figure. This form fitted the other empirically assessed points very well. Since parameters b and c are positive, this utility function is monotonically decreasing and risk averse.

Similarly, in assessing $u_Z(0, z)$, the conditional utility function for Z, $\langle(0, 10), (0, 0)\rangle$, was found indifferent to $(0, 5.5)$, $\langle(0, 5.5), (0, 0)\rangle$ indifferent to $(0, 3)$, and $\langle(0, 10), (0, 5.5)\rangle$ indifferent to $(0, 8)$. Thus, by scaling

$$u_Z(0, 0) = 0 \qquad (5.99)$$

and

$$u_Z(0, 10) = -1, \qquad (5.100)$$

the points on the utility function shown in Fig. 5.22b were determined. Again, by fitting curves, this utility function was

$$u_Z(0, z) = \frac{1}{.492}(1 - e^{.04z}). \qquad (5.101)$$

ASSESSING THE SCALING CONSTANTS. The next step of the assessment involved the consistent scaling of $u_Y(y, 0)$ and $u_Z(0, z)$. It was determined that $(0, 10)$ was preferred to $(10, 0)$, $(2, 0)$ was preferred to $(0, 10)$, and finally that $(0, 10)$ was indifferent to $(4.75, 0)$. Now, it is possible to scale the utility function for (y, z), which will be denoted by $u(y, z)$, as follows. First, set

$$u(0, 0) = 0 \tag{5.102}$$

and

$$u(10, 10) = -1, \tag{5.103}$$

and define k_Y and k_Z by

$$u(10, 0) = k_Y \tag{5.104}$$

and

$$u(0, 10) = k_Z. \tag{5.105}$$

From (5.96), (5.97), (5.102), and (5.104), it follows that

$$u(y, 0) = -k_Y u_Y(y, 0). \tag{5.106}$$

Similarly, from (5.99), (5.100), (5.102), and (5.105),

$$u(0, z) = -k_Z u_Z(0, z). \tag{5.107}$$

Also, $u(4.75, 0) = u(0, 10)$ or, by substituting from (5.100), (5.106), and (5.107),

$$-k_Y u_Y(4.75, 0) = -k_Z u_Z(0, 10) = k_Z. \tag{5.108}$$

Using (5.98), $u_Y(4.75, 0) = -.32$, which can be substituted into (5.108) to yield

$$k_Z = .32 k_Y. \tag{5.109}$$

Because of mutual utility independence between Y and Z, $u(y, z)$ is of the form*

$$u(y, z) = u(y, 0) + u(0, z)$$
$$+ \frac{u(10, 10) - u(0, 10) - u(10, 0)}{u(10, 0)u(0, 10)} u(y, 0)u(0, z). \tag{5.110}$$

Substituting (5.98), (5.101), (5.106), (5.107), and (5.109) into (5.110), we find that

$$u(y, z) = \frac{-k_Y}{2.67}(1 - e^{.13y}) - \frac{.32k_Y}{.492}(1 - e^{.04z}) - \frac{(1 + 1.32k_Y)}{(2.67)(.492)}$$
$$\times (1 - e^{.13y})(1 - e^{.04z}). \tag{5.111}$$

---

* Proof of this result is identical to Theorem 5.2 with the scale of u from minus one to zero rather than zero to plus one as in the theorem.

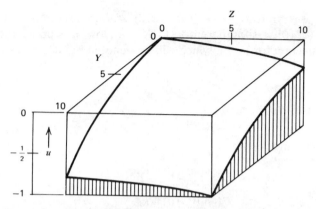

Fig. 5.23.   The utility function for shortage and outdating.

The only parameter needed in (5.111) to completely specify $u(x, y)$ is k_Y. To calculate k_Y it was established that the decision maker was indifferent between $\langle(10, 10), (0, 0)\rangle$ and $(6, 6)$. Then using (5.102) and (5.103),

$$u(6, 6) = \tfrac{1}{2}u(10, 10) + \tfrac{1}{2}u(0, 0) = -\tfrac{1}{2}. \qquad (5.112)$$

Equation (5.111) now can be evaluated at $(6, 6)$ and equated to (5.112) to yield

$$k_Y = -.87. \qquad (5.113)$$

We obtain the desired utility function, shown in Fig. 5.23, by substituting (5.113) into (5.111):

$$u(y, z) = .32(1 - e^{.13y}) + .57(1 - e^{.04z}) + .107(1 - e^{.13y})(1 - e^{.04z}). \qquad (5.114)$$

CHECKING FOR CONSISTENCY.   Two types of consistency checks were conducted on this utility function. First, an alternative procedure was used to determine whether the conditional utility functions were risk averse as previously found. The decision maker felt that $(i, 0)$ was preferred to $\langle(i+1, 0), (i-1, 0)\rangle$ for $i = 1, 2, \ldots, 9$, and thus $u(y, 0)$ was indeed risk averse. The same procedure resulted in a similar conclusion for $u(0, z)$.

The second check involved pairwise comparisons of consequences R, S, T, U, V, W, and P as defined in Fig. 5.24. In response to questioning, the decision maker said $R > S$, $T > R$, $U > R$, $V > W$, and $P > V$ where $>$ is read "is preferred to." In the table of Fig. 5.24, the utilities of these consequences, calculated using (5.114), are shown. A check shows them to be consistent with the decision maker's comparisons. This is true

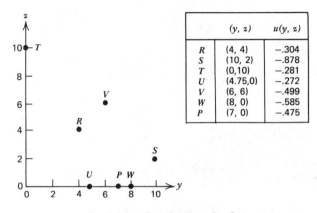

	(y, z)	$u(y, z)$
R	(4, 4)	−.304
S	(10, 2)	−.878
T	(0,10)	−.281
U	(4.75,0)	−.272
V	(6, 6)	−.499
W	(8, 0)	−.585
P	(7, 0)	−.475

Fig. 5.24.   Consistency checks.

despite the fact that only one of the comparisons was simple, that is, an almost obvious choice. The particular outcome of the pairwise comparisons is due, at least partially, to chance. Nevertheless, this method for checking consistency is important.

5.10.3   Conclusions

By exploiting general characteristics of the preferences structure, such as utility independence, some of the difficulties of obtaining multiattribute utility functions are overcome. This reduces the actual amount of subjective information needed to specify the utility function. The procedure described here is operational both for identifying the utility independence characteristics of the preference structure and for assessing the multiattribute utility function.

Two concluding observations of the assessment process are noteworthy. First, the decision maker was interested and enthusiastic about what was being done, and she was willing to think hard about her preferences. This cooperation allowed the assessment procedure to go very smoothly and resulted in a utility function that seemed to represent *her* preferences accurately. Second, the decision maker had a degree in liberal arts, along with her nursing credentials, but no formal education in the quantitative areas. This did not hinder the assessment in any way. We speculate from this that open-mindedness and willingness to think hard about the consequences are more important for correctly assessing preferences than any formal quantitative education.

Multiattribute Preferences Under Uncertainty: More Than Two Attributes

This chapter parallels that of Chapter 5 with the distinction that here we are concerned with multiattribute utility functions with more than two arguments. The problem discussed in this chapter (as well as in Chapter 5) was outlined in section 5.1. Also in that section we discussed procedures for assessing a multiattribute utility function *without* first specifying the functional form. As indicated there, these procedures are valid for two- and more-than-two-attribute problems. Therefore, we illustrate here how various sets of additive independence, preferential independence, and utility independence assumptions among the attributes X_i, $i = 1, \ldots, n$, imply a utility function of the form

$$u(x_1, x_2, \ldots, x_n) = f[u_1(x_1), u_2(x_2), \ldots, u_n(x_n)], \qquad (6.1)$$

where x_i is a specific amount of X_i, f is a scalar-valued function, and u_i is a utility function over X_i. These results generalize forms of (6.1) that have been derived for specific sets of preference assumptions by Fishburn (1965a, 1966, 1971), Keeney (1968, 1972a, 1974), Meyer (1970), Pollak (1967), and Raiffa (1969).

6.1 OVERVIEW OF THE CHAPTER

The results in this chapter are important for applications in that the assumptions are reasonable and operationally verifiable for many problems, and furthermore the assessment of the resulting utility function in

282

such a case is greatly simplified. Several fundamental theoretical relationships between various independence conditions are also presented. These have practical importance in that they provide us with simpler sets of necessary and/or sufficient conditions for specific functional forms of the utility function.

6.1.1 Notation

In this chapter, it is convenient to introduce a few new bits of notation to streamline the presentation. For reference, the important notation in this chapter is cataloged here:

ATTRIBUTES. The basic attributes in most of our constructions will be $X_1, X_2, \ldots, X_{n'}$ where X_i may be either a vector attribute or a scalar attribute. Beginning in Section 6.7, we introduce an additional attribute X_0, which plays a role that is distinct from the other X_i, $i = 1, 2, \ldots, n$.

SETS OF ATTRIBUTES. The set of attributes X is defined as $\{X_1, X_2, \ldots, X_n\}$. When we use X_0, it also is in X. If Y is a subset of X, we will refer to the set of attributes in Y simply as attribute Y.

COMPLEMENTARY SETS. If two sets of attributes, call them Y_1 and Y_2, partition X, then we will refer to Y_1 and Y_2 as complements of each other. Often the complement of Y will be written $\bar{Y}$.

PREFERENTIAL INDEPENDENCE AND UTILITY INDEPENDENCE. Instead of repeatedly saying that Y_1 is utility independent of its complement $\bar{Y}_1$ or that Y_2 is preferentially independent of its complement, we will write Y_1 is UI and Y_2 is PI, respectively. This is done when no ambiguity can result, and it should be understood that UI or PI is implied relative to the complement.

CONSEQUENCES. The consequence space $X_1 \times X_2 \times \cdots \times X_n$ represents a rectangular subset of finite-dimensional Euclidean space. Consequences are designated by $x \equiv (x_1, x_2, \ldots, x_n)$ where x_i designates a specific amount of X_i for $i = 1, 2, \ldots, n$. When referring to a subset Y of X and its complement $\bar{Y}$ we shall often designate x by $(y, \bar{y})$; thus, for example, if $n = 5$ and $Y = \{X_1, X_3\}$, then $y = (x_1, x_3)$ and $\bar{y} = (x_2, x_4, x_5)$.

UTILITY FUNCTIONS. As in previous chapters, we assume throughout Chapter 6 that a set of assumptions, such as von Neumann and Morgenstern's (1947), implying the existence of a utility function, are appropriate. The utility function u is assumed to be continuous in each x_i and bounded. We will write $u(x)$ or $u(x_1, x_2, \ldots, x_n)$ or $u(y, \bar{y})$ interchangeably.

284   MULTIATTRIBUTE PREFERENCES UNDER UNCERTAINTY

SCALING.   The symbol $x^* \equiv (x_1^*, x_2^*, \ldots, x_n^*) \equiv (y^*, \bar{y}^*)$ designates the most desirable consequence and $x^o \equiv (x_1^o, x_2^o, \ldots, x_n^o) \equiv (y^o, \bar{y}^o)$ designates the least desirable. The utility function is scaled by $u(x^o) = 0$ and $u(x^*) = 1$. Instead of repeating many superscript zeros, we sometimes take the liberty and write, for instance, $u(x_1, x_2^o, x_3^o, \ldots, x_n^o)$ and $u(x_1^o, x_2, x_3^o, x_4, x_5^o, x_6^o)$ as $u(x_1)$ and $u(x_2, x_4)$, respectively. That is, all attribute levels not explicitly denoted as arguments of a function are at their least desirable level. Granted, the symbolism is not entirely consistent, but the context should dispel any confusion. At least we hope so.

6.1.2 Independence Concepts

Now the concepts of preferential independence and utility independence introduced in previous chapters must be generalized.

Definition. Attribute Y, where $Y \subset X$, is preferentially independent of its complement $\bar{Y}$ if the preference order of *consequences* involving only changes in the levels in Y does not depend on the levels at which attributes in $\bar{Y}$ are held fixed.

Preferential independence implies that the conditional indifference curves over Y do not depend on attributes $\bar{Y}$. The concept concerns the decision maker's preferences for consequences where no uncertainty is involved. Symbolically, Y is PI if and only if for any consequences $y', y'', \bar{y}^+$,

$$(y', \bar{y}^+) \gtrsim (y'', \bar{y}^+) \Rightarrow (y', \bar{y}) \gtrsim (y'', \bar{y}), \quad \text{for all } \bar{y}. \quad (6.2)$$

Utility independence, on the other hand, concerns preferences for lotteries that do involve uncertainty.

Definition. Attribute Y is utility independent of its complement $\bar{Y}$ if the conditional preference order for *lotteries* involving only changes in the levels of attributes in Y does not depend on the levels at which attributes in $\bar{Y}$ are held fixed.

Symbolically, Y is UI if and only if for any lotteries $\tilde{y}', \tilde{y}''$, and consequence $\bar{y}^+$,

$$(\tilde{y}', \bar{y}^+) \gtrsim (\tilde{y}'', \bar{y}^+) \Rightarrow (\tilde{y}', \bar{y}) \gtrsim (\tilde{y}'', \bar{y}), \quad \text{for all } \bar{y}. \quad (6.3)$$

By definition, it follows that if Y is UI, then Y is PI. The converse is not necessarily true. This relationship can be seen by noting that degenerate lotteries, those involving no uncertainty, are the same things as a consequence. Hence, the preferential independence condition could be stated in terms of the preference order for degenerate lotteries only, and since the utility independence condition holds for all lotteries, the former is implied by the latter. Utility independence is the stronger condition.

If Y is preferentially independent of $\bar{Y}$, given utility function u it follows that

$$[u(y', \bar{y}^+) \geqslant u(y'', \bar{y}^+)] \Rightarrow [u(y', \bar{y}) \geqslant u(y'', \bar{y})], \qquad \text{for all } \bar{y}, \qquad (6.4)$$

where $\bar{y}^+$ is any fixed level of $\bar{y}$. Similarly, if Y is utility independent of $\bar{Y}$, then since utility functions are unique up to positive linear transformations

$$u(y, \bar{y}) = f(\bar{y}) + g(\bar{y})u(y, \bar{y}'), \qquad \text{for all } y \text{ and } \bar{y}, \qquad (6.5)$$

where g is always positive and $\bar{y}'$ is arbitrarily chosen specific amount of $\bar{Y}$. Functions f and g, in general, will depend on the specific value of $\bar{y}'$ but not on the variable y.

As indicated, throughout this chapter we choose for simplicity to scale the utility function from 0 to 1. Thus,

$$u(y^o, \bar{y}^o) = 0$$

and

$$u(y^*, \bar{y}^*) = 1,$$

where y^o and $\bar{y}^o$ are least preferred levels of Y and $\bar{Y}$ and y^* and $\bar{y}^*$ are the most preferred levels. Then, by evaluating (6.5) at y^o, we find

$$f(\bar{y}) = u(y^o, \bar{y}),$$

so condition (6.5) can be written as

$$u(y, \bar{y}) = u(y^o, \bar{y}) + g(\bar{y})u(y, \bar{y}^o), \qquad (6.6)$$

where we have chosen to set $\bar{y}'$ in (6.5) equal to $\bar{y}^o$. Equations (6.4) and (6.6) will be used in our proofs.*

6.1.3   Organization

The next section presents a number of representation theorems for three attributes. This (1) indicates some of the issues involved in assessing utility functions with more than two attributes, (2) illustrates the type of results to be expected, and (3) helps motivate the rest of the chapter. Functional forms of n-attribute utility functions that follow from various sets of preferential and utility independence conditions are presented in Sections 6.3–6.5, and assessment of such utility functions follows. Sections 6.7–6.10 generalize and tie together the concepts of preferential independence and utility independence. The extension of our results to

---

* Preferential independence and utility independence can be generalized to allow for reversals of preferences as indicated in Appendix 6A.

hierarchical structures of attributes using conditional preference assumptions is the topic of Section 6.11. An understanding of Sections 6.1–6.6, excluding proofs, should enable the reader to proceed to the later chapters.

6.2 UTILITY FUNCTIONS WITH THREE ATTRIBUTES

Here we state and illustrate four results concerning utility functions with three attributes. Proofs are not included since all of these results are special cases of theorems presented and proven later in this chapter. The results are stated with the most restrictive case (in the sense of the strength of the requisite assumptions) first, and then the second most restrictive, the third, and finally the most general case.

Result 1. If preferences over lotteries on X_1, X_2, and X_3 depend only on their marginal probability distributions for these attributes and not on their joint probability distribution, then

$$u(x_1, x_2, x_3) = k_1 u_1(x_1) + k_2 u_2(x_2) + k_3 u_3(x_3). \qquad (6.7)$$

This result is the additive utility function of three attributes. The utility functions u, u_1, u_2, and u_3 can all be scaled from 0 to 1 and the k_i's are scaling constants. Using a weaker set of assumptions, we have

Result 2. If X_1 is utility independent of $\{X_2, X_3\}$, and if $\{X_1, X_2\}$ and $\{X_1, X_3\}$ are preferentially independent of X_3 and X_2, respectively, then

$$u(x_1, x_2, x_3) = k_1 u_1(x_1) + k_2 u_2(x_2) + k_3 u_3(x_3)$$
$$+ kk_1 k_2 u_1(x_1) u_2(x_2) + kk_1 k_3 u_1(x_1) u_3(x_3)$$
$$+ kk_2 k_3 u_2(x_2) u_3(x_3) + k^2 k_1 k_2 k_3 u_1(x_1) u_2(x_2) u_3(x_3).$$
$$(6.8)$$

Each of u, the u_i's, and the k_i's in (6.8) have the same meaning as in (6.7). In addition, k is an additional scaling constant. Clearly if $k = 0$, then (6.8) reduces to the additive form (6.7). If $k \neq 0$, then by multiplying each side of (6.8) by k, adding 1, and factoring, we obtain the multiplicative utility function

$$ku(x_1, x_2, x_3) + 1 = \prod_{i=1}^{3} [kk_i u_i(x_i) + 1]. \qquad (6.9)$$

There are two important things to note about Result 2: it uses both utility independence and preferential independence assumptions, and these assumptions concern "overlapping" sets of attributes. Both of these characteristics are very important in specifying multiattribute utility functions with many attributes. Since we use the notation u_2 and u_3 in this result, we implicitly imply that it can be proved that X_2 and X_3 are each utility independent of its complementary set of attributes.

Becoming more general, we get

Result 3. If each of X_1, X_2, and X_3 are utility independent of their respective complements, then

$$u(x_1, x_2, x_3) = k_1 u_1(x_1) + k_2 u_2(x_2) + k_3 u_3(x_3)$$
$$+ k_{12} k_1 k_2 u_1(x_1) u_2(x_2) + k_{13} k_1 k_3 u_1(x_1) u_3(x_3)$$
$$+ k_{23} k_2 k_3 u_2(x_2) u_3(x_3) + k_{123} k_1 k_2 k_3 u_1(x_1) u_2(x_2) u_3(x_3).$$
$$(6.10)$$

Again, the utility functions u, u_1, u_2, and u_3 and the scaling constants k_1, k_2, and k_3 are defined as before. In addition, we need to assess the additional scaling constants k_{12}, k_{13}, k_{23}, and k_{123}. Expression (6.10) is referred to as the multilinear utility function in three attributes. It should be clear that both the multiplicative and additive utility functions are special cases of the multilinear.

As the most general case considered in this section we have

Result 4. If X_2 and X_3 are utility independent of their respective complements $\{X_1, X_3\}$ and $\{X_1, X_2\}$, then

$$u(x_1, x_2, x_3) = k_1 u_1(x_1) + f_2(x_1) u_2(x_2) + f_3(x_1) u_3(x_3)$$
$$+ f_{23}(x_1) u_2(x_2) u_3(x_3), \qquad (6.11)$$

where

$$f_2(x_1) = u(x_1, x_2^*, x_3^o) - u(x_1, x_2^o, x_3^o),$$
$$f_3(x_1) = u(x_1, x_2^o, x_3^*) - u(x_1, x_2^o, x_3^o),$$
$$f_{23}(x_1) = u(x_1, x_2^*, x_3^*) - u(x_1, x_2^*, x_3^o) - u(x_1, x_2^o, x_3^*) + u(x_1, x_2^o, x_3^o).$$

In (6.11), again each of the utility functions is scaled from 0 to 1, with (x_1^*, x_2^*, x_3^*) being the best consequence and (x_1^o, x_2^o, x_3^o) the worst. If f_2, f_3, and f_{23} are of certain forms, then it is easy to see that (6.7), (6.8), or (6.10) result, and thus the additive, multiplicative, and multilinear utility functions are all special cases of (6.11).

If we consider the attributes as scalar attributes, then we can graphically illustrate what must be empirically assessed using each of the above results. This is done in Fig. 6.1, where the dark lines and points indicate consequences which must be assessed on a common scale.

The remainder of this chapter develops results for n-attribute utility

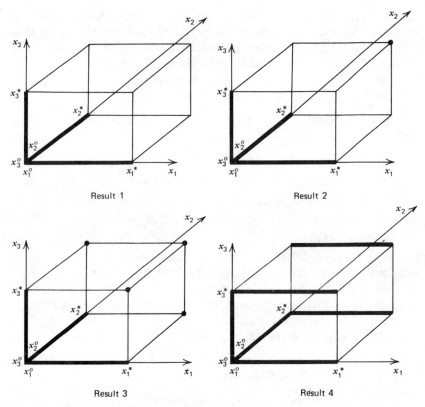

Fig. 6.1. Empirical assessment required to specify certain three-attribute utility functions.

functions similar to those in this section. Once there are three or more attributes, it is possible to have overlapping sets of utility independence and preferential independence assumptions without having them contained in each other. This was not possible with just two attributes. As hinted at by the requisite assumptions for Result 2, it turns out to be very fruitful to look at the implications of such overlapping independence conditions. In the next three sections we begin to explore these implications by proving general theorems for n-attribute utility functions.

6.3 THE MULTIPLICATIVE UTILITY FUNCTION*

One of the most important results of multiattribute utility theory specifies conditions that enable one to conclude that a utility function is

* Material in this section is adapted from Keeney (1974).

either multiplicative or additive. Let us first define mutual utility independence, which is a sufficient condition for the fundamental result. After stating and proving this result, we will suggest several weaker sets of assumptions that imply mutual utility independence.

Definition. Attributes $X_1, X_2, \ldots, X_n$ are *mutually utility independent* if every subset of $\{X_1, X_2, \ldots, X_n\}$ is utility independent of its complement.

Theorem 6.1. *If attributes $X_1, X_2 \ldots, X_n$ are mutually utility independent, then*

$$u(x) = \sum_{i=1}^{n} k_i u_i(x_i) + k \sum_{\substack{i=1 \\ j>i}}^{n} k_i k_j u_i(x_i) u_j(x_j)$$

$$+ k^2 \sum_{\substack{i=1 \\ j>i \\ \ell>j}}^{n} k_i k_j k_\ell u_i(x_i) u_j(x_j) u_\ell(x_\ell)$$

$$+ \cdots + k^{n-1} k_1 k_2 \cdots k_n u_1(x_1) u_2(x_2) \cdots u_n(x_n), \quad (6.12)$$

where

1. *u is normalized by $u(x_1^o, x_2^o, \ldots, x_n^o) = 0$ and $u(x_1^*, x_2^*, \ldots, x_n^*) = 1$.*
2. *$u_i(x_i)$ is a conditional utility function on X_i normalized by $u_i(x_i^o) = 0$ and $u_i(x_i^*) = 1$, $i = 1, 2, \ldots, n$.*
3. *$k_i = u(x_i^*, \bar{x}_i^o)$.*
4. *k is a scaling constant* that is a solution to*

$$1 + k = \prod_{i=1}^{n} (1 + kk_i).$$

Remark Before Proof. When $\sum_{i=1}^{n} k_i = 1$, then $k = 0$ and (6.12) reduces to the additive utility function

$$u(x) = \sum_{i=1}^{n} k_i u_i(x_i). \quad (6.13)$$

On the other hand, when $\sum_{i=1}^{n} k_i \neq 1$, then $k \neq 0$, so we can multiply each side of (6.12) by k, add one to each, and factor to obtain

$$ku(x) + 1 = \prod_{i=1}^{n} [kk_i u_i(x_i) + 1]. \quad (6.14)$$

---

* Procedures for choosing the correct value of k are given in the Appendix 6B at the end of this chapter.

When k is positive in (6.14), then $u'(x) \equiv 1 + ku(x)$ and $u_i'(x_i) \equiv 1 + kk_i u_i(x_i)$ are utility functions over the appropriate domains and

$$u'(x) = \prod_{i=1}^{n} u_i'(x_i).$$

When k is negative, note that $u'(x) \equiv -[ku(x) + 1]$ and $u_i'(x_i) \equiv -[1 + kk_i u_i(x_i)]$ are utility functions over X and X_i, respectively, so

$$-u'(x) = (-1)^n \prod_{i=1}^{n} u_i'(x_i).$$

Thus we can refer to form (6.14) as a multiplicative utility function.

Proof. Mutual utility independence by definition implies that $\bar{X}_i$ is UI for $i = 1, 2, \ldots, n-1$, which implies

$$u(x) = u(x_i) + c_i(x_i)u(\bar{x}_i), \qquad i = 1, 2, \ldots, n-1. \tag{6.15}$$

Setting all $x_i = x_i^o$ except x_1 and x_j, $j = 2, 3, \ldots, n-1$, we get the equality

$$u(x_1, x_j) = u(x_1) + c_1(x_1)u(x_j) = u(x_j) + c_j(x_j)u(x_1)$$

or

$$\frac{c_j(x_j) - 1}{u(x_j)} = \frac{c_1(x_1) - 1}{u(x_1)} \equiv k, \qquad j = 2, 3, \ldots, n-1, \qquad u(x_j) \neq 0, \tag{6.16}$$

where k is some constant. If $u(x_j) = 0$, clearly $c_j(x_j) = 1$, so it follows that

$$c_i(x_i) = ku(x_i) + 1, \qquad \text{for all } i = 1, 2, \ldots, n-1. \tag{6.17}$$

We can repeatedly use (6.15) to obtain

$$u(x) = u(x_1) + c_1(x_1)u(x_2, x_3, \ldots, x_n)$$
$$= u(x_1) + c_1(x_1)[u(x_2) + c_2(x_2)u(x_3, x_4, \ldots, x_n)]$$

$$\vdots$$

$$= u(x_1) + c_1(x_1)u(x_2) + c_1(x_1)c_2(x_2)u(x_3)$$
$$+ \cdots + c_1(x_1) \cdots c_{n-1}(x_{n-1})u(x_n). \tag{6.18}$$

Substituting (6.17) into (6.18) yields

$$u(x) = u(x_1)$$
$$+ [ku(x_1) + 1]u(x_2)$$
$$+ [ku(x_1) + 1][ku(x_2) + 1]u(x_3)$$

$$\vdots$$

$$+ [ku(x_1) + 1] \cdots [ku(x_{n-1}) + 1]u(x_n),$$

or, in more symbolic fashion,

$$u(x) = u(x_1) + \sum_{j=2}^{n} \prod_{i=1}^{j-1} [ku(x_i) + 1]u(x_j). \tag{6.19}$$

When $k = 0$, (6.19) becomes the additive utility function

$$u(x) = \sum_{i=1}^{n} u(x_i). \tag{6.20}$$

When $k \neq 0$ we can multiply both sides of (6.19) by k, then add 1 to each, and rearrange terms to find

$$ku(x) + 1 = \prod_{i=1}^{n} [ku(x_i) + 1]. \tag{6.21}$$

Recall that $u(x_i)$ actually means $u(x_1^o, \ldots, x_{i-1}^o, x_i, x_{i+1}^o, \ldots, x_n^o)$. Hence we can define

$$u(x_i) \equiv k_i u_i(x_i)$$

so that $u_i(\cdot)$ can be scaled from 0 to 1. Then (6.20) and (6.21) become, respectively, (6.13) and (6.14), which completes the proof. ◀

Notice that the results in Section 5.4 showing that the two-attribute utility function $u(x_1, x_2)$ is either multiplicative or additive if X_1 and X_2 are mutually utility independent is a special case of the above result.

Given that the conditions of Theorem 6.1 do hold, it is important to know whether the utility function is additive or multiplicative. One procedure is to pick any two attributes, for instance, X_1 and X_2. Then, choose two amounts of X_1, call them x_1' and x_1'', between which the decision maker has a preference, and similarly, choose two amounts of X_2, for instance, x_2' and x_2''. Next, fix the amounts of all attributes other than X_1 and X_2 at some convenient level. Let us designate this as $\bar{x}_{12}^+$. Now we state without proof the following corollary.

Corollary. *If, in addition to the requisite assumptions of Theorem 6.1, the decision maker is indifferent between a lottery yielding either $(x_1', x_2', \bar{x}_{12}^+)$ or $(x_1'', x_2'', \bar{x}_{12}^+)$ with equal probability or a lottery yielding either $(x_1', x_2'', \bar{x}_{12}^+)$ or $(x_1'', x_2', \bar{x}_{12}^+)$ with equal probability, the utility function must be additive. If he is not indifferent between these two lotteries, then the utility function must be multiplicative.*

If the indifference or preference condition between the lotteries holds for one $\bar{x}_{12}^+$, it can be shown to hold for all $\bar{x}_{12}$ because $\{X_1, X_2\}$ is UI. Thus, it is not necessary to worry about the value of $\bar{x}_{12}^+$ in ascertaining whether the assumption is appropriate.

6.3.1   Weaker Conditions Implying Mutual Utility Independence

There are several sets of weaker conditions that imply mutual utility independence. These are important because they drastically reduce the number of conditions that need to be verified in order to utilize Theorem 6.1. Given a set of n attributes $\{X_1, X_2, \ldots, X_n\}$ there are $2^n - 2$ subsets that must be UI if mutual utility independence holds. For $n = 10$, this means that in the absence of weaker conditions, 1022 assumptions would need to be verified to ascertain mutual utility independence. The weaker conditions require, at most, n assumptions.

Theorem 6.2.   *Given attributes* $X_1, X_2, \ldots, X_n$, *the following are equivalent:*

1. *Attributes* $X_1, X_2, \ldots, X_n$ *are mutually utility independent.*
2. $\bar{X}_i$ *is UI*, $i = 1, 2, \ldots, n$.
3. $\{X_i, X_{i+1}, \ldots, X_n\}$ *is UI*, $i = 2, 3, \ldots, n$, *and* $\{X_1, X_2, \ldots, X_{n-1}\}$ *is UI.*
4. $\{X_i, X_{i+1}\}$ *is UI*, $i = 1, 2, \ldots, n-1$; $n \geq 3$.
5. X_1 *is UI* and* $\{X_1, X_i\}$ *is PI*, $i = 2, 3, \ldots, n$; $n \geq 3$.

Notice that by definition, case 1 implies cases 2–5. The reverse implications are proven in Section 6.9. There a procedure for generating sets of assumptions implying mutual utility independence is given. Cases 2, 3, and 4 are all special cases of this general result. The proof that (5) implies (1) also requires a fundamental relationship between preferential independence and utility independence derived in Section 6.7. Pollak (1967) used condition 2 and Meyer (1970) condition 3 to prove that the resulting utility function must be either multiplicative or additive. For conditions 4 and 5, note that there must be at least three attributes, otherwise the conditions do not apply as their meaning is transparent.

With conditions 2, 3, 4, and 5, the number of assumptions increases linearly with the number of attributes. However, the sets 2, 3, and 4 require the decision maker to express preferences over lotteries with from two to $n - 1$ attributes varying at a time. This turns out to be a very taxing task for a decision maker. The assumptions of 5 require only preferences over consequences with two attributes varying and preferences over lotteries involving one attribute. These latter conditions seem reasonable for many problems and have been shown in practice to be operationally verifiable; see Chapters 7 and 8.

---

*Condition 5 can be generalized to require that any single attribute, not necessarily X_1, is UI.

6.4 THE MULTILINEAR UTILITY FUNCTION*

The multilinear utility function with n attributes is a generalization of the three-attribute Result 3 discussed in Section 6.2 and a generalization of both the additive and multiplicative utility functions. The result is given in the following theorem.

Theorem 6.3. *Given the set of attributes* $X \equiv \{X_1, X_2, \ldots, X_n\}$ *with* $n \geq 2$, *if* X_i *is utility independent of* $\bar{X}_i$ $i = 1, 2, \ldots, n$, *then*

$$u(x) = \sum_{i=1}^{n} k_i u_i(x_i) + \sum_{i=1}^{n} \sum_{j>i} k_{ij} u_i(x_i) u_j(x_j)$$

$$+ \sum_{i=1}^{n} \sum_{j>i} \sum_{\ell>j} k_{ij\ell} u_i(x_i) u_j(x_j) u_\ell(x_\ell)$$

$$+ \cdots + k_{123\ldots n} u_1(x_1) u_2(x_2) \cdots u_n(x_n), \qquad (6.22)$$

where

1. u *is normalized by* $u(x_1^o, x_2^o, \ldots, x_n^o) = 0$ *and* $u(x_1^*, x_2^*, \ldots, x_n^*) = 1$.
2. $u_i(x_i)$ *is a conditional utility function on* X_i *normalized by* $u_i(x_i^o) = 0$ *and* $u_i(x_i^*) = 1$.
3. *The scaling constants can be evaluated† by*

$$k_i = u(x_i^*, \bar{x}_i^o), \qquad (6.23a)$$

$$k_{ij} = u(x_i^*, x_j^*, \bar{x}_{ij}^o) - k_i - k_j$$

$$= u(x_i^*, x_j^*, \bar{x}_{ij}^o) - u(x_i^*, \bar{x}_i^o) - u(x_j^*, \bar{x}_j^o), \qquad (6.23b)$$

$$k_{ij\ell} = u(x_i^*, x_j^*, x_\ell^*, \bar{x}_{ij\ell}^o) - k_{ij} - k_{i\ell} - k_{j\ell} - k_i - k_j - k_\ell$$

$$= u(x_i^*, x_j^*, x_\ell^*, \bar{x}_{ij\ell}^o) - u(x_i^*, x_j^*, \bar{x}_{ij}^o) - u(x_i^*, x_\ell^*, \bar{x}_{i\ell}^o)$$

$$- u(x_j^*, x_\ell^*, \bar{x}_{j\ell}^o) + u(x_i^*, \bar{x}_i^o) + u(x_j^*, \bar{x}_j^o) + u(x_\ell^*, \bar{x}_\ell^o), \qquad (6.23c)$$

and, finally,

$$k_{123\ldots n} = u(x^*) - \sum_i k_{1\ldots(i-1)(i+1)\ldots n} - \cdots - \sum_{i,j>i} k_{ij} - \sum_i k_i$$

$$= 1 - \sum_i u(x_i^o, \bar{x}_i^*) + \cdots + (-1)^{n-2} \sum_{i,j>i} u(x_i^*, x_j^*, \bar{x}_{ij}^o)$$

$$+ (-1)^{n-1} \sum_i u(x_i^*, \bar{x}_i^o). \qquad (6.23d)$$

---

*The results of this section have been generalized in Fishburn (1973b) and Farquhar (1975). The latter work includes decompositions with nonseparable interaction terms.

† To simplify expressions, we extend our notation so that, for instance, when we write $(x_1, x_2, \bar{x}_{12})$, the symbol $\bar{x}_{12}$ will designate levels of all attributes except X_1 and X_2.

Proof. Because of the utility independence assumptions, from (6.6)

$$u(x) = u(\bar{x}_i) + c_i(\bar{x}_i)u(x_i), \qquad c_i > 0, \qquad i = 1, 2, \ldots, n, \qquad (6.24)$$

where u is scaled from 0 to 1. Let us define u_i to be a utility function over X_i scaled from 0 to 1. Then, noting that $u(x_i) = k_i u_i(x_i)$ for some positive constant k_i, we can define $d_i(\bar{x}_i) = k_i c_i(\bar{x}_i)$ and rewrite (6.24) as

$$u(x) = u(\bar{x}_i) + d_i(\bar{x}_i)u_i(x_i), \qquad d_i > 0, \qquad i = 1, 2, \ldots, n. \qquad (6.25)$$

To evaluate the d's, set x_i at its most desirable level x_i^* and evaluate (6.25), yielding

$$u(x_i^*, \bar{x}_i) = u(x_i^o, \bar{x}_i) + d_i(\bar{x}_i)u_i(x_i^*),$$

and since $u_i(x_i^*) = 1$,

$$d_i(\bar{x}_i) = u(x_i^*, \bar{x}_i) - u(x_i^o, \bar{x}_i), \qquad i = 1, 2, \ldots, n. \qquad (6.26)$$

Substituting (6.26) into (6.25) and rearranging, we find

$$u(x) = u_i(x_i)u(x_i^*, \bar{x}_i) + [1 - u_i(x_i)]u(x_i^o, \bar{x}_i), \qquad i = 1, 2, \ldots, n. \qquad (6.27)$$

The proof is conceptually simple, although algebraically tedious, from here. We repeatedly substitute (6.27) into itself for $i = 1, 2, \ldots, n$ and rearrange terms to get the result. We indicate the first step, where (6.27) with $i = 2$ is substituted into (6.27) with $i = 1$:

$$
\begin{aligned}
u(x) &= u_1(x_1)u(x_1^*, \bar{x}_1) + [1 - u_1(x_1)]u(x_1^o, \bar{x}_1) \\
&= u_1(x_1)[u_2(x_2)u(x_1^*, x_2^*, \bar{x}_{12}) + [1 - u_2(x_2)]u(x_1^*, x_2^o, \bar{x}_{12})] \\
&\quad + [1 - u_1(x_1)][u_2(x_2)u(x_1^o, x_2^*, \bar{x}_{12}) + [1 - u_2(x_2)]u(x_1^o, x_2^o, \bar{x}_{12})] \\
&= u(x_1^o, x_2^o, \bar{x}_{12}) + [u(x_1^*, x_2^o, \bar{x}_{12}) - u(x_1^o, x_2^o, \bar{x}_{12})]u_1(x_1) \\
&\quad + [u(x_1^o, x_2^*, \bar{x}_{12}) - u(x_1^o, x_2^o, \bar{x}_{12})]u_2(x_2) \\
&\quad + [u(x_1^*, x_2^*, \bar{x}_{12}) - u(x_1^*, x_2^o, \bar{x}_{12}) - u(x_1^o, x_2^*, \bar{x}_{12}) \\
&\quad + u(x_1^o, x_2^o, \bar{x}_{12})]u_1(x_1)u_2(x_2).
\end{aligned}
\qquad (6.28)
$$

Repeating the procedure, we get the desired result (6.22) and (6.23). ◀

That equation (6.22) is a generalization of the multiplicative and additive utility functions can be seen by comparing the results of Theorems 6.1 and 6.3. With the multilinear utility function (6.22), there are $2^n - 1$ scaling constants but, since $u(x^*) = 1$, we know that the sum of all these constants must equal 1 so only $2^n - 2$ are independent. Using (6.23), these can be evaluated from the utilities of the "corner" consequences in X.

6.5 THE ADDITIVE UTILITY FUNCTION

In this section, we are interested in the n-attribute additive utility function. Much of the work in additive utility theory has been done by Fishburn (1964, 1965a, 1965b, 1966, 1967a, 1967b, 1967c, 1970, 1971, 1972). He has derived necessary and sufficient conditions for additive utility functions in many situations, including whole product sets, denumerable products sets, incomplete product sets, and interdependencies among some attributes. Pruzan and Jackson (1963) and Pollak (1967) also present necessary and sufficient conditions for a utility function to be additive.

With n attributes, Fishburn's additive independence condition can be defined as follows.

Definition. Attributes $X_1, X_2, \ldots, X_n$ are *additive independent* if preferences over lotteries on $X_1, X_2, \ldots, X_n$ depend only on their marginal probability distributions and not on their joint probability distribution.

With this condition we can state a fundamental result of additive utility theory.

Theorem 6.4 (Fishburn).   *The n-attribute additive utility function*

$$u(x) = \sum_{i=1}^{n} u(x_i, \bar{x}_i^o) = \sum_{i=1}^{n} k_i u_i(x_i) \qquad (6.29)$$

is appropriate if and only if the additive independence condition holds among attributes $X_1, X_2, \ldots, X_n$, where:

1. *u is normalized by $u(x_1^o, x_2^o, \ldots, x_n^o) = 0$ and $u(x_1^*, x_2^*, \ldots, x_n^*) = 1$.*
2. *u_i is a conditional utility function of X_i normalized by $u_i(x_i^o) = 0$ and $u_i(x_i^*) = 1$, $i = 1, 2, \ldots, n$.*
3. *$k_i = u(x_i^*, \bar{x}_i^o)$, $i = 1, 2, \ldots, n$.*

Proof. The proof follows from repeated use of the derivation of the two-attribute additive utility function in Theorem 5.1. If we define Y as $\{X_2, X_3, \ldots, X_n\}$, from Theorem 5.1,

$$u(x_1, x_2, \ldots, x_n) = k_1 u_1(x_1) + k_Y u_Y(x_2, x_3, \ldots, x_n). \qquad (6.30)$$

Then to break down u_Y, we define $Z \equiv \{X_3, X_4, \ldots, X_n\}$ and invoke Theorem 5.1 again to yield

$$u_Y(x_2, x_3, \ldots, x_n) = k_2 u_2(x_2) + k_Z u_Z(x_3, x_4, \ldots, x_n). \qquad (6.31)$$

We proceed in this manner and then substitute (6.31) into (6.30), and so on, to yield the result (6.29). The converse follows directly from calculating the expected utility of any lottery using the additive utility function.

◀

Pollak's (1967) formulation of necessary and sufficient conditions for additive utility functions leads to the following theorem.

Theorem 6.5.   (Pollak).   *An individual's utility function is additive if and only if his preference between any two lotteries*

$$L_1 \equiv \langle (x_i \bar{x}'_i), (x^a_i, \bar{x}^a_i) \rangle \qquad \text{and} \qquad L_2 \equiv \langle (x_i, \bar{x}''_i), (x^b_i, \bar{x}^b_i) \rangle$$

is the same for all x_i for any $\bar{x}'_i$, $\bar{x}''_i$, x^a_i, $\bar{x}^a_i$, x^b_i, and $\bar{x}^b_i$.

[*Remark Before Proof.* Pollak's basic assumption is illustrated in Fig. 6.2, where L_1 is $\langle A, B \rangle$ and L_2 is $\langle C, D \rangle$. Note that consequences A and C have the same amount of attribute X_i. Pollak's assumption says that whatever preference we have between L_1 and L_2, we must also have if the level x_i in A and C is changed. That is, if A and C are slid horizontally to A' and C', the preference between $L'_1 \equiv \langle A', B \rangle$ and $L'_2 \equiv \langle C', D \rangle$ must be the same as between L_1 and L_2].

Proof.   If u is additive, the expected utilities of the above lotteries (using 6.29) are, respectively,

$$E[u(L_1)] = \tfrac{1}{2}u(x_i, \bar{x}^o_i) + \tfrac{1}{2}u(x^o_i, \bar{x}'_i) + \tfrac{1}{2}u(x^a_i, \bar{x}^a_i)$$

and

$$E[u(L_2)] = \tfrac{1}{2}u(x_i, \bar{x}^o_i) + \tfrac{1}{2}u(x^o_i, \bar{x}''_i) + \tfrac{1}{2}u(x^b_i, \bar{x}^b_i).$$

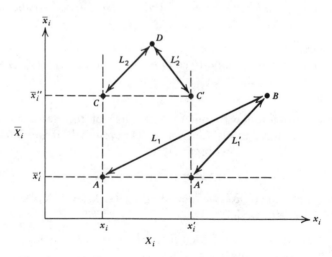

Fig. 6.2.   An illustration of Pollak's additivity condition.

Subtracting $E[u(L_2)]$ from $E[u(L_1)]$, it is clear that preferences between L_1 and L_2 would not depend on x_i.

Now assume preferences between L_1 and L_2 do not depend on x_i. Let us set $\bar{x}_i^b = \bar{x}_i'$, $\bar{x}_i^a = \bar{x}_i''$, and $x_i^a = x_i^b = x_i^o$. Then $L_1 = \langle (x_i, \bar{x}_i'), (x_i^o, \bar{x}_i'') \rangle$ and $L_2 = \langle (x_i, \bar{x}_i''), (x_i^o, \bar{x}_i') \rangle$. For one value of x_i, that is, x_i^o, lotteries L_1 and L_2 are equally preferable. Therefore, from the condition of the theorem, this must be the case for any x_i. It now follows directly from repeated application of Theorem 5.1 that u is additive. ◀

The main advantage to the additive utility function is its relative simplicity. The assessment of the n-attribute utility function is reduced to the assessment of n one-attribute utility functions and $n-1$ independent scaling constants. Any of the techniques discussed in this book could be used to assess the one-attribute utility functions. The problem of evaluating scaling constants is discussed in Section 6.6.

A major shortcoming of the additive utility function is the restrictiveness of the necessary assumptions. We could often expect the utility of a lottery to depend not only on the marginal probability distributions of the respective attributes, but also on their joint probability distribution. In addition, it is difficult to determine whether the requisite assumptions would be reasonable in a specific real-world problem. This difficulty arises because the assumptions are stated in terms of the decision maker's preferences for probability distributions over consequences, with more than one attribute simultaneously varying.

6.6 ASSESSING MULTIATTRIBUTE UTILITY FUNCTIONS*

With the additive, multiplicative, and multilinear utility functions, preferential independence and utility independence have been used to reduce the assessment of an n-attribute utility function to the assessment of n one-attribute utility functions, which can be designated as $u_1, u_2, \ldots, u_n$, and some scaling constants k_j, $j = 1, 2, \ldots, r$. And so we have

$$u(x_1, x_2, \ldots, x_n) = f[u_1(x_1), u_2(x_2), \ldots, u_n(x_n), k_1, k_2, \ldots, k_r], \quad (6.32)$$

where f is a scalar function. Each of the u_i can be assessed independently, since the scaling constants are meant to insure consistent scaling among

---

*Three publications with discussions concerning the assessment of multiattribute utility functions are Fishburn (1967d), Huber (1974b), and Kneppreth et al. (1974). Boyd (1970, 1973) discusses an interactive routine for multiattribute utility assessment.

the u_i's. Thus, except for the fact that there are more of them, the problem of assessing the u_i's is no more involved than in the two-attribute case considered in Section 5.8. Therefore, we do not discuss this topic here. However, the problems of verifying the independence conditions and assessing the k_j's are more involved with more attributes. The approach remains the same as in the two-attribute case, but operationally the problem is more complicated.

In terms of the required assessments and general robustness, the additive and multiplicative utility functions appear to be the practical ones for $n \geq 4$, for instance. Even when the requisite assumptions do not precisely hold over the domains of all the attributes, it may be a good approximation [see von Winterfeldt and Edwards (1973)] to assume they do, or it may be reasonable to integrate different additive and multiplicative utility functions over separate regions of these attributes. Furthermore, by nesting one multiattribute utility function inside another, a technique described in the next paragraph, additional flexibility in the preference structure can be achieved. The result of this is special cases of the multilinear utility function.

The results of Theorem 6.1 (multiplicative utility function) and Theorem 6.4 (additive utility function) are valid regardless of whether the X_i's are scalar attributes or vector attributes. This means that the x_i's can be either scalars or vectors. In the former case, the component utility functions u_i are single-attribute utility functions, whereas in the latter case, u_i is itself a multiattribute utility function. If X_i is a vector attribute, it is possible, subject to satisfying the requisite assumptions, to reuse Theorem 6.1 or 6.4 in structuring u_i. In such a case, we say that u_i is a *nested* multiattribute utility function. That is, u_i is a multiattribute utility function nested within the multiattribute utility function u.

Nesting multiplicative forms provides an extra degree of freedom in the problem by having an extra independent scaling constant. Without nesting, using the multiplicative utility function, the number of independent scaling constants is equal to the number n of attributes. However, suppose the last single utility function u_n is a multiplicative utility function nested within the overall utility function and that u_n has three single attributes. Then we would need n scaling constants for the "outer multiplicative utility function" and three for the "inner multiplicative utility function" for a total of $n + 3$, even though there are only $n + 2$ single attributes: $X_1, \ldots, X_{n-1}$ and the three single attributes in u_n. The degree of freedom afforded by the extra parameter permits tradeoffs between two attributes to depend on a third. This allows for some violation of the preferential independence conditions. By various nesting schemes, enough extra constants could be provided to model situations where tradeoffs between many pairs of attributes depend on the level of other attributes. The additive and multiplicative utility functions are simple enough to be tractable and yet, especially with nesting, robust enough to adequately quantify preferences for many problems. In practice, however, assessing and using these multiattribute functions is easier said than done.

6.6.1 Verifying Preferential Independence and Utility Independence Conditions

Partition X into Y and $\bar{Y}$. To check whether Y is preferentially independent of $\bar{Y}$, we proceed as follows. First choose $\bar{y}^+$ with all components at a relatively undesirable level and choose y' and y'' such that $(y', \bar{y}^+)$ is indifferent to $(y'', \bar{y}^+)$. Then pick another point $\bar{y}'$ with all components at a relatively desirable level and ask the decision maker if $(y', \bar{y}')$ is indifferent to $(y'', \bar{y}')$. This must be true if Y is preferentially independent of $\bar{Y}$. If the decision maker's answer was affirmative, repeat the same procedure for other pairs of y consequences with $\bar{y}$ fixed at various levels. If the answers to these questions still indicate preferential independence, then ask the decision maker, "If you are indifferent between $(y', \bar{y})$ and $(y'', \bar{y})$ for some particular $\bar{y}$, does this imply the same indifference would hold for every choice of $\bar{y}$?" A positive answer strongly suggests that Y is preferentially independent of $\bar{Y}$. We must, in addition, check the orientation of the components of Y. If $(y_1, \bar{y})$ is preferred to $(y_2, \bar{y})$ for one level of $\bar{y}$, then the same orientation must hold (i.e., preferences cannot reverse) for any other level of $\bar{y}$. This condition, together with the fact that indifference curves over Y, given $\bar{Y}$ is fixed, are the same, implies that Y is PI of $\bar{Y}$.

Because it is so important to verify independence conditions and because there are various approaches to do this, we present a short dialogue below that illustrates an alternate procedure.

Partition X into Y and $\bar{Y}$. To check whether Y is preferentially independent of $\bar{Y}$ we might proceed along the lines of this hypothetical interview between the analyst and the assessor:

ANALYST. I would now like to investigate how you feel about various Y values when we hold fixed a particular value of $\bar{Y}$. For example, on the first page of this questionnaire [this is shown to the assessor] there is a list of 25 paired comparisons between Y evaluations; each element of the pair describes levels on the Y attributes alone. On this first page it is assumed that, throughout, the $\bar{Y}$ evaluations are all the same, that is, $\bar{y}^{(1)}$ [values for components of all $\bar{Y}$ are shown to the assessor.] Is this clear?

ASSESSOR. Crystal clear, but you are asking me for a lot of work.

ANALYST. Well, I have a devious purpose in mind and it will not take as much time as you think to find out what I want. Now on the second page of the questionnaire [this is shown to the assessor] the identical set of 25 paired comparisons are repeated but now the fixed, common level on the $\bar{Y}$ attributes is changed from $\bar{y}^{(1)}$ to $\bar{y}^{(2)}$ [values are shown to the assessor]. Are you with me?

ASSESSOR. All the way.

ANALYST. On page 3, we have the same 25 paired comparisons but now the common value of the $\bar{Y}$ values is $\bar{y}^{(3)}$ [shown to the assessor].

ASSESSOR. You said this would not take long.

ANALYST. Well now, here comes the punchline. Suppose that you painstakingly respond to all 25 paired comparisons on page 1 where $\bar{y}^{(1)}$ is fixed. Now when you go to the next page would your responses change to these same 25 paired comparisons?

ASSESSOR. Let's see. In the second page all paired comparisons are the same except $\bar{y}^{(1)}$ is replaced by $\bar{y}^{(2)}$. What difference should that make?

ANALYST. Well, you tell me. If we consider this first comparison [pointed to on the questionnaire] does it make any difference if $\bar{Y}$ values are all fixed at level $\bar{y}^{(1)}$ or $\bar{y}^{(2)}$? There could be some interaction concerning how you view the paired comparison depending on the common value of the $\bar{Y}$ values.

ASSESSOR. I suppose that might be the case in some other situation but in the first comparison I prefer the left alternative to the right no matter what the $\bar{Y}$ values are . . . as long as they are the same.

ANALYST. Okay. Would you now feel the same if you consider the second paired comparison?

ASSESSOR. Yes. And the third and so on. Am I being naive? Is there some trick here?

ANALYST. No, not at all. I am just checking to see if the $\bar{y}$ values have any influence on your responses to the paired comparisons. So I gather that you are telling me that your responses on page 1 would carry over to page 2.

ASSESSOR. That's right.

ANALYST. And to page 3, where the $\bar{Y}$ values are held fixed at $\bar{y}^{(3)}$ [shown to assessor]?

ASSESSOR. Yes.

ANALYST. Well, on the basis of this information I now pronounce that for you the attribute set Y is preferentially independent of the attribute set $\bar{Y}$.

ASSESSOR. That's nice to know.

ANALYST. That's all that I wanted to find out.

ASSESSOR. Aren't you going to ask me to fill out page 1?

ANALYST. No. That's too much work. There are less painful ways of getting that information.

Of course, once the analyst and the assessor go through this procedure to check preferential independence of Y from $\bar{Y}$, there are obvious shortcuts if the analyst wants to check other preferential independence relations. There is a danger, however, of shortcutting the procedure on the first round since these ideas, although terribly simple once you know them, do give trouble at first.

We could go through a similar procedure to check whether Y is utility independent of $\bar{Y}$. On page 1 of the questionnaire we keep $\bar{Y}$ fixed at level $\bar{y}^{(1)}$ but now, instead of paired comparisons between simple consequences involving y's, there would be paired comparisons between one 50-50 lottery and either another 50-50 lottery or a single certainty consequence. Of course, all the consequences in the paired comparisons are described in the Y-attribute space. Throughout, $\bar{Y}$ attributes are held fixed at $\bar{y}^{(1)}$ on page 1. Similarly, they are held fixed at $\bar{y}^{(2)}$ on page 2, and so on. The analyst can now go through the same routine as before, and if the assessor sees no reason why the paired comparisons should depend on the value of $\bar{y}$, then we can conclude that Y is UI.

In practice, if such a condition were verified for approximately four different values of $\bar{y}$ covering the range of $\bar{Y}$, we would usually be justified in assuming that Y is utility independent of $\bar{Y}$.

6.6.2 Evaluating Scaling Constants

The basic objective to be followed in evaluating k_1 to k_r should be obvious from Section 5.8. We want to obtain a set of r independent equations that have the k_j's as r unknowns. These are then solved to get the k_j's. The set of equations can be generated from certainty considerations, probabilistic considerations, or a combination of both. For example, if consequences x and y are equally preferred by the decision maker, then clearly $u(x) = u(y)$ or, from (6.32),

$$f[u_1(x_1), \ldots, u_n(x_n), k_1, \ldots, k_r] = f[u_1(y_1), \ldots, u_n(y_n), k_1, \ldots, k_r]. \quad (6.33)$$

Once the u_i's have been assessed, $u_i(x_i)$ and $u_i(y_i)$ are just numbers, so (6.33) is one equation with at most r unknowns. Also, for example, if $x \sim \langle w, p, w \rangle$, then substituting (6.32) into

$$u(x) = pu(w) + (1-p)u(z)$$

gives us another equation with r unknowns at most.

There are operational problems of concern: (1) How do we guarantee that the equations are independent? (2) What should we do with more than r independent equations when they are inconsistent?

In practice, our understanding of the problem and knowledge of the functional form of the utility function are probably the best guards against a large number of redundant equations. Even so, it is interesting to think about one approach that can be used to avoid any redundancy with the multilinear utility function since it involves the most scaling constants of any of our functional forms. Recall that for this case we need $2^n - 2$ scaling constants, where n is the number of attributes. There are 2^n "corner" consequences of the form $(x'_1, x'_2, \ldots, x'_n)$, where $x'_i = x^*_i$ or x^o_i, and where $u(x^*_1, x^*_2, \ldots, x^*_n) = 1$ and $u(x^o_1, x^o_2, \ldots, x^o_n) = 0$ are used to scale u. If each corner consequence is evaluated in terms of these two reference consequences, or other previously assessed consequences, we will get an independent set of $2^n - 2$ equations. The most obvious— although not necessarily the best—way to do this is equate each corner consequence to a lottery of the form $\langle (x^*_1, x^*_2, \ldots, x^*_n), p, (x^o_1, x^o_2, \ldots, x^o_n) \rangle$ by assessing the appropriate p. When redundancies do occur in a set of equations, we must empirically generate additional equations relating the k_j's until we do have a set of r independent equations. See the example illustrating this in Section 5.8.

Concerning overdetermination with inconsistencies, the desire is clearly to have the decision maker reflect on the inconsistencies which perhaps can be illuminated by the analyst and change some responses to imply a consistent set of preferences. If this is impossible because of time considerations or other factors, then perhaps sensitivity analysis using the different sets of implied scaling factors would indicate the same alternative was best. Or at least, it may be possible to drop some options from further consideration. Of these remaining, we should be able to identify which parameters are critical to the decision, and from this, develop a procedure to specify these parameter values.

6.6.3   Scaling the Conditional Utility Functions

As it will become apparent in this section, the problem of scaling conditional utility functions is very similar to that of scaling conditional value functions addressed in Section 3.7. The techniques discussed for assessing scaling factors in the value function context are directly applicable to our current problem. However, in the utility context, the additional possibility of scaling by using probabilistic questioning is appropriate.

The additive, multiplicative, and multilinear utility functions can be written

$$u(x_1, x_2, \ldots, x_n) = \sum_{i=1}^{n} k_i u_i(x_i) + \text{POT}, \qquad (6.34)$$

where POT designates "possible other terms." With the additive form, there are no other terms, whereas the opposite is true with the multiplicative and multilinear forms. In each case, when the u_i and u are scaled from 0 to 1 by

$$u(x^*_1, x^*_2, \ldots, x^*_n) = 1, \qquad u(x^o_1, x^o_2, \ldots, x^o_n) = 0 \qquad (6.35)$$

and

$$u_i(x_i^*) = 1, \; u_i(x_i^o) = 0, \qquad \text{for all } X_i, \tag{6.36}$$

then

$$u(x_i^*, \bar{x}_i^o) = k_i, \qquad i = 1, 2, \ldots, n. \tag{6.37}$$

The problem of interest in this subsection is assessing the scaling factors for the conditional utility functions in (6.34), which is done by specifying the k_i's for $i = 1, \ldots, n$. This requires n independent equations with the unknown k_i's to be generated.

Because the difficulty in manually solving n equations (which are not necessarily linear) with n unknowns is tedious to say the least, current practice in assessing the k_i's usually requires sets of equations that are simple to evaluate. This basically limits the questions to two types.

Question I.   For what probability p are you indifferent between:

1. the lottery giving a p chance at x^* and a $1 - p$ chance at x^o
and
2. the consequence $(x_1^o, \ldots, x_{i-1}^o, x_i^*, x_{i+1}^o, \ldots, x_n^o)$.

If we define the decision maker's answer as p_i, then using (6.35), the expected utility of the lottery is p_i, and from (6.37) the utility of the consequence is k_i. Equating the expected utilities, we find $k_i = p_i$. We could then clearly generate the values of each of the k_i's in this fashion.

The second type of question is illustrated by

Question II.   Select a level of X_i (e.g., x_i') and a level of X_j (e.g., x_j') so that, for any fixed levels of all other attributes, you are indifferent between:

1. a consequence yielding x_i' and x_j^o together
and
2. a consequence yielding x_j' and x_i^o together.

Using (6.35) and (6.36), the utilities of these two indifferent consequences can be equated to yield

$$k_i u_i(x_i') = k_j u_j(x_j'). \tag{6.38}$$

Once the single-attribute utility functions u_i and u_j are assessed, both $u_i(x_i')$ and $u_j(x_j')$ are easily found, so (6.38) is a simple linear equation. Suppose in addition, for example, that $x_i' = x_i^*$; then by (6.36), the relationship between k_i and k_j given by (6.38) is even simpler.

A major shortcoming of questions of both types I and II is the use of the extreme levels of the attributes, that is, the x_i^*'s and x_i^o's. Since the range from x_i^o to x_i^* must cover all the possible x_i's, the implications of, and preferences for, the extreme levels are usually very difficult for a decision maker to assess. A further difficulty with Question I is that the effect resulting from varying all n attributes simultaneously must be considered. Therefore, for computational ease, we must force the decision maker to respond to questions that are much more difficult to evaluate than would be theoretically necessary. A computer program developed to eliminate this necessity is discussed in Appendix 6C.

A common practice in assessing the k_i's would be to first rank them, then to use Question I to evaluate the largest k_i, and finally to use type II questions to evaluate the magnitude of the other k_j's relative to the largest k_i. Once we have the k_i's, the additive form must hold if they sum to one. Otherwise, the k_i's are substituted into (6.34) to use in evaluating k for the multiplicative form or the other constants in the multilinear form. This task in itself can be difficult.

It should not be a particularly difficult task to order the k_i's. This can be done, for instance, by asking the decision maker whether he prefers $(x_1^*, \bar{x}_1^o)$ or $(x_2^*, \bar{x}_2^o)$. Using (6.37) if the former is preferred, then $k_1 > k_2$; if the latter is preferred, then $k_2 > k_1$ and if they are equally preferable, then $k_1 = k_2$. Repeating this for other binary comparisons, we would get a complete ranking of the k_i's. At most it would require $(n^2 - n)/2$ such comparisons for a complete ranking, but judicious choice of the order could reduce this to only $n - 1$ comparisons. For instance, it is not unreasonable to present the decision maker with a list of consequences and ask him to rank them. Using this ranked list as a beginning, we could check its consistancy by asking the $n - 1$ binary choices between now adjacent consequences. The ideas of how we might order the k_i's should now be clear. Asking a decision maker to rank the k_i's before actually assessing them serves to introduce him to the tradeoff considerations that he must make without initially overwhelming him with complexity.*

Example 6.1. Suppose we ascertain that $k_1 > k_2 > k_3$ although, for future purposes in this example, we only need to know the largest k_i. Next we ask the decision maker for an x_1 (call it x_1') so that (x_1', x_2^o, x_3^o) and (x_1^o, x_2^*, x_3^o) are equally preferable. From (6.34), it follows that

$$k_1 u_1(x_1') = k_2, \tag{6.39}$$

where $u_1(x_1')$ is just a number between 0 and 1. Similarly, we ask for another x_1 (call it x_1'') so that $(x_1'', x_2^o, x_3^o) \sim (x_1^o, x_2^o, x_3^*)$. Equating utilities

---

* As discussed in Section 5.8, the k_i cannot be interpreted as indicators of the relative importance of the attributes X_i.

gives us

$$k_1 u_1(x_1'') = k_3. \tag{6.40}$$

Note that our information is identical to that used in Chapter 3 to scale value functions.

If our utility function is additive, then from (6.29) for consistency, we know

$$k_1 + k_2 + k_3 = 1. \tag{6.41}$$

The set of equations (6.39), (6.40), and (6.41) can easily be solved to yield the appropriate values of the k_i's. And of course for consistency, k_3 must be less than k_2.

If our utility function is multiplicative, then from (6.14) for consistency,

$$k + 1 = (kk_1 + 1)(kk_2 + 1)(kk_3 + 1). \tag{6.42}$$

Equations (6.39), (6.40), and (6.42) together have four unknowns: k_1, k_2, k_3, and k, so we must generate another equation. Using probabilistic scaling, we might determine p_1 so that (x_1^*, x_2^o, x_3^o) is indifferent to $\langle (x_1^*, x_2^*, x_3^*), p_1, (x_1^o, x_2^o, x_3^o) \rangle$. Using the three-attribute multiplicative utility function and equating expected utilities, we find

$$k_1 = p_1. \tag{6.43}$$

This equation, together with (6.39), (6.40), and (6.42), can be solved to yield the scaling constants. ∎

6.6.4 Scaling the Additive Utility Function

To make a specific point, let us turn our attention to the k_i's in an n-attribute additive utility function. Note that we need only to assess empirically $n-1$ of the k_i factors since the nth can be specified from these and the consistency requirement

$$\sum_{i=1}^{n} k_i = 1. \tag{6.44}$$

Although the use of questions of type I and II for assessing the k_i's is simple procedurally, it may not be so simple operationally. The decision maker may, in fact, find some of the questions asked of him using this method very difficult. Unfortunately we must introduce more notation before discussing ways to get around such difficulties. For any subset T of the indices $\{1, 2, \dots n\}$, let x_T be the x point where the ith attribute is x_i^* if i belongs to T and is x_i^o if i does not belong to T. Thus for $n = 5$ and $T = \{1, 2, 4\}$, then

$$x_T = x_{\{1,2,4\}} \equiv (x_1^*, x_2^*, x_3^o, x_4^*, x_5^o). \tag{6.45}$$

Also let us define

$$k_T = \sum_{i \in T} k_i, \tag{6.46}$$

and p_T as the probability such that the decision maker is indifferent between lottery $L_T \equiv \langle x^*, p_T, x^o \rangle$ and consequence x_T. Using this notation, if we assess p_T for any particular T, then $u(x_T)$ must equal the expected utility of L_T. The expected utility of L_T is clearly p_T and $u(x_T) = k_T$, so

$$k_T = p_T, \quad \text{for all } T. \tag{6.47}$$

From (6.46), we see that k_T can be obtained for any subset T from the individual k_i's. However, our motivation here is that it may be easier for the decision maker to obtain the k_i's from some k_T's. This can be done using (6.46) and (6.47).

Example 6.2.   Again let $n = 5$ and suppose $T = \{1, 2, 4\}$ and $R = \{1, 2\}$. Then if we empirically assess p_T and p_R, it follows from (6.46) and (6.47) that

$$k_T = k_1 + k_2 + k_4 = p_T$$

and

$$k_R = k_1 + k_2 = p_R.$$

Clearly then, for this example,

$$k_4 = p_T - p_R. \tag{6.48}$$

There are obviously many consistency checks that can be performed to verify our assignment of k_4. For instance, suppose we assess p_Q for $Q = \{1, 2, 3, 5\}$. Then since from (6.47), it follows that

$$k_1 + k_2 + k_3 + k_5 = p_Q$$

and from (6.45)

$$k_1 + k_2 + k_3 + k_4 + k_5 = 1,$$

we know

$$k_4 = 1 - p_Q.$$

Another obvious consistency check on k_4 is to assess it directly, as previously indicated, by obtaining p_4.   ■

An alternative approach to assessing the k_i factors is suggested by the following idea from probability theory. In assigning probabilities to a finite set of mutually exclusive and collectively exhaustive events $\{E_1, E_2, \ldots, E_r\}$, it is often natural to make an assignment first to a subset of these events and then to use conditional probability considerations to further subdivide this assignment. We might find it helpful to proceed in an analogous manner in the present context.* To this end suppose S is a

---

* A similar procedure for the certainty problem is found in Section 3.7.

subset of T. We want to find what portion of the weight of k_T should be assigned to S. Letting $p_{S|T}$ be the probability such that x_S is indifferent to $\langle x_T, p_{S|T}, x^o \rangle$, and equating expected utility,

$$u(x_S) \underset{?}{=} p_{S|T} u(x_T).$$

From this, we establish the rule that

$$p_S = p_{S|T} p_T, \qquad S \subset T, \tag{6.49}$$

which is analogous to the multiplication rule of probability theory.

How we finally choose to assess the k_i's, whether directly or indirectly by using (6.49), depends on which procedure seems most natural in the context of the real problem under consideration.

6.6.5   Scaling the Multiplicative Utility Function*

Techniques for evaluating the scaling constants k_i in the multiplicative utility function were addressed in Subsection 6.6.3. However, the scaling constant k is special to the multiplicative form, therefore it is considered now. If Theorem 6.1 holds and $\sum_{i=1}^{n} k_i = 1$, then the additive utility function is appropriate. If $\sum_{i=1}^{n} k_i \neq 1$, the utility function is multiplicative and the additional constant k in (6.14) can be found from the k_i values.

In this case, we can evaluate (6.14) at x^* to find

$$1 + k = \prod_{i=1}^{n} (1 + kk_i). \tag{6.50}$$

If $\sum_{i=1}^{n} k_i > 1$ then, using (6.14) and (6.50), the utility independence properties of the utility function (6.14) can only be preserved given that $-1 < k < 0$. In this case, by iteratively evaluating (6.50) given the k_i, $i = 1, 2, \ldots, n$, we can converge to the appropriate value of k (call it k^*). First set $k = k'$ and substitute this into (6.50). If the right-hand side (r.h.s.) is smaller than the left-hand side (l.h.s.), then $k^* < k'$. If the r.h.s. is greater than the l.h.s., then $k^* > k'$.

When $\sum_{i=1}^{n} k_i < 1$, it follows from similar reasoning that $k^* > 0$. Let us arbitrarily set $k = k'$ in (6.50). If the r.h.s. > l.h.s., then $k^* < k'$, whereas if the l.h.s. > r.h.s., then $k^* > k'$.

6.6.6   An Example†

To illustrate some of the ideas of this section, let us consider the problem of selecting a job. And, just to keep matters simple, let us

---

* The assertions in this subsection are proven in Appendix 6B at the end of this chapter.

† This section illustrates concepts introduced earlier in this section in a simplistic example. It can be skipped.

Table 6.1

Measurement Scales for Attributes

	Attribute	Measurement Scale
X_1 $\begin{cases} Y_1 \\ \\ Y_2 \end{cases}$	Starting salary	Starting annual income in dollars
	Future increases in salary	Annual salary after five years in dollars
X_2	Commuting travel time	Door-to-door travel time from work to job in minutes
X_3	Degree of urbanization	Metropolitan area population

assume there are three attributes to be considered about each job: monetary compensation, commuting travel time, and degree of urbanization of the area. These will be designated by X_1, X_2, and X_3, respectively. Furthermore, we will assume that monetary compensation is broken down into starting salary and future prospects for increases, which we will designate as Y_1 and Y_2, respectively. Thus, $X_1 = Y_1 \times Y_2$. The measurement scales for each of the attributes are summarized in Table 6.1.

We must next establish best and worst possible outcomes under any job for each of the attributes. Let us assume these are found as shown in Table 6.2. Now we can define $y_1^o = 12,000$ and $y_2^o = 12,000$ so that $x_1^o \equiv (y_1^o, y_2^o) = (12,000; 12,000)$. Similarly, let $x_2^o = 60$ and $x_3^o = .5$. Then choose $x_1^* = (18,000; 25,000)$, $x_2^* = 0$, and $x_3^* = 15$. Notice that x_2^* was set equal to zero minutes travel time even though the best condition required at least 10 minutes. This is legitimate for our purposes since the only condition on x_2^* was that it be at least as good as the best possible consequence.

Now suppose that the additive independence assumptions have been verified for all the X_i terms, and that this condition does *not* hold for Y_1

Table 6.2

Range of Measurement Scales

			Range	
			Best	Worst
X_1 $\begin{cases} Y_1 \\ Y_2 \end{cases}$	Starting salary		$18,000	$12,000
	Future salary increases		$25,000	$12,000
X_2		Commuting travel time	10 min	60 min
X_3		Degree of urbanization	15 million	.5 million

and Y_2. Then, according to Theorem 6.4, the utility function $u(x_1, x_2, x_3)$ is additive. We can write from (6.29) that

$$u(x_1, x_2, x_3) = k_1 u_1(x_1) + k_2 u_2(x_2) + k_3 u_3(x_3), \qquad (6.51)$$

where

$$u_i(x_i^o) = 0, \qquad u_i(x_i^*) = 1, \qquad \text{for all } i. \qquad (6.52)$$

The manner in which we would assess the u_2 and u_3 functions subject to the convention of (6.52) was extensively covered in Chapter 4, so nothing more will be said here. But the utility function u_1 is a utility function for more than one scalar attribute, that is, Y_1 and Y_2. And, as we stated, the decision maker is unwilling to accept the additive independence assumption for these two attributes, so a simple additive function is not appropriate. Perhaps we could use some of the substitution schemes discussed in Chapter 3, which essentially reduce a two-dimensional representation to a unidimensional representation before the conversion to utilities is effected. But what if we are not so lucky? Alternatively, some of the methods to assess two-attribute utility functions discussed in Chapter 5 may be appropriate.

Now let us return to the scaling constants of (6.51). It is possible to ask the decision maker some meaningful qualitative questions about k_i's to get some "feeling" for their values. For instance: "Imagine that each of the performance measures are at the state x_i^o. Would you rather have attribute X_1 pushed to x_1^* than both attributes X_2 and X_3 pushed to x_2^* and x_3^*?" A yes answer would imply $k_1 > k_2 + k_3$, which means $k_1 > .5$. We then ask, "Would you rather have attribute X_2 pushed from x_2^o to x_2^* than X_3 pushed from x_3^o to x_3^*?" And if this question received an affirmative answer we would know that $k_2 > k_3$. If there exists a subset T of attributes such that $x_T \sim x_{\bar{T}}$, then we can infer that $k_T = k_{\bar{T}} = 1/2$.

The larger the set of attributes, the easier it becomes to group attributes in a way that permits the analyst to infer properties of the k_i's without asking probabilistic questions. At any stage of an analysis such as this, the sophisticated analyst would use sensitivity checks to determine whether he need probe any further. Perhaps the crude qualitative measures already obtained suffice to resolve the original problem.

Another methodological point that needs clarification is the idea of consistency. When questions are asked one way, it might turn out that $k_1 > .3$, for example, and when asked another way, $k_1 < .3$. This will happen, and when it does the decision maker will just have to think harder about the issues and modify some of his assumptions or evaluations in order to attain consistency. This is psychologically painful and time consuming and, once again, this step should be preceded by a sensitivity analysis to determine whether the inconsistency is worth resolving.

Let's proceed. Suppose that we assess $k_1 = .6$, that is, the decision maker is indifferent between (x_1^*, x_2^o, x_3^o) and the lottery $\langle(x_1^*, x_2^*, x_3^*), .6, (x_1^o, x_2^o, x_3^o)\rangle$. Then, of course, $k_2 + k_3 = .4$ and we ask, for instance, "What is the value of p so that you are indifferent between (x_1^o, x_2^*, x_3^o) and $\langle(x_1^o, x_2^*, x_3^*), p, (x_1^o, x_2^o, x_3^o)\rangle$?" If the decision maker's response is .7, from (6.49) we have

$$k_2 = p(k_2 + k_3) = (.7)(.4) = .28.$$

Then clearly, $k_3 = .12$ so the utility function is

$$u(x_1, x_2, x_3) = .6u_1(x_1) + .28u_2(x_2) + .12u_3(x_3), \qquad (6.53)$$

where each of the utility functions is scaled from 0 to 1. Expression (6.53) is then appropriate for evaluating decisions under uncertainty. Of course, we might want to run sensitivity tests on those aspects of the assessment procedure that appear to be most unstable.

6.6.7   Consistency Checks

As with all phases of assessing utility functions, it is important to include consistency checks to develop some confidence in our representation of the decision maker's preferences. Clearly, when we check the consistency of the overall utility function, we are also checking the appropriateness of the scaling constants. It is also prudent to include consistency checks specifically for these scaling constants. In all of these checks, we simply set up additional equations that have some scaling constants in them. But since we have already evaluated these constants, we can plug in their values to check the original assessment. The different approaches for evaluating scaling constants can obviously be used as checks of each other. In most situations, the imagination of the analyst will not be stretched in an attempt to develop efficient and effective consistent checks for the scaling constants.

6.7   A FUNDAMENTAL RELATIONSHIP BETWEEN PREFERENTIAL INDEPENDENCE AND UTILITY INDEPENDENCE*

We now begin to introduce general results that allow us to weaken the assumptions necessary to invoke theorems such as those in Sections

---

* The remainder of this chapter concerns important theoretical and operational results. The reader interested mainly in applications can proceed to Chapters 7 and 8.

6.3–6.5. The result of this section relates our two independence conditions concerning cardinal and ordinal preferences over the consequence space X. It allows us to build "higher-order" utility independence conditions from the weaker preferential independence conditions of the same-order and lower-order utility independence conditions.* Decision makers find it very difficult to think about lotteries involving more than one attribute because they must consider simultaneously both tradeoffs between different levels of the attributes and the probabilities that the various consequences occur. However, one can reasonably specify a preference order for lotteries involving only one attribute. Although it is not easy, one can also accurately indicate the tradeoffs between two attributes under certainty with all the levels of the other attributes fixed. By completing each of these tasks separately, the assumptions necessary to invoke Theorems 6.1–6.4 implying specific forms of the multiattribute utility function can be verified.

The general case of our main result can be proven with $X \equiv \{X_0, X_1, X_2\}$ since the X_i's can be vector attributes. The attribute X_0 introduced is distinct from the other X_i's. Throughout this chapter, it will never be assumed or implied that X_0 is either PI or UI. Hence, it will never be the case that preferences for X_0 will ever be independent in any sense of $\bar{X}_0$. We are interested in the utility function $u(x_0, x_1, x_2)$, which is assumed to be continuous, with each argument of u having a definite effect on preferences. It is assumed that preferences over X are bounded and (x_0^*, x_1^*, x_2^*) will designate the most desirable and (x_0^o, x_1^o, x_2^o) the least desirable consequence.

Theorem 6.6.[†]   *Given three attributes $\{X_0, X_1, X_2\}$, if $\{X_1, X_2\}$ is preferentially independent of X_0 and if X_1 is utility independent of $\{X_0, X_2\}$, then $\{X_1, X_2\}$ is utility independent of X_0.*

[*Remark Before Proof.* This result says preferential independence of $\{X_1, X_2\}$ from its complement can be strengthened to *utility independence*, provided that either X_1 or X_2 is UI. Theorem 6.6 provides necessary conditions for a "second-order" utility independence assumption in terms of a "second-order" preferential independence assumption and a "first-order" utility independence assumption.

---

* Let $Y \subset X \equiv \{X_1, \ldots, X_n\}$. If Y is UI or PI, the order of the assumption is the number of X_i's in Y. Thus, for example, the assumption that $Y \equiv \{X_2, X_3\}$ is UI is a second-order assumption.

† This result does not require boundedness and the independence conditions can be weakened to allow for reversals of preferences over various attributes as proven in Fishburn and Keeney (1974).

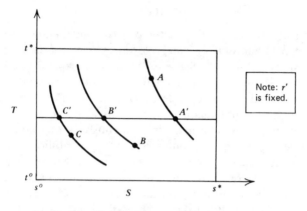

Note: r' is fixed.

(a) Conditional indifference curves in $S \times T$

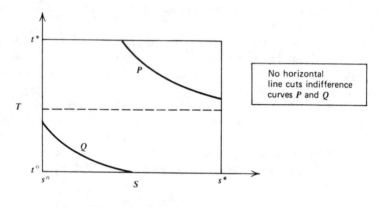

No horizontal line cuts indifference curves P and Q

(b) Complicating case

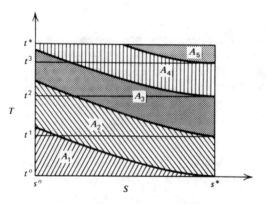

(c) Constructing the domain of utility independence

Fig. 6.3. Illustration of the proof for Theorem 6.6.

The proof of Theorem 6.6 is fairly involved, but the presentation can be simplified with a special notation. To avoid subscripts where unnecessary, we will define attributes $R \equiv X_0$, $S \equiv X_1$, and $T = X_2$. Thus, for instance, s will be a specific amount of S, and the utility function of interest will be written as $u(s, t, r)$.]

[*Idea of Proof.* The mode of the proof can be illustrated by taking s and t as scalars. Let r' be any fixed value of R and consider the three isopreference or indifference curves shown in Fig. 6.3a. These same conditional indifference curves are appropriate for any other value of r since $\{S, T\}$ is PI. Suppose that given r', we know that $B \sim \langle A, C \rangle$. The essence of the proof is to show that given any other value of R (e.g., r'') then it still holds that $B \sim \langle A, C \rangle$.

One of the fundamental axioms of utility theory is the *subsitution principle*: a lottery is not made better or worse by substituting equivalent (or indifferent) prizes. Hence given r' or r'' we know that $\langle A, C \rangle \sim \langle A', C' \rangle$ and $B \sim B'$. But since S is UI we know that $B' \sim \langle A', C' \rangle$ given r' implies that it still is valid given r''. This demonstrates the essence of the proof, and it is simple to clean up the details of the proof if each indifference curve would cut a single horizontal line. But what happens if we have two indifference curves P and Q as shown in Fig. 6.3b? In this case we have to modify our previous argument and build up the domain of applicability in stages. It is first shown (see Fig. 6.3c) that the condition for $\{S, T\}$ to be utility independent of R holds for all r and (s, t) pairs in A_1. Then, because the line $t = t^1$ overlaps with A_1, we can show the condition holds for all (s, t^1). Since each (s, t) pair in A_2 is indifferent to some pair (s, t^1), the necessary utility independence condition can be extended to include A_2. Then an amount t^2 is chosen such that the line $t = t^2$ overlaps A_2, and the procedure is repeated. Eventually, one of the A_i's (A_4 in Fig. 6.3c) will overlap with the line $t = t^*$ so the utility independence condition can be proven valid on that line and extended to A_5. Since the A_i's cover all (s, t) pairs, the utility independence condition is valid for all s, t, and r.]

Proof.* We can represent the condition that S is utility independent of $\{T, R\}$ by

$$u(s, t, r) = u(t, r) + b(t, r)u(s), \qquad b > 0. \tag{6.54}$$

Also, since $\{S, T\}$ is preferentially independent of R, from (6.4) we know that

$$[u(s, t, r^o) = u(s^+, t^+, r^o)] \Rightarrow [u(s, t, r) = u(s^+, t^+, r)], \qquad \forall r. \tag{6.55}$$

---

* In this proof, when an attribute is at its least desirable amount, designated as s^o, for example, we may delete it in the function when no ambiguity will result. Thus, rather than write $u(s^o, t^o, r)$, $u(s^o, t, r)$, and $b(t^o, r)$, we will use $u(r)$, $u(t, r)$, and $b(r)$.

For each pair (s, t) in A_1 defined by

$$A_1 \equiv \{(s, t) : u(s, t, r^o) \le u(s^*, t^o, r^o)\}, \tag{6.56}$$

there exists an s' such that

$$u(s, t, r^o) = u(s', t^o, r^o), \qquad (s, t) \in A_1. \tag{6.57}$$

From (6.55) and (6.57), it follows that

$$u(s, t, r) = u(s', t^o, r), \qquad \forall r, \quad (s, t) \in A_1. \tag{6.58}$$

Evaluating (6.58) with (6.54), we find

$$u(s, t, r) = u(r) + b(r)u(s'), \qquad \forall r, \quad (s, t) \in A_1, \tag{6.59}$$

which, combined with (6.57), gives us

$$u(s, t, r) = u(r) + b(r)u(s,t), \qquad \forall r, \quad (s, t) \in A_1. \tag{6.60}$$

Equation (6.60) says that $\{S, T\}$ is utility independent of R for $(s, t) \in A_1$ and all r. We want to extend this condition to all possible (s, t) pairs.

Choose a t^1 such that

$$u(s^o, t^o, r^o) < u(s^o, t^1, r^o) < u(s^*, t^o, r^o).$$

Since $(s^o, t^1) \in A_1$, from (6.60)

$$u(s^o, t^1, r) = u(r) + b(r)u(t^1), \qquad \forall r. \tag{6.61}$$

Evaluating (6.54) at $t = t^1$ and $r = r^o$ yields

$$u(s, t^1) = u(t^1) + b(t^1)u(s), \qquad \forall s. \tag{6.62}$$

Setting $t = t^1$ in (6.60) gives us

$$u(s, t^1, r) = u(r) + b(r)u(s, t^1), \qquad (s, t^1) \in A_1, \tag{6.63}$$

which can be combined with (6.62) to yield

$$\begin{aligned} u(s, t^1, r) &= u(r) + b(r)[u(t^1) + b(t^1)u(s)] \\ &= u(t^1, r) + b(r)b(t^1)u(s), \qquad \forall r, \quad (s, t^1) \in A_1. \end{aligned} \tag{6.64}$$

Comparing (6.64) to (6.54) with $t = t^1$ shows

$$b(t^1, r) = b(r)b(t^1), \qquad \forall r. \tag{6.65}$$

Substituting (6.61) and (6.65) into (6.54) with $t = t^1$ yields

$$\begin{aligned} u(s, t^1, r) &= u(t^1, r) + b(t^1, r)u(s) \\ &= u(r) + b(r)[u(t^1) + b(t^1)u(s)], \qquad \forall s, r, \end{aligned} \tag{6.66}$$

which can be combined with (6.62) to give

$$u(s, t^1, r) = u(r) + b(r)u(s, t^1), \qquad \forall s, r. \qquad (6.67)$$

To extend result (6.67), let us define A_2 by

$$A_2 \equiv \{(s, t) : u(s^*, t^o, r^o) < u(s, t, r^o) \le u(s^*, t^1, r^o)\}.$$

For any $(s, t) \in A_2$, there exists an s'' such that

$$u(s, t, r^o) = u(s'', t^1, r^o), \qquad (s, t) \in A_2, \qquad (6.68)$$

so from (6.55), it follows that

$$u(s, t, r) = u(s'', t^1, r), \qquad \forall r, \quad (s, t) \in A_2. \qquad (6.69)$$

Evaluating the right-hand side of (6.69) with (6.67) gives

$$u(s, t, r) = u(r) + b(r)u(s'', t^1)$$

which, combined with (6.68), gives us

$$u(s, t, r) = u(r) + b(r)u(s, t), \qquad (s, t) \in A_2. \qquad (6.70)$$

Equation (6.70) says $\{S, T\}$ is utility independent of R for (s, t) pairs in A_2.

The process from (6.61) on is now repeated by choosing an amount t^2 such that

$$u(s^o, t^1, r^o) < u(s^o, t^2, r^o) < u(s^*, t^1, r^o),$$

and then proving that (6.67) holds with t^2 substituted for t^1. Then (6.70) is extended to include all (s, t) pairs such that

$$u(s^*, t^1, r^o) < u(s, t, r^o) \le u(s^*, t^2, r^o).$$

Because of the continuity assumptions on u and the fact that S is essential [i.e., $u(s)$ is not a constant and $b(t, r)$ is positive], by repeating this process with a more preferred t on each iteration, we will eventually prove

$$u(s, t^*, r) = u(r) + b(r)u(s, t^*)$$

so that for any (s, t) pair such that

$$u(s, t, r^o) = u(s', t^*, r^o)$$

for some s', the utility independence expression similar to (6.70) will follow. More formally, let us define

$$h = \min_{t,r} [u(s^*, t, r) - u(s^o, t, r)]$$

so that it follows from (6.54) that

$$h = \min_{t,r} [b(t, r)]$$

which is positive. Then in choosing the series $t^1, t^2, \ldots$, if t^k is such that $u(s^o, t^*, r^o) < u(s^*, t^k, r^o)$, choose $t^{k+1} = t^*$. Otherwise select t^{k+1} such that

$$u(s^o, t^{k+1}, r^o) = u(s^o, t^k, r^o) + \frac{h}{2}.$$

Since $u(s^o, t^*, r^o)$ must by definition, be less than 1, the series $t^1, t^2, \ldots, t^*$ will require, at most $1/(h/2) = 2/h$ members.

By the manner in which the A_i's are defined, collecting all the equations similar to (6.60), (6.70), and so on, will prove that

$$u(s, t, r) = u(r) + b(r)u(s, t), \qquad \forall s, t, r, \tag{6.71}$$

which is the desired result.   ◀

6.8 RELATIONSHIPS AMONG UTILITY INDEPENDENCE ASSUMPTIONS

Let us look at some implications of different sets of utility independence conditions. In particular, we will be interested in implying higher-order utility independence conditions from lower-order conditions. The results included in this section are requisite for the general theorems that follow in the next sections. Here our result concerns the implications of two overlapping utility independence assumptions.

Definition. Let Y_1 and Y_2 be subsets of $X \equiv \{X_1, X_2, \ldots, X_n\}$. Attributes Y_1 and Y_2 *overlap* if their intersection is not empty and if neither contains the other.

Theorem 6.7. *Let Y_1 and Y_2 be overlapping attributes contained in $X \equiv \{X_0, X_1, \ldots, X_n\}$. If Y_1 and Y_2 are each UI then*

  (i) $Y_1 \cup Y_2$, *the union of Y_1 and Y_2, is UI.*
  (ii) $Y_1 \cap Y_2$, *the intersection of Y_1 and Y_2, is UI.*
  (iii) $(Y_1 \cap \bar{Y}_2) \cup (\bar{Y}_1 \cap Y_2)$, *the symmetric difference of Y_1 and Y_2, is UI.*
  (iv) $Y_1 \cap \bar{Y}_2$ *and* $\bar{Y}_1 \cap Y_2$, *the differences, are each UI.*

Proof. Since X_i can designate a vector attribute, the general case can be proven by considering the special case where $X = \{X_0, X_1, X_2, X_3\}$, $Y_1 = \{X_1, X_2\}$, and $Y_2 = \{X_2, X_3\}$, and where Y_1 and Y_2 are each assumed to be UI.

We must show in this case that (i) $\{X_1, X_2, X_3\}$ is UI, (ii) X_2 is UI, (iii) $\{X_1, X_3\}$ is UI, and (iv) X_1 is UI and X_3 is UI. From (6.6), our hypotheses can be written respectively as

$$u(x) = u(x_0, x_1, x_2, x_3) = u(x_0, x_3) + c(x_0, x_3)u(x_1, x_2) \quad (6.72)$$

and

$$u(x) = u(x_0, x_1, x_2, x_3) = u(x_0, x_1) + d(x_0, x_1)u(x_2, x_3), \quad (6.73)$$

where as before we have taken the liberty to delete arguments of u, c, and d when they are at their least preferred levels and no misunderstanding can result. Hence, for instance $u(x_1, x_2)$ and $d(x_0)$ will denote $u(x_0^o, x_1, x_2, x_3^o)$ and $d(x_0, x_1^o)$ respectively. Note, however, from (6.72) and (6.73) that

$$c(x_0^o, x_3^o) = 1 \quad \text{and} \quad d(x_0^o, x_1^o) = 1. \quad (6.74)$$

Part (i). Substituting (6.73) into (6.72) and then (6.72) into (6.73) gives us, respectively,

$$u(x) = u(x_0) + d(x_0)u(x_3) + c(x_0, x_3)[u(x_1) + d(x_1)u(x_2)] \quad (6.75)$$

and

$$u(x) = u(x_0) + c(x_0)u(x_1) + d(x_0, x_1)[u(x_3) + c(x_3)u(x_2)]. \quad (6.76)$$

Equating (6.75) and (6.76) with $x_3 = x_3^o$ indicates

$$d(x_0, x_1) = c(x_0)d(x_1), \quad (6.77)$$

which, together with (6.76), implies that

$$u(x) = u(x_0) + c(x_0)[u(x_1) + d(x_1)u(x_2, x_3)]. \quad (6.78)$$

Evaluating (6.73) at $x_0 = x_0^o$, we see

$$u(x_1, x_2, x_3) = u(x_1) + d(x_1)u(x_2, x_3),$$

and so, from (6.78), it follows that

$$u(x) = u(x_0) + c(x_0)u(x_1, x_2, x_3). \quad (6.79)$$

Expression (6.79) says that $\{X_1, X_2, X_3\}$ is utility independent of X_0.

Part (ii). Substituting (6.73) into (6.72) yields

$$u(x) = u(x_0, x_3) + c(x_0, x_3)[u(x_1) + d(x_1)u(x_2)], \quad (6.80)$$

which can be evaluated at $x_2 = x_2^o$ giving

$$u(x_0, x_1, x_3) = u(x_0, x_3) + c(x_0, x_3)u(x_1). \quad (6.81)$$

Combining (6.80) and (6.81) and denoting $c(x_1, x_3)d(x_1)$ as $f(x_0, x_1, x_3)$, we find

$$u(x) = u(x_0, x_1, x_3) + f(x_0, x_1, x_3)u(x_2), \quad (6.82)$$

which says X_2 is utility independent of $\{X_0, X_1, X_3\}$.

Part (iii). Setting $x_0 = x_0^o$ and $x_2 = x_2^o$ in (6.72) and (6.73) and equating gives

$$u(x_3) + c(x_3)u(x_1) = u(x_1) + d(x_1)u(x_3), \qquad (6.83)$$

which can be rearranged to yield

$$\frac{c(x_3) - 1}{u(x_3)} = \frac{d(x_1) - 1}{u(x_1)} = k, \qquad u(x_i) \neq 0, \qquad i = 1, 3, \qquad (6.84)$$

where k is a constant, since (6.84) has a function of x_3 equal to a function of x_1. If $u(x_1) = 0$, from (6.83), it follows that $d(x_1) = 1$ and similarly $c(x_3) = 1$ when $u(x_3) = 0$. Thus, from (6.84), we see that

$$c(x_3) = ku(x_3) + 1 \qquad (6.85)$$

and

$$d(x_1) = ku(x_1) + 1, \qquad (6.86)$$

which can be substituted into (6.75) with $x_0 = x_0^o$, yielding

$$u(x_1, x_2, x_3) = u(x_3) + [ku(x_3) + 1][u(x_1) + [ku(x_1) + 1]u(x_2)]$$
$$= u(x_2) + [ku(x_2) + 1][u(x_1) + u(x_3) + ku(x_1)u(x_3)]. \qquad (6.87)$$

Combining (6.87) and (6.79), it follows that

$$u(x) = u(x_0) + c(x_0)[u(x_2) + [ku(x_2) + 1]u(x_1, x_3)]$$
$$= u(x_0, x_2) + g(x_0, x_2)u(x_1, x_3), \qquad (6.88)$$

where $g(x_0, x_2) = c(x_0)[ku(x_2) + 1]$. Expression (6.88) proves the desired result that $\{X_1, X_3\}$ is utility independent of $\{X_0, X_2\}$.

Part (iv). We are given that $\{X_1, X_2\}$ is utility independent of its complement and part (iii) has shown $\{X_1, X_3\}$ is utility independent of its complement. Hence, from part (ii), it follows that the intersection X_1 is utility independent of its complement $\{X_0, X_2, X_3\}$. Similarly it follows that X_3 is utility independent of $\{X_0, X_1, X_2\}$. ◀

Theorem 6.7, which assumes utility independence conditions and concerns preferences for lotteries, closely parallels a result of Gorman (1968a) concerning preferences for consequences derived from preferential independence conditions. If each designation of the term utility independence in Theorem 6.7 were replaced by preferential independence, we would essentially have Gorman's result, which was presented in Chapter 3.*

---

* Since UI implies PI we could have exploited Gorman's results (see Theorem 3.7) in the proof of Theorem 6.7. But UI is such a strong condition that it enables us to present a straightforward algebraic proof directly.

6.9 DECOMPOSITION OF MULTIATTRIBUTE UTILITY FUNCTIONS

Roughly speaking, the more utility independence properties we can identify, the simpler the assessment of the utility function becomes. It is important to specify the simplest functional form of the multiattribute utility function consistent with an arbitrary set of utility independence assumptions. With this in mind, we want to generalize the results of Section 6.8 by constructing a "chaining theorem" using Theorem 6.7 as the building block. Let us illustrate with a simple example.

Example 6.3. Let $X \equiv \{X_1, X_2, X_3, X_4, X_5, X_6\}$ and suppose $Y_1 = \{X_1, X_2\}$ and $Y_2 = \{X_2, X_3, X_4\}$ are each UI. Then, by invoking Theorem 6.7 repeatedly, we can show possible unions of X_1, X_2, and $\{X_3, X_4\}$ are also UI. In particular, we know that $\{X_1, X_2, X_3, X_4\}$ is UI.

Now, in addition, suppose that we find out that X_4 is UI. This may eventually help us assess a utility function, but since X_4 does not overlap, as distinct from being contained in, any of the existing sets of UI attributes, the implications of X_4 being UI cannot be further exploited. We may also find out that X_6 is UI, but since it does not overlap any UI attributes, it cannot be used to imply additional utility independence conditions.

However, if in addition it is determined that $Y_3 = \{X_4, X_5\}$ is UI, many implications follow from Theorem 6.7. Because $\{X_3, X_4\}$ is UI also, we know X_3, X_4, and X_5 are each UI. And as can be verified, given that Y_1, Y_2, and Y_3 are UI, each possible union of the elements $X_1, X_2, \ldots, X_5$ is also UI. ∎

Given an arbitrary set of utility independence assumptions (e.g., Y_j is UI of $\bar{Y}_j$, $j = 1, 2, \ldots, J$), we want to exploit this to the maximum extent possible in structuring the resulting utility function. If $J = 2$, three possibilities relating Y_1 and Y_2 exist:

1. Y_1 and Y_2 overlap.
2. Y_1 and Y_2 are disjoint.
3. Y_1 or Y_2 is contained in the other.

The previous section studied case 1. Here we want to investigate the generalization of this case when $J \geq 3$. The implication of cases 2 and 3 for $J \geq 3$, as well as combinations of all three cases, will be considered in the remainder of the chapter.

Definition. A *utility independent chain* is a collection of $\{Y_1, \ldots, Y_R\}$, where (1) Y_j is UI, $j = 1, \ldots, R$, and (2) there is an ordering of Y_1

through Y_R such that each Y_j (other than the first in the ordering) overlaps at least one of its predecessors in the ordering.

We want to find utility independent chains that consist of as many sets as possible. This will allow us to exploit the utility independence properties to the fullest extent in simplifying the implied functional form of the utility function.

Definition. Let $\{Y_1, \ldots, Y_J\}$ be a set such that Y_j is UI, $j = 1, \ldots, J$ and let $\{Y_1, \ldots, Y_R\}$, $R \le J$ be a utility independent chain. This chain is a *maximal utility independent chain* if no Y_k, $k = R + 1, \ldots, J$ overlaps any Y_j, $j = 1, \cdots, R$.

To gain some insight into this definition, let us construct a maximal utility independent chain from a collection of sets $\{Y^j : j = 1, \ldots, J\}$ where each Y^j is UI. We use superscripts because we shall shortly rearrange and relabel these Y^j's with subscripts. Select some Y^i that is not contained in any of the other Y^j, $j \ne i$. Label this set Y_1. Next we search for a Y^i in the remaining collection of sets that overlaps Y_1. If no such set exists, then Y_1 by itself is a maximal utility chain. If such a set exists, relabel it Y_2. Then $\{Y_1, Y_2\}$ is a utility independent chain. The process now repeats.

Suppose that the process continues and we have drawn R sets from the original collection $\{Y^j : j = 1, \ldots, J\}$ and suppose that these R sets have been relabeled $\{Y_1, \ldots, Y_R\}$ and form a utility independent chain. We now seek a Y^i from the remaining collection $\{Y^j : j = 1, \ldots, J\} - \{Y_1, \ldots, Y_R\}$ such that Y^i overlaps one of the sets $Y_1, \ldots, Y_R$. If no such Y^i exists, $\{Y_1, \ldots, Y_R\}$ is a maximal utility independent chain. If such a Y^i exists, relabel it Y_{R+1}, and then $\{Y_1, \ldots, Y_R, Y_{R+1}\}$ is a utility independent chain, and so on. Note that more than one maximal utility independent chain can be selected from the original collection.

Definition. Let $\{Y_1, Y_2, \ldots, Y_R\}$ be a maximal utility independent chain. Each Y_j, $j \le R$, partitions $X \equiv \{X_1, X_2, \ldots, X_n\}$ into Y_j and $\bar{Y}_j$. There are 2^R possible subsets of X created by taking intersections formed with either Y_j or $\bar{Y}_j$ for each $j \le R$. Thus, for instance, if $R = 3$, we have $Y_1 Y_2 Y_3$, $Y_1 Y_2 \bar{Y}_3$, $Y_1 \bar{Y}_2 Y_3$, and so on. Each intersection, except for $\bigcap_{j=1}^{R} \bar{Y}_j$, is defined to be an *element* of the maximal utility independent chain $\{Y_1, \ldots, Y_R\}$ if it is not empty.

An example should help illustrate our definitions.

Example 6.4. Consider the set $X = \{X_1, X_2, \ldots, X_8\}$, and suppose Y_j is UI, $j = 1, 2, \ldots, 5$, where

$$Y_1 \equiv \{X_1, X_2, X_3\}, \qquad Y_2 \equiv \{X_3, X_4, X_5\}, \qquad Y_3 \equiv \{X_2, X_3\},$$
$$Y_4 \equiv \{X_5\}, \qquad \text{and} \qquad Y_5 \equiv \{X_7, X_8\}.$$

Note that Y_2 overlaps Y_1, therefore $\{Y_1, Y_2\}$ is a utility independent chain. Now Y_3 is contained in Y_1 but Y_3 does overlap Y_2. Thus, Y_3 is added to $\{Y_1, Y_2\}$ forming $\{Y_1, Y_2, Y_3\}$, another utility independent chain. Checking Y_4, we see it is completely contained in Y_2 and distinct from both Y_1 and Y_3. Thus, the attribute Y_4 does not overlap any of Y_1, Y_2, or Y_3, so it does not enter the maximal utility independent chain we are constructing. Also Y_5 does not overlap any of Y_1, Y_2, or Y_3 implying that the collection of sets $\{Y_1, Y_2, Y_3\}$ is a maximal utility independent chain on X. In addition, Y_5 is itself another maximal utility independent chain on X.

To identify the *elements* of the maximal utility independent chain $\{Y_1, Y_2, Y_3\}$, we note that $Y_1 Y_2 Y_3 = \{X_3\}$, $Y_1 \bar{Y}_2 Y_3 = \{X_2\}$, $Y_1 \bar{Y}_2 \bar{Y}_3 = \{X_1\}$, $\bar{Y}_1 Y_2 \bar{Y}_3 = \{X_4, X_5\}$, and $Y_1 Y_2 \bar{Y}_3$, $\bar{Y}_1 Y_2 Y_3$, and $\bar{Y}_1 \bar{Y}_2 Y_3$ are empty. Thus there are four elements of the chain, that is, X_1, X_2, X_3, and $\{X_4, X_5\}$. For the maximal utility independent chain Y_5, there is the one element $\{X_7, X_8\}$. ∎

Let us return to the general case and state an important result.

Theorem 6.8.* *Each possible union of the elements in a maximal utility independent chain defined on $X = \{X_0, X_1, \ldots, X_n\}$ is utility independent of its complement in X.*

[*Remark Before Proof.* The proof follows in three parts. Let us assume there are L elements $\{W_1, \ldots, W_L\}$ of the maximal utility independent chain $\{Y_1, \ldots, Y_R\}$ and define $Z \equiv \bigcup_{j=1}^{R} Y_j$, which can be thought of either as a collection of the X_i's, which are members of any Y_j, $j = 1, \ldots, R$, or as the set of elements $\{W_1, \ldots, W_L\}$. We first show the set Z is utility independent of its complement. Next, each subset of $L-1$ of the elements is shown to be utility independent of its complement. Then, using the intersection part of Theorem 6.7, it follows that each union of the elements is utility independent of its complement in X. The proof concerns maximal utility independent chains with three or more elements. The only other possibility involves chains with one element, in which case the theorem is valid by definition.]

Proof. Part 1. Let $\{Y_1, \ldots, Y_R\}$ be a maximal utility independent chain. By the manner in which the chain was constructed, Y_{k+1} intersects $\bigcup_{j=1}^{k} Y_j$ and hence, using the union part of Theorem 6.7, it follows that $\bigcup_{j=1}^{k+1} Y_j$ is UI. By induction we see that $Z \equiv \bigcup_{j=1}^{R} Y_j$ is UI.

---

* This result, which explores the implications of maximal utility independent chains, repeatedly invokes Theorem 6.7. A similar construction, using Theorem 3.7 as a basic tool, could have proven analogous implications for what we might have referred to as maximal preferential independent chains and their corresponding elements.

Part 2. To prove that each union of $L-1$ elements of the chain is UI, let us renumber the Y_j's so that the typical element of the chain, call it W, is defined by $W \equiv \bigcap_{j=1}^{r} Y_j \bigcap_{j=r+1}^{R} \bar{Y}_j$, where $1 \le r \le R$ and $[\bigcup_{j=1}^{t-1} Y_j] \cap Y_t$, $t = 2, \ldots, R$, is not empty. This renumbering will always be possible because of the manner in which Z was constructed. We wish to prove that $Z - W$ is utility independent of its complement.

Either $\bigcap_{j=1}^{r} Y_j$ must be equivalent to W or it must be equivalent to $\{W, M_1, \ldots, M_s\}$ where $M_1, \ldots, M_s$ designate other elements. Allowing the M's to be null sets, the general case is $\bigcap_{j=1}^{r} Y_j = \{W, M_1, \ldots, M_s\}$. Consider two cases $r \ge 2$ and $r = 1$.

For $r \ge 2$, define $T_j = (Y_j \cup Y_{j+1}) - (Y_j \cap Y_{j+1})$, for $j = 1, 2, \ldots, r-1$. By the symmetric difference part of Theorem 6.7, each T_j, $j = 1, 2, \ldots, r-1$, is UI. Also, each T_{j+1} overlaps T_j because of the way they are defined. Thus, the union part of Theorem 6.7 implies that

$$\bigcup_{j=1}^{r-1} T_j = \left[\bigcup_{j=1}^{r} Y_j - \{W, M_1, \ldots, M_s\} \right]$$

is UI.

If the M's are null sets, then clearly $[\bigcup_{j=1}^{r} Y_j - W]$ is UI. Since no Y_j, $j = r+1, \ldots, R$ overlaps W, the construction $[\bigcup_{j=1}^{r} Y_j - W] \cup Y_{t+1}$ is equal to $\bigcup_{j=1}^{t+1} Y_j - W$, for all $t = r, \ldots, R-1$.

Taking successive unions in this manner and, since $\bigcup_{j=1}^{t} Y_j$ overlaps Y_{t+1}, invoking the union part of Theorem 6.7, we find that the final construction $[\bigcup_{j=1}^{R} Y_j - W]$ is utility independent of its complement.

If $\{M_1, \ldots, M_s\}$ is not the null set, we again take successive unions using the Y_j's, $j = r+1, \ldots, R$, beginning with the original construction $[\bigcup_{j=1}^{r} Y_j - \{W, M_1, \ldots, M_s\}] \cup Y_{r+1}$. None of the Y_j's, $j = r+1, \ldots, R$ can overlaps W. However collectively $\bigcup_{j=r+1}^{R} Y_j$ must contain $\{M_1, \ldots, M_s\}$ since

$$W \equiv \bigcap_{j=1}^{r} Y_j \bigcap_{j=r+1}^{R} \bar{Y}_j = \{W, M_1, \ldots, M_s\} \bigcap_{j=r+1}^{R} \bar{Y}_j,$$

implying $\bigcap_{j=r+1}^{R} \bar{Y}_j$ does not contain $\{M_1, \ldots, M_s\}$. Taking the successive unions as described, we will again find $[\bigcup_{j=1}^{R} Y_j - W]$ is UI.

For $r = 1$, we have $W = Y_1 \bigcap_{j=2}^{R} \bar{Y}_j$ and since Y_j must contain at least two elements by the manner in which the chain was constructed, the general case is where $Y_1 = \{W, M_1, \ldots, M_s\}$. Each element M_k, $k = 1, \ldots, s$, must be contained in some Y_j, $j = 2, \ldots, R$. Otherwise, for instance, M_1 would only be in Y_1 so $\{W, M_1\} = Y_1 \bigcap_{j=2}^{R} \bar{Y}_j$, which implies W is not an element.

Thus each element M_k, $k = 1, \ldots, s$, is in at least two Y_j's, $j = 1, \ldots, R$, and we have shown for this case that $\{Z - M_k\}$ is UI, $k = 1, \ldots, s$. Using the intersection part of Theorem 6.7,

$$\bigcap_{k=1}^{s} \{Z - M_k\} = \{Z - \bigcup_{k=1}^{s} M_k\}$$

is UI. Now $\{Z - \bigcup_{k=1}^{s} M_k\} \cap Y_1 = W$, so by the symmetric difference part of Theorem 6.7, we findd $\{Z - W\}$ is UI since $\{Z - \bigcup_{k=1}^{s} M_k\} \cup Y_1 = Z$.

Part 3. From Part 2, each subset of $L - 1$ of the elements $\{W_1, W_2, \ldots, W_L\}$ is utility independent of its complement in X. Thus, any proper subset of these W's is identical to the intersection of the appropriate sets of size $L - 1$, and so by the intersection part of Theorem 6.7, all subsets of elements are utility independent of their complements. ◄

The relevance of Theorem 6.8 in structuring multiattribute utility functions will be shown in the next section. To illustrate the power of Theorem 6.8, let us use it to prove Theorem 6.2 given in Section 6.3. For reference, the result is repeated here.

Theorem 6.2. *Given attributes* $X_1, X_2, \ldots, X_n$, *the following are equivalent:*

1. *Attributes* $X_1, X_2, \ldots, X_n$ *are mutually utility independent.*
2. $\bar{X}_i$ *is UI,* $i = 1, 2, \ldots, n$.
3. $\{X_i, X_{i+1}, \ldots, X_n\}$ *is UI,* $i = 2, 3, \ldots, n$ *and* $\{X_1, X_2, \ldots, X_{n-1}\}$ *is UI.*
4. $\{X_i, X_{i+1}\}$ *is UI,* $i = 1, 2, \ldots, n - 1, n \geq 3$.
5. X_1 *is UI and* $\{X_1, X_i\}$ *is PI,* $i = 2, \ldots, n, n \geq 3$.

Proof. By definition, (1) implies (2)–(5). To prove the converses, we wish to show that $X_1, X_2, \ldots, X_n$ are each elements of a *maximal utility independent chain* encompassing $\{X_1, \ldots, X_n\}$ given any condition (2)–5). Then the result directly follows from Theorem 6.8.

$(2) \Rightarrow (1)$. Note that $\bar{\bar{X}}_i = X_i$. Then $(\bigcap_{j \neq i} \bar{X}_i) \cap X_i = X_i$ is an element of the chain $\{\bar{X}_1, \bar{X}_2, \ldots, \bar{X}_n\}$.

$(3) \Rightarrow (1)$. The collection of sets $Y_i \equiv \{X_i, X_{i+1}, \ldots, X_n\}$, $i = 2, 3, \ldots, n - 1$, and the set $Y_n \equiv \{X_1, X_2, \ldots, X_{n-1}\}$ make a maximal utility independent chain. Note that

$$\left(\bigcap_{j=2}^{i} Y_j \right) \cap \left(\bigcap_{j=i+1}^{n-1} \bar{Y}_j \right) \cap Y_n = X_i, \qquad i = 2, \ldots, n - 1,$$

is an element. Also $X_n = (\bigcap_{j=2}^{n-1} Y_j) \cap \bar{Y}_n$ and $X_1 = Y_n \cap (\bigcap_{j=2}^{n-1} \bar{Y}_j)$ are elements.

$(4) \Rightarrow (1)$. Let us define $Y_i = \{X_i, X_{i+1}\}$, $i = 1, 2, \ldots, n - 1$, so that

$\{Y_1, Y_2, \ldots, Y_{n-1}\}$ is a maximal utility independent chain. Then clearly $X_1 = Y_1 \cap (\cap_{j=2}^{n-1} \bar{Y}_j)$, and

$$X_i = Y_{i-1} \cap Y_i \cap \left(\underset{j \neq i, i-1}{\cap} \bar{Y}_j \right), \qquad i = 2, 3, \ldots, n-1,$$

and

$$X_n = \left(\overset{n-2}{\underset{j=1}{\cap}} \bar{Y}_j \right) \cap Y_{n-1}$$

are elements.

$(5) \Rightarrow (1)$. By Theorem 6.6, $\{X_1, X_i\}$ is UI, $i = 2, 3, \ldots, n$. Define $Y_i = \{X_1, X_i\}$, $i = 2, \ldots, n$, so that $\{Y_2, Y_3, \ldots, Y_n\}$ is a maximal utility independent chain. Then $X_1 = \cap_{i=2}^n Y_i$ and $X_i = Y_i \cap (\cap_{j \neq i} \bar{Y}_i)$, $i = 2, \ldots, n$, are elements of the chain. ◀

6.10 ADDITIONAL REPRESENTATION THEOREMS*

In the last three sections, we have looked at the implications of (1) a utility independence condition together with a preferential independence condition, (2) two overlapping utility independence conditions, and (3) an arbitrary number of utility independence conditions. Implications of (1) can be used to invoke (2) or (3) and implications of (2) can be utilized with (3). In this and the following sections, we shall try to integrate some of these ideas and present some special results that are important. Proofs will usually not be given in detail since they either follow directly from or are similar to earlier ones. First we will look at extensions of the multiplicative and multilinear utility function.

6.10.1 Extension of the Multiplicative Form

The following is a straightforward extension of Theorem 6.1.

Theorem 6.9. *Given the set of attributes $X \equiv \{X_0, X_1, \ldots, X_n\}$ where X_i, $i = 1, 2, \ldots, n$, are elements of a maximal utility independent chain (this excludes X_0!), then*

$$u(x_0, \bar{x}_0) = u(x_0, \bar{x}_0^o) + [u(x_0, \bar{x}_0^*) - u(x_0, \bar{x}_0^o)] u(x_0^o, \bar{x}_0),$$

and either (if $\sum_{i=1}^n k_i = 1$),

$$u(x_0^o, \bar{x}_0) = \sum_{i=1}^n u(x_i, \bar{x}_i^o) = \sum_{i=1}^n k_i u_i(x_i),$$

*This section contains specialized results that can be omitted at first reading.

or (*if* $\sum_{i=1}^{n} k_i \neq 1$)

$$1 + ku(x_0^o, \bar{x}_0) = \prod_{i=1}^{n} [1 + ku(x_i, \bar{x}_i^o)] = \prod_{i=1}^{n} [1 + kk_i u_i(x_i)],$$

where

1. $\bar{x}_i = (x_0, x_1, \ldots, x_{i-1}, x_{i+1}, \ldots, x_n)$, $\quad i = 0, 1, \ldots, n$.
2. $u(x_0^o, x_1^o, \ldots, x_n^o) = 0$, $\quad u(x_0^o, x_1^*, x_2^*, \ldots, x_n^*) = 1$.
3. $u_i(x_i^o) = 0$, $\quad u_i(x_i^*) = 1$, $\quad i = 1, 2, \ldots, n$.
4. $k_i = u(x_i^*, \bar{x}_i^o)$, $\quad i = 1, 2, \ldots, n$.

and

5. k *is a scaling constant,** *which is a solution to*

$$1 + k = \prod_{i=1}^{n} (1 + kk_i).$$

Proof. Using Theorem 6.1, plus the additional assumption that $\{X_1, X_2, \ldots, X_n\}$ is utility independent of X_0, implying

$$u(x_0, x_1, \ldots, x_n) = u(x_0) + c(x_0)u(x_1, x_2, \ldots, x_n), \quad c > 0,$$

leads one directly to conclude either

$$u(x) = k_0 u_0(x_0) + [u(x_0, \bar{x}_o^*) - u(x_0, \bar{x}_0^o)]\left[\sum_{i=1}^{n} k_i u_i(x_i)\right], \quad (6.89)$$

or

$$u(x) = k_0 u_0(x_0) + [u(x_0, \bar{x}_0^*) - u(x_0, \bar{x}_0^o)]$$
$$\times \left[\frac{1}{k}\left\{\left[\prod_{i=1}^{n} [1 + kk_i u_i(x_i)]\right] - 1\right\}\right], \quad (6.90)$$

which is the desired result. ◄

6.10.2 Extension of the Multilinear Form

Expressions (6.89) and (6.90) provide forms of the utility function when there is one maximal utility independent chain. However, there are situations where more than one maximal utility independent chain may exist among the same set of attributes. For instance, let X be partitioned into $\{Z_0, Z_1, Z_2\}$ and suppose Z_i is utility independent of $\bar{Z}_i$, $i = 1, 2$. That is, Z_1 and Z_2 are maximal utility independent chains. We can derive

---

* Procedures for choosing the correct value of k are given in Appendix 6B at the end of this chapter.

functional forms of utility functions involving more than one such chain by considering sets of utility independence assumptions over nonoverlapping attributes. With regard to this, we have the following theorem.

Theorem 6.10. Let $X = \{X_1, X_2, \ldots, X_n\}$ be partitioned into $\{Z_0, Z_1, \ldots, Z_M\}$ where Z_m, $m = 1, 2, \ldots, M$, is utility independent. Then the utility function $u(x)$ can be represented by

$$u(x) = g[z_0, u_1(z_1), u_2(z_2), \ldots, u_M(z_M)], \tag{6.91}$$

where u_m, $m = 1, 2, \ldots, M$, is a utility function over Z_m. The specific result is

$$u(x) = u(z_0) + \sum_{m=1}^{M} f_m(z_0) u_m(z_m) + \sum_{\substack{m=1 \\ m < j \le M}}^{M} f_{mj}(z_0) u_m(z_m) u_j(z_j)$$

$$+ \cdots + f(z_0) u_1(z_1) \cdots u_M(z_M), \tag{6.92}$$

where

$$f_m(z_0) = u(z_0, z_m^*, \bar{z}_{0m}^o) - u(z_0, z_m^o, \bar{z}_{0m}^v), \tag{6.93a}$$

$$f_{mj}(z_0) = u(z_0, z_m^*, z_j^*, \bar{z}_{0mj}^o) - u(z_0, z_m^*, z_j^o, \bar{z}_{0mj}^o)$$
$$- u(z_0, z_m^o, z_j^*, \bar{z}_{0mj}^o) + u(z_0, z_m^o, z_j^o, \bar{z}_{0mj}^o), \tag{6.93b}$$

$$\vdots$$

$$f(z_0) = u(z_0, \bar{z}_0^*) - \sum_{m=1}^{M} u(z_0, z_m^o, \bar{z}_{0m}^*) + \sum_{\substack{m=1 \\ m < j \le M}}^{M} u(z_0, z_m^o, z_j^o, \bar{z}_{0mj}^*)$$

$$- \sum_{\substack{m=1 \\ m < j \le M \\ j < k \le M}}^{M} u(z_0, z_m^o, z_j^o, z_k^o, \bar{z}_{0mjk}^*) + \cdots + (-1)^M u(z_0, z_1^o, \ldots, z_M^o). \tag{6.93c}$$

Theorem 6.10 is the natural extension of the multilinear utility function. The distinction is that Z_0 is not assumed to be utility independent of its complement.

One of the important facts to remember about Theorems 6.9 and 6.10 is that they can be used repeatedly in simplifying the expression for a multiattribute utility function. That is, the attributes designated by X_i in (6.89) and (6.90) and by Z_m in (6.92) may be vector attributes and possess utility independent properties among their respective components. If this is the case, then of course Theorems 6.9 and 6.10 can be used in specifying the relevant utility function $u_i(x_i)$ in (6.89) and (6.90) or $u_m(z_m)$ in (6.92). An example should help illustrate this, in addition to clarifying our definitions.

Example 6.5. Suppose we want to assess a utility function u over the set of attributes $X \equiv \{X_1, X_2, \ldots, X_9\}$. Furthermore, suppose that it has been verified that Y_j is utility independent of $\bar{Y}_j$, $j = 1, 2, \ldots, 6$, where

$$Y_1 = \{X_2, X_3\},$$
$$Y_2 = \{X_4, X_5, X_6\},$$
$$Y_3 = \{X_5\},$$
$$Y_4 = \{X_5, X_6, X_7, X_8\},$$
$$Y_5 = \{X_8\},$$
$$Y_6 = \{X_8, X_9\}.$$

By our definition, there are two maximal utility independent chains in X: $\{Y_1\}$ and $\{Y_2, Y_4, Y_6\}$. Attributes Y_3 and Y_5 are not in the second chain because $Y_3 \cap Y_j$ for $j = 2, 4, 6$ is either Y_3 itself or empty. The same is true for Y_5, so by the definition of a utility independent chain, Y_3 and Y_5 are excluded. Thus, we can define $Z_1 = Y_1$ and $Z_2 = Y_2 \cup Y_4 \cup Y_6$ and use (6.92) to write

$$u(x) = u(z_0) + f_1(z_0)u_1(z_1) + f_2(z_0)u_2(z_2) + f_{12}(z_0)u_1(z_1)u_2(z_2), \quad (6.94)$$

where u, u_1, and u_2 are scaled from 0 to 1.

There is clearly only one element $\{X_2, X_3\}$ in Y_1 but $\{Y_2, Y_4, Y_6\}$ has five elements: X_4, $\{X_5, X_6\}$, X_7, X_8, and X_9. We can use Theorem 6.9 to specify $u_2(z_2)$ further. For this purpose, we can assume that $x_0 = x_0^o$ in (6.89) and (6.90) so $u_0(x_0) = 0$ and $c_0(x_0) = 1$, and either

$$u_2(z_2) = k_4 u_4'(x_4) + k_{56}u_{56}'(x_5, x_6) + k_7 u_7'(x_7) + k_8 u_8'(x_8) + k_9 u_9'(x_9), \quad (6.95)$$

or

$$u_2(z_2) = \frac{1}{k}\left\{\left[\prod_{i \in T}[1 + kk_i u_i'(x_i)]\right] - 1\right\}, \quad (6.96)$$

where

$$T = \{4, (5, 6), 7, 8, 9\}.$$

Considering only the attributes $\{X_5, X_6\}$, there is another utility independent chain, that is, $Y_3 = \{X_5\}$. Thus, by Theorem 6.10,

$$u_{56}'(x_5, x_6) = u_6'(x_6) + f_6(x_6)u_5'(x_5), \quad (6.97)$$

which can be substituted back into (6.95) or (6.96). The original assumption that Y_5 is utility independent of $\bar{Y}_5$ is redundant for this problem since $Y_5 = \{X_7\}$ is an element in the maximal utility independent chain

$\{Y_2, Y_4, Y_6\}$, and by Theorem 6.8, each element of such a chain is utility independent of its complement. Combining (6.94)–(6.97) permits us to break down $u(x)$ as far as possible consistent with the specified assumptions. ∎

6.10.3 Special Multilinear Forms of the Utility Function

As we might expect, there are many sets of assumptions that are stronger than the utility independence assumptions of Theorem 6.3 and yet weaker than mutual utility independence assumption of Theorem 6.1. Let us illustrate the usefulness of exploring the additional restrictions placed on the utility function by various assumptions. As we will show, additional assumptions reduce the amount of empirical information necessary to specify u. Related results follow in Section 6.11 when we discuss preferences in hierarchical structures of attributes.

Throughout this subsection, we will assume that $X \equiv \{X_1, X_2, \ldots, X_n\}$ and each X_i is UI, $i = 1, 2, \ldots n$, so that, from Theorem 6.3, we know the utility function $u(x_1, x_2, \ldots, x_n)$ can be assessed from the n one-attribute utility functions $u_i(x_i)$ and $2^n - 2$ scaling constants. We could have been a bit more general and looked at the effect of additional assumptions used in connection with the assumptions of Theorem 6.10. However, since the ideas are analogous to that of adding additional assumptions to those of Theorem 6.3, and since the latter case is notationally more convenient, we chose it for illustration.

Y IS UTILITY INDEPENDENT OF $\bar{Y}$. Let us assume that $Y \equiv \{X_1, X_2, \ldots, X_m\}$. If Y is utility independent of $\bar{Y}$, then the attributes Y, $X_{m+1}, X_{m+2}, \ldots, X_n$ are set of attributes, each of which is UI. Thus, Theorem 6.3 applies so the overall utility function can be assessed from $(n - m + 1)$ one-attribute utility functions: $u_Y(y)$, $u_{m+1}(x_{m+1}), \ldots, u_n(x_n)$, and $2^{n-m+1} - 2$ scaling constants. But $u_Y(y)$ can be assessed by again applying Theorem 6.3 since each of $X_1, X_2, \ldots, X_m$ is utility independent. Therefore, the m utility functions $u_1(x_1), u_2(x_2), \ldots, u_m(x_m)$ and $2^m - 2$ scaling constants will specify $u_Y(y)$. Putting this together, the original utility function of interest $u(x_1, x_2, \ldots, x_n)$ is now specified by the n one-attribute utility functions and $(2^{n-m+1} + 2^m - 4)$ scaling constants.

The usefulness of the additional assumption should be clear: it allows us to specify u with fewer scaling constants. This is so, since the assumption that Y is UI puts a set of consistency restrictions on the scaling constants of the multilinear form.

Y AND $\bar{Y}$ ARE MUTUALLY UTILITY INDEPENDENT. Using the same notation as before, let us assume that Y and $\bar{Y}$ are mutually utility independent. From Theorem 5.2, we know the utility function can be specified

Table 6.3

Number of Scaling Constants Required to Assess n-Attribute Utility Functions Given X_i is UI, $i = 1, 2, \ldots, n$

n	No Additional Assumptions (Multilinear Utility Function)	Assuming $Y \equiv \{X_1, X_2, \ldots, X_m\}$ is UI			Assuming $Y \equiv \{X_1, X_2, \ldots, X_m\}$ and $\bar{Y}$ are each UI			Assuming $X_1, X_2, \ldots, X_n$ Are Mutually Utility Independent (Multiplicative Utility Function)
		$m=2$	$m=3$	$m=5$	$m=2$	$m=3$	$m=5$	
n	$2^n - 2$	2^{n-1}	$2^{n-2}+4$	$2^{n-4}-28$	$2^{n-2}-2$	$2^{n-3}+6$	$2^{n-5}+30$	n
3	6	4			4			3
4	14	8	8		6	8		4
5	30	16	12		10	10		5
6	62	32	20	32	18	14	32	6
7	126	64	36	36	34	22	34	7
8	254	128	68	44	66	38	38	8
9	510	256	132	60	130	70	46	9
10	1022	512	260	92	258	134	62	10

from $u_Y(y)$ and $u_{\bar{Y}}(\bar{y})$ and two scaling constants. Then from Theorem 6.3, it follows that $u_Y(y)$ is specified by m one-attribute utility functions: $u_1(x_1), \ldots, u_m(x_m)$, and $2^m - 2$ scaling constants. Similarly, $u_{\bar{Y}}(\bar{y})$ can be expressed from $u_{m+1}(x_{m+1}), \ldots, u_n(x_n)$ and $2^{n-m} - 2$ scaling constants. Therefore, subject to the additional mutual utility independence assumption, the utility function $u(x_1, x_2, \ldots, x_n)$ is given by $u_1(x_1)$, $u_2(x_2), \ldots, u_n(x_n)$ and $2^m + 2^{n-m} - 2$ scaling constants.

With the multiplicative and multilinear utility function, as well as the two cases considered above, the utility function u was specified by the n utility functions $u_1, u_2, \ldots, u_n$ and some number of scaling constants. The additional assumptions above allowed us to assess u with less constants than required in the multilinear case. Table 6.3 compares the number of constants required with and without the additional assumptions for some representative values of n and m, and thus gives an indication of the additional simplification in the assessment of u provided. In all cases we assume that X_i is UI, $i = 1, 2, \ldots, n$.

OTHER SETS OF ASSUMPTIONS. The additional assumptions that we have considered so far are the ones that would necessarily be "building blocks" for more involved sets of utility independence assumptions. To give just one more illustration, let us define Y as before and define Z as $\{X_r, X_{r+1}, \ldots, X_n\}$. Now let us assume that Y and Z are utility independent of their complementary sets of attributes. There are three separate cases to consider—those where $r \leq m$, $r = m + 1$, and $r > m + 1$. We will just consider the most involved case where $r \leq m$ and there is some "overlapping" in our utility independence assumptions. Let us define the following notation to simplify our discussion:

$$Y_1 \equiv \{X_1, X_2, \ldots, X_{r-1}\},$$
$$Y_2 \equiv \{X_r, X_{r+1}, \ldots, X_m\}, \quad \text{and}$$
$$Y_3 \equiv \{X_{m+1}, X_{m+2}, \ldots, X_n\}.$$

In terms of this notation, we are assuming that $\{Y_1, Y_2\}$ is utility independent of Y_3 and $\{Y_2, Y_3\}$ is utility independent of Y_1, in addition to the original assumption that X_i is UI, $i = 1, 2, \ldots, n$. When these assumptions hold, it follows from Theorem 6.1 that the utility function $u(y_1, y_2, y_3)$ is either additive or multiplicative, and thus we must assess utility functions over each of the Y_j's and assess three independent scaling constants. But the component attributes of each of the Y_j's are each UI, so the $u_j(y_j)$ terms can be assessed from a utility function for each component X_i in Y_j and $2^{b_j} - 2$ scaling constants, where b_j is the number of X_i's in Y_j.

Example 6.6. To illustrate the power of this result, suppose we have nine original attributes denoted by $X_1, X_2, \ldots, X_9$ and $Y_1 \equiv \{X_1, X_2, X_3\}$, $Y_2 \equiv \{X_4, X_5, X_6\}$, and $Y_3 \equiv \{X_7, X_8, X_9\}$. Then when our assumptions hold, we need to assess $u_1(y_1)$, $u_2(y_2)$, and $u_3(y_3)$ and three scaling constants. But each $u_j(y_j)$ requires that we assess the respective three utility functions over the respective X_i's and $2^3 - 2 = 6$ scaling constants. Therefore, the overall utility function u requires that we assess the nine-component utility functions and 21 scaling constants. This can be compared to the 510 scaling constants necessary when only X_i is UI, $i = 1, 2, \ldots, 9$. ∎

6.10.4   The Additive Value Function and Multiplicative Utility Function*

It is interesting to relate the additive value function of Section 3.6 to the multiplicative utility function of Section 6.3 since necessary and sufficient conditions for the *additive value function* are necessary for the *multiplicative utility function*.

Theorem 6.11.   Given.

1. *Preferences over $X_1 \times X_2 \times \cdots \times X_n$ are compatible with an additive value function v.*

---

* The ideas of the result in this section were generated by Richard F. Meyer and John W. Pratt.

2. *Some X_i is UI (let it be X_1).*

3. $n \geq 3$.

then the utility function u must have one of the following three forms:

$$u(x) \sim -e^{-cv(x)}, \quad c > 0, \tag{6.98a}$$

$$u(x) \sim v(x), \tag{6.98b}$$

$$u(x) \sim e^{cv(x)}, \quad c > 0. \tag{6.98c}$$

[*Note Before Proof:*. This result says that the utility function over the scalar attribute V, which measures value by v, must have constant risk aversion.]

Proof. Let us write v as

$$v(x_1, x_2, \ldots, x_n) = \lambda_1 v_1(x_1) + \lambda_2 v_2(x_2) + \cdots + \lambda_n v_n(x_n) \tag{6.99}$$

and scale v by

$$v(x_1^*, x_2^*, \ldots, x_n^*) = 1, \quad v(x_1^o, x_2^o, \ldots, x_n^o) = 0, \tag{6.100}$$

and similarly scale the v_i's by

$$v_i(x_i^*) = 1, \quad v_i(x_i^o) = 0, \quad i = 1, 2, \ldots, n, \tag{6.101}$$

so of course

$$\sum_{i=1}^{n} \lambda_i = 1. \tag{6.102}$$

The idea of the proof is simple: we deduce a utility function for the V attribute and show that it must have constant risk aversion (see Theorem 4.15) from which the forms (6.98) follow.

Let $y \equiv (x_2, \ldots, x_n)$; in this notation we have $x = (x_1, y)$ and X_1 is UI of Y. For attribute X_1 let $\hat{x}_1 \sim \langle x_1^*, x_1^o \rangle$ and therefore $(\hat{x}_1, y) \sim \langle (x_1^*, y), (x_1^o, y) \rangle$ for all y. In terms of the V attribute, this means that

$$[\lambda_1 v_1(\hat{x}_1) + \bar{v}(y)] \sim \langle \lambda_1 + \bar{v}(y), \bar{v}(y) \rangle, \tag{6.103}$$

where

$$\bar{v}(y) = \sum_{i=2}^{n} \lambda_i v_i(x_i).$$

In other words, adding $\bar{v}(y)$ to the prizes of the lottery $\langle \lambda_1, 0 \rangle$ increases the certainty equivalent by $\bar{v}(y)$, for all $\bar{v}(y)$. This implies constant risk aversion for V to be shown. ◀

Theorem 6.11 is interesting for two reasons:

1. It provides for a simple procedure to obtain a multiattribute utility function given that the necessary assumptions hold and given that an additive value function has been assessed.

2. The analysts can independently assess both a multiplicative (or additive) utility function and an additive value function and use one to check against the other.

It is important to note that if the utility function is additive, then (6.98b) must hold, whereas if the utility function is multiplicative, either (6.98a) or (6.98c) must be valid.

Given v, the assessment of u is straightforward. Simply assess the certainty equivalent $\hat{x}_1$ for the lottery $\langle x_1^*, x_1^o \rangle$. Then if

$$v_1(\hat{x}_1) = \tfrac{1}{2} v_1(x_1^*) + \tfrac{1}{2} v_1(x_1^o),$$

the utility function must be the additive case (6.98b). If

$$v_1(\hat{x}_1) \neq \tfrac{1}{2} v_1(x_1^*) + \tfrac{1}{2} v_1(x_1^o), \tag{6.104}$$

then (6.98a) is the proper form if the left-hand side of (6.104) is less than the right-hand side and case (6.98c) is the appropriate utility function when the right-hand side is smaller. In either case, by setting the utility of $\hat{x}_1$ equal to $\langle x_1^*, x_1^o \rangle$ using (6.98a) or (6.98c) and solving, the scaling constant c is determined.

6.11 HIERARCHICAL STRUCTURES AND CONDITIONAL PREFERENCES

Suppose that the attributes for a particular problem have been structured as shown in Fig. 6.4. Furthermore, suppose that Y_1 and Y_2 are mutually utility independent. Then from Theorem 5.2, we know that

$$u(y_1, y_2) = k_1 u_1(y_1) + k_2 u_2(y_2) + k_{12} u_1(y_1) u_2(y_2), \tag{6.105}$$

where all utility functions are scaled from 0 to 1. Note that by evaluating (6.105) at y_1^o and at y_2^o, the respective least preferable amounts of Y_1 and

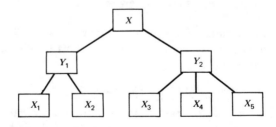

Fig. 6.4. A hierarchy of attributes for a hypothetical problem.

Y_2, we find

$$u_1(y_1) = \frac{u(y_1, y_2^o)}{k_1} \quad \text{and} \quad u_2(y_2) = \frac{u(y_1^o, y_2)}{k_2}.$$

The point is that u_1 and u_2 are actually conditional utility functions over their respective domains given a fixed level of the other attribute. Because of utility independence, the conditional utility function over Y_1, for example, is the same regardless of the level of Y_2. That is why we only need one conditional utility function for Y_1 in specifying $u(y_1, y_2)$.

The logical next step in assessing u would be to try to identify functions f_1 and f_2 such that

$$u_1(y_1) = f_1[u_1'(x_1), u_2'(x_2)]$$

and

$$u_2(y_2) = f_2[u_3'(x_3), u_4'(x_4), u_5'(x_5)],$$

where the u's are utility functions over their respective domains. Using previous results, this could be done if X_i is UI, $i = 1, 2, \ldots, 5$. However, because of the dimensionality, it might be difficult to verify such assumptions. Fortunately, we do not need such strong assumptions. Because Y_1 is utility independent of Y_2, we can just worry about whether X_1 is conditionally utility independent of X_2 given that Y_2 is set at y_2^o, for instance.

More generally, in all the formulations of the previous two chapters, once we have determined that a subset of attributes Y is utility independent of $\bar{Y}$, we could then speak of preferences and utility functions over subsets of attributes included in Y without considering the levels of the attributes within $\bar{Y}$. The latter can be specified at some convenient level. With this motivation, we can define a number of useful conditional preference concepts.

6.11.1 Conditional Independence Assumptions

We are interested in concepts of conditional independence for three reasons:

1. Simplifying the structure of a multiattribute utility function provided that certain conditional independence assumptions are met.
2. Representing necessary conditions for independence assumptions to hold, and thus, in some cases, requiring less empirical questioning to find in fact that they do not hold.
3. Representing sufficient conditions for independence conditions to hold, thus providing for weaker assumptions, and consequently less verification, to imply utility functions of particular forms.

After defining our terms, we will expand on each one.

To formalize these ideas, consider the set of attributes $X \equiv \{X_1, X_2, \ldots, X_n\}$ that will be partitioned into three nonempty subsets Y_1, Y_2, and Y_3. We will say Y_1 is *conditionally preferentially independent* of Y_2 given y_3^+ if the preference order for consequences involving only changes of attribute levels in Y_1 does not depend on the level of Y_2 when Y_3 is fixed at y_3^+. Mathematically this condition can be expressed as follows: for any y_1', y_1'', y_2',

$$[(y_1', y_2', y_3^+) \gtrsim (y_1'', y_2', y_3^+)] \Rightarrow [(y_1', y_2, y_3^+) \gtrsim (y_1'', y_2, y_3^+)], \forall y_2. \quad (6.106)$$

Similarly, we define Y_1 to be *conditionally utility independent* of Y_2 given y_3^+ if the preference order for lotteries involving only changes of attribute levels in Y_1 does not depend on the level of Y_2 when Y_3 is fixed at y_3^+. This condition can be represented mathematically as follows: for any lotteries $\tilde{y}_1'$, $\tilde{y}_1''$, and any y_2',

$$[(\tilde{y}_1', y_2', y_3^+) \gtrsim (\tilde{y}_1'', y_2', y_3^+)] \Rightarrow [(\tilde{y}_1', y_2, y_3^+) \gtrsim (\tilde{y}_1'', y_2, y_3^+)], \forall y_2. \quad (6.107)$$

These definitions follow naturally from our original ones of preferential and utility independence.

Given a utility function u, expression (6.106) holds if and only if

$$[u(y_1', y_2', y_3^+) \geq u(y_1'', y_2', y_3^+)] \Rightarrow [u(y_1', y_2, y_3^+) \geq u(y_1'', y_2, y_3^+)], \forall y_2.$$
$$(6.108)$$

Similarly, expression (6.107) holds if and only if

$$u(y_1, y_2, y_3^+) = c(y_2) + d(y_2)u(y_1, y_2', y_3^+), \, d(y_2) > 0, \quad (6.109)$$

where y_2' is arbitrarily chosen. Both (6.108) and (6.109) are useful in deriving implications of conditional independence assumptions.

There is a generalization of each of these definitions. We say that Y_1 is conditionally preferentially independent of Y_2 given Y_3 if the preference order for consequences involving only changes in attribute levels in Y_1 does not depend on the level of Y_2 when Y_3 *is fixed at any level.* In the same manner, we define Y_1 to be conditionally utility independent of Y_2 given Y_3 if the preference order for lotteries involving only changes of attribute levels in Y_1 does not depend on the level Y_2 when Y_3 is fixed at any level. These conditional preference assumptions can be written respectively as: for any y_1', y_1'', y_2'

$$[(y_1', y_2', y_3) \gtrsim (y_1'', y_2', y_3)] \Rightarrow [(y_1', y_2, y_3) \gtrsim (y_1'', y_2, y_3)], \forall y_2, y_3$$
$$(6.110)$$

and for any lotteries $\tilde{y}_1'$, $\tilde{y}_1''$, and any y_2'

$$[(\tilde{y}_1', y_2', y_3) \gtrsim (\tilde{y}_1'', y_2', y_3)] \Rightarrow [(\tilde{y}_1', y_2, y_3) \gtrsim (\tilde{y}_1'', y_2, y_3)], \forall y_2, y_3$$
$$(6.111)$$

As before, given utility function u, (6.110) holds if and only if

$$[u(y_1', y_2', y_3) \geq u(y_1'', y_2', y_3)] \Rightarrow [u(y_1', y_2, y_3) \geq u(y_1'', y_2, y_3)], \forall y_2, y_3. \quad (6.112)$$

and expression (6.111) holds if and only if

$$u(y_1, y_2, y_3) = f(y_2, y_3) + g(y_2, y_3)u(y_1, y_2', y_3), \ g(y_2, y_3) > 0, \quad (6.113)$$

where y_2' refers to an arbitrary but fixed level of Y_2.

It is clear that (6.112) implies (6.108) and (6.113) implies (6.109), so the latter conditional preference conditions are stronger than the former. Note that the relative preferences over Y_1 given y_3' need not be the same as the relative preferences over Y_1 given y_3'' for condition (6.113) to hold. If Y_1 is conditionally utility independent of Y_2 given Y_3 and if the relative preferences over Y_1 are the same for all values of Y_3, then we find, in fact, that Y_1 is utility independent of $\{Y_2, Y_3\}$. Hence for any y_2' and y_3',

$$u(y_1, y_2, y_3) = d_1(y_2, y_3) + d_2(y_2, y_3)u(y_1, y_2', y_3').$$

In Fig. 6.5 we try to graphically illustrate how utility independence and conditional utility independence relate to each other. Condition (6.109), that Y_1 is conditionally utility independent of Y_2 given y_3^+, means that the

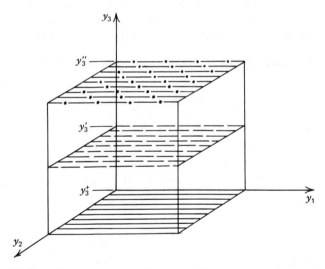

Fig. 6.5. Relationships among conditional utility independence assumptions and utility independence.

relative preferences over each of the heavy *solid* lines in Fig. 6.5 are strategically equivalent. This means the conditional utility functions over each of these solid lines are the same except for positive linear transformations. This condition does not mean the relative preferences over the heavy *dashed* lines must be the same. However, they may be. The condition (6.113) that Y_1 is conditionally utility independent of Y_2 given Y_3 means, for instance, that the relative preferences over each of the heavy solid lines must be the same, that the relative preferences over each of the heavy dashed lines must be the same, and that the relative preferences over each of the dot–dash lines must be the same. It does not require that the relative preferences over the solid lines be the same as those over the dashed lines or the dot–dash lines. When in fact, the relative preferences over each of the heavy lines—solid, dashed, and dot-dash—are the same, then it is very likely that Y_1 is utility independent of $\{Y_2, Y_3\}$. "Very likely" is used here since the condition must also hold for all planes not drawn in the figure in addition to those where y_3 is y_3^+, y_3', or y_3'' in order for Y_1 to be utility independent of $\{Y_2, Y_3\}$.

Finally let us define conditional additive independence. Attributes Y_1 and Y_2 are *conditionally additive independent given* y_3' if preferences over lotteries on Y_1 and Y_2 given that Y_3 is fixed at y_3' depend only on their marginal conditional probability distributions and not on their joint conditional probability distribution. And similar to the previous cases, we define attributes Y_1 and Y_2 to be conditionally additive independent given Y_3 if preferences over lotteries on Y_1 and Y_2, given any fixed level of Y_3, depend only on their marginal conditional probability distributions and not on their joint conditional probability distribution.

6.11.2 Simplifying the Structure of Multiattribute Utility Functions

Now we examine the usefulness of the conditional preference assumptions. For most of the theorems using preferential, utility, or additive independence, analogous results could be derived with the corresponding conditional independence assumptions. We state a few of these without proofs since they are very similar to proofs found earlier in the book. For example, corresponding to Theorem 5.2, we have the following result.

Theorem 6.12. *If Y_1 and Y_2 are conditionally utility independent of each other given y_3^o, then*

$$u(y_1, y_2, y_3^o) = u(y_1, y_2^o, y_3^o) + u(y_1^o, y_2, y_3^o) + ku(y_1, y_2^o, y_3^o)u(y_1^o, y_2, y_3^o),$$

where $u(y_1^o, y_2^o, y_3^o) = 0$ and k is an empirically evaluated constant.

The proof is analogous to that of Theorem 5.2.

Aside from those results with direct analogies using utility independence, additional results can be proven, such as the following:

Theorem 6.13. *If Y_1 and Y_2 are conditionally utility independent of each other given Y_3, then $u(y_1, y_2, y_3)$ can be specified by assessing $u_1(y_1, y_2^o, y_3)$ $u_2(y_1^o, y_2, y_3)$, and $u_3(y_1^*, y_2^*, y_3)$ for arbitrary $y_1^o, y_1^*, y_2^o, y_2^*$, subject to consistent scaling of the u_i.*

The result allows us to assess a three-attribute utility function by assessing three conditional utility functions—one with one attribute and two with two attributes. The reasoning behind Theorem 6.13 is illustrated in Fig. 6.6, where it is assumed that Y_1, Y_2, and Y_3 are scalar attributes. The consequences whose preferences must be assessed are shaded in the figure. Suppose we want to get the utility of an arbitrary point (y_1', y_2', y_3'), illustrated as point A. Since Y_1 is conditionally utility independent of Y_2 given y_3', the utility of A can be expressed in terms of the utilities of B and C since the relative preferences between A, B, and C, are the same as those between A', B', and C', and the latter are known. The utility of C is also known, but the utility of B is not. However, since Y_2 is conditionally utility independent of Y_1 given y_3', the utility of B can be expressed in terms of the utilities of B' and D since the relative preferences between B', B, and D are the same as those between C', C, and D' and the latter are known. Since the utilities of B' and D are assessed, we can calculate the utility of B and, thus, the utility of an arbitrary consequence A.

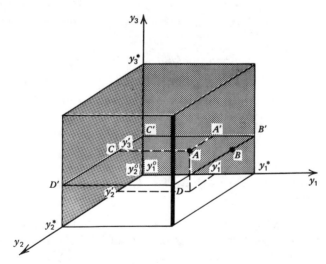

Fig. 6.6. Illustration of a proof for Theorem 6.13.

Let us state one more result indicative of the usefulness of conditional independence concepts in specifying the structure of a utility function.

Theorem 6.14. *If Y_1 and Y_2 are conditionally additive independent given Y_3, then*

$$u(y_1, y_2, y_3) = u(y_1, y_2^o, y_3) + u(y_1^o, y_2, y_3) - u(y_1^o, y_2^o, y_3), \quad (6.114)$$

where

$$u(y_1^o, y_2^o, y_3^o) = 0.$$

The proof is very similar to that of Theorem 5.1. This result allows us to specify the three-attribute utility function from two consistently scaled two-attribute utility functions. If Y_1, Y_2, and Y_3 each represent scalar attributes, then (6.114) says we only need to assess a utility function over the two shaded planes of Fig. 6.6 in order to completely specify u.

6.11.3 Necessary Conditions for Independence Assumptions

There is a second area in which conditional independence assumptions are useful. The ideas discussed here are trivial analytically, but helpful practically, so they are included. It may be quite difficult in some situations to determine whether or not Y_1 is utility independent of $\{Y_2, Y_3\}$. However, if we hold the value of Y_3 fixed and check relative preferences over Y_1 for various values of Y_2 given y_3^+ and if these relative preferences are not the same, then clearly the relative preferences over Y_1 cannot be the same for all (y_2, y_3) pairs. Thus Y_1 could not be utility independent of $\{Y_2, Y_3\}$. The following simple result formalizes this.

Theorem 6.15. *A necessary condition for Y_1 to be utility independent of $\{Y_2, Y_3\}$ is that Y_1 be conditionally utility independent of Y_2 given Y_3.*

In a similar spirit, we state the following without proof.

Theorem 6.16. *A necessary condition for Y_1, Y_2, and Y_3 to be additive independent is that Y_1 and Y_2 be conditionally additive independent given Y_3.*

6.11.4 Sufficient Conditions for Independence Assumptions

A third use of conditional utility independence is that it provides tools to state sufficient sets of assumptions about preference independence properties. Thus less empirical validation is necessary to verify that a particular form of utility function is appropriate for a particular problem.

Theorem 6.17. *If Y_1 is conditionally utility independent of Y_2 given Y_3 and if Y_1 is conditionally utility independent of Y_3 given y_2^+, then Y_1 is utility independent of $\{Y_2, Y_3\}$.*

Proof. Since Y_1 is conditionally utility independent of Y_2 given Y_3, from (6.113) for arbitrary Y_2, which we will choose as y_2^+,

$$u(y_1, y_2, y_3) = d_1(y_2, y_3) + d_2(y_2, y_3)u(y_1, y_2^+, y_3). \qquad (6.115)$$

And since Y_1 is conditionally utility independent of Y_3 given y_2^+, from (6.109)

$$u(y_1, y_2^+, y_3) = c_1(y_3) + c_2(y_3)u(y_1, y_2^+, y_3^+). \qquad (6.116)$$

Substituting (6.116) into (6.115), we find

$$u(y_1, y_2, y_3) = d_1(y_2, y_3) + d_2(y_2, y_3)[c_1(y_3) + c_2(y_3)u(y_1, y_2^+, y_3^+)]$$
$$= f_1(y_2, y_3) + f_2(y_2, y_3)u(y_1, y_2^+, y_3^+), \qquad (6.117)$$

where

$$f_1(y_2, y_3) = d_1(y_2, y_3) + d_2(y_2, y_3)c_1(y_3)$$

and

$$f_2(y_2, y_3) = d_2(y_2, y_3)c_2(y_3).$$

Equation (6.117) implies that Y_1 is utility independent of $\{Y_2, Y_3\}$. ◄

A particularly important class of problems concern those with a hierarchical structure of attributes. Some useful results pertaining to this follow.

Theorem 6.18. *If $\{Y_1, Y_2\}$ is utility independent of Y_3 and if Y_1 is conditionally preferentially independent of Y_2 given y_3', then Y_1 is preferentially independent of $\{Y_2, Y_3\}$.*

Proof. The utility independent condition implies that

$$u(y_1, y_2, y_3) = u(y_3) + c(y_3)u(y_1, y_2, y_3^o), \qquad (6.118)$$

and the conditional preferential independence assumption means that

$$[u(y_1', y_2', y_3') \geq u(y_1'', y_2', y_3')] \Rightarrow [u(y_1', y_2, y_3') \geq u(y_1'', y_2, y_3')]. \qquad (6.119)$$

Evaluating the right-hand side of (6.119) with (6.118) yields

$$u(y_1', y_2, y_3^o) \geq u(y_1'', y_2, y_3^o) \qquad (6.120)$$

Thus it follows by substituting (6.120) into (6.118) that

$$u(y_1', y_2, y_3) \geq u(y_1'', y_2, y_3), \qquad \forall y_2, y_3, \qquad (6.121)$$

which means that Y_1 is preferentially independent of $\{Y_2, Y_3\}$. ◄

There is the analogous result involving utility independence.

Theorem 6.19. *If $\{Y_1, Y_2\}$ is utility independent of Y_3 and Y_1 is conditionally utility independent of Y_2 given y_3', then Y_1 is utility independent of $\{Y_2, Y_3\}$.*

Proof. The assumptions mean that

$$u(y_1, y_2, y_3) = f(y_3) + g(y_3)u(y_1, y_2, y_3''), \qquad (6.122)$$

where y_3'' is arbitrarily chosen, and

$$u(y_1, y_2, y_3') = c(y_2) + d(y_2)u(y_1, y_3'). \qquad (6.123)$$

Setting $y_3'' = y_3'$, substituting (6.123) into the right-hand side of (6.122), and rearranging terms yields

$$u(y_1, y_2, y_3) = f(y_3) + g(y_3)c(y_2) + g(y_3)d(y_2)u(y_1, y_3'). \qquad (6.124)$$

Evaluating (6.124) at (y_1, y_2^o, y_3^o), solving for $u(y_1, y_3')$, and substituting this result back into (6.124) proves the desired result. ◀

The previous two results allow us to focus independently on the decision maker's preferences over utility-independent chains and their elements without worrying about the levels of the other attributes once they have been fixed at any convenient level. For instance, in Example 6.5, Section 6.10, we did not need the condition that X_5 was utility independent of $\bar{X}_5$ in order to arrive at (6.97). By using Theorem 6.19, we only needed that X_5 was conditionally utility independent of X_6 given $\bar{X}_{56}$ was fixed at some convenient level $\bar{x}_{56}$. This latter condition would be much easier to verify than the former.

Concerning additive independence, we have the following:

Theorem 6.20. *If (1) Y_1 and Y_2 are conditionally additive independent given Y_3, (2) Y_1 and Y_3 are conditionally additive independent given y_2^o, and (3) Y_2 and Y_3 are conditionally additive independent given y_1^o, then Y_1, Y_2, and Y_3 are additive independent.*

Proof. Conditions 2 and 3 imply, respectively, that

$$u(y_1, y_2^o, y_3) = u(y_1, y_2^o, y_3^o) + u(y_1^o, y_2^o, y_3) \qquad (6.125)$$

and

$$u(y_1^o, y_2, y_3) = u(y_1^o, y_2, y_3^o) + u(y_1^o, y_2^o, y_3), \qquad (6.126)$$

where

$$u(y_1^o, y_2^o, y_3^o) = 0.$$

Thus, substituting (6.125) and (6.126) into (6.114), which follows from condition 1, we find that

$$u(y_1, y_2, y_3) = u(y_1, y_2^o, y_3^o) + u(y_1^o, y_2, y_3^o) + u(y_1^o, y_2^o, y_3). \qquad (6.127)$$

Expression (6.127) is the additive utility function from which additive independence directly follows.   ◀

6.11.5   An Example Illustrating the Hierarchical Structure

We introduce a simplified version of a regulation problem typical of those facing the various segments of government to illustrate some of the ideas introduced here. In particular, suppose a state is considering passing legislation requiring that seat belts be worn by all state highway users. The overall objective of such a program is stated to "improve the well-being" of motorists in the state. Subobjectives are to minimize physical harm to motorists and to keep monetary costs as low as possible. Thus we might define our overall attribute X as "well-being," where Y_1 is "physical harm" and Y_2 is "monetary costs." Furthermore, suppose that Y_1 is broken into attributes X_1 and X_2, representing deaths and serious injuries, respectively, and that Y_2 is broken into attributes X_3 and X_4, representing costs to motorists and costs to the state, respectively. The measures of effectiveness that will be used for each of the attributes are listed in Table 6.4. Figure 6.7 should be useful in illustrating the hierarchical structure of the attributes.

Our next step in an analysis, and the step of interest here, is to assess a utility function $u(x)$. Clearly $u(x)$ can also be written as $u(y_1, y_2)$ or $u(x_1, x_2, x_3, x_4)$. A reasonable place to begin to structure u might be with the additive independence assumption discussed in Section 5.3. The first place we check is whether this condition holds for attributes Y_1 and Y_2. Suppose it does not. But we do verify that Y_1 is preferentially independent of Y_2 and that X_1 is utility independent of $\{X_2, Y_2\}$. Then from Theorem 6.6, Y_1 is utility independent of Y_2. Suppose we also find that

Table 6.4
Attributes and Measures for the Seat Belt Problem

Attribute	Measure of Effectiveness
$X_1 \equiv$ motorist deaths	Annual number of highway deaths in state
$X_2 \equiv$ motorist serious injuries	Annual number of highway serious injuries
$X_3 \equiv$ monetary costs to motorists	Dollar cost to install seat belts in a car
$X_4 \equiv$ monetary costs to state	Annual dollar cost to maintain program

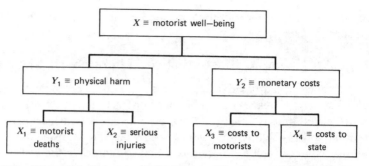

Fig. 6.7. Hierarchical structure of attributes for the seat belt problem.

Y_2 is utility independent of Y_1 so, from Theorem 5.2,

$$u(y_1, y_2) = u(y_1, y_2^o) + u(y_1^o, y_2) + ku(y_1, y_2^o)u(y_1^o, y_2), \quad (6.128)$$

where

$$u(y_1^o, y_2^o) = 0.$$

We wish to go further if possible and simplify both $u(y_1, y_2^o)$ and $u(y_1^o, y_2)$. Taking these in order, suppose we ascertain that X_1 and X_2 are conditionally mutually utility independent given y_2^o. From the fact X_1 was utility independent of $\{X_2, Y_2\}$, we knew this held for X_1. It follows from Theorem 6.12 that

$$u(y_1, y_2^o) \equiv u(x_1, x_2, y_2^o)$$
$$= u(x_1, x_2^o, y_2^o) + u(x_1^o, x_2, y_2^o) + k_1 u(x_1, x_2^o, y_2^o)u(x_1^o, x_2, y_2^o),$$
$$(6.129)$$

where the origin is still set by $u(y_1^o, y_2^o) \equiv u(x_1^o, x_2^o, y_2^o) = 0$. Notice that the scaling of u has not yet been specified.

Now we go on to $u(y_1^o, y_2)$, which for our purposes will be written $u(y_1^o, x_3, x_4)$. After checking, suppose we can conclude that only X_4 is conditionally utility independent of X_3 given y_1^o. This means a result analogous to Theorem 5.6 in Section 5.6 is valid and

$$u(y_1^o, x_3, x_4) = u(y_1^o, x_3, x_4^o)[1 - u(y_1^o, x_3^o, x_4)]$$
$$+ u(y_1^o, x_3, x_4')u(y_1^o, x_3^o, x_4), \quad (6.130)$$

where the origin and scale are set by $u(y_1^o, x_3^o, x_4^o) = 0$ and $u(y_1^o, x_3^o, x_4') = 1$.

Since the three utility functions of (6.128), (6.129), and (6.130) all have the same origin and the scale is only specified in (6.130), we can directly substitute (6.129) and (6.130) into (6.128) to get an expression for $u(x_1, x_2, x_3, x_4)$ in terms of $u(x_1, x_2^o, x_3^o, x_4^o)$, $u(x_1^o, x_2, x_3^o, x_4^o)$,

$u(x_1^o, x_2^o, x_3, x_4^o)$, $u(x_1^o, x_2^o, x_3^o, x_4)$, $u(x_1^o, x_2^o, x_3, x_4')$, k, and k_1 where the origin and scale of u are set by

$$u(x_1^o, x_2^o, x_3^o, x_4^o) = 0$$

and

$$u(x_1^o, x_2^o, x_3^o, x_4') = 1,$$

respectively. Thus, in this example, by exploiting independence and conditional independence conditions, the assessment of the four-attribute utility function u has been simplified to the consistent assessment of five one-attribute conditional utility functions and two additional scaling constants. This means seven scaling constants are required in all—one each to specify a second point on each of the conditional utility functions that already have the same origin plus k and k_1.

6.12 SUMMARY

This chapter develops representation theorems that are suitable for a decision maker's utility function given various sets of assumptions about his basic preferences. Relationships among various assumptions are investigated with two purposes in mind: (1) to weaken the assumptions necessary to imply particular forms of utility function, and (2) to understand and exploit fully all the implications of an arbitrary set of preference assumptions. An oversimplified summary of the results of Chapters 3, 5, and 6 is given in Table 6.5.

As we begin to generalize the two-attribute results of Chapter 5 to more than two attributes, one fact is apparent. In three or more dimensions, the richness of possible sets of preferential and utility independence assumptions increases greatly for two reasons: (1) the existence of independence conditions over overlapping attributes, and (2) the existence of *conditional* preferential and utility independence assumptions. We have illustrated this richness by our results.

For most real problems, we would expect that, collectively, the techniques presented in Chapters 3–6 should significantly help to specify a "reasonable" representation of the decision maker's preferences, provided that the problem has been structured with meaningful objectives and attributes in the sense discussed in Chapter 2. A number of researchers (including Yntema and Torgerson (1961), Fischer (1972, 1973), von Winterfeldt and Edwards (1973a, 1973b), and Dawes and Corrigan (1974)) have results supporting this claim. The cases discussed in Chapters 7 and 8 provide additional supporting evidence.

Table 6.5

Independence Assumptions in Multiattribute Utility Theory Given Consequences $x \equiv (x_1, x_2, \ldots, x_n) \equiv (y, z)$

Assumption	Preferential Independence (PI)	Utility Independence (UI)	Additive Independence (AI)
Concerns	Preferences for consequences (y, z) with z held fixed	Preference for lotteries over $(\tilde{y}, z)$ with z held fixed	Preferences for lotteries over $(\tilde{y}, \tilde{z})$ with both y and z varying
Definition	Y is PI of Z if preferences for consequences (y, z') with z' fixed do not depend on the amount z'	Y is UI of Z if preferences for lotteries on $(\tilde{y}, z')$ with z' fixed do not depend on the amount z'	Y and Z are AI preferences for lotteries $(\tilde{y}, \tilde{z})$ depend only on the marginal probability distributions on y and z
Mathematical implication of definition	$[u(y^a, z') > u(y^b, z')] \rightarrow [u(y^a, z) > u(y^b, z)]$, all z	$u(y, z) = f(z) + g(z)u(y, z^o)$, $g > 0$, all z	$\langle (y', z'), (y^o, z^o) \rangle \sim \langle (y', z^o), (y^o, z') \rangle$, all y', z'
Note	PI is not reflexive; Y PI Z does not imply Z PI Y	UI is not reflexive	AI is reflexive
Main results: two attributes		If Y UI Z and Z UI Y, then $u(y, z) = k_Y u_Y(y) + k_Z u_Z(z)$ $+ k k_Y k_Z u_Y(y) u_Z(z)$	If Y and Z are AI, then $u(y, z) = k_Y u_Y(y) + k_Z u_Z(z)$
Main results: n attributes	If $\{X_1, X_i\}$ PI $\bar{X}_{1i}$, $i = 2, 3, \ldots, n$, then $v(x) = \sum_{i=1}^{n} v_i(x_i)$ where v's are all value functions	If X_i UI $\bar{X}_i$, $i = 1, 2, \ldots, n$, then $u(x) = \sum k_i u_i(x_i) + \sum_{j>1} k_{ij} u_i(x_i) u_j(x_j)$ $+ \cdots + k_{1 \cdots n} u_1(x_1) \cdots u_n(x_n)$	If X_i AI $\bar{X}_i$, $i = 1, 2, \ldots, n$, then $u(x) = \sum_{i=1}^{n} k_i u_i(x_i)$
Combining PI and UI	If $\{X_1, X_i\}$ PI $\bar{X}_{1i}$, $i = 2, 3, \ldots, n$, and X_1 UI $\bar{X}_1$, then either $(1)\ 1 + ku(x) = \prod_{i=1}^{n} [1 + k k_i u_i(x_i)]$ or $(2)\ u(x) = \sum_{i=1}^{n} k_i u_i(x_i)$		

344

Generalization of Preferential Independence and Utility Independence

Suppose that we have vector attributes Y and Z, and that given Z is z^o, there is a definite preference for different levels of Y. If this is quantified by the value function $v(y, z)$, then if

$$[v(y', z^o) \geq v(y'', z^o)] \Rightarrow [v(y', z) \geq v(y'', z)], \quad \forall z,$$

we define Y to be preferentially independent of Z. Thus, given a z, the conditional preference order of y is the same regardless of the z chosen. If the reverse order on y occurs for some z', that is,

$$[v(y', z^o) \geq v(y'', z^o)] \Rightarrow [v(y'', z') \geq v(y', z')],$$

we say that conditional preferences on y given z^o and z' are reversals of each other. We could also have indifference on Y given Z is some other level z''. Y is *generalized preferentially independent* of Z if, given any two levels of Z, say z' and z'', the two orderings of y are either identical, reversals of each other, or indifference exists among the y. A bit more mathematically, Y is generalized preferentially independent of Z if

$$v(y, z) = f(z)[v(y, z^o)],$$

where the only restriction of $f(z)$ is that it is scalar valued. If $f > 0$, we have the case where Y is preferentially independent of Z.

Similarly, we can have reversals of preferences among lotteries over Y for different amounts of Z. If Y is *generalized utility independent* of Z, then

$$u(y, z) = g(z) + h(z)u(y, z^o),$$

345

where z^0 is chosen so that there is a definite conditional preference on Y given z^o and h can be negative, zero, or positive. If $h(z')$ is negative, then preferences over lotteries on Y given z' are a reversal of the order on these lotteries given z^o. Of course, when $h > 0$, then we have the utility independent case considered in detail in the chapter.

Fishburn and Keeney (1974, 1975) show that results analogous to many results in this chapter can be derived using the weaker generalized preferential independence and generalized utility independent condition rather than preferential and utility independence. Some results, however, do not follow due to the reversals of preferences.

Evaluating the Scaling Constant k in the Multiplicative Utility Function

Taking $x = x^*$ in (6.14) yields

$$k + 1 = \prod_{i=1}^{n} (1 + kk_i). \tag{6B.1}$$

By evaluating (6.12) at x_i^* and $\bar{x}_i^*$ we have $k_i = u(x_i^*)$, and

$$ku(\bar{x}_i^*) + 1 = \prod_{j \neq i} (1 + kk_j) = \frac{k+1}{kk_i + 1}$$

or

$$1 = k_i + [1 + kk_i]u(\bar{x}_i^*). \tag{6B.2}$$

Since $k_i < 1$ and the u value above is positive, it follows from (6B.2) that

$$1 + kk_i > 0. \tag{6B.3}$$

Comparing the signs of the two sides of (6B.1), we infer that

$$k > -1. \tag{6B.4}$$

Now let $S = \sum_{i=1}^{n} k_i$, and introduce the polynomial

$$f(q) = 1 + q - \prod_{i=1}^{n} (1 + k_i q), \qquad (-1 < q < \infty), \tag{6B.5}$$

so that (6B.1) says that $f(k) = 0$; note also that $f(-1) < 0$. Differentiating (6B.5) gives

$$1 - f' = \sum_{i=1}^{n} k_i \prod_{i \neq j} (1 + k_j q), \tag{6B.6}$$

which shows that $1 - f'$ is an increasing function and, therefore f' is decreasing.

347

First suppose that $S = 1$, that is, $f'(0) = 0$. Then, since f' is decreasing in $(-1, \infty)$, it is positive in $(-1, 0)$ and negative in $(0, \infty)$. Thus $q = 0$ is the only root of $f(q) = 0$ in $(-1, \infty)$, and so $S = 1$ implies $k = 0$ and corresponds only to the additive utility function.

Next suppose that $S < 1$, that is, $f'(0) > 0$. Then since f' is decreasing, it is positive in $(-1, 0)$, so that $f(q) = 0$ has no root between (-1) and the root at 0. It follows from (6B.6) that $f'(\infty) = -\infty$, and so $f'(q) = 0$ has a unique root q^* in $(0, \infty)$. Since $f(0) = 0$ and $f' > 0$ in $(0, q^*)$, $f(q) = 0$ has no root in $(0, q^*)$. Since $f(q^*) > 0$, and f' is negative and decreasing to $(-\infty)$ in (q^*, ∞), $f(q) = 0$ has a unique root k in (q^*, ∞); moreover, $f > 0$ in $(0, k)$ and $f < 0$ in (k, ∞), so that the iterative method described in the text works provided the search for k is confined to $(0, \infty)$.

Finally, suppose that $S > 1$, that is, $f'(0) < 0$. Since f' is decreasing, it is negative in $(0, \infty)$, so that $f(q) = 0$ can have no root to the right of the root at $q = 0$. Since $f > 0$ immediately to the left of this root, while $f(-1) < 0$, there must be at least one root k of $f(q) = 0$ in $(-1, 0)$; since f' is decreasing and $f(0) = 0$, there can be at most one such root, and the iterative method described in the text is valid, provided the search for k is confined to $(-1, 0)$.

An Interactive Computer Program for Assessing and Using Multiattribute Utility Functions*

Section 6.6 discussed and illustrated the considerations necessary for assessing multiattribute utility functions. The task is difficult, and the current state of unaided empirical assessment (i.e., with the lack of direct computer support) has some shortcomings. The most important of these are as follows:

1. The necessity of asking "extreme-value" questions to keep the computational requirements for specifying a utility function at a manageable level.
2. The tedium of calculating the component utility functions and scaling constants even in this case.
3. The lack of immediate feedback to the decision maker of the implications of his preferences.
4. The absence of an efficient procedure to "update" the decision maker's preferences and conduct sensitivity analysis.

This section briefly describes the major features of a computer package designed to alleviate the above shortcomings with existing methods for the assessment and use of multiattribute utility functions. The package is referred to by the mnemonic MUFCAP, standing for "multiattribute utility

---

* This section was adapted from Keeney and Sicherman (1976). In Section 9.7, an analogous interactive computer program that is designed for intertemporal tradeoffs is described.

function calculation and assessment package." Presently, some of the subroutines in the package are rather crude. However, the package is operational and, as a first try, indicates a worthwhile direction to proceed.

In the following, we will assume that the assumptions implying that the multiattribute utility function is either additive or multiplicative have been verified. Also, since the procedures for assessing the basic components, the u_i's and k_i's, of both the multiplicative and additive utility functions are essentially the same, there is no need to consider the cases separately. Recall that the extra constant k in the multiplicative form is calculated directly from the k_i's. For illustration, the multiplicative form will be used for both the overall utility function u and any nested utility function. In the remainder of this section, we summarize the MUFCAP package. Details and a listing of the program are found in Sicherman (1975). The abbreviation MUF means a multiattribute utility function of either multiplicative or additive form.

COMMANDS TO STRUCTURE THE UTILITY FUNCTION

Structuring a utility function consists of specifying a functional form, its attributes, and the ranges for each of the attributes. MUFCAP requests a name for the utility function and asks for the number of attributes that are arguments of this function. The package then requests a name and a range for scalar attributes. For vector attributes, the program requests the number of attributes that are arguments of this nested MUF. For each of these a name and range will be solicited. Further levels of nesting could be specified if desired and the information requested would be analogous to the above material.

MUFCAP has commands for adding or deleting attributes to or from the utility function. It also has a command for switching the order of the attributes in a utility function. In this way, attributes may be conveniently "regrouped" to alter the model for the problem in terms of different nesting schemes.

COMMANDS TO SPECIFY THE SINGLE-ATTRIBUTE UTILITY FUNCTIONS

The next step in assessing a MUF involves specifying the u_i's for the single attributes. As noted in Chapter 4, sophisticated computer programs do exist for assessing single-attribute (scalar) utility functions. These could be incorporated into MUFCAP. Initially, however (for simplicity in the current package), a subroutine for assessing unidimensional utility functions (referred to as UNIF) was developed.

MUFCAP has available commands to specify conveniently three types of unidimensional utility functions: linear, exponential, and piecewise linear. These three functions allow the user to conveniently specify his preferences for many situations. MUFCAP also has several commands that enable a user to display any assessed unidimensional utility function to check its appropriateness.

COMMANDS TO SPECIFY THE
SCALING CONSTANTS

Once u_i's have been evaluated, the package has several commands useful for assessing the k_i's in any particular MUF. The command INDIF2 takes as input two pairs of two indifference consequences each. These consequences can vary only in terms of the two attributes, for example X_j and X_m. Their scaling constants k_j and k_m are the object of assessment. Using the MUF and the single-attribute utility functions, the program computes the relative value of k_j and k_m implied by the indifference pairs. With INDIF2, the user is not limited to choosing consequences that have one attribute at a least desireable level in order to determine the relative k_i's.

Given the information from INDIF2, indifference curves over attributes X_j and X_m can be calculated with the command IMAP. IMAP permits a user to get immediate feedback on the implications of the relative k_i's that he has specified. He can quickly see if the points "claimed" to be indifferent really appear so to him. If not, the relative k_i's can be changed until they represent the user's preferences for tradeoffs between those attributes.

Once we know the relative k_i's the command INDIF1 takes as input a single pair of indifference consequences and computes the k and the absolute magnitude of the k_i's implied by that pair and the relative k_i's. For consistency checks, a new indifference pair of consequences can be input into INDIF1, which then computes the factor by which the current k_i's need to be multiplied to be consistent with the indifference point just given. MUFCAP provides a routine that allows the user to multiply the currently assigned k_i's for any MUF by any factor. In this way, INDIF1 enables the calculation of the magnitude of the k_i's using an indifference relation instead of a lottery over all the attributes at once.

COMMANDS FOR EVALUATING ALTERNATIVES
AND SENSITIVITY ANALYSIS

Once the u_i's and k_i's have been set, the utility function is completely specified and can be used. To help explore the implications of the utility function, and to perform rough analysis, MUFCAP has commands for specifying two kinds of alternatives; those with certainty and those with uncertainty. For "certainty" alternatives, which are simply consequences, uniattribute amounts are solicited until the alternative is completely described. For "uncertainty" alternatives, at present, MUFCAP assumes probabilistic independence and requests a probability distribution function for each single attribute.* The probability distribution function currently used is a piecewise linear approximation to the cumulative probability distribution for X_i. Then MUFCAP calculates the expected utilities for probabilistic alternatives.

By specifying a group of alternatives differing slightly in some feature, we can conduct a sensitivity analysis of the probabilistic inputs. Also, we can conduct a sensitivity analysis of the preference structure by varying such parameters as the scaling constants in the multiattribute utility function. In this way, different utility functions of members of a decision-making group can be used to evaluate and rank the alternatives. This might clarify differences of opinion and suggest certain creative compromises if needed.

SUMMARY

The current version of MUFCAP provides the basic features necessary to assess and use multiattribute utility functions on complex decision problems. In particular, it permits us to use realistic and simple questions in assessing the decision maker's preferences, rather than the "difficult to think about" types of questions previously used for computational reasons. MUFCAP provides for (1) a variety of immediate feedback of implications of the decision maker's responses, (2) evaluation of alternatives and sensitivity analysis, and (3) analyzing differences of preferences and judgments among various individuals in a decision-making group.

The present MUFCAP should be considered a first edition, a basis on which to improve. Some possible improvements of existing routines have

---

* It is easy to use Monte Carlo techniques to find the expected utility values for dependent probability distributions. The Monte Carlo routine would generate a sequence of $\{x^\alpha : \alpha = 1, 2, \ldots\}$ and we would then compute $1/T \sum_{\alpha=1}^{T} u(x^\alpha)$ for T large.

been suggested in this section, such as a more sophisticated single-attribute utility function assessment technique and potential for evaluating alternatives where probabilistic independence need not be assumed. The program could then be easily coupled with simulation models producing such probability distributions. Other important improvements would include the addition of new routines (1) to help in verifying preferential and utility independence assumptions, (2) to simplify sensitivity analysis and feedback, perhaps with the aid of graphical displays, and (3) to conduct conflict analyses in problems involving more than one decision maker.

CHAPTER 7

Illustrative Applications

We are dealing in this book with a nonvacuous problem: many difficult, real-world decision problems do involve multiple objectives. Consequently, many of the concepts we have introduced are relevant and must be applied in either a formal or informal analysis of the alternatives. If we choose to analyze multiple objectives and value or utility tradeoffs in a *formal* manner, then we immodestly believe that the ideas and procedures discussed in this book can often be of considerable use. This chapter and Chapter 8 support this contention by illustrating many cases where multiattribute preferences have been formalized. This chapter, in a variety of settings, focuses exclusively on the preference assessments themselves whereas Chapter 8, which concerns the site selection of an airport for Mexico City, presents a complete case including probability assessments, analysis of alternatives, interactions with the decision makers, and so on, as well as multiattribute preference assessments.

The applications discussed in this chapter cover the range of topics presented in Chapters 2–6. Section 7.1 discusses the generation of objectives and the specification of measures of effectiveness for an air pollution problem. Section 7.2 discusses the allocation of resources for an educational program and the value functions of the members of a local school board and other local education officials are formalized. Next, a five-attribute utility function for response times of various fire trucks is assessed. This problem typically arises in planning operations of emergency services. Section 7.4 discusses the problem of structuring corporate preferences. In Sections 7.5 and 7.6, we discuss preliminary work on the quantification of multiattribute preferences concerning decisions involving the selection of computer systems and decisions about the siting and licensing of nuclear power facilities.

Sections 7.1–7.6 relate experiences that we and others have had in assessing multiattribute preferences. Section 7.7 gives brief surveys of a

354

number of other problems where formal analyses have explicitly considered multiple objectives using concepts discussed in earlier chapters. These include utilization of frozen blood, sewage sludge disposal, safety of landing aircraft, choice of a job, shipments of hazardous materials, and medical and surgical treatment of cleft lip and palate.

We contend that the concepts and procedures introduced in this book are not just theoretically but also operationally interesting and they can be—and have been—utilized to make contributions in a variety of important contexts. Many analysts are currently applying decision analysis to such crucial problems as those discussed in this chapter and the inventory of case studies is growing rapidly.

7.1 AIR POLLUTION CONTROL*

In New York City, the mayor must decide whether he should approve a proposed major addition to Consolidated Edison's electric power generating station in Astoria, Queens. If this addition is approved, city residents would be reasonably assured of receiving the growing quantity of electricity they will demand over the next several years at reasonable cost. However, approval would result in increased air pollution, particularly sulfur dioxide, particulates, and nitrogen oxides. Should this addition be approved?

In both Boston and New York City, the respective city councils must decide whether to pass legislation that would place stringent limits on the sulfur content of fuels that are burned. If passed, the legislation would lead to a definite improvement in the city's air quality, especially due to a reduction of sulfur dioxide. However, passage of this legislation would require residents to incur added annual costs for heating and electricity to pay for the more expensive fuels with low sulfur contents. Should the respective city councils pass such legislation?

In Washington, D.C., Congress must decide whether to establish very stringent emission standards for carbon monoxide, hydrocarbons, and nitrogen oxides for all motor vehicles manufactured and sold in the United States. Establishment of these standards would contribute toward improving the air quality. On the other hand they would require the public to pay significantly more money for new automobiles. Should Congress adopt these stringent standards?

---

* This section draws heavily on the dissertation of Ellis (1970) and adapts material from Ellis and Keeney (1972). A related dissertation by Mead (1973) goes into more depth on the Astoria problem. Both dissertations were supervised in part by Raiffa.

Each of these decision problems is faced presently or has been faced recently by public officials. Moreover, they represent similar problems that public officials increasingly confront. The basic question is, "Should government adopt a specific, proposed program intended to improve the air quality?" With each such investigation there is the additional question, "What should the air quality standard be?"

The major focus of this book has described how a decision maker, in this case a public official, can utilize decision analysis to help make up his mind: how to select a desirable course of action from the many alternatives. In this section, we focus our attention on the selection of a set of objectives and measures of effectiveness for analyzing governmental programs designed to control air pollution better. We draw heavily on the concepts discussed in Chapter 2.

As an illustration of our suggestions, focus is placed on one specific problem faced by one particular individual, the mayor of New York City. Obviously, we would not expect the mayor of New York to spend his time working on details of the air pollution problem. It would be reasonable, however, to expect members of the mayor's staff in the Environmental Protection Administration and the Department of Air Resources to do so. These individuals and the mayor might then review the results and implications of such analyses in formulating and supporting air pollution control programs for New York City.

In the next subsection, we present a brief overview of the air pollution control problem in New York City, along with an introduction to the sulfur dioxide problem. Then we generate objectives and measures of effectiveness to analyze the problem. To avoid leaving the reader in midstream, the final subsection briefly sketches other aspects of this problem.

7.1.1 The Air Pollution Control Problem of New York City

A general model of the process by which many air pollution control programs are designed and evaluated is shown in Fig. 7.1. The main problem with the overall process as it is currently practiced in most municipal governments is that the outputs are usually not explicitly considered in choosing air pollution policy. The reason is, of course, understandable. There are simply too many difficulties: in defining appropriate output measures, in establishing the relationships between pollution concentrations and these measures, and in specifying preferences for the various possible outputs. But, since action must be taken, in most instances the feedback loop goes directly from the measured air pollution concentrations to the control mechanism. In a sense, the process

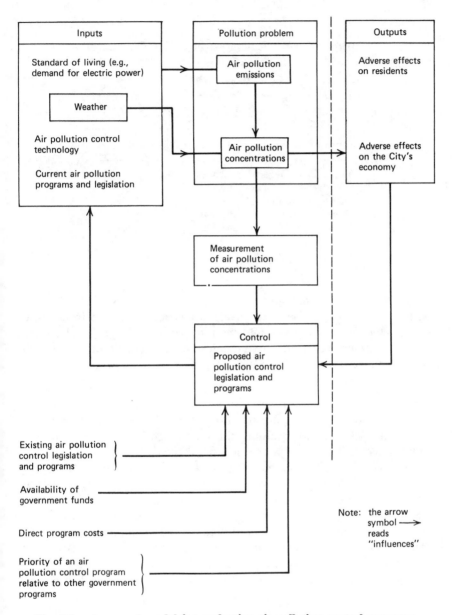

Fig. 7.1. A general model for evaluating air pollution control programs.

Table 7.1

Estimated 1972 Emissions of Sulfur Dioxide in New York City (N.Y.C. Department of Air Resources, 1969)

	Emissions of Sulfur Dioxide	
Source of Emissions	Tons	Percent of Total
Incineration of refuse	2,500	0.6
Motor vehicles	20,400	5.1
Industrial processes	9,900	2.5
Space heating	195,300	49.2
Power generation	169,500	42.6
Total	397,600	100.0

can be thought of as being short circuited at the dashed line in Fig. 7.1. Whenever this occurs the decision-making process excludes from formal analysis the most important information necessary for rational control. Our suggestions are meant to eliminate the short circuit and include the outputs explicitly in the decision-making process in order to improve formal analysis.

THE SULFUR DECISION PROBLEM.   A survey of air pollution problems and current air pollution control programs in New York is given in Eisenbud (1970). In 1970 a major decision still to be made in New York City's air pollution control program concerned sulfur dioxide. Table 7.1 presents a breakdown of the estimated 1972 emissions of sulfur dioxide from sources within the city (as viewed from 1969). These estimates accounted for all provisions of existing laws enacted through the middle of 1971.

Since over 90 percent of these emissions arise from the burning of fuels for space heating and power generation, and since the only current, practical way to reduce emissions from these sources is to lower the sulfur content of the fuels burned, one important decision faced by the city was whether the legal limit on the sulfur content of fuels burned in the city (then 1 percent) should be lowered.

7.1.2 Identification of Major Objectives

In almost every decision problem faced by the mayor of New York City, his most fundamental objective is to improve the well-being of his constituents. However, we must spell out in more detail what is meant by this objective as it pertains to air pollution. Precisely what would the mayor want to accomplish by his actions concerning air pollution? After serious thought, Ellis, through an evolutionary process, divided the overall objective regarding air pollution into five subobjectives:

1. Decrease the adverse health effects on the residents.
2. Decrease the adverse economic effects on the residents.
3. Decrease the adverse effects on the residents' psychological well-being.
4. Decrease the net costs to the city government.
5. Achieve as desirable a political "solution" as possible.

These objectives require little justification. However, note that the second objective includes costs of the air pollution control program in addition to costs of pollution itself. The net costs alluded to in objective 4 include all the direct costs (such as the costs of an air pollution control program), indirect costs (such as those resulting from migration of businesses and industry from the city and less tourism), and tax revenue losses resulting from employee absences due to sickness caused by air pollution.

Do these five objectives include all the issues of importance to the mayor? For instance, nothing has been said about the overall consequences of the various alternatives on New York State, on the federal government, on businesses, or on nonresidents of New York City. Should these factors be included in a complete analysis of proposed air pollution control programs? Of course, the mayor is concerned about these issues. However, note that some aspects of these consequences, such as economic effects due to tourism and businesses moving to the city, are included in the objective "decrease the net costs of air pollution to the city government." Benefits to nonresidents from any air pollution program, for example, are probably highly correlated with the benefits to residents, and therefore could be ignored in a first approximation. All in all, Ellis felt that explicit consideration of any of these additional objectives would not alter the optimal strategy, and therefore they were initially excluded from his list of objectives. However, after a preliminary analysis, he did reexamine these exclusions, albeit in an informal manner.

7.1.3 Assigning Attributes to Each Objective

The next task is to identify for each of the objectives suitable attributes that clearly indicate the degree to which the associated objective is achieved.

HEALTH EFFECTS ON RESIDENTS.   Several possible attributes immediately come to mind for the objective "decrease the adverse effects of air pollution on the health of residents." These include the annual number of deaths attributable to air pollution, the annual number of man-days of morbidity attributable to air pollution, and a subjectively assessed health index that includes consideration of both morbidity and mortality.

There are important objections against each attribute. The annual number of deaths attributable to air pollution is not comprehensive in that it does not account at all for what is believed to be the more prevalent effect of air pollution on health: its effect on morbidity. Similarly, the annual number of man-days of morbidity does not account at all for the extremely serious effect of air pollution on health in terms of mortality.

Thus, it seems clear that no single measure of effectiveness, aside from possibly a subjective health index, can be identified for this objective. However, because such an index lacks a physical interpretation, it is not particularly desirable in terms of the measurability criterion discussed in Chapter 2. Thus the alternative of specifying the major objective in more detail was chosen. Health considerations were divided into two detailed objectives: "decrease mortality" and "decrease morbidity."

For the first of these, two of the possible measures of effectiveness are the "annual number of deaths attributable to air pollution" and the inversely oriented scale, "per capita increase in the number of days of remaining lifetime due to improved air quality." The first equally weighs the death of an old person and the death of a child, whereas the second measure weighs the death of a young person more heavily. The latter measure was chosen since it was felt that, in this case, it more adequately described the impact of a program alternative with respect to "decrease mortality."

For the objective "decrease morbidity," the "per capita decrease in the number of days of bed disability per year due to improved air quality" was chosen as the attribute. Obviously, this does not include such effects as sore eyes, which would not force anyone to a bed. Part of the consequence of sore eyes is psychological, which can be accounted for by the third major objective. However, the physical aspects of sore eyes intuitively seem important enough to be formally included in the analysis. To do this we suggest calibrating a number of days of bed disability per year that would be equivalent to having sore eyes of different levels of severity during the year. Then, for each program alternative, the effects resulting from sore eyes would be included in the analysis by adding an "equivalent number of bed-days disability" to our measure of the degree to which "decrease morbidity" is met.

ECONOMIC EFFECTS ON RESIDENTS.   No single attribute could be identified for the objective "decrease the adverse economic effects of air pollution on residents of New York City," because the mayor would want to consider the economic impact on residents at various income levels. As a compromise Ellis considered a dichotomy: the economic effects on low-income residents and on other residents. Per capita annual net cost to residents was used as the measure of effectiveness for each group.

PSYCHOLOGICAL EFFECTS ON RESIDENTS. There seems to be no direct measure of effectiveness for the objective "decrease the adverse effects of air pollution on the psychological well-being of the residents." We could, however, define some subjective index and perhaps interview residents about their feelings for various levels of air quality. But Ellis chose a simpler approach, which used the daily concentration of sulfur dioxide as a proxy attribute for "psychological well-being."* It seems reasonable to assume that "psychological well-being" is closely related to the concentration levels.

ECONOMIC EFFECTS TO THE CITY. As a measure of effectiveness for the fourth objective, "decrease the net costs of air pollution to the City government" Ellis used "annual net costs." As mentioned previously, this includes both direct and indirect costs.

POLITICAL IMPLICATIONS. The fifth objective, "achieve the best political solution to the air pollution problem," has no specific objective measure of effectiveness and a subjective index was used. Considerations used to measure the index included the possibility of court suits brought by landlords or homeowners who are forced to pay higher fuel prices for heating, the mayor's relations with the City Council and with Con Edison and with other political groups in the city, and the support of the general public for various program alternatives. All of these have a potential effect on the mayor's political future, which also should be taken into account.

7.1.4   The Final Set of Objectives and Attributes

Figure 7.2 exhibits the hierarchy of objectives and their associated measures of effectiveness used by Ellis in his study of air pollution control in New York City.

Of course, there may be important objectives that Ellis did not think about that are consequently not included in his analysis. However, if we cannot identify such omissions before utilizing the implications of the analysis, the same omissions might have occurred if any less formal procedure for guiding the decision-making process were followed. And in

---

* It is important to emphasize that this concentration level is to be viewed as a proxy for psychological well-being *only* and not for the other objectives.

362

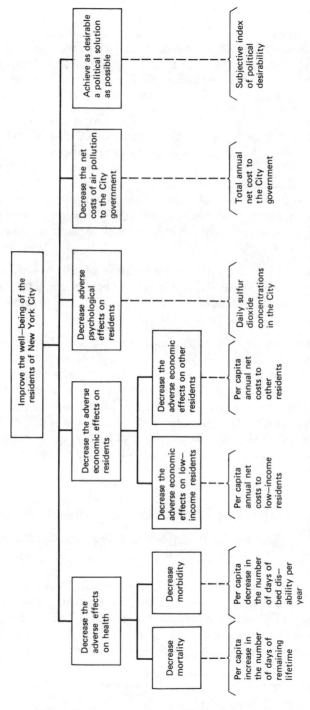

Fig. 7.2. The complete set of objectives and attributes for choosing an air pollution control program for New York City.

this case we would be no worse off using formal analysis than not. Admittedly, with an informal analysis, we might think intuitively or subconsciously about objectives that we might not be able to articulate. In addition, a formal analysis may inhibit this mysteriously creative way of thinking. But on the other hand, this type of unstructured introspective analysis is so very private that others cannot share in the process and suggest additions or modifications they deem appropriate.

7.1.5 Decision Analysis of the Sulfur-Dioxide Decision Problem

Since the purpose of this section was to develop objectives and attributes for the sulfur-dioxide decision problem, the ensuing analysis will only be briefly mentioned. The interested reader may refer to Ellis (1970) for details of the assessments or to Ellis and Keeney (1972) for an overview.

Since Ellis's work was done as a doctoral thesis designed to illustrate the methodology, only two alternatives were explicitly evaluated. These were the status quo, which entailed maintaining a 1 percent legal limit on the sulfur content of oil and coal used in New York City, and an alternative that lowered the legal limit to 0.37 percent for oil and 0.7 percent for coal. To analyze the full range of alternatives would require a team of researchers rather than one individual.

The alternatives were evaluated in terms of the seven attributes defined as follows:

$X_1 \equiv$ per capita increase in the number of days of remaining lifetime.

$X_2 \equiv$ per capita decrease in the number of days of bed disability per year.

$X_3 \equiv$ per capita annual net costs to low-income residents.

$X_4 \equiv$ per capita annual net costs to other residents.

$X_5 \equiv$ daily sulfur-dioxide concentrations in parts per million.

$X_6 \equiv$ total annual net cost to city government.

$X_7 \equiv$ subjective index of political desirability.

Joint probability functions describing the possible impact of the two alternatives were assessed using probabilistic independence, conditional probability assessments, and a small simulation model. Exploiting utility independence assumptions that were deemed to be appropriate on the basis of discussions with staff members in the Department of Air Resources, a seven-attribute utility function was structured.

It is interesting to note that Ellis' did *not* conclude that the mayor of New York would view each attribute as utility independent of its complement. The main reason for this was the feeling that the mayor would likely be more risk averse in terms of attributes X_1, X_2, X_4, and X_5 if the political effects were at an undersirable level than he would be given desirable political effects. From his interaction with the Department of Air Resources, Ellis did conclude that for the ranges of the possible consequences, the attributes X_3, X_6, and X_7 were each individually utility independent of their respective complements. Also, he felt that given any fixed level of attributes X_7, the attributes X_1, X_2, X_4, and X_5 would each be conditionally utility independent of the remaining attributes. With these assumptions, the assessment of the complete utility function required (1) assessing 11 one-attribute conditional utility functions, and (2) assessing 18 scaling constants to insure that the seven utility functions were properly scaled. No assessments of the utility function were completed, although details about the functional form of the utility function and the reasonableness of the utility independence are given in Ellis (1970). Appropriate techniques for performing each of the necessary assessments are found in earlier chapters of this book.

7.1.6 Impact of This Work

The ideas and results expressed in this section may have had some influence on the thinking of individuals responsible for air pollution control programs in New York City. Although no claim of causality can be made, the following events have occurred:

The results of this work, concerning the range of possible effects of a program that lowered the legal limits of oil and coal used in the city from the present 1 percent to 0.37 and 0.7 percent, respectively, were made available to the New York City Environmental Protection Administration, which was in the process of preparing a new air pollution control code for the city. This group included, as one of the key provisions in its recommended code to the City Council, a program that was essentially the same program as the one Ellis analyzed.

These same results, as well as the methods of analysis upon which these results are based, were presented by Howard M. Ellis in testimony before the New York City Council in its legislative hearings on the proposed new air pollution control code. The code was approved by the City Council and became law in 1971. Ellis continued to consult with the city after his thesis was completed.

The present authors suspect that, as is the case with many analyses of this type, the detailed quantitative work involved in doing the full-scale study probably helped the investigator to better understand the *qualitative* implications of the problem, and it was this *qualitative* understanding that helped him influence the governmental officials. Perhaps this level of sophistication could have come about through other means, but we should not underestimate the important intellectual and emotional impact that arises when we are forced to express vexing tradeoffs in unambiguous quantitative terms. It forces us to think harder than we are ordinarily accustomed to especially if we then have to defend our assessments in front of other experts.

7.2   PREFERENCE TRADEOFFS AMONG INSTRUCTIONAL PROGRAMS

Roche* considers the problem faced by a decision maker who must choose, from alternative budget allocations, diverse activities that compete for the same scarce resource. He is concerned about the role played by the decision maker caught "in the middle," that is, a decision maker who is in the position where he must obtain funds from some approving authority and, at the same time, approve the budgets for programs directed by professionals in his employ. With a constrained budget he can increase the budget of one program only at the expense of other programs. He must take from Peter to pay Paul and convince his overseers of the reasonableness of it all. Roche wanted to see whether our type of formal preference analysis could help such a man to crystallize his own tradeoffs and communicate this process to the body that controls the dispensation of funds.

Roche studied the budget allocation problem of a small school district. The school superintendent was the decision maker in the middle, Roche's principal client; the people below the superintendent were the school principal and the coordinators of various educational programs; the people above the superintendent were the school board that acted as the funding agency for the town. School boards in New England have a great deal of fiscal autonomy and can impose financial obligations on the town. But, of course, these school board members are themselves elected officials so that the ultimate responsibility does reside in the collectivity of town citizens.

Roche was indeed fortunate—but it was far from all luck—to find a chairman of a school board and a superintendent who were initially interested in pursuing a pilot test of Roche's ideas. It is a credit to Roche that the initial curiosity of these cooperating individuals bloomed into full-scale enthusiastic cooperation and, as we shall see, he was skillful

---

* In this section, we summarize and review the work of Roche (1971). His doctoral thesis, which was supervised by Raiffa, makes extensive use of the material in Chapter 3 on tradeoffs under certainty.

enough in his personal relations to involve other individuals in the measurement exercise. Roche, in his thesis, disguised the name of the town, which he fictitiously called "Somerstown," and he also disguised the names of the people that participated in the exercise. However, many of the dialogues recorded in the thesis are verbatim reports of actual measurement sessions. We also point out, as background material, that Somerstown is a small homogeneous community whose educational program was deemed comparatively stable and free of the many frictions that plagued other educational systems at that tumultuous time.

7.2.1   Refining the Problem

Somerstown began a program budgeting effort in September 1969, several years before Roche's work. One of the school board members was a business school professor, and it was through his intervention that the superintendent recast the traditional line-item budget into a program format. At the junior high school level, the basic program format was segregated according to subject matter. The superintendent and the business school professor admitted, however, that to their disappointment the program budgeting effort had practically no effect whatsoever on the reallocation of funds to different school-subject programs. Each year, the funds were allocated like the year before except perhaps for a uniform percentage increase. This history may partially explain the receptive audience that Roche received when he approached Somerstown authorities with the idea of examining fundamental tradeoffs among the funding of different subjects.

Roche concentrated on the allocation process for four subject programs at the junior high school level:

1. English/language arts.
2. Science.
3. Mathematics.
4. Social studies.

The Somerstown schools have a coordinator for each of these programs and they prepare an annual budget for their respective areas. Each coordinator feels a responsibility to do better each year than the year before and each tries to get increases in funding for his or her program— the usual advocacy procedure. When Mr. A asks for an increase, he seldom feels obliged—nor would it be considered good form—to argue that the money he is seeking should come from Mr. B's program. It is the superintendent's task to juggle these requests and to suggest a compromise among them in a fashion that maintains the loyalty of his staff and at the same time gains the acceptance of the school committee.

The first half of the thesis is concerned with the creation of a suitable production function: the transformation of financial and personnel inputs to educational outputs—no mean task! For a long time before Roche started his probing, the Somerstown school authorities worried about educational indices. Several indicators could be chosen but many are highly correlated and for convenience of the exercise, Roche and his collaborators chose for each of the four programs the index, "percentage of students achieving at or above grade level on the standardized achievement test."

Toward the end of his thesis Roche discusses the inadequacy of this output measure. He defends his use of it, however, on pragmatic grounds and he also discusses what other researchers might do if they chose other output indices. We feel that the chosen index is far from a good surrogate for educational performance and we feel that it is not an elementary task to suggest how Roche's analysis could proceed using a more sensitive set of output indices. But for the time being we are stuck with the index used and let us get on with the story even though it is marred by the exclusive use of this oversimplified output index.

7.2.2 Relating Program Costs to Output

Let us look at the process Roche followed in confronting the science coordinator. The science budget for the existing year was $81,000 and 59 percent of the students performed at or better than their specified grade level. Roche first inquired about the effects of dropping the science program altogether. The coordinator conceded that many of the students would continue to perform at or above the grade level. He then inquired about the effect of a 10 percent increase, (i.e., an increase of $8100). "What would I be allowed to do with the money?" Dave Flaherty queried.

"It's up to you," responded Roche. "The essential point is, Dave, that none of us knows how to use an additional $8100 in science better than you do. Once you decide what you would do with the $8100 I will ask you to assess what impact those additional funds would have on the students in the same way we did before. That is, we shall ask: What would you do with the increased funds? Which levels or sections in which grades would be effected? What would you expect the effect would be along the dimension of number of students achieving at or above grade level in science?"

Roche told Dave Flaherty to think about the questions posed. He encouraged the science coordinator to examine the past data, to think about the increased money not in the abstract but in terms of what it would buy in the form of additional teaching help or additional audio-visual facilities, and to think about the effect on individual students. He posed such questions as: "If you do X, would this really help Mary Jane over the hurdle?"

The production function ideally should have been probabilistically assessed, but all Roche had the time to do was to elicit a median value in each case, that is, a value for which the assessor thought the true value would be equally likely to fall above or below the estimated value. He formalized the assessment procedure in terms of a written protocol with several pages of work sheets that the coordinator took many hours over a period of days to answer.

The end product that Roche sought from the science coordinator was a curve that plotted estimated performance (percent at or above grade level) on the vertical axis against budgetary values on the horizontal axis. This curve, the assessed production function, was to go through a pivot point at the status quo level, that is, a budget of $81,000 produces a performance of 59 percent.

After Flaherty completed Roche's work sheets he was presented with the following task: "Now that you (Flaherty) have completed the assessment questions, we would like to probe your qualitative judgement about the possible shapes of a performance function for the Somerstown Junior High Science Program." Roche then showed Flaherty several shaped curves as shown in Fig. 7.3 and they discussed the qualitative meaning of

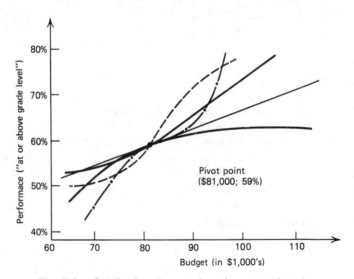

Fig. 7.3. Qualitative shapes of performance functions.

each. After Flaherty seemed to understand the implications of each shape, he was asked to select one of the shapes presented or to invent a shape that reflected his true feelings.

Roche discussed with Flaherty some of his responses and pointed out inconsistencies among the answers he recorded, but he tried to do this in a manner such that Flaherty would not be embarrassed at these inconsistencies. The important thing was to have Flaherty think about these inconsistencies and then try to modify some of his earlier assessments so that the revised set of responses would be internally consistent. And, what is perhaps more important, the revised answers should be felt to accurately portray the current best assessments Flaherty could have made in light of his new level of understanding.

All we can do in this summary is describe the way in which Roche generated a performance function from each of the four coordinators. The superintendent, Dr. Nelson, had his own views about these performance assessments and felt compelled in some circumstances to modify the assessments of his subordinates. Dr. Nelson remarked, however, that if this assessment process were repeated each year he would be able to calibrate his coordinators on the basis of a track record. The school committee, which monitored the entire exercise, felt that it was most appropriate for the superintendent to modify these performance functions in collaboration with his coordinators, since the school committee superintendent had to take full responsibility for the finally recorded performance functions. The committee explicitly stated that their deliberations would be based primarily on the superintendent's own assessments, which would be based partly on the inputs he received from his coordinators.

7.2.3 Assessing a Value Function

Now we discuss the second part of the thesis dealing with preference structures. Roche investigated the preference structures of several concerned individuals for different performance profiles. A typical profile is a four-tuple $(x_{LA}, x_S, x_M, x_{SS})$, which refers to performance scores on language arts, science, mathematics, and social sciences respectively, and where x_{LA}, for example, represents the percentage of students at or above grade level in language arts.

As is evident in Fig. 7.4 each performance range was restricted to a subinterval of the theoretically feasible range from 0 to 100 percent. For example, mathematics performance was restricted from the worst case of 65 percent to the best case of 85 percent. These restricted ranges were ample enough to accommodate budgetary changes that could realistically be recommended. It was critical to restrict these ranges so that various

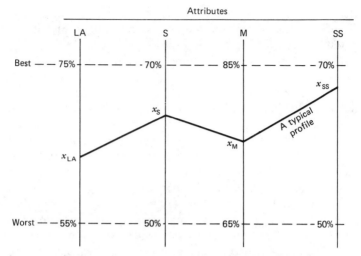

Fig. 7.4.   Performance ranges and a typical profile.

preferential independence assumptions could be adopted. We shall expand on this point shortly.

Because of the considerable support Roche received from Dr. Nelson, the superintendent, and Mrs. Humphrey, the chairwoman of the school committee, Roche was able to field test preference assessments with every single administrator and policy maker involved in the decision-making process of the junior high school. These involved the principal and assistant principal of the junior high school, the superintendent and assistant superintendent, and all five members of the Somerstown school committee. Absent from this listing are the citizens and the parents of school children. In addition, the preference procedure was also field tested on a group of 18 doctoral students in educational administration.

It was surprisingly easy to verify the reasonableness of pairwise preferential independence. For example, Roche set x_M and x_{SS} at low levels of 70 and 55 percent, respectively, and then probed conditional preference tradeoffs between x_{LA} and x_S. After he thoroughly engaged his subjects in this problem he asked parenthetically whether any of the tradeoff responses between x_{LA} and x_S would be altered if x_M and x_{SS} were not set at 70 and 55 percent, respectively. Practically all of his subjects felt that these tradeoffs would certainly not be influenced by such modifications of the fixed levels of x_M and x_{SS}. Some subjects, including the superintendent, emphasized that the tradeoffs would not depend on the fixed levels of x_M and x_{SS} *provided that these levels were within the specified bounds.* He felt for example, that if x_M were set at 30 percent this would be such a shock to the system that his tradeoffs between x_{LA} and x_S would be affected.

For all subjects, Roche felt that the necessary pairwise preferential independence assumptions were satisfied to legitimize adopting a value function of the form

$$v(x_{LA}, x_S, x_M, x_{SS}) = k_{LA}v_{LA}(x_{LA}) + k_S v_S(x_S) + k_M v_M(x_M) + k_{SS}v_{SS}(x_{SS})$$

$$(7.1)$$

where the component v's were normalized respectively at 0 and 1 for the worst and best consequences (e.g., $v_{LA}(55) = 0$, $v_{LA}(75) = 1$, etc.), where the k's were nonnegative, and where

$$k_{LA} + k_S + k_M + k_{SS} = 1. \qquad (7.2)$$

Roche followed the assessment procedure described in Section 3.7. For each subject he assessed the component value functions by the midvalue technique: for each component function he first found the .50-value point, next the .25 and the .75 points, then he checked the .50 point against the .25 and .75 points, and finally he discussed the general shape of the v-component functions. Next he sought the k weights. He asked these questions: "Suppose we consider a disastrous profile such as (55, 50, 65, 50) where all performance measures are at their worst levels. Now suppose you could push one of these worst scores up to the best level, which would you choose? Would you prefer to push language arts up from 55 to 75, science from 50 to 70, mathematics from 65 to 85, or social science from 50 to 70?" He thus probed each respondent for rankings of the k's. Next, he followed the technique discussed in Section 3.7 and determined precise numerical values for the k weights. Figure 7.5 depicts the assessments of Superintendent Nelson and his assistant, Mr. Elliot. Table 7.2 summarizes some salient data collected from the nine principal actors involved in the exercise. Roche not only obtained Nelson's assessments but he had Nelson guess at what some of his associates would record. It's fascinating to read how Nelson rationalized some of the recorded assessments of members of his staff and the school committee members. There are striking differences of opinion!

As regards the 18 students in the doctoral seminar in educational administration, all of whom were subjected to the same assessment procedure, we quote from Roche:

"There is little to be gained at this point in the study from exhibiting the 18 structures. However, the following summary information might be of interest.

1. With respect to the Language Arts program, 11 of the curves were concave, 5 were linear, and 2 S shaped about the current performance level.

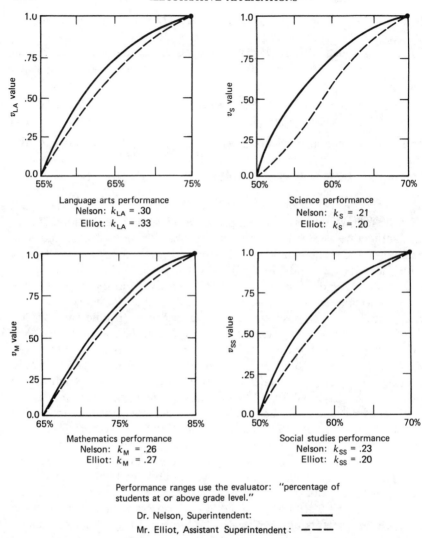

Performance ranges use the evaluator: "percentage of
students at or above grade level."

Dr. Nelson, Superintendent: ————
Mr. Elliot, Assistant Superintendent: – – – –

Fig. 7.5. Value functions assessed by the Superintendent and Assistant Superintendent of the Somerstown School System.

2. In the Science program, 8 were concave, 2 were linear, 4 were S shaped about current performance, and 4 were convex. Thus, there was much less concern with poor performance in Science than in Language Arts.
3. Interestingly enough, all 18 of the curves were concave in the mathematics program. That is, there was unanimous concern with poor performance in Mathematics.

Table 7.2

Assessed k Values and .50 Midvalue Points of Principal Subjects

Name	k Values				(.50) Midvalue Points			
	LA	S	M	SS	LA	S	M	SS
Administration								
(1) Mrs. Carter (Principal)	.20	.25	.22	.33	60.5	54.5	70	54
(2) Mrs. MacGregor (Asst. Principal)	.21	.24	.23	.32	61	54.5	68	53.5
(3) Dr. Nelson (Superintendent)	.30	.21	.26	.23	60.5	55	71.5	55
(4) Mr. Elliot (Asst. Superintendent)	.33	.20	.27	.20	62	59	72	57
School Committee:								
(1) Mrs. Humphrey (Chairwoman)	.36	.13	.30	.21	62	63	69	57.5
(2) Mrs. Clark	.22	.26	.23	.29	65	59	67.5	57
(3) Mr. Cowles	.53	.10	.27	.10	65	62	70	63
(4) Mrs. Oscar	.47	.11	.35	.07	65	62	69	60
(5) Mr. MacMillan	.29	.23	.28	.20	59	55	68	54.5
Lowest midvalue point assessed:					59	54.5	67.5	53.5
Highest midvalue point assessed:					65	63	72	63

Key: Each row contains (1) the scale factor for each program, which indicates the subject's tradeoffs *among* programs; and (2) the "global" midvalue point for each program, which gives an indication of the subject's tradeoffs *within* a program. A low midvalue point indicates a strong aversion to poor performance.

4. In the Social Studies program, 11 of the curves were concave, 3 were linear, 2 were S shaped about current performance, and 2 were convex.

"It is of interest to note that the doctoral students, like the subjects in Somerstown, basically fell into two groups: (1) the educators who were essentially concave in all programs (eight of the students fell into this group); and, (2) the policy makers who were either concave or linear in Language Arts, concave in Mathematics, and S shaped or convex in either/or Science and Social Studies (eight of the students fell into this group). Only two of the students did not fall into either of these groups. This was because these two students were S shaped about current performance in Language Arts. It may be coincidental, but one of the students whose structure very closely approximated the typical school committee member's structure in Somerstown, had just recently run for election to the Boston School Committee.

"Of even more interest to the analyst was the fact that *no* student was linear in all the programs. Therefore, without knowing it, the students demonstrated that the typical 'priority list' approach, i.e., the constant linear form, would be inappropriate for analyses of their preferences among programs. When this evidence is added to the data generated in Somerstown, it suggests that the analyst should be extremely careful about using the constant linear form.

"With respect to the determination of scale factors during the second part of the assessment procedure, the vast majority of the students behaved as did the Somerstown superintendent and a majority of the Somerstown School Committee. That is, 15 out of the 18 students chose Language Arts as that program they would want to "push-up" first. Science was picked by 2 students, and one chose the Social Studies program. Although none of the students picked Mathematics as the 'base' program, 9 of them chose this program as the second program they would like to see 'pushed-up.' The remaining 9 students all chose Social Studies as the second program."

After Roche obtained the full assessments from his subjects he asked each of four of the School Board members plus the assistant superintendent to suggest budgetary alternatives that would either be most appealing to themselves and would have some chance of being accepted by the group or be of a type that they would welcome seeing evaluated. Five alternatives besides the no-change position were thus generated. Again we quote from Roche:

"The 'no-change' alternative for the Junior High School Core Program was as follows: allocate $92,000 to the Language Arts program, $81,000 to the Science program, $76,000 to the Mathematics program, and $75,000 to the Social Studies program. The alternative allocations (expressed as changes to the 'no-change' case) are listed below with the names of the individuals who suggested them.

1. The *Humphrey* alternative. Take $6000 from Science, and $6000 from Social Studies. Increase Language Arts by $10,000 and increase Mathematics by $2000.
2. The *Oscar* alternative. Take $7000 from Science, and $2000 from Social Studies. Increase Language Arts by $6000, and increase Mathematics by $3000.
3. The *Elliot* alternative. Take $7000 from Science, and $1000 from Social Studies. Increase Language Arts by $3000, and increase Mathematics by $5000.
4. The *Cowles* alternative. Take $3000 from Language Arts, and $6000 from Mathematics. Increase Science by $4000, and increase Social Studies by $5000.
5. The *Clark* alternative. Take $2000 from Language Arts, $2000 from Science, and $1000 from Mathematics. Apply all $5000 to Social Studies."

Table 7.3

Preference of Each Individual for Each Budget Alternative Generated
by the Educational Value Function

Administrators and Board Members	Alternative Budget Allocations					
	No Change	Humphrey	Oscar	Elliot	Cowles	Clark
Dr. Nelson	.730	.743	.737	.743	.730	.727
Mr. Elliot	.642	.650	.643	.646	.646	.637
Mr. Carter	.771	.778	.778	.777	.793	.785
Mr. MacGregor	.765	.771	.771	.771	.784	.775
Mrs. Humphrey	.667	.697	.686	.686	.668	.667
Mrs. Clark	.638	.647	.629	.628	.676	.632
Mr. Cowles	.584	.647	.624	.608	.563	.570
Mrs. Oscar	.608	.647	.650	.631	.588	.597
Mr. MacMillan	.813	.816	.807	.809	.816	.809

Key: In each row, the preference or value number as determined by each subject's
preference structure is presented for each alternative budget allocation.

Using the performance functions as generated by the program coordinators and modified by Superintendent Nelson, and using the preferences of each of the four administrators and five board members, it was
possible to evaluate the six suggested proposals. These preferences are
shown in Table 7.3 and comparative rankings are shown in Table 7.4. We
can readily see that the Humphrey alternative strictly dominates the
"no-change" alternative and the Elliot alternative. Furthermore, when

Table 7.4

Rankings of the Alternatives for Each Individual Developed from the
Preference Numbers in Table 7.3

Administrators and Board Members	Alternative Budget Allocations					
	No Change	Humphrey	Oscar	Elliot	Cowles	Clark
Dr. Nelson	3	1	2	1	3	4
Mr. Elliot	4	1	3	2	2	5
Mr. Carter	5	3	3	4	1	2
Mr. MacGregor	4	3	3	3	1	2
Mrs. Humphrey	4	1	2	2	3	4
Mrs. Clark	3	2	5	6	1	4
Mr. Cowles	4	1	2	3	6	5
Mrs. Oscar	4	2	1	3	6	5
Mr. MacMillan	2	1	4	3	1	3

power realities are also considered, the Humphrey alternative essentially overpowers the Clark and Oscar alternatives as well. This leaves a contest between the Humphrey and the Cowles proposals. Again, however, looking at the personalities and the strengths of preferences we are tempted to single out the Humphrey proposal as the obvious winner.

Roche raises the question whether the above described procedure could seriously be implemented for group decision making. He writes:

> "Under normal conditions, I don't believe it would be reasonable to expect that policy makers would allow their own preference structures to be communicated. Recall that Dr. Nelson said that he would usually want to keep his own preference structure private. The administrators and policy makers in Somerstown are rather unusual. They willingly cooperated in this effort in order to further research on decision making. Additionally, there are no major educational problems in Somerstown. That is, there are no sensitive issues at stake. Therefore, no individual felt threatened by having his or her preference structure recorded. In such a case, decisions would of the fine tuning variety, rather than the sensitive policy decisions."

Roche developed a computer program that takes the performance functions and the preference structure of a single decision maker—he used Nelson's as an example—and generates the optimum allocation for a given overall budget level. It is essentially a resource-allocation type of dynamic program. Given this program it is easy to generate the program implications of various overall budget levels. Roche, however, did not choose to formalize tradeoffs between money and the four indices of scholastic performance. If he had, undoubtedly the set of four scholastic attributes would have been preferentially independent of the monetary attribute so that all of Roche's work would also be relevant and appropriate in the extended framework. The computer program also makes it relatively easy to investigate various sensitivity studies: for example, dependence on the k weights or on changes in performance functions.

We conclude this section with a quote from Roche:

> "Although this research demonstrates that these new techniques could be used to examine budgetary alternatives among programs, the demonstration was within a very narrow context. There may be problems in attempting to use these formal techniques elsewhere. The local educational setting served as a 'laboratory' for the investigation of these techniques. I believe that this setting is representative of numerous non-profit organizations. However, on the basis of this research we cannot say that these formal techniques should be used *everywhere*, but, rather, that they could be used *somewhere*."

7.3 FIRE DEPARTMENT OPERATIONS*

In any analysis of fire department policy a classical question is, "How much is a minute of response time† worth?" Clearly the value for any particular fire depends on the detailed circumstances of that fire. It is not feasible to treat individually each of the several thousand serious fires that the New York Fire Department extinguishes each year. Instead, we focus on the "typical" New York structural fire.

By exploiting the concepts and results of utility theory discussed in earlier chapters, we present an initial attempt to quantify the experience of some New York City Fire Department officials and investigate means of using this information for evaluating Fire Department policies. This first step involves the preferences of one deputy chief of the New York City Fire Department. A five-attribute utility function is assessed specifying the value of response time to a "typical" fire as a function of the particular piece of equipment, the response times of the other fire-fighting vehicles, and whether it is the difference between a two- and a three-minute response or the difference between a seven- and an eight-minute response. The attributes of this utility function are the response times of the first three engines and first two ladders arriving at a structural fire.

7.3.1 An Overview

Let us step back and try to get an overall picture of where this work fits into Fire Department decision making. It would be desirable to evaluate proposed Fire Department policies and programs in terms of such fundamental objectives as "maximize the quality of fire service provided" and "minimize its cost." Annual cost of the Fire Department measured in dollars might be an appropriate attribute for the second objective, but there is no clear attribute for the first one. Thus, it may be necessary to divide this objective into such lower-level objectives as "minimize loss of life," "minimize injuries," "minimize property damage," "minimize psychological anxiety of the citizens," and so on. Reasonable attributes for these first three objectives are, respectively, the annual number of

---

* The work discussed in this section was done for the New York City–Rand Institute by Keeney, who was employed as a consultant. He thanks Deputy Chief Francis J. Ronan of the New York Fire Department and Edward H. Blum of the New York City–Rand Institute for their important contributions to this work. The effort represents part of the joint work by the Fire Department and the Institute to understand and improve the bases for deploying fire department resources. This section utilizes material originally published in Keeney (1973c).

† The response time for a particular piece of equipment is defined as the time elapsed after the apparatus leaves the fire house and before it arrives at the location of the incident.

deaths, the annual number of injuries caused by fire, and the annual dollar value of lost property, whereas a subjective index would likely be required for the attribute dealing with psychological anxieties. However, these first three attributes are not exactly ideal. It is very difficult to determine what fatalities, injuries, and damage is attributable to the service of the Fire Department and what is not. For example, an individual who causes a fire by falling asleep while smoking in bed might die before the fire is reported. This and similar fatalities should not reflect on Fire Department services. Such problems with the available data, coupled with the fact that little is known quantitatively about the fire-fighting process, contribute to the insufficiency of these measures. In addition, there are problems about the relative seriousness of different injuries and difficulties of directly placing a value on the life of an individual that further complicate matters.

Fortunately, the response times of the various apparatus responding to fires provide a natural set of proxy attributes for evaluating the level of service for such problems. Figure 7.6 is a simplified model of the fire service system illustrating that response times are inputs to the fire-fighting process, whereas objectives concerning loss of life and property damage relate to outputs.

Firemen are accustomed to thinking in terms of response times in informally evaluating their preferences for various alternative courses of action. In doing this, they use their experience in gauging both the likelihoods of the various possible response times given a particular policy and the effects these response times have on the more fundamental service objectives of the department. Aside from their interpretative appeal, data exist for specifying the probabilities of the response times conditional on a particular course of action. Beginning in the early 1960's, the New York Fire Department kept extensive records on particular aspects of fire occurrence. These data have been analyzed, providing the necessary input information for developing a simulation model of Fire Department operations, an early version of which is described in Carter and Ignall (1970). This model generates probability density functions for the response times of any prescribed operational policy.

Our aim is to relate the various possible response times to the accomplishment of the Fire Department's objectives for fundamental services. We want to distill years of experience of some Fire Department officials by quantifying their subjective preferences for response times to fires in a manner useful for improving the fire fighter's decision making process. Thus, we are essentially asking the offical to consider the implications of a particular set of response times (e.g., the first engine responds in three minutes, the second in five minutes, . . . , the first ladder responds in two

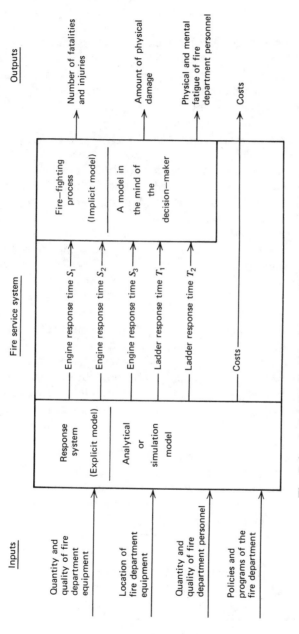

Fig. 7.6. A simplified model of a fire department service system.

379

minutes, . . .) on the outputs, and then to evaluate his preferences for various sets of response times in light of the respective implications. The result is a subjective model—based on experience—for the fire-fighting process, its consequences, and the relative undesirabilities of these consequences.

Whose preferences should be assessed? By virtue of their experience, it was decided that the operating chiefs were best suited to understand the many implications of various combinations of response times. As a logical first step, the preferences discussed here are those of one deputy chief of the New York Fire Department.

7.3.2 Use of the Response-Time Utility Function

The original motivation for assessing a utility function for response times was to develop a model for the escalation of fires. If the originally delegated units cannot control a fire, additional units must be requested, and the fire is said to escalate. Since such events are very important to the Fire Department's performance, it would be useful to model the escalation phenomenon and include it in the simulation model. Specifically, we want to know when poor Fire Department service leads to escalation. Since the probability of escalation is clearly related to the quality of deployment, and since this quality can be measured by the response-time utility function, it may be desirable to assess the conditional probability of escalation given the quality of the response as summarized by its utility.

The utility function for response times can be useful for guiding decisions concerning operational policy of the department. Examples of such policies concern variation in initial response patterns and dispatching of vehicles, alteration of the areas of responsibility between different pieces of equipment, introduction of "special squads" during high-demand hours, and temporary relocation of equipment into areas where resources are almost all working at fires. The simulation mentioned earlier and other models generate probability distributions for response times for any given policy. Thus, given an appropriate utility function, we can evaluate policies according to expected utility.

Let R denote the vector attribute dealing with response time service levels and let C denote the cost attribute. Then $u'(c, \mathbf{r})$ is the overall utility for cost c and the response vector $\mathbf{r}$. Assuming that R is utility independent of C (a most reasonable assumption), we can define a utility function $u(\mathbf{r})$ and, from the results in Chapter 5,

$$u'(c, \mathbf{r}) = f[c, u(\mathbf{r})].\tag{7.3}$$

In our discussion, we shall confine our remarks to the assessment of $u(\mathbf{r})$.

Before proceeding to the assessment of the response-time utility function, we suggest that the general ideas presented here are relevant to other emergency services such as law enforcement agencies and emergency ambulance systems. In such systems, Larson (1972), Savas (1969), and Stevenson (1972) among others, use response times to evaluate alternative proposed policies. In all such cases, the question arises, "How much is a minute of response time worth?" The work discussed here is an initial attempt to address such questions.

7.3.3 Assessing the Response-Time Utility Function

During 1970, Deputy Chief Francis J. Ronan of the New York Fire Department and Keeney held a number of discussions to specify Chief Ronan's preferences for response times to fires. These usually lasted between one and two hours each.

Historically the traditional "standard response" in New York City has involved three engines and two ladders, so it was decided to assess a utility function over five attributes: the response times of the first and second ladders arriving at a fire and the response times of the first three arriving engines. Let us designate these attributes respectively by T_i, $i = 1$, 2, and S_j, $j = 1, 2, 3$, and let t_i and s_j represent specific amounts of T_i and S_j, respectively. Thus, we are interested in the response-time utility function $u(t_1, t_2, s_1, s_2, s_3)$.

In discussing the assessment of Chief Ronan's utility function, we will follow the guidelines for the assessment procedure suggested in Chapter 5. Thus, the discussion differentiates into five activities:

1. Familiarization.
2. Verifying the assumptions.
3. Assessing conditional utility functions.
4. Evaluating scaling constants of u.
5. Checking for consistency.

The presentation here illustrates how the response-time utility function was assessed and what input information was necessary.

FAMILIARIZATION. Before beginning on this problem, Chief Ronan and Keeney had worked together on a very simple decision-analytical model of a fire-response problem. Also, at an earlier time, Keeney had roughly assessed Chief Ronan's utility function for the response time of the first engine arriving at a fire. The main purpose of this preliminary exercise was to examine the reasonableness of the objective "minimize the *expected* response time of the first engine arriving at a fire." In most

382 ILLUSTRATIVE APPLICATIONS

analytical studies dealing with emergency services, this linearity assumption (i.e., minimize expected response time) is used implicitly. As a result of this initial exposure, the Chief was introduced to the basic concepts of utility theory. After the first two assessment sessions, which turned out to be learning experiences for both analyst and respondent, the discussions became more productive.

VERIFYING THE ASSUMPTIONS. To exploit the theory of Chapters 5 and 6, it was necessary to check whether requisite utility independence assumptions were appropriate for this problem.*

Specifically, it was verified that it was reasonable[†] to assume:

1. Engine response times $\{S_1, S_2, S_3\}$ and the ladder response time $\{T_1, T_2\}$ were utility independent of each other.
2. First ladder response T_1 and second ladder response T_2 were utility independent of each other.
3. The jth engine response S_j was utility independent of the other engine responses, for $j = 1, 2, 3$.

Because of Theorem 5.3 and assumption (1), the assessment of u was broken into two parts: assessments of an engine utility function and a ladder utility function. Analogously, these two utility functions could be broken down into component parts because of (2) and (3).

Let us illustrate the verification procedure with an example. To check if T_1 was utility independent of T_2, Chief Ronan was asked "If the response time of the second arriving ladder is fixed at 6 minutes, what response time t_1 for the first arriving ladder would be indifferent to having a 50–50 chance that the first ladder responds in either 1 or 5 minutes?" Notice that if $t_2 = 6$, then $t_1 < 6$, and this restricts the domain conveniently. A response that $t_1 = 3.4$ minutes was eventually chosen using a "convergence" technique discussed in Section 4.9.

Next we asked the same question, only the second ladder response time was fixed at 8 rather than 6 minutes. Again, the indifference response was 3.4 minutes, leading us to believe that the relative preferences for changes in the response time of the first ladder did not depend on the

---

* Strictly speaking we need a generalization of utility independence since, for example, the domain of T_1 depends on the value of T_2. Consider two response times t_2' and t_2'' and let u_1' and u_1'' be the conditional utility functions on T_1 given t_2' and t_2'', respectively. Then we assume, in this example, that $u_1' \sim u_1''$ for the domain $0 \le t_1 \le \min(t_2', t_2'')$. The representation theorems that are employed in the section can be shown to hold for the above generalization of utility independence.

[†] The following independence assumptions were deemed to be approximately valid after considerable probing. Some of the dependencies were so slight—contrary to what was first expected—that independence was taken as an innocuous idealization.

fixed response time of the second ladder. By additional questioning similar to the above, this speculation was confirmed. Thus, it seemed appropriate to assume that T_1 was utility independent of T_2.

ASSESSING CONDITIONAL UTILITY FUNCTIONS. In view of the above assumptions, utility functions were needed for each of the five response-time attributes. Actually these are conditional utility functions, since they concern preferences over a single response time given that the other response times are held fixed. However, because of the utility independence conditions, the particular amounts of these other responses are not important, since the utility function should be the same in any case. To illustrate the approach, let us assess $u_1^T(t)$, the conditional utility function for the first arriving ladder.

It was decided to scale u_1^T from -1 to 0. The response times ranged from 0 to 20 minutes, which implied that

$$u_1^T(0) = 0 \tag{7.4}$$

and

$$u_1^T(20) = -1. \tag{7.5}$$

Through questioning, we found that a 2.2-minute response of the first arriving ladder was indifferent to a 50–50 chance at either a 1- or 3-minute response. Similarly, 4.2 minutes was indifferent to a 50–50 chance at 3 or 5 minutes, and 6.2 minutes was indifferent to a 50–50 chance at 5 or 7 minutes. In general, a 50–50 chance at either a t or a $(t+2)$-minute response was indifferent to a $(t+1.2)$-minute response for certain. As indicated in Chapter 4, such preferences imply that the utility function must be of the form

$$u_1^T(t) = d + b(-e^{ct}) \tag{7.6}$$

where d, b, and $c > 0$ are constants.

We could have specified d, b, and c using (7.4), (7.5), and the certainty equivalent from any one of the above responses. However, for parameter estimation, it is better to use a wider range lottery as discussed in Chapter 4. Thus, a 4.5-minute response time for the first ladder was found to be indifferent to a 50–50 lottery yielding either 1 or 7 minutes. Hence u_1^T must be such that

$$u_1^T(4.5) = \tfrac{1}{2}u_1^T(1) + \tfrac{1}{2}u_1^T(7). \tag{7.7}$$

Substituting (7.6) into (7.4), (7.5), and (7.7) yields three equations with three unknowns, which can easily be solved to give

$$u_1^T(t) = .0998(1 - e^{.12t}). \tag{7.8}$$

Similar procedures were used to obtain the other four conditional utility functions.

EVALUATING SCALING CONSTANTS OF u. Given the individual utility functions for the five response times, the next step is to put them together in the appropriate manner to obtain the overall utility function for response times. This requires assessing the scaling constants, that is, the k's, of Theorems 5.2 and 6.3. To illustrate the method, let us use the ladder-response utility function

$$u_L(t_1, t_2) = k_1 u_1^T(t_1) + k_2 u_2^T(t_2) + [k_1 + k_2 - 1] u_1^T(t_1) u_2^T(t_2). \qquad (7.9)$$

Chief Ronan was asked for the response time t_2 of the second ladder where he would be indifferent between the two ladders arriving in 3 and 8 minutes, respectively, denoted by $(3, 8)$, and the response $(4, t_2)$. His answer was $t_2 = 5.7$, indicating a willingness to give up 1 minute of first ladder response in exchange for decreasing second ladder response by 2.3 minutes, given that he started from $(3, 8)$. This implied that

$$u_L(3, 8) = u_L(4, 5.7). \qquad (7.10)$$

Similarly, we found $(2, 6)$ indifferent to $(3, 4.2)$, therefore

$$u_L(2, 6) = u_L(3, 4.2). \qquad (7.11)$$

Using (7.9) and the individual utility functions to evaluate both sides of (7.10) and (7.11) gives us two equations with two unknowns, the parameters k_1 and k_2, which when solved, yields

$$u_L(t_1, t_2) = .66 u_1^T(t_1) + .19 u_2^T(t_2) - .15 u_1^T(t_1) u_2^T(t_2). \qquad (7.12)$$

Other parameters of the overall utility function were evaluated in similar ways as covered in Section 6.6. The general idea is to ask questions to obtain equations containing the unknown parameters, and then to solve the set of equations for the parameter values.

CHECKING FOR CONSISTENCY. Checking the utility function for consistency and reasonableness is obviously very important, because the assessment is inherently a subjective process and because the synthesis required to obtain the overall utility function can result in the introduction of "errors." It was important to make sure that the implications of the utility function agreed with the chief's preferences.

The most important checks concern the conditional utility functions and tradeoffs between the various response times. This involved discussing the implications of the utility function and using the utility function for providing answers to questions like those asked in the assessment process. In all cases where there was a major discrepancy between the implications of the utility function and the chief's preferences, part of the assessment procedure was repeated and his utility function adjusted accordingly. Many parts of the utility function were adjusted in light of consistency checks. The final utility function appears to represent Chief Ronan's responses quite closely.

7.3.4 The Response-Time Utility Function

In this section, we present the final form of the first-cut utility function and discuss its implications. From our assessments, we found that

$$u(\mathbf{t}, \mathbf{s}) = .24u_L(\mathbf{t}) + .16u_E(\mathbf{s}) - .6u_L(\mathbf{t})u_E(\mathbf{s}), \tag{7.13}$$

where

$$u_L(\mathbf{t}) \equiv u_L(t_1, t_2) = .66u_1^T(t_1) + .19u_2^T(t_2) - .15u_1^T(t_1)u_2^T(t_2), \tag{7.14}$$

with

$$u_1^T(t_1) = .0998[1 - e^{.12t_1}], \tag{7.15}$$

and

$$u_2^T(t_2) = .143[1 - .5e^{.08t_2} - .5e^{.12t_2}], \tag{7.16}$$

and where

$$\begin{aligned} u_E(\mathbf{s}) \equiv u_E(s_1, s_2, s_3) = &.63u_1^S(s_1) + .18u_2^S(s_2) + .09u_3^S(s_3) \\ &- .06u_1^S(s_1)u_2^S(s_2) - .03u_1^S(s_1)u_3^S(s_3) \\ &- .01u_2^S(s_2)u_3^S(s_3), \end{aligned} \tag{7.17}$$

with

$$u_1^S(s_1) = .0845[1 - .4e^{.10s_1} - .6e^{.14s_1}], \tag{7.18}$$

$$u_2^S(s_2) = .156[1 - e^{.10s_2}], \tag{7.19}$$

and

$$u_3^S(s_3) = .253[1 - e^{.08s_3}]. \tag{7.20}$$

For illustrative purposes, the utility function in (7.15) is shown in Fig. 7.7 and the indifference map implied by (7.14) is given in Fig. 7.8.

It was decided to evaluate preferences in the unit hypercube from (0, 0, 0, 0, 0) to (20, 20, 20, 20, 20), Thus, for each of the equations above, the variables may only range from 0 to 20 minutes. Furthermore, by definition, we have $t_1 \le t_2$ and $s_1 \le s_2 \le s_3$.

PROPERTIES OF THE UTILITY FUNCTION. The utility function u in (7.13) has several properties that are intuitively appealing and that appear to represent Chief Ronan's preferences. Some of these pertain to u as a whole, some to the utility function for ladders u_L or the utility function for engines u_E, and some to the utility functions of the individual units.

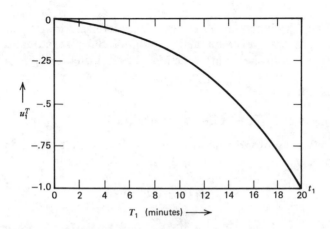

Fig. 7.7. Utility function for first ladder response time.

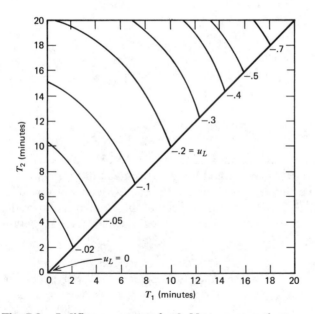

Fig. 7.8. Indifference curves for ladder response times.

386

Taking the latter first, we have:

1. u is decreasing in each t_i and s_j. This means that the sooner a particular unit arrives, the better, if the response time of other units are fixed.

2. Each minute of delay of the first arriving engine is more important* than a corresponding minute for the second arriving engine, which itself is more important than the corresponding delay of the third arriving engine. Similarly, each minute of delay of the first ladder is more important than a corresponding delay of the second ladder. These properties are indicated by the relative values of the coefficients of the u_i^T terms in (7.14) and the u_j^S terms in (7.17).

3. The conditional utility function for each attribute is risk averse regardless of the values of the other attributes. This means, for instance, that for T_1, a sure $(t_1'' + t_1')/2$ minute response is preferred to a 50–50 lottery yielding either t_1'' or t_1'. Or, the average response time is preferred to the lottery. When this is the case, for each unit, each additional minute of delayed response is more important than the former minute.

Concerning the utility function for ladders, we have:

4. The relative importance of the response time of the ith ladder increases as the response time of the other ladder increases. This means that the slower the first ladder is in arriving, the more important it is that the second ladder arrive soon after. This property is accounted for by the fact that the product term in (7.14) has a negative coefficient.

Similarly, for engines, there is an analogous property:

5. The relative importance of the response time of the jth engine increases as the response times of the other engines increase. This property is accounted for by the negative coefficients of the product terms in (7.17).

The last two properties concern the entire utility function. They are:

6. A one-minute delay in the arrival of the ith ladder is more important than the corresponding minute delay on the ith engine. Thus,

---

* To clarify the meaning of *more important*, recall the utility function (7.3) for cost and response times $u'(c, \mathbf{r}) = u'(c, t_1, t_2, s_1, s_2, s_3)$ and assume the cost attribute C and the set of response attributes $R \equiv \{T_1, T_2, S_1, S_2, S_3\}$ are utility independent of each other. Now select any base level cost c_0 and consider changes $\mathbf{r}'$ to $\mathbf{r}''$ and $\hat{\mathbf{r}}$ to $\hat{\hat{\mathbf{r}}}$, each of which is assumed to be for the better. We say that the change $\mathbf{r}'$ to $\mathbf{r}''$ is more important than the change $\hat{\mathbf{r}}$ to $\hat{\hat{\mathbf{r}}}$ if $c_1 > c_2$, where c_1 and c_2 are defined by $u'(c_0, \mathbf{r}') = u'(c_1, \mathbf{r}'')$ and $u'(c_0, \hat{\mathbf{r}}) = u'(c_2, \hat{\hat{\mathbf{r}}})$. That is, we must be willing to pay more in cost to make the *more important* change.

for example, using two-minute response for both the first engine and the first ladder as a base, we would prefer to have the first ladder respond in two minutes and the first engine in three than to have the first engine respond in two minutes and the first ladder in three. This property is indicated by the fact that the coefficient of u_L in (7.13) multiplied by the coefficient of u_1^T in (7.14) is larger than the coefficient of u_E in (7.13) multiplied by the coefficient of u_1^S in (7.17).

7. The relative importance of the response times of ladders increases as the response times of engines increase. This means the importance of the first arriving engine is less when a ladder has already arrived than it is when no ladders have arrived. The negative coefficient of the product term in (7.13) indicates that this property holds.

These properties, each of which is intuitively reasonable, go a long way toward specifying the utility function. That is, the manner in which the shape of the utility function (7.13) can be altered without violating one or more of the above conditions is severely restricted. This fact lends some additional confidence to our assessments.

Although the complexity of assessing a multiattribute utility function increases rapidly as the number of measures of effectiveness increase, the opportunity for "consistency checks" involving properties such as those above also greatly increases. In order to meaningfully represent our preferences in these complex situations, it is important to exploit such intuitively appealing attitudes toward preference to the fullest extent possible.

7.3.5 Conclusions

The main result of this work is a first-cut utility function over five response-time attributes, that is, those associated with the first two ladders and the first three engines arriving at a fire. This gives us some way of determining the relative values of a minute of response time for the various pieces of equipment. By looking at the coefficients of the single u_i terms of (7.13), we can get a very rough idea of the relative values of a minute of response time for the different pieces of apparatus. Doing this, if we set the relative value for a minute of response time of the first ladder at 10, the corresponding value for first engine is 7, the second ladder is 3, the second engine is 2, and the third engine is 1.

However, as we have mentioned, the worth of a minute of response time of a specific vehicle depends on the response times of the other pieces of equipment and the time since the alarm was reported. For instance, using a (2, 4; 2, 4, 6) response* as a base, the partial derivatives of u with respect to the five response times are in a ratio of $10:4:5:3:2$, implying that if the relative value of a minute of response time of the first ladder is set at 10, the corresponding value of the second ladder is 4, the first engine is 5, and the second engine is 3, and the third engine is 2, showing that the relative values depend on the base response.

The assessment procedure was too time consuming and too complex. Since it was impractical to develop a computer program to help assess one utility function, calculations were done by hand. Thus, there was a lack of immediate feedback to Chief Ronan concerning the implications of his preferences. Often this caused small differences in the Chief's responses during different sessions due to the slight variation of his preferences from time to time. But, of course, the involvement over a considerable time span has its merits too. We would like the assessed utility structure to be somewhat stable over time. In the future, an interactive computer program, such as the one discussed in Appendix 6C, would likely help maintain interest as well as assess the utility function much more quickly with many more consistency checks.

By asking Chief Ronan about his preferences for responses to the "typical" structural fire, we essentially asked him to synthesize in his mind all the possible implications of each response aggregated over the possible types of structural fires. This understandably caused some discrepancies in the answers to our questions, because of the tendency to focus on particular types of incidents at different times. The main purpose of our work was to develop a rough first-cut preference model that was reasonable for examining structural fires. For this, the aggregation requirement seemed appropriate. Further efforts could differentiate between types of structural fires.

We ultimately want to obtain a utility function appropriate for the use of the New York Fire Department. This section reports a first step: assessing a utility function of one deputy chief of that department. However, the Chief's preferences are his and not necessarily those of the Fire Department, and they should not be interpreted as such. Furthermore, although a serious attempt was made not to lead the Chief to any specific answers, his responses to questions could have partly been shaped by the questioning process, and the results should be interpreted with this possibility in mind.

This assessment exercise was done about five years ago, and if the exercise were to be repeated again, we probably would now proceed

---

* The first ladder responds in 2 minutes, the second ladder in 4 minutes, the first, second, and third engines in 2, 4, and 6 minutes, respectively.

somewhat differently. We would establish broad, basic, underlying principles that seemed to govern Chief Ronan's responses, and then deduce more of the structure of his utility function from these basic principles. Essentially we would model his motivations based on interviews that would probe more deeply on qualitative matters. This, of course, is easier said than done, and we would like someday to be able to report a good example of this technique.

7.4 STRUCTURING CORPORATE PREFERENCES FOR MULTIPLE OBJECTIVES*

Every corporation periodically asks itself: "How *should* we run our business?" More specifically, this raises the following questions: In view of the complex social, economic, technological, and political characteristics of our society, which management policies should we adopt now? Are these policies consistent with our personal objectives, with the desires of our shareholders, and with our social value structure? If we choose policy A, will it be possible to account for the contingencies that may arise in the near future and adapt accordingly? How can we best maintain the leadership position in our field and simultaneously, keep the vitality of our organization? All of these are crucial questions that deny the simple dollars-and-cents answers that are mythically supposed to be appropriate for almost all "business" decisions.

Since early 1972, Woodward-Clyde Consultants, a holding firm for several professional-service consulting firms has used some innovative approaches based on ideas discussed in this book to help them examine questions like the above-mentioned ones.[†] Although this effort is still in progress, it is sufficiently interesting and informative to include here. Two aspects of this effort seem to be unique. First, multiattribute utility functions over attributes measuring fundamental objectives of the corporation have been assessed for several executives at Woodward-Clyde. Second, this work was done *not* to evaluate a specific decision but,

---

* We thank the management of Woodward-Clyde Consultants for its permission to discuss this work in our book. The assistance of Dr. Keshavan Nair of Woodward-Clyde in writing this section is greatly appreciated. Material in this section appeared in Keeney (1975).

[†] In November, 1974, Woodward-Clyde made some very broad organizational changes. It is no longer a holding firm but, instead, a consulting firm with five regional divisions. The work described in this section was done from 1972 through October 1974; the organizational structure that prevailed during that period is described. The subsequent organizational changes are briefly summarized at the end of the section.

instead, to:

- Aid communication among the decision makers.
- Grapple with fundamental issues of the firm.
- Determine and examine differences of opinion in a quantitative fashion.
- Aid in generating creative alternatives in solving corporate problems.

The affiliate consulting firms of Woodward-Clyde Consultants operate mainly in the geotechnical engineering and environmental areas. Problems they examine include design of earth dams, siting and design of nuclear power plants, geotechnical and environmental studies associated with pipeline systems (e.g., the Trans-Alaska pipeline), and design of structures for earthquake-prone regions. None of the affiliates build any products (e.g., roads, dams, power plants); they are exclusively professional-service consulting firms. Collectively, their fees received in 1973 were approximately $25 million and, historically, this has increased at approximately 20 percent annually. All the shareholders of Woodward-Clyde must be senior professionals on the staff of one of the affiliates.

In 1972, Richard J. Woodward, Chairman of the Board of Woodward-Clyde Consultants, appointed a long-range planning committee whose assignment included "the development of a long-range plan for Woodward-Clyde Consultants that includes quantified objectives and is responsive to the Statement of Purpose and Standing Policies." After this original committee reported, the 1973 and 1974 Long-Range Planning Committees have successively updated the objectives of Woodward-Clyde and examined policy alternatives in terms of these objectives. Douglas C. Moorhouse was the chairman of each of these three committees. Dr. Keshavan Nair, a Vice President of Woodward-Lundgren and Associates, one of the affiliates of Woodward-Clyde, was also a member of these committees.

Much of the work discussed here (specifically Subsections 7.4.2–7.4.5) was done jointly by Dr. Nair and Ralph L. Keeney, working as a consultant to Woodward-Clyde. Subsection 7.4.1 discusses the original Long-Range Planning Committee's work, which has served as an excellent basis on which to build. The final subsection, 7.4.6, surveys some of the specific uses being made of Woodward-Clyde's utility function. The purpose in assessing a utility function was *not* to help management choose among action alternatives in a formal manner—probabilistic analysis was not done in accompaniment of utility analysis—but instead to help management articulate some of its basic assumptions and to facilitate communications among the executive group. This largely was and is being accomplished through use of the formal assessment procedures described below.

7.4.1   The 1972 Objectives and Measures of Effectiveness

The basic approach taken by the 1972 Long-Range Planning Committee to fulfill its mission was to (1) establish the primary objective of the firm, (2) divide this into subobjectives, and (3) conduct a deficiency analysis indicating discrepancies between present state and desired state on each objective. By weighting the various objectives, the deficiencies were ranked in order of importance and policies recommended for eliminating these deficiencies.

The overall objective of Woodward-Clyde was provided by a sentence in their Statement of Purpose: "The combined efforts of Woodward-Clyde Consultants and its affiliates are directed toward the creation and maintenance of an environment in which their employees can realize their personal, professional, and financial goals." They felt that growth was essential in the achievement of this objective.

The hierarchy of objectives developed by the 1972 Long-Range Planning Committee is presented in Fig. 7.9. This hierarchy has been adaptively revised since then. The numbers in parentheses in the box with each objective indicates the original division of weight among subobjectives (see subsection 3.7.4). In Table 7.5, the weights of each of the attributes associated with the lowest-level objectives and the range of each attribute are identified.

It was implicitly assumed that an additive value function

$$v(x_1, x_2, \ldots, x_{12}) = \sum_{i=1}^{12} k_i v_i(x_i),$$

where the x_i's represent levels of the attributes, each v_i is a value function over the ith attribute, v and the v_i's are scaled 0 to 1, and the weights, that is, the k_i's sum to 1, was appropriate. For each attribute, component value functions were constructed and present states and desired states, defined as the practical maximum felt to be achievable, were identified. Deficiency on each of these lowest-level objectives was then calculated by multiplying the weight of the objective times the difference in the value of its present and desired states. This indicated "areas" where improvement was needed.

Four shortcomings of the 1972 "quantification of objectives" are categorized as follows:

1. The weights were assigned to each objective without explicitly considering the range of the associated attributes.

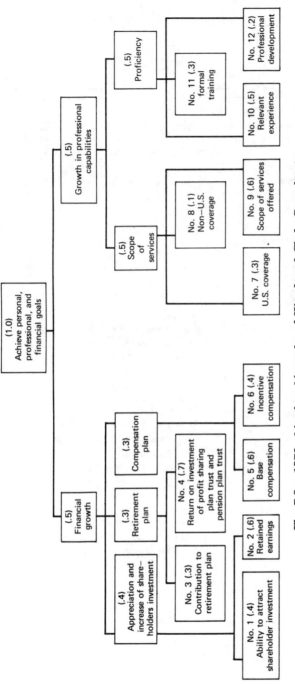

Fig. 7.9. 1972 objectives hierarchy of Woodward-Clyde Consultants.

393

Table 7.5
1972 Attributes for Woodward-Clyde Consultants

Attribute	Measurement Unit	Range	Attribute Weight
Ability to attract shareholders investment	$\dfrac{\text{Number of shares requested}}{\text{fees}}$ %	0–5	.08
Retained earnings	% of fees	0–8	.12
Contribution to retirement plan	% of fees	0–10	.045
Return on investment for retirement plan	% of investment	0–20	.105
Base compensation	% annual increase	0–20	.09
Incentive compensation	% of fees	0–8	.06
U.S. coverage	$\left(\dfrac{\text{Geographic centers adequately covered}}{\text{Centers where relevant work can be generated}}\right)$ %	25–100	.075
Non-U.S. coverage	$\left(\dfrac{\text{Geographic centers adequately covered}}{\text{Centers where relevant work can be generated}}\right)$ %	0–50	.025
Scope of services offered	$\left(\dfrac{\text{Number of disciplines having threshold capability}}{\text{Number of synergistic disciplines required by society}}\right)$ %	25–100	.15
Relevant experience	$\left(\dfrac{\text{Existing man-years experience}}{\text{Required man-years experience}}\right)$ %	25–100	.125
Formal training	Number of degrees per professional staff member	1–3	.075
Professional development	% of fees	0–2	.05

2. The component value functions were estimated by a direct value estimation technique independent of each other.
3. The overall objective function, being a value function, was not appropriate for examining policies with uncertain consequences.
4. The additive value structure did not lend itself to investigating overlap among the objectives.

Even with these weaknesses, the Long-Range Planning Committee and the Board of Directors felt that this quantification of objectives was a big improvement over informally articulated objectives. This set of objectives and measures has proved to be an excellent basis for modification and improvement, the substance of which we begin to describe in the next subsection.

Before proceeding, we briefly remark on aspects of the attributes and their measurement units that may not be clear from Table 7.5. For the first attribute, using the number of shares requested divided by fees implicitly assumes that the cost of a share is known in order to make the measure readily interpretable. The measure of the scope of services offered is an index indicating breadth in handling the interdisciplinary projects increasingly requested by society. With relevant experience, the idea is to have the staff available to do quality work on those projects which the Woodward-Clyde affiliates would like to do. For formal training, the number of degrees per professional staff member is defined as follows: a doctorate is three, a masters degree two, and a bachelors one. Professional development includes attending management or technical seminars, holding in-house study sessions, and so on.

7.4.2 Clarifying the Measures of Effectiveness

One of the first issues Nair and Keeney jointly considered was whether the measures of effectiveness met the comprehensiveness and measurability criteria discussed in Chapter 2. For each objective, the question "Can a better attribute be found?" was asked. In several cases, the answer was "yes." Let us discuss some examples.

ABILITY TO ATTRACT SHAREHOLDERS INVESTMENT.   The measurement unit for this attribute was changed to the dollar value of shares requested divided by the fees. Thus in interpreting trends, and simply in evaluating various levels of the attributes, we do not need to keep the value of the shares implicitly in mind.

SCOPE OF NON-U.S. COVERAGE.   The 1974 Long-Range Planning Committee changed this measure to percentage of the U.S. business in terms of fees received. It was the Committee's viewpoint that the major reason for

Table 7.6
An Aid for Evaluating Preferences for the Attribute Formal Training as Measured by the Degrees per Professional Staff Member.

Degrees per Professional Staff Member	5% PhD BS MS PhD	10% PhD BS MS PhD	15% PhD BS MS PhD	20% PhD BS MS PhD	25% PhD BS MS PhD	30% PhD BS MS PhD	35% PhD BS MS PhD	40% PhD BS MS PhD	45% PhD BS MS PhD	50% PhD BS MS PhD
1.5	55, 40, 5	60, 30, 10	65, 20, 15	70, 10, 20	75, 0, 25	Not possible	Not possible	Not possible	Not possible	Not possible
1.6	45, 50, 5	50, 40, 10	55, 30, 15	60, 20, 20	65, 10, 25	70, 0, 30	Not possible	Not possible	Not possible	Not possible
1.7	35, 60, 5	40, 50, 10	45, 40, 15	50, 30, 20	55, 20, 25	60, 10, 30	65, 0, 35	Not possible	Not possible	Not possible
1.8	25, 70, 5	30, 60, 10	35, 50, 15	40, 40, 20	45, 30, 25	50, 20, 30	55, 10, 35	60, 0, 40	Not possible	Not possible
1.9	15, 80, 5	20, 70, 10	25, 60, 15	30, 50, 20	35, 40, 25	40, 30, 30	45, 20, 35	50, 10, 40	55, 0, 45	Not possible
2.0	5, 90, 5	10, 80, 10	15, 70, 15	20, 60, 20	25, 50, 25	30, 40, 30	35, 30, 35	40, 20. 40	45, 10, 45	50, 0, 50
2.1	Not possible	0, 90, 10	5, 80, 15	10, 70, 20	15, 60, 25	20, 50, 30	25, 40, 35	30, 30, 40	35, 20, 45	40, 10, 50
2.2	Not possible	Not possible	Not possible	0, 80, 20	5, 70, 25	10, 40, 30	15, 50, 35	20, 40, 40	25, 30, 45	30, 20, 50
2.3	Not possible	Not possible	Not possible	Not possible	Not possible	0, 70, 30	5, 60, 35	10, 50, 40	15, 40, 45	20, 30, 50
2.4	Not possible	Not possible	Not possible	Not possible	Not possible	Not possible	Not possible	0, 60, 40	5, 50, 45	10, 40, 50
2.5	Not possible	Not possible	Not possible	Not possible	Not possible	Not possible	Not possible	Not possible	Not possible	0, 50, 50

expanding overseas was to reduce the consequences of a possible reces-
sion in the United States and to take advantage of current foreign
opportunities. Since Woodward-Clyde will remain primarily a U.S. operation in the foreseeable future, the new measure both is more easily
quantifiable than the previous one, and it also more directly indicates
vulnerability to domestic recessions.

RELEVANT EXPERIENCE AND PROFESSIONAL DEVELOPMENT.   As demand for
Woodward-Clyde services increases, the need to increase their relevant
experience grows. The 1972 measure of relevant experience indicated the
level at any given time, as opposed to focusing on the increase of relevant
experience. Increased relevant experience is funded out of the Professional Development budget and usually consists of opportunities for
employees to work on projects under experienced personnel at company
expense and to take specialized courses in areas of their practice. Because
it is the increase in relevant experience that is currently important at
Woodward-Clyde, the measure was changed to percent of fees committed
to the relevant experience program.

This change of the relevant experience measure required a redefinition
of the components of the professional development measure. In 1972, the
latter measure included fees used for obtaining relevant experience.
However, with the new relevant experience measure, the professional
development measure must explicitly exclude the fees used for acquiring
relevant experience.

FORMAL TRAINING.   The measure remained the same for formal training
but the desirability of particular levels has greatly changed. The value
function in this case is interesting in that it is not monotonic. It is low at a
level of 1, since all professionals then only have a bachelor's degree, and
increases to a peak and then falls rapidly as the level of degrees increases.
With a level of 3, the firm would consist entirely of professionals with
doctorates. In 1972, the desired state was identified as 2.25, the peak of
the value function. On further examination, this level seemed high. If just
25 percent of the professionals of Woodward-Clyde had only a bachelor's
degree, a minimum of 50 percent would have to have a doctorate to get
the average level to the "desired state" 2.25.

As an aid to thinking about the implications of different levels of
"degrees per professional," Table 7.6 was constructed. For evaluating
preferences over average degree levels, an individual selects the best
distribution of degrees for each average level, and then compares these
"best" distributions.

7.4.3   Checking for Independence Conditions

To structure a utility function over the 12 attributes of Table 7.5, modified as indicated in the previous subsection, the process began by examining whether pairs of attributes were preferentially independent of their complements.* In most cases it seemed appropriate to assume preferential independence, but we will indicate three situations where this was not so.

In examining preferential independence assumptions involving the attribute "ability to attract shareholder investment," the Long-Range Planning Committee came to the agreement that it was redundant based on present policy. This attribute indicated the ability and desirability of the principals to invest in the corporation. The Committee felt that the desirability aspect was adequately captured by retained earnings. On the other hand, the ability to invest was measured by both incentive compensation and base compensation. For these reasons, the "ability to attract shareholder investment" was dropped from the list of attributes.

In another case it first seemed advantageous to subdivide the objective concerning base compensation into three groups: senior principals, junior principals and associates, and associate candidates. In effect, the current attribute "base compensation" would have been replaced by three attributes: base compensation for senior principals, base compensation for junior principals and associates, and base compensation for associate candidates. It was found that any of these attributes, taken together with a different attribute (e.g., retained earnings), was not preferentially independent of its complement. The reason was that the rate at which retained earnings would be substituted for base compensation for associate candidates depended on the level of base compensation increases to the principals and associates. If these latter groups received large increases in base compensation, it seemed reasonable to give up more retained earnings to bring increases in base compensation for associate candidates up to a comparable level, than one would give up to make the same increase for associate candidates if, in fact, the other groups received low increases in base compensation. The concept of equity among the three groups made it inappropriate to assume preferential independence in this case.

There were two other possibilities investigated. Each pair of the three base compensation attributes was found to be conditionally preferentially independent of the third, given all other attributes are fixed at an arbitrary level. This would have allowed us to construct an additive

---

* Initial assessments were done using Dr. Nair's preferences. Subsequently, Dr. Nair has assessed the preferences of other members of the Long-Range Planning Committee.

component value function over the three attributes. The alternative was to use the original aggregated base compensation attribute. It was felt that members of the Long-Range Planning Committee could keep the equity considerations in mind when using the aggregated attribute. Therefore, since it is simpler to use one attribute than the three-component attributes, the former was chosen.

Base compensation and incentive compensation do have some overlap in purpose and, because of this, the incentive compensation paired with retained earnings, for instance, is not exactly preferentially independent of its complement. However, the overlap is not great since the function of the base compensation is to provide a solid salary for competent work within the "normal" call of duty, whereas the function of the incentive compensation is to provide motivation and reward for efforts beyond the call of duty. Thus, after considerable checking, it was decided that it was a reasonable approximation to assume the preferential independence condition. This "appropriateness" decision was taken in conjunction with the decision to eliminate the attribute "ability to attract shareholder investment" from the list in Table 7.5.

It was decided that the two attributes concerning retirement plan should be aggregated into one called "growth in retirement plan," since in fact both seemed to meet the same fundamental objective. Woodward-Clyde wanted any participant in their retirement plan to receive a combined amount from the plan and Social Security equal to 50 percent of his or her last five years average salary. The new measure for "growth of retirement plan" is the annual increase of assets in the retirement plan. Its range is 0 to 30 percent, and it should be clear that this excludes the Social Security benefits. In effect, this change is simply moving up the objectives hierarchy of Fig. 7.9 for a quantiative assessment of retirement plan consequences.

7.4.4   The 1974 Objectives and Measures of Effectiveness

The objectives and attributes updated from the original 1972 list are given in Table 7.7. After considerable examination, Dr. Nair felt that it was appropriate to assume that, for the ranges given in the table, each pair of attributes was preferentially independent of its complement. The reasonableness of this assumption was accepted by each of the other members on the 1974 Long-Range Planning Committee.

7.4.5   Assessing the Utility Function

The preferential independence conditions imply that an additive value function exists over the 10 attributes in Table 7.7. From Theorems 6.1 and 6.2, by verifying that just one attribute is utility independent of its

Table 7.7

1974 Attributes for Woodward-Clyde Consultants

Attribute	Measurement unit	Range
$X_1 \equiv$ retained earnings	% of tees	0–8
$X_2 \equiv$ growth in retirement plan	% of existing assets	0–30
$X_3 \equiv$ base compensation	% annual increase	0–30
$X_4 \equiv$ incentive compensation	% of fees	0–8
$X_5 \equiv$ U.S. coverage	$\left(\dfrac{\text{Geographic centers adequately covered}}{\begin{array}{c}\text{Centers where rele-}\\\text{vant work can be}\\\text{generated}\end{array}} \right)$	25–100%
$X_6 \equiv$ non-U.S. coverage	% of U.S. business	0–50
$X_7 \equiv$ scope of services offered	$\left(\dfrac{\begin{array}{c}\text{No. of disciplines}\\\text{having threshold}\\\text{capability}\end{array}}{\begin{array}{c}\text{no. of synergistic}\\\text{disciplines re-}\\\text{quired by society}\end{array}} \right)$	25–100%
$X_8 \equiv$ relevant experience (annual increment)	% of fees	0–1
$X_9 \equiv$ formal training	No. of degrees per professional staff member	1.5–2.5
$X_{10} \equiv$ professional development (excluding relevant experience)	% of fees	0–1

complement, either a mutiplicative or additive utility function is appropriate to quantify preferences. It was verified that retained earnings was, in fact, utility independent of its complement, and utility independence was also verified for other attributes to serve as consistency checks. For future reference, it turned out, the final utility function over the attributes in Table 7.7 was multiplicative and thus expressible in the form

$$1 + ku(\mathbf{x}) = \prod_{i=1}^{10} [1 + kk_i u_i(x_i)], \qquad (7.21)$$

where u and the u_i's are scaled 0 to 1, $0 < k_i < 1$, and k is a nonzero scaling constant greater than -1 that can be evaluated from the k_i's.

The task remaining was to assess the component utility functions, assess their scaling factors, and then evaluate the k value for the multiplicative form.

ASSESSING THE COMPONENT UTILITY FUNCTIONS. All the 10 utility functions were assessed on a 0 to 1 scale using the techniques discussed in

Chapter 4. Let us briefly consider those for retained earnings and formal training, attributes X_1 and X_9 in Table 7.7.

The range of retained earnings is 0 to 8 percent. Thus, since preferences are monotonically increasing, we set

$$u_1(0) = 0, \qquad u_1(8) = 1,$$

where u_1 is the utility function for retained earnings. Next, by checking certainty equivalents for a number of lotteries, we verified that Dr. Nair was risk averse in terms of retained earnings. It was found that $2 \sim \langle 0, 8 \rangle$ $.75 \sim \langle 0, 2 \rangle$, $4 \sim \langle 2, 8 \rangle$, $5.5 \sim \langle 4, 8 \rangle$, and for a check, that 4 for certain was indifferent to a .75 chance at 8 and a .25 chance at zero. The utility function consistent with these assessments is shown in Fig. 7.10.

The assessment of the utility function for formal training led to some surprises. What was not a surprise was that preferences for levels of this attribute are not monotonic—they increase up to a maximum point and then decrease. Originally, we wanted to assess preferences from 1 to 3 degrees per professional staff member. However, once we began this task, it became clear that with levels between 1 and 1.3 and 2.7 and 3, Woodward-Clyde could not exist in a form similar to the present. Hence our viable range was changed from 1.5 to 2.5, which were practical limits for the foreseeable future.

Next, by using the Table 7.6, it became clear that the previously felt optimum level of 2.25 was too high and 2.1 was chosen as an alternative after some consideration. Dr. Nair also felt that the undesirability of 1.5 or 2.5 degrees per professional was about equally as bad so u_9, the utility function for formal training, was scaled by

$$u_9(1.5) = u_9(2.5) = 0, \qquad u_9(2.1) = 1.$$

Again with the aid of Table 7.6, Dr. Nair concluded that $1.7 \sim \langle 1.5, 2.1 \rangle$, $1.8 \sim \langle 1.7, 2.1 \rangle$, and $2.3 \sim 1.8$. The resulting utility function is shown in Fig. 7.10.

ASSESSING THE RELATIVE SCALING FACTORS. The ranking of the 10-attribute scaling constants of the multiplicative utility function—that is, the k_i's in (7.21)—is given in Table 7.8. To specify their relative magnitude, Dr. Nair considered the relative desirability of consequences with one attribute at its most preferred level and all other attributes at their worst levels. He decided that the one he would most like to have at its best level was retained earnings. Thus the scaling factor associated with retained earnings is the largest. The attribute he would next prefer to have alone at its most desirable level was formal training, thus its scaling factor is second largest. Repeating this procedure led to the ranking of the scaling factors indicated in Table 7.8.

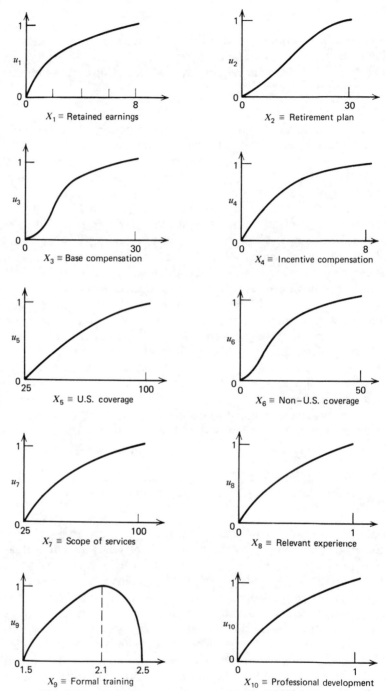

Fig. 7.10. Woodward-Clyde's component utility functions.

Table 7.8

Evaluating the Scaling Factors in Woodward-Clyde's Utility Function

Attribute	Ranking of Scaling Factor	Range	Indifference Equivalent	Relative Scaling Factor	Scaling Factor
$X_1 \equiv$ retained earnings	1	0-8	—	k_1	.67
$X_2 \equiv$ retirement plan	7	0-30	30 of $X_2 \sim 3$ of X_1	$k_2 = .66k_1$	.44
$X_3 \equiv$ base compensation	5	0-30	30 of $X_3 \sim 4$ of X_1	$k_3 = .77k_1$	.517
$X_4 \equiv$ incentive compensation	9	0-8	8 of $X_4 \sim 2.5$ of X_1	$k_4 = .58k_1$	.391
$X_5 \equiv$ U.S. coverage	6	25-100	100 of $X_5 \sim 3.5$ of X_1	$k_5 = .72k_1$	.482
$X_6 \equiv$ non-U.S. coverage	10	0-50	50 of $X_6 \sim 50$ of X_5	$k_6 = .5k_5$	.241
$X_7 \equiv$ scope of services	3	25-100	55 of $X_7 \sim 100$ of X_5	$k_5 = .75k_7$	.634
$X_8 \equiv$ relevant experience	4	0-1	1 of $X_8 \sim 50$ of X_5	$k_8 = .5k_5$	.241
$X_9 \equiv$ formal training	2	1.5-2.5	2.1 of $X_9 \sim 7$ of X_1	$k_9 = .97k_1$	.647
$X_{10} \equiv$ professional development	8	0-1	1 of $X_{10} \sim 50$ of X_5	$k_{10} = .5k_5$	.241
					4.505

To establish the relative values of the scaling factors quantitatively, tradeoffs between pairs of attributes were explicitly assessed. Dr. Nair was asked, for nine pairs of attributes, questions such as:

"Assume all attributes other than retained earnings and retirement plan are fixed at convenient levels. Now, how high would retained earnings have to be, given the retirement plan is at its lowest level, in order for you to be indifferent between this option and an alternative option with the retirement plan, at its most desirable level of 30 and retained earnings fixed at its lowest level?"

The responses are shown in Table 7.8 in the column labeled "indifference equivalent." Thus if we designate the scaling factor of X_1 as k_1, the scaling factor for X_2, for instance, must be $.66k_1$ since, using u_1 in Fig. 7.10, the utility of a retained earnings of 3 percent is .66. This follows since the utility of 3 percent retained earnings, with the growth in retirement plan at its least desirable level, must equal the utility of 30 percent growth in retirement plan, with retained earnings at its minimum level. Because of the preferential independence assumptions, the levels of the attributes other than retained earnings and retirement plan do not matter. The relative values of the scaling constants are also shown in Table 7.8.

SELECTING A UTILITY FUNCTION. We felt fairly confident about the relative values of the scaling constants, but to get their absolute magnitudes requires the answer to a difficult question. Dr. Nair was asked:

"For what probability π_1 would you be indifferent between option 1 yielding retained earnings at 8 percent and all other attributes at their least desirable levels and an alternative option 2 consisting of a lottery yielding all attributes at their most desirable level with probability π_1 or otherwise all attributes at their least desirable level?"

Those two options are illustrated in Fig. 7.11. Using the "converging method" discussed in Section 4.9, a value of 2/3 for π_1 was selected. This implied that the scaling factor k_1 should be .67, from which the values of the other scaling factors indicated* in Table 7.8 follows.

Since the sum of the scaling factors is 4.505, we knew that the multiplicative utility function was appropriate to express Dr. Nair's preferences. Evaluating (7.21) for the most desirable consequences we find that

$$1 + k = \prod_{i=1}^{10} (1 + kk_i), \tag{7.22}$$

* The sensitivity of the analysis to π_1 is discussed shortly.

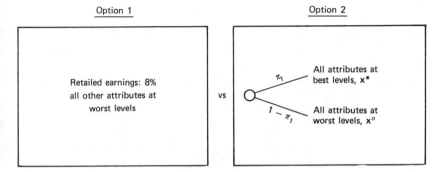

Fig. 7.11. Adjust π_1 to get indifference.

which was solved using the routine of Appendix 6B to yield $k = -.998$. Such a low level for k (it must be greater than -1) indicates a high level of complementarity among preferences for the attributes. It is the general feeling of the Long-Range Planning Committee that if retained earnings is at a high level, the other attributes can be "taken care of" if proper policies are implemented. However, this feeling weakens as the time frame of reference increases. That is, if our attributes represent one-year levels, Woodward-Clyde could stand a bad year with most attributes and make it up in the next year. On the other hand, if the attributes of Table 7.8 designate five-year averages, the desirability of waiting five years to "redistribute" high retained earnings to attributes at their lowest levels is understandably much less. This situation, which became apparent during the assessment process, is clearly important to recognize in discussions of options affecting the future vitality of Woodward-Clyde. The original preference assessments were made using a one-year period. The results reported here are made using annual averages over a three-year period.*

SENSITIVITY ANALYSIS. Because of the importance of the probability π_1 assessed to specify k_1, a small sensitivity analysis was made of this parameter using the same relative values of the scaling constants in Table 7.8. Recall that $\mathbf{x}^*$ defines the consequence with all attributes at their best levels and $\mathbf{x}^o$ the consequence with all attributes at their worst levels. To assist in examining the implications of the various π_1 values, let us make two definitions:

$\pi' \equiv$ the probability such that a lottery with a π' chance at $\mathbf{x}^*$ and a $(1 - \pi')$ chance at $\mathbf{x}^o$ is indifferent to a consequence with retained earnings and formal training at their best lévels and all other attributes at their worst levels.

* For reference, the indifference probability π_1 for the options in Fig. 7.11 was .75 when a one-year period was considered, whereas it was .67 for the three-year period.

Table 7.9

A Sensitivity Analysis of the Scaling
Factor k

π_1	$\sum k_i$	k	π'	$\hat{\pi}$
.87	5.86	−.999	.98	.973
.74	4.96	−.999	.925	.947
.67	4.5	−.998	.884	.928
.60	4.06	−.996	.836	.903
.47	3.15	−.979	.714	.835
.34	2.25	−.900	.561	.733

$\hat{\pi} \equiv$ the probability such that $\langle \mathbf{x}^*, \hat{\pi}, \mathbf{x}^o \rangle$ is indifferent to the sure consequence with each attribute at its level of 0.5 utility.

The results, which were calculated using the computer program discussed
in Appendix 6C, are shown in Table 7.9, where π_1 is first specified. Then,
using the relative scaling factors from Table 7.8, the individual k_i's are
fixed. From these, k, π', and $\hat{\pi}$ were calculated. Further reflection and
examination of Table 7.9 led Dr. Nair to stay with his original estimate of
$\pi_1 = 0.67$ for the three-year period. Thus, the final scaling constants are
those shown in the last column of Table 7.8.

7.4.6 Uses of Woodward-Clyde's Utility Function

Since the original assessments, Dr. Nair has essentially repeated the
assessment procedure just described with each member of the 1974
Long-Range Planning Committee. These assessments included verifying
the assumptions, assessing single-attribute utility functions, and specifying
scaling constants. This resulted in some minor changes to Dr. Nair's
utility function (already integrated into the previous subsections) to
achieve what may be referred to as a consensus corporate utility function.
This obviously does not mean the Board of Woodward-Clyde will blindly
make decisions with this utility function. It is being used to *facilitate*
communication among officers of Woodward-Clyde and to *help* professional intuition.

The assessment process forced individuals to be a bit more precise in
deciding why they felt certain levels of specific attributes were important.
As previously mentioned, the assessment process indicated how tradeoffs
among attributes depended on the time frame of reference. The general
feeling of those involved in the utility function assessment is summed up
by the comment of one individual, "I've had to make tradeoff decisions
like this all my life, but until now the process has always been somewhat

fuzzy and left me with the feeling that I didn't completely comprehend all the implications of my subjective judgements. The use of utility theory and explicit tradeoffs helps considerably. With a better understanding of our own tradeoffs and preferences, it is obviously easier to communicate these and discuss the issues with our colleagues."

The process of assessing a utility function has also led to minor (but important) modifications in the overall evaluation process for long-range plans. Some objectives have been deleted or aggregated, and in other cases, several attributes have been altered to better indicate the concerns of Woodward-Clyde. Changing the attribute measure for relevant experience to reflect the yearly increase in experience is one such example.

Since several of the attributes concern distribution of income available (i.e., percent of fees), it is a simple task to use the utility function to help select the best distribution among salaries, retained earnings, incentive compensation, professional development, relevant experience, and contribution to retirement plan. With any fixed percentage of fees available, the technically feasible surface of fee distribution, as well as the distribution with maximum utility, is easily specified.

As before, the component utility functions can still be used to conduct a deficiency analysis by indicating the difference between the present state and a desired state, representing what is technically feasible in a specified time span. A bit more broadly, by calculating the gradient of the utility function in each attribute for the present state position and combining this with subjectively assessed changes in the state of each attribute for an equivalent amount of effort (time and money), one gets an indicator of policies that may be particularly fruitful to pursue.

The utility function discussed here will no doubt go through additional metamorphosis in the future years, as needs and preferences of individuals at Woodward-Clyde adjust to better reflect their position in society, the external environment, and so on. For example, the Pension Reform Act of 1974, because of certain provisions with regard to the ability of Pension and Profit Sharing Plan Trusts to invest in company stock, is likely to alter the present relative value of the attribute "growth in retirement plan" among the attributes. Woodward-Clyde Consultants is presently examining the effect of this and other external changes on the utility functions for the various individual attributes and the tradeoffs between the attributes. This will be a continuing activity.

The current function does overcome the original shortcomings on the 1972 quantification of objectives outlined in Subsection 7.4.1. It is being used to examine present decisions that effect the future existence of the company. In addition, the Woodward-Clyde objectives hierarchy partially provides an underlying and unifying basis for evaluating long-range plans and operational activities of the affiliated firms. It is not an overstatement to say that several individuals at Woodward-Clyde find the multiattribute utility concept interesting and helpful. Perhaps more importantly, they are enthusiastic about potential future uses. In this regard, partially as a result of the work discussed here, a special group within Woodward-Clyde Consultants has been set up and funded to begin to transfer the concepts and techniques of decision analysis into their professional practice.

To summarize, in 1974, Woodward-Clyde Consultants reorganized its operations from that of a holding company subsidiary relationship to an operating company with five regional divisions, each division having geotechnical and environmental capabilities. The more significant reasons given for this reorganization were to better serve its clients in terms of providing integrated geotechnical and environmental capability, establish a one-company image for improved marketing, and increase efficiencies by eliminating various subsidiary management structures. In evaluating the desirability of the organizational changes, many members of the Board of Directors made a subjective determination as to whether the changes would increase the companies ability to improve their level of performance over the various attributes. The explicit statement of attributes made it possible to make this evaluation.

7.5 EVALUATING COMPUTER SYSTEMS

How should management select a computer system? How should the management of a computer facility evaluate the quality of its service? When and how should a time-sharing system be altered to provide better service to its users and to attract additional users? These are representative questions facing various participants, including both managers and users in today's computer industry. Responsible answers to such questions require the consideration of a number of factors: availability of the system, its reliability, response times to different requests, costs, and many less tangible aspects. These problems are inherently multidimensional.

In this section we report on some of Grochow's work (1972, 1973), which deals with the questions using the concepts and methodology discussed earlier in this book. Grochow assessed a three-attribute utility function for users of time-sharing systems. To illustrate the usefulness of such information for decision making by the management of these systems, we first describe what Grochow did and then discuss its relevance to the questions posed at the beginning of this section.

7.5.1   Preferences of Systems Programmers

Grochow interviewed several users of general time-sharing systems to determine their usage patterns and objectives. His subjects were computer system programmers concerned mainly with the input and editing of programs and their compilation and testing. The subjects ratio of editing sessions to compiling and testing sessions was approximately five to one. Four attributes of the system important to this class of users were:

1. Response time to trivial requests (i.e., editing).
2. Response time to compute-bound requests (i.e., compiling)
3. Availability.
4. Reliability.

Grochow assessed utility functions over the first three of these attributes conditional on reliability being at a high level.

Before beginning the assessment process, Grochow discussed the basic ideas of utility theory with each user and presented a plan indicating the importance of the three attributes and establishing that reliability was at a high level. For measures of effectiveness he used, for the first two attributes, the average number of seconds to satisfy requests and for the third, the percentage of successful log-ins.

By assessing various conditional utility functions over one attribute at a time given that the other two attributes were held fixed, he established the appropriateness of different utility independence conditions and restricted the form of the utility function. Let us define attributes:

$X \equiv$ average response time to trivial requests in seconds.
$Y \equiv$ average response time to compute-bound requests in seconds.
$Z \equiv$ percentage of successful log-ins.

In terms of this notation, the conditions that Grochow verified as appropriate for the class of users under consideration were:

1. X is conditionally utility independent of Y given Z.
2. X is conditionally utility independent of Z given Y.
3. Y is conditionally utility independent of Z given X.

It follows directly from Theorem 6.17 in Subsection 6.11.4 that conditions 1 and 2 imply that:

4. X is utility independent of $\{Y, Z\}$.

Using Theorem 5.6, from condition 4, we know that

$$u(x, y, z) = u_X(x, y^\circ, z^\circ)u(x^*, y, z) + [1 - u_X(x, y^\circ, z^\circ)]u(x^\circ, y, z), \qquad (7.23)$$

where u and u_X are scaled from 0 to 1 with superscripts ^{o} and * indicating, the least and most desirable level of an attribute, respectively. Then using condition 3 and the analogous result to Theorem 5.6 for conditional utility functions, we further break down (7.23) to yield

$$
\begin{aligned}
u(x, y, z) = u_X(x, y^o, z^o)[&u_Y^*(x^*, y, z^o)u(x^*, y^*, z) \\
+&\{1 - u_Y^*(x^*, y, z^o)\}u(x^*, y^o, z)] \\
+[1 - u_X(x, y^o, z^o)][&u_Y^o(x^o, y, z^o)u(x^o, y^*, z) \\
+&\{1 - u_Y^o(x^o, y, z^o)\}u(x^o, y^o, z)],
\end{aligned}
\tag{7.24}
$$

where u_Y^* and u_Y^o are also scaled from 0 to 1.

We note that, given these scaling conventions,

$$
u_X(x, y^o, z^o) \equiv \frac{u(x, y^o, z^o)}{u(x^*, y^o, z^o)},
\tag{7.25a}
$$

$$
u_Y^o(x^o, y, z^o) \equiv \frac{u(x^o, y, z^o)}{u(x^o, y^*, z^o)},
\tag{7.25b}
$$

$$
u_Y^*(x^*, y, z^o) \equiv \frac{u(x^*, y, z^o) - u(x^*, y^o, z^o)}{u(x^*, y^*, z^o) - u(x^*, y^o, z^o)}.
\tag{7.25c}
$$

If we substitute (7.25) into (7.24) we see that (x, y, z) is completely specified by assessing the seven consistently scaled one-attribute conditional utility functions illustrated by heavy lines in Fig. 7.12.

The actual verification of conditions 1, 2, and 3 was iterative in nature. Each additional conditional utility function contributed to a better understanding of the overall structure of the utility function $u(x, y, z)$. The implications of these functions were discussed with the user throughout the assessment procedure. Whenever there were inconsistencies in the responses of a user, they were pointed out and part of the procedure was

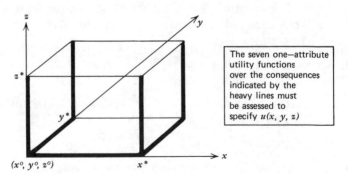

The seven one–attribute utility functions over the consequences indicated by the heavy lines must be assessed to specify $u(x, y, z)$

Fig. 7.12. Assessments required for evaluating a utility function for a time-sharing computer system.

redone. In all, the utility independence conditions 1, 2, and 3 were verified for eight different individuals in the class of users described earlier.

An actual utility function was assessed for only one user. The general procedure discussed in Chapters 5 and 6 was used for this purpose. The utility function was assessed over the space $2 \le x \le 9$ (seconds), $2 \le y \le 120$, and $10 \le z \le 100$ (percent).

It turned out that Z was *not* utility independent of $\{X, Y\}$ or conditionally utility independent of either X or Y. Grochow states the reason for this: when either response time is at an unfavorable value, for instance, the programmer will be spending most of his or her time contending with the slow response, and consequently will not be as concerned about logging in as when response times are at more desirable levels. The stated reason why Y is not conditionally utility independent of X given Z is that the users may set their relative preferences for response time to compute-bound requests in terms of the response time to trivial requests they are experiencing.

7.5.2   Uses of the Utility Function

Suppose our user tried to choose among different time-sharing facilities that differed not only in terms of X, Y, and Z, but also in terms of their reliability R and their monthly subscription cost S. A proper evaluation here would require a utility function $u'(r, s, x, y, z)$ for the user. However, if $\{X, Y, Z\}$ is utility independent of $\{R, S\}$, then, of course, from Theorem 5.6, u' can be expressed as a function of r, s, and u so

$$u'(r, s, x, y, z) = f[r, s, u(x, y, z)].$$

The original utility function u can be used in a similar fashion if $\{R, S\}$ is utility independent of $\{X, Y, Z\}$ and $\{X, Y, Z\}$ is not utility independent of $\{R, S\}$. Given this assumption, Theorem 5.6 says that u' may be expressed as a function of one utility function over $\{R, S\}$ and two utility functions over $\{X, Y, Z\}$ given different levels of $\{R, S\}$. One of these utility functions can be $u(x, y, z)$.

Going one step further, suppose our user (or firm) must decide whether to *buy* or *rent* a computer. If the choice is made to buy, there are many options. Clearly, such a decision would involve a time horizon of at least a few years. To remain simple, let us assume that attributes X, Y, and Z and a cost attribute are sufficient for the decision. With a five-year span, this cost attribute might be $C \equiv \{C_1, C_2, \ldots, C_5\}$ where C_i represents costs in the ith year. Then, as before, with necessary utility independence assumptions between C and $\{X, Y, Z\}$, the original utility function u can be used.

Switching gears, suppose the management of a time-sharing service has two objectives: maximize profits and provide the best possible service to customers. Some may consider the latter objective partially as a proxy objective for long-term profits. Regardless of motivation, a reasonable measure of the quality of service to a user may be the user's function over attributes X, Y, and Z. Hence, given many users, the firm may select a utility function that is a function of annual profits, for instance, and the individual utility functions of its users.

By including potential users' utility functions as arguments of its utility function, the firm may have a tool to help select pricing and service policy. That is, if prices are too high, many users will select competitors and thus reduce the firm's profit. If the subscription prices are too low, the firm will also do poorly financially. By maximizing its expected utility, the firm can find the "optimal" price.*

7.6 SITING AND LICENSING OF NUCLEAR POWER FACILITIES

The siting of nuclear power facilities is an extremely complex process. There are many concerned interest groups trying to influence the decision-making process, each with their own set of multiple objectives. The stakes are large, involving hundreds of millions of dollars, possible energy shortages and "blackouts," the possibilities of severe environmental damage and, in some situations, heavy dependency on foreign fuels, to mention a few of the relevant considerations.

In the United States a power company has to prepare its case advocating a particular site or sites and submit these plans for review by governmental regulatory authorities (e.g., nuclear power, environmental impact). These groups try to reach a decision by weighing the available data, considering the broad tradeoffs, and examining diverse viewpoints of the power company, of environmentalist groups, of the public as energy consumers, and of local groups, such as the communities near the suggested sites. How can these government authorities rationally integrate all the available information in a manner useful for aiding their decision process?

The power companies themselves have difficulties in dealing with the multiple objectives they face. They are, however, mainly concerned with

---

* This brief discussion has neglected actions by competitors. The utility functions discussed are applicable in conjunction with game theory, a discipline concerned with these competitive aspects. A basic introduction and survey of game theory is Luce and Raiffa (1957). A more recent survey is Shakun (1972).

competitive business positions and engineering factors, such as transmission facilities design and network reliability, which directly affect their financial returns. But when a power company is asked its position on broader questions such as the impacts of its proposals on the environment and local communities by the regulatory boards, it, too, must deal with a broader set of objectives, and often their analyses depend on informal and intuitive reasoning. Perhaps with a better understanding and presentation of the fundamental tradeoffs among the conflicting objectives necessitated by each of the alternatives under consideration, the power company might be in better position to select the best alternative in view of its economic objectives, its public responsibility, and the public's requirements. A formal analysis of these considerations may contribute toward reducing the required time of the now-lengthy process necessary for approval of nuclear power facilities. What are the characteristics of such an analysis, and how is it done? The literature on this subject is voluminous, but of direct relevance to the techniques and framework introduced in this book, we single out the works by Gros (1974), Papp et al. (1974), Nair et al. (1975), and Keeney and Nair (1975).

In this section, we do two things:

1. Speculate on the appropriateness of multiattribute utility theory for examining the questions raised in the preceding paragraphs.
2. Discuss the work of Jacques Gros, who quantifies preferences for nuclear siting problems using results discussed in this book.

The work described below is far from definitive; perhaps it could more appropriately be described as "suggestive research." We do not dwell on important issues, such as whether the attribute set is complete, whose preferences should be assessed, how one introduces political relevancies, or how the analysis helps (or hinders) conflict resolution. We want to focus on the concepts of the suggestions and not worry about their pragmatic implementation. We speculate on possible uses of a theoretical nature in a so-called "applications" chapter because we believe that the ideas introduced here are important and that the framework of analysis may be appropriate to carry out in practice. In this regard, we feel that efforts of Ovi (1973) and Gros (1974) and experience by Woodward-Clyde Consultants [see Woodward-Clyde Consultants (1975) and Keeney and Nair (1976)] are encouraging. Undoubtedly there are other groups doing similar work.

7.6.1 Objectives for Nuclear Power Siting

Each group interested in siting nuclear power facilities has its own objectives. By and large, however, in each case these objectives might fall

Table 7.10

Some Objectives for Siting Nuclear Power Facilities

Attribute	Category	Objective	Parties Primarily Concerned[a]
X_1	Environmental	Minimize pollution	E, L
X_2	Environmental	Provide aesthetically pleasing facilities	E, L
X_3	Human safety	Minimize human health hazards	E, L, P, S, F
X_4	Consumer well-being	Provide necessary power	C, E, P, S
X_5	Consumer well-being	Minimize consumer power costs	C, S
X_6	Economic	Maximize economic benefits to local community	L
X_7	Economic	Maximize utility company profits	P
X_8	Economic	Maximize state revenues	S
X_9	Economic	Improve balance of payments	F
X_{10}	National interest	Reduce dependency on foreign fuels	F

[a] C, consumers; E, environmentalists; L, local communities; P, power company; S, state agency; F, federal agency.

under five categories: environmental, human safety, consumer well-being, economic, and national interest. Let us suppose that the set of objectives listed in Table 7.10 is sufficient for analysis by any of the interested parties, although there is clearly an overlap in this crude list and all of these objectives are not needed by all of the parties. Those objectives of primary interest to the concerned parties are indicated in the table. Also, for future reference, the associated attribute—possibly a vector attribute—is designated notationally. No attempt is made to list specific attributes at this time.

7.6.2 A Conceptual Framework for Analyses by the Interested Parties

The utility functions briefly discussed here are intended mainly to suggest a conceptual framework for thinking about crucial preference aspects of the nuclear power siting problem and for communicating these preferences to other interested parties. For brevity, we skip a discussion of the utility functions of the consumers, environmentalists, and local community interests. These are, in theory, more straighforward than the cases we do consider.

THE POWER COMPANY'S POINT OF VIEW.   We might simply say that a power company is concerned only with maximizing its own profits. If this were true, it would be appropriate to assess the company's utility function $u_P(x_7)$ over attribute X_7 and use this in evaluating the power company's alternatives. However, in this era of broader corporate interest and responsibility, it is more likely the case that the company is also interested in satisfying its consumers preferences for energy, minimizing the detrimental environmental impact of its facilities, and maximizing the net benefits of its facilities on local communities in which facilities are to be built.* Let us designate attributes for these three additional objectives as U_C, U_E, and U_L, respectively, and note that they can be measured by the respective utility functions u_C, u_E, and u_L. The power company, at least informally, is concerned with its utility function $u_P(x_7, u_C, u_E, u_L)$ over four attributes in order to analyze which of its possible options is most attractive to pursue. Conceptually, one might define utility u_L to be a function of $u_1, \ldots, u_l, \ldots, u_N$, where u_l is the lth community's utility function and N communities are considered as possible sites. The power company must weigh its subjective judgements about the relative desirability that community 1 has for proposed plant A against the relative desirability that community 2 has for proposed plant B. Such tradeoffs, although terribly difficult, must be formally or informally addressed by the power company.

THE STATE AGENCY'S POINT OF VIEW.   Let us oversimplify once again and assume there is only one stage agency concerned with licensing nuclear power facilities, whose main responsibility is nuclear safety. Thus, the objectives of the agency might be to minimize danger due to nuclear radiation, to provide state revenue, and to satisfy the interested groups. Attributes X_3 and X_8 from Table 7.10 may be useful for measuring the first two objectives, whereas U_C, U_E, U_L, and U_P might do for indicating interest group satisfaction. Thus, the state agencies preferences might be conceptualized by $u_S(x_3, x_8, u_C, u_E, u_L', u_P)$, where u_L' is the state agencies' aggregation of the N communities' utility functions.

---

* One could cynically say that the concern of the utility company for consumers, environmentalists, and local communities is just good business, that these concerns are a surrogate for future profits. This observation, whether true or not, does not invalidate our development.

THE FEDERAL AGENCIES' POINT OF VIEW. The main federal agency concerned with nuclear power plants in the United States is the Nuclear Regulatory Commission. Its problem is quite similar to that of the state agency just outlined. The major difference might be the federal concern for the balance of payments, indicated by attribute X_9, and the national dependency on foreign fuels, measured by attribute X_{10}. It may be useful for the federal agency to conceptualize its preferences with the utility function $u_F(x_3, x_9, x_{10}, u_C, u_E, u_L'', u_P)$, where u_L'' measures the federal agencies' concern for the local community impact of nuclear facilities.

7.6.3 Empirical Assessments

Gros (1974) studies nuclear facility siting from a slightly different viewpoint. Specifically Gros investigates the usefulness of what he refers to as *Paretian environmental analysis* in nuclear siting decisions. He was not interested in choosing a single best alternative for the group. Rather he wanted to identify alternatives where all parties can improve their positions over the status quo. His ultimate aim was to characterize the set of Paretian alternatives—each such alternative has the property that, relative to this alternative, improvements can be made for some parties only at the expense of other parties. The set of Paretian alternatives contains, in general, many (usually an infinite number) alternatives and the problem remains of how best to select an alternative within this domain. This problem is considered further in Chapter 10. However, just the identification of alternatives leading to *joint gains* (i.e., gains by all, relative to the status quo) is a practical and important accomplishment in conflict resolution.

To illustrate his approach, Gros examines the deployment of 1000-megawatt nuclear baseload units to possible sites along the New England coast. Gros assessed multiattribute utility functions for four parties involved in nuclear power plant siting in New England: power companies, environmentalists, regulatory agencies, and local groups. These utility functions were each assessed over four attributes:

$Y_1 \equiv$ Capacity at a site, measured by the number of 1000 megawatt units at a coastal site.

$Y_2 \equiv$ Incremental dollar costs, measured by the cost of thermal abatement equipment plus transmission costs expressed as a percent of the minimum cost facility.

$Y_3 \equiv$ Radiation hazard, measured by the population within 15 miles of the nuclear facility times the number of units at the site.

$Y_4 \equiv$ Thermal pollution level, measured in degrees Fahrenheit at the outfall of the nuclear facility.

These attributes were generated after interviewing individuals who had previously participated in siting controversies. We would prefer attributes that are more closely related to the fundamental objectives, but rather than focus on whether or not this set of attributes is appropriate for the problem, let us consider the assessment procedure.

For each of the four interest groups, a knowledgeable observer, who had an intimate knowledge of many of the group members' preferences, was chosen based on recommendations of group members. The knowledgeable observer's utility function was assessed and his preferences were used as those of the appropriate representative group. The results were verified for reasonableness with other group members. For each of the four utility functions, necessary utility independence conditions were verified to invoke Theorem 6.1 implying the appropriateness of either the multiplicative or additive utility functions.

Gros was also interested in preferences over the 40-year design span. For each of the knowledgeable observers he verified that preferences for lotteries in any individual year were utility independent of preferences for lotteries over the other years. Also he found preferences in each pair of years to be preferentially independent of preferences in other years. Hence the 40-attribute utility function, representing the 40-year period, was again either multiplicative or additive. Because of the desire on the part of the knowledgeable observers to spread risks over the years, the multiplicative form was selected as appropriate.*

Gros' efforts and empirical assessments are an important first step toward characterizing utility functions directly useful in making nuclear power siting decisions. The task is difficult and the effort required to obtain these preferences is substantial. However, to avoid these problems relegates the crucial tradeoff issues and the preference evaluation of the risks involved to informal analysis.

7.7 OTHER APPLICATIONS

Experience with formal quantification of preferences in multiattribute contexts is growing. Let us briefly mention a number of decision problems, in addition to those in earlier sections in this chapter, where the concepts of Chapters 2–6 were utilized.

---

* A discussion of preferences over time indicating some of these issues is found in Chapter 9.

7.7.1 The Safety of Landing Aircraft

The safety of landing an aircraft depends on many factors: wind, visibility, ceiling, other aircraft in the vicinity, and so on. Yntema and Klem (1965) attempted to quantify the safety of various situations that differed in terms of ceiling, visibility, and amount of fuel that would remain at touchdown given a normal landing. Other relevant factors were fixed at a standard value.

The decision makers for this study consisted of 20 Air Force pilots, each of whom had a good deal of experience in landing aircraft under a wide variety of situations. Using the three-attribute multilinear utility function discussed in Result 2 of Section 6.2, utility functions over the attributes ceiling, visibility, and remaining fuel were assessed. In the attribute space, ceiling varied from 100 to 5000 feet, visibility from 0.25 to 5 miles, and remaining fuel from 15 to 250 gallons. Each decision maker was also presented with 40 pairs of consequences and asked to pick the preferable one of each pair. These responses were compared with the implications of each decision maker's utility function. Yntema and Klem concluded that the results were satisfactory.

It should be pointed out that the utility independence assumptions requisite for Result 2 of Section 6.2 were not empirically verified. In fact, the assessments of Yntema and Klem were completed a few years before the formal theory was developed. In spite of this, the resulting utility functions did seem appropriate to represent the preferences of the pilots. Yntema and Klem's pioneering effort gave some support to the contention that it was reasonable and practical to quantify preferences in multiattribute situations.

7.7.2 Strategic and Operational Policy Concerning Frozen Blood

Should a hospital blood bank or system of blood banks invest in expensive blood freezing equipment? And for systems with such capabilities, what are the most desirable proportions of frozen and nonfrozen blood? These questions were addressed in a thesis by Bodily (1974). He also conducted a preliminary investigation of national strategies in blood research and in the usage of frozen blood.

First, after considerable consultation with blood bankers, objectives and measures of effectiveness were specified for evaluating frozen blood issues. The resulting list, given in Table 7.11, indicates the depth at which preferences and probabilities were initially going to be assessed. However, to help the respondent's thinking about the implications of various

Table 7.11
Objectives of a Hospital Blood Bank

Objectives	Measures of Effectiveness
Meet all requests for blood	Average delay or frequency of delay above some acceptable cutoff
Provide high-quality blood	Average age at transfusion
Minimize disease	Rate of hepatitis
Minimize cost	Cost per unit
Minimize transfusion reactions	Rate of transfusion reaction
Minimize wastage	Outdating plus processing loss
Provide bloods for special uses	Fraction of special needs that are met with frozen blood or an equivalent unit

levels of the attributes, the objectives hierarchy was developed and qualitatively extended as illustrated in Fig. 7.13.

In analyzing the problem of what proportion of frozen blood should be selected for a particular blood bank and the problem of whether or not such a bank should invest in blood freezing equipment, Bodily used a variety of approaches to obtain reasonable probability distributions over the attributes for each alternative. These approaches included utilizing empirical information from blood banks, projections using simple mathematical models of the operations of such blood banks, judgmental estimation of experts, and statistical data available in journal articles, and so on.

Bodily tried to assess preferences over the six attributes labeled X_i, $i = 1, 2, \ldots, 6$ in Fig. 7.13 for a number of individuals concerned with blood banking. A first conclusion was that attribute X_6 could be eliminated in considering the question of proportion of blood to freeze. The reasoning was that if a blood bank froze any blood, it would certainly freeze enough to satisfy special needs, and so the objective "meet special needs" would be equally satisfied with all the viable alternatives. Hence, it could be dropped from the list.

Next, attributes X_1, X_2, and X_3 were aggregated since each pair of these was preferentially independent of its complement and substitution rates were constants. Wastage and delay were translated into economic terms using a simple additive value function

$$v(x_1, x_2, x_3) = x_1 + dx_2 + wx_3,$$

where d is the equivalent cost per unit of blood delayed and w is the cost

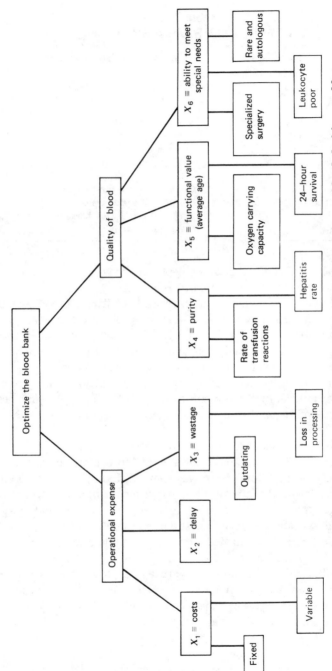

Fig. 7.13. A possible configuration for aggregation of attributes for a frozen blood decision problem.

per unit wastage. If attribute Y is defined as $X_1 + dX_2 + wX_3$, then what is needed is a utility function $u(y, x_4, x_5)$ over Y, X_4, and X_5.

In the assessment process, it became clear that blood bankers considered the possible range of the average age transfused much less important than the ranges of economic and purity considerations. Hence X_5 was dropped and a utility function $u(y, x_4)$ was completely assessed for one blood banker and for one individual with a public health graduate degree and a knowledge of decision analysis. In both cases Y and X_4 were mutually utility independent and so, from Theorem 5.2, the multilinear utility function was appropriate. In addition, Bodily ascertained that, in a paired comparison of two simple lotteries with identical marginal probability distributions, the blood banker was indifferent. Thus from Theorem 5.4, it follows that the respondent's utility function was additive. Details of these assessments are found in Bodily (1974).

Many of the concepts of Chapters 2–6 were explicitly used in the overall assessment process. First, a first-cut hierarchy of objectives was articulated as discussed in Chapter 2, and one objective was then dropped since it was not important enough to influence decisions. Then using preferential independence conditions and the concepts of Chapter 3, a value function over three of the attributes was specified to achieve an aggregation and reduction of dimensionality. Next, quantitative considerations led to the exclusion of attribute X_5. Finally, utility independence and the unidimensional assessment techniques surveyed in Chapter 4 were used to specify the final utility functions.

This case illustrates well a typical evolutionary process that starts from a listing of objectives—in this case the specification of subobjectives extended further down the hierarchy than the quantitative analysis—and terminates with the quantification of the final utility function.

7.7.3 Sewage Sludge Disposal in the Metropolitan Boston Area

In Boston, the Metropolitan District Commission (MDC) has responsibility for water and sewage works for the 43 cities and towns within its jurisdiction. As of 1971, 100 tons of sewage sludge was being discharged daily into Boston Harbor by the treatment plants of the MDC. Because of increasing public concern and the interest of the U.S. Environmental Protection Agency, the Division of Water Pollution Control of the Massachusetts Department of Natural Resources requested the MDC to make a comprehensive study of new and better alternatives to the present sludge disposal practice. The MDC organized a committee named the Boston Harbor Pollution Task Force (BHPTF) to study the problem and make recommendations. At the suggestion of the Massachusetts Office of

Environmental Affairs, and with the consent of the BHPTF, Dennis Horgan, then a graduate student at M.I.T., worked with this task force and conducted an independent decision analysis of the sludge disposal alternatives. This subsection briefly surveys Horgan's work.

The viable alternatives for Boston sludge disposal could be categorized as being either marine disposal or land disposal. In marine disposal, one could either barge sludge to a dumping ground 10 miles offshore or extend a submerged sludge line approximately 7 miles out to sea. In land disposal, one could spread the sludge directly on available land and till it into the soil or, alternately, the sludge could first be incinerated, thus reducing its volume approximately 70 percent, and then disposed of at a land site. There are variations of these four basic alternatives, such as different processes of incineration, and the like but these were felt to be second-order considerations and not explicitly considered in the analysis.

The analysis by Horgan specified four major objectives: minimize costs, minimize water pollution, minimize land pollution, and minimize air pollution. Thus, the classic question concerning tradeoffs of one kind of pollution against another was explicitly addressed. The net present value of costs was used as the measure of effectiveness of the cost objective. Air pollution was measured in tons of particulate matter and gases resulting from sludge incineration, and land pollution was measured in terms of the total area required for sludge disposal sites. To indicate water quality, Horgan defined a subjective index, as discussed in Section 2.3, scaled from 0 to 10, based on state water-quality standards.

Exploiting probabilistic independence properties where appropriate, probability distributions were specified over the four variables for each of the four basic alternatives.* Concerning preferences, Horgan verified with members of the BHPTF that each of the four attributes was utility independent of its respective complement and, also, that pairs of attributes were *not* preferentially independent of their complements. There fore, by Theorem 6.3, the multilinear utility function was appropriate. The specific utility function and probability assessments, as well as sensitivity analysis of the results, are found in Horgan (1972).

7.7.4 Selecting a Job or Profession

A critical decision facing each of us from time to time concerns the selection of a job. This problem is different in one important respect from many of the other illustrations in this book in that it is essentially a

---

* For an incineration alternative, air pollution and land pollution, for example, were not probabilistically independent since they both depend on the volume of sludge; Horgan's model explicitly included such dependencies.

personal decision. Most of the other problems dealt with a decision maker as representative of his company or as representative of a branch of the government. Here we will briefly summarize two philosophical approaches to job selection, both of which utilize the general ideas discussed in earlier chapters. The works of Miller (1966, 1970) and Teweles (1972) serve as models for our discussion.

Miller developed and tested a procedure for evaluating the "worth" of various situations described by multiple attributes. One of the problems to which it has been applied involved a graduate student faced with numerous employment offers immediately following graduation. After preliminary analysis, this number was reduced to four viable contenders. The objectives hierarchy and attributes associated with each of the lowest-level objectives that were identified by the graduate student are illustrated in Fig. 7.14.

An additive value function,*

$$v(x).= \sum_i k_i v_i(x_i), \qquad (7.26)$$

where v_i measures the worth of an amount x_i of attribute X_i, was used to evaluate the alternatives on a 0 to 1 scale. The scaling factors k_i were determined using conditional assessments as described in Section 3.7. For instance, first weights of .33, .17, .17, and .33 were assigned to monetary compensation, geographical location, travel requirements, and nature of work, respectively. Then, for instance, of the monetary compensation, a .7 weight went to immediate compensation and .3 to future compensation. Of the future compensation, .65 and .35 went to anticipated three-year salary and anticipated five-year salary, respectively. Then, the total effective weight assigned to anticipated three-year salary was (.33)(.3)(.65) or .064. These effective weights were then adjusted to account for the degree to which the attribute actually measured achievement on an objective. Finally, for each of the 15 attributes, individual value functions v_i were determined.

The four alternatives were then each represented as a 15-attribute vector and the value of each calculated using (7.26). Uncertainties were not explicitly considered in the problem.

Notice that all the attributes in Miller's problem are, in some sense, proxy attributes. Presumably, they are proxy for the quality of the decision maker's life. Because of this it was possible to identify many objective measures for these attributes.

Teweles' approach was very different in this respect. He attempted to establish a more direct set of attributes to indicate the desirability of

---

* Miller used the expression "worth function" rather than "value function."

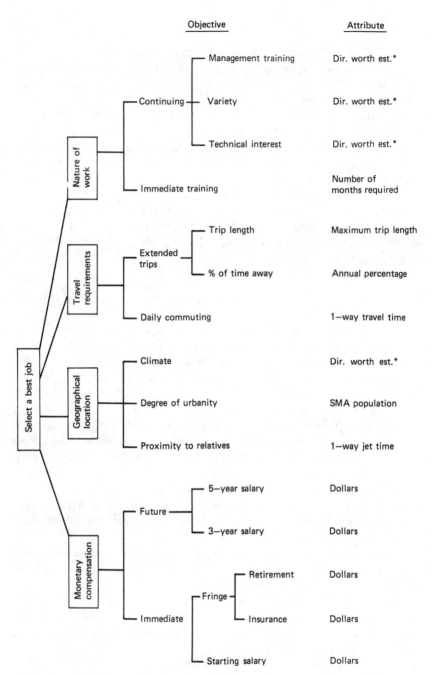

	Objective	Attribute

(*Direct worth estimate: a subjective assessment)

Fig. 7.14. Miller's objectives for evaluating employment options.

Table 7.12

Teweles' Objectives for Evaluating Professions

Job satisfaction—Enjoyment derived from doing the type of work you have chosen. Direct benefits of a job such as the opportunity for travel, meeting interesting people, and means of self-expression are included in this factor.

Wealth—The financial remuneration that can be expected from working and the accumulation of capital that can be earned from investment of excess funds. Since money is, in a sense, a means of obtaining other goods and services, the utility of these products can be substituted for wealth in determining its value.

Security—A condition of relative safety that results from being able to continue your job if you wish to do so. Also included in this factor is the risk to one's health associated with a particularly dangerous occupation.

Family considerations—This factor is an amalgamation of the possible influence a particular career might have on the other members of your family. A wife's attitude, mother's sentiment, child's future, or other considerations should be accounted for in career planning.

Independence—The ability you have to be your own boss and schedule your own activities. Independence also refers to the short-term flexibility to do what is most important to you at a particular time.

Self-esteem—The self-respect you gain from your own achievements. The self-esteem you could anticipate from a job is very dependent on your ability to be successful at your work.

Prestige—The reputation you acquire within a group as the result of competence, character, power, wealth, and the like. The professional respect of one's colleagues may be an important factor to some individuals.

---

various alternative careers. Teweles' objectives are given in Table 7.12 along with a short description of the meaning of each.

For each of the above objectives, except wealth, a subjective index was defined, ranging from 0 to 100, which was used to indicate the degree to which the corresponding objective was achieved.*

The job alternatives evaluated by Dr. Teweles† were (1) a private general dentist, (2) a military dentist, (3) an orthodontic dental specialist, (4) an investment analyst, and (5) a management consultant. These five occupations were evaluated using an additive utility function. Using available data on various professions in addition to personal judgement, Teweles was able to assess probabilities about the degree to which each

---

* Miller's and Teweles' work illustrates a tendency mentioned in Chapter 2: as the attributes become more direct indicators of fundamental objectives—as opposed to proxy attributes—it is more difficult to identify suitable objective measures, and one must define subjective indices.

† Dr. Teweles is a dentist, and at the time he wrote his paper, he was completing a Masters of Science in Business Administration and reaching the end of his initial military commitment.

objective would be met conditional on each alternative. Expected utilities were calculated for each alternative and sensitivity analyses performed.

In Dr. Teweles' report, he states, "The major difficulty in all career planning decisions is for an individual to gain sufficient insight into his own future goals and then learn enough about each alternative to evaluate it." Among Dr. Teweles' conclusions is the following: "As a result of my career analysis, I feel more capable of making the proper career decision at this time. There is no doubt that I understand the factors which motivate me a little better than I did before the analysis." We know of many cases where similar personal analyses have been conducted. Some of these resulted in similar conclusions as Dr. Teweles'; other self-analyses, as you might expect, were abortive and useless. We also know of one medical doctor who used this personal self-evaluation technique on a mental patient in a hospital and he reported a surprising success. This doctor took our vernacular phrase, "a framework for straightening out one's mind," quite literally.

7.7.5 Transport of Hazardous Substances

During the past decade there has been a large growth in the type and the amount of hazardous materials transported within the United States. Shipment of such materials is achieved via all ground modes—rail, highway, water, and pipeline. Private citizens, industry, and governmental agencies have become increasingly concerned about the risks associated with transporting these hazardous materials. Aspects of the risk might be divided into two factors:

1. The likelihoods of various accidents occurring.
2. The damage caused by an accident that does occur.

Too often, we have a tendency to assume that "reducing the risks" can always be accomplished by reducing the probability of an accident occurring.* However, we must clearly also include the possible consequences when attempting to reduce risk. Said another way, the *risk* of the circumstance "There is one chance in 1,000,000 that a gas leak will lead to a moderate-sized explosion in a populated area next year" seems much greater intuitively than the circumstance "There are 4 chances in 1,000,000 that a gas leak will lead to a large explosion in the desert next year."

Some work of Brooks and Kalelkar at Arthur D. Little attempted to measure the relative undesirability of the consequences of various accidents that may result from transporting hazardous materials. In addition,

---

* One can investigate "fail-safe" as well as "safe-fail" techniques.

Table 7.13

Environmental Effects from Hazardous Chemical Spills

1. No effect.
2. Residual surface accumulation of harmless material such as sugar or grain.
3. Aesthetic pollution (odor-vapors).
4. Residual surface accumulation of removable material such as oil.
5. Persistent leaf damage (spotting, discoloration) but foliage remains edible for wildlife.
6. Persistent leaf damage (loss of foliage) but new growth in following year.
7. Foliage remains poisonous to animals (indirect cause of some death upon ingestion).
8. Animals become more susceptible to predators because of *direct* exposure to chemicals and resulting physical debilitation.
9. Death to most smaller animals.
10. Short-term (one season) loss of foliage with emigration of specific animals that eat the foliage. Eventual reforestation.
11. Death to foliage and emigration of animals.
12. Death to foliage and animals.
13. Sterilization of total environment with no potential for reforestation or immigration of species.

Note. This scale applies equally well to water and to land.

they investigated which modes of transport are safer for which specific substances.

The aspect of Brooks and Kalelkar's efforts of most interest here concerns their attempts to assess a three-attribute utility function over the attributes human deaths, property damage, and environmental damage. The first attribute ranged from 0 to 1200, and the second attribute ranged from 0 to $10 million. The third attribute was measured by a subjective index scaled from 1 to 13, as defined in Table 7.13.

The person whose preferences were assessed was an experienced worker in the field of safety who attempted to take the viewpoint of society as a whole in indicating preferences. It was verified that each of the single attributes was utility independent of the remaining two. Thus, Theorem 6.3 held and the three one-attribute utility functions and the requisite scaling constants necessary for specifying the three-attribute utility function were assessed. The three utility functions are illustrated in Fig. 7.15. Details of these assessments are found in Kalelkar et al. (1974).

This analysis raises deep ethical concerns and should be examined critically and constructively by analysts concerned with such problems. At least Kalelkar articulates a utility structure that others can criticize, and this is a step forward. Pious, vacuous rhetoric does not help in making such horrendous tradeoffs. We feel that in cases such as the one

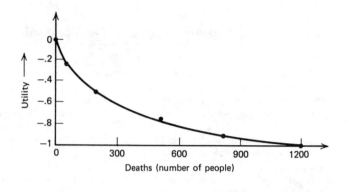

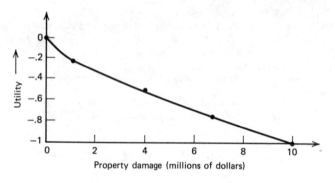

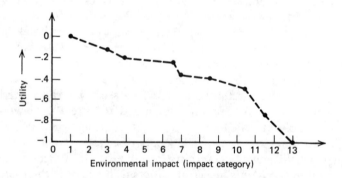

Fig. 7.15. Utility functions for evaluating the transportation of hazardous substances.

428

examined by Kalelkar, the value and utility structures that are used either implicitly or explicitly should be of public concern and should be articulated and publicly discussed.

7.7.6   Treatment for Cleft Lip and Cleft Palate*

Cleft lip and cleft palate is the second most common congenital deformity in the United States. Treatment for this condition is very involved: it requires many different medical specialists, coordinating from birth to adulthood, not only to correct surgically the physiological defect, but also to deal with the child's psychological, social, and mental development. The effects of the treatment of clefts and the effects of the clefts themselves are not completely distinguishable. Both are serious and should be considered in selecting an approach for treatment. With this, a critical issue surfaces: What is the best procedure for treatment in a given situation? Value judgments are essential in answering this question, but because survival of the child is not a factor, various concerned individuals—parents and professionals—often disagree more in their value structures in this situation than in cases where survival is an issue. The best treatment should depend on a number of characteristics, such as the physical features of the child after treatment, the cost, the effects on hearing and speech, and so on. Path-breaking results of Jeffrey Krischer (1974) constitute a very interesting attempt to address some of the critical value issues concerning treatment of cleft lip and cleft palate. Here, we briefly describe his work.

In discussing the importance of cleft lip and cleft palate, Krischer states, "Rarely are there defects so handicapping to the child or so disturbing to the family, yet so amenable to treatment." One major objective of treatment is to correct the physical deformities and provide a normal-looking lip and nose. There are usually uncertainties about the surgical success a patient will have in this process and there is always the possibility of resulting scars. Defective speech often accompanies those with cleft palate, which can be attributed to both physical and psychological factors. Another complication is the possibility of hearing loss. Thus, clearly two other important objectives of treatment are to improve future speech skills and to improve hearing.

Krischer has quantified the preferences of over 100 people, including surgeons, orthodontists, speech therapists, audiologists, pediatricians, and parents of children with clefts, all of whom are actively involved with

---

* Roughly speaking, a cleft lip is a failure of the upper lip to grow together. It usually results in a gap in the lip approximately below one nostril. Cleft palate refers to a split in the palate at birth.

Table 7.14
Krischer's Objectives for Evaluating Treatment of
Cleft Lip and Palate

Objective	Attribute	Range
Provide normal looking lip and nose	Pictorial	(See text)
Improve speech	Percent word intelligibility	35–90
Improve hearing	Hearing aid required	Yes or no
Minimize treatment costs	Dollars	0–10,000

individuals having clefts. The four objectives and associated attributes that he explicitly considered are given in Table 7.14 along with the range of these attributes. One unique aspect of these assessments was the attribute evaluating physical effects. Krischer had segments of children's faces showing the nose and mouth area superimposed on a sketched face of a child. These pictures illustrated various degrees of physical deformity after treatment for the cleft. The individuals were asked to assess subjectively their preferences for these pictorial displays. Also note that the hearing attribute only had two values. This, of course, could be generalized. For speech, word intelligibility was measured as the percent of words accurately identified by a group of listeners with normal hearing. Here 90 percent is completely adequate, 75 percent causes mild difficulty in understanding, 50 percent requires frequent repetition, and 35 percent is unintelligible.

Once these objectives and attributes were specified, Krischer, working with medical specialists concerned with clefts, developed a questionnaire to assess preferences over the four attributes. This was mailed to medical specialists at numerous cleft lip and cleft palate treatment facilities in the United States and through these facilities to some parents of children with clefts. Part of the questionnaire concerned utility independence assumptions and the conditional utility functions for the four attributes and another part concerned preferential independence assumptions and tradeoffs among attributes. Of the first 125 responses, approximately 75 percent appear to have accepted requisite assumptions to invoke Theorem 6.1 for formalizing preferences with either a multiplicative or additive utility function. Details of these assessments, a copy of the questionnaire, and an interesting discussion of individual differences of preferences are found in Krischer (1974).

7.7.7   Development of Water Quality Indices

Recent work by O'Connor (1973) illustrates some important considerations relevant to specifying and using social indices. O'Connor utilized a modified Delphi procedure [Dalkey (1969)] to combine the judgments of several experts in constructing two separate indices of water quality. One concerned the quality of water to be used as a public water supply and the other described the quality of water for sustaining fish and wildlife populations. Eight experts* were used to (1) specify attributes that should be included in each of the water quality indices and (2) prescribe a value function over these attributes that would indicate water quality. Since these indices are value functions, they have the property that higher values indicate higher water quality. However, it is not necessarily appropriate to use the expected value of these indices in making decisions when uncertainty is involved.

O'Connor sent questionnaires to and personally visited each of the experts to discuss the attributes that should be explicitly included in some aggregate water quality index and the form of this aggregation function. An additive model was chosen for both the public water supply and fish and wildlife indices. O'Connor emphasizes that an additive model is not

Table 7.15
O'Connor's Final Attributes in the
Water Quality Indices

Public Water Supply	Fish and Wildlife
Fecal coliforms	Dissolved oxygen
Phenols	Temperature
Dissolved solids	pH
pH	Phenols
Fluorides	Turbidity
Hardness	Ammonia
Nitrates	Dissolved solids
Chlorides	Nitrates
Alkalinity	Phosphates
Turbidity	
Dissolved oxygen	
Color	
Sulfates	

* O'Connor describes the experts as follows: "Eight experts were chosen from an initial set of 20 contacted. Two experts were high-ranking members of The Environmental Protection Agency. Two members were heads of state engineering services departments, and four were university professors in the areas concerned with environmental quality."

appropriate, for instance, when certain toxic substances enter the water at an unacceptable level or when some of the other attributes, such as pH, reach extreme levels. Thus O'Connor's models are meant to be valid subject to the condition that toxic substances are under recommended limits and other attributes are within specified ranges. However, many normal situations probably meet these restrictions. The final attributes used in the public water supply index and in the fish and wildlife index are given in Table 7.15. Details about procedures used and the final value functions are in O'Connor (1973).

7.7.8 Examining Foreign Policy

What are the advantages and disadvantages to the United States of a Mideast agreement sought to ensure the continued availability of Mideast oil and an increased production to meet the world demand? An exploratory policy analysis done by Decisions and Designs, Inc.* examined how a multiattribute decision analysis might clarify the reasoning and simplify the presentation of conclusions for such a complex problem.

The first phase of the analysis produced a flexible decision model and used it initially to examine three sharply different negotiating strategies regarding a possible Mideast agreement. A "base option" involving no change now or later in U.S.–Mideast policies was used primarily as a reference point for purposes of comparison. A maximum option involved an agreement that went most of the way toward what certain Mideast oil-producing countries want. A moderate option was an intermediate strategy reflecting a moderate change in U.S. policy, which would be attractive to the Mideast oil-producing countries but not politically difficult for the United States.

The decision model evaluated the impact of various negotiating postures on Mideastern oil supply and the associated political and economic costs and gains to the United States. Specifically, the attributes concerned balance of payments, the way Western Europe and Japan would perceive a Mideast agreement, the impact on U.S. foreign relations, the resulting public sentiment in the United States and, finally the effect an agreement would have on other oil producers.

Various submodels were used to elicit probabilistic judgments and preference assessments at differing levels of complexity and aggregation. The uncertainty analysis was based on judgments elicited from policy makers and substantive experts. The preferences used in the problem

---

* Decisions and Designs, Inc. is an independent research and development company located in McLean, Virginia.

were solicited from policy analysts charged with making recommendations. For a first analysis, the utility function chosen was additive.

The next phase of the ongoing decision analysis used the model developed, with several variations, to explore a much richer set of realistic options and to update continually the inputs in the light of changing circumstances or perceptions of individual decision makers. More details can be found in Brown and Peterson (1975).

7.7.9   Forest Pest Management

The forests of New Brunswick, Canada have been frequently attacked by an insect pest known as the spruce budworm. Historical evidence taken from the trees themselves indicate that with great regularity the forests have been periodically devastated for more than 500 years. When a major outbreak of budworm began in the late 1940s, DDT and other insecticides were introduced to minimize the disruption to the important lumber industry. Spraying has continually been used since that time. However, in the ensuing 25 years, spraying costs have spiraled, the lumbering industry has become more important to the overall economy, and information and concern about insecticides has greatly increased. In addition, the spraying has grown less and less effective, and a major outbreak of budworm is underway in 1975. The Canadian government is reviewing the problem and examining policy options. How should the cutting and spraying of trees prevent a severe outbreak of the budworm, and hence, both maintain a viable lumber industry and preserve the forest for recreational purposes?

As part of the attempt to answer this question, a detailed simulation model of the New Brunswick forests has been built at the Institute for Resource Ecology of the University of British Columbia and at the International Institute for Applied Systems Analysis [see Holling et al. (1974)].* This model examines the impacts that different alternatives might have on several critical variables such as the environmental quality of the forest, indicated by the percentage of trees in certain stages of growth and health, the existence of budworm in varying stages of their life cycle, lumber company profits, and employment due to the lumbering industry. Given all this information, the problem is to "make sense of it" to aid policy makers in reaching a responsible decision.

Bell (1974b) reports in detail the steps taken to derive relevant attributes from the several output variables and to assess a value function

---

* The models were designed under the leadership of Professor Buzz Holling. Team members included Bill Clark, Ray Hilborn, Dixon Jones, Zafar Rashid, Carl Walters, and Ralph Yorque.

reflecting the preferences of one member of the simulation project for the condition of the forest and economy. The attributes were profit (calculated from the dollar value of timber logged minus expenses including spraying costs), unemployment (the measure was percentage of mill capacity unused), and the recreational value of the forest (indicated by two subjective indices representing the areas of "good" and "bad" recreational potential in the forest).

Subsequently, Bell (1975b) also assessed a utility function for these four attributes over time. It was established that the decision maker's preference for the time stream of recreation and the two streams of profit and unemployment were mutually utility independent. Thus, Theorem 5.2 allowed one to separately assess utility functions for the recreational component and the profit-unemployment component of the overall utility function.

To assess the recreational utility function over the several periods, the utility independence assumptions implying the appropriateness of the multiplicative utility function of Theorem 6.1 were verified. The recreational utility function could then be derived using only consistently scaled marginal utility functions for the areas of "good" and "bad" forest in a single period. It is of interest to note that simple discounting of the temporal stream of recreational indices (or transforms of these indices) was found to be an inadequate representation of the assessor's judgments.

The assessment of a utility function over profit and unemployment streams was more complex. It was necessary to account for interdependencies of preference in adjacent time periods, since achieved levels in period i set up aspiration levels for period $i+1$. The decision maker proved to be risk prone in uncertain situations involving either levels of employment that were lower than the level in the previous year or employment levels that were much lower than the following period; otherwise he was risk averse. This complication was handled using assumptions based on conditional utility independence introduced in Section 6.10. Chapter 9, largely based on the work of Richard Meyer, generalizes Bell's (1975a) formulation for handling utility dependencies of time streams.

Work is continuing on the forest-pest management problem and the utility functions, assessed by Bell, are being used in conjunction with the simulation model to evaluate various strategies.

7.7.10 Other Applications

As you can see from the examples described, there is a wide variety of settings in which multiattribute value or utility analysis is being employed.

Still our collective experience is not large enough for the theory and art of such analyses to be anywhere near standardized. Indeed, practically each new analysis contributes to the art of assessing multiattribute preferences, if not to the theoretical aspects as well. For space considerations, we have unfortunately not been able to review many such interesting ground-breaking analyses.

Some of these are Bauer and Wegener's (1975) examination of urban development plans, Gearing, Swart, and Var's (1973, 1974) measure of tourist attractiveness and selection of touristic projects for the Turkish Ministry of Tourism, Lorange and Norman's (1973) investigation of risk attitudes of Scandinavian shipowners, Gustafson and Holloway's (1974) development of a severity of pain index, Boyd, Howard, Matheson, and North's (1971) decision of whether to seed hurricanes, Dyer, Farrell, and Bradley's (1973) development of curriculum planning information for elementary school principles, and Collins' (1974) evaluation of solid waste disposal alternatives in Southeastern Michigan. Huber (1974a) reviews a number of studies that used multiattribute utility models. Two more general articles that survey the applications of decision analysis in industry are Brown (1970) and Longbottom and Wade (1973).

CHAPTER 8

Airport Development for Mexico City: A Case Study*

This chapter applies decision analysis to a large-scale public decision problem: selection of a strategy for developing the major airport facilities of the Mexico City metropolitan area. There are two purposes in discussing this study here. First, many of the techniques and procedures developed in earlier chapters of this book are utilized on a very important "typical" problem. Of course, it's typical of those one-of-a-kind strategic decisions that always concern many atypical aspects. Second, although the analysis stresses the value side of the multiattribute problem, it also deals with structuring the problem, aspects of modeling the possible impacts of various alternatives, and the larger framework within which the analysis occurred.

Many people contributed significantly to the study. It was done in the summer of 1971 for the Government of Mexico under the auspices of the Secretaria de Obras Publicas (Ministry of Public Works, SOP) and directed by F. J. Jauffred, Director of the Center for Computation and Statistics, and F. Dovali, Head of the Department of Airports. Richard deNeufville of the Massachusetts Institute of Technology and we authors were consultants assisting SOP on the project. The total time spent by the consultants on the project was 50 man-days.

8.1 THE PROBLEM

Rapid growth in the demand for air travel, combined with increasingly difficult operating conditions at the existing airport facilities, compelled

* This chapter closely follows the development in, and at times takes sections almost verbatim from deNeufville and Keeney (1972) and Keeney (1973a).

the Mexican Government to ask: "How should the airport facilities of Mexico City be developed to assure adequate service for the region during the period from now to the year 2000?" This was the overall question examined by the study team.

Our initial problem was not this one, however. Two previous studies for developing the airport facilities of Mexico City had recommended very different alternatives. One concluded that the current airport, 5 miles from the city center should be greatly expanded,* whereas the other suggested moving all aircraft operations to a new airport to be built 25 miles north of the city.† Our initial charter was to evaluate the various alternatives, in light of this discrepancy, and to recommend the most effective program for airport development.

For this more limited development decision, we were concerned with the following:

1. The location of the airport (or airports)
2. The operational policy defining which services were to be performed and where they were to be located
3. The timing for development of different airport facilities.

Because of severe environmental constraints, the two sites previously mentioned were the only ones adequate for a large international airport in the Mexico City metropolitan area. The configurations possible at either site, with respect to the runways for example, were not really significant in this particular problem.

Many different ways of operating the airports (with substantial differences in the quality of service provided) were possible, however. In particular, it was necessary to decide what kinds of aircraft activity (international, domestic, military, or general) should be operating at each of the two sites.

The question of timing was very important, since failure to act at a given time may preclude future options. For example, land available now may not be available for development in the future. On the other hand, premature action can significantly increase total costs to the nation. The timing issue and operational policies were the most important aspects of this initial airport problem.

8.2 BACKGROUND INFORMATION

The existing airport is about 5 miles east of the central part of Mexico City, but still within the city limits on the edge of Lake Texcoco. The other

* See Ipesa Consultores and the Secretaria de Communicaciones y Transportes (1970).
† See Secretaria de Obras Publicas (1967) or Wilsey y Ham de Mexico (1967).

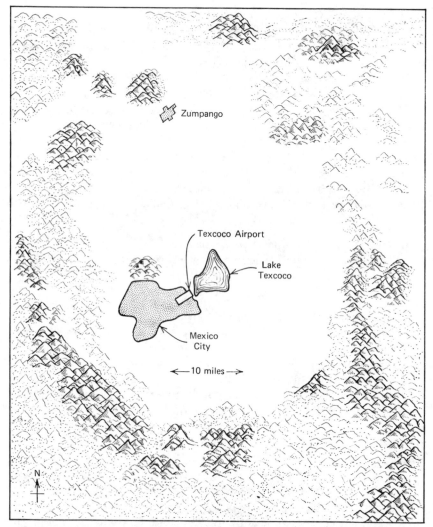

Fig. 8.1. General geography of the Mexico City Metropolitan Area.

site is 25 miles north of the city in an undeveloped farming area, near the village of Zumpango. The relative location of the two feasible sites is indicated in Fig. 8.1.

8.2.1 The Physical Environment in Mexico City

Mexico City is situated at an altitude of about 7400 feet in a valley ringed with high mountains ranging to over 17,000 feet above sea level.

The mountains are very high in all directions except the northeast, where the range lowers to around 10,000 feet. Most flights entering or leaving the Mexico City area fly over these lower mountains to the northeast, although some do proceed through a smaller and higher pass to the south.

The maneuverability of the aircraft at high altitudes is low, especially in hot climates. This requires that the flight patterns over Mexico City be broader than usual and prevents aircraft from safely threading their way through mountainous regions. Thus there are considerable restrictions on the usable airspace around Mexico City. This constraint, which principally affects the capacity of the Texcoco site, is serious since Mexico City already handles over two million passengers a year and ranks among the the busiest airports on the continent.

When the Texcoço Airport was organized in the 1930s, it was out in the country, but the population of the metropolitan area has grown at the rate of about 5 percent a year, passing from five million in 1960, to eight million in 1970. During this time, Texcoco has been surrounded on three sides by mixed residential and commercial sections. This has created problems of noise, social disruption, and safety.

Should a major accident occur on landing or takeoff toward the city, it would likely cause hundreds of casualties. The area is densely populated and, for example, a large school is located under a flight path only 500 feet from the end of a runway. Since the approach pattern passes directly over the central parts of the city, high noise levels affect many thousands of people. These noise levels are bound to persist for at least the next 15 years until "quiet" engines are developed and installed on all aircraft. In addition, major expansion at Texcoco could result in displacing almost 200,000 people. A compensating advantage for the Texcoco site is that major facilities already exist. However, they do not meet the standards found in the major airports of other large developed countries.

The location of Mexico City on a former lake bed makes construction especially expensive at Texcoco. Heavy facilities such as runways not only sink rapidly, but at different rates in different locations, depending on their loads. Each of the two major existing runways at Texcoco require leveling and resurfacing every two years. Such repairs closed down half the airport for four months when they were done in 1971. Because the Zumpango site is on higher and firmer ground, it is not expected to have the same kind of difficulties.

Access to the airport by ground transportation appears to be reasonable for both sites. The Texcoco site is near the main peripheral highway, which can distribute traffic around the suburbs. It is not, however, especially well connected to the center of the City, to which one has to proceed through congested city streets. The Zumpango site has the clear disadvantage of being further away, but it can be linked directly to the tourist and business areas via an existing north–south expressway.

8.2.2 The Institutional Setting

The government of Mexico has been in the hands of a single party, the Partido Revolucionario Institucional, for almost 40 years. Political power tends to be concentrated in the federal government and, for major decisions such as the location of the capital's airport, in the President himself. Any decision about a new airport during 1970–76 will require the approval of President Luis Echeverria. The debate about this decision has been carried on by three major governmental bodies:

1. The Secretaria de Obras Publicas, SOP (the Ministry of Public Works).
2. The Secretaria de Communicaciones y Transportes, SCT (the Ministry of Communication and Transport).
3. The Secretaria de la Presidencia, a body with functions similar to those of the Office of Management and Budget in the United States.

8.2.3 Previous Studies

Both SOP and SCT have commissioned rival large-scale studies of the airport problem within the past few years. The SOP study [SOP (1967), Wilsey y Ham de Mexico (1967)], done for its Department of Airports between 1965 and 1967, recommended that a new airport be built at Zumpango and that all commercial flights be shifted to this facility. The master plan then proposed was not adopted at that time.

The study commissioned by SCT in 1970 [Ipesa Consultores and SCT (1970)] resulted in a master plan for expanding the airport at Texcoco by adding new runway and terminal facilities. Interestingly, this report assumed that aircraft could take off away from the city toward the east, and could land coming into the city from the east in opposing streams of traffic aimed at adjacent parallel runways. While this proposal "solves" the noise and displacement problems, its implications for safety are extremely serious at any significant level of traffic, and are unlikely to be acceptable for the expected volumes. This report assumed that "quiet" engines would completely eliminate any noise problems outside the airport boundaries by 1990. The SCT study was prepared and submitted during the closing months of the 1964–1970 administration of the previous President; it was not accepted in 1970. The government of Mexico did, however, wish to resolve the issue. In early 1971 the new administration committed itself to a restudy. As stated by President Echeverria in his State of the Union Message of September 1, 1971, "Construction of a new international airport in the metropolitan area (of Mexico City) is also under study at this time." The study referred to is the one presented here.

8.3 EVOLUTION OF THE ANALYSIS

During the short three-month period (the summer of 1971) in which we were associated with the airport problem, it took on many forms. Much of the time was used in defining the problem, but it seemed to be more than this. There wasn't a single problem, but many interrelated problems: What is the best manner to provide acceptable air service for Mexico City? How can one contribute to a reconciliation of differences of judgment, "facts," and opinion of independent government agencies concerned with airport development, in order to improve quality of information available to the decision makers? What strategies for developing the airport facilities are best in light of the financial and political realities facing the government? The focus of the analysis shifted as the Secretaria de Obras Publicas became more sensitized to issues we felt might be important, as we became more familiar with the total environment in which this analysis was situated, and as segments of the study felt to be important were completed.

Because of the conflicting recommendations of previous reports, the original directive given to our colleagues in SOP was to evaluate various master plans for developing Texcoco and Zumpango. Therefore, this aspect of the problem had to be completed first. Before we entered the scene, SOP had been formulating this problem for a few months. The alternatives were specified and objectives and preliminary measures of effectiveness were defined. Our main effort in helping SOP concerned (1) synthesizing the volumes of relevant information in the previous reports, as well as results from additional studies, and indicating the degree to which various alternatives met objectives, (2) meaningfully aggregating the effects occurring in different time periods, (3) quantifying a value structure appropriate for the problem, and (4) developing a system for doing sensitivity analysis and for reporting results.

As this work progressed, the original problem began to be "solved," thus meeting the original directive and freeing the team to address other important issues. Perhaps the most crucial issue was to attempt to reconcile the differences of viewpoint held by various parties, especially SOP and SCT, involved in airport development and operation.

8.3.1   An Attempt at Reconciliation Through Shared Analysis

It is expected that impartial experts might disagree on many aspects of a complex analysis. It is crucial to know what aspects of the problem they agree or disagree on and why. For instance, there may be agreement on the structuring of the problem, but disagreement on the possible impacts of the various alternatives and disagreement on the value structure. The reasons may simply be that different experts have incomplete information or conflicting information or that traditional viewpoints due to political and professional orientation have been "cast in concrete." The decision analysis model, along with a graphical input–output display developed to assist in the analysis, seemed to offer a useful framework for analyzing these differences of opinion.

Input–output consoles were installed in offices of the study team, the Secretary and Undersecretary of SOP, the Presidencia, and the President's own office. Our hope was that both SOP and SCT would agree on the basic framework for analyzing the airport problem and that this framework could then help highlight just where fundamental disagreements lay. The Presidencia would then be in a position to better understand the root causes of the different viewpoints, hear the rationalizations of each side, and then commission its own studies if required to clarify critical aspects of the problem. The SOP felt sure that if this reconciliation process were carried out, they would be shown to be right and they were prepared to be quite open, even about their uncertainties on some inputs. A major problem, of course, lay in the fact that it was SOP who was suggesting the framework (not the Presidencia) and, understandably (but regretfully from our point of view), the reconciliation process was never engaged.

Hence SOP had to proceed in a new direction. Clearly their minds were made up about the merits of Zumpango and now their efforts turned to amassing an argument that would convince the President and the Presidencia, over and above the objections of the SCT. We thus proceeded in the preparation of an advocacy document that was meant to be impressively scientific. Some strange things happened.

8.4   THE STATIC MODEL

Because of the history of the previous studies, the alternatives, objectives, and measures of effectiveness for the static analysis were firmly specified by our clients, the Secretaria de Obras Publicas.

8.4.1 The Alternatives

The alternatives specified what types of aircraft would operate at each of the two possible sites for the rest of the century. In abstracting these, because of similarities in operating characteristics and functions, SOP had categorized aircraft as follows: International (I), domestic (D), general (G), and military (M). It was assumed that at any one time, each category of aircraft could operate at only one of the two sites.

To account for changes in operating arrangements over the 30-year period while keeping the problem manageable, we focused on the years 1975, 1985, and 1995 as times when changes in the classes of aircraft operating at a site could occur. Thus, an alternative might be "develop the Zumpango site and move general aircraft to it in 1975, shift international to Zumpango in 1985, and operate all classes of aircraft at Zumpango in 1995." Of course, this discreteness into three time elements was done solely to keep the analysis tractable, and the actual timing of moves would not be so constrained in implementation. We are still discussing a rough-cut level of analysis with presumably more refined tuning coming at a later stage.

Notice that this gives us $(2^4)^3 = 4096$ alternatives. However, many of these were very similar in nature since, for instance, military operations accounted for less than 5 percent of the aircraft volume. Other alternatives defined as above were unreasonable. We would not move all operations from Texcoco to Zumpango in 1975 and back again in 1985, for example. In the final analysis, the total number of alternatives that were evaluated was approximately 100.

8.4.2 Objectives and Measures of Effectiveness

To evaluate the alternatives, we needed to specify some measures of effectiveness that explicitly described their possible impacts on each of the important groups concerned about the problem. For this problem, the groups were (1) the government, as builder and operator of the airports, (2) users of the air facilities, and (3) nonusers. Based on the previous reports of SOP and SCT and lengthy discussions the following six objectives were selected by SOP.

1. Minimize total construction and maintenance *costs*.
2. Provide adequate *capacity* to meet the air traffic demands.
3. Minimize the *access time* to the airport.
4. Maximize the *safety* of the system.
5. Minimize *social disruption* caused by the provision of new airport facilities.
6. Minimize the effects of *noise* pollution due to air traffic.

Although there is obviously much overlap, the first two objectives account for the government's stake as operator; objectives 2, 3, and 4 for the user's; and the last three objectives for the nonusers. Measures of effectiveness for these objectives were defined as follows:

$X_1 \equiv$ total cost in millions of pesos; with "suitable" discounting.

$X_2 \equiv$ the practical capacity in terms of the number of aircraft operations per hour.

$X_3 \equiv$ access time to and from the airport in minutes, weighted by the number of travelers from each zone in Mexico City.

$X_4 \equiv$ number of people (including nonpassengers) seriously injured or killed per aircraft accident.

$X_5 \equiv$ number of people displaced by airport development.

$X_6 \equiv$ number of people subjected to a high noise level, in this case to 90 CNR or more.*

Clearly, these six measures of effectiveness are not unique or completely comprehensive. For instance, air pollution considerations are absent. However, SOP felt the list did include all the important factors (other than political factors, prestige, and the like, which we will discuss later in this chapter) for evaluating effectiveness of the proposed alternatives.

8.4.3 The Basic Decision Model

The basic model is illustrated by the decision tree in Fig. 8.2. An alternative was specified by defining the classes of aircraft that would operate at which site in each of the three time elements. As a result of the alternative chosen and events that occurred (e.g., demand changes), a consequence $(x_1, x_2, \ldots, x_6)$ eventually resulted. However, at the time the decision was made, uncertainties about this consequence for each possible alternative was quantified by a probability distribution over the consequences.

The most important point to note about this model is that the alternatives were master plans. They were not designed to adapt to the unfolding of critical events (e.g., demand changes, technological changes, increasing environmental concerns of citizens, and so on) that might occur over the 30-year period formally considered in the model. Clearly, such considerations were essential to any analysis purporting to assist the government of Mexico in deciding which actions to take in airport development. This was done in the dynamic analysis of options available in 1971 described

---

* The composite noise rating, CNR, is a standard index of noise that combines decibel level and frequency of occurrence. The 90 level was selected by the SOP Department of Airports.

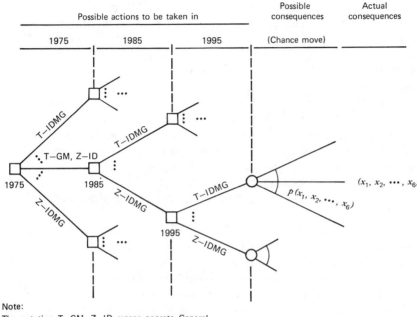

Fig. 8.2. The basic decision model.

in Section 8.8. There were two main reasons for first completing a formal analysis of this static problem:

1. The original request to study the "airport problem" required identifying discrepancies between previous studies, both of which were static analyses.

2. Without such a study, SOP was very vulnerable to potential criticism of the analysis for excluding the details of such considerations.

The complete description of the probabilistic assessments are given in Section 8.5, the preference structure is described in Section 8.6, and the computer input–output along with the results of the analysis are given in Section 8.7.

8.5 SPECIFYING THE POSSIBLE IMPACTS OF EACH ALTERNATIVE

The probabilistic assessments were made using the volumes of relevant information from previous studies, the results of parallel studies being conducted by SOP, and the professional judgment of administration within the Mexican government connected with airport construction, operation, and maintenance. Both reports for SOP [SOP (1967), Wilsey y Ham de Mexico (1967)] and SCT [Ipesa Consultores and SCT (1970)] contain many volumes including detailed demand studies for future air travel, soil mechanics and engineering studies at possible sites, pollution studies considering noise effects, analysis of ground traffic and airport access interaction, cost estimates and projections for various considered airport alterations, and so forth. To help in the cost estimates, for each of the 16 arrangements for aircraft operation at the two possible sites, in 1975, 1985, and 1995, general construction plans were outlined indicating where runways, support facilities, and access facilities would have to be built. These plans translated the feasible alternatives specified in Section 8.4 into designs meaningful to airport planners and government officials.

To gain insight on the impacts of alternatives, various experiments were conducted by the SOP. One, that gathered data on access times, divided Mexico City into 10 zones on the basis of residents' pattern of airport patronage, and then studied the driving times to the two airport sites from each zone in different weather conditions at different times of day, and so on. These data on travel times and usage characteristics provided the information necessary to assess reasonable distributions for access times for the various alternatives.

Similarly, detectors were located at various spots in the city to determine the noise levels caused by aircraft. By analyzing current and projected flight paths, superimposed on aerial photos of the city, and the population densities of the affected areas, we acquired a good indication of the noise impacts of various alternatives. These alternatives assessed distributions for the number of people subjected to specified noise levels.

By superimposing the various plans for construction on aerial photos of the city, we could easily identify the areas in which people would have to be relocated if a particular alternative were adopted. The population of those areas was tabulated providing information for assessing the number of people who would be displaced.

The results of all the previous studies and the data of the concurrent experiments of SOP had to be integrated to provide meaningful estimates of the impacts of various plans. This integration was done using the professional judgment and experience of members of the Secretaria de Obras Publicas, including the Director of Airports, who is responsible for building and maintaining all the airports in the country of Mexico, the director of the Center for Computation and Statistics, and members of their staffs. The assessments were made in group sessions, where differences in judgments were discussed to arrive at a consensus. The fact that there were no problems in reaching a consensus can probably be attributed to a number of factors: all the professionals had the same information available, all had similar technical training in engineering, they were accustomed to working with each other and each knew how the others thought, and the subordinates tended to agree with their superiors.

Having indicated how the probabilistic assessments were conducted, we now get to the specifics. First, the single-year assessments will be described, and then the time effects will be accounted for.

8.5.1 One-Year Assessments

The probability density functions were assessed using the fractile method described in Raiffa (1968). We use Fig. 8.3 to illustrate the method by example. Consider the possible 1975 noise impact of the operating arrangement "all classes of aircraft at Texcoco." First, the maximum and minimum number of people subjected to 90 CNR or greater was specified as 800,000 and 400,000. Next the .5 fractile was evaluated as 640,000. This meant, in the judgment of SOP, that the

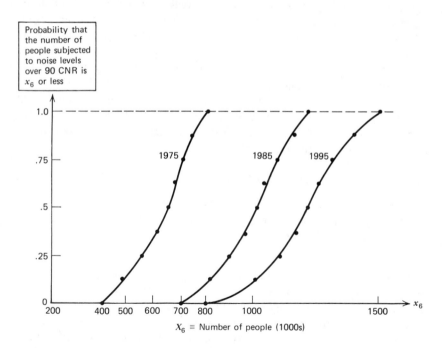

Fig. 8.3. Assessed distributions of the number of people subjected to noise levels over 90 CNR with the "all Texcoco" option.

probability that the number of people impacted by 90+ CNR, denoted by X_6^{75}, would be less than 640,00 is one-half. Or, said another way, it is equally likely that the number of people subjected to the high noise level will be less than or greater than 640,000. The interval between 400,000 and 640,000 was then divided into equally likely parts by choosing the .25 fractile as 540,000. The .75 fractile was 700,000. Finally, each quartile was divided into equally likely parts in a similar manner.

The fractiles that were assessed are indicated by the dots on Fig. 8.3 and the smooth lines are the cumulative probability distributions describing possible noise impacts for the "all Texcoco" option in 1975, 1985, and 1995. For any given year, the probability that the impact is between any two adjacent fractile points should be the same, that is, .125. Thus, to check consistency of the assessments, we asked SOP if, in fact, their judgmental probabilities of falling into any of the eight ranges of impact were the same. SOP adjusted their assessments until no more discrepancies could be found. Figure 8.3 indicates the final adjusted curves.

What are the basic uncertainties that must be considered when assessing the possible noise influence of each airport? First, there is the uncertainty of the population in the flight path area. Current population is known rather accurately, but there is more uncertainty about the population in the future. There is uncertainty about when noise suppressors for jet engines will become operational and incorporated on most jets and about the level of impact of such suppressors. And there is uncertainty about the volume of air traffic in future years. Previous SOP and SCT studies, census figures, SOP experiments, and so on, all provided useful information on these basic uncertainties. This information was both formally and informally used by SOP in making their combined assessments for the possible noise impacts.

8.5.2   Incorporating Time Effects

Each of the measures of effectiveness needed to account for the impact over the 30-year period to the year 2000. Different adjustments seemed appropriate for different measures as indicated.

COSTS.   The costs that were considered in the model included building and maintenance, but excluded operating costs since it was felt these would be approximately the same for any alternative. As is normal practice for SOP, the present value of the costs was taken as the time-dependent attribute of importance. The discount rate used was 12 percent, the standard for the Mexican government. Sensitivity analysis indicated the choice of a discount rate was not critical for identifying effective strategies.

NOISE.   For noise, the average number of people annually subjected to aircraft noise levels above 90 CNR was used as the measure of effectiveness. This assumes that it is equally undesirable to have one person subjected to these noise levels for two years or to have two different people subjected in the different years. Furthermore, it assumes the undesirability to an individual of a certain noise level in any year is the same.

SAFETY.   As previously mentioned, safety is measured in terms of the number of people killed or seriously injured per air crash. To adapt this, we chose the average number of people killed or seriously injured per crash averaged over the 30-year period. Clearly this measure does not account for the different likelihoods of crashes with various arrangements. SOP was aware of this and of the need to make adjustments to account for this factor. However, they felt it was not prudent to formally include the likelihood of crashes in the model and chose, instead to make adjustments of the impact per crash in the sensitivity analysis to indicate the effect of differential crash likelihoods.

ACCESS TIME.   For access time, an average of the possible access times in the various years weighted by the expected number of users in those years was used. This assumes each trip to or from the airport by any individual in any year is as important as any other such trip and that one's preferences for the various access times are stationary over time.

SOCIAL DISRUPTION.   By reasoning that, on the average, it would be just as undesirable for a random individual to be moved from his home because of airport development in one year as any other year, we chose the total number of such people displaced to be the measure of social disruption for the analysis.

CAPACITY.   Capacity (maximum possible operations per hour) could not be aggregated in any reasonable way to combine impacts in the different years. This is mainly because the relative desirability of various levels of capacity would be very different in different years since demand would probably be larger in later years. Increasing capacity from 80 to 100 in 1975 may be worth very little, since the additional capacity would rarely be needed. However, this same change in 1995 could be extremely important. Thus in the 30-year model, separate measures of effectiveness for the capacity of 1975, 1985 and 1995 were included.

8.5.3 The Thirty-Year Assessments

By aggregating the three yearly assessed impacts for each measure of effectiveness, except capacity, in the manner just described, we could

calculate the probability density functions over the measures to account
for impact over time. With noise, for instance, if we define

$$X_6 \equiv \frac{X_6^{75} + X_6^{85} + X_6^{95}}{3} \tag{8.1}$$

where X_6^i is the number of people subjected to noise levels over 90 CNR
in year i, then by using the probability distributions assessed for the X_6^i
for a particular strategy, it is easy to derive the probability distribution for
X_6. This represents what we have taken to be the overall impact of a
particular strategy in terms of noise.

8.5.4   Probabilistic Independence Assumptions

In conducting the assessments over one attribute at a time, we explicitly
assumed that, for each alternative, the six attributes were probabilistically
independent. For some of the attributes, this assumption seemed appropriate.
For instance, for any given alternative, noise and access time
considerations were probably independent of the other attributes. On the
other hand, safety considerations depended on capacity, for instance. The
lower the capacity, the more often the airport will be operating under
hazardous conditions.

The most important assumption with regard to these assessments was
that impacts in separate years were probabilistically independent conditional
on the given alternative. This is clearly not true. For instance, for
the "all Texcoco" alternative, if we found that 800,000 people were
subjected to high noise levels in 1975, we would likely feel that more
people will be affected by noise in 1985 than we would have if 400,000
had high noise levels in 1975.

Our analysis was designed in an iterative fashion. First, simplifying assumptions
(e.g., probabilistic independence) were adopted with the intention
at a later stage of recycling back with more realistic assumptions. It
turned out, however, that the delicacy taken in modeling the probabilistic
part of our analysis was not a critical factor since other considerations
dominated. If we had had more time, we would have dressed up the
probabilistic analysis to be more credible to the reader. But it would have
been mere "window dressing" because the action recommendations we
finally suggested could not have been reversed by acknowledging the joint
dependence of the random variables involved. It would not have been too
difficult to incorporate this complexity, if not analytically, at least
through a simulation mode of analysis. It simply was not worth it in this
case.

In view of the oversimplifying probabilistic assumptions and the insensitivities, it might have been just as accurate and simpler to use point estimates of the impacts rather than probability distributions. In retrospect, this seems quite reasonable. However, this does not avoid any of the assumptions made in our analysis, and in addition, no account is made for the possible uncertainty of impact for the single attributes. Our approach forces an explicit recognition of this uncertainty by the decision makers. Also, before our analysis, the lack of sensitivity of the types of effective strategies to the attribute levels was not known. A sensitivity analysis using point estimates could have indicated this, however. The strongest reason for using probability distributions was that SOP wanted to avoid potential criticism of the analysis because of exclusion of the uncertainties.

8.6 ASSESSING THE MULTIATTRIBUTE UTILITY FUNCTION

Once we had probability assessments that adequately described the impact of alternative strategies in terms of our six measures of effectiveness, we next assessed a utility function $u(x_1, x_2, \ldots, x_6) \equiv u(\mathbf{x})$ over these measures. Proceeding as suggested in Section 6.6, we began by exploring the decision maker's preference structure in a qualitative manner. This was to build up SOP's and our own experience in thinking directly about $(x_1, x_2, \ldots, x_6)$ consequences but, more importantly, to ascertain whether any of the preferential independence or utility independence assumptions discussed in earlier chapters were appropriate for this problem. Then we formally verified a sufficient set of such assumptions that allowed us to define for each i, $i = 1, 2, \ldots, 6$, a conditional utility function u_i over X_i and then to construct u as a function of the conditional utility functions. That is,

$$u(\mathbf{x}) = f[u_1(x_1), u_2(x_2), \ldots, u_6(x_6)], \tag{8.2}$$

where f is scalar valued. To specify $u(\mathbf{x})$, the six u_i's and necessary scaling factors were assessed.

The utility assessments incorporated the best professional judgments of both the SOP Director at Airports and the SOP Director of the Center for Computation and Statistics, and members of their staffs. A serious attempt was made to analyze the problem from the point of view of the government of Mexico.

8.6.1   The Assumptions

Let us briefly and informally review the concepts of preferential independence and utility independence. Recall that preferential independence concerns only ordinal preferences and no probabilistic elements are involved. Partition the set of attributes into Y and Z. If the rankings of consequences, which differ only in the level of attribute Y, are the same regardless of the fixed level of attribute Z, then Y is preferentially independent of Z.

Utility independence, on the other hand, concerns the cardinal preferences of the decision maker. If the rankings of all lotteries, which differ only in the possible levels of Y that may occur, are the same regardless of the fixed levels of Z, then Y is utility independent of Z.

8.6.2   Verifying the Assumptions

Let us illustrate how we verified the preferential independence assumptions used in our work. As an example, consider whether safety X_4 and noise X_6 are preferentially independent of the other attributes. First, we fixed the other attributes at a desirable level and asked what amount of safety x_4 was such that $(x_4; 2500)$ was indifferent to $(1; 1,500,000)$. That is, x_4 people seriously injured or killed given an accident and 2500 people subjected to high noise levels is indifferent to one person seriously injured or killed and 1,500,000 subjected to a high noise level. After "converging," the amount of x_4 was chosen as 300. The exact number is not important for verifying the assumptions; we want to know whether it changes as the other four attributes vary. So we next set these four attributes at undesirable levels and asked the same question and again elicited 300 as a response.

Then we asked if this would generally be true for any values of the other four attributes, and the response was, "The answer would always be the same given that the other attributes were in a static condition." In fact, the respondent stated this would be the case concerning any tradeoffs between safety and noise. Thus, we concluded safety and noise were preferentially independent of the other attributes.

By using identical procedures, we verified that capacity and cost were preferentially independent of the remaining attributes, as were displacement and access time. By this time, the man answering the questions, an assistant to the Director of Airports, stated that ordinal preferences over any two attributes did not depend on the amounts of the other attributes. These conditions were then also verified with other staff members of SOP, including the Director of Airports.

The same general approach was used in verifying the utility independence assumptions, that X_i was utility independent of its complementary set $\bar{X}_i$ for all $i = 1, 2, \ldots, 6$. For example, consider whether access time X_3 was utility independent of $\bar{X}_3$. The other five attributes were set at desirable levels, and the conditional utility function over access time from 12 to 90 minutes (the range originally specified by SOP) was assessed. We found 62 minutes indifferent to a 50–50 lottery yielding either 12 or 90 minuutes. Then we changed the amounts of the $\bar{X}_3$ attributes to less preferred amounts and repeated the question. Again, an access time of 62 minutes was indifferent to a 50–50 lottery yielding either 12 or 90 minutes. A general question indicated this would be true for any fixed amounts of $\bar{X}_3$. We found that relative preferences for any consequences and lotteries involving uncertainties only about access time were indeed independent of the other five attributes.

This condition was verified for all six attributes with both the Director of Airports and members of his staff. In all of these verification procedures, an attempt was made not to lead the respondent to answers he would not have arrived at otherwise. Our opinion is that this was done successfully. Since preferences may vary with time, such questioning of the same people may lead to different conclusions at another point in time. However, the preferences indicated by the individuals questioned appeared to represent their "true" preferences at that time, and thus the assumptions we made were deemed appropriate for the problem.

8.6.3   Forms of the Utility Function

The main theoretical results used in obtaining the utility function were Theorems 6.1 and 6.2 given in Section 6.3. Informally, these results state that if each pair of attributes is preferentially independent of its complement, and if each attribute is utility independent of its complement, then $u(x_1, x_2, \ldots, x_6)$ is either an additive or a multiplicative function of the component utility functions $u_1(x_1), u_2(x_2), \ldots, u_6(x_6)$. Actually, as indicated in Section 6.3, this same result is implied by a much weaker set of assumptions, that is, only one attribute X_i needs to be utility independent of its complement and each pair of attributes including X_i needs to be preferentially independent of its complement. Therefore, many of the assumptions that were verified are redundant, and they can be thought of as consistency checks on the appropriateness of our results.

The exact form of the utility function u, scaled 0 to 1, is

$$
u(x_1, x_2, \ldots, x_6) = \sum_{i=1}^{6} k_i u_i(x_i) + k \sum_{i=1}^{6} \sum_{j>i} k_i k_j u_i(x_i) u_j(x_j)
$$
$$
+ k^2 \sum_{i=1}^{6} \sum_{j>i} \sum_{n>j} k_i k_j k_n u_i(x_i) u_j(x_j) u_n(x_n)
$$
$$
+ \cdots + k^5 k_1 k_2 k_3 k_4 k_5 k_6 u_1(x_1) u_2(x_2) \cdots u_6(x_6), \quad (8.3)
$$

where u_i is a utility function over X_i scaled from 0 to 1, k_i is a scaling factor for u_i, and k is another scaling constant. Each k_i must be between 0 and 1 and can be interpreted as the utility u assigned to a consequence with all its attributes except X_i set at their least preferable amount and X_i set at the most preferable amount.

The value of k can be found from the values of the k_i's. When $\sum k_i = 1$, then $k = 0$ and (8.3) reduces to the additive form

$$u(x_1, x_2, \ldots, x_6) = \sum_{i=1}^{6} k_i u_i(x_i). \tag{8.4}$$

When $\sum k_i \neq 1$, then $k \neq 0$ so we can multiply each side of (8.3) by k, add 1 to the results, and factor to get the multiplicative form

$$ku(x_1, x_2, \ldots, x_6) + 1 = \prod_{i=1}^{6} [kk_i u_i(x_i) + 1]. \tag{8.5}$$

8.6.4   Assessing the u_i's

Each single-attribute utility function was assessed using the techniques discussed in Chapter 4. Let us illustrate this by assessing preferences for access time.

First we obtained maximum and minimum values for access time. From probabilistic assessments of SOP, we found that the range should go from 12 minutes to 90 minutes, where shorter access times were preferred to longer ones. Thus, to remain consistent with our scaling convention where the utility functions ranged from 0 to 1, we set

$$u_3(90) = 0 \tag{8.6}$$

and

$$u_3(12) = 1. \tag{8.7}$$

From questions that were previously used to check whether X_3 was utility independent of $\bar{X}_3$, we found that 62 minutes was indifferent to a lottery, which we will denote by $\langle 12, 90 \rangle$, yielding either 12 or 90 minutes, each with probability 1/2. Hence, the utility assigned to 62 minutes, the certainty equivalent for the lottery, is

$$u_3(62) = .5u_3(12) + .5u_3(90) = .5 \tag{8.8}$$

Since 62 is greater than the expected access time 51 of the lottery $\langle 12, 90 \rangle$, this original assessment indicated that the utility function might exhibit risk aversion. In this context, risk aversion means that the expected amount $(x_3 + x_3')/2$ of any lottery $\langle x_3, x_3' \rangle$ would be preferred to that lottery. By asking several questions including specific lotteries, and then one concerning the general case, we found that the decision makers were

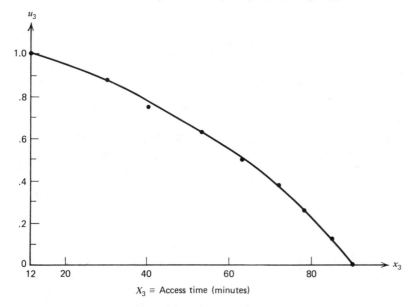

Fig. 8.4.   The utility function for access time.

risk averse in the attribute access time. This implied the utility function would be concave as indicated in Fig. 8.4.

By asking more questions to find certainty equivalents of additional lotteries, other points on u_3 were specified. For instance, we found 40 minutes indifferent to $\langle 12, 62 \rangle$ and 78 minutes indifferent to $\langle 62, 90 \rangle$, therefore

$$u_3(40) = .5u_3(12) + .5u_3(62) = .75, \qquad (8.9)$$

and

$$u_3(78) = .5u_3(62) + .5u_3(90) = .25. \qquad (8.10)$$

Then an exponential utility curve was fitted to the empirically assessed points.

At this stage, we did not immediately try to ascertain and exploit "higher-order" risk properties such as decreasing risk aversion. Such properties represent rather fine tunings in a multiattribute utility function relative to the scaling constants "weighting" the levels of the different attributes and more basic properties such as monotonicity and risk aversion of the separate u_i's. If, later in the analysis, it had turned out that the precise form of some of the u_i's were important, we would have returned to this aspect and reiterated our evaluation of alternatives. This did not happen to be the case.

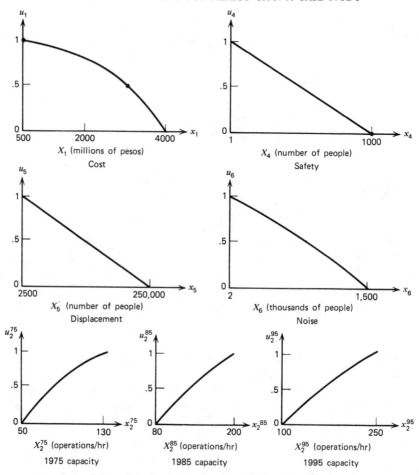

Fig. 8.5. The utility functions for the Mexico City Airport study.

Procedures similar to those described above were also used to assess utility functions for cost, safety, displacement, and noise. The results are illustrated in Fig. 8.5. However, as mentioned earlier, no single measure was found to combine capacities in different years. Thus, it was necessary to assess the capacity utility function u_2 differently.

Although the general shapes of the utility functions for access time, cost, and noise seem intuitive, the fact that the curves for safety and displacement are linear is not. For instance, concerning safety, we might expect that since governments usually abhor large numbers of deaths resulting from single tragedies the utility function for safety would be risk averse. The reason for this attitude is usually the political impact resulting from such tragedies. However, our measure of effectiveness in this problem was not meant to capture these political factors. Roughly speaking, if we say that each life is equally important, then alternatives with the same expected number of people killed or seriously injured should be equally undesirable in this respect. This was the attitude taken by SOP in the assessments, and so u_4 is linear.

It was important, before proceeding, to do consistency checks on the reasonableness of the exponential and linear utility functions. We did this by asking additional questions about the decision maker's preferences, and comparing his responses to the implications of the "fit" utility function. When they were consistent with each other, we developed more confidence in the utility function. When they were inconsistent, the inconsistencies were discussed, and part or all of the assessment repeated.

8.6.5 The Capacity Utility Function

Capacity x_2 is a vector $(x_2^{75}, x_2^{85}, x_2^{95})$, where x_2^{75} is the capacity in 1975, and so on.

The first step in assessing u_2 was to identify the minimum and maximum possible airport capacities for 1975, 1985, and 1995. There were 50, 80, 100 and 130, 200, 250 operations per hour, respectively. Clearly more capacity in any given year was preferred to less capacity, so to scale u_2 from 0 to 1, we set

$$u_2(50, 80, 100) = 0 \tag{8.11}$$

and

$$u_2(130, 200, 250) = 1. \tag{8.12}$$

We verified that each pair of capacity attributes was preferentially independent of the third, and that each attribute was utility independent of the other two.

Thus we know from Theorems 6.1. and 6.2. that either

$$u_2(x_2^{75}, x_2^{85}, x_2^{95}) = \sum_{j=75,85,95} c_i u_2^j(x_2^j) \tag{8.13}$$

or

$$cu_2(x_2^{75}, x_2^{85}, x_2^{95}) + 1 = \prod_{j=75,85,95} [cc_j u_2^j(x_2^j) + 1], \tag{8.14}$$

where the u_2^j are the utility functions over X_2^j assessed on a 0 to 1 scale as illustrated in Fig. 8.5 and c and the c_j are scaling constants. Notice that the forms of (8.13) and (8.14) are analogous to the utility functions expressed in (8.4) and 8.5). Since the following discussion concerns how the k_i's and k in (8.5) are assessed, we will not indicate the assessment of the c_j's and c in (8.14) since the procedures are identical.

8.6.6 Assessing the k_i Scaling Factors

To illustrate the technique for assessing the k_i scaling factors, let us take cost X_1 as an example. We asked the decision makers to compare a consequence with cost at its most preferred amount, and all the attributes at their least preferred amount, to a lottery yielding the consequences with all attributes at their most preferred amount with probability p or the consequence with all attributes at their least preferred amount with probability $1-p$. The object is to find the value of p, call it p_1, such that the decision maker is indifferent between the lottery and the consequence. Then, as shown in Section 6.6, by using $u(\mathbf{x})$ from either (8.4) or (8.5) and equating expected utilities, k_1 must equal p_1.

Using this procedure involving questions concerning lotteries, we arrived at an initial estimate for the k_i values. Then we used nonprobabilistic questions as consistency checks. For example, we set all attributes at their least desirable level and asked, "Would you prefer to have capacity or cost changed to its most desirable level?" Capacity was the response implying k_2, the coefficient of capacity utility, had to be greater than k_1, the coefficient of cost utility. Then we found a level of capacity, call it x_2^I, that was indifferent to the best level of cost, denoted by x_1^*. Then using either (8.4) or (8.5), we see that $k_2 u_2(x_2^I)$ must equal k_1. Since we assessed u_2, this gives us a relationship between k_1 and k_2. Pairwise comparison of the k_i's in this manner provided many consistency checks, redundant with others, and forced a readjustment of the k_i values. After several iterations, we ended up using the values of k_i indicated in Table 8.1.

Table 8.1
Scaling Factors for the Mexico City Airport Study

Attribute X_i	Scaling Factor k_i
$X_1 = $ cost	.48
$X_2 = $ capacity	.60
$X_3 = $ access time	.10
$X_4 = $ safety	.35
$X_5 = $ displacement	.18
$X_6 = $ noise	.18

8.6.7   Assessing Parameter k

Since the sum of the k_i is 1.89, we know the utility function is multiplicative rather than additive; it is additive only if $\sum k_i = 1$. Therefore the value of k in (8.5) must be determined by evaluating (8.5) at $(x_1^*, x_2^*, \ldots, x_6^*)$ where x_i^* is the most preferred amount of X_i. This gives us

$$ku(x_1^*, x_2^*, \ldots, x_6^*) + 1 = \prod_{i=1}^{6} [kk_i u_i(x_i^*) + 1], \qquad (8.15)$$

but, from our scaling conventions, we know both $u(x_1^*, x_2^*, \ldots, x_6^*)$ is 1 and the $u_i(x_i^*)$ are all 1 so

$$k + 1 = (kk_1 + 1)(kk_2 + 1) \cdots (kk_6 + 1). \qquad (8.16)$$

Since the k_i are known, parameter k can be evaluated by solving (8.16). As shown in the Appendix 6B, since $\sum k_i > 1$, the value that k must assume is the solution to (8.16) such that $-1 < k < 0$. Using the k_i values from Table 8.1, we found $k = -.877$. Of course, if this were redone from scratch a new k would be found. But it would probably fall closer to $-.80$ than to $.00$ or to $+.80$. In the final analysis, it is important to do sensitivity studies on k and the k_i's.

8.6.8   The Utility Function

Procedures identical to those just illustrated were used to evaluate the c_j and c in (8.14). It was found that $c_1 = .3$, $c_2 = .5$, $c_3 = .4$, and $c = -.46$. These parameters, together with Table 8.1 and $k = -.877$ and the utility functions illustrated in Fig. 8.4 and 8.5, represent the information necessary to specify the utility function $u(x_1, x_2, \ldots, x_6)$. Section 8.7 describes how it was used.

8.7   THE ANALYSIS

A computer was programmed to assist in evaluating the alternatives. Computationally, the program was quite simple: given any set of probability distributions and a utility function, it calculated the expected utility for specified alternatives.

To keep the calculations at a reasonable number, as mentioned earlier, many alternatives were eliminated before going through expected utility calculations. For instance, since military aircraft represent a relatively insignificant amount of the total air traffic, most alternatives differing only in terms of the airport for military operations were not considered separately. Second, alternatives that shifted certain types of aircraft from the Texcoco site to Zumpango and back again at a later date were excluded.

8.7.1 The Input–Output Display

Graphical input–output consoles were used as an efficient and accessible system for sensitivity analyses and communicating results of the study. This capability was used by the Secretaria de Obras Publicas, and could also be used by the other interested parties to examine the relative merits of alternative developmental policies. The input–output system allowed any user to use his own probability and utility estimates for evaluating any specified alternatives. There were two options for doing this. Option 1 provided the standard estimates that the SOP used in evaluating the alternatives on the console screen. To change these, one just typed in the changes over the SOP estimates. This option was particularly useful for sensitivity analyses. Option 2 allowed the user to enter his own estimates without seeing any others.

The probabilistic estimates of possible impact could be altered by changing the upper and lower bounds on these impacts. For instance, as illustrated in Fig. 8.3, SOP's lower and upper bounds on the possible number of people subjected to noise above 90 CNR (composite noise rating) in 1975 were 400,000 and 800,000, respectively. Merely by typing on the console, the overall effect on strategy could be seen if these were 600,000 and 1,200,000.

To alter the utility function, we changed the scaling factors listed in Table 8.1. Because the meaning of these constants can be easily misunderstood (as discussed in Section 5.9), and because of the difficulty in specifying a consistent set of estimates, a short subroutine was developed to assist the user. This routine essentially asked the user on the screen the same questions that we asked SOP in initially assessing the scaling constants. Once a reasonable consistency was achieved among the k_i's, the constant k in (8.3) was calculated. If $k = 0$, the additive form (8.4) was used, and if $k \neq 0$, the multiplicative utility function was used to evaluate strategies. As was the case with the general shape of the probability densities, the individual utility functions u_i could not be changed by graphical input–output. These changes required adjustments in the programs. However, although important, these changes represent fine tunings relative to the options provided for graphically.

Another particularly useful feature of the computer program was a routine that calculated certainty equivalents. Using this routine, the overall possible impact of any alternative could be reduced to an equivalent impact described by a vector of certainty equivalents. Since we assumed probabilistic independence* and first-order utility independence (i.e., each X_i is utility independent of its complementary set), from the marginal probability distribution of X_i and the component utility function u_i, it is possible to define the certain equivalent $\hat{x}_i$ by

$$u_i(\hat{x}_i) = E[u_i(\tilde{x}_i)], \qquad i = 1, 2 \ldots, 6. \tag{8.17}$$

Notice that the certainty equivalent $\hat{x}_i$ is independent of the possible impacts on other attributes. Also notice that the certainty equivalent vector $\hat{\mathbf{x}} = (\hat{x}_1, \ldots, \hat{x}_6)$ does not commit one to any determination of the scaling constants k_i's or k.

If two alternatives A and B are reduced to certainty equivalent vector impacts $\hat{\mathbf{x}}_A$ and $\hat{\mathbf{x}}_B$, it is easy to check for dominance. Also, for example, one could investigate exactly how large a change in the impact on attribute X_i of alternative A would be required before it would be less preferred than alternative B.

8.7.2 Effective Strategies

Of the alternatives we did evaluate using expected utility, the top 10, according to SOP, are indicated in Table 8.2. In the table, the expected utilities are calculated on a scale from 0 to 100, where zero utility was assigned to a hypothetical alternative generated by taking the least desirable probability distribution for each attribute from the set of all alternatives. The utility value of 100 units was assigned to a hypothetical alternative generated by taking the most desirable probability distribution for each attribute from the set of all alternatives. On this scale, the alternative of keeping all aircraft in Texcoco in all three years has an expected utility 5.20.

By looking at Table 8.2, it is clear that two types of strategies are effective. One type might be categorized as the "all Zumpango" alternative and represents building a major new airport at Zumpango as soon as possible. The alternatives in the table involving both international and domestic aircraft operating at Zumpango in all three years make up this category. The other type of effective strategy is the "phased development at Zumpango" characterized by either international or domestic aircraft

---

* If $k = 0$ (or close to zero), then u can be taken to be (approximately) additive and only the marginal probability distributions are of relevance. If $k \neq 0$, and joint probabilistic dependence is warranted, then the analysis by certainty equivalents must be considerably modified. We could, however, employ the concept of "*conditional* certainty equivalence" to some advantage. This was not done.

Table 8.2

The Best Ten Alternatives

Alternative							
1975		1985		1995		Expected	
Z	T	Z	T	Z	T	Utility	Ran
D	IMG	ID	MG	ID	MG	91.23	1
IDMG	—	IDMG	—	IDMG	—	90.90	2
I	DMG	ID	MG	ID	MG	90.79	3
ID	MG	ID	MG	ID	MG	89.30	4
ID	MG	IDMG	—	IDMG	—	88.10	5
ID	MG	ID	MG	IDMG	—	86.75	6
I	DMG	IDMG	—	IDMG	—	86.55	7
IG	DM	IDMG	—	IDMG	—	86.19	8
DG	IM	IDMG	—	IDMG	—	86.17	9
D	IMG	IDMG	—	IDMG	—	85.60	10

To help read the table, the alternative ranked 1 is *D*omestic aircraft at *Z*umpango with *I*nternation
*M*ilitary, and *G*eneral aircraft at *T*excoco in 1975; and *I*nternational and *D*omestic at *Z*umpan
with *M*ilitary and *G*eneral at *T*excoco in 1985 and 1995.

operating in Zumpango in 1975 and then both by 1985 and 1995. All
strategies that included keeping a part of the international or domestic
traffic operating out of Texcoco through 1985 did not appear competitive
in terms of effectiveness with the two types of strategies outlined above.
Of course, these expected utility evaluations depend on two types of
judgmental inputs: probability and utility assessments. The ones we used
were those of officials of SOP and presumably, if the same analysis were
to be made with inputs from officials of the Secretaria de Communicaciones y Transportes, another ranking of strategic alternatives
would result. We will discuss more about these reconciliation problems
later.

8.7.3 Use of the Analysis

As we indicated earlier in the chapter, the original purpose of the work
described here was to identify effective strategies (as measured by our six
measures of effectiveness) for developing the airport facilities of Mexico
City. It was not to indicate what action should be taken by the government of Mexico in 1971 to meet its needs. Once the "effective strategies"
had been identified, the problem shifted to this second question: What
action should be initially implemented?

So far, the formal analysis has included only master plans defining actions for a 30-year period. A more appropriate course would be to make some initial decision and then, based on subsequent events, to revise strategies as necessary. Furthermore, any study that is designed to aid in the selection of an airport development policy for Mexico City must include factors such as political preferences and community priorities. This was the task undertaken in a dynamic analysis of development strategies to be discussed in Section 8.8.

8.8 THE DYNAMIC ANALYSIS

The purpose of the dynamic model was to decide what governmental action should be taken in 1971 that would best serve the overall objective of providing quality air service to Mexico City for the remainder of the century. This model assumed that the second step in the decision process could be taken in 1975 or 1976, at the end of the current president's six-year term. The action taken then would depend both on the action taken in 1971 and the critical events that might occur in the interim. Our analysis of the dynamic model was much less formal than the one developed for the static model, primarily because of time pressures and the general complexity of the situation.

8.8.1 Alternatives for 1971

We first identified (using common sense) the reasonable alternatives available to the government in 1971. These alternatives differed in the degrees of commitment to immediate construction at the two sites. We chose only four levels of commitment (minimum, low, moderate, and high) giving us the 16 alternatives exhibited in Fig. 8.6. Actually, each nominal case in the figure represents a class of specific alternatives. We wanted to do a first-cut analysis to decide which classes of alternatives were sufficiently viable to be examined in more detail. Note that the two strategies defined by the static analysis could be compatible with all the nominal dynamic options except 11, 12, 15, and 16.

Next, we defined the alternatives in greater detail. Briefly, the alternatives at Texcoco (for the period 1971–1975) were defined as follows:

Minimum: Maintain and introduce safety equipment only.

Low: Extend the runways, upgrade support facilities (such as terminals), do all routine maintenance, and introduce new safety equipment.

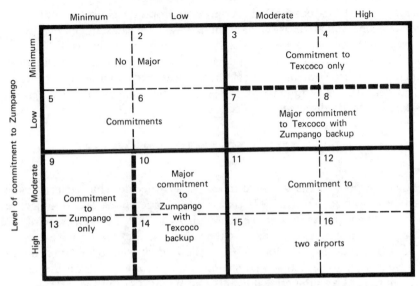

Fig. 8.6. The 16 nominal dynamic alternatives for 1971.

Moderate: In addition to that done with a low strategy, buy and prepare land for building a. new runway and expand passenger facilities.

High: Build a new runway and passenger facilities, improve the airport access—in short, build a totally new airport at Texcoco.

Similarly, for Zumpango, we defined the commitment levels:

Minimum: At most, buy land at Zumpango.

Low: Buy land, build one jet runway and very modest passenger facilities.

Moderate: Buy land, build a first jet runway and plan others, build major passenger facilities, and construct an access road connection to the main Mexico City highway.

High: Build multiple jet runways, major passenger facilities, and access roads; that is, build a large new airport at Zumpango.

8.8.2 Objectives

We identified four major objectives that were important in choosing a strategy for airport development: effectiveness, political consequences, externalities, and flexibility of the various alternatives. The components of the "effectiveness" attribute are indicated by the six measures of effectiveness covered in the static model. The political consequences were those important to the President, since he was the principal decision maker, involving the political effects that would be felt by SOP, SCT, and the Presidencia. Flexibility concerned the range of options open to the President at the second stage of the decision-making process: What freedom would he realistically have at the end of his tenure in modifying his earlier 1971 stance after learning about the intervening uncertain events? Finally, all other important considerations were lumped together as "externalities." These included the amount of access roads needed, the distribution of federal expenditures between the Mexico City region and the rest of the country, the distribution of expenditures for airports and other uses, regional development away from central Mexico City, and the national prestige associated with new airport facilities.

8.8.3 Possible Scenarios

To gain insight into the meanings and implications of each of the classes of alternatives, detailed scenarios were outlined for each. These included (1) the consideration of important and critical events that could occur in the period 1971–1976, and possibly affect the best strategy in 1976, (2) the likelihood of their occurrences, (3) the strategic reaction to each intervening event complex, and (4) the possible eventual consequences for each act–event–reaction path. The events involved safety factors and air disasters; shifts in demand in terms of both passengers and aircraft; technological innovations, such as noise suppressors, better runway construction on marshy ground; changes in citizen attitudes toward the environment; and changes in priorities, such as national willingness to have government funds used for major airport construction. Figure 8.7 depicts a schematic representation of one possible scenario.

In each of the scenarios, the manner in which the 1971 strategy should be altered in 1976 to account for the critical events listed above was defined. For instance, if we originally chose strategy 6, then a reasonable response to increased numbers of landings and thus decreased safety, in addition to increased consideration about the impact of noise and air pollution in Mexico City, would be to hasten the building at Zumpango and make it the Mexico City International Airport. On the other hand, response to a rather constant demand on the Texcoco facilities and a shift in public priorities toward more medical and educational support from the government, might be to postpone additional construction at Zumpango until a later date.

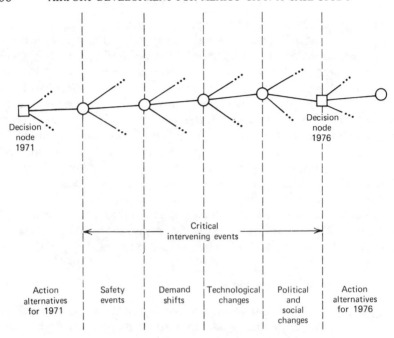

Fig. 8.7. Schematic representation of a typical scenario.

Suppose that strategy 13 was initially chosen in 1971, and that air demand greatly increased, environmental concerns of citizens grew, and no technological innovations were developed favorable to Texcoco (e.g., runway technology). Then in 1976, the government could either easily switch to a two-airport option or continue to develop and expand Zumpango. However, if strategy 13 were chosen and demand did not increase as predicted, and so on, the govenment might find by 1976 that it had a "white elephant" in that a new airport existed but was not needed or used. The political effects might be very bad and little flexibility would be available for "correcting" the situation.

The main purpose of these exercises was to indicate better what the overall impact of the 1971 decision might be. This was very important before beginning the evaluation process described next. It should be obvious that certain options in 1971 eliminate the possibility of other options in 1976, regardless of the events that occur in the interim.

8.8.4   First Evaluation of Nominal Alternatives

The 16 alternatives, defined in Fig. 8.6, were evaluated in a series of extensive discussions among the Directors of the Department of Airports and of the Center for Computation and Statistics, other staff members in SOP, and ourselves.

A preliminary evaluation indicated that 7 of the 16 alternatives could be discarded. Alternative 1 did not provide for maintaining the present service levels due to anticipated increases in demand. Alternatives 7, 8, 11, 12, 15, and 16 were undesirable because a high level of commitment to Texcoco in 1971 would make it the major airport for the near future and remove the need for simultaneous construction at Zumpango. Finally, since the location of the new runway specified by the moderate Texcoco commitment would require new passenger facilities, option 3 was essentially the same as option 4. Hence, they were coalesced into a single alternative, which we label 4.

The next stage of the analysis involved having the members of SOP rank the remaining broadly defined alternatives on the attributes of flexibility, political effects, externalities and effectiveness, as described before. The particular rankings, which were reached by open discussions, represent the consensus judgment. When some alternatives were "indistinguishable" on a particular attribute, they were assigned the same ranking. For the political considerations and externalities, the assessments on the components were first carried out, and then the overall ranking for these attributes was established.* The ranking of the alternatives according to effectiveness was provided directly by results of the static model.

The results of the first ranking effort are shown in Table 8.3, where the smaller numbers represent the better rankings. From this table it can be seen that alternatives 4, 9, 13, and 14 are each dominated by others on the basis of their overall rankings for the four main measures of effectiveness. Alternative 6, for instance, is better than alternative 14 in terms of all four of the measures. Therefore alternative 14, and similarly, alternatives 4, 9, and 13, can be dropped from further consideration. The alternatives that were not dominated are those represented by the nominal cases 2, 5, 6, and 10. It is important to note here, however, that before we actually discarded dominated alternatives we engaged in a devil's advocate procedure: we tried to give the benefit of reasonable doubt to the impending noncontenders to see whether they could be resurrected to a place of contention: they could not.

---

* Unfortunately it is not clear how the overall rankings on political and externality effects are related to the component rankings for these composite attributes. There are several reasons for this: first, the component attributes are not complete; second, rankings mask intensities of preference; third, several people were involved in the process and because of lack of time, not enough attention was paid to the component rankings. With more time we would have examined those details in more depth.

Table 8.3

Preliminary Evaluation of Plausible Governmental Options for 1971 by Rank Order

Attributes

Alter-native	Flexi-bility	Political Effects on				Externalities due to					Effectiveness
		Presi-dencia	SOP	SCT	Overall	Pres-tige	Reg. Dev.	Bal. of Fed. Exp.	Roads	Overall	
2	1	1	8	2	3	4	4	1	1	3	7
4ᵃ	7	4	5	1	4	1	4	6	3	7	8
5	2	3	6	4	3	3	3	2	1	1	3
6	3	2	7	3	2	3	3	3	1	3	1
9ᵃ	4	6	3	6	5	2	2	4	2	2	4
10	5	5	4	5	1	2	2	5	2	4	5
13ᵃ	6	8	1	8	7	1	1	6	4	5	2
14ᵃ	8	7	2	7	6	1	1	7	4	6	6

ᵃ Alternatives dominated by 2, 5, 6, or 10 on overall ranking of four major attributes.

8.8.5· Final Analysis of Dynamic Options

To refine the analysis of the possible governmental decisions, it was necessary to define the remaining contending alternatives more precisely. This was done as follows:

2. At Zumpango, do no more than buy land for an airport. At Texcoco, extend the two main runways and the aircraft apron; construct freight and parking facilities, and a new control tower. Do not build any new passenger terminals.

5A. Build one jet runway, some terminal facilities and a minor access road connection at Zumpango. Buy enough land for a major international airport. At Texcoco, perform only routine maintenance and make safety improvements.

5B. Same as alternative 5A, except buy just enough land for the current Zumpango construction.

6. Extend one runway at Texcoco and make other improvements enumerated in alternative 2. Buy land for a major international airport at Zumpango, and construct one runway with some passenger and access facilities.

10. Same implications for Texcoco as alternative 6. Build two jet runways with major passenger facilities and access roads to Zumpango.

These five alternatives were examined more closely and reranked. The results are given in Table 8.4. Proceeding as before, we can quickly see that alternative 6 dominates 10, and alternatives 2, 5A, and 6 all dominate 5B. Thus the three remaining viable alternatives are 2, 5A, and 6.

Table 8.4

Final Evaluation of Governmental Options for 1971

Alternative	Attributes			
	Flexi-bility	Political Effects	Exter-nalities	Effec-tiveness
2	1	4	4	3
5A	2	3	3	3
5B[a]	4	5	5	4
6	3	1	1	1
10[a]	5	2	2	1

[a] Alternatives dominated by 2, 5A, or 6 on overall ranking of four major attributes.

The relative advantages of these three options were, finally, subjectively weighed by the SOP personnel as follows. Alternative 6 ranks better on effectiveness, externalities, and political considerations than either 2 or 5A, Although it is worse in terms of relative flexibility, it does allow the President to react effectively to all the critical events that might occur between 1971 and 1976, when the second stage of the airport decision could be made. Thus, in the opinion of the members of SOP working on this problem, alternative 6 was chosen as the best strategy.

8.9   IMPACT OF THE RESULTS

Based on the 1965–1967 study by SOP that recommended moving the International Airport to Zumpango as soon as possible, as well as indications early in this study, it was clear that some members of SOP believed that a major move to Zumpango was still the most effective strategy. The static analysis, using SOP's own estimates and preferences, indicated that a phased development involving a gradual shift toward Zumpango appeared equally as good. Once political considerations, flexibility of the policy, and externalities were accounted for along with effectiveness in the dynamic analysis of alternatives open to the government in 1971, it was evident that the "phased development at Zumpango" policy was better than an "all Zumpango" policy.

Looking at the implications of *their* evaluations, the SOP staff was very surprised and bewildered. Using their own preferences over measures of effectiveness that they knew were relevant for a realistic set of options, they agreed that alternatives 13 and 14, which were most consistent with their strongly held position, were completely dominated. Note also that the position of SCT, being most consistent with alternative 4 was also dominated.

This glaring inconsistency had a profound impact on many individuals within SOP. They rethought their position, analyzing in their own minds how this "strange" implication came about. As they understood the implication better, they gained some confidence in the result. With the final analysis of nondominated alternatives and additional group discussions of the dynamic analysis, SOP adopted a new flexible position, exemplified by an initial choice of option 6 in 1971. Thus a very strange thing happened: an analysis undertaken for advocacy purposes (i.e., to justify going all-out to Zumpango) turned out to convince the sponsors of the analysis that perhaps a more flexible stance was really in the best interest of Mexico.

8.9.1   The Ensuing Political Process

SOP recommended a "phased development" strategy to the President in December 1971. Specifically, it was suggested that land be acquired at Zumpango, that a major runway and modest terminal facilities be planned for construction during President Echeverria's term. It was also proposed that he reserve until 1976 a more detailed decision on how the airport facilities for Mexico City should be developed. This recommendation represented a major change in SOP's posture from the 1967 study. The previous recommendations of SOP were for master plans specifying what should be done at various points in time over the next 30 years without regard to the unfolding of relevant uncertain events. Thinking in terms of adaptive dynamic strategies rather than in terms of master plans played a pivotal role in our analysis.

As the last stage of our consulting activities, we, in collaboration with our clients, examined in some detail the steps that had to be taken in order to *implement* the newly developed stance of SOP. This required developing a strategy for the planning of technical documents, informal presentations to key government agencies, private meetings, and possible public announcements. Since we were not certain of the reactions of SCT and the Presidencia we mapped out some contingency plans that themselves were more in the spirit of an adaptive dynamic analysis than of a master plan. We are sure that you will understand that this chapter, however, is not the place to discuss the details of these politically sensitive considerations.

The analyses described in this chapter were completed in early September 1971. In late 1971, Ing. Jauffred and Ing. Dovali, together with Secretary Bracamontes of SOP, presented the basic ideas of this study to the President of Mexico. Members of SCT and the Presidencia, including the respective secretaries of these ministries, were also present at this meeting.

The meeting did not eliminate all differences of opinion concerning the two basic points of view—remain at Texcoco or move to Zumpango— positions that had long been established. After the meeting, the President requested that SOP, SCT, and the Presidencia work out philosophical disagreements on the airport issue, as well as technical and financial details of further developing the airport facilities of the Mexico city area. Because of its complexity and importance, the process of working out the details was very time consuming. By the middle of 1974, no concrete decision had been made. However, it was a different situation in 1974 than in 1971. In 1971, the basic issue was whether the main Mexico City Airport should be at Texcoco or Zumpango. In 1974, the issue seemed to be when the Zumpango site would be the main airport—next year, in 5 years, or 20. Support for this came from the fact that land for an airport at Zumpango was expropriated by SOP, who holds this authority, in early 1974. Presumably, whatever decision evolves by the government of Mexico will be done with greater awareness of the relative influence of the different attributes and of the dynamic issues.

ACKNOWLEDGMENT

It was a pleasure for us to work with F. J. Jauffred, Director of the Center for Computation and Statistics, and F. Dovali, Head of the Department of Airports, and their staffs in the Secretaria de Obras Publicas, and with Richard deNeufville of M. I. T., who added both engineering know-how as well as prodigious language skills to our consulting team. We felt that our colleagues in SOP contributed greatly to the integrity of the study by weighing seriously their answers to vexing value questions. Throughout they demonstrated a healthy skepticism at critical points, demanded meaningful explanations of the process of analysis, and were flexible enough to modify previously advocated positions.

CHAPTER 9

Preferences over Time

by Richard F. Meyer*

The consequences of a decision often do not all occur simultaneously. Thus a decision maker may have to consider his preferences for some consequence x at a time t_1, and a consequence y at a time t_2. This indicates the distinguishing characteristic of time preferences: the consequences accrue at two or more points in the future. A typical example is the stream of income and cash flow resulting from a long-term investment. In this case it may be natural to divide time into discrete periods (e.g., months or quarters), and to use $(x_1, x_2, \dots, x_n)$ to indicate a time stream of consequences, where x_i indicates the consequences in time period i. Alternatively, we may have a continuous stream of consequences, which we shall denote by $x(\cdot)$, where $x(t)$ is the consequence at time t. For example, in consumption problems $x(t)$ might represent a decision maker's rate of consumption at time t for each component of a commodity bundle. Because (1) many continuous-time problems can be reasonably formulated as discrete-time problems without oversimplifying the issues involved, and (2) the development of procedures for analyzing continuous-time problems are analogous to those for discrete ones, we emphasize the discrete-time problems in this chapter.

Two important features affecting time preferences are (1) the timing of the resolution of uncertainties and (2) the horizon to be used. Both of these considerations, discussed in Section 9.1, influence greatly the appropriateness of a given approach for specifying one's preferences. The most common method of ranking temporal flows is to discount at a standard interest rate. This method, its pros and cons, and some generalizations are considered in Section 9.2. In our terminology, these methods provide a value function. Next, in Sections 9.3–9.7, we discuss utility

* Sections 9.1 to 9.3 draw heavily on an unpublished manuscript by Ralph Keeney and Howard Raiffa.

functions for multiperiod consequences, including uncertain-horizon problems. These value functions and utility functions seem appropriate for classes of problems where all the uncertainties are resolved immediately after the decision is made, but in certain cases of deferred resolution, some important elements may be missing in these formulations. These are emphasized in Section 9.8 on the time resolution of uncertainty. Throughout the chapter, much of the discussion will focus on attributes that are monetary in nature or on consumption. However, at times we will examine the appropriateness of the existing methodology for formalizing time preferences for other attributes, such as environmental impacts or health consequences, which are inherently nonmonetary.

There is no attempt in this chapter to review systematically the literature on preferences over time. The interested reader may refer to Koopmans (1960), Koopmans et al. (1964), Lancaster (1963), Pollard (1969), and Bell (1974a) for a variety of other approaches to the problem, as well as a guide to further references.

9.1 CHARACTERISTICS OF THE TIME PROBLEM

The time problem is abstracted as follows. The decision maker must choose among alternatives, each of which will eventually result in a time stream of consequences. We designate X_1 as a vector attribute useful for describing consequences in the current period, period one. Similarly $X_2, X_3, \ldots$ denote vector attributes for periods 2, 3, and so on. A specific consequence of any decision can then be designated as $\mathbf{x} = (x_1, x_2, x_3, \ldots)$.

An important characteristic of the temporal problem is the horizon: How far into the future should we take the consequence stream into account? The answer depends a great deal on the decision maker and on the context of the problem. For instance, if a 60-year-old corporation president is considering a merger decision, the overall impact of the decision may be felt long after he has retired from his post, although the impact on him may end with his retirement. However, the firm may be expected to "last forever" and thus, as the representative of the firm in the merger decision, he may effectively want to consider an infinite time horizon. Consequences in 50 years may be very important. Other examples of problems with very long, effectively infinite, horizons are decisions by governments on the licensing and siting of nuclear power plants or the licensing of various drugs.

This same company president may be faced with a decision how to expand his marketing activities into a new area. He could either build a manufacturing facility in the new area now and make the area more or less self-sufficient or else import products from the current manufacturing facilities now and build a plant in the new market area in a few years. He and all his "advisors" feel it is a foregone conclusion that before five years are up, they will be operating a separate manufacturing facility in the new area. Furthermore, exactly when, in the next four years, this facility is built will not affect future marketing performance of the company in either their current market or the new one, although it may affect the productive life of the new plant, for example, through changes in technology. Subject to all these conditions, it is very appropriate to use a finite horizon of five years in evaluating the different alternatives. Thus, a consequence might be $\mathbf{x} = (x_1, x_2, \ldots, x_5, x_6)$, where x_5 denotes the consequences in the fifth year from now, which ends in five years' time, and x_6 is an end-position "state," reflecting for example the technology and age of the new plant.

Often it is easier, for one reason or another, to replace a finite horizon by an infinite horizon, or vice versa. In some of these cases, simply truncating an infinite time stream or extending a finite one in some specified manner may have little impact on the results of the analysis. In deciding whether to use such an approximation, we should, of course, conduct a sensitivity analysis of the impact of changes of the horizon.

The crucial problem of the time resolution of uncertainty can be well illustrated with a simple example. A fair coin will be tossed: heads you will receive $10,000 five years from now and tails you receive nothing. How much would you have to be paid *now* for certain in lieu of the option? Clearly it would matter to most people whether the coin were tossed tomorrow, providing immediate resolution of the uncertainties, or tossed five years from now, giving delayed resolution. Most individuals would rather have immediate than delayed resolution, and in fact, earlier resolution of the lottery would generally be preferred to later resolution in all cases. Surely an analysis of this problem must consider more than the monetary consequences ($10,000 or $0) and the probabilities (.5 and .5) since these are the same in both the immediate and delayed resolution versions of the problem.

Obviously the time of resolution of uncertainty is important in more complex problems involving in each time period multiattribute consequences and multiple-action alternatives. This stems from two factors. First of all, if there is a difference between the time of resolution and the time the consequences are felt, we can take measures to prepare for the consequences to come. Second, we no longer have to worry about uncertainties once they are resolved, and so earlier resolution shortens the period of anxiety.

An issue related to the time of resolution of uncertainty is the "present perception of future utility." How can we account for our imperfect knowledge of changing tastes? This problem is very important in personal decision making as well as in firms and governments. For example, an airport built near a city to satisfy demands for easy access in the 1950s may face tremendous public relations problems with residents due to noise and pollution in the 1970s. A closely related problem is how to account for the ever-changing perception of future opportunities: the choice of job after college may limit our future options and lead to closed doors in a field only discovered to be interesting at a later date. Clearly one approach to the problem is to express explicitly the uncertainty of future preferences at the time the decision is made. Large uncertainties about future preferences for consequences, as well as about the consequences themselves, increase the importance of providing for future flexibility in actions taken now.

9.2 THE CERTAINTY CASE: VALUE FUNCTIONS OVER TIME STREAMS

Let us assume that a decision maker has to choose between two alternatives, one leading to consequence $x = (x_1, x_2, \ldots, x_n)$ and the other to consequence $y = (y_1, y_2, \ldots, y_n)$, where x_i (and y_i) indicates the consequence in the ith year from now. The fact that we have assumed n time periods for both x and y is no limitation, since the consequence in a given year can be assumed to be empty. The question of which alternative to choose boils down to whether x is preferred to y. In general, as indicated previously, the consequence in any given year may include many nonmonetary factors as well as monetary ones. However, for discussion purposes, let us assume that all the necessary assumptions for "costing-out" nonmonetary variables discussed in Chapter 3 hold, so x and y can be considered as streams of monetary payments and rewards, that is, cash flows. Then, if a cash flow in a given period is positive, the decision maker may use part of this cash flow for consumption (or for dividend payments and bonuses in the case of a corporation, or for grants in the case of a foundation) and part for further investment.

The usual suggested procedure is to discount the stream, using some standard interest rate or (opportunity) cost of capital and the justification of the procedure is based on the observation that money today can be used to make money tomorrow (sometimes supplemented with the specious argument that consumption today is sweeter than consumption tomorrow). If the x_i's and y_j's are uncertain, then several different techniques are suggested in practice: (1) discount the expected cash flows in each period, with possibly a higher discount rate to account for uncertainty, (2) discount certainty equivalents at the certainty discount rate, (3) discount utilities at some rate, (4) discount the various possible certainty streams that could arise at the certainty rate, assess a utility for such present values, and weight these utilities by the respective probabilities of the streams. These approaches will now be discussed from the vantage point of the results developed in this book.

9.2.1 The Net Present Value

A first step in evaluating time streams under certainty might be to assess a value function over all possible streams. Then, of course, if he had perfect information, a decision maker should choose the alternative leading to the largest value. Even when there is uncertainty—and this is the usual case—a value function can be a very useful part of the procedure to obtain a utility function as illustrated in Section 5.1. Let us therefore assume certainty and proceed with an example to illustrate the net present value concept.

Suppose we have the monetary stream $\mathbf{x} \equiv (x_1, x_2, x_3, x_4)$, where x_1 indicates the flow this year, x_2 the flow next year, and so on. We can engage in the procedure of successive reductions discussed earlier in Chapter 3. If x_4 is reduced to zero, what compensating change must be made in x_3 to maintain indifference? In other words, we ask for a number $\hat{x}_3$ so that the two streams

$$(x_1, x_2, x_3, x_4) \quad \text{and} \quad (x_1, x_2, \hat{x}_3, 0) \tag{9.1}$$

are indifferent. Presumably $\hat{x}_3$ will depend on x_3 and x_4; but it also may depend on x_1 and x_2. Suppose $x_4 > 0$ and $(\hat{x}_3 - x_3) > 0$. We could use some of the excess $(\hat{x}_3 - x_3)$ for investment in year 3 and some for consumption. Now even if the x_i's are certain, we may *not be certain* about the investment opportunities in year 3. Furthermore, even if the two streams in (9.1) are indifferent it does not follow that the decision maker would follow the same consumption and investment choice in year 2—yes we mean 2!

All these observations notwithstanding, we can still ask the decision maker to come up with a number $\hat{x}_3$ that makes him indifferent, but we must recognize that this assessment might involve consideration by the decision maker of external factors in the environment that are themselves *uncertain.*

Next we seek a number $\hat{x}_2$ such that

$$(x_1, x_2, \hat{x}_3, 0) \quad \text{and} \quad (x_1, \hat{x}_2, 0, 0)$$

are indifferent. Again $\hat{x}_2$ may depend on the possibly uncertain investment opportunities available in year 2. Finally we get an $\hat{x}_1$ such that

$$(x_1, \hat{x}_2, 0, 0) \qquad \text{and} \qquad (\hat{x}_1, 0, 0, 0)$$

are indifferent. By transitivity we now have indifference between

$$(x_1, x_2, x_3, x_4) \qquad \text{and} \qquad (\hat{x}_1, 0, 0, 0).$$

The amount $\hat{x}_1$ will be referred to as the (generalized) *net present value* of the certain stream (x_1, x_2, x_3, x_4). If we accept the very weak assumption that more money is preferred to less money, the generalized net present value is itself a value function for the entire time stream.

Note that we have not made any special assumptions in obtaining $\hat{x}_1$ concerning the manner one trades off consequences in periods i and $i+1$. However, if there are many streams to be evaluated, which is almost always the case when uncertainty is present, the effort of obtaining a net present value for each stream is hopelessly large unless some simplifying preferential assumptions of the type introduced in Chapter 3 are exploited. The usual manner in which this is done is to assume discounting of money in the future, usually at a constant rate. We shall investigate this procedure in the next subsection, but let us first discuss a couple of variations on the above theme of successive reductions.

In the above discussion we sought to find a value of $\hat{x}_3$ such that

$$(x_1, x_2, \hat{x}_3, 0) \sim (x_1, x_2, x_3, x_4).$$

We transformed x_4 into a so-called base-case value of zero and adjusted x_3 accordingly to sustain indifference. We could have chosen some preassigned base-case value other than zero, b_4, and then sought a value $\bar{x}_3$, such that

$$(x_1, x_2, \bar{x}_3, b_4) \sim (x_1, x_2, x_3, x_4).$$

Continuing this procedure we could have introduced other base-case values b_3 and b_2 and by successive, iterated indifferences have generated a value $\bar{x}_1$ such that

$$(\bar{x}_1, b_2, b_3, b_4) \sim (x_1, \bar{x}_2, b_3, b_4) \sim (x_1, x_2, \bar{x}_3, b_4) \sim (x_1, x_2, x_3, x_4).$$

If for another stream $\mathbf{y} \equiv (y_1, y_2, y_3, y_4)$, we have

$$(\bar{y}_1, b_2, b_3, b_4) \sim (y_1, y_2, y_3, y_4),$$

then comparison of streams $\mathbf{x}$ and $\mathbf{y}$ boils down to the comparison of $\bar{x}_1$ and $\bar{y}_1$.

It is often more convenient, especially when dealing with streams of *consumption* in contrast to cash flows, to use nonzero base-case values.

Nothing prevents us, of course, from choosing $b_2 = b_3 = b_4$ for convenience.

In some circumstances one might seek to find a *constant stream* (say of consumption) that is indifferent to an initial nonconstant stream $\mathbf{x} = (x_1, x_2, x_3, x_4)$. Thus for example, one might try to find successively values x_3', x_2', and x_1' such that

$$(x_1, x_2, x_3', x_3') \sim (x_1, x_2, x_3, x_4),$$
$$(x_1, x_2', x_2', x_2') \sim (x_1, x_2, x_3', x_3'),$$
$$(x_1', x_1', x_1', x_1') \sim (x_1, x_2', x_2', x_2').$$

If we proceeded in an analogous manner with stream $\mathbf{y} = (y_1, y_2, y_3, y_4)$ and showed that

$$(y_1', y_1', y_1', y_1') \sim (y_1, y_2, y_3, y_4),$$

then once again comparison of $\mathbf{x}$ and $\mathbf{y}$ would reduce to comparison of x_1' and y_1'.

All this is rather obvious and not at all deep from a theoretical point of view, but nevertheless it is a technique that is often appropriate and easily understood and applied.

9.2.2 Discounting Monetary Amounts at a Constant Rate

The net present value $\hat{x}_1$ of an income stream $(x_1, x_2, \ldots, x_n)$ calculated with a constant effective interest rate r is

$$\hat{x}_1 = \sum_{i=1}^{n} \frac{x_i}{(1+r)^{i-1}} = \sum_{i=1}^{n} \alpha^{i-1} x_i \tag{9.2}$$

where $\alpha \equiv (1+r)^{-1}$ and $r > 0$. This, of course, assumes that an amount x_i in period i is worth $x_i/(1+r)$ in period $i-1$ and $(1+r)x_i$ in period $i+1$, for all periods. Using such a criterion, it follows that $(x_1, x_2, \ldots, x_n)$ is preferred to $(y_1, y_2, \ldots, y_n)$ if and only $\hat{x}_1$ is greater than $\hat{y}_1$, the respective net present values calculated using (9.2). Also, these streams are indifferent if $\hat{x}_1 = \hat{y}_1$. Let us investigate some of the properties satisfied by constant-rate discounting.

1. DOMINANCE. Stream $\mathbf{x} = (x_1, x_2, \ldots, x_n)$ *dominates* $\mathbf{y} = (y_1, y_2, \ldots, y_n)$ if $x_i \geq y_i$, for all i, and $x_i > y_i$, for at least one i. It is easy to prove that if $\mathbf{x}$ dominates $\mathbf{y}$, then $\hat{x}_1 > \hat{y}_1$ for any discount rate. The converse is not true, since there are cases where $\hat{x}_1 > \hat{y}_1$ for all $r > 0$ but where $\mathbf{x}$ does not dominate $\mathbf{y}$. For example, let $\mathbf{x} = (1, 0)$ and $\mathbf{y} = (0, 1)$.

2. SUCCESSIVE PAIRWISE PREFERENTIAL INDEPENDENCE. This property holds if the preferential comparison of two streams $\mathbf{x}$ and $\mathbf{y}$ that differ only in periods i and $i+1$ does not depend on the common values held by $\mathbf{x}$ and $\mathbf{y}$ in any period j other than i or $i+1$ (for all $i = 1, 2, \ldots$). This concept was discussed in detail in Chapter 3, but let us illustrate its meaning in our present context.

Consider the stream $\mathbf{x} = (-5, -3, 5, 6, 2, 4, 1)$. Now suppose $\mathbf{x}$ is modified by adding an amount λ in period 4 and by reducing the amount in period 5 by one unit, giving us $\mathbf{y} = (-5, -3, 5, 6+\lambda, 1, 4, 1)$. Notice that the amounts in periods 1, 2, 3, 6, and 7 remain fixed. If λ is 0 then clearly (by dominance) $\mathbf{x}$ is preferred to $\mathbf{y}$. For some large value of λ it will likely be true that $\mathbf{y} > \mathbf{x}$. We are concerned with the fundamental question: How large does λ have to be so that $\mathbf{x}$ is indifferent to $\mathbf{y}$?

This question involves tradeoffs between amounts in periods 4 and 5. When you think about such tradeoffs, is it important to keep in mind the actual specific flows in periods other than 4 and 5? Should the value of λ that makes $\mathbf{x}$ indifferent to $\mathbf{y}$ depend on the size of the flows in periods 1, 2, 3, 6, and 7, respectively (in this case, the numbers -5, -3, 5, 4, 1)?

If the choice between $\mathbf{x}$ and $\mathbf{y}$ is based on the constant discount rate criterion, the answer to the last question is "No." Both $\hat{x}_1$ and $\hat{y}_1$, the net present values of $\mathbf{x}$ and $\mathbf{y}$, respectively, will have identical contributions from periods 1, 2, 3, 6, and 7. The constant-discount-rate criterion satisfies the successive pairwise preferential independence assumption.

We remark parenthetically that when (9.2) is employed as a value function for the ordering of streams not only is it true that any successive pair of indices $(i, i+1)$ is preferentially independent of the remaining indices, but this is also true of *any pair* (i, j) where j is not necessarily $i+1$.

3. CONSTANT PAIRWISE SUBSTITUTION RATE. A criterion for choice among streams that satisfies the successive pairwise preferential assumption will be said to have a constant substitution rate if, for any i, the indifference curves over amounts x_i and x_{i+1} are parallel straight lines. With a constant discount rate r, meaning one unit in period i is worth $1+r$ units in period $i+1$, the property of constant pairwise substitution is satisfied. We can allow for the case where r depends on i.

4. PAIRWISE INVARIANCE. If the indifference curves in the i, $i+1$ space are the same for all $i < n$, then we shall say that preferences are pairwise invariant. The criterion using the net present value with a constant discount rate satisfies this property also.

We have now introduced the properties necessary to illustrate an interesting result.

Theorem 9.1. *The only evaluation criterion that satisfies properties 1, 2, 3, and 4 is the net present value using a constant discount rate r.*

Table 9.1

Discounting at a Constant Rate[a]

	Time Period				
Stream	1	2	3	4	5
x	−5	−3	8	5	3
x′	−5	−3	8	7.78	0
x″	−5	−3	14.20	0	0
x‴	−5	9.14	0	0	0
x⁗	3.46	0	0	0	0

[a] The discount rate used in the table is $r = .08$.

Instead of formally proving this result, let us demonstrate its validity by means of an example. We begin with the time stream **x** shown in Table 9.1. Suppose we keep the flows in the first three periods (i.e., −5, −3, 8) fixed and ask how we should change the flow in period 4 to compensate for a reduction in period 5 from 3 units to 0 units? We are asking: How large does b have to be such that the two streams exhibited below are equally desirable?

$$\textbf{x:} \quad -5 \quad -3 \quad 8 \quad 5 \quad 3$$

$$\textbf{x}': \quad -5 \quad -3 \quad 8 \quad b \quad 0$$

If we invoke the principle of pairwise *preferential independence*, then b should not depend on −5, −3, and 8. If we invoke the principle of *constant substitution* rates, then the indifference curves that show our preferences for flows in periods 4 and 5 are parallel straight lines. Suppose the appropriate discount rate $r = .08$, to take a concrete example. Then

$$b = 5 + \frac{3}{1 + .08} = 7.78.$$

Thus, in Table 9.1, we have $\mathbf{x} \sim \mathbf{x}'$.

Now let us look for a value c such that the streams exhibited below are equally desirable.

$$\textbf{x}': \quad -5 \quad -3 \quad 8 \quad 7.78 \quad 0$$

$$\textbf{x}'': \quad -5 \quad -3 \quad c \quad 0 \quad 0$$

By the two above-mentioned principles, c must only depend on the flows in periods 3 and 4. If we invoke the principle of *pairwise invariance*, the indifference curves for period 3 versus period 4 flows must be identical to those for period 4 versus period 5 flows. Hence

$$c = 8 + \frac{7.78}{1 + .08} = 14.20.$$

Following this line of argument $\mathbf{x}' \sim \mathbf{x}''$, $\mathbf{x}'' \sim \mathbf{x}'''$, and $\mathbf{x}''' \sim \mathbf{x}''''$. By transitivity of indifference, we learn that the original stream $\mathbf{x}$ is indifferent to the degenerate stream with net present value $\hat{x}_1$ equal to 3.46. It is trivial to show that

$$3.46 = -5 + \frac{-3}{1 + .08} + \frac{8}{(1 + .08)^2} + \frac{5}{(1 + .08)^3} + \frac{3}{(1 + .08)^4}.$$

In other words, 3.46 is the net present value of the stream $\mathbf{x}$ at the constant rate $r = .08$.

Once we committed ourselves to the number 7.78 in stream $\mathbf{x}'$ we had no choice but to choose the numbers 14.20, 9.14 and 3.46—no choice, that is, if we wanted to satisfy the principles of pairwise preferential independence, constant substitution rates, and pairwise invariance.

Now suppose we must choose between streams $\mathbf{x}$ and $\mathbf{y}$. We know that $\mathbf{x}$ is indifferent to the stream $(3.46, 0, 0, \ldots, 0)$, and if $\mathbf{y}$ has a net present value $\hat{y}_1$ of 3.23, at the discount rate of 8 percent, then $\mathbf{y}$ will be indifferent to the stream $(3.23, 0, 0, \ldots, 0)$. Instead of comparing $\mathbf{x}$ and $\mathbf{y}$, we can now compare $(3.46, 0, 0, \ldots, 0)$ and $(3.23, 0, 0, \ldots, 0)$.

By the principle of *dominance* the former stream must be preferred to the latter stream.

This concludes the demonstration that the principles of dominance, successive pairwise preferential independence, constant substitution rates, and pairwise invariance imply the criterion of net present value at a constant rate. Since we also illustrated the converse we can say that these principles *characterize* the criterion of net present value at a constant rate.

One can generalize (9.2) in several ways:

1. By using a variable discount factor, for example,

$$\sum_{i=1}^{n} \gamma_i x_i, \tag{9.3}$$

where γ_i is not necessarily of the form α^{i-1}. It might be convenient to express

$$\gamma_i = \alpha_1 \cdot \alpha_2 \cdots \alpha_i, \qquad i = 1, 2, \ldots, \qquad \alpha_1 = 1,$$

and think of α_i (for $i > 1$) as the factor that discounts the cash flow in period i to period $i-1$. Criterion (9.3) satisfies properties of dominance, successive pairwise preferential independence, and constant substitution rate but not pairwise invariance.

2. By using an additive value function of the form

$$\sum_{i=1}^{n} v_i(x_i).$$

In this case the criterion is characterized by monotonicity and pairwise preferential independence (all pairs, not only successive ones). We might wish to constrain the v_i functions to obtain pairwise invariance. For example, as discussed in the next subsection, we might choose

$$v_i(x_i) = \alpha^i v^*(x_i), \qquad (9.4)$$

where there is no subscript on the v^* function.

9.2.3 Preference Orderings for Infinite Streams with a Stationary Assumption

Let us briefly review some of the pioneering work by Tjalling Koopmans (1972), who examined a set of assumptions giving rise to (9.4). Further references to allied work are cited in this paper.

Professor Koopmans structured preferences for time streams with infinite horizons. He labeled the generic stream $\mathbf{x} = (x_1, x_2, \ldots, x_t, \ldots)$ where x_t can be thought of as the consumption in time period t. The consumption x_t can be vector valued, but its range must be a connected subset of finite-dimensional Euclidean space. He posits the existence of a complete preference ordering ($\gtrsim$) over the space of such infinite streams. The expression $\mathbf{x} \gtrsim \mathbf{y}$ is interpreted as stream $\mathbf{x}$ is preferred or indifferent to stream $\mathbf{y}$. For mathematical purposes he requires that this preference ordering be continuous in the following sense: for any $\mathbf{x} > \mathbf{y}$, all $\mathbf{z}$ sufficiently close to $\mathbf{x}$ (i.e., such that no component of z_t differs from the corresponding component of x_t by more than a small value $\delta > 0$) will be preferred to $\mathbf{y}$, and all $\mathbf{z}$ sufficiently close to $\mathbf{y}$ will be less preferred to $\mathbf{x}$. He then ruled out the uninteresting cases where all streams are indifferent to each other and where preferences between any two streams are solely dictated by the long-run asymptotic behavior of the two streams. He wanted, for example, to allow consumptions in the next 100 years or so to influence the preference ordering, which is quite reasonable. But now we come to the less innocuous assumptions.

Very roughly, Koopmans next introduced a set of assumptions that collectively implied (in our terminology) pairwise preferential independence, and from this he established the existence of an additive value function. But he was more sparing than we are in his assumptions and merely assumed:

1. Consumption in period 1 is preferentially independent of consumption in other periods.
2. Consumption in period 2 is preferentially independent of consumption in other periods.
3. Consumption in periods 1 and 2 is pairwise preferentially independent of consumption in other periods.
4. Stationarity. (This is the most powerful and therefore the most controversial of Koopmans' assumptions.) If two streams have identical first-period consumption, then the modified streams obtained by deleting the first-period consumption and advancing the timing of all subsequent consumption by one period are ordered in the same ways as the original streams. For example, the streams

$$(5, 7, 9, 3, 8, \ldots) \quad \text{and} \quad (5, 8, 2, 6, 1, \ldots)$$

are ordered in the same way as the streams

$$(7, 9, 3, 8, \ldots) \quad \text{and} \quad (8, 2, 6, 1, \ldots).$$

This is appealing, but far from innocuous!

Using this powerful stationarity assumption together with the rather limited pairwise preferential independence assumption, which only deals with consumptions in periods 1 and 2, he proved complete pairwise preferential independence and he therefore established the existence of an additive value function v, which takes the form

$$v(\mathbf{x}) = v_1(x_1) + v_2(x_2) + \cdots.$$

But now we invoke stationarity again and again to relate the v_t's and prove that

$$v_{t+1}(x) = \beta_{t+1} + \alpha v_t(x), \qquad \alpha > 0.$$

Since the β_{t+1}'s are unimportant for orderings we can choose a v^*, without a subscript, and take

$$v_{t+1}(x) = \alpha^t v^*(x)$$

so that v becomes expressible as

$$v(\mathbf{x}) = v^*(x_1) + \alpha v^*(x_2) + \alpha^2 v^*(x_3) + \cdots.$$

Koopmans then invokes the continuity assumption to argue that $0 < \alpha < 1$. This is truly a remarkable result. If we are persuaded by the reasonableness of the behavioral assumptions—as we are in *some applied settings!*—then we merely have to assess the component value function v^* and the so-called discounting factor α.

We could, for example, assess v^* by the midvalue scaling technique (if the component entities x_t for $t = 1, 2, \ldots$ are themselves unidimensional) or else by a multidimensional generalization found in Chapter 3. Once v^* is assessed we can seek two streams of the form

$$(x_1, x_2, z_3, z_4, \ldots) \quad \text{and} \quad (y_1, y_2, z_3, z_4, \ldots)$$

that are indifferent even though $v^*(x_2) \neq v^*(y_2)$ and then we can calculate an operational α by solving (for α) the equation

$$v^*(x_1) + \alpha v^*(x_2) = v^*(y_1) + \alpha v^*(y_2).$$

9.2.4 Other Situations Leading to Discounting

There are numerous other situations in which some form of discounting may be appropriate. We illustrate this below through two paradigms.

PARADIGM A. The following situation captures important aspects of certain real-world problems: A decision maker must choose one project from a set of prespecified projects and each project gives rise to a flow of monetary penalties (negative values) and rewards (positive values). At each discrete time interval the decision maker can spend (i.e., consume) some of the resources at his disposal and any excess he can reinvest. For simplicity, let us assume that all reinvestments along the way are of only one standard kind (e.g., short-term bonds). Let us also assume that he can borrow from a unique source at a single specified schedule of rates. The decision maker wants to choose a project and a compatible consumption stream to maximize his preferences. In this deterministic, simplistic world we assume that his fundamental preferences are for consumption streams and that the temporal streams of monetary rewards and penalties associated with the selection of any project is of interest merely as a means to various consumption ends. With the appropriate interpretation of consumption, this paradigm could apply equally well to a corporation or society as to a particular individual.

Now for some notation. Let A denote the set of available projects, with a representing a generic project. For any a in A, let $\mathbf{x}(a) = [x_1(a), x_2(a), \ldots]$ represent the sequence of monetary flows, and associated to each $\mathbf{x}(a)$ stream let $T[\mathbf{x}(a)]$ be the set of possible consumption streams* compatible with $\mathbf{x}(a)$ and the financial environment that enables transfers of monetary flows from one period to an earlier or later period. The transformation T is a one-to-many mapping—the *one* monetary flow stream to the *many possible consumption streams*—that characterizes this financial environment. A typical element of the set $T[\mathbf{x}(a)]$ will be a consumption stream $\mathbf{c} \equiv (c_1, c_2, \ldots)$. A project a' is preferred to a project a'' if, from the set $T[\mathbf{x}(a')]$, we can find a consumption stream that is preferred to any consumption stream of the set $T[\mathbf{x}(a'')]$. In this manner we can deduce a preference ordering on the $\mathbf{x}$ streams via a well-specified preference ordering on $\mathbf{c}$ streams and knowledge of the transformation T.

Now comes the punch line that is well-known to most economists. There may be quite diverse preference functions on the $\mathbf{c}$'s that get translated (via T) into the same (or nearly the same) preference function on the $\mathbf{x}$'s. For example, if we can lend or borrow at the same rate, that is, translate monetary amounts forward and backward at a given discount rate, then we can simply show that, regardless of the fundamental orderings on the $\mathbf{c}$'s, the induced ordering on the $\mathbf{x}$'s is given by simple discounting at this given rate. All that we need to justify this result is the elementary theorem: If $\mathbf{c}$ is compatible with $\mathbf{x}$, meaning that the discounted present value of $\mathbf{c}$ is less than that of $\mathbf{x}$, and if the net present value of $\mathbf{x}$ is greater than that for $\mathbf{x}'$, then $\mathbf{c}$ is compatible with $\mathbf{x}'$. We could say that "the market assumes command and the market rate prevails for monetary flows" even though we might not have chosen to express our preference for consumption streams through discounting.

PARADIGM B. This paradigm captures another aspect of reality that we feel is of some relevance in this highly complicated field. Let us assume that each act a gives rise to a stream of pairs of consequences: (x_1, e_1), $(x_2, e_2), \ldots, (x_i, e_i), \ldots$ where in the ith period, x_i refers to a monetary amount and e_i to a summary description of environmental effects. We could think of e_i as a vector quantity comprising several attributes. The essence of our problem is to make paired comparisons between two streams $\{(x_i', e_i') : i = 1, 2, \ldots\}$ and $\{(x_i'', e_i'') : i = 1, 2, \ldots\}$. For example, in forest management, a government agency might be concerned with the sequence of net monetary flows and the sequence of environmental states.

---

* Consumption streams, as used throughout the remainder of this chapter, indicate the monetary amount used for consumption in the various time periods. Here, and in the next section, we use the more suggestive notation $(c_1, c_2, \ldots)$, rather than the neutral $(x_1, x_2, \ldots)$, to designate a consumption stream. In this subsection, the notation is meant to differentiate consumption streams from streams of monetary flows. In Section 9.3, it is done because the specific discussion concerns mainly streams of consumption.

If we are prepared to argue that each pair of attributes $\{X_i, E_i\}$ is preferentially independent of other pairs, then we can price out each E-attribute in terms of the X attribute. In particular, we can specify a base case e^* and substitute for each (x_i, e_i) pair an indifferent pair of the form $(\hat{x}_i, e^*)$. Doing this for all i, we can find for each sequence $\{(x_i, e_i): i = 1, 2, \ldots\}$ an indifferent sequence $\{(\hat{x}_i, e^*): i = 1, 2, \ldots\}$. We are then led to consider the sequence $\hat{\mathbf{x}} = (\hat{x}_1, \hat{x}_2, \ldots)$ with the understanding that there is a constant associated environmental stream $(e^*, e^*, \ldots)$. Now if we can justify treating the $\hat{\mathbf{x}}$-sequence by discounting, we can summarize the desirability of the original sequence by the pair $(\sum_i \alpha^{i-1} \hat{x}_i, e^*)$. If, in addition, we can express

$$\hat{x}_i = x_i + f(e_i, e^*, x_i)$$

where f has *no subscript*, then we can think of $f(e_i, e^*, x_i)$ as the price we are paid for converting e_i to e^*, when the monetary component is at level x_i. In this case we have

$$\sum_i \alpha^{i-1} \hat{x}_i = \sum \alpha^{i-1} x_i + \sum \alpha^{i-1} f(e_i, e^*, x_i)$$

and once again we see that the financial rate of discount α applies to the environmental effects as well. Of course, this result depends on a string of strong assumptions that are often dubious in real settings. An even more restricted case would occur if $f(e_i, e^*, x_i)$ did not depend on the level of x_i.

Now let us back up and consider other assumptions. If the set of X attributes as a totality were preferentially independent of the E attributes then we could try to order the monetary stream by some value function (e.g., by discounting). If we now assume that the set of E attributes is preferentially independent of the X attributes, then we are led to the problem of structuring our preferences for streams of the form $\mathbf{e} = (e_1, e_2, \ldots)$. With a few assumptions, akin to those used by Koopmans described in the previous section, we could find a justification for evaluating preferences for $\mathbf{e}$ streams by a value function of the form $\sum_i \beta^{i-1} v(e_i)$. In this case the discount factor β would not generally be the same as the financial discount rate α. The stream $\{(x_i, e_i: i = 1, 2, \ldots\}$ might be then summarized in terms of the pair

$$\left(\sum \alpha^{i-1} x_i, \sum \beta^{i-1} v(e_i) \right)$$

We suspect that however nice the above reduction seems, in practice it might be difficult to accept the assumptions that would lead to discounting of the $v(e_i)$'s. The stumbling block for us would be our feeling that the pair of attributes E_i and E_{i+1} are not preferentially independent of the remaining E attributes. More intuitively, at any time period i, our preferences for the future might depend on the past (and vice versa). This dependence need not be total, however. It could be that there is some reasonable Markovian condition, for example, that the future depends on the past only through the present, or perhaps more generally, through a simple summary of the past and present (e.g., an exponentially smoothed index of the form

$$\sum_{t=1}^{i-1} \gamma^{t-1} \nu(e_{i-t})$$

or a variation). More will be said about this in Section 9.6.

9.3 THE UNCERTAINTY CASE: UTILITY FUNCTIONS OVER TIME STREAMS

Most problems where time considerations are important do involve uncertainties, since it is a difficult task to forecast perfectly the future. Hence we would like to obtain a utility function u for the time stream $(x_1, x_2, \ldots, x_n)$. Then the expectation of u can be used in making decisions involving uncertainty. When the requisite assumptions for any of the results in Chapters 5 and 6 hold, then clearly it is appropriate to use them in structuring u. These results would generally allow us to structure the multiperiod utility function from single-period utility functions. However, there are no restrictions on the dimensionality of the single-period consequences. They can be multiattributed.

Our primary concern is to assess utility functions over time streams of consumption $\mathbf{c} = (c_1, c_2, \ldots, c_n)$, where c_i represents the amount of consumption in period i. We may think of c_n as a legacy rather than consumption, the amount left to heirs. For scaling convenience, a base case of consumption $\mathbf{c}^o = (c_1^o, c_2^o, \ldots, c_n^o) = (c^o, c^o, \ldots, c^o)$ and an "upper bound" $\mathbf{c}^* \equiv (c_1^*, c_2^*, \ldots, c_n^*) = (c^*, c^*, \ldots, c^*)$ are specified.

In what follows, we first discuss the two period case in order to illustrate the fundamental ideas. Then this is generalized to n period and continuous-consumption streams.*

9.3.1 The Two-Period Case

Let C_1 and C_2 denote the consumption attributes in periods 1 and 2, respectively. A typical consumption stream will then be $\mathbf{c} = (c_1, c_2)$. First let us investigate the implications of mutual utility independence. From

---

* This presentation is based on Meyer (1970).

Theorem 5.3, it follows that

$$u(c_1, c_2) = k_1 u_1(c_1) + k_2 u_2(c_2) + k k_1 k_2 u_1(c_1) u_2(c_2), \tag{9.5}$$

where

$$u(c_1^o, c_2^o) = 0, \qquad u_1(c_1^o) = 0, \qquad u_2(c_2^o) = 0, \tag{9.6}$$

and

$$u(c_1^*, c_2^*) = 1, \qquad u_1(c_1^*) = 1, \qquad u_2(c_2^*) = 1. \tag{9.7}$$

The scaling constants k_1 and k_2 are positive and

$$k = \frac{1 - k_1 - k_2}{k_1 k_2}. \tag{9.8}$$

Now let us add the assumption of stationarity, which says that preferences are stable over time. More formally, this means that if $\hat{c}$ is indifferent to the lottery $\langle c', p, c'' \rangle$ yielding a p chance at c' and a $(1-p)$ chance at c'', where all the consequences accrue in period 1, then $\hat{c}$ must be indifferent to the same lottery in period 2. This, along with the scaling convention of (9.6) and (9.7), implies that the utility function in each period is identical. Let us label this utility function $u^*(c)$ so

$$u^*(c) = u_1(c) = u_2(c). \tag{9.9}$$

Combining this with the previous result (9.5) yields

$$u(c_1, c_2) = k_1 u^*(c_1) + k_2 u^*(c_2) + k k_1 k_2 u^*(c_1) u^*(c_2). \tag{9.10}$$

There are three cases to consider: k is zero, positive, and negative. If $k = 0$, then (9.10) reduces to an additive utility function,

$$u(c_1, c_2) = k_1 u^*(c_1) + k_2 u^*(c_2) \tag{9.11}$$

where, in addition, $k_2 < k_1$ if the consumption stream (c', c'') is preferred to (c'', c') whenever $c' > c''$, that is, if greater consumptions are preferred sooner. In such a case, expression (9.11) is effectively discounting of utilities.

Now suppose k is not zero. Then we can multiply both sides of (9.10) by k and add 1 to each to find

$$1 + k u(c_1, c_2) = [1 + k k_1 u^*(c_1)][1 + k k_2 u^*(c_2)]. \tag{9.12}$$

When k is positive, then $1 + ku$, $1 + kk_1 u^*$, and $1 + kk_2 u^*$ are each utility functions over their respective domains so we can consider (9.12) a multiplicative utility function,

$$u(c_1, c_2) \sim u_1^*(c_1) u_2^*(c_2), \tag{9.13}$$

and when k is negative, then the expression reduces to

$$-[u(c_1, c_2)] \sim [u_1^*(c_1)][u_2^*(c_2)] \tag{9.14}$$

where $u_1^*(c_1) \equiv 1 + kk_1 u^*(c_1)$ and $u_2^*(c_2) \equiv 1 + kk_2 u^*(c_2)$ in both (9.13) and (9.14). Expression (9.14) will be called the negative form of the multiplicative utility function since $-u$, u_1^*, and u_2^* are each "disutility" functions.

Let us explore what behavioral properties might distinguish (9.11), (9.13), and (9.14). Consider preferences for consumption streams (c, c) where consumption in each period is identical (so-called level streams). In particular, let us suppose that the level consumption c^α is such that (c^α, c^α) is indifferent to $\langle (c', c'), 1/2, (c'', c'') \rangle$. Compare this c^α to the one-period case and ask: what amount c^β is indifferent to the lottery $\langle c', 1/2, c'' \rangle$, where c^β, c', and c'' are all consumed in the same period. Would c^α be equal, less than, or greater than c^β? If $c^\alpha = c^\beta$, then the additive form (9.11) must hold provided the other conditions that imply the additive or multiplicative form are satisfied. If $c^\alpha > c^\beta$, the positive multiplicative utility function (9.13) holds, and if $c^\alpha < c^\beta$, the negative multiplicative form (9.14) is appropriate.

It seems natural, in many cases, that c^α be less than c^β. To illustrate, suppose $c' = \$10,000$ and $c'' = \$50,000$. In any one period (e.g., one year) the certainty equivalent for $\langle \$50,000; 1/2; \$10,000 \rangle$ might be $\$25,000$; we are not greatly risk averse, because if the lottery were chosen and $\$10,000$ resulted, we are only stuck with the result for one year, and next year is a new ball game. However, in finding the certainty equivalent for the two-period lottery $\langle (\$50,000, \$50,000); 1/2; (\$10,000, \$10,000) \rangle$, we might choose $(\$22,000, \$22,000)$ because the prospect of the lower consumption of $\$10,000$ per year for *both* years in a row is quite unappealing. This type of attitude would imply $c^\alpha < c^\beta$ in our preceding discussion.

Let us define the induced utility function u^o over level streams of consumption by

$$u^o(c) \equiv u(c, c), \tag{9.15}$$

where from (9.6) and (9.7), $u^o(c^*) = 1$ and $u^o(c^o) = 0$. If one is risk averse in single periods, meaning $c^\beta \le (c' + c'')/2$ for all c' and c'', then we can conclude that one is more risk averse for two-period constant consumption streams if $c^\alpha < c^\beta$. In this case the risk aversion* $r(c)$ for single-period consumption is always less than $r^o(c)$, the risk aversion for two-period constant consumption. The scaling constant k is an indicator of our risk attitudes in multiple-period situations. The smaller k is, the more risk averse we will be for constant consumption streams [see Richard (1975)].

---

* Recall from Chapter 4 that the risk aversion $r(x)$ of the utility function $u(x)$ is defined as $-u''(x)/u'(x)$ where u' and u'' are the first and second derivatives of $u(x)$ with respect to x.

Consider one more two-period situation: let the decision maker be faced with the choice of lottery $L_1 \equiv \langle (c^*, c^o), 1/2, (c^o, c^*) \rangle$ or lottery $L_2 \equiv \langle (c^*, c^*), 1/2, (c^o, c^o) \rangle$. With each lottery, there is a 50–50 chance of receiving the worst or best consequence in each of the periods. However, in L_1, we get the worst in one period and the best in the other regardless of the outcome, whereas in L_2, either both periods are good or both are bad. Many people state a preference for L_1 over L_2, which from the discussion in Section 5.4 indicates that $k < 0$, and hence one is more risk averse for level consumption streams than for single-period consumption.

9.3.2 The Multiple-Period Case

Now let us generalize the preceding ideas and results to the n-period-plus-legacy situation for a consumption stream $\mathbf{c} = (c_1, c_2, \ldots, c_n)$, where c_n designates the legacy. Let us designate the future-consumption vector $\vec{c}_m \equiv (c_m, c_{m+1}, \ldots, c_n)$ and the past consumption vector $\tilde{c}_m \equiv (c_1, c_2, \ldots, c_m)$, $m = 1, 2, \ldots, n$. Suppose it is behaviorally acceptable to the decision maker (1) to make his decisions about the future (in each period) without regard to his past consumption stream, and (2) to make his decisions affecting only his lifetime stream $\tilde{c}_{n-1}$ without regard to the legacy c_n he will actually bequeath. We then have

Theorem 9.2. *If $\vec{C}_m$ is utility independent of $\vec{C}_{m-1}$ for all $m = 2, 3, \ldots, n$, and if $\tilde{C}_{n-1}$ is utility independent of C_n, then $u(\mathbf{c}) \equiv u(c_1, c_2, \ldots, c_n)$ must either be of the form*

$$u(\mathbf{c}) = \sum_{i=1}^{n} k_i u_i(c_i), \qquad if \sum_{i=1}^{n} k_i = 1, \tag{9.16}$$

or

$$1 + k u(\mathbf{c}) = \prod_{i=1}^{n} [1 + k k_i u_i(c_i)], \qquad if \sum_{i=1}^{n} k_i \neq 1, \tag{9.17}$$

where

1. *$u(\mathbf{c})$ is normalized by $u(\mathbf{c}^o) = 0$ and $u(\mathbf{c}^*) = 1$,*
2. *$u_i(c_i)$, $i = 1, 2, \ldots, n$, is a single-period utility function on C_i normalized by $u_i(c_i^o) = 0$ and $u_i(c_i^*) = 1$,*
3. *$k_i = u(c_1^o, \ldots, c_{i-1}^o, c_i^*, c_{i+1}^o, \ldots c_n^o)$, $i = 1, 2, \ldots, n$,*
4. *k is the nonzero solution to $1 + k = \prod_{i=1}^{n} (1 + k k_i)$ with $k > -1$.*

We have already shown in Chapter 6, Theorem 6.2, that these assumptions imply that the attributes $C_1, C_2, \ldots, C_n$ are mutually utility independent, by which it follows from Theorem 6.1 that u can be expressed in the additive or multiplicative form.

As illustrated in the two-period case, if we assume that preferences for lotteries in period i are the same as preferences in period j for the identical lotteries, then we can define a common utility function

$$u^*(c) \equiv u_i(c), \qquad i = 1, 2, \ldots, n.$$

With this assumption, the additive and multiplicative form of (9.16) and (9.17) become

$$u(\mathbf{c}) = \sum_{i=1}^{n} k_i u^*(c_i) \qquad (9.18)$$

and

$$1 + ku(\mathbf{c}) = \prod_{i=1}^{n} [1 + kk_i u^*(c_i)], \qquad (9.19)$$

respectively.

The constant k plays the same role in (9.19) as it did in (9.12). Suppose we look at preferences for level consumption streams of the form $(c, c, \ldots, c)$. Then, if the level certainty equivalent $\mathbf{c}^\alpha \equiv (c^\alpha, c^\alpha, \ldots, c^\alpha)$ for the lottery $\langle \mathbf{c}', 1/2, \mathbf{c}'' \rangle$ is such that c^α is less than c^β, the one-period certainty equivalent for the lottery $\langle c', 1/2, c'' \rangle$ in that period, we must have $\sum_{i=1}^{n} k_i > 1$ so, as shown in Appendix 6B, $-1 < k < 0$. In these cases, we are more risk averse for level consumption streams than for one-period consumption, which could be proven by calculating the risk-aversion functions of the induced utility function

$$u^o(c) \equiv u(c, c, \ldots, c) = u(\mathbf{c})$$

and the one-period utility function $u^*(c)$.

Also, as argued in the two-period case, if k is negative, and if we have a choice between lotteries L_1 and L_2 over periods i and j, where $L_1 \equiv \langle (c^o, c^o), 1/2, (c^*, c^*) \rangle$ and $L_2 \equiv \langle (c^o, c^*), 1/2, (c^*, c^o) \rangle$ with (c_i, c_j) designating the consumption in periods i and j, then L_2 will be preferred. This seems intuitively reasonable since both two-period consequences in L_2 have a period of high consumption that might partially compensate for the period of low consumption. If the decision maker were indifferent between L_1 and L_2, this would imply the additive utility function (9.16). And if L_1 is preferred to L_2, the multiplicative form (9.17) is valid with $\sum_{i=1}^{n} k_i < 1$ and $k > 0$. In this case, we are less risk averse for lotteries for n-period level income streams than for one-period lotteries.

9.3.3 Continuous-Consumption Streams*

Most of the results of Sections 9.2 and 9.3 can be extended to continuous streams. When time is continuous, it is more natural to deal

---

* This subsection can be omitted without loss of continuity to other sections.

with consumption rates; therefore, let $c(t)$ denote the rate of consumption at time t, so that $c(t)\Delta t$ is the actual consumption in the time interval $(t, t + \Delta t)$. Let t range over $(0, T)$. Then we can extend (9.16) and (9.17) by dividing $(0, T)$ into n equal intervals, each with $\Delta t = T/n$ and bounded by $t_i = iT/n$, and taking the limit as n approaches infinity. The result will be an "additive" and a "multiplicative" utility *functional* $u\{c(\cdot)\}$. We recognize that k_i, since it is the value of $u\{\cdot\}$ when $c(\cdot)$ is at its base value throughout $(0, T)$ except for a single interval of duration Δt, must be of order Δt, so that instead of k_i we write $k(t_i)\Delta t$. We also replace $u_i(c_i)$ by $\hat{u}(t_i, c(t_i))$, so that (9.16) becomes

$$u\{c(\cdot)\} = \operatorname*{Lim}_{n \to \infty} \sum_{i=1}^{n} k(t_i)\hat{u}(t_i, c(t_i))\Delta t$$

$$= \int_0^T k(t)\hat{u}(t, c(t)) \, dt. \tag{9.20}$$

Similarly, (9.17) becomes

$$1 + ku\{c(\cdot)\} = \operatorname*{Lim}_{n \to \infty} \prod_{i=1}^{n} \exp\left[kk(t_i)\hat{u}(t_i, c(t_i))\Delta t\right]$$

$$= \exp\left[k\int_0^T k(t)\hat{u}(t, c(t)) \, dt\right]. \tag{9.21}$$

The additive form (9.20) has been widely used by economists, especially in the stationary case when $k(t)$ is exponential and $\hat{u}(t, c)$ is independent of t. The multiplicative form (9.21) has been used in applications by Meyer (1970), Richard (1972), and Pye (1973).

9.4 RELAXING THE INDEPENDENCE ASSUMPTIONS

In Sections 6.4 and 6.9 we explored in the context of multiattribute utility what utility structures resulted from weakening the independence assumptions so that they were no longer sufficient to yield the purely additive or multiplicative forms. In particular, we saw that the assumption "X_i utility independent of $\bar{X}_i$ for all i" resulted in the multilinear form, and we are therefore tempted to examine this generalization in the temporal setting.

Unfortunately, it is not an appropriate generalization in the context of time preferences, for the following reason. The idea that X_t is utility independent focuses on a particular time period in contrast to the rest of time.* The length of such a single period, in public and private decision problems where the extent of time is important, may range from one month to 10 years, although it typically is of the order of 1 year. Why is this the appropriate duration of a single period? Well, because economic consequences, even severe ones, that last only days are, on the human time scale, easily accepted (e.g., to live at a subsistence level for a week is not serious, even with your whole family; to do so for a year is quite grim). Yet, the unit of time, that is, the length of the period, must not be chosen.so long that the detailed pattern within a single period matters much.

Given that these kinds of imprecise considerations determine the length of an appropriate unit period, it makes little sense to assume rigidly that a single period's consequence, measured by attribute X_t, is utility independent of its complement, but that two successive periods' consequences, measured by X_t and X_{t+1}, are *not* utility independent of their complement. Now, if in addition to assuming that each single period is utility independent of its complement, we assume that *any* sequence $X_t, X_{t+1}, \ldots, X_{t+T}$ of successive periods is utility independent of its complement, then once again we have mutual utility independence, and hence we are back to the additive or multiplicative form.

It is more useful, in the temporal setting, to generalize the results of Section 9.3 by removing the last condition of Theorem 9.2, so that we assume only that the future is utility independent of the past, that is, $\vec{X}_t$ is utility independent of $\breve{X}_{t-1}$ for all t. Note that this assumption:

1. Will not generally imply the existence of unconditional single-period utilities; that is, we can not make single-period decisions in isolation since each X_i is not utility independent of the complementary set.
2. Is the most general assumption that still permits us to solve decision problems by backward induction without having to introduce an additional "state descriptor" that represents those features of the past consequence stream that influence our liking for future consequences.

The assumption that $\vec{X}_t$ is utility independent of $\breve{X}_{t-1}$ does imply the existence of utilities $\vec{u}_t(\vec{\mathbf{x}}_t)$ for $t = 0, 1, \ldots, n$, but only $\vec{u}_n$ is a single-period utility. It also follows from this assumption that

$$\vec{u}_t(\vec{\mathbf{x}}_t) = a_t(x_t) + b_t(x_t)\vec{u}_{t+1}(\vec{\mathbf{x}}_{t+1}), \quad \text{for } t = 1, 2, \ldots, n, \quad (9.22)$$

where $b_t(\cdot) > 0$.

---

* Throughout the remainder of this chapter, all time streams of consequences, including consumption streams, will be designated by **x**.

If we scale $\vec{u}_t(\cdot)$ in the usual manner to range from 0 to 1 as $\vec{x}_t$ ranges from $\vec{x}_t^o$ to $\vec{x}_t^*$, it follows from (9.22) that

1. $a_t(x_t^o) = 0$ [since $\vec{u}_t(\vec{x}_t^o) = \vec{u}_{t+1}(\vec{x}_{t+1}^o) = 0$].

2. $a_t(x_t^*) + b_t(x_t^*) = 1$ [since $\vec{u}_t(\vec{x}_t^*) = \vec{u}_{t+1}(\vec{x}_{t+1}^*) = 1$].

3. We must assess *two* univariate functions, $a_t(\cdot)$ and $b_t(\cdot)$, for each period except the last one, for which we need to assess only one function $\vec{u}_n$. The functions $a_t(\cdot)$ have the properties of (unscaled) univariate utility functions, since they are the utilities for x_t given that $\vec{x}_{t+1} = \vec{x}_{t+1}^o$. The functions $b_t(\cdot)$ are ≤ 1, since $b_t > 1$ together with $\vec{u}_{t+1} = 1$ would imply $a_t < 0$, which is false. We may therefore interpret (9.22) as follows: to calculate $\vec{u}_t$ discount $\vec{u}_{t+1}$ by a discount factor b_t (which depends on x_t) and then add the single-period "base" utility $a_t(x_t)$ which, after all, is the utility of the stream $(x_t, \vec{x}_{t+1}^o)$.

4. If we rename $\vec{u}_n = a_n$ in order to standardize notation, then (9.22) has the solution

$$u(\mathbf{x}) = \vec{u}_1(\vec{x}_1) = \sum_{t=1}^{n} a_t(x_t)\left(\prod_{\tau=1}^{t-1} b_\tau(x_\tau)\right) \tag{9.23}$$

where we employ the usual convention that the empty product

$$\prod_{\tau=1}^{0} b_\tau(x_\tau) = 1.$$

We shall call the utility structure given in (9.23) *semiseparable*, since in general single-period decisions are no longer fully separable. Equation (9.23) contains as particular cases the additive form [when $b_\tau(\cdot)$ is constant for all τ], the multiplicative form [when $a_t(\cdot) = 0$ for $t = 1, 2, \ldots, n-1$], and a special subset of the multilinear form [when $a_t(\cdot)$ is constant for $t = 1, 2, \ldots, n-1$, or else when b_τ, $\tau = 1, 2, \ldots, n-1$, can be interpreted as a single-period unconditional utility function]. These are the only instances of (9.23) where unconditional single-period utilities exist. In all other cases, (9.22) shows that the utility for x_t is dependent on the future stream $\vec{x}_{t+1}$; however, it depends on the future *only* through our utility $\vec{u}_{t+1}(\vec{x}_{t+1})$ for this future, so that we may think of $\vec{u}_{t+1}$ as a univariate descriptor of our liking for future prospects which, if known, is a sufficient descriptor of the future to permit us to state our preferences for the current single period.

We may generalize this idea by dividing time into an "immediate" future and a "distant" future: $\vec{x}_1 = (x_1, x_2, \ldots, x_m, x_{m+1}, \ldots, x_n) = (\vec{x}_m, \vec{x}_{m+1})$. Think of the "immediate" future as those "years" for which the decision problem can be reasonably well structured, and of the "distant" future as the vague and ill-perceived years beyond this "horizon." Since the utility independence of $\tilde{X}_{m+1}$ from $\tilde{X}_m$ implies that

$$\vec{u}_1(\tilde{\mathbf{x}}_1) = a(\tilde{\mathbf{x}}_m) + b(\tilde{\mathbf{x}}_m)\vec{u}_{m+1}(\tilde{\mathbf{x}}_{m+1}), \tag{9.24}$$

it follows that we may in principle proceed with the analysis of such decision problems in the following way:

1. Structure the problem up to the horizon of the "immediate" future, and assess the functions $a(\cdot)$ and $b(\cdot)$; more precisely, assess the univariate functions $a_t(\cdot)$ and $b_t(\cdot)$ for $t = 1, 2, \ldots, m$, which permits the construction of $a(\cdot)$ and $b(\cdot)$ by means of (9.23).
2. Assess, for each end position on the tree, the expected value of $\vec{u}_{m+1}$, that is, the expected utility of the "distant" future given that end position of the "immediate" future.
3. Then use (9.24) as the utility function.

The utility function given by (9.23) is especially convenient to use in sequential decision problems under uncertainty that can be described as follows: at each time period t an investment and consumption decision is made and then an uncertain event is revealed; the utility value of a path through the tree depends solely on the consumption stream (and legacy). For this class of decision problems, the utility function (9.23) is the most general utility function that permits backward induction to be used without the burden of utility-state descriptors. Backward induction is particularly simple when the underlying probabilistic structure of the uncertain environment is Markovian. General results for this class of problems are reported in Oksman (1974).

Just as for the additive and multiplicative utility functions, we again want to introduce the idea of stationarity. Now, however, this becomes a more subtle concept, since we cannot simply require that all single periods are strategically equivalent when single-period decisions depend on the future, and the future is surely different, if only in duration, for each single period of a finite horizon stream. To overcome this problem we introduce the concept of *equivalent futures*. Let us suppose x_t ranges from x^o to x^*, that is, the same range in each period, and let $t < t'$. We shall then require that for any future $\tilde{\mathbf{x}}_{t'+1}$, there exists an (equivalent) future $\tilde{\mathbf{x}}_{t+1}$ such that the conditional single-period utility for x_t given $\tilde{\mathbf{x}}_{t+1}$ is *strategically equivalent* to the conditional single-period utility for x_t, given $\tilde{\mathbf{x}}_{t'+1}$ for the entire range (x^o, x^*). This generalized stationarity condition is sufficient to imply that the two sets of functions $a_t(\cdot)$ and $b_t(\cdot)$

of (9.22) are each independent of t [see Oksman (1974)]. Defining $\alpha = a_t$, for all t, and $\beta = b_t$, for all t, the stationary version of (9.22) becomes

$$\vec{u}_t(\vec{\mathbf{x}}_t) = \alpha(x_t) + \beta(x_t)\vec{u}_{t+1}(\vec{\mathbf{x}}_{t+1}). \tag{9.25}$$

9.5 UNCERTAIN HORIZON

Thus far in this chapter we have regarded the horizon time n as fixed and known. Although many decision problems are appropriately structured using a fixed horizon, there are others that clearly demand the use of a variable or uncertain horizon. Private long-term decisions such as career choice, pension plan and life-time savings decisions, major medical decisions, and so on are typical examples where the natural problem horizon, that is, the time of death of the individual, is uncertain. The same is true for certain public or corporate decisions, for example, decisions whose natural horizon is the time at which a technological breakthrough will occur. In the latter case the horizon time may be partly (or even entirely) under the decision maker's control: by allocating necessary resources he may be able to affect the time of the breakthrough.

If the horizon is not fixed and known, we shall have to deal with preferences for streams $\mathbf{x}^n = (x_1, x_2, \ldots, x_n)$ of unequal lengths. In the foregoing we have developed a framework for the comparison of lotteries for streams of equal lengths; we shall now proceed to extend our methodology to streams of different lengths.

Let the horizon attribute N range from n^o to n^*, the minimum and maximum possible horizons for the decision problem at hand. In principle, we can assess the *conditional* utility functions $u(\mathbf{x}^n \mid n)$ for each value of n. This merely requires the approach described in the preceding sections to be applied for each value of n separately: we fix n and assess our preference for all possible streams $\mathbf{x}^n$ of that length. This yields the function $u(\cdot \mid n)$, and we now repeat the process for a different value of n, until we have the family of conditional utilities $\{u(\cdot \mid n), n^o \le n \le n^*\}$.

In order to make decisions involving different values of n, however, these conditional utilities are not adequate, because they do not describe our relative preference for different n's. Hence we need the *joint* utilities $u(\mathbf{x}^n, n)$, which describe our preference for a stream $\mathbf{x}^n$ *and* a horizon n. Since $u(\mathbf{x}^n, n)$ for any given n must be strategically equivalent to $u(\mathbf{x}^n \mid n)$ for decisions affecting $\mathbf{x}^n$ only, it follows that $u(\mathbf{x}^n, n)$ must be a positive linear function of $u(\mathbf{x}^n \mid n)$ with coefficients that may depend on n but not on $\mathbf{x}^n$:

$$u(\mathbf{x}^n, n) = \eta(n) + \theta(n)u(\mathbf{x}^n \mid n), \qquad \text{where } \theta(n) > 0. \qquad (9.26)$$

Equation (9.26) is a basic instrument for decision analysis with uncertain horizons. It remains for us to explore how to assess $\eta(\cdot)$ and $\theta(\cdot)$, and to examine the special utility structures that follow from simplifying independence assumptions.

Consider a decision problem where we must choose one from a set of lotteries $\{L_k, k = 1, 2, \ldots\}$. Let the kth lottery result in the stream $\mathbf{x}^n$ with joint probability density $f_k(\mathbf{x}^n, n)$, so that we should select that lottery which maximizes the expected utility

$$\bar{u}(k) = \sum_{n=n^0}^{n^*} \int f_k(\mathbf{x}^n, n)u(\mathbf{x}^n, n) \, d\mathbf{x}^n. \qquad (9.27)$$

We can now distinguish two classes of decision problems:

1. Those problems in which the horizon time, although uncertain, is entirely outside of our control. This corresponds to the statement that each lottery L_k must have the same marginal probability distribution for n, that is,

$$\int f_k(\mathbf{x}^n, n) \, d\mathbf{x}^n = f(n), \qquad \text{for all } k = 1, 2, \ldots. \qquad (9.28)$$

2. Those problems in which our choice of lottery can affect the horizon time, that is, (9.28) does not hold for all available lotteries.

For problems of class 1 above, the function $\eta(\cdot)$ occurring in (9.26) does not affect our decision, and therefore need not be assessed. To see this, substitute (9.26) in (9.27), and apply (9.28). It follows that the expected utility $\bar{u}(k)$ for lottery k depends on $\eta(\cdot)$ only through an additive constant, $\sum_n f(n)\eta(n)$, irrespective of k. The function $\eta(\cdot)$ therefore has no strategic impact in such situations: it impacts only those decision problems where the horizon time can be affected by our decision.

The implications of the above for the assessment of $\eta(\cdot)$ and $\theta(\cdot)$ are clear: it should be possible to assess $\theta(\cdot)$ by asking for indifferences between lotteries where we cannot affect the horizon time, but to assess $\eta(\cdot)$ we shall have to make tradeoffs between the *level* of streams and their *lengths*. There are, of course, many ways to do this, but as a concrete example consider the following approach, which might make sense in situations where $x_t^* = x^*$ and $x_t^o = x^o$, where it is natural to think in terms of level streams, and where, *ceteris paribus*, a longer horizon is preferred to a shorter.

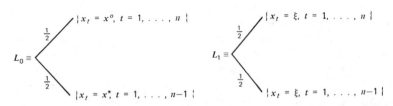

Fig. 9.1. Assessing preferences for lotteries involving varying horizon times.

First, for each $n > n^o$, consider two lotteries, L_0 and L_1, as shown in Fig. 9.1. Both lotteries give an equal chance $1/2$ at horizon times $n-1$ and n. In L_0 we receive the best consequence x^* as a level stream if the horizon time is $n-1$, and the worst consequence x^o as a level stream if the horizon time is n. In L_1 we receive some intermediate consequence ξ as a level stream for either horizon. The relevant assessment question to ask is, "What amount of ξ makes you indifferent between L_0 and L_1?" If we answer this question for every $n > n^o$, thus assessing a set of indifference consequences $\{\xi_n, n^o < n \leq n^*\}$, we can calculate $\theta(\cdot)$, but for a multiplicative constant, as follows. The expected utilities calculated using (9.26) for L_0 and L_1 are, respectively,

$$\bar{u}_0 = \tfrac{1}{2}[\eta(n-1) + \theta(n-1)] + \tfrac{1}{2}\eta(n),$$
$$\bar{u}_1 = \tfrac{1}{2}[\eta(n-1) + \theta(n-1)u(\xi_n \mid n-1)] + \tfrac{1}{2}[\eta(n) + \theta(n)u(\xi_n \mid n)].$$

Since ξ_n was assessed in order to make $\bar{u}_0 = \bar{u}_1$, it follows that

$$\theta(n) = \theta(n-1)\frac{1 - u(\xi_n \mid n-1)}{u(\xi_n \mid n)}, \qquad n^o < n \leq n^*. \qquad (9.29)$$

This determines $\theta(\cdot)$ completely up to a multiplicative constant, for example, $\theta(n^o) = \theta_0$.

We may now assess $\eta(\cdot)$ by asking for the simplest possible tradeoffs between the level of x and the horizon time n under certainty. Consider the two streams

$$\mathbf{x}^n = \{x_t = x^o, t = 1, \ldots, n\} \quad \text{and} \quad \mathbf{x}^{n-1} = \{x_t = \zeta, t = 1, \ldots, n-1\}.$$

We ask, for each $n > n^o$, for a level of ζ that makes us indifferent between these two streams. This results in a set of indifference consequences $\{\zeta_n, n^o < n \leq n^*\}$ such that

$$\eta(n) = \eta(n-1) + \theta(n-1)u(\zeta_n \mid n-1), \qquad n^o < n \leq n^*. \qquad (9.30)$$

Since we have calculated $\theta(\cdot)$ from (9.29), we can now obtain $\eta(\cdot)$ from (9.30), but for an additive constant which we may call $\eta(n^\circ) = \eta_0$. To determine η_0 and θ_0, we apply the normalization conditions $u(\mathbf{x}^*, n^*) = 1$ and $u(\mathbf{x}^\circ, n^\circ) = 0$. This completes the assessment process.*

Finally it remains to explore the consequences of utility independence assumptions when the horizon is variable or uncertain. In Sections 9.3 and 9.4 we considered situations where, for a fixed horizon, decisions about the "future" $\tilde{\mathbf{x}}_t$ are independent of the "past" $\tilde{\mathbf{x}}_{t-1}$. Now let us extend these conditions in the most natural way to the case of variable horizons, and require that our joint preference for $\tilde{\mathbf{x}}_t^n = (x_t, x_{t+1}, \ldots, x_n)$ and the horizon time n is utility independent of $\tilde{\mathbf{x}}_{t-1}$ for every t. We can then derive generalizations of the results of Sections 9.3 and 9.4. For example, the multiplicative form of Theorem 9.2 as given in (9.17) may be shown [Richard (1972)] to generalize as follows:

Let $\{\tilde{X}_t^n, N\}$ be utility independent of $\tilde{X}_{t-1}$ for $2 \le t \le n \le n^*$, and let $\tilde{X}_{n-1}^n$ be utility independent of X_n given the horizon is n for $n^\circ \le n \le n^*$. Then

$$1 + ku(\mathbf{x}^n, n) = g(n) \prod_{t=1}^{n-1} [1 + kk_t u_t(x_t)][1 + kl_n w_n(x_n)] \qquad (9.31)$$

for $n^\circ \le n \le n^*$ if $\sum_{t=1}^{n-1} k_i + l_n \neq 1$.

The implications of this result are extremely interesting. Note first of all that the functions $u_t(\cdot)$ do not depend on the horizon time n, so that they may be assessed by asking questions about tradeoffs in period t *regardless* of n. The functions $w_n(\cdot)$ correspond to "end-position" utilities; for example, for individual economic decisions they correspond to the utility for the legacy left behind at time of death. One such legacy utility function must be assessed for each possible time of death.

Second, note that (9.31) does not contain an additive function of n, in the sense of $\eta(n)$ in (9.26). This implies that all functions in (9.31) *can* be assessed *without* asking any questions that involve tradeoffs between the level of consumption streams and their length n. Yet, once fully assessed, (9.31) can be used to *answer* questions that do involve such tradeoffs! In other words, without ever making choices between alternatives that affect our length of life, we are nonetheless providing information that indicates how much consumption we would be willing to forego to increase our lifespan—*if* we believe the independence assumptions leading to (9.31).

---

* Of course, admittedly, many of these assessments are difficult to make and, in practice, we would want to run various sensitivity studies. Furthermore, if $n^* - n^\circ$ were large, we would ask questions for only a few representative n's and interpolate for other n-values.

This shows how far-reaching such independence assumptions can be, and how careful we must be in checking whether *all* their implications are acceptable.

The semiseparable results that were examined in Section 9.4 may be generalized similarly, and lead to remarkable properties analogous to those indicated above. If the second condition leading to (9.31) is dropped, it is shown in Appendix 9A that the joint utility function for X^n and N is of the form

$$u(\mathbf{x}^n, n) = \sum_{t=1}^{n-1} a_t(x_t) \prod_{\tau=1}^{t-1} b_\tau(x_\tau) + w_n(x_n) \prod_{\tau=1}^{n-1} b_\tau(x_\tau), \quad \text{for } n^o \le n \le n^*. \quad (9.32)$$

The assessment problem reduces to the assessment of two functions, $a_t(\cdot)$ and $b_t(\cdot)$, for each possible year of "life" $1 \le t < n^*$, and the assessment of one function, $w_n(\cdot)$, for each possible year of "death" $n^o \le n \le n^*$.

9.6 STATE-DEPENDENT UTILITIES*

All multivariate structures that we have thus far derived for $u(\mathbf{x})$ have assumed that preferences about the "distant" future $\vec{X}_{t+1}$ are utility independent from the "immediate" future $\vec{X}_t$ for all $1 \le t < n$. Yet, in many cases, we would not expect people to want to act in so superrational a manner. For example, we may become accustomed to the standard of living recently experienced, and adjust our aspiration levels and the scale of our risk aversion to conform to this recent experience.† Or else, we may feel that we appreciate a high standard of living more after a period of relative deprivation, and vice versa that we mind a (temporary) low standard of living less when we know that it will be followed by a period of affluence. These are all examples of utility dependence: our preferences for the future are affected by our past experience, or else our preferences for the immediate future depend on what the distant future holds in store. This section focuses on the special utility structures appropriate in such cases.

9.6.1 Efficient Backward and Forward State Descriptors

Consider $u(\vec{\mathbf{x}}_t, \vec{\mathbf{x}}_{t+1})$ as a utility function for $\vec{X}_{t+1}$ ("the future") when $\vec{X}_t$ ("the past") is given. Since $\vec{X}_{t+1}$ is utility *dependent* on $\vec{X}_t$, that is, the past

---

* The reader may wish at this point to skip directly to Section 9.7. This section briefly outlines a subject at the forefront of research.

† To account explicitly for such aspiration levels in a particular context, Bell (1975a) derives functional forms of utility functions for time streams involving preference dependencies between adjacent periods. See Section 7.7.9.

does matter, $u(\bar{\mathbf{x}}_t, \bar{\mathbf{x}}_{t+1})$ when viewed as a function of $\bar{\mathbf{x}}_{t+1}$ is not strategically equivalent to $u(\bar{\mathbf{x}}_t', \bar{\mathbf{x}}_{t+1})$ for all $\bar{\mathbf{x}}_t'$. Another way of saying this is to observe that our utility for $\bar{\mathbf{x}}_{t+1}$ may be affected only by certain features of the past, and not necessarily by all the detail contained in the full description $\bar{\mathbf{x}}_t$ of the past. It is therefore natural to introduce a state descriptor of the past, $\bar{s}_t(\bar{\mathbf{x}}_t)$, where $\bar{s}_t(\cdot)$ may itself be vector-valued, although presumably of lower dimension than $\bar{\mathbf{x}}_t$, and has the property that two different pasts, $\bar{\mathbf{x}}_t$ and $\bar{\mathbf{x}}_t'$, that have the same $\bar{s}_t$ [that is, $\bar{s}_t(\bar{\mathbf{x}}_t) = \bar{s}_t(\bar{\mathbf{x}}_t')$] will lead to strategically equivalent utilities for the future. We may then regard the conditional utility of $\vec{X}_{t+1}$ given $\vec{X}_t$ as a function of $\bar{s}_t$ instead of $\bar{\mathbf{x}}_t$, and shall denote it as $\vec{u}_{t+1}(\bar{\mathbf{x}}_{t+1} \mid \bar{s}_t(\bar{\mathbf{x}}_t))$, that is, the "forward" utility for streams starting in period $t+1$.

Thus far we have only required that $\bar{s}_t(\cdot)$ be a more economical description of the past than $\bar{\mathbf{x}}_t$, but still adequate for decisions regarding $\bar{\mathbf{x}}_{t+1}$. Now we ask whether $\bar{s}_t(\cdot)$ is, in some sense, as *economical a descriptor as possible* for this purpose. We therefore define $\bar{s}_t(\cdot)$ to be an *efficient* backward state descriptor if and only if for any past state $\bar{s}_t$ the strategic equivalence of $\vec{u}_{t+1}(\cdot \mid \bar{s}_t)$ and $\vec{u}_{t+1}(\cdot \mid \bar{s}_t')$ implies that $\bar{s}_t = \bar{s}_t'$. Another way of stating this is to require that *all* $\bar{\mathbf{x}}_t$, which lead to strategically equivalent (with respect to $\vec{X}_{t+1}$) $u(\bar{\mathbf{x}}_t, \cdot)$, be assigned the same $\bar{s}_t$.

Analogously, we can define forward-state descriptors, $\vec{s}_{t+1}(\bar{\mathbf{x}}_{t+1})$, that permit a less detailed, more economic description of the distant future to serve as a conditioning variable for decisions affecting only the near term future $\bar{\mathbf{x}}_t$. And again, we may introduce the concept of an efficient descriptor; that is, $\vec{s}_{t+1}(\cdot)$ is efficient if $\bar{u}_t(\bar{\mathbf{x}}_t \mid \vec{s}_{t+1}) \sim \bar{u}_t(\bar{\mathbf{x}}_t \mid \vec{s}_{t+1}')$ implies that $\vec{s}_{t+1} = \vec{s}_{t+1}'$.

A number of interesting results about these efficient state descriptors have been proven [Meyer (1975)] but since the theory itself is still not in a fully operational state, we prefer merely to summarize informally a few of these results.

Most importantly, efficient state descriptors are *updatable*. Thus, for example, $\bar{s}_t(\cdot)$ is a function of $\bar{s}_{t-1}(\cdot)$ and x_t only. Similarly, $\vec{s}_t(\cdot)$ is a function of $\vec{s}_{t+1}(\cdot)$ and x_t only.

Next, if $t < t'$, and we are interested in the conditional utility function defined over the partial stream $(x_{t+1}, \ldots, x_{t'})$ given the past $\bar{\mathbf{x}}_t$ and the future $\bar{\mathbf{x}}_{t'+1}$, then the dependence on $\bar{\mathbf{x}}_t$ and $\bar{\mathbf{x}}_{t'+1}$ will occur only through $\bar{s}_t(\bar{\mathbf{x}}_t)$ and $\vec{s}_{t'+1}(\bar{\mathbf{x}}_{t'+1})$.

Finally, an examination of consistency requirements leads to the discovery of a limited number of special structures involving updating of the state descriptors that are, at the same time, flexible for analytical work and applicable in domains where utility independence assumptions would be inappropriate. These results indicate that a great richness of temporal preference modeling is available to us through the use of efficient state descriptors.

9.7   PROBLEMS OF APPLICATION

Thus far this chapter has explored special utility structures for temporal problems. But temporal decision-making problems differ from ordinary, static, multiattribute utility theory in two other respects:

1. The number of univariate functions that must be assessed is typically very large. For example, a midcareer person with a maximum of 50 years more of life, must, if he uses the year as the basic time period, and if the rather strong assumptions leading to (9.31) apply to him, assess two functions for each year (a consumption utility and a legacy utility), so a total of 100 subjectively assessed univariate functions!

2. The univariate functions involved in temporal problems typically have special properties. The attributes involved (consumption, profit, legacy, pollution) have utilities that usually exhibit positive risk aversion, in fact decreasing positive risk-aversion, over broad ranges. These qualitative properties should be taken into account in their assessment as well as their interpolation.

We shall treat these two aspects in the reverse order.

9.7.1   Univariate Assessment and Fairing

The simplest families of univariate utilities are single-parameter families such as the exponential family $u(x) = -e^{-rx}$, where $r > 0$ if we are to have positive risk aversion. (See Section 4.6.) This family has constant risk aversion, in the sense that the risk premium we would be willing to pay to insure against the risk entailed in a lottery $\tilde{x}$ depends only on the incremental lottery $(\tilde{x} - \bar{x})$ and not at all on the mean level $\bar{x}$. For attributes such as consumption and assets we probably do not feel that this behavior reflects our feelings, since most of us would feel that our risk premium for a given incremental lottery decreases as $\bar{x}$ increases. It has therefore often been suggested that of all the single-parameter families the constant-proportional risk-aversion family $u(x) = -x^{-\rho}$ where $\rho > 0$, is the most appropriate. (See Section 4.7.) This family has the property that proportional lotteries have a proportional risk premium. In other words, if $\tilde{x}$ is a lottery in which we gain or lose a given percentage of $\bar{x}$ then our risk premium is expressible as a percentage of $\bar{x}$, for any $\bar{x}$. There is some appeal to the belief that, if faced for example with a lottery with equal chances at ± 10 percent of next year's consumption, we would settle for an insurance premium of a given percentage of $\bar{x}$, for example, 2 percent of $\bar{x}$, to avoid the risk, *for any level of* $\bar{x}$. In fact, however, the following turns out to be true experimentally for a broad class of subjects:

1. A single assessment question, asking for the certainty equivalent for a 50–50 lottery, yields a value for ρ. These ρ values for actual subjects are perilously* close to $\rho = 0$. Now, the family $-x^{-\rho}$ approaches, as $\rho \to 0$, the logarithmic utility $\ln x$. This utility has the property that 50–50 chances at equal logarithmic changes (e.g., doubling or halving) of the annual consumption leave us indifferent to what we have for sure. In other words, a subject whose typical level of consumption† is around \$10,000 per year might, for a single year, be indifferent between \$10,000 per year for sure or a fair lottery between \$5000 and \$20,000.

2. For gambles that are well above his normal experience, a typical subject tends to be less than proportionally risk averse. For example, the above subject, for a fair lottery between \$10,000 and \$40,000 annual consumption, might want over \$20,000 for sure to be indifferent. As a result, it appears that the constant-proportional risk-aversion family, although probably the best single-parameter family that is available, is not sufficiently adaptable to model typical subject feelings over a wide enough range of consumption.

We are therefore led to look farther afield for faithful and simple representations of univariate utilities. First, let us examine the properties we would like such a utility to have. If the attribute is consumption, there should be a (vaguely known) subsistence level at which the utility drops off very steeply, and we can idealize this by saying it drops off vertically. On the right, for very large x, we would expect the utility to remain bounded, for the following reason. Suppose you are facing a 50–50 gamble on your annual consumption for next year. If you lose, your consumption will be exactly \$5000 per year, with no hope of anything better. If you win, the payoff will be simply enormous, \$$10^8$ or \$$10^9$ or more if you wish, but you must consume it all next year. Call this payoff x^*. In such a situation, most of us will gladly settle for \$$10^6$ per year for sure instead of the lottery, and we feel that way irrespective of how large

---

* We shall argue below that we want $u(x)$ to be bounded for large x, which requires $\rho > 0$.

† We should really speak here of "consumption in excess of the minimum subsistence level," and all references to consumption are to be taken in that sense in the above discussion.

x^* becomes. What we are saying is that for us $.5[u(5000)+u(x^*)]<$ $u(10^6)$ regardless of the size of x^*, so that clearly $u(x^*)$ must be finite (hence bounded) for arbitrarily large x^*.

Since $u(x)$ is bounded on the right, and drops vertically on the left,* it is convenient to choose it everywhere negative, and to let $u \to 0$ as $x \to \infty$. This is particularly true for univariate utilities in multiplicative structures such as (9.31), for there we have a product of single-period factors none of which *must ever change sign*! To see this, suppose that the factor corresponding to x_t changed sign at $x_t = x_t^o$. Then, if $u(\mathbf{x})$ is an increasing function of $x_{t'}$, $t' \neq t$, when $x_t > x_t^o$, it will be a decreasing function of $x_{t'}$ when $x_t < x_t^o$, and such a reversal in the direction of increasing preference for all $x_{t'}$, $t' \neq t$, is clearly unacceptable, especially when it purportedly results from a negligible change in x_t (from $x_t^o - \epsilon$ to $x_t^o + \epsilon$, where $|\epsilon|$ is arbitrarily small).

Note that the general shape derived above for univariate consumption utilities also applies for attributes very different from consumption, for example, air purity. If we were to use the pollutant concentration (e.g., particles per cubic centimeter) as our attribute, it would have the unpleasant property that higher values of the attribute are less desirable. We therefore use the inverse of the pollutant level, the air purity described by the number of cubic centimeters of pure air per particle. Call this measure of air purity X. Then there is a vague lower bound on x below which the air is too impure for human survival. Subsistence ceases, hence near this vague lower bound the utility drops off very steeply and once again we can idealize by saying "vertically." Similarly, on the right, for very large x, we will approach an upper bound for much the same reason as before: given a 50–50 lottery between dirty air and infinitely pure air, we would settle for some finite value of air purity for sure. Also, the utility may be expected to be risk averse, as the following example will show.

Consider a 50–50 gamble between air purities of 2 and 10 cc/particle, respectively. The "average" purity is 6 cc/particle. It seems as if most people would prefer the "average" purity for sure to the lottery. To see this, consider the same choice in terms of pollutant *concentrations*, that is willingness to risk a one-half chance of an increase of 1/3 particles/cc (i.e., from 1/6 to 1/2) for a one-half chance at a 1/15 particles/cc decrease (i.e.,

---

* We also feel that, strictly speaking, the utility function should be bounded on the left, that is, if x^o represents ruin, $u(x^o)$ should not be taken as $-\infty$. The argument goes as follows: let x^o be ruin and let $x^o < x' < x''$; the certainty value x' can always be made (for us!) preferable to the lottery that yields x^o with probability p and x'' with probability $(1-p)$ by making p sufficiently small. This implies $u(x^o) \neq -\infty$. If $u(x^o)$ is taken as a finite value, then it is possible to choose $u(\cdot)$ as nonnegative. However, it is more convenient for many applications to let $u(\cdot)$ be unbounded on the left and in this case we must choose $u(\cdot)<0$.

from 1/6 to 1/10). Such a willingness seems unlikely. A preference for the sure 1/6 implies risk aversion in the *purity* attribute.

If the assessor deems it appropriate to use a family of positive decreasing risk aversion utility functions, then we remind the reader of the versatility of the "sum of exponentials" form

$$u(x) = -e^{-ax} - ce^{-bx}, \qquad a > b. \tag{9.33}$$

These so-called sumex functions turn out to be reasonably satisfactory fits to utilities over the intervals we are interested in. The numerical problems associated with fitting them are described in Schlaifer (1971), and these programs have been extensively used for fitting purposes. We should like, however, to remark here that sumex functions can prove inadequate when their range becomes large, and that a more theoretically sound interpolation theory would be desirable, even though we can manage in a numerical engineering sense with sumex functions.

9.7.2 Multivariate Assessment

We shall illustrate the problems of assessment of multiattribute temporal utilities by describing the assessment process for a utility for lifetime consumption and legacy streams. The utility structure shall be taken to satisfy (9.31); complete details of the assessment process are given in Richard (1972).

Suppose that, in the spirit of the preceding subsection, we take the individual utilities $u_t(\cdot)$ to be sumex functions, so that three certainty equivalent assessments will determine each utility function. If we are now 40 years old, have a maximum actuarial life of 100, and use the year as our period, there are 120 functions to be determined, that is, 360 certainty equivalent assessments, which is surely more than necessary to express our feelings about these matters! To reduce this burden a little, we recognize that our feelings will only vary slowly from year to year, so that assessing our utilities once every five years is probably adequate. The intervening years we can either assume our utilities to stay the same, or else we can smoothly interpolate the three parameters a, b, and c in (9.33) from year to year. This reduces the number of certainty equivalents to be assessed to $3 \times 24 = 72$, which is more manageable.

Over what range should these 24 utilities be assessed? Experience shows that:

1. Lotteries presented to a subject should be sufficiently wide to feel uncomfortable; we are interested in risk-taking behavior "in the large."
2. Lotteries should jointly span the entire range of consumption and legacy levels that the subject is likely to encounter in reality.

In order to know where to place these lotteries, a series of questions is first asked of the subject that establish the general magnitude of consumption levels throughout that person's life. Next, an extended "conversation" with the subject (using a time-shared computer program) proceeds through a sequence of six types of questions:

1. SPREADING A LUMP SUM. Suppose you had $600,000 of consumption (in present real terms, free of inflation) to spread over the remaining 60 years of your life (you are *sure* you will live to be 100). How would you spread these $600,000? *Note.* This is *consumption*, so you do not get any return on money not spent. Whatever spending pattern you come up with, it must add up to $600,000. The answer to this question is a sequence that we shall call $\hat{\mathbf{x}} = \{\hat{x}_1, \ldots, \hat{x}_{60}\}$. Of course we need an answer only every five years, and can interpolate in between.

2. CONSUMPTION-COMPATIBLE LEGACIES. Suppose that you die before you are 100, specifically, suppose you die at the end of year t from now, and you know this now. Suppose that you will enjoy the consumption stream $\{\hat{x}_1, \hat{x}_2, \ldots, \hat{x}_t\}$, which you assigned in question 1, until your death. What legacy, $\hat{z}_t$, would you consider compatible with this lifetime consumption stream in the following sense: that if $\hat{z}_t$ has been earmarked for your heirs (after taxes), and you are now given the opportunity to shift some moneys from the stream $\hat{x}_1, \ldots, \hat{x}_t$ to $\hat{z}_t$ or vice versa, you would not wish to do any shifting because you feel the balance between your lifetime consumption stream and your legacy is just right. This question yields a sequence $\hat{\mathbf{z}} = \{\hat{z}_1, \ldots, \hat{z}_{60}\}$.

3. CONSUMPTION UTILITIES. For any fifth year, the interactive program helps to assess a sumex utility function for consumption. First, one must determine a minimum subsistence level for this year, typically a level somewhat below the official "poverty" levels, for example, $3000 or $4000 for a family of four. The first lottery proposed to the subject is typically chosen to run from a little above the subsistence level to several times (2 or 3 times) the $\hat{x}_t$ he allocated to the relevant year, so it is a very wide lottery. The two other lotteries then subdivide this interval in the usual way as discussed in Section 4.9.

The result is a sequence of sumex utilities $\{u_t(\cdot), t = 1, \ldots, 60\}$. In the conversational time-shared programs that have been written to aid the assessment process the resulting utilities are required to be risk averse.

4. LEGACY UTILITIES. The assessment procedure of question 3 above is repeated to obtain a sequence of sumex legacy utilities $\{w_t(\cdot), t = 1, \ldots, 60\}$. The assessment ranges are pegged about the sequence $\hat{\mathbf{z}}$, and usually a minimum legacy level (the analog of subsistence) of zero is used, although this is not essential.

5. TEMPORAL RISK-AVERSION. The lotteries presented in question 3 above referred to consumption during a single year. How much more risk averse would you be if the lottery outcome determined your consumption for a longer period, say 5 or 10 years? Specifically, the program chooses a midlife period of five years, and presents the widest lottery used in question 3 for the representative year in that period, with the additional provision that the lottery outcome will be your level of consumption for all five years. How much do you lower your certainty equivalent? This single question determines the "temporal risk aversion" as measured by k in (9.31).

6. SPREADING CONSUMPTION OVER AN UNCERTAIN LIFETIME. This is the hardest type of question, both to explain and to answer. Its purpose is to assess the function $g(n)$ in (9.31). The discussion following (9.31) makes clear that $g(n)$ can be assessed by asking consumption-spreading questions over an uncertain lifetime. In this spirit we ask every fifth year the following question (refer to Fig. 9.2 to understand the question better).

"Consider two successive five-year periods following t_0. You will have a 50 percent chance of dying at time $t_1 = t_0 + 5$, and a 50 percent chance of dying at time $t_2 = t_0 + 10$, so you will be dead for sure at the end of the 10-year period. Up to time t_0 you will enjoy the consumption stream $(\hat{x}_1, \ldots, \hat{x}_{t_0})$ you assigned in response to question 1. If you die at t_1, your heirs will receive a legacy $\hat{z}_{t_1}$, and if you die at t_2 a legacy $\hat{z}_{t_2}$, just as you determined in response to question 2. For the 10 years from t_0 to t_2 you will have total consumption $x = \sum x_t$ (where t ranges from $t_0 + 1$ to $t_0 + 10$) available to consume. You have to decide *now*

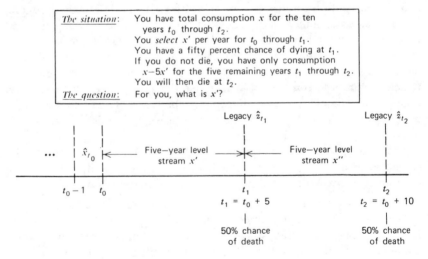

Fig. 9.2. **Spreading consumption over an uncertain lifetime.**

how much of x to consume each of the first five years. Call this amount x' per year, that is, a level stream of consumption totaling $5x'$ for the five years. Clearly $5x'$ must be less than the available total x. The remainder, $x - 5x'$, is automatically allocated to a level stream $x'' = .2x - x'$ for each of the last five years, if you survive past t_1. If you die at t_1, the amount $5x'' = x - 5x'$ of consumption is forfeited, so you are asked to trade off the forfeiture of $5x''$ if you die at t_1 against having to live at an undesirably low level of consumption if you survive."

Since this is a difficult question to answer, the conversational program provides some feedback regarding the implications of your answer for the value you attach to an additional year of life. It was pointed out in the discussion following (9.31) that, under the restrictive assumptions made there, consistent tradeoff decisions affecting length of life could be inferred from assessments involving only allocations of consumption over uncertain lifetime. In the conversational assessment programs we make full use of these properties.

These assessment programs are running on the DEC System 10 computer at the Harvard Business School, and have been used to assess lifetime utility functions for a wide variety of subjects. Research continues in determining optimal economic decision-making patterns for these individuals. Some of this research has been reported in Richard (1972).

9.8 TIME RESOLUTION OF UNCERTAINTY

We have already discussed briefly in Section 9.1 the group of problems that fall under this rubric. Here we should like to go into them more deeply. There are, in fact, three distinct kinds of issues that relate to the delayed (as opposed to immediate) resolution of uncertainty:

1. The evolution of our utility over time, as our experience and preferences change.
2. The anxiety that accompanies unresolved uncertainty.
3. The need to hedge in order to maintain the flexibility to condition future actions on intervening information.

We shall treat each in turn.

9.8.1 Evolving Utility

Suppose as before that we are going to take actions that will affect (probabilistically!) a consequence stream $\tilde{x}$. Suppose furthermore that our liking for $\mathbf{x}$, that is, our utility function, will depend on some other uncertain events, which may also be a stream over time and which we shall denote as $\tilde{\boldsymbol{\theta}}$, and which are uninfluenced by our actions affecting $\mathbf{x}$. To render this more concrete, consider the following two examples.

1. We're now in midcareer. Let $\tilde{\mathbf{x}}$ be the stream of retirement income we'll receive subsequent to age 65. It clearly depends on career, savings, and investment actions we'll take in the future. Let $\boldsymbol{\theta}$ indicate whether, at age 65, our tastes have developed toward gardening or toward traveling, toward hot climates or cold ones. Clearly our liking for $\mathbf{x}$ will depend on what $\boldsymbol{\theta}$ turns out to be. Observe that we'll learn about $\boldsymbol{\theta}$ gradually, hence we can think of the stream $\boldsymbol{\theta}$ as our gradually increasing stream of knowledge about the ultimate $\boldsymbol{\theta}$.

2. Let $\mathbf{x}$ denote our consumption stream, and $\boldsymbol{\theta}$ the sequence of family statuses we pass through. We might start out single, become married, have k children, divorce, remarry, acquire one more child, and so on. Clearly our utility for $\mathbf{x}$ will depend on $\boldsymbol{\theta}$, even though our decisions affecting $\mathbf{x}$ may well not influence $\boldsymbol{\theta}$.

The proper formulation of such a problem requires in general that we use our joint utility $u(\mathbf{x}, \boldsymbol{\theta})$ for $\mathbf{x}$ and $\boldsymbol{\theta}$, even though our decisions do not influence $\boldsymbol{\theta}$. A special example of this already occurred in Section 9.5, where $\boldsymbol{\theta}$ was the uncertain length of life. An analogous problem was also discussed in Section 4.12. Naively one might think that, if $f(\boldsymbol{\theta})$ is the probability density function for $\boldsymbol{\theta}$ and is unaffected by our actions, then

$$u^*(\mathbf{x}) = \int f(\boldsymbol{\theta})u(\mathbf{x}, \boldsymbol{\theta})\, d\boldsymbol{\theta} \qquad (9.34)$$

should do as a utility for actions affecting $\mathbf{x}$. This would indeed be true if no additional information regarding $\boldsymbol{\theta}$ were received until all actions affecting $\mathbf{x}$ had been taken. If, however, the stream $\boldsymbol{\theta}$ is revealed gradually and simultaneously with the unfolding of $\mathbf{x}$, we need to proceed more carefully. Suppose that at time t we have had $\tilde{\mathbf{x}}_t$ and $\tilde{\boldsymbol{\theta}}_t$ revealed, and must make decisions about $\vec{\mathbf{x}}_{t+1}$ in the face of residual uncertainty about $\vec{\boldsymbol{\theta}}_{t+1}$. An appropriate utility function would be

$$\vec{u}(\vec{\mathbf{x}}_{t+1} \mid \tilde{\mathbf{x}}_t, \tilde{\boldsymbol{\theta}}_t) = \int f(\vec{\boldsymbol{\theta}}_{t+1} \mid \tilde{\boldsymbol{\theta}}_t)u(\tilde{\mathbf{x}}_t, \vec{\mathbf{x}}_{t+1}; \tilde{\boldsymbol{\theta}}_t, \vec{\boldsymbol{\theta}}_{t+1})\, d\vec{\boldsymbol{\theta}}_{t+1}$$

which cannot be derived from $u^*(\mathbf{x})$ in (9.34) simply by substituting the revealed sequence $\tilde{\mathbf{x}}_t$.

Although the correct procedure, as outlined above, is conceptually clear enough, it may be hard to apply in practice. What consequence streams besides $\mathbf{x}$ have to be included in our utility function when making decisions affecting $\mathbf{x}$ only? The operational answer: all those streams that will provide information on which, at some future time, we may significantly want to condition our future actions affecting **x**. Returning to the consumption–investment decisions examined in Section 9.7, this surely means that information streams regarding such matters as family status and health must be included to get a realistic model.

9.8.2 Anxiety Along the Way

Now let us suppose that **x** includes all consequence streams that matter in the sense of Section 9.8.1, so that $u(\mathbf{x})$ is all we need to consider even when we include the effect of changing perceptions of utility. Also, suppose all decisions are made at the outset, so that the rate of resolution of uncertainty cannot affect the information available at the time of decision. We must then still face the differences in anxiety along the way caused by differences in *when* uncertainties regarding $\tilde{\mathbf{x}}$ are resolved. If these uncertainties are resolved early, the period of anxiety is short, and we will generally prefer this to extended periods of anxiety (unless, of course, we love the suspense). In other words, we have utility for the duration and intensity of the anxiety associated with **x**, as well as for **x** itself.

Let us try to formalize this idea. Suppose the state of anxiety or stress caused by uncertainty about the future stream **x** can be quantified by the stream **s**. In some cases we experience "joy of anticipation" rather than anxiety and we will consider this included in **s**. Clearly, **s** is a functional of two kinds of data:

1. The probability density function $f(\mathbf{x})$.
2. The time schedule according to which this uncertainty in **x** is (gradually) resolved. Note that x_t will normally* be fully known by time t, but it may, of course, be fully or partially revealed much earlier.

In a simple-minded way we think of **s** as the stream of "sleepless nights." Next, we assess a utility for **x** and **s** (call it $u(\mathbf{x}, \mathbf{s})$ and choose the act that maximizes† $E_{\mathbf{x}} u(\tilde{\mathbf{x}}, \mathbf{s})$. Note that in this formulation our utility for **x** depends on the probability of **x** through the timing of the resolution of uncertainty and the magnitude of this uncertainty! In static utility theory the independence of the utility of **x** from the probability distribution of **x** is an essential consequence of the axioms. Here, in a dynamic, temporal

---

* In some cases the true x_t might be revealed only long after the fact, for example, the number of fetuses that were malformed in an early month of pregnancy may only be revealed at birth. But this situation is uncommon.

† For a given act the stream **s** may also be uncertain and then one must maximize $E_{\mathbf{x},\mathbf{s}}[u(\tilde{\mathbf{x}}, \tilde{\mathbf{s}})]$.

setting it seems that we must introduce such a dependence in order to deal with anxiety. The extent to which such a formulation can or cannot be made self-consistent is still inadequately understood.*

9.8.3 Hedging and Anticipating

Suppose that the consequence stream **x** includes, to whatever extent necessary,

1. Any experience relevant for the time-evolution of utility, designated θ in Section 9.8.1.
2. Any anxiety along the way that affects our utility, designated **s** in Section 9.8.2.

The resulting $u(\mathbf{x})$ may then be used to choose among alternatives on an expected utility basis. The time resolution of uncertainty still has an additional impact in this analysis, beyond the θ and **s** streams already accounted for: it affects the degree to which we must hedge in our early acts in order for us to be able to use information acquired later on to adjust direction.

If uncertainty is resolved very early, we should be able to anticipate the future very well and act in an anticipatory way. If uncertainty is resolved late, but there are "recourse" acts that permit last-minute adjustments, we will want to hedge early on. However, this type of problem·is not in any way different from the usual decision-tree analysis. First a tree structure of acts and events is established. This tree must include all informational events, in the right temporal sequence. Next, we evaluate endpositions based on the $u(\mathbf{x})$ associated with the stream **x** leading to each end position. Backward induction will then automatically produce the correct strategy, including the proper degree of hedging and anticipating.† The only reason to emphasize this point here is that frequently, especially in simulations, the gradual resolution of uncertainty is treated improperly and early actions are taken as if future information were already available.

---

* If we let $\mathbf{s}^o$ represent a state of absence of anxiety or of an absence of joy from anticipated suspense, then we ask the admittedly difficult question: Given the combined stimulus $(\mathbf{x}, \mathbf{s})$, what stream $\mathbf{x}'$ would make you indifferent between $(\mathbf{x}, \mathbf{s})$ and $(\mathbf{x}', \mathbf{s}^o)$? How much would we pay to get rid of those sleepless nights?

† Admittedly, this is easier said than done, since the decision tree can become awfully complicated very quickly. Once again we pose the simple-sounding question: What is your certainty equivalent now for a 50–50 lottery that yields nothing or $100,000 deliverable in 10 years' time if the resolution of the uncertainty takes place in 10 years? If we structure this problem carefully we might be forced to consider hedging actions and external uncertainties along the way. Should we contemplate going into debt in anticipation of a favorable outcome? Can the lottery be used as a collatoral for loans? Many business investment decisions involve analogous considerations.

Derivation of a Utility Function for Consumption and Lifetime

We want to show that (9.32) follows from the conditions:

1. $(\vec{X}_t^n, N)$ is utility independent from $\vec{X}_{t-1}$ for $2 \le t \le n$, $n^o \le n \le n^*$;
2. $\vec{u}_t(\vec{x}_t^n \mid n)$ depends on $\vec{x}_t^n$ for any given t and n, that is, we can obtain at least two values for $\vec{u}_t$ by varying $\vec{x}_t^n$ over its entire range, while holding t and n fixed.

First, we observe that condition 1 implies that $\vec{u}_t(\vec{x}_t^n, n)$ and $\vec{u}_{t+1}(\vec{x}_{t+1}^n, n)$ both exist, and that they must be strategically equivalent for decisions regarding $(\vec{x}_{t+1}^n, n)$ if we set x_t to any specific value. Hence

$$\vec{u}_t(\vec{x}_t^n, n) = a_t(x_t) + b_t(x_t) \vec{u}_{t+1}(\vec{x}_{t+1}^n, n) \qquad \text{for } 1 \le t < n, \quad n^o \le n \le n^* \quad (9A.1)$$

where $a_t(\cdot)$ and $b_t(\cdot)$ do not depend on n or on $\vec{x}_{t+1}^n$.

Second, we recognize from (9.26) that

$$\vec{u}_t(\vec{x}_t^n, n) = \eta_t(n) + \theta_t(n) \vec{u}_t(\vec{x}_t^n \mid n) \qquad \text{for } 1 \le t \le n, \quad n^o \le n \le n^*. \quad (9A.2)$$

Third, condition 1 implies that $\vec{X}_t^n$ is utility independent of X_{t-1} for any given n and for $2 \le t \le n$, so that, by analogy with (9.22) and (9.23),

$$\vec{u}_t(\vec{x}_t^n, n) = \lambda_t(x_t \mid n) + \mu_t(x_t \mid n) \vec{u}_{t+1}(\vec{x}_{t+1}^n \mid n)$$

$$\text{for } 1 \le t < n, \quad n^o \le n \le n^*, \quad (9A.3)$$

and

$$u(\mathbf{x}^n \mid n) = \sum_{t=1}^{n} \lambda_t(x_t \mid n) \prod_{\tau=1}^{t-1} \mu_\tau(x_\tau \mid n) \qquad \text{for } n^o \le n \le n^*, \quad (9A.4)$$

where $\lambda_n(x_n \mid n) = u_n(x_n \mid n)$.

We are now ready to prove (9.32). Substitute (9A.2) on both sides of (9A.1) to obtain

$$\eta_t(n) + \theta_t(n) \vec{u}_t(\vec{x}_t^n \mid n) = a_t(x_t) + b_t(x_t)[\eta_{t+1}(n) + \theta_{t+1}(n) \vec{u}_{t+1}(\vec{x}_{t+1}^n \mid n)]$$

$$\text{for } 1 \le t < n, \quad n^o \le n \le n^*. \quad (9A.5)$$

Substitute (9A.3) on the left-hand side of (9A.5), and collect terms that multiply $\vec{u}_{t+1}(\cdot \mid \cdot)$; this yields

$$\eta_t(n) + \theta_t(n)\lambda_t(x_t \mid n) - a_t(x_t) - b_t(x_t)\eta_{t+1}(n)$$
$$= [b_t(x_t)\theta_{t+1}(n) - \theta_t(n)\mu_t(x_t \mid n)]\vec{u}_{t+1}(\vec{x}_{t+1}^n \mid n).$$

But since $\vec{u}_{t+1}$ may be varied independently of the rest, the left-hand side, as well as the bracketed expression on the right, must equal zero. Hence we find, for $t < n$ and for all n, that

$$\theta_t(n)\lambda_t(x_t \mid n) = a_t(x_t) + b_t(x_t)\eta_{t+1}(n) - \eta_t(n)$$

$$\mu_t(x_t \mid n) = \frac{b_t(x_t)\theta_{t+1}(n)}{\theta_t(n)}. \tag{9A.6}$$

We now want to substitute (9A.6) in (9A.4). First, notice that

$$\prod_{\tau=1}^{t-1} \mu_\tau(x_\tau \mid n) = \frac{\theta_t(n)}{\theta_1(n)} \prod_{\tau=1}^{t-1} b_\tau(x_\tau), \qquad \text{for } 1 < t \le n.$$

We substitute this in (9A.4), separating the term corresponding to $t = n$ in the summation since (9A.6) only holds for $t < n$. This yields, after some cancellation of terms,

$$u(\mathbf{x}^n \mid n) = \frac{1}{\theta_1(n)}\left[\sum_{t=1}^{n-1} a_t(x_t) \prod_{\tau=1}^{t-1} b_\tau(x_\tau) - \eta_1(n)\right.$$

$$\left. + (\eta_n(n) + \lambda_n(x_n \mid n)\theta_n(n)) \prod_{\tau=1}^{n-1} b_\tau(x_\tau)\right] \text{ for } n^\circ \le n \le n^*. \tag{9A.7}$$

We now substitute (9A.7) in (9A.2) for the desired result:

$$u(\mathbf{x}^n, n) = \eta_1(n) + \theta_1(n)\vec{u}_1(\mathbf{x}^n \mid n)$$

$$= \sum_{t=1}^{n-1} a_t(x_t) \prod_{\tau=1}^{t-1} b_\tau(x_\tau) + w_n(x_n) \prod_{\tau=1}^{n-1} b_\tau(x_\tau) \tag{9A.8}$$

where $w_n(x_n) = \eta_n(n) + \lambda_n(x_n \mid n)\theta_n(n)$.

CHAPTER 10

Aggregation of Individual Preferences

A decision maker may be concerned about the effects of his or her actions on other individuals. There may be altruistic or malevolent motives involved, but, since we prefer to think positively, we shall concentrate our attention on the prototypical higher-level, benevolent, executive decision maker. Let us refer to this individual decision maker simply as the "Decision Maker"—that person who wishes to incorporate the feelings, values, preferences, and utilities of others into her own value assessments. She wants to make *everyone* happy but, alas, tradeoffs will have to be made.* These concerns will be the subject matter of this chapter but before we delve into details, let us put this problem into a broader perspective: that of the *group decision problem*. We must be careful, however, since we believe there is no such thing as *the* group decision problem. We should talk in the plural about group decision problems.

From a *descriptive* point of view, as contrasted to a *prescriptive* point of view, most actions taken by decision makers, both private and public, can only be explained in terms of a panoply of various interacting forces and actions taken by many individuals acting through a mixture of motives. Just imagine how a bill gets through the U.S. Congress. This is truly a group effort. One can theorize about such complex group processes and investigate how such processes "really" work, how they can be made to work better given political realities, how ideal systems should be designed to be fair, resilient, and responsive to popular will, how such processes

---

* Throughout this chapter, we refer to the Decision Maker as a she and to the others whose preferences she is concerned about as he's. This will help to keep clear references to his and her in the chapter. Soon we will name the model with the Decision Maker as the Supra Decision Maker Model, so an ardent MCP can just assume she is short for supra he. Astute readers will *note* that this is a classical method—deception—of addressing problems with multiple interests.

can attract the responsible involvement of the citizenry, and so on. The list of so-called group decision problems is practically unending. The vast literature of political economy, of sociology, of anthropology, and the like, deals with group decision processes. Closer to our concern in this chapter is the literature emanating from the monumental work of John von Neumann in the theory of games and the work of Kenneth Arrow on social choice and individual values.

We could argue that no decision is ever an *individual's* decision; in some cases it may appear to be superficially so, but when we probe further we recognize how interrelated all decisions are with one another and any decision is the result of group interactions. On the other hand, since the human mind is the synthesizer in the decision-making process, we could argue that each group choice is determined by individual's decisions—perhaps by many—and that there are no *group* decisions. In our opinion, attempting to "resolve" this philosophical issue would not contribute toward improved decision making.

In this book we have concentrated on *the individual decision maker* and this will continue to be our orientation in this chapter. We shall be concerned with how a given individual could systematically incorporate the views of others into her own decision making framework. As we develop our point of view we shall make frequent asides to the work of others who consider similar problems from the perspective of the participatory group rather than from a single individual.

10.1 THE DECISION MAKER AS SYNTHESIZER OR AMALGAMATOR

As usual, we assume that the Decision Maker must choose one of several alternatives. Her decision will have an impact on a number of people whose feelings and preferences she is concerned about. Our problem is, "How can we help her think about the issues involved?" In particular, the focus is on structuring *her* preferences—but we reiterate the main point once again: her preferences depend on the preferences of others. However, we do not take a fully interactive viewpoint, that is, we do *not* assume that the preferences of those "others" depend on the preferences of our "supra" decision maker.

10.1.1 The Pure Cases

The essence of our Decision Maker's decision problem can be illustrated with a couple of "pure cases." Assume that the consequences x of her decision can be described in terms of attributes $X_1, X_2, \ldots, X_M$, and suppose that her overall objective is to "maximize the well-being of N specified individuals." We can divide this into N lower-level objectives that are of the form "maximize the well-being of individual i." Further subdividing is of course the problem of specifying an individual's objectives, which was considered in some detail in Chapter 2. Two useful attributes, call them V_i and U_i, which measure the degree to which individual i's well-being is maximized, are provided by his value function v_i and his utility function u_i for the consequences $\mathbf{x}$ of the possible alternatives. We focus on two versions of our protagonist's decision problem: the *certainty* model and the *uncertainty* model.

THE CERTAINTY MODEL. With no uncertainty, the Decision Maker's value function v over the consequences $\mathbf{x}$ is sufficient to select an alternative. Because the fundamental objective of the Decision Maker is to "maximize the well-being of the N individuals," it may be desirable to investigate functional relationships relating the individuals' value functions to the Decision Maker's. Specifically, if $V_1, V_2, \ldots, V_N$ designate N attributes measured by the respective individuals' value functions $v_1, v_2, \ldots, v_N$ we will want to investigate forms of v_D such that

$$v(\mathbf{x}) = v_D[v_1(\mathbf{x}), v_2(\mathbf{x}), \ldots, v_N(\mathbf{x})], \qquad (10.1)$$

where both v and v_D are value functions of the Decision Maker. Expression (10.1) functionally illustrates the pure certainty case of the Decision Maker's problem. This formulation has some strong implicit assumptions. The first is that the Decision Maker's preferences for consequences $\mathbf{x}$ are entirely captured through the v_i's, with due allowance, of course, to consideration of scales.* A second is that individual i's preference structure is completely specified by v_i, for all i. Third, (10.1) implicitly assumes that the Decision Maker knows the v_i's, for if she did not, the decision problem would become one of uncertainty.

THE UNCERTAINTY MODEL. In the uncertainty case, we need the Decision Maker's utility function u over the consequences $\mathbf{x}$. Reasoning analogously to the certainty case, we define $U_1, U_2, \ldots, U_N$ as the N attributes measured by the individuals' utility functions $u_1, u_2, \ldots, u_N$. The pure uncertainty model requires that we find an appropriate form of u_D such that

$$u(\mathbf{x}) = u_D[u_1(\mathbf{x}), u_2(\mathbf{x}), \ldots, u_N(\mathbf{x})]. \qquad (10.2)$$

---

*Since each v_i is meaningful up to a positive monotonic transformation, care must be taken in norming the scales before interpersonal comparisons can be made.

This model also has strong implicit assumptions. Most importantly, it assumes that the Decision Maker's concern about the x's is captured through the u_i's. Also, this implies that individual i's preference structure is represented by u_i, for all i. Unlike model (10.1), we do not have to assume that the Decision Maker knows the u_i for certain, although specific forms of (10.2) that we will investigate will utilize this assumption.

A simple example might help to clarify some possible misconceptions. Let the (supra) Decision Maker be concerned with the welfare of just two individuals, 1 and 2. Each individual has preferences for the (certainty) consequences of the problem and we assume that these preferences are encoded in a utility function. Now suppose that the Decision Maker has a choice between (certainty) consequence C and a lottery L with (certainty) consequences A and B. The Decision Maker ascertains that:

$$u_1^A = 1, \qquad u_1^B = 0, \qquad u_1^C = .4,$$
$$u_2^A = 0, \qquad u_2^B = 1, \qquad u_2^C = .4.$$

For the lottery L, the Decision Maker may or *may not* only be interested in each individual's expected utility for the lottery. For example, if the Decision Maker feels that A and B are equally likely she would *not necessarily* want to evaluate the lottery L by the pair of numbers $Eu_1(L) = .5$ and $Eu_2(L) = .5$. Rather, at this point we assume that she will view the choice as being between the lottery $\langle(1,0),(0,1)\rangle$ and the certainty $(.4, .4)$. As one possible additional assumption to be imposed at a later stage we might require her to be indifferent between $\langle(1,0),(0,1)\rangle$ and $(.5, .5)$ but this is not required at this point. To make this assumption prematurely would miss the main points of this chapter. In (10.2), you should think of the term $u_1(x)$ as 1's utility for the *certainty* consequence x and at this point his feelings for x may include his malevolent or benevolent attitudes toward the other individuals.

The formulations (10.1) and (10.2) are identical to our multiattribute formulations of an individual decision maker's problem, which has been the consideration of much of this book. Thus, the formalizations of preference structures provided by the results in Chapters 3–6 are appropriate, provided the requisite assumptions can be justified. The main distinction, at this point, is the types of considerations required by the Decision Maker to formalize her preference structure.

Let us be clear about this point: u is the Decision Maker's utility function and the u_i are the utility functions of individuals or groups whom the Decision Maker wishes to consider in making her decision. The final responsibility to select an alternative remains with the Decision Maker, and she must consider the tradeoffs among impacts on individuals $i = 1$,

$2, \ldots, N$. *These individuals have no authority in the decision making process. She* is the one who will be making the interpersonal comparisons of utilities.

AN ADDITIONAL ASSUMPTION.   In all the specific models of either (10.1) or (10.2) that we investigate in this chapter, one additional assumption will be explicitly made or implied by other assumptions. This can best be illustrated with an example. Suppose, for concreteness, that the Decision Maker's utility function could be written additively as

$$u(\mathbf{x}) = \sum_{i=1}^{N} \lambda_i u_i^*[u_i(\mathbf{x})], \tag{10.3}$$

where u_i^* is her utility function over attribute U_i and the λ_i's are scaling factors. This formulation assumes a marginal utility function u_i^* does exist for each attribute. In addition, we wish to assume that the Decision Maker is willing to use the ith individual's utility function itself as her own marginal utility function over U_i. In mathematical terms, this means

$$u_i^*[u_i(\mathbf{x})] = u_i(\mathbf{x}), \qquad \text{for } i = 1, 2, \ldots, N,$$

so that (10.3) would simplify to

$$u(\mathbf{x}) = \sum_{i=1}^{N} \lambda_i u_i(\mathbf{x}).$$

Similarly, our formulations under certainty will assume that the Decision Maker's single marginal value function v_i^* over V_i exists, and that it is strategically equivalent to individual i's own value function v_i.

10.1.2   Complications

There are numerous ways in which reality violates our pure models. The Decision Maker may have an interest in the consequences $\mathbf{x}$ above and beyond their implications on the v_i's or u_i's. Sometimes it may be appropriate that she just considers herself as an additional one of the affected individuals. In this case we can clearly include an argument $u_{N+1}(\mathbf{x})$ that represents the Decision Maker's personal desires (leaving out desire to incorporate the feelings of others) and the formulation may still be relevant in this case.

We assume in the above pure cases that the Decision Maker knows each of the individual's preferences. This crucial assumption implies first that the individuals themselves are capable of articulating their preferences in the format necessary for the respective model, and second that the individuals are honest in formally expressing these.

The models we investigate in this chapter assume that the preferences of *all* the N individuals can be assessed. While this may be reasonable if N is small and perhaps possible with, for example, elaborate questionnaires for modest sized groups, it is certainly not possible for large groups. However, in all branches of the government, as well as in many large private organizations, "benevolent dictators" are routinely making decisions affecting large numbers of people. In order to use some of the formal techniques suggested in this book, we might incorporate some largely to-be-developed sampling techniques or use representative experts. This latter approach, where the preferences of suitably chosen experts are used to account for the impacted individuals, was utilized in all the governmental decisions discussed in Chapters 7 and 8, but this feature is particularly illustrated in Sections 7.2 and 7.5 by Roche's and Gros' assessments, respectively.

Whenever it is unreasonable to obtain all the v_i's or u_i's—and this may generally be the case in practice—we might resort to the use of various social indices that are, for this case, proxy or surrogate attributes. O'Connor's work on the establishment of water quality indices discussed in Section 7.7 is an example of an important contribution along this line. The establishment of a suitable measure for "quality of life" is another such example, which we shall briefly consider in Section 10.7.

10.1.3 The Participatory Group

As we have said, in order to remain consistent with the theme of this book, "helping a specified individual understand and articulate his or her preference structure," we are focusing on the problem of the Decision Maker who is concerned about the preferences of others. A related model assumes that a group of individuals collectively shares the responsibility for making a particular decision. We feel that many of the results discussed in this chapter are relevant in examining this *participatory group problem*, and from time to time, reference will be made to this interpretation of the results. The main distinctions between the models focusing on the participatory group versus the single, supra Decision Maker involve such questions as, "Who verifies the necessary assumptions?" And, once verified, "Whose preferences provide the requisite input information?"

In the participatory group model, the individuals $i = 1, 2, \ldots, N$ are the members of the decision-making group. With this model, u in (10.2) is, for example, this group's utility function and the group as a whole must address the tradeoff and equity considerations to its members. Each u_i specifies individual i's utility function for consequences. Effectively, the group is creating a "benevolent dictator incarnate" and then, thinking collectively for "her."

When the decision maker is a group, then members of the group may have different probability distributions for describing the alternatives. Procedures by which these distributions get aggregated into what may be referred to as a group probability distribution are obviously important. However, as we have done with the uncertainty aspects of the multiattribute decision problem, we will neglect this issue and concentrate on the preference question. Some considerations relevant to aggregating individual's probabilities are discussed in Raiffa (1968). For our purposes in this chapter, it may be helpful for the reader to assume that the individual members of the group are in unanimous agreement on the probability distributions.

10.1.4 Related Work

Nowhere in this chapter do we even begin to survey the many important contributions in the vast literature dealing with problems of social welfare. This chapter indicates the relevance of multiaatribute utility analysis—and, even more narrowly, mainly the results discussed in Chapters 3–6 —for the aggregation of individual preferences as viewed from the perspective of a unitary supra Decision Maker. Three recent books that include discussions of a wider range of work on group decision processes are Sen (1970), Pattanaik (1971), and Fishburn (1973a). These books plus Luce and Raiffa (1957) have useful bibliographies for exploring the general area. Before getting on to the main results of this chapter, let us draw some connections to the existing literature.

Consider first analogous problems in game theory. To be concrete, let us take a case where the number, N, of affected individuals is 2 and let us suggestively call these individuals players. In two-person game theory the outcome of a "game" depends jointly on actions taken by each of the two players and the players scale the outcomes in terms of utility functions u_1 and u_2. In two-person, non-zero-sum games, where there is an element of cooperative behavior involved, there is no generally accepted prescriptive theory of what the players should do, except perhaps that they should not be content with a non-Pareto-optimal outcome, an outcome where there is a possibility of improvement by both players. There have been attempts in the literature that try to characterize what a "fair" or "reasonable" solution should be [see Luce and Raiffa (1957) Chapter 6, for a survey of this literature]. Some of these attempts create a new function u with arguments u_1 and u_2 and then proceed to maximize u, an approach not unlike the one we described earlier in this chapter. The question arises: Where does this new function u come from? Raiffa (1951, 1953) examines the problem from the vantage point of an arbiter, who, for the sake of analogy with our present chapter, can be thought of as a single supra Decision Maker, whose utility depends on the utilities of the two players. The arbiter wants to do right by both players, but tradeoffs have to be made. The analogy to the problem of our present chapter is a bit fuzzy at points because in the game-theory context the Decision Maker (or arbiter) also wants her chosen action to reflect the strategic realities of the game context, for example, threat power, and therefore, in order to bring out the analogy most clearly we would have to make the supra Decision Maker's utility function depend not only on u_1 and u_2 but on extraneous attributes that could partly be captured by those $\mathbf{x}$ arguments displayed in (10.2). Hence it should not be a surprise to those of you who know the works of Nash (1950, 1953), Harsanyi (1961, 1967, 1968), Zeuthen (1930), Braithwaite (1955), and Rapoport (1974)—authors who have written extensively on the bargaining problem and on the cooperative, two-person, non-zero-sum game problem—that what we shall have to say in subsequent sections of this chapter is related somewhat to this literature.

Of closer concern to the problem we pose in this chapter is the work of Arrow (1951, 1963) on social choice and individual values. In Arrow's seminal work, however, he considers only a finite number of alternatives and each affected individual simply rank orders the outcomes according to his preference. The problem as formulated by Arrow does not bring in the individual's "strengths of preferences" as captured by a full utility function. Luce and Raiffa (1957) review Arrow's work and in Section 14.6 of their book they discuss (as of 1957) some attempts [notably that of Hildreth (1953)] that modify Arrow's work to include strengths of preferences as data inputs. In Section 10.2 we review Arrow's work once again because we want to examine a modification of his problem from the vantage point of the theory developed here.

10.1.5 Orientation

Specific formulations of the supra Decision Maker's preference are investigated in the next two sections. The general approach is the same as that taken in Chapters 3–6 with the development of multiattribute value and utility functions. We will make assumptions about the Decision Maker's preference structure, and then derive the restrictions these assumptions place on her value or utility function. In Sections 10.4 and 10.5, the implications and reasonableness of these assumptions are explored in detail. Section 10.6 suggests procedures for the assessment of these "preference" functions. Our last section suggests some of the uses of multiattribute utility analysis in decisions that impact a large number of individuals.

10.2 AGGREGATING INDIVIDUALS' PREFERENCES UNDER CERTAINTY

Much of the work on decision models that incorporate preferences of several individuals confines itself to the certainty domain, and uncertainty is not explicitly considered. In this section we will first briefly describe Arrow's Impossibility Theorem, which is perhaps the best-known work on such group preferences. This result has had a significant impact on practically all the work on the group preferences in the past two decades. Following this we will interpret the results of Chapter 3 in the context of a problem faced by a Decision Maker concerned about the welfare of others.

10.2.1 Arrow's Impossibility Theorem

Arrow's problem is roughly as follows: Given the rankings of a set of alternatives by each individual in a decision making group, what should the grouping ranking for these alternatives be? He postulated some very reasonable assumptions concerning the aggregation of individual's rankings, and then he investigated their composite implications, which turned out to be quite surprising and disturbing. These assumptions are as follows.

Assumption A (Complete Domain).   There are at least two individual members in the group, at least three alternatives, and a group ordering is specified for all possible individual members' orderings.

Assumption B (Positive Association of Social and Individual Orderings).   If the group ordering indicates alternative A is preferred to alternative B for a certain set of individual rankings, and if (1) the individual's paired comparison between alternatives other than A are not changed, and (2) each individual's paired comparison between A and any other alternative either remains unchanged or is modified in A's favor, *then* the group ordering must imply A is still preferred to B.

Assumption C (Independence of Irrelevant Alternatives).   If an alternative is eliminated from consideration and the preference relations for the remaining alternatives remain invariant for all the group members, then the new group ordering for the remaining alternatives should be identical to the original group ordering for these same alternatives.

Assumption D (Individual's Sovereignty).   For each pair of alternatives A and B, there is some set of individual orderings such that the group prefers A to B.

Assumption E   (Nondictatorship).   There is no individual with the property that whenever he prefers alternative A to B, the group will also prefer A to B regardless of the other individuals' preferences.

Arrow (1951) proved that there is no rule for combining the individual's rankings that is consistent with the seemingly innocuous Assumptions A through E. More precisely, we have the following theorem:

Theorem 10.1.   (*Arrow's Impossibility Theorem*).   *Assumptions A, B, C, D, and E are inconsistent.*

Thus, we conclude that our Decision Maker can find no procedure that can combine several individual's rankings of alternatives to obtain her ranking and that will simultaneously satisfy these five assumptions.

One interpretation of Arrow's Impossibility Theorem is that, in general, there is no procedure for combining individual rankings into a group ranking that does not explicitly address the question of interpersonal comparison of preferences. This result is generalized in Sen (1970) where it is proven that there is no procedure for quantifying a group's preference structure that is consistent with both the spirit of Arrow's assumptions and either formulation (10.1) or (10.2) that does not include interpersonal comparison of preferences. The results in the next subsection and in Section 10.3 do require utilization of individual's strengths of preferences and the necessary interpersonal comparisons of preferences are clearly identified.

10.2.2   Additive Group Value Functions

Let us return to the problem (10.1) where we want to obtain a value function v for the Decision Maker who is given individual value functions v_i, $i = 1, 2, \ldots, N$, where $N \geq 3$, as arguments. We assume that a v_D exists such that

$$v(\mathbf{x}) = v_D[v_1(\mathbf{x}), v_2(\mathbf{x}), \ldots, v_N(\mathbf{x})],$$

and make two further assumptions.

Assumption 1   (Preferential Independence).   The attributes $\{V_i, V_j\}$ are preferentially independent of their complement $\bar{V}_{ij}$, for all $i \neq j$, $N \geq 3$.

Assumption 2   (Ordinal Positive Association).   Let certain alternatives A and B be equally preferred by the group. If A is modified to alternative A' in such a manner that some individual i prefers A' to A but all other individuals remain indifferent, then A' is preferred to B by the group.

Let us try to clarify the meaning of these assumptions. Assumption 1 implies that, for any two individuals i and j, $j \neq i$, if all other $N-2$ individuals are indifferent between a pair of consequences, then the preferences of the Decision Maker for these consequences should be governed only by the preferences of individuals i and j and, in particular, should not depend on the level of preferences of the other individuals.

To be more concrete, consider a three-person group and start with consequences $\mathbf{x}'$ and $\mathbf{x}''$. Now suppose that $\mathbf{x}'$ is deemed to be indifferent to $\mathbf{x}''$ by individual 3. Assumption 1 says, among other things, that the group preference of $\mathbf{x}'$ versus $\mathbf{x}''$ by the supra Decision Maker should not depend on whether individual 3 thinks $\mathbf{x}'$ and $\mathbf{x}''$ are awful or delightful. The Decision Maker's ranking of $\mathbf{x}'$ versus $\mathbf{x}''$ should depend *only* on the feelings of individuals 1 and 2.

Assumption 2 says that v_D in (10.1) is a positive monotonic function of each of its arguments. That is if the value to individual i, $i = 1, 2, \ldots, N$, indicated by v_i, increases while all other v_j, $j \neq i$, are held fixed, then the value v_D to the Decision Maker increases. Note that it is in the same spirit as Arrow's Assumption B, positive association of social and individual orderings. Given these assumptions, we might suspect, from the results of Chapter 3, that an additive value function results.

Theorem 10.2.   *Given $N \geq 3$, Assumption 1 (preferential independence) and Assumption 2 (ordinal positive association) hold if and only if*

$$v(\mathbf{x}) = \sum_{i=1}^{N} v_i^*[v_i(\mathbf{x})] = \sum_{i=1}^{N} v_i^+(\mathbf{x}), \qquad (10.4)$$

where, for all i,

1. v_i *is a value function for individual i scaled from 0 to 1.*
2. v_i^*, *a positive monotonic transformation of its argument v_i, is the Decision Maker's value function over V_i, reflecting her interpersonal comparison of the individuals preferences.*
3. v_i^+ *defined as $v_i^*(v_i)$ is another value function for individual i consistently scaled to reflect the Decision Maker's interpersonal comparison of preference.*

Proof.   Let us assume that v_i designates a value function over consequences $\mathbf{x}$ for individual i. These v_i's can all be scaled independently from 0 to 1.

From Theorem 3.6 it follows, given Assumption 1, that

$$v(\mathbf{x}) = \sum_{i=1}^{N} v_i^*[v_i(\mathbf{x})], \qquad (10.5)$$

where v_i^* is the Decision Maker's value function over the attribute V_i measured in amounts v_i. Assumption 2 implies that v_i^* is a positive monotonic function, which implies

$$v_i^*[v_i(\mathbf{x})] = v_i^+(\mathbf{x}), \qquad i = 1, 2, \ldots, N, \qquad (10.6)$$

where the v_i^+'s are consistently scaled from the Decision Maker's viewpoint. Combining (10.5) and (10.6) proves the result. The converse follows directly from (10.4). ◄

In a sense, the result of Theorem 10.2 seems to contradict Arrow's result stated in Theorem 10.1, because once the additive value function (10.4) is assessed, it appears to satisfy five assumptions analogous to Arrow's when individual's values, taken from their value functions, for the alternatives, are substituted for rankings. This *is* true. However, we have implicitly added an element to our formulation that Arrow wanted to exclude. This is the interpersonal comparison of preferences introduced by the functions v_i^* in (10.4). In Arrow's work these considerations would be ruled out by the very formulation of his problem.

The intensity of preference is given formal expression in our model by a conjoint scaling technique that is accomplished exogenously by the Decision Maker. Not only does the Decision Maker have to scale intensities of preference for each of the individuals, but the process requires interlinking the scales of the individuals and hence it involves extraneous interpersonal comparisons.

We can obtain interesting, and perhaps useful, aggregations of individual's preferences, *but* in general, this *demands* the consideration of interpersonal comparison of preferences. A more detailed discussion of this in relation to Arrow's result is found in Luce and Raiffa (1957).

It should be clear, again from results in Chapter 3, that if $\{V_1, V_2\}$ is preferentially independent of $\bar{V}_{12}$, and if $\{V_1, V_3\}$ is preferentially independent of $\bar{V}_{13}$, then $\{V_2, V_3\}$ is preferentially independent of $\bar{V}_{23}$. By repeatedly using this result, the requisite conditions needed to verify Assumption 1 can be reduced in number to $N-1$. For instance, if $\{V_1, V_i\}$ is preferentially independent of $\bar{V}_{1i}$ for $i = 2, 3, \ldots, N$, then Assumption 1 must be true.

Fleming (1952) investigated a set of assumptions, whose crucial assumption was essentially the same as Assumption 1, that led to the additive value function (10.4). More recently, Fishburn (1969) also postulated necessary and sufficient conditions for this result. The assessment of additive value functions will be considered in both the supra Decision Maker and participatory group contexts in Section 10.6.

10.3 AGGREGATING INDIVIDUALS' PREFERENCES UNDER UNCERTAINTY*

In this section, we concern ourselves with structuring the Decision Maker's utility function u defined over component utility functions u_i, $i = 1, 2, \ldots, N$, for the individuals concerned. Thus, in all the results of this section, we will assume the existence of u_D such that

$$u(\mathbf{x}) = u_D[u_1(\mathbf{x}), u_2(\mathbf{x}), \ldots, u_N(\mathbf{x})]. \qquad (10.7)$$

10.3.1 Additive Group Utility Functions

Harsanyi (1955) postulated a set of necessary and sufficient conditions that indicate when a group utility function u must be a weighted average of the individual group members utility functions u_1 to u_N. That is,

$$u(\mathbf{x}) = \sum_{i=1}^{N} \lambda_i u_i(\mathbf{x}).$$

This has a clear interpretation for the case of our supra Decision Maker. In addition to (10.7), Harsanyi's critical condition is:

Assumption H. If two alternatives, defined by probability distributions over the consequences $\mathbf{x}$, are indifferent to each individual, then they are indifferent for the group as a whole.

Assumption H is not concerned with the "balance" among individuals but only how each individual feels in isolation. Note that Assumption H is very similar in concept to the basic assumption used by Fishburn (1965a) in deriving additive utility functions over multiattribute consequences for individual decision makers. (See Sections 5.3 and 6.5.) Recognizing this, let us consider the implications of two assumptions stated in our terminology of earlier chapters.

Assumption 3 (Additive Independence). The set of attributes U_1, $U_2, \ldots, U_N$ is additive independent.

Assumption 4 (Strategic Equivalence). The Decision Maker's conditional utility function u_i^* over the attribute U_i designating individual i's utility is strategically equivalent to individual i's utility function u_i.

The relationship between Assumption 3 and Harsanyi's Assumption H will become clear in our proof of Theorem 10.3. However, let us briefly consider Assumption 4. This assumption is an honesty assumption. The

---

* Parts of Sections 10.3–10.6 are adapted from Keeney and Kirkwood (1975).

Decision Maker, because she believes individual i honestly represented his preferences, is willing to use the utility function of individual i as her own utility function to measure the impact on individual i.

Theorem 10.3. *For $N \geq 2$, Assumptions 3 (additive independence) and 4 (strategic equivalence) hold if and only if*

$$u(\mathbf{x}) = \sum_{i=1}^{N} \lambda_i u_i(\mathbf{x}) \qquad (10.8)$$

where u_i, $i = 1, 2, \ldots, N$, is a utility function for individual i scaled from 0 to 1, the λ_i's are positive scaling constants, and $\mathbf{x}$ is a consequence.

Proof. Given assumption 3, it follows from Theorem 6.4 that

$$u(\mathbf{x}) = \sum_{i=1}^{N} \lambda_i u_i^*[u_i(\mathbf{x})], \qquad \lambda_i > 0, \qquad (10.9)$$

where u_i^*, $i = 1, 2, \ldots, N$ is the Decision Maker's utility function over U_i scaled from 0 to 1. Given that we have also scaled the individual u_i from 0 to 1, Assumption 4 implies that

$$u_i^*[u_i(\mathbf{x})] = u_i(\mathbf{x}), \qquad i = 1, 2, \ldots, N,$$

from which the theorem directly follows.   ◄

Comparing (10.8) with (10.9), the difference between the additive independence assumption and Harsanyi's Assumption H is clear. In fact, by the result of Theorem 10.3, we can see that Assumption H and the pair of assumptions 3 and 4 together are equivalent. The Decision Maker's interpersonal comparison of the individual's preferences is required to assess the λ_i scaling factors. The fact that the λ_i's are positive insures the ordinal positive association of the Decision Maker's and individual's preferences in the sense of Assumption 2. Actually a stronger positive association is implied by (10.8) as we shall see in the next subsection.

10.3.2 More General Group Utility Functions

Consider the following assumption, which we know from Chapter 6 is weaker than Assumption 3 and which seems to be reasonable for some decision problems.

Assumption 5 (Utility Independence). Attribute U_i, $i = 1, 2, \ldots, N$, is utility independent of the other attributes $\bar{U}_i$.

From the definition of utility independence, Assumption 5 implies

$$u_D(u_1, \ldots, u_i, \ldots, u_N) = g_i(\bar{u}_i) + f_i(\bar{u}_i) u_i^*(u_i), \qquad \text{for all } i, \quad (10.10)$$

where $\bar{u}_i \equiv (u_1, \ldots, u_{i-1}, u_{i+1}, \ldots, u_N)$, the f_i's are positive, and u_i^* is the Decision Maker's conditional utility function over attribute U_i. Now we can state the following:

Theorem 10.4. *For $N \geq 2$, Assumptions 4 (strategic equivalence) and 5 (utility independence) imply*

$$u(\mathbf{x}) = u_D(u_1, u_2, \ldots, u_N)$$

$$= \sum_{i=1}^{N} \lambda_i u_i(\mathbf{x}) + \sum_{\substack{i=1 \\ j > i}}^{N} \lambda_{ij} u_i(\mathbf{x}) u_j(\mathbf{x}) + \cdots + \lambda_{12\cdots N} u_1(\mathbf{x}) u_2(\mathbf{x}) \cdots u_N(\mathbf{x})$$

$$(10.11)$$

where u and the u_i's are scaled from 0 to 1, the λ's are scaling constants, and $0 < \lambda_i < 1$ for all i.

Proof. Given Assumption 4, the form (10.11) follows directly from Theorem 6.3 only with u_i^*, the Decision Maker's utility function over U_i, in place of u_i. However, from Assumption 4,

$$u_i^*[u_i(\mathbf{x})] = u_i, \qquad i = 1, 2, \ldots, N, \qquad (10.12)$$

since u_i^* and u_i are both scaled 0 to 1, from which (10.11) immediately follows.   ◀

An alternate condition—the stronger positive association referred to in the last subsection—implying (10.11) is interesting to consider.

Assumption 6   (Cardinal Positive Association). Let A, B, and C be three certain consequences such that all individuals other than i are indifferent among all three. The Decision Maker's preference for a lottery involving A and B versus C is determined by her own probabilities and by i's utilities for the alternatives.

Illustration. Let u_i^A, u_i^B, u_i^C be i's utilities for consequences A, B, C respectively; and let $u_j^A = u_j^B = u_j^C$ for all $j \neq i$. The Decision Maker prefers $\langle A, B \rangle$ to C provided that $.5u_i^A + .5u_i^B > u_i^C$.

Assumption 6 implies that u_D, as a function of its ith argument u_i, is a positive linear transformation of u_i. In particular,

$$u_D(u_1, \ldots, u_i, \ldots, u_N) = g_i(\bar{u}_i) + f_i(\bar{u}_i) u_i, \qquad \text{for all } i, \qquad (10.13)$$

where g_i and f_i are defined as in (10.10).

If (10.13) were not true, we could easily construct a contradiction to Assumption 6. To see this, suppose that (10.13) did not hold for some i. Then we could find a lottery of the form

$$\langle (u_1^o, \ldots, u_{i-1}^o, u_i', u_{i+1}^o, \ldots, u_N^o), (u_1^o, \ldots, u_{i-1}^o, u_i'', u_{i+1}^o, \ldots, u_N^o) \rangle$$

and a consequence $(u_1^o, \ldots, u_{i-1}^o, \hat{u}_i, u_{i+1}^o, \ldots, u_N^o)$ such that individual i would have a different preference than that suggested by u_D.

Comparing equations (10.10) and (10.12) to (10.13), it should be clear that *the cardinal positive association assumption is equivalent to the assumptions of utility independence and strategic equivalence.*

Let us consider Assumption 1 in Section 10.2, which says all pairs of attributes $\{V_i, V_j\}$ are preferentially independent of their complements. Note, from the definition of value functions and utility functions, that this is equivalent to the following:

Assumption 1A (Preferential Independence). The attributes $\{U_i, U_j\}$ are preferentially independent of their complement $\bar{U}_{ij}$ for all $i \neq j$, $N \geq 3$.

Now we can state a strong result.

Theorem 10.5. *For $N \geq 3$, Assumptions 1 or 1A (preferential independence), 4 (strategic equivalence), and 5 (utility independence) imply*

$$u(\mathbf{x}) = u_D(u_1, u_2, \ldots, u_N)$$
$$= \sum_{i=1}^{N} \lambda_i u_i(\mathbf{x}) + \lambda \sum_{\substack{i=1 \\ j>i}}^{N} \lambda_i \lambda_j u_i(\mathbf{x}) u_j(\mathbf{x}) + \cdots$$
$$+ \lambda^{N-1} \lambda_1 \lambda_2 \cdots \lambda_N u_1(\mathbf{x}) u_2(\mathbf{x}) \cdots u_N(\mathbf{x}), \quad (10.14)$$

where u and the u_i's are scaled from 0 to 1, the λ's are scaling constants, $0 < \lambda_i < 1$ for all i, and $\lambda > -1$.

Proof. Given Assumptions 1 and 5, as proven in Theorem 6.1 the form (10.14) holds only with u_i^*, the Decision Maker's utility function over U_i, replacing u_i. From Assumption 4, we know that $u_i^* = u_i$, $i = 1, 2, \ldots, N$ proving the result.   ◄

Note that when only two individuals compose the group, Assumption 1 has no meaning. However, in this case, by Theorem 10.4, we conclude with the form of (10.14) directly from Assumptions 4 and 5.

As must be the case because of the requisite assumptions, (10.14) is a special case of (10.11). Furthermore, notice that special cases of both (10.11) and (10.14) result in the additive group utility function

$$u(\mathbf{x}) = \sum_{i=1}^{N} \lambda_i u_i(\mathbf{x}). \quad (10.15)$$

In particular, this results from (10.14) when $\lambda = 0$. If λ is not 0, we can multiply both sides of (10.14) by λ and add 1 to obtain

$$\lambda u(\mathbf{x}) + 1 = \prod_{i=1}^{N} [\lambda \lambda_i u_i(\mathbf{x}) + 1], \tag{10.16}$$

which is a multiplicative group utility function. The different implications of the additive and multiplicative utility functions are considered in Sections 10.4 and 10.5.

10.3.3   A Specialization Leading to the Additive Form

The following assumption may be appropriate for structuring certain group utility functions.

Assumption 7   (Universal Agreement).   If all the members of a group have the same utility function, then the group utility function should be the common utility function.

Combining this with previous assumptions we have:

Theorem 10.6.   For $N \geq 2$, Assumptions 1 or 1A (preferential independence), 4 (strategic equivalence), 5 (utility independence), and 7 (universal agreement) hold if and only if the group utility function is the additive form

$$u(\mathbf{x}) = \sum_{i=1}^{N} \lambda_i u_i(\mathbf{x}). \tag{10.17}$$

Proof.   The proof is straightforward. Because Assumptions 4 and 5 hold, the group utility function $u(\mathbf{x})$ is given by (10.14). Now consider the special case where $u_1 = u_2 = \cdots = u_N$ and call the common function u_0. Combining this with (10.14), we then have

$$u(\mathbf{x}) = u_0(\mathbf{x}) \sum_{i=1}^{N} \lambda_i + [u_0(\mathbf{x})]^2 \lambda \sum_{\substack{i=1 \\ j>i}}^{N} \lambda_i \lambda_j + \cdots + [u_0(\mathbf{x})]^N \lambda^{N-1} \lambda_1 \lambda_2 \cdots \lambda_N.$$

$$\tag{10.18}$$

But by Assumption 7,

$$u(\mathbf{x}) = a + b u_0(\mathbf{x}), \tag{10.19}$$

where a and $b > 0$ are unspecified constants. Equations (10.18) and (10.19) are compatible only if $u(\mathbf{x})$ is the additive form (10.17). Conversely, Assumptions 1, 4, 5, and 7 follow directly from (10.17).   ◀

10.4 ADDITIVE UTILITY AND EQUITY CONSIDERATIONS

Let us briefly appraise the main assumptions used in this chapter. This section concentrates on the issue of equity or "fairness" to the individuals involved and, specifically, will investigate the different implications of additive and multiplicative utility functions. An interesting and thought-provoking discussion of many of these same issues is found in Harsanyi (1974).

10.4.1 Prior Versus Posterior Equity

Let us consider a simple example. Suppose the Decision Maker is interested in the preferences of two individuals and her utility function is

$$u(\mathbf{x}) = u_D(u_1(\mathbf{x}), u_2(\mathbf{x})) = .5u_1(\mathbf{x}) + .5u_2(\mathbf{x}), \qquad (10.20)$$

where u_i designates the utility for individual i scaled from 0 to 1; and let $(.4, .6)$ designate, for example, the alternative where $u_1 = .4$ and $u_2 = .6$. Now consider these alternatives:

Alternative A: $(1, 0)$,

Alternative B: $\langle (1, 0), (0, 1) \rangle$,

Alternative C: $\langle (1, 1), (0, 0) \rangle$.

Using (10.20), the Decision Maker must be indifferent between alternatives A, B, and C, since they all have an expected utility of .5.

Diamond (1967) remarks that if equal utilities have the same meaning for each individual, then, because the Decision Maker is indifferent between A and B, the decision-making process seems to be unfair to individual 2. With alternative A, he has no chance of receiving his preferred outcome (i.e., $u_2 = 1$), whereas he does have a chance with alternative B. Thus, in order to give individual 2 a "fair shake," Diamond feels the Decision Maker should prefer alternative B.

Even in situations where all the individuals get a fair shake, the additive group utility function may lead to undesirable results for the group. For example, with both alternatives B and C, each individual has a 50–50 chance of obtaining his preferred consequence. However, in some situations, it seems reasonable that the Decision Maker should prefer alternative C to alternative B. With C, either both individuals receive their preferred consequences or both receive their less preferred consequence, each of which is an "equitable" result. On the other hand, with alternative B there will always be an inequity in the consequences received: one individual will receive his preferred consequence while the other will receive his less preferred one.

Both alternatives B and C are *a priori* equitable, in some sense, whereas alternative A is not. Here the qualifier "in some sense" is used since we have not explicitly compared absolute utilities of the individuals. For instance, if a consequence with $u_1 = 1$ somehow brings the same amount of pleasure to individual one as the consequence with $u_2 = 0$ brings to the second individual, we might conclude that alternative A was equitable. However, in terms of the alternatives offered, A gives individual 1 his best consequence and individual 2 his worse consequence. In view of our convention of scaling the utilities of consequences from 0 to 1 for each individual, we have termed alternative A as relatively inequitable. In terms of posterior equity, C is clearly more equitable, given the options, than either B or A. Each of the latter is, roughly speaking, equally inequitable *a posteriori*.

The additive group utility function (10.20) cannot differentiate preferences among alternatives A, B, and C. Thus it does not promote prior or posterior equity of the type of which we have just spoken.

The more general utility functions of Theorems 10.4 and 10.5 can promote posterior equity. To illustrate, consider again two individuals and the Decision Maker's utility function

$$u(\mathbf{x}) = \lambda_1 u_1(\mathbf{x}) + \lambda_2 u_2(\mathbf{x}) + \lambda_{12} u_1(\mathbf{x}) u_2(\mathbf{x}), \qquad (10.21)$$

where

$$\lambda_1 + \lambda_2 + \lambda_{12} = 1 \qquad (10.22)$$

since u, u_1, and u_2 must all be scaled from 0 to 1. Suppose, for example, that $\lambda_1 = \lambda_2 = .4$ so $\lambda_{12} = .2$ and (10.21) becomes

$$u(\mathbf{x}) = .4u_1(\mathbf{x}) + .4u_2(\mathbf{x}) + .2u_1(\mathbf{x}) u_2(\mathbf{x}). \qquad (10.23)$$

Then the Decision Maker's expected utilities for the alternatives A, B, and C are .4, .4, and .5, respectively. Since A and B are still indifferent, Diamond's objection to the additive group utility function concerning prior equity is not met by (10.23). However, alternative C is preferred to B, because constant λ_{12} is positive. This provides a formal consideration of the posterior equity of the distribution of utilities among group members that is not possible with the additive form.

An important issue with respect to posterior equity for the Decision Maker in specifying her utility function is the degree of familiarity that the concerned individuals have with the decision process. If they are aware and feel the Decision Maker is trying to be fair, an inequitable final consequence might be attributed to happenstance. On the other hand, if one individual receives what he considers to be the rough end of an "unfair" outcome and is not aware of the process, he may feel the Decision Maker is responsible and therefore of questionable integrity.

10.4.2 Pareto Optimality

A cornerstone of most social welfare theory is the Pareto optimality principle. A Pareto optimal alternative is one for which no individual can increase his preference without simultaneously decreasing the preferences of another affected individual. The Pareto optimality principle then states that an alternative that is not Pareto optimal should never be chosen— since it would then be possible to improve the satisfaction of some without the consequent diminution of satisfaction of others.

To consider the reasonableness of this condition in the Decision Maker choice situation, let us add a fourth alternative:

$$\text{Alternative } D: \ (.48, .48).$$

We will assume that these levels of u_1 and u_2 each come from a certain consequence. Using (10.20), the expected utility for alternative D is clearly .48, so in this case alternative B, with expected utility of .5, is preferred to alternative D. However, the reverse is true using the utility function (10.23). In this case, it is easily verified that the expected utility of alternative D is .425, which is greater than the Decision Maker's .4 expected utility of alternative B. This latter conclusion seems defendable in certain situations. The Decision Maker may prefer to make both individuals somewhat happy, as opposed to making one very happy and one sad.

However, note that the utility function (10.23) will sometimes lead to alternatives that are not Pareto optimal. In our previous example, the Decision Maker prefers alternative D to alternative B, even though both individuals 1 and 2 clearly should prefer alternative B to alternative D. If we broaden our definition of Pareto optimality to include individual 3 (i.e., the Decision Maker), then since she is concerned about the equity aspects of the problem, she prefers D to B: so in this more generalized sense, D would not be dominated by B. The Decision Maker is faced with the tradeoff of amount of equity versus degree to which the narrow interpretation of Pareto optimality is violated.

10.4.3 Appraisal of Assumption 7, Universal Agreement

If we reject the additive group utility function for a specific problem, we must also be rejecting Assumption 3. The last two subsections have essentially reviewed the implications of Assumption 3. However, as we have seen from Theorem 10.6, Assumptions 1, 4, 5, and 7 together are equivalent to Assumption 3. The appropriateness of Assumptions 4 and 5 is considered in the next section, but let us comment on considerations that may lead to rejection of Assumption 7.

There are situations where Assumption 7 may not be as reasonable as it appears on the surface. For example, suppose the board of directors of a company is considering various business ventures with monetary payoffs being the only consequences of importance to any of the board members. However, further suppose the responsibility for the decision rests with one individual, the chairman* of the board, our Decision Maker. Then even if all the individual board members have identical risk-averse utility functions for money, it might be reasonable for the chairman's utility function to be less risk averse than the individual functions. This may result from the fact that the responsibility for the decision is being shared by all the group members, as opposed to falling entirely on herself. In the latter case, if a very undesirable consequence happened to result from the decision, the chairman may "feel terrible" about the situation she had "caused." However, she might not have felt as bad if the original decision had been supported by the entire group. The moral and emotional responsibility for the decision is, in more sense, divided among the members, whereas the entire monetary consequences accrue to the group as a whole.

This reasoning is appropriate when considering Assumption 7 for a participatory group. In general, whenever all the individuals have the same utility functions, the eventual consequence of any decision will affect them in the same manner. Hence because "misery loves company" and the individuals are all in the same boat together, the undesirable consequences will not seem so bad. Therefore, the group may be willing (i.e., prefer) to act less risk averse than any of them would individually. In this situation the individual views receiving the undesirable consequence alone and receiving the same undesirable consequence as a member of a group as being two different consequences. One might adapt the original individual utility functions to include an attribute indicating the "number of companions in the same situation" and then accept Assumption 7 using these new utility functions. An alternative is to use the original individual utility functions but violate Assumption 7 to incorporate the individuals' preferences for companionship.

In both the supra Decision Maker and the participatory group models, posterior equity is automatically ensured if the individual's utility functions are identical. Whatever consequence x eventually occurs will have

---

* To be perfectly consistent we should use "chairwoman," but consistency is not a compelling desideratum in this context, notwithstanding the fact that the desire for consistency is the cornerstone of formal utility theory.

the same utility, on a 0-to-1 scale, for each individual. Prior equity is also ensured in the case of the benevolent dictator because she has only one probability distribution over the consequences for each alternative. However, in the participatory group model, the various individuals may disagree on these probability distributions for the different alternatives. This may result in perceived inequities by some individuals prior to the consequences of a decision being known.

10.5 APPRAISAL OF THE INDEPENDENCE ASSUMPTIONS

The assumptions that are implicit in equations (10.1) and (10.2) are basic for our discussions and essentially define our problem domain in this chapter. Without these, the other assumptions that we have used make no sense at all. Here we are going to concentrate on the reasonableness of these other assumptions in situations where (10.1) and (10.2) are appropriate. Since the implications of Assumptions 3 and 7 have already been considered and we have shown that Assumption 6 is equivalent to Assumptions 4 and 5, our remarks will be limited to Assumptions 1, 2, 4, and 5, which will be considered in reverse order.

The reasonableness of all four of these assumptions depends, among other things, on which individuals have a knowledge of how the overall utility function is constructed. Often, in the participatory group problem, if events occur that yield favorable consequences for some individuals in the group and unfavorable consequences for the others, they should realize that this did not result from an unfair group utility function. However, when a supra Decision Maker has final responsibility in making the decisions, the situation is different. In this case the individuals receiving unfavorable consequences may not have been involved in structuring the group utility function. Thus, they may not interpret the outcome as due to chance, but rather as due to unfairness on the part of the Decision Maker.

10.5.1 Appraisal of Assumption 5, Utility Independence

To illustrate the point above, consider two situations where all but one individual is indifferent between the consequences. In one case all the individuals that are indifferent between alternatives are impacted in a very undesirable manner and in the other case all such individuals are very desirably impacted. According to Assumption 5, the group utility function should count only the preferences of the individual who is not indifferent in both cases. However, if everyone else's utility is low then, because of pressures among the individuals, the Decision Maker may prefer consequences where that individual also receives an undesirable consequence rather than a desirable one. On the other hand, the situation may be reversed if all the other individuals have a high utility.

If such distinctions are important then Assumption 5 is violated so Theorems 10.3–10.6 do not hold. In such situations, it may be appropriate to use generalized utility independence (see Appendix 6A), which allows for reversals of preferences. This would model certain cases where, for instance, from the position of the Decision Maker taking preferences of individuals 1 and 2 into account, (1) the group utility increases when individual 1's utility is increased from low to high if individual 2's utility is high, and (2) the group utility decreases when individual 1's utility is increased from low to high if individual 2's utility is low. The underlying rationale is a concern for equity.

Another situation where utility independence would not be appropriate would be where the Decision Maker might be less "risk averse" concerning impact to a given individual knowing that many of the other individuals would receive high utilities than she would be when she knew these other individuals would receive low utilities. The reasoning is that the Decision Maker had done reasonably well for her constituents and so she could afford to gamble.

10.5.2 Appraisal of Assumption 2, Ordinal Positive Association, and Assumption 4, Strategic Equivalence

Assumptions 2 and 4 are similar in spirit since they require the Decision Maker to take individual i's preferences to be her own. In general, this seems appropriate for many problems. However, the Decision Maker may not accept this assumption if she feels that any one of the following three statements is true.

1. Some individuals have not been honest in communicating their preferences.
2. Some individuals do not know what is best for themselves.
3. Because of gross inequity, it is preferred to reduce the utility of an individual with very high utility, while holding the others' utilities fixed.

10.5.3 Appraisal of Assumption 1, Preferential Independence

Now consider the preferential independence assumption, which is formalized by both Assumptions 1 and 1A. If all the members of a group are somehow equal in "importance" or "stature" or "involvement in the decision process," the assumption may be appropriate. If the group has no control over the consequences accruing to $N-2$ of the individuals, it may be reasonable to try to obtain as much equity (i.e., distribution of value or utility) as possible between the two remaining individuals. If this search for equity did not depend on the preferences of the others, Assumption 1 would be appropriate.

To illustrate this situation suppose we had three individuals labeled 1, 2, and 3, with utility functions u_1, u_2, and u_3. Furthermore, suppose individual 1 was "very important," and clearly in a different class—as far as the decision to be made is concerned—from the others, who are roughly equal in importance to each other. Then we might agree that $\{U_2, U_3\}$ is preferentially independent of U_1. If U_1 were high, for instance, $u_1 = 1$, the tradeoffs between u_2 and u_3 might be the same as when $u_1 = 0$. Equity among individuals 2 and 3 is important and does not depend on u_1. However, now consider whether $\{U_1, U_2\}$ is preferentially independent of U_3. Suppose that $u_1 = 1$, $u_2 = .5$, and $u_3 = 1$. Then the participatory group or the Decision Maker, depending on the context, might consider it appropriate to reduce u_1 quite a lot to get u_2 up to $u_2 = 1$. On the other hand, if $u_1 = 1$, $u_2 = .5$, and $u_3 = .5$, either "decision maker" might only reduce u_1 slightly to increase u_2 to $u_2 = 1$. In the latter situation an inequity is created between individuals 2 and 3, whereas in the former an equity is promoted. The supra Decision Maker can account for different equity requirements among different sets of individuals by suitably manipulating the λ's in expression (10.11); however, the more restrictive form (10.14) does not afford her with suitable degrees of freedom.

An additional comment of the use of Assumption 1 is in order. Suppose our decision making group has seven individuals of which the first three individuals are in one class, call it I, and the other four in a different class, II. Now, it may be reasonable to assume that the sets of attributes $\{U_1, U_2, U_3\}$ and $\{U_4, U_5, U_6, U_7\}$ are mutually utility independent. Hence the results in Section 5.4 suggest forms for the group utility u_D as a function of a utility function u_I, for individuals in class I, and a utility function u_{II}, for individuals in class II. That is,

$$u_D[u_1, u_2, \ldots, u_7] = f[u_I(u_1, u_2, u_3), u_{II}(u_4, u_5, u_6, u_7)].$$

Now Assumption 1 may be reasonable for structuring either or both utility functions u_I and u_{II}. In this same manner, we might creatively use any of the results in Chapter 3–6 in structuring group utility functions.

10.6 ASSESSING GROUP UTILITY FUNCTIONS

Results such as Theorems 10.2–10.6 are theoretically interesting. However, if we wish to utilize them, answers must be provided to questions raised earlier in this chapter:

1. Who must verify the assumptions?
2. Whose value functions or utility functions are to be used?
3. Who assesses the scaling constants?

The answers to these depend on how the results are to be used.

10.6.1 The Supra Decision Maker Model

For the supra Decision Maker model of group decisions, all of the answers are the individual decision maker, the supra Decision Maker, who has the power to make the decision. The v in Theorem 10.2 and the u in Theorems 10.3, 10.4, 10.5, and 10.6 are the Decision Maker's value function and utility function, respectively. Verification of the independence assumptions directly follows the procedures suggested in Chapters 3, 5, and 6. If the Decision Maker is interested in the welfare of individual i, then it seems reasonable to use the utility of individual i as an attribute, and it may be reasonable to measure this by individual i's utility function u_i. In this case, each u_i obviously becomes the conditional utility function over attribute U_i for the Decision Maker.

The scaling constants, that is, the λ's in (10.8), (10.11), and (10.14), are assessed by the Decision Maker. Her answers involve trading off utility to one individual or group, as measured by u_i, against another individual or group, as measured by u_j. This involves consideration of two issues: (1) the inherent value of the different measured utilities to each individual (interpersonal comparison of utility) and (2) the relative weight that the Decision Maker wishes to give to the preferences of the different individuals.*

In making the interpersonal comparisons of utility, it will likely prove advantageous to go back to the original consequences $\mathbf{x}$ in order to make decisions about equity. The Decision Maker must consider such questions as the happiness brought to individual 1 by a consequence $\mathbf{x}_1$ relative to the happiness of individual 2 due to consequence $\mathbf{x}_2$. Such questions are not easy, but they represent the essence of the interpersonal comparison of utility issue and must be faced either explicitly or implicitly in almost all group decision processes.

---

* This problem is considered in detail in Kirkwood (1972).

With the group value function v of (10.4), consistent scaling is much more difficult than with the group utility functions. At each stage of construction of each v_i^*, an interpersonal comparison of value must be made by the Decision Maker. The difficulty arises because v_i provides only an ordinal ranking of consequences. Thus, for instance, if the Decision Maker concludes it is equally desirable to have v_1 increase from 0 to 1 as to have v_2 increase from 0 to 1, it does not necessarily follow that increases of v_1 or v_2 from 0 to .5 are equally desirable. If v_1 and v_2 in this situation are also utility functions, this implication does follow using the results of Theorems 10.3–10.6. With individual utility functions u_i, all interpersonal comparison of utility can be inferred from interpersonally comparisons of two points on each u_i scale. As with the scaling procedures discussed in Chapter 3, the v_i's can only be consistently assessed by a simultaneous conjoint scaling technique, which essentially involves many separate, but intertwined, interpersonal comparisons of the individual's preferences.

10.6.2   The Participatory Group Decision

If we have a participatory group decision process, the group as a whole must verify the assumptions and assess the scaling constants, whereas the value functions v_i and utility functions u_i can be assessed by respective individual members in the group. For the assumptions and scaling constants, a consensus would be needed in order to proceed. This may be relatively easy in the case of verifying the assumptions necessary for the special structures of group preferences. Each individual in the group can be checked separately.

Agreement on the scaling constants in some circumstances would likely be difficult to achieve. This follows since in (10.8), (10.11), and (10.14) the larger λ_i is and the smaller the other λ_j's are, the more power individual i has in influencing decisions made using u. This effect can be moderated in (10.14) by λ and in (10.11) by the λ's other than the λ_i's. As previously indicated, these constants can promote equity among group members and provide an opportunity for the group to reasonably insure that individual members are protected from receiving all the undesirable effects of a decision while other members receive all the benefits. The ability to incorporate such characteristics formally into the group utility structure should facilitate necessary compromises in assessing the λ's.

Even when a consensus cannot be reached on the λ's, all is not in vain. It may be that with each of the sets of λ's advocated by any individual, the implications for decision making are the same. Then, after a responsible sensitivity analysis (which should be conducted, constraints permitting, in all circumstances), the group might select the alternative they all agree is best. If this is not the case, they may agree on alternatives that should be eliminated from further consideration.

Having identified a basic disagreement should, at least, provide a base point from which to proceed to constructive compromise through arbitration, generation of new alternatives, or whatever. Unfortunately, we have no magical solutions here—the nature of the problem makes it very difficult. However, a little ingenuity on the part of group members may help considerably. For instance, a second-level consensus may be possible. Suppose a group of 10 directors was divided in opinion into two subgroups, call them I and II, of three and seven, respectively. Within each subgroup, there was complete agreement on what the group utility function should be. Now the group as a whole may address a new decision of reaching a constructive compromise with objectives "to please subgroup I" and "to please subgroup II." Measures of the degree to which the objectives are achieved would obviously be the two subgroups utilities for the group given by $u_I(u_1, u_2, \ldots, u_{10})$ and $u_{II}(u_1, u_2, \ldots, u_{10})$, respectively. The overall group utility function u_G would then be a function of the two subgroups' utilities, that is, $u_G(u_I, u_{II})$. If the subgroups can agree on a specific u_G, the original problem can be solved.

10.6.3 Hierarchies of Group Decisions and Other Complications

Many problems have group decision aspects that we have focused on here. Some of these are pure, in that they have only the supra Decision Maker aspects or only the participatory group decision aspects. An example of the former might be the operating officer of a company whose objectives is to please each of the directors on the board, whereas the small group of four who incorporate and jointly own and manage their own company might be an example of the latter. Many decisions have both aspects.

Consider, for example, the board of directors of a large firm, each of whom wishes to include the attitudes of various other individuals within the company in his decisions. Here each director alone has a "benevolent dictator" problem, and then collectively they have a participatory group decision. Adding one more complication, each of the directors may be concerned with the impact of the decision on several groups within the company. Thus, the arguments of each director's utility function will be the utilities of the various groups. These various groups, if they are organized, may quantify their preferences by methods suggested for the participatory group. Thus, since the company utility function is generated through a participatory group decision process using the utility function of each of the directors as arguments, and since each director's utility function is generated using the supra Decision Maker model, where the impacted group's utility functions are the arguments, the overall model has three levels in the hierarchy of preferences.

COMPLICATIONS.   A decision maker or a group may be concerned with several attributes, only some of which represent the preferences of impacted individuals or groups. Let us use $\{X_1, \ldots, X_M, U_1, \ldots, U_N\}$ to represent the set of all attributes where the U's represent the preference attributes. A utility function $u(x_1, \ldots, x_M, u_1, \ldots, u_N)$ is needed, where the small letters represent specific amounts of the attributes. If the sets $\{X_1, \ldots, X_M\}$ and $\{U_1, \ldots, U_N\}$ are utility independent of each other, the problem is simplified since u can be written as a function of a utility function u_X over the X attributes and another utility function u_P over the preference attributes U. Then, of course, the ideas in this chapter, as well as those in Chapters 3–6, can be directly used in constructing u.

An interesting situation arises when one individual in a decision making group *explicitly* wishes to consider the utility of another individual in the group. With two people concerned about an attribute X, we may write the group utility written functionally as $u[u_1(x, u_2), u_2(x, u_1)]$. Kirkwood (1972) has some preliminary findings on this problem.

10.7   USES OF MULTIATTRIBUTE UTILITY ANALYSIS FOR GROUPS

Many of the applications in Chapters 7 and 8 were "group" decisions, as we have used the term in this chapter. For instance, Roche's work with a local educational system (Section 7.2), Gros' examination of siting of nuclear power plants (Section 7.5), the analysis of Woodward-Clyde Consultants on long-range planning (Section 7.4), O'Connor's water quality index (Section 7.7), and the Mexico City Airport Study (Chapter 8), have each explicitly assessed preferences of a variety of individuals and/or preferences impacting many individuals. What was not involved in any of the efforts cited was an explicit interpersonal comparison of preferences of different individuals or groups.

Throughout this chapter, our focus has been on assessing a preference structure, explicitly including interpersonal comparison of preferences, to use directly for decision making purposes. To this end we concentrated on the assessment of a supra Decision Maker's utility function defined over utility levels of her constituents. The results clarify issues that should be considered in group decisions processes, and in some instances, may be directly applicable to selecting a best alternative. There are, however, in group-decision contexts, other important uses of multiattribute utility analysis.

10.7.1 Some Pragmatic Alternatives

If N is large, it is impossible to obtain $u_1, \ldots, u_N$. This is difficult to do even if N is small. The discussion in previous sections was more a theoretical ideal than a practical option. What can be done in practice in case of the supra Decision Maker? She could sample to obtain information about the u_i's, or she could use representative groups, but more often, we suspect, she will not formalize these steps but synthesize these considerations informally and incompletely in her mind. She will use information about the X attributes as proxy attributes. Let us examine this more closely.

Suppose the supra Decision Maker is really concerned about the preferences and feelings of others and she has some feelings about their attitudes. She might start by structuring a hierarchy of attributes that would capture the concerns of the relevant impacted individuals and groups. Let the elemental attributes at the lower end of the hierarchy be $X_1, \ldots, X_M$. First, suppose M is a manageable size. When the Decision Maker thinks about her tradeoffs between X_α and X_β (keeping other attributes fixed at some level), she must keep in mind what the implications of these tradeoffs are to the impacted individuals. Qualitatively in some circumstances this might be easy to do. In other circumstance she might call in experts to help her or she might informally or formally try to get the concerned citizenry to articulate their views. But somehow, some way, she might be able to force herself to formalize her preferences for tradeoffs between X_α and X_β under the realization that they are proxies for the nonavailable u_i's. It is a mammoth task to synthesize these diverse elements, but real Decision Makers do it all the time. Decisions have to be made.

We can formalize this procedure at many levels. If the X's are structured in a hierarchy, the decision Maker can quantify her preferences and attitudes starting at any level of the hierarchy. She can, of course, react only at the very highest level of the hierarchy, which in a sense we all do when we make complicated decisions without any formal quantitative analysis.

Now let us return to the case where the number of basic lower-level attributes is large. We might, keeping in mind the constituent individuals and groups who will be affected by the actions of the supra Decision Maker, try to synthesize the large number of attributes into a few summary indices. For example, in economic affairs, we might look at the GNP, inflation rate, gross unemployment, and balance of trade. These may be summaries of thousands of lower-level attributes that we might want to monitor for a deeper understanding of the problem. It may be important to keep the lower-level attributes informally in mind when making preferential tradeoffs among the composite indices.

What we are trying to say is that formalization can take place at many different levels and it is not the case that the Decision Maker must choose either between a complete nonquantitative, intuitive analysis and an analysis that gets bogged down into hopeless minutiae.

10.7.2   Advantages of Partial Formalization

What is involved in obtaining the supra Decision Maker's utility function? If we do not complete the task of finding the decision Maker's u function, are there any advantages in completing part of the process?

Oversimplifying, we might say that in the group context there are three steps that the Decision Maker follows in order to articulate her utility function:

1. Objective and attributes $X_1, \ldots, X_M$ must be specified.
2. Individual utility function $u_1, \ldots, u_N$ over the X_j's must be assessed.
3. The aggregate utility function u over the u_i's must be assessed.

This entire book has addressed the first two steps; it is only in this chapter that step 3 has been included. Carrying out step 3 requires interpersonal comparison of preferences, a topic that has a very long history of controversy [see Arrow (1951), Harsanyi (1955), and Luce and Raiffa (1957)]. The completion of steps 1 and 2 is often very difficult, although, comparatively speaking, not philosophically controversial. Here we want briefly to state some of the advantages that result from even a partial formalization of these first two steps.

The detailed specification of objectives and associated attributes should lead to a clearer articulation of the substantive issues of a problem, and it should sensitize the different individuals to a better understanding of these issues as well. Furthermore, it may help to identify decomposable parts of the overall problem and facilitate effective communication among the group members and between the group members and the Decision Maker. Given some information about individual preferences, an analyst might be able to isolate differences in the judgements and in the preferences of individuals. An understanding of these differences, as well as an understanding of the points of agreement, could provide a firm basis on which to begin a constructive process of conflict resolution. This analytical process might help generate creative alternatives that might otherwise be overlooked.*

The next two subsections elaborate on these considerations.

10.7.3   Generating Creative Alternatives

In Chapter 1 we talked about the importance of generating imaginative alternatives but then we said that in this book we would not stress this point, no matter how important it may be. However, we feel compelled to return to this issue in the group context.

Let us imagine that a public administrator has to choose among alternatives that affect groups of individuals, $1, \ldots, i, \ldots, N$. Let the ith group have a composite utility function u_i and let the status quo point have a utility value $u_i(\text{status quo}) = \hat{u}_i$. If an alternative is chosen other than the status quo whose utility for group i is below $\hat{u}_i$, a most natural aspiration level, then we might expect that group i will be unhappy— perhaps enough so to become obstreperous or to try to exert pressure on the system. In many public policy problems a public agency would like to be able to generate a legitimate alternative, A, say, such that $u_i(A) \geq \hat{u}_i$ for all i. This may not be easy to do, but by examining the details that contribute to the composite final evaluation for each individual—and this means not only the fine structure on the value or utility side of the analysis but the probabilistic side as well—an astute analyst might discover the key that can open up meaningful negotiations. For example, if the ith group falls far below $\hat{u}_i$ because of the low utility score on the jth attribute that it highly prizes, then perhaps the analyst can modify an existing alternative in a manner that would make it more palatable on the jth attribute to the ith group.†

Life can get more complicated. There may be many ways of simultaneously achieving the aspiration levels, the u_i's, of all the groups and, in this case, there then will be a problem of finding a choice principle to decide among them. But often in complex problems the real issue is to find some

---

* An excellent application illustrating many of the advantages summarized in this paragraph is presented in Dyer and Miles (1974). The problem concerned selecting trajectories for the Mariner Jupiter–Saturn 1977 Project. Ten teams of scientists, representing disciplines with different scientific interests, were the "individuals" in this group-decision process. Each team provided cardinal utilities for 32 alternatives, which were analyzed and used in resolving potential conflicts, creating new and better alternatives, and reaching a constructive compromise on an overall "best" alternative.

† Even when an alternative does exist that is "acceptable" to all groups 1 through N, a multiattribute utility analysis of the type described here may help generate better alternatives. Peterson (1974) has investigated such uses in connection with optimizing treaty negotiations between countries.

operational alternative that is judged by all concerned groups to be an improvement over the status quo. Formal multiattribute utility analysis might, in some circumstances help. Indeed, it may be the single most important way it can help.

10.7.4   Social Indices and the Quality of Life*

Let us focus on one specific, but very important, problem: measuring the "quality of life." Note that with model (10.2),

$$u(\mathbf{x}) = u_D[u_1(\mathbf{x}), u_2(\mathbf{x}), \ldots, u_N(\mathbf{x})],$$

if we interpret the X_j's, $j = 1, 2, \ldots, M$, which are collectively measured by $\mathbf{x}$, as a complete set of social indicators, then u_i has the interpretation of being a measure of individual i's quality of life and u can be interpreted as a measure of society's quality of life. In this context, it admittedly is clearly unreasonable to assess u as a function of all the individuals' u_i's.

As an alternative, the Decision Maker might attempt to assess her aggregate utility function $u(\mathbf{x})$ directly, that is, to treat $\mathbf{x}$ as a proxy (vector) variable. Actual assessment of u in this "direct" manner obviously requires that the societal Decision Maker balances subjectively and implicitly her concern for the feelings of various individuals comprising the societal group and she must do this by vicariously thinking about what they are thinking or feeling.

The process of attempting to formalize a quality-of-life measure has many important side benefits from multiattribute utility analysis. The one most relevant to the theme of this book is its use in making decisions. For each policy alternative, the resulting consequences could be described in terms of their possible impact on the several social indices of importance, perhaps in a probabilistic manner. With a utility function u aggregating these, one can then calculate the expected utility of each alternative and select the one with the highest value. This same analysis, even if incompletely done, may be used for communication purposes. If we wish to advocate or describe a certain position, it may be appropriate to indicate the desirability of the alternative in terms of its anticipated effects on the social indices. Such communication, which attempts to describe impacts and preference judgements in quantitative terms, is often less ambiguous than communication in a less quantitative fashion. In this manner, the several individuals working on a problem may be

---

*This brief section in no way attempts to summarize the large literature on social indicators and the quality of life. See, for example, Bauer (1966), Dalkey (1972), and Liu (1974).

better able to focus discussion and/or debate on issues of misunderstanding and disagreement. In addition, if required, this may lead to more effective compromises.

Even if no decisions are to be made in the near future, it may be important to utilize social indices in monitoring the quality of life. By monitoring many social indices, it may be possible to identify problem areas where certain aspects of life are low or degrading and this in turn may help one in generating alternatives appropriate for improving the circumstances.

Can decision makers effectively use social indicators together with analytical tools such as decision analysis in their decision making? Sawhill (1969), Szanton (1972), and Charnes et al. (1973), among others, have made recent suggestions in this direction. The essence of the problem facing the decision makers is to create an order out of a morass of diverse, often conflicting, noncertain, noncommensurable social indices. We believe that decision analysis, employing multiattribute utility theory, is an appropriate methodological handle to grapple with this problem and we hope that its use will contribute towards our common ultimate objective: better and better decisions and an improving quality of life.

Bibliography

The following bibliography includes only those items referenced in the text. It is far from complete. For additional references on topics covered in the book, extensive bibliographies are found in the following: Edwards (1954), Luce and Raiffa (1957), Fishburn (1968), Sen (1970), Krantz et al. (1971), and Cochrane and Zeleny (1973).

Acton, J. P. (1970). Evaluation of a life-saving program: The case of heart attacks. Unpublished doctoral dissertation, Harvard University, Cambridge, Mass.

Arrow, K. J. (1951) (2nd ed. 1963). *Social Choice and Individual Values*. Wiley, New York.

Arrow, K. J. (1971). *Essays in the Theory of Risk-Bearing*. Markham Publishing Company, Chicago.

Bauer, R. A., ed. (1966). *Social Indicators*. M.I.T. Press, Cambridge, Mass.

Bauer, V. and M. Wegener. (1975). Simulation, evaluation, and conflict analysis in urban planning. *Proceedings of the IEEE*, **63**, 405–413.

Becker, G. M., M. H. DeGroot, and J. Marschak. (1964). Measuring utility by a single-response sequential method. *Behavioral Science*, **9**, 226–232.

Bell, D. E. (1974a). Evaluating time streams of income. *Omega*, **2**, 691–699.

Bell, D. E. (1974b). Defining and quantifying goals for measuring the state of an ecosystem. RR-74-26, International Institute for Applied Systems Analysis, Laxenburg, Austria.

Bell, D. E. (1975a). A utility function for time streams having inter-period dependencies. RR-75-22, International Institute for Applied Systems Analysis, Laxenberg, Austria.

Bell, D. E. (1975b). A decision analysis of objectives for a forest pest problem. RR-75-43, International Institute for Applied Systems Analysis, Laxenburg, Austria.

Blumstein, A. (1959). The landing capacity of a runway. *Operations Research*, **7**, 752–763.

549

Bodily, S. E. (1974). The utilization of frozen red cells in blood banking systems: a decision theoretic approach. Technical report No. 94, Operations Research Center, M.I.T., Cambridge, Mass.

Boyd, D. W. (1970). A methodology for analyzing decision problems involving complex preference assessments. Stanford Research Institute, Menlo Park, Cal.

Boyd, D. W. (1973). Interactive preference assessment for decisions with multiattribute outcomes. Fourth research conference on subjective probability, utility, and decision making. Rome, Italy.

Boyd, D. W., R. A. Howard, J. E. Matheson, and D. W. North. (1971). Decision analysis of hurricane modification. Final report. Stanford Research Institute, Menlo Park, Cal.

Braithwaite, R. B. (1955). *Theory of Games as a Tool for the Moral Philosopher.* Cambridge University Press, Cambridge, England.

Brown, R. V. (1970). Do managers find decision theory useful? *Harvard Business Review,* **48,** 78–89.

Brown, R. V., A. S. Kahr, and C. Peterson. (1974). *Decision Analysis for the Manager.* Holt, Rinehart and Winston, New York.

Brown, R. V. and C. Peterson. (1975). An analysis of alternative mideastern oil agreements. Technical report, Decisions and Designs, Incorporated, McLean, Virginia.

Carter, G. and E. L. Ignall. (1970). A simulation model of fire department operations: design and preliminary results. *IEEE Transactions on Systems Science and Cybernetics,* **SSC-6,** 282–293.

Charnes, A., W. W. Cooper, and G. Kozmetsky. (1973). Measuring, monitoring, and modeling quality of life. *Management Science,* **19,** 1172–1188.

Cochrane, J. L. and M. Zeleny, eds. (1973). *Multiple Criteria Decision Making.* University of South Carolina Press, Columbia, S.C.

Collins, J. P. (1974). The development of a solid waste environmental evaluation procedure. Unpublished doctoral dissertation, University of Michigan, Ann Arbor, Mich.

Dalkey, N. C. (1969). The Delphi Method: an experimental study of group opinion. RM-5888-PR, The Rand Corporation, Santa Monica, Cal.

Dalkey, N. C. (1972). *Studies in the Quality of Life: Delphi and Decision-Making.* D. C. Heath and Company, Lexington, Mass.

Davidson, D., P. Suppes, and S. Siegel. (1957). *Decision Making: An Experimental Approach.* Stanford University Press, Stanford, Cal.

Dawes, R. M. and B. Corrigan. (1974). Linear models in decision making. *Psychological Bulletin,* **81,** 95–106.

Debreu, G. (1960). Topological methods in cardinal utility theory. In *Mathematical Methods in the Social Sciences, 1959,* K. J. Arrow, S. Karlin, and P. Suppes, eds. Stanford University Press, Stanford, Cal.

de Neufville, R. and R. L. Keeney. (1972). Use of decision analysis in airport development for Mexico City. In *Analysis of Public Systems,* A. W. Drake, R. L. Keeney, and P. M. Morse, eds. M.I.T. Press, Cambridge, Mass.

Diamond, P. A. (1967). Cardinal welfare, individualistic ethics, and interpersonal comparison of utility: comment. *Journal of Political Economy,* **75,** 765–766.

Dole, S. H., H. G. Campbell, D. Dreyfuss, W. D. Gosch, E. D. Harris, D. E. Lewis, T. M. Parker, J. W. Ranftl, and J. String, Jr. (1968a). Methodologies for analyzing the comparative effectiveness and costs of alternate space plans. RM-5656-NASA, Volume 1 (Summary), The Rand Corporation, Santa Monica, Cal.

Dole, S. H., H. G. Campbell, D. Dreyfuss, W. D. Gosch, E. D. Harris, D. E. Lewis, T. M. Parker, J. W. Ranftl, and J. String, Jr. (1968b). Methodologies for analyzing the comparative effectiveness and costs of alternate space plans. RM-5656-NASA, Volume 2, The Rand Corporation, Santa Monica, Cal.

Dyer, J. S. (1972). Interactive goal programming. *Management Science*, **19**, 62–70.

Dyer, J. S., W. Farrel, and P. Bradley. (1973). Utility functions for the test performance. *Management Science*, **20**, 507–519.

Dyer, J. S. and R. F. Miles, Jr. (1974). Trajectory selection for the Mariner Jupiter/Saturn 1977 Project. Technical memorandum 33-706, Jet Propulsion Laboratory, California Institute of Technology, Pasadena, Cal.

Edwards, W. (1954). The theory of decision-making, *Psychological Bulletin*, **51**, 380–417.

Edwards, W. (1961). Behavioral decision theory. *Annual Review of Psychology*, **12**, 473–492.

Eisenbud, M. (1970). Environmental protection in the city of New York. *Science*, **170**, 706–712.

Ellis, H. M. (1970). The application of decision analysis to the problem of choosing an air pollution control program for New York City. Unpublished doctoral dissertation, Graduate School of Business Administration, Harvard University, Cambridge, Mass.

Ellis, H. M. and R. L. Keeney. (1972). A rational approach for government decisions concerning air pollution. In *Analysis of Public Systems*. A. W. Drake, R. L. Keeney, and P. M. Morse, eds. M.I.T. Press, Cambridge, Mass.

Farquhar, P. H. (1975). A fractional hypercube decomposition theorem for multiattribute utility functions. *Operations Research*, **23**, 941–967.

Feller, W. (1966). *An Introduction to Probability Theory and Its Applications*, Volume 2. Wiley, New York.

Fischer, G. W. (1972). Four methods for assessing multiattribute utilities: an experimental validation. Technical report, Engineering Psychology Laboratory, University of Michigan, Ann Arbor, Mich.

Fischer, G. W. (1973). Multidimensional utility models for riskless and risky decision making: theory and experimental application. Duke University, Durham, N.C.

Fischer, G. W. and W. Edwards. (1973). Technological aids for inference, evaluation, and decision-making: a review of research and experience. Technical report, Engineering Psychology Laboratory, University of Michigan, Ann Arbor, Mich.

Fishburn, P. C. (1964). *Decision and Value Theory*. Wiley, New York.

Fishburn, P. C. (1965a). Independence in utility theory with whole product sets. *Operations Research*, **13**, 28–45.

Fishburn, P. C. (1965b). Markovian dependence in utility theory with whole product sets. *Operations Research*, **13**, 238–257.

Fishburn, P. C. (1966). Additivity in utility theory with denumerable product sets. *Econometrica*, **34**, 500–503.

Fishburn, P. C. (1967a). Interdependence and additivity in multivariate, unidimensional expected utility theory. *International Economic Review*, **8**, 335–342.

Fishburn, P. C. (1967b). Additive utilities with incomplete product sets: application to priorities and assignments. *Operations Research*, **15**, 537–542.

Fishburn, P. C. (1967c). Additive utilities with finite sets: applications in the management sciences. *Naval Research Logistics Quarterly*, **14**, 1–13.

Fishburn, P. C. (1967d). Methods of estimating additive utilities. *Management Science*, **13**, 435–453.

Fishburn, P. C. (1968). Utility theory. *Management Science*, **14**, 335–378.

Fishburn, P. C. (1969). Preferences, summation, and social welfare functions. *Management Science*, **16**, 179–186.

Fishburn, P. C. (1970). *Utility Theory for Decision Making*. Wiley, New York.

Fishburn, P. C. (1971). Additive representations of real-valued functions on subsets of product sets. *Journal of Mathematical Psychology*, **8**, 382–388.

Fishburn, P. C. (1972). Interdependent preferences on finite sets. *Journal of Mathematical Psychology*, **9**, 225–236.

Fishburn, P. C. (1973a). *The Theory of Social Choice*. Princeton University Press, Princeton, N.J.

Fishburn, P. C. (1973b). Bernoullian utilities for multiple-factor situations. In *Multiple Criteria Decision Making*, J. L. Cochrane and M. Zeleny, eds. University of South Carolina Press, Columbia, S.C.

Fishburn, P. C. (1974). Von Neumann–Morgenstern utility functions on two attributes. *Operations Research*, **22**, 35–45.

Fishburn, P. C. (1975). Nondecomposable conjoint measurement for bisymmetric structures. *Journal of Mathematical Psychology*, **12**, 75–89.

Fishburn, P. C. and R. L. Keeney. (1974). Seven independence concepts and continuous multiattribute utility functions. *Journal of Mathematical Psychology*, **11**, 294–327.

Fishburn, P. C. and R. L. Keeney. (1975). Generalized utility independence and some implications. *Operations Research*, **23**, 928–940.

Fleming, M. (1952). A cardinal concept of welfare. *Quarterly Journal of Economics*, **66**, 366–384.

Fried, C. (1970). *An Anatomy of Values*. Harvard University Press, Cambridge, Mass.

Gearing, C. E., W. W. Swart, and T. Var. (1973). Determining the optimal investment policy for the tourism sector of a developing country. *Management Science*, **20**, 487–497.

Gearing, C. E., W. W. Swart, and T. Var. (1974). Establishing a measure of touristic attractiveness. *Journal of Travel Research*, 1–8.

Geoffrion, A. M., J. S. Dyer, and A. Feinberg. (1972). An interactive approach for multi-criterion optimization, with an application to the operation of an academic department. *Management Science*, **19**, 357–368.

Gorman, W. M. (1968a). The structure of utility functions. *Review of Economic Studies*, **35**, 367–390.

Gorman, W. M. (1968b). Conditions for additive separability. *Econometrica*, **36**, 605–609.

Grayson, C. J. (1960). *Decisions Under Uncertainty: Drilling Decisions by Oil and Gas Operators*. Division of Research, Harvard Business School, Boston, Mass.

Grochow, J. M. (1972). A utility theoretic approach to evaluation of a time-sharing system. In *Statistical Computer Performance Evaluation*, W. Frieberger, ed. Academic Press, New York.

Grochow, J. M. (1973). On user supplied evaluations of time-shared computer systems. *IEEE Transactions on Systems, Man and Cybernetics*, **SMC-3**, 204–205.

Gros, J. G. (1974). A paretian environmental approach to power plant siting in New England. Unpublished doctoral dissertation, Harvard University, Cambridge, Mass.

Gustafson, D. H. and D. C. Holloway. (1974). A decision theory approach to measuring severity in illness. Unpublished report, University of Wisconsin, Madison, Wis.

Hammond, J. S. III (1965). Bringing order into the selection of a college. *Personnel and Guidance Journal*, 654–660.

Hammond, J. S. III (1974). Simplifying the choice between uncertain prospects where preference is nonlinear. *Management Science*, **20**, 1047–1072.

Harsanyi, J. C. (1955). Cardinal welfare, individualistic ethics, and interpersonal comparisons of utility. *Journal of Political Economy*, **63**, 309–321.

Harsanyi, J. C. (1961). On the rationality postulates underlying the theory of cooperative games. *Journal of Conflict Resolution*, **5**, 179–196.

Harsanyi, J. C. (1967). Games with incomplete information played by "Bayesian" players. Part I. *Management Science*, **14**, 159–182.

Harsanyi, J. C. (1968). Games with incomplete information played by "Bayesian" players. Parts II and III. *Management Science*, **14**, 320–334 and 486–502.

Harsanyi, J. C. (1974). Nonlinear social welfare functions. *Theory and Decision*, **7**, 61–82.

Hatry, H. P. (1970). Measuring the effectiveness of nondefense public programs. *Operations Research*, **18**, 772–784.

Hildreth, C. (1953). Alternative conditions for social orderings. *Econometrica*, **21**, 81–94.

Holling, C. S., D. E. Bell, W. C. Clark, G. B. Dantzig, M. B. Fiering, D. D. Jones, Z. Rashid, H. Velimirovic, C. J. Walters, and C. Winkler. (1974). Project status report: ecology and environment project. SR-74-2-EC, International Institute for Applied Systems Analysis, Laxenburg, Austria.

Horgan, D. N., Jr. (1972). A decision analysis of sewage sludge disposal alternatives for Boston harbor. Unpublished masters thesis, Department of Electrical Engineering, M.I.T., Cambridge, Mass.

Howard, R. A. (1968). The foundations of decision analysis. *IEEE Transactions on Systems Science and Cybernetics,* **SSC-4,** 211–219.

Howard, R. A., J. E. Matheson, and D. W. North. (1972). The decision to seed hurricanes. *Science,* **176,** 1191–1202.

Huber, G. P. (1974a). Multi-attribute utility models: a review of field and field-like studies. *Management Science,* **20,** 1393–1402.

Huber, G. P. (1974b). Methods for quantifying subjective probabilities and multiattribute utilities. *Decision Sciences,* **5,** 430–458.

Huber, G. P., V. Sahney, and D. Ford. (1969). A study of subjective evaluation models. *Behavioral Science,* **14,** 483–489.

Ipesa Consultores and the Secretaria de Communicaciones y Transportes (1970). Estudio de ampliacion del aeropuerto internacional de la ciudad de Mexico. Mexico City, Mexico.

Jennings, J. B. (1968). An analysis of hospital blood bank whole blood inventory control policies. *Transfusion,* **8,** 335–342.

Kalelkar, A. S., L. J. Partridge, and R. E. Brooks. (1974). Decision analysis in hazardous material transportation. *Proceedings of the 1974 National Conference on Control of Hazardous Material Spills,* American Institute of Chemical Engineers, San Francisco, Cal.

Kaufman, G. M. (1963). *Statistical Decision and Related Techniques in Oil and Gas Exploration.* Prentice-Hall, Englewood Cliffs, N.J.

Keeney, R. L. (1968). Quasi-separable utility functions. *Naval Research Logistics Quarterly,* **15,** 551–565.

Keeney, R. L. (1971). Utility independence and preferences for multiattributed consequences. *Operations Research,* **19,** 875–893.

Keeney, R. L. (1972a). Utility functions for multiattributed consequences. *Management Science,* **18,** 276–287.

Keeney, R. L. (1972b). An illustrated procedure for assessing multiattributed utility functions. *Sloan Management Review,* **14,** 37–50.

Keeney, R. L. (1973a). A decision analysis with multiple objectives: the Mexico City airport. *Bell Journal of Economics and Management Science,* **4,** 101–117.

Keeney, R. L. (1973b). Concepts of independence in multiattribute utility theory. In *Multiple Criteria Decision Making,* J. Cochrane and M. Zeleny, eds. University of South Carolina Press, Columbia, S.C.

Keeney, R. L. (1973c). A utility function for the response times of engines and ladders to fires. *Urban Analysis,* **1,** 209–222.

Keeney, R. L. (1973d). Risk independence and multiattributed utility functions. *Econometrica,* **41,** 27–34.

Keeney, R. L. (1974). Multiplicative utility functions. *Operations Research,* **22,** 22–34.

Keeney, R. L. (1975). Examining corporate policy using multiattribute utility analysis. *Sloan Management Review,* **17,** 63–76.

Keeney, R. L. and C. W. Kirkwood. (1975). Group decision making using cardinal social welfare functions. *Management Science,* **22,** 430–437.

Keeney, R. L. and K. Nair. (1975). Decision analysis for the siting of nuclear power plants—the relevance of multiattribute utility theory. *Proceedings of the IEEE*, **63**, 494–501.

Keeney, R. L. and K. Nair. (1976). Evaluating potential nuclear power plant sites in the pacific northwest using decison analysis. PP-76-1, International Institute for Applied Systems Analysis, Laxenburg, Austria.

Keeney, R. L. and H. Raiffa. (1972). A critique of formal analysis in public decision making. In *Analysis of Public Systems*, A. W. Drake, R. L. Keeney, and P. M. Morse, eds. M.I.T. Press, Cambridge, Mass.

Keeney, R. L. and A. Sicherman. (1976). An interactive computer program for assessing and analyzing preferences concerning multiple objectives. *Behavioral Science*, to appear.

Kirkwood, C. W. (1972). Decision analysis incorporating preferences of groups. Technical report No. 74, Operations research Center, M.I.T., Cambridge, Mass.

Kirkwood, C. W. (1976). Parametrically dependent preferences for multiattributed consequences. *Operations Research*, **24**, 92–103.

Knepperth, N. P., D. H. Gustafson, R. P. Leifer, and E. M. Johnson. (1974). Techniques for the assessment of worth. Technical paper 254, U.S. Army Research Institute for the Behavioral and Social Sciences, Arlington, Va.

Koopmans, T. C. (1960). Stationary ordinal utility and impatience. *Econometrica*, **28**, 287–309.

Koopmans, T. C. (1972). Representation of preference orderings over time. In *Decision and Organization*, C. B. McGuire and R. Radner, eds. North-Holland Publishing Company, Amsterdam.

Koopmans, T. C., P. A. Diamond, and R. E. Williamson. (1964). Stationary utility and time perspective. *Econometrica*, **32**, 82–100.

Kornbluth, J. S. H. (1973). A survey of goal programming. *Omega*, **1**, 193–205.

Krantz, D. H. (1964). Conjoint measurement: the Luce–Tukey axiomatization and some extensions. *Journal of Mathematical Psychology*, **1**, 248–277.

Krantz, D. H., R. D. Luce, P. Suppes, and A. Tversky. (1971). *Foundations of Measurement*, Volume 1. Academic Press, New York.

Krischer, J. P. (1974). An analysis of patient management decisions as applied to cleft palate. TR-12-74. Center for Research in Computing Technology, Harvard University, Cambridge, Mass.

Lancaster, K. J. (1963). An axiomatic theory of consumer time preference. *International Economic Review*, **4**, 221–231.

Larson, R. C. (1972). *Urban Police Patrol Analysis*. M.I.T. Press, Cambridge, Mass.

Leontief, W. (1947a). Introduction to a theory of the internal structure of functional relationships. *Econometrica*, **15**, 361–373.

Leontief, W. (1947b). A note on the interrelation of subsets of independent variables of a continuous function with continuous first derivatives. *Bulletin of the American Mathematical Society*, **53**, 343–350.

Liu, B. (1974). Quality of life indicators: a preliminary investigation. *Social Indicators Research*, **1**, 187–208.

Longbottom, D. and G. Wade. (1973). An investigation into the application of decision analysis in United Kingdom companies. *Omega*, **1**, 207–215.

Lorange, P. and V. D. Norman. (1973). Risk preference in Scandinavian shipping. *Applied Economics*, **5**, 49–59.

Luce, R. D. (1966). Two extensions of conjoint measurement. *Journal of Mathematical Psychology*, **3**, 348–370.

Luce, R. D. and H. Raiffa. (1957). *Games and Decisions*. Wiley, New York.

Luce, R. D. and J. W. Tukey. (1964). Simultaneous conjoint measurement: a new type of fundamental measurement. *Journal of Mathematical Psychology*, **1**, 1–27.

MacCrimmon, K. R. (1969). Improving the system design and evaluation process by the use of trade-off information: an application to northeast corridor transportation planning. RM-5877-DOT, The Rand Corporation, Santa Monica, Cal.

MacCrimmon, K. R. and J. K. Siu. (1974). Making trade-offs. *Decision Sciences*, **5**, 680–704.

MacCrimmon, K. R. and M. Toda. (1969). The experimental determination of indifference curves. *The Review of Economic Studies*, **36**, 433–451.

Manheim, M. L. and F. Hall. (1967). Abstract representation of goals: a method for making decisions in complex problems. In *Transportation: A Service*. Proceedings of the Sesquicentennial Forum, New York Academy of Sciences–American Society of Mechanical Engineers, New York.

Matheson, J. E. and W. T. Roths. (1967). Decision analysis of space projects. *Proceedings of the National Symposium, Saturn/Apollo and Beyond*, American Astronautical Society.

McKean, R. N. (1958). *Efficiency in Government Through Systems Analysis*. Wiley, New York.

Mead, R. H. (1973). The Astoria problem: a systems analysis of an electric power versus air quality conflict. Unpublished doctoral dissertation, Harvard University, Cambridge, Mass.

Meyer, R. F. (1970). On the relationship among the utility of assets, the utility of consumption, and investment strategy in an uncertain, but time invariant world. In *OR 69: Proceedings of the Fifth International Conference on Operational Research*, J. Lawrence, ed. Tavistock Publications, London.

Meyer, R. F. (1975). State-dependent time preference. In *Proceedings of the Workshop on Decision Making with Multiple Conflicting Objectives*, International Institute for Applied Systems Analysis, Laxenburg, Austria.

Meyer, R. F. and J. W. Pratt. (1968). The consistent assessment and fairing of preference functions. *IEEE Systems Science and Cybernetics*, **SSC-4**, 270–278.

Miller, J. R. III (1966). The assessment of worth: a systematic procedure and its experimental validation. Unpublished doctoral dissertation, Massachusetts Institute of Technology, Cambridge, Mass.

Miller, J. R. III (1969). Assessing alternative transportation systems. RM-5865-DOT, The Rand Corporation, Santa Monica, Cal.

Miller, J. R. III (1970). *Professional Decision Making*. Praeger Publishers, New York.

Moore, M. H. (1973). Policy towards heroin use in New York City. Unpublished doctoral dissertation, Harvard University, Cambridge, Mass.

Mosteller, F. and P. Nogee. (1951). An experimental measurement of utility. *Journal of Political Economy*, **59**, 371–404.

Nair, K., G. E. Brogan, L. S. Cluff, I. M. Idriss, and K. T. Mao. (1975). An approach to the siting of nuclear power plants. In *Siting of Nuclear Facilities*, International Atomic Energy Agency, Vienna, Austria.

Nash, J. F. (1950). The bargaining problem. *Econometrica*, **18**, 155–162.

Nash, J. F. (1953). Two-person cooperative games. *Econometrica*, **21**, 128–140.

New York City Department of Air Resources (1969). Emissions inventory.

O'Connor, M. F. (1973). The application of multiattribute scaling procedures to the development of indices of water quality. Report 7339, Center for Mathematical Studies in Business and Economics, University of Chicago, Chicago.

Odoni, A. (1972). Efficient operation of runaways. In *Analysis of Public Systems*, A. W. Drake, R. L. Keeney, and P. M. Morse, eds. M.I.T. Press, Cambridge, Mass.

Oksman, W. (1974). Markov decision processes with utility independent objective functions. Unpublished doctoral dissertation, Harvard University, Cambridge, Mass.

Ovi, A. (1973). Decision analysis applied to nuclear versus fossil alternatives for electric energy production. Unpublished masters thesis, Department of Nuclear Engineering, M.I.T., Cambridge, Mass.

Papp, R., P. E. McGrath, L. D. Maxim, and F. X. Cook, Jr. (1974). A new concept in risk analysis for nuclear facilities. *Nuclear News*, November 62–65.

Pattanaik, P. K. (1971). *Voting and Collective Choice*. Cambridge University Press, Cambridge, England.

Peterson, C. (1974). Optimizing negotiations. Unpublished manuscript, presented at the ORSA/TIMS Conference, San Juan, Puerto Rico, October.

Pollak, R. A. (1967). Additive von Neumann–Morgenstern utility functions. *Econometrica*, **35**, 485–494.

Pollak, R. A. (1973). The risk independence axiom. *Econometrica*, **41**, 35–39.

Pollard, A. B. (1969). A normative model for joint time/risk preference decision problems. Stanford Research Institute, Menlo Park, Cal.

Pratt, J. W. (1964). Risk aversion in the small and in the large. *Econometrica*, **32**, 122–136.

Pratt, J. W., H. Raiffa, and R. O. Schlaifer. (1965). *Introduction to Statistical Decision Theory*. McGraw-Hill, New York.

Pruzan, P. M. and J. T. R. Jackson. (1963). On the development of utility spaces for multi-goal systems. *Saertryk af Erhvervsøkonomisk Tidsskrift*, **4**, 257–274.

Pye, G. (1973). Lifetime portfolio selection in continuous time for a multiplicative class of utility functions. *The American Economic Review*, **63**, 1013–1016.

Raiffa, H. (1951). Arbitration schemes for generalized two-person games. Report M720-1, R30, Engineering Research Institute, University of Michigan, Ann Arbor, Mich.

Raiffa, H. (1953). Arbitration schemes for generalized two-person games. In *Contributions to the Theory of Games, II*, H. W. Kuhn and A. W. Tucker, eds. Princeton University Press, Princeton, N.J.

Raiffa, H. (1968). *Decision Analysis.* Addison-Wesley, Reading, Mass.

Raiffa, H. (1969). Preferences for multi-attributed alternatives. RM-5868-DOT/RC, The Rand Corporation, Santa Monica, Cal.

Rapoport, A., editor (1974). *Game Theory as a Theory of Conflict Resolution.* D. Reidel Publishing Company, Dordrecht, Holland.

Richard, S. F. (1972). Optimal life insurance decisions for a rational economic man. Unpublished doctoral dissertation, Graduate School of Business Administration, Harvard University, Cambridge, Mass.

Richard, S. F. (1975). Multivariate risk aversion, utility independence and separable utility functions. *Management Science,* **22,** 12–21.

Roche, J. G. (1971). Preference tradeoffs among instructional programs: an investigation of cost-benefit and decision analysis techniques in local educational decision making. Unpublished doctoral dissertation, Graduate School of Business Administration, Harvard University, Cambridge, Mass.

Roy, B. (1971). Problems and methods with multiple objective functions. *Mathematical Programming,* **1,** 239–266.

Savage, L. J. (1954). *The Foundations of Statistics.* Wiley, New York.

Savas, E. S. (1969). Simulation and cost-effectiveness analyses of New York's emergency ambulance service. *Management Science,* **15,** B608–B627.

Sawhill, I. V. (1969). The role of social indicators and social reporting in public expenditure decisions. In *The Analysis and Evaluation of Public Expenditures: the PPB System.* U.S. Government Printing Office, Washington, D.C., 473–485.

Schimpeler, C. C., N. R. Baker, and W. L. Grecco. (1969). Criteria weighting: inter-method stability and consistency of preference in an urban planning application. Louisville Metropolitan Comprehensive Transportation and Development Program, Louisville, Ken.

Schlaifer, R. O. (1969). *Analysis of Decisions Under Uncertainty.* McGraw-Hill, New York.

Schlaifer, R. O. (1971). *Computer Programs for Elementary Decision Analysis.* Division of Research, Graduate School of Business Administration, Harvard University, Cambridge, Mass.

Schroeder, R. G. (1974). Resource planning in university management by goal programming. *Operations Research,* **22,** 700–710.

Schwartz, W. B., G. A. Gorry, J. P. Kassirer, and A. Essig. (1973). Decision analysis and clinical judgement. *The American Journal of Medicine,* **55,** 459–472.

Secretaria de Obras Publicas (1967). Aeropuerto internacional de la ciudad de Mexico. Mexico City, Mexico.

Sen, A. K. (1970). *Collective Choice and Social Welfare.* Holden-Day, San Francisco.

Shakun, M., ed. (1972). *Game Theory and Gaming.* Special issue of *Management Science,* **18.**

Sicherman, A. (1975). An interactive computer program for assessing and using multiattribute utility functions. Technical report No. 111, Operations Research Center, M.I.T., Cambridge, Mass.

Slovic, P. and S. Lichtenstein. (1971). Comparison of bayesian and regression approaches to the study of information processing in judgement. *Organizational Behavior and Human Performance*, **6**, 649–744.

Spetzler, C. S. (1968). The development of a corporate risk policy for capital investment decisions. *IEEE Transactions on Systems Science and Cybernetics*, **SSC-4**, 279–300.

Stanford Research Institute (1968). Decision analysis of nuclear plants in electrical systems expansion. Report on Project 6496, Menlo Park, Cal.

Stevenson, K. A. (1972). Emergency ambulance transportation. In *Analysis of Public Systems*, A. W. Drake, R. L. Keeney, and P. M. Morse, eds. M.I.T. Press, Cambridge, Mass.

Swalm, R. O. (1966). Utility theory—insights into risk taking. *Harvard Business Review*, **44**, 123–136.

Szanton, P. L. (1972). Analysis and urban government. In *Analysis of Public systems*, A. W. Drake, R. L. Keeney, and P. M. Morse, eds. M.I.T. Press, Cambridge, Mass.

Teweles, R. B. (1972). The use of risk analysis techniques in career planning. Unpublished manuscript.

Ting, H. M. (1971). Aggregation of attributes for multiattributed utility assessment. Technical report No. 66, Operations Research Center, M.I.T., Cambridge, Mass.

Toda, M. (1974). A computational procedure for obtaining additive utility functions from observed indifference curves. HRP-3-74-15, Department of Psychology, Hokkaido University, Sapporo, Japan.

Toy, N. E. (1971). Analysis of financial decisions for retirement: an exploration of several methodologies where there is uncertainty of investment returns and mortality. Unpublished doctoral dissertation, Graduate School of Business Administration, Harvard University, Cambridge, Mass.

Tribus, M. (1969). *Rational Descriptions, Decisions, and Designs*. Pergamon Press, New York.

Tversky, A. (1967). A general theory of polynomial conjoint measurement. *Journal of Mathematical Psychology*, **4**, 1–20.

Tversky, A. (1975). On the elicitation of preferences: descriptive and prescriptive considerations. In *Proceedings of the Workshop on Decision Making with Multiple Conflicting Objectives*, International Institute for Applied Systems Analysis, Laxenburg, Austria.

von Neumann, J. and O. Morgenstern. (1947). *Theory of Games and Economic Behavior*. 2nd ed. Princeton University Press, Princeton, N.J.

von Winterfeldt, D. and W. Edwards. (1973a). Evaluation of complex stimuli using multiattribute utility procedures. Technical report, Engineering Psychology Laboratory, The University of Michigan, Ann Arbor, Mich.

von Winterfeldt, D. and W. Edwards. (1973b). Flat maxima in linear optimization models. Technical report, Engineering Psychology Laboratory, The University of Michigan, Ann Arbor, Mich.

Wilsey y Ham de Mexico, S.A. de C.V. (1967). Aeropuerto internacional de la ciudad de Mexico. Mexico City, Mexico.

Winkler, R. L. (1972). *An Introduction to Bayesian Inference and Decision.* Holt, Rinehart and Winston, New York.

Woodward-Clyde Consultants (1975). Final report to the Washington Public Power Supply System. San Francisco, Cal.

Yntema, D. B. and L. Klem. (1965). Telling a computer how to evaluate multidimensional situations. *IEEE Transactions on Human Factors in Electronics,* **HFE-6,** 3–13.

Yntema, D. B. and W. S. Torgenson. (1961). Man–computer cooperation in decisions requiring common sense. *IEEE Transactions on Human Factors in Electronics,* **HFE-2,** 20-26.

Zeleny, M. (1974). *Linear Multiobjective Programming.* Springer-Verlag, Berlin.

Zeuthen, F. (1930). *Problems of Monopoly and Economic Warfare.* G. Routledge & Sons, London.

Zionts, S. and J. Wallenius. (1976). An interactive programming method for solving the multiple criteria problem. *Management Science,* **22,** 652–663.

Index

Acton, J. P., 20, 549
Additive independence, 229, 263, 295, 527
  conditional, 336, 337
  definition, 230, 295
  in the group context, 527, 532
  verification of, 263
Additive utility function, 231, 238, 250,
  286, 295, 305, 489
  assessment of, 305
  definition, 231
  group, 528
Additive value function, 90, 105, 111, 330,
  371, 392, 483, 484
  assessment of, 92, 96, 106, 117
  definition, 91
  group, 525
Advocacy, 9, 442
Aggregation of individual preferences:
  under certainty, 523
  rankings, 526
  under uncertainty, 527
Air pollution, 1, 32, 355
Airport location, 2, 437
Alternatives:
  adaptive, 11, 471
  generation of, 11, 374, 545
  process-oriented, 11
Analyst, role of, 9, 190
Anxiety, 511
Approximations, 100, 253, 461
Arrow, K. J., 131, 159, 516, 522, 544, 549
Arrow's Impossibility Theorem, 523
Arthur D. Little, 426
Aspiration level, 21, 72, 78, 136, 545

Assessment:
  bias, 212
  direct, 222, 257
  scaling constants, 121, 267, 301,
    384, 458
  utility functions:
    conditional, 216, 266, 383
    group, 539
    multiattribute, 261, 297, 505
    single attribute, 188, 503
  value functions, 92, 95, 96, 106, 117, 369
Assumptions:
  additive independence, 230, 295
  conditional independence, 333
  group preference, 536
  parametric dependence, 259
  preferential independence, 101, 284
  state dependence, 214, 502
  utility independence, 226, 284
  verification of, 191, 276, 382, 398, 452
    additive independence, 263
    preferential independence, 299
    risk aversion, 192
    utility independence, 264, 299
Attributes, 283, 359
  characteristics of, 38
  complementary sets, 283
  comprehensiveness, 38
  decomposability, 51
  definition of, 32, 67
  importance of, 272
  measurability, 39
  nonuniqueness, 53
  objective, 40, 45

operational, 51
overlapping sets, 112, 316
properties of, 50
proxy, 55, 61, 543
redundancy of, 51
scalar, 32, 224
specification of, 38
subjective, 40, 45, 427
vector, 32, 224
visual, 430

Baker, N. R., 558
Bauer, R. A., 546, 549
Bauer, V., 435, 549
Becker, G. M., 188, 549
Behavioral decision theory, 8
Bell, D. E., 260, 433, 434, 474, 501, 549
Benevolent dictator, 520
Bias, 212
Blood bank preferences, 210, 275
Blum, E. H., 377
Blumstein, A., 139, 549
Bodily, S. E., 418, 550
Bounded utility, 311, 505
Boyd, D. W., 127, 297, 435, 550
Bracamontes, Secretary, 2, 471
Bradley, P., 435, 551
Braithwaite, R. B., 522, 550
Brogan, G. E., 557
Brooks, R. E., 426, 554
Brown, R. V., 5, 433, 435, 550
Business decisions, 4, 206, 390
Buying price, 143

Campbell, H. G., 551
Cardinal utility functions, 220
Carter, G., 58, 378, 550
Cases:
  air pollution, 355
  cleft lip and palate, 429
  computer systems, 408
  corporate preferences, 390
  fire department operations, 377
  foreign policy, 432
  forest pest management, 433
  frozen blood, 418
  hospital blood bank, 210, 273
  instructional programs, 365
  landing aricraft, 418
  Mexico City airport, 436

nuclear power, 412
oil wildcatting, 204
selecting a job, 422
selecting a profession, 422
sewage sludge disposal, 421
transporting hazardous substances, 426
water quality, 431
Cash equivalent, 143
Centainty equivalent, 142, 193, 242, 252,
  460
  conditional, 216
Chance nodes, 6
Charnes, A., 547, 550
Clark, W. C., 433, 553
Cleft lip and palate, 429
Cluff, L. S., 557
Cochrane, J. L., 550
Collins, J. P., 435, 550
Communication, 9, 391, 406, 546
Complement, 283
Completeness, 50
Comprehensiveness, 38
Computer programs, 209, 349, 460, 509
Conditional additive independence, 336, 337
Conditional preferences, 100, 109, 214, 332,
  497
Conditional preferential independence, 334,
  339
Conditional utility functions, 227, 243, 497
  scaling of, 302, 458
Conditional utility independence, 334, 336,
  339, 342, 409
Conflict resolution, 10, 442
Conjoint scaling:
  lock-step procedure, 91
  midvalue splitting technique, 94, 120
Consequence, 7, 31, 283, 473
  description of, 14
Consistency checks, 198, 270, 280, 310, 384
Constant proportional risk aversion, 178
Consumption streams, 486
  continuous, 492
  discrete, 491
Cook, F. X., Jr., 557
Cooper, W. W., 550
Corporate preferences, 207, 390
Corresponding tradeoffs condition, 91
Corrigan, B., 343, 550
Cost-benefit analysis, 19
Cost-effectiveness analysis, 20

Criteria, *see* Attributes

Dalkey, N. C., 431, 546, 550
Dantzig, G. B., 553
Davidson, D., 188, 204, 550
Dawes, R. M., 343, 550
Debreu, G., 68, 105, 111, 130, 550
Decision analysis:
  implementation, 13
  iterative nature of, 10, 466
  paradigm, 5
  personal, 50, 425
Decision making:
  advocacy, 9, 46
  descriptive, 8, 18
  descriptive versus prescriptive, 8, 515
  formal versus informal, 12
  group, 8, 26
  individual, 8, 18
  personal, 50, 425
  prescriptive, 8
  reconciliation, 9, 46, 442
  social welfare, 20
  strategic versus repetitive, 13
Decision nodes, 6
Decisions and Designs, Inc., 432
Decomposability:
  of attributes, 51
  of preferences, 319
Decreasing marginal utility, 88, 150, 214
Decreasing risk aversion, 166, 173, 185
DeGroot, M. G., 188, 549
Delphi, 431
de Neufville, R., 436, 472, 550
Derived utility function, 56
Differentially value-equivalent, 94
Diamond, P. A., 532, 550
Dimensionality, 52, 311
  reduction of, 102
Direct preference measurements, 61
Discounting, 24, 479, 485
  generalizations, 482
Dole, S. H., 36, 41, 551
Dominance, 69, 117, 128, 461, 479
  extended, 128
  probabilistic, 135
Double counting, 51
Dovali, F., 436, 472
Dreyfuss, D., 551
Dyer, J. S., 72, 435, 545, 551

Echeverria, President Luis, 2, 440, 471
Educational programs, 365
Edwards, W., 8, 298, 343, 551
Efficient frontier, 70
  exploration of:
    using artificial constraints, 72
    using linear-weighted averages, 74
Eisenbud, M., 358, 551
Ellis, H. M., 43, 355, 364, 551
Energy problems, 412
Environmental problems, 486
  air pollution, 355
  forest pest management, 433
  nuclear power siting, 412
  transporting hazardous substances, 426
  water quality, 431
Equity, 532
  posterior, 533
  prior, 532
Equivalent futures, 496
Essentiality, 104
Essig, A., 4, 558
Expected utility, 7, 16, 131, 133, 220
  calculations, 200
Exponential transforms, 201, 202
Exponential utility function, 145, 167, 186
Extended dominance, 128

Farquhar, P. H., 293, 551
Farrell, W., 435, 551
Feinberg, A., 72, 552
Feller, W., 164, 551
Fiering, M. B., 553
Fire department operations, 377
Fischer, G. W., 8, 343, 551
Fishburn, P. C., 111, 130, 131, 231, 258,
  259, 282, 293, 295, 297, 346, 521,
  526, 551
Fleming, M., 526, 552
Flexibility, 465, 509
Ford, D., 40, 554
Forest pest management, 433
Fried, C., 25, 552
Frozen blood, 418

Game theory, 412, 521
Gearing, C. E., 41, 435, 552
Generating alternatives, 11, 374, 545
Geoffrion, A. M., 72, 552
Goals, 33, 34

Gorman, W. M., 68, 107, 112, 116, 130, 318, 553
Gorry, G. A., 4, 558
Gosch, W. D., 551
Government decisions:
    air pollution, 355
    airport location, 436
    educational programs, 365
    fire department operations, 377
    foreign policy, 432
    forest pest management, 433
    nuclear power siting, 412, 415
    sewage sludge disposal, 421
Grayson, C. J., 18, 158, 194, 204, 553
Grecco, W. L., 558
Grochow, J. M., 408, 553
Gros, J. G., 413, 416, 520, 553
Group decisions, 26, 515, 520
    versus individual decisions, 8, 515
Group utility functions, 527
Group value functions, 525
Gustafson, D. H., 54, 435, 553

Hall, F., 41, 556
Hammond, J. S., III, 20, 198, 553
Harris, E. D., 551
Harsanyi, J. C., 522, 527, 544, 553
Hatry, H. P., 60, 553
Harvard Business School, 209, 509
Health effects, 359
Hedging, 512
Heroin addiction, 3
Hierarchical structure, 41, 332, 341,
Hilborn, R., 433
Hildreth, C., 522, 553
Holling, C. S., 433, 553
Holloway, D. C., 54, 435, 553
Horgan, D. N., Jr., 422, 553
Horizon, 474, 483
    uncertain, 497
Howard, R. A., 5, 127, 435, 554
Huber, G. P., 40, 297, 435, 554
Hypothetical questions, 18, 40, 190, 207

Idriss, I. M., 557
Ignall, E. L., 58, 378, 550
Illustrations:
    air pollution, 32
    emergency ambulance service, 57
    Louisville, 36

    medical treatment, 53
    NASA, 35
    Northeast Corridor, 41, 48
    postal service, 33
    seat belts, 341
    selecting a job, 307
Implementation, 13
Independence:
    additive, 229, 263, 295, 527
    conditional, 333
    preferential, 101, 109, 310, 484, 524, 537
    probabilistic, 242, 450
    utility, 224, 310, 528, 536
Indifference curves, 79
    linear, 85, 480
    see also Isopreference curves
Induced utility function, 56
Instructional programs, 365
Insurance premium, 153
Interest rate, 473
Intergenerational tradeoffs, 23
Interpersonal comparison:
    of preferences, 517, 526, 544
    of utilities, 519
Ipesa Consultores, 437
Isopreference curves, 236, 246, 249. See also
    Indifference curves

Jackson, J. T. R., 68, 87, 111, 295, 557
Jauffred, F. J., 436, 472
Jennings, J. B., 274, 554
Job selection, 307, 422
Johnson, E. M., 555
Jones, D. D., 433, 553

Kahr, A. S., 5, 550
Kalelkar, A. S., 426, 554
Kassirer, J. P., 4, 558
Kaufman, G. M., 205, 554
Keeney, R. L., 12, 51, 226, 243, 282, 288,
    311, 346, 349, 355, 390, 413, 436, 527,
    554
Kennedy, President John, 34
Kirkwood, C. W., 259, 260, 527, 539, 542,
    555
Klem, L., 418, 560
Knepperth, N. P., 54, 297, 555
Koopmans, T. C., 474, 483, 555
Kornbluth, J. S. H., 72, 555
Kozmetsky, G., 550

Krantz, D. H., 68, 105, 111, 130, 555
Krischer, J. P., 429, 555

Lancaster, K. J., 474, 555
Landing aircraft, 418
Larson, R. C., 58, 139, 381, 555
Leifer, R. P., 555
Leontief, W., 68, 112, 130, 555
Lewis, D. E., 551
Lexicographical ordering, 77
Lichtenstein, S., 8, 559
Lintner, J., 15
Liu, B., 546, 555
Logarithmic utility function, 169, 205
Longbottom, D., 435, 555
Lorange, P., 435, 556
Lottery, 7, 140, 242
  nondegenerate, 149
Louisville objectives, 36
Luce, R. D., 68, 91, 130, 131, 412, 521, 544, 556

MacCrimmon, K. R., 35, 41, 83, 556
McGrath, P. E., 557
McKean, R. N., 52, 556
Manheim, M. L., 41, 556
Mao, K. T., 557
Marginal rate of substitution, 82
Marginal utility, 88, 150
Marschak, J., 188, 549
Master plans, 444, 471
Matheson, J. E., 127, 435, 556
Maxim, L. D., 557
Maximal utility independent chain, 320, 323, 325
Mead, R. H., 355, 556
Mean-variance criterion, 136, 168
Means-ends, 41, 52
Measurable, 39
Medical decisions:
  ambulance service, 57
  blood bank inventory, 273
  cleft lip and palate, 429
  diagnostics, 4
  frozen blood, 418
  treatment, 4, 53
Mellin transform, 201
Mexico City airport, 2, 436
  dynamic analysis, 463
  static model, 442

surroundings, 438
uncertainties, 445
utility functions, 451
Meyer, R. F., 131, 197, 214, 260, 282, 292, 330, 473, 488, 493, 502, 556
Midvalue point, 94, 120
Miles, R. F., Jr., 545, 551
Miller, J. R., III, 41, 62, 423, 556
Monotonicity, 141
Monte Carlo techniques, 352
Moore, M. H., 3, 556
Moorhouse, D. C., 391
Morgenstern, O., 131, 283, 559
Mosteller, F., 188, 203, 557
Multilinear utility function, 233, 250, 287, 293, 325
  with additional assumptions, 328
  group, 529
Multiplicative utility function, 238, 286, 288, 324, 330, 453, 489
  group, 530
  scaling of, 307, 347, 401, 459
Mutual preferential independence, 111
Mutual utility independence, 229, 232, 289
  equivalent assumptions, 292

Nair, K., 390, 391, 413, 557
NASA objectives, 35
Nash, J. F., 522, 557
Nesting, 298, 457
Net present value, 477
New York City Department of Air Resources, 358
New York City Fire Department, 377
New York City - Rand Institute, 377
Nightmares, methodological, 19
Nogee, P., 188, 203, 557
Norman, V. D., 435, 556
North, D. W., 127, 435, 550
Northeast Corridor, 41, 48
Nuclear power siting, 412

Objectively correct preferences, 190
Objectives, 34
  clarification of, 395
  generation of, 34, 41, 358, 392, 443
  hierarchy, 41, 332, 341
  how far to formalize, 43, 44
  lower-level, 32
  nonuniqueness, 47

structuring of, 31
Objectivism, 12, 46
O'Connor, M. F., 431, 520, 557
Odoni, A., 139, 557
Oil Wildcatters, 204
Oksman, W., 214, 496, 557
Operational, 51
Ordinal utility functions, 220
Overlapping attributes, 112, 316
Ovi, A., 413, 557

Pairwise preferential independence, 105,
    479, 481
Papp, R., 413, 557
Parametric dependence, 259
Paretian environmental analysis, 416
Pareto optimality, 70, 521, 534
Parker, T. M., 551
Participatory group, 520, 540
Partridge, L. J., 554
Pattanaik, P. K., 521, 557
Personal decisions, 50, 425, 497, 509
Peterson, C. R., 5, 433, 545, 557
Political implications, 351, 465
Pollak, R. A., 226, 282, 292, 295, 296, 557
Pollard, A. B., 474, 557
Pollution:
    air, 1, 32, 355
    land, 422
    water, 421, 431
Pratt, J. W., 131, 159, 163, 197, 212, 330,
    557
Preanalysis, 5, 10
Preference complements, 240
Preference substitutes, 241
Preferences:
    over time, 417, 457, 473
    reversals, 258, 345, 536
Preferential independence, 101, 109, 310,
    484, 524, 537
    conditional, 334, 339
    definition of, 101, 284
    generalization of, 345
    in the group context, 524, 537
    mutual, 111
    pairwise, 105, 479, 481
    verification of, 114, 299
Present perception of future utility, 476
Present value, 24
Pricing out, 125

Probability assessment, 1, 6
    with simulation models, 378
    subjective, 445
    over time, 448
Proportional risk aversion, 174
    definition of, 178
Proportional risk premium, 178
Proxy attribute, 55, 61, 543
Pruzan, P. M., 68, 87, 111, 295, 557
Pye, G., 493, 557

Quadratic utility function, 168, 186
Quality of life, 546

Raiffa, H., 5, 7, 12, 28, 41, 51, 131, 133,
    143, 282, 412, 447, 521, 544, 557
Ranftl, J. W., 551
Rapoport, A., 522, 558
Rashid, Z., 433, 553
Reconciliation, 9, 10, 47, 442
Reduction of dimensionality, 102
Response time, 57, 139, 377
Response time utility functions, 380, 385
    assessment of, 381
    properties of, 385
    use of, 380
Revealed preferences, 18
Reversing preferences, 258, 345, 536
Richard, S. F., 214, 490, 493, 500, 506,
    509, 558
Risk, 126
Risk aversion, 148, 180
    constant, 167, 185
    constant proportional, 178
    decreasing, 166, 173, 185
    definition of, 149, 160
    increasing, 169, 185
    measure of, 159, 183
    proportional, 174
    temporal, 490, 508
Risk aversion function, 161
Risk premium, 151
Risk proneness, 150, 157, 173
Roche, J. G., 117, 365, 520, 558
Ronan, F. J., 377, 381, 389
Roths, W. T., 127, 556
Roy, B., 72, 558

Sahney, V., 40, 554
Savage, L. J., 131, 558

Savas, E. S., 57, 139, 381, 558
Sawhill, I. V., 547, 558
Scalar attribute, 32, 224
Scaling constants, 271, 301
  assessment of, 121, 267, 278, 301, 384,
    401, 458
  interpretation of, 271
  misinterpretation of, 271
Scenarios, 465
Schimpeler, C. C., 36, 41, 558
Schlaifer, R. O., 5, 131, 138, 196, 209, 506,
  558
Schroeder, R. G., 72, 558
Schwartz, W. B., 4, 558
Secretaria de Communicaciones y Transportes,
  436, 554
Secretaria de Obras Publicas, 436, 558
Selling price, 143
Semiseparability, 495
Sen, A. K., 521, 524, 558
Sensitivity analysis, 100, 125, 201, 405, 460
Sewage sludge disposal, 421
Sex, 50, 69
Shakun, M., 412, 558
Sicherman, A., 349, 350, 558
Siegel, S., 188, 204, 550
Simulation models, 378
Siu, J. K., 83, 556
Slovic, P., 8, 559
Social indices, 544, 546
Social welfare, 20, 516
Spetzler, C. S., 207, 559
Spruce budworm, 433
Stanford Research Institute, 127, 559
State dependent preferences, 214, 501
State descriptors, 214, 260, 494
  efficient, 502
  updatable, 502
Stationarity, 484
Stevenson, K. A., 57, 381, 559
Strategically equivalent, 81, 144, 527
  utility functions, 144, 160
  value functions, 81
String, J., Jr., 551
Subjective index, 40, 45, 427, 544
Substitution rates:
  constant, 85, 480
  constant with transformed variable, 86
Sulfur-dioxide decision problem, 358, 363
Suppes, P., 130, 188, 204, 550

Swalm, R. O., 206, 559
Swart, W. W., 435, 552
Szanton, P. L., 547, 559

Temporal tradeoffs, 22
Test of importance, 43, 359
Teweles, R. B., 423, 559
Time horizon, 474, 483, 497
Time preference, 22, 417, 434, 437, 473
  assessment of, 499, 506
  quantification, of utility functions, 488
    of value functions, 476
Time resolution of uncertainty, 475, 509
Time sharing computer systems, 408
Ting, H. M., 68, 115, 130, 559
Toda, M., 83, 559
Torgenson, W. S., 343, 560
Toy, N. E., 212, 559
Tradeoffs:
  intergenerational, 23
  interpersonal, 543
  performance, 367
  technological, 76
  temporal, 22
  value, 15, 66, 365
Transformations:
  multiple attribute, 256, 486
  single attribute, 184
  time streams, 486
Transporting hazardous substances, 426
Tribus, M., 5, 559
Tukey, J. W., 68, 91, 130, 556
Tversky, A., 130, 212, 559

Uncertainty:
  quantification of, 6, 378, 445, 448
Uncertainty analysis, 6
Utility analysis, 16
Utility assessment, 261, 297
  cases, 210, 273, 377, 399, 410, 451
  computer programs, 209, 349, 509
  consistency checks, 198, 270, 280, 310,
    384
  direct, 140, 222, 257
  hypothetical questions, 18, 190, 207
  illustrations, 203, 307
  multiattribute, 261, 297
  of time preferences, 499, 506
  over value attribute, 220
  parameter estimation, 178

preliminaries, 189, 261
questionnaire, 430
single attribute, 188, 503
Utility dependence, 260, 434
Utility functions:
  additive, 231, 238, 250, 286, 295, 305, 489
  approximation of, 253
  cardinal, 220
  conditional, 227, 243, 383
  decomposition of, 319
  derived, 56
  exponential, 145, 167, 186
  group, 527
  induced, 56
  logarithmic, 147, 169
  multiattribute, 282, 488
  multilinear, 233, 250, 287, 293, 325
  multiplicative, 238, 286, 288, 324, 330, 453, 489
  nested, 298, 457
  nonmonotonic, 142, 179, 187, 397
  ordinal, 68, 220
  parametric family, 197
  partial formalization, 544
  semiseparable, 495
  single attribute:
    assessment, 188, 503
    exponential, 145, 167, 186
    logarithmic, 147, 169
    monotonic, 141
    nonmonotonic, 142, 179
    power, 175
    quadratic, 168, 186
    risk averse, 149
    risk prone, 150, 157
    weighted exponential, 170, 506
  strategic equivalence, 144, 160
  sum of exponentials, 170, 506
  three attribute, 286
  over time streams, 488
  two attribute, 219
  over value, 137, 220, 221, 330
Utility independence, 224, 310, 528, 536
  conditional, 334, 336, 339, 342, 409
  definition of, 225, 284
  generalization of, 345
  in the group context, 528, 536
  interpreting, 227
  mutual, 229, 232, 289

  over subsets, 257
  verification of, 264, 299
Utility independent chain, 319
  element of, 320, 323
  maximal, 320, 323, 325
Utility theory, 132
  conditional, 214

Value assessment, 91, 96, 117
  cases, 365, 419
Value functions, 68, 80, 476
  additive, 90, 105, 111, 371, 392, 483, 484
  assessment of, 87, 92, 95, 96, 106, 117, 369
  assessment of component value function, 96, 120
  assessment of scaling constants, 98, 121, 123
  for three attributes, 100, 105
  for two attributes, 82
  group, 525
  more than three attributes, 111
  over time streams, 476, 483
  partial additivity, 116
  strategic equivalence, 81
Value of a life, 25
Value problem, 15
Value tradeoffs, 66, 365
Values, subjective, 12
Var, T., 435, 552
Vector attribute, 32, 224
Velimirovic, H., 553
von Neumann, J., 131, 283, 516, 559
von Winterfeldt, D., 298, 343, 559

Wade, G., 435, 555
Wallenius, J., 74, 560
Walters, C. J., 433, 553
Water quality index, 431
Wegener, M., 435, 549
What is quantifiable?, 12
Williamson, R. E., 555
Willingness to pay, 84, 125
Wilsey y Ham de Mexico, 437, 559
Winkler, C., 553
Winkler, R. L., 5, 560
Woodward-Clyde Consultants, 390, 413, 560
Woodward, R. J., 391
Worth function, 423

Yntema, D. B., 343, 418, 560
Yorque, R., 433

Zeleny, M., 74, 560
Zeuthen, F., 522, 560
Zionts, S., 74, 560

Decisions
Multiple

Library